DATE DUE

SOMETHING ABOUT THE AUTHOR®

Something about
the Author *was named
an* **"Outstanding
Reference Source,"**
*the highest honor given
by the American
Library Association
Reference and Adult
Services Division.*

ISSN 0276-816X

SOMETHING ABOUT THE AUTHOR®

Facts and Pictures about Authors
and Illustrators of Books for Young People

VOLUME 112

GALE GROUP

TM

Detroit
New York
San Francisco
London
Boston
Woodbridge, CT

STAFF

Editor: Alan Hedblad

Associate Editors: Sara L. Constantakis, Melissa Hill, Motoko Fujishiro Huthwaite
Assistant Editors: Kristen A. Dorsch, Tom Schoenberg, Mark Springer, Erin E. White

Managing Editor: Joyce Nakamura
Literature Content Coordinator: Susan M. Trosky

Research Manager: Victoria B. Cariappa
Research Specialists: Gary J. Oudersluys, Cheryl L. Warnock
Project Coordinator: Corrine A. Boland
Research Associates: Patricia Tsune Ballard, Tamara C. Nott, Tracie A. Richardson
Research Assistants: Phyllis J. Blackman, Tim Lehnerer, Patricia L. Love

Permissions Manager: Maria L. Franklin
Permissions Associates: Edna Hedblad, Sarah Tomasek

Composition Manager: Mary Beth Trimper
Manufacturing Manager: Dorothy Maki
Buyer: Stacy Melson

Graphic Artist: Gary Leach
Image Database Supervisor: Randy Bassett
Imaging Specialists: Robert Duncan, Michael Logusz
Imaging Coordinator: Pamela A. Reed

Library of Congress Catalog Card Number 72-27107

ISBN 0-7876-3221-X
ISSN 0276-816X

Printed in the United States of America

10 9 8 7 6 5 4 3 2 1

Contents

Authors in Forthcoming Volumes vii
Introduction ix
Acknowledgments xi

Authors in Forthcoming Volumes

Below are some of the authors and illustrators that will be featured in upcoming volumes of *SATA*. These include new entries on the swiftly rising stars of the field, as well as completely revised and updated entries (indicated with *) on some of the most notable and best-loved creators of books for children.

*Aliki Brandenberg: Greek-American author-illustrator Aliki Brandenberg, most commonly known as "Aliki," is widely respected for her ability to convey information to children and young readers in a variety of ways. Aliki has enjoyed acclaim for her work in many genres, as evidenced by her award-winning biography *William Shakespeare and the Globe* and the well-received tale *Marianthe's Story.*

*Carolyn B. Cooney: A prolific and popular novelist, Cooney has written scores of books for young adults. One of her more recent works, *The Voice on the Radio,* was named an American Library Association Notable Book in 1996.

Andrew McLean: Andrew McLean and his wife, author and teacher Janet McLean, have created many popular books for children. Their collaboration has resulted in such efforts as *Dog Tales* and *Cats' Whiskers,* which depict lively, expressive animal characters.

Pat Moon: An English author of poems, novels, and picture books, Moon combines humor and mystery to create works that are highly regarded. Her young adult novels, including such works as *The Spying Game* and *Nathan's Switch,* confront realistic issues that teenagers often face, particularly the subjects of bullying and divorce.

Nick Park: A recipient of dozens of film and animation awards, Park, who hails from England, is an internationally esteemed English writer and director. His wildly popular duo, Wallace and Gromit, have appeared in many of his works and have inspired books, toys, and clothing.

Andrea Davis Pinkney: Pinkney draws on African-American family traditions in many of her works, most notably *Seven Candles for Kwanzaa.* She received the Coretta Scott King award in 1999 for her well-researched biography *Duke Ellington: The Piano Prince and His Orchestra.*

*Maurice Sendak: Sendak is a celebrated author and illustrator whose remarkable work has captivated generations. His more recent efforts include illustrations for James Marshall's *I Saw Esau: The Schoolchild's Pocketbook* and *Swine Lake.*

Angela Sommer-Bodenburg: German author Sommer-Bodenburg has captured the attention of budding horror fans with her popular character, "der kleine Vampir." Written in her native tongue, the "Little Vampire" series as well as others of her stories have been translated into thirty languages.

*James Stevenson: Well known for his antic touch and light humor, Stevenson is a prolific author and illustrator of scores of books as well as cartoons and novels for young readers.

*William Taylor: *Jerome,* a novel recently published by New Zealand author Taylor, has been the subject of critical debate in both the United States and in New Zealand due to its focus on the controversial subjects of homosexuality and suicide.

Sheri S. Tepper: In addition to addressing a variety of human issues in her more than two dozen science fiction and fantasy novels, Tepper has also produced two successful mystery series, the "Jason Lynx" mysteries and the "Shirley McClintock" series.

Erico Verissimo: One of Brazil's most beloved authors, Verissimo was a writer of popular fiction for both adults and children. Before his death in 1975, Verissimo penned nearly fifty works during a career that spanned five decades.

Introduction

Something about the Author (*SATA*) is an ongoing reference series that examines the lives and works of authors and illustrators of books for children. *SATA* includes not only well-known writers and artists but also less prominent individuals whose works are just coming to be recognized. This series is often the only readily available information source on emerging authors and illustrators. You'll find *SATA* informative and entertaining, whether you are a student, a librarian, an English teacher, a parent, or simply an adult who enjoys children's literature.

What's Inside SATA

SATA provides detailed information about authors and illustrators who span the full time range of children's literature, from early figures like John Newbery and L. Frank Baum to contemporary figures like Judy Blume and Richard Peck. Authors in the series represent primarily English-speaking countries, particularly the United States, Canada, and the United Kingdom. Also included, however, are authors from around the world whose works are available in English translation. The writings represented in *SATA* include those created intentionally for children and young adults as well as those written for a general audience and known to interest younger readers. These writings cover the entire spectrum of children's literature, including picture books, humor, folk and fairy tales, animal stories, mystery and adventure, science fiction and fantasy, historical fiction, poetry and nonsense verse, drama, biography, and nonfiction.

Obituaries are also included in *SATA* and are intended not only as death notices but also as concise overviews of people's lives and work. Additionally, each edition features newly revised and updated entries for a selection of *SATA* listees who remain of interest to today's readers and who have been active enough to require extensive revisions of their earlier biographies.

New Autobiography Feature

Beginning with Volume 103, *SATA* features three or more specially commissioned autobiographical essays in each volume. These unique essays, averaging about ten thousand words in length and illustrated with an abundance of personal photos, present an entertaining and informative first-person perspective on the lives and careers of prominent authors and illustrators profiled in *SATA*.

Two Convenient Indexes

In response to suggestions from librarians, *SATA* indexes no longer appear in every volume but are included in alternate (odd-numbered) volumes of the series, beginning with Volume 57.

SATA continues to include two indexes that cumulate with each alternate volume: the Illustrations Index, arranged by the name of the illustrator, gives the number of the volume and page where the illustrator's work appears in the current volume as well as all preceding volumes in the series; the Author Index gives the number of the volume in which a person's biographical sketch, autobiographical essay, or obituary appears in the current volume as well as all preceding volumes in the series.

These indexes also include references to authors and illustrators who appear in Gale's *Yesterday's Authors of Books for Children, Children's Literature Review,* and *Something about the Author Autobiography Series.*

Easy-to-Use Entry Format

Whether you're already familiar with the *SATA* series or just getting acquainted, you will want to be aware of the kind of information that an entry provides. In every *SATA* entry the editors attempt to give as complete a picture of the person's life and work as possible. A typical entry in *SATA* includes the following clearly labeled information sections:

- *PERSONAL:* date and place of birth and death, parents' names and occupations, name of spouse, date of marriage, names of children, educational institutions attended, degrees received, religious and political affiliations, hobbies and other interests.

- *ADDRESSES:* complete home, office, electronic mail, and agent addresses, whenever available.

- *CAREER:* name of employer, position, and dates for each career post; art exhibitions; military service; memberships and offices held in professional and civic organizations.

- *AWARDS, HONORS:* literary and professional awards received.

- *WRITINGS:* title-by-title chronological bibliography of books written and/or illustrated, listed by genre when known; lists of other notable publications, such as plays, screenplays, and periodical contributions.

- *ADAPTATIONS:* a list of films, television programs, plays, CD-ROMs, recordings, and other media presentations that have been adapted from the author's work.

- *WORK IN PROGRESS:* description of projects in progress.

- *SIDELIGHTS:* a biographical portrait of the author or illustrator's development, either directly from the biographee—and often written specifically for the *SATA* entry—or gathered from diaries, letters, interviews, or other published sources.

- *FOR MORE INFORMATION SEE:* references for further reading.

- *EXTENSIVE ILLUSTRATIONS:* photographs, movie stills, book illustrations, and other interesting visual materials supplement the text.

How a SATA Entry Is Compiled

A *SATA* entry progresses through a series of steps. If the biographee is living, the *SATA* editors try to secure information directly from him or her through a questionnaire. From the information that the biographee supplies, the editors prepare an entry, filling in any essential missing details with research and/or telephone interviews. If possible, the author or illustrator is sent a copy of the entry to check for accuracy and completeness.

If the biographee is deceased or cannot be reached by questionnaire, the *SATA* editors examine a wide variety of published sources to gather information for an entry. Biographical and bibliographic sources are consulted, as are book reviews, feature articles, published interviews, and material sometimes obtained from the biographee's family, publishers, agent, or other associates.

Entries that have not been verified by the biographees or their representatives are marked with an asterisk (*).

Contact the Editor

We encourage our readers to examine the entire *SATA* series. Please write and tell us if we can make *SATA* even more helpful to you. Give your comments and suggestions to the editor:

BY MAIL: Editor, *Something about the Author,* The Gale Group, 27500 Drake Rd., Farmington Hills, MI 48331-3535.

BY TELEPHONE: (800) 877-GALE

BY FAX: (248) 699-8054

Acknowledgments

Grateful acknowledgment is made to the following publishers, authors, and artists whose works appear in the volume.

ADAMS, PAM. Adams, Pam, illustrator. From an illustration in her *Mrs. Honey's Hat.* Child's Play International, Ltd., 1990. (c) M. Twinn 1980. Reproduced by permission. / Adams, Pam, illustrator. From an illustration in *Old Macdonald Had a Farm.* Child's Play International Ltd., 1998. (c) 1975 M. Twinn. Reproduced by permission.

ARCHAMBAULT, JOHN. Rand, Ted, illustrator. From an illustration in *Barn Dance!* by Bill Martin Jr. and John Archambault. Text copyright (c) 1986 by Bill Martin Jr. and John Archambault. Illustrations copyright (c) 1986 by Ted Rand. Reproduced by permission of Henry Holt and Company, LLC. / Ehlert, Lois, illustrator. From an illustration in *Chicka Chicka Boom Boom* by Bill Martin Jr. and John Archambault. Simon & Schuster Books for Young People, 1989. Illustrations copyright (c) 1989 by Lois Ehlert. Reproduced by permission of Simon & Schuster Macmillan.

AZARIAN, MARY. Azarian, Mary, illustrator. From an illustration in *Snowflake Bentley* by Jacqueline Briggs Martin. Houghton Mifflin Company, 1998. Illustrations copyright (c) 1998 by Mary Azarian. All rights reserved. Reproduced by permission of Houghton Mifflin Company. / Azarian, Mary, illustrator. From an illustration in *Barn Cat* by Carol P. Saul. Little, Brown and Company, 1998. Illustrations copyright (c) 1998 by Mary Azarian. Reproduced by permission of Little, Brown and Company.

BAMBARA, TONI CADE. Bambara, Toni Cade, 1977, photograph by Sandra L. Swans. Reproduced by permission. / Taddei, Richard, illustrator. From a cover of *Gorilla, My Love* by Toni Cade Bambara. Vintage Contemporaries, 1992. All rights reserved. Reproduced by permission of Vintage Books, a division of Random House, Inc. / Taddei, Richard, illustrator. From a cover of *The Salt Eaters* by Toni Cade Bambara. Vintage Contemporaries, 1992. All rights reserved. Reproduced by permission of Vintage Books, a division of Random House, Inc.

BATEMAN, TERESA. Bateman, Teresa, photograph. Reproduced by permission. / Rayyan, Omar, illustrator. From an illustration in *The Ring of Truth* by Teresa Bateman. Holiday House, 1997. Illustrations copyright (c) 1997 by Omar Rayyan. All rights reserved. Reproduced by permission of Holiday House, Inc.

BELLOC, HILAIRE. Belloc, Hilaire, photograph. The Library of Congress.

BERNARDIN, JAMES. Bernardin, James, illustrator. From an illustration in *Giants!* by Paul Robert Walker. Harcourt Brace & Company, 1995. Illustrations copyright (c) 1995 by James Bernardin. All rights reserved. Reproduced by permission of Harcourt, Inc.

BLACKLOCK, DYAN. Kelly, Geoff, illustrator. From a cover of *Comet Vomit* by Dyan Blacklock. Little Ark Books, 1995. Reproduced by permission of Allen & Unwin Pty Ltd.

BRIMBER, LARRY DANE. All personal photographs reproduced with permission from the author.

BROOKS, BRUCE. Brooks, Bruce, photograph. Reproduced by permission.

CONLY, JANE LESLIE. Conly, Jane Leslie, photograph by J. Brough Schamp. Reproduced by permission. Natale, Vince, illustrator. From a cover of *Crazy Lady* by Jane Leslie Conly. HarperTrophy, 1995. Copyright (c) 1993 by Jane Leslie Conly. Cover art (c) 1995 by Vince Natale. Reproduced by permission of HarperCollins Publishers. / From a cover of *Trout Summer* by Jane Leslie Conly. Scholastic Inc., 1995. Copyright (c) 1995 by Jane Leslie Conly. Reproduced by permission.

DUNNAR, JOYCE. Blythe, Gary, illustrator. From a cover of *This Is the Star* by Joyce Dunbar. Harcourt Brace & Company, 1996. Cover illustration copyright (c) 1996 by Gary Blythe. Reproduced by permission of Harcourt, Inc. In the British Empire by permission of Transworld Publishers. / Craig, Helen, illustrator. From an illustration in *The Bowl of Fruit* by Joyce Dunbar. Candlewick Press, 1999. Illustrations copyright (c) 1999 by Helen Craig. All rights reserved. Reproduced by permission of Walker Books Ltd. Published in the U.S. by Candlewick Press, Inc., Cambridge, MA. /

sOMETHING ABOUT THE AUTHOR

ADAMS, Pam 1919-

Personal

Born in 1919, in Swindon, Wiltshire, England. *Education:* Attended Swindon Art College and the Central School of Art in London.

Career

Author and illustrator. Worked as a graphic artist for various advertising agencies during the 1950s and 60s. *Military service:* Worked as a driver for RAF Wroughton during World War II.

Writings

AUTHOR AND ILLUSTRATOR

There Was an Old Lady Who Swallowed a Fly, Child's Play, 1973.
I Thought I Saw, illustrated with Ceri Jones, Child's Play, 1974.
This Old Man, Child's Play, 1974.
Old Macdonald Had a Farm, Child's Play, 1975.
Old MacDonald, Child's Play, 1978.
The Child's Play Museum, Child's Play, 1979.
Mrs. Honey's Hat, Child's Play, 1980.
Wally Whale and Friends, Child's Play, 1981.
(With Michael Twinn) *The Lady Who Loved Animals,* Child's Play, 1981.
The Gingerbread Man, Child's Play, 1981.
Noah's Ark, Child's Play, 1981.
If I Weren't Me ... Who Would I Be?, Child's Play, 1981.

Pam Adams's ebullient illustrations capture the playfulness of the traditional song. (From Old Macdonald Had a Farm, *written and illustrated by Adams.)*

Baby Bubbles, Child's Play, 1981.
Froglet's Bathtime, Child's Play, 1981.
Dolly Dolphin's Play School, Child's Play, 1981.
Tingaling, Child's Play, 1981.
Owl's Number School, Child's Play, 1983.
The Ocean, Child's Play, 1984.

An alley cat
saw Mrs Honey's hat
through the window.
"That ribbon might help **me**
to win a prize," he thought.

So he pulled it from the hat
and left some fish bones behind.

But Mrs Honey didn't notice.

As several creatures remove things from Mrs. Honey's hat and leave new items behind, the hat goes through a drastic change, unknown to the cheerful woman. (From Mrs. Honey's Hat, *written and illustrated by Adams.*)

The Fairground, Child's Play, 1984.
Ups and Downs, Child's Play, 1985.
The Frog, Child's Play, 1985.
The Green-Eyed Monster, Child's Play, 1985.
The Red-Eyed Monster, Child's Play, 1985.
The Helpful Shoelace, Child's Play, 1987.
(With Michael Twinn) *Rabbit's Golden Rule Book,* Child's Play, 1988.
Ten Beads Tall, Child's Play, 1988.
Who Cares about Elderly People?, Child's Play, 1989.
Who Cares about Disabled People?, Child's Play, 1989.
What on Earth?, Child's Play, 1989.
Magic Shoelaces, Child's Play, 1989.
On a Cold and Frosty Morning, Child's Play, 1990.
Six in a Bath, Child's Play, 1990.
Child's Play Day Dreams: An Imagination Book, Child's Play, 1990.
The Mystery Express, Child's Play, 1990.
Who Cares about Law and Order?, Child's Play, 1991.
Playmates, Child's Play, 1991.
Mr. Lion's I-Spy ABC, Child's Play, 1992.
Mrs. Honey's Dream, Child's Play, 1992.
Mrs. Honey's Holiday, Child's Play, 1992.
Mrs. Honey's Glasses, Child's Play, 1992.
Lift the Lid, Child's Play, 1995.
Great Pal Mouse, Child's Play, 1996.
First Day, Child's Play, 1996.
First Noel, Child's Play, 1996.
Gloria, Hosanna in Excelsis!, Child's Play, 1996.
Sing a Song of Sixpence, Child's Play, 1998.
Croaky, Child's Play, 1999.
Lucky, Child's Play, 1999.
There Was an Old Lady, Child's Play, 1999.

ILLUSTRATOR

This Is the House That Jack Built, Child's Play, 1972.
A Book of Ghosts, Child's Play, 1974.

Angels, Child's Play, 1974.
The Best Things, Child's Play, 1974.
What Is It? Child's Play, 1975.
How Many?, Child's Play, 1975.
Same and Different, Child's Play, 1975.
Letters and Words, Child's Play, 1975.
Magic, Child's Play, 1978.
I-Spy ABC, Child's Play, 1978.
Day Dreams, Child's Play, 1978.
Oh Soldier, Soldier, Won't You Marry Me?, Child's Play, 1978.
There Were Ten in the Bed, Child's Play, 1979.
All Kinds: Who Cares about Race and Colour?, Child's Play, 1989.
Yogesh Patel, *Magic Glasses,* Child's Play, 1995.

ILLUSTRATOR; BY MICHAEL TWINN

Alf 'n Bet, Child's Play, 1992.
Alf 'n Bet Learn Their ABC, Child's Play, 1992.
Alf 'n Bet's Handwriting Book, Child's Play, 1993.
Emily Elephant and Her Friends, Child's Play, 1995.
Henry the Helpful Elephant, Child's Play, 1995.
Away in a Manger, Child's Play, 1996.

ILLUSTRATOR; "POCKET PALS" SERIES; BY MICHAEL TWINN

Pocket Pal: Bunny, Child's Play, 1995.
... *Frog,* Child's Play, 1995.
... *Kitten,* Child's Play, 1995.
... *Puppy,* Child's Play, 1995.
... *Chameleon,* Child's Play, 1996.
... *Earwig,* Child's Play, 1996.
... *Fox,* Child's Play, 1996.
... *Koala,* Child's Play, 1996.
... *Mouse,* Child's Play, 1996.
... *Panda,* Child's Play, 1996.
... *Pony,* Child's Play, 1996.

... *Python,* Child's Play, 1996.
... *Dolphin,* Child's Play, 1997.
... *Penguin,* Child's Play, 1997.
... *Polar Bear,* Child's Play, 1997.
... *Seahorse,* Child's Play, 1997.

ILLUSTRATOR; "GREAT PALS" SERIES; BY MICHAEL TWINN

Great Pals: Seahorse, Child's Play, 1997.
... *Penguin,* Child's Play, 1997.
... *Polar Bear,* Child's Play, 1997.
... *Dolphin,* Child's Play, 1997.
... *Bunny,* Child's Play, 1997.
... *Panda,* Child's Play, 1997.
... *Kitten,* Child's Play, 1997.
... *Puppy,* Child's Play, 1997.

A number of Adams's books have been translated into Welsh and Gaelic.

Sidelights

Pam Adams has been a children's book author and illustrator since the 1970s, producing more than a hundred titles distributed by the international publisher Child's Play in both her native England and the United States. Author Michael Twinn, the founder of Child's Play and Adams's frequent collaborator, commented on his partnership with Adams in an interview with Marianne Adey in *Carousel:* "Although she had never worked on children's books before, her attractive art work, sense of humour and great versatility soon made her an invaluable member of the team." Adams's first self-illustrated book, *There Was an Old Lady Who Swallowed a Fly,* is based on the folk song about a woman who swallows a fly, then a spider to catch the fly, then a bird to catch the spider, and so forth, each time consuming a larger animal to catch the smaller one that preceded it. Child's Play's 1973 edition of *There Was an Old Lady* was one of the first books to incorporate holes in the pages as part of the book's design. Adams used the same method to create versions of *This Old Man,* based on the traditional children's counting song; and *Old Macdonald,* which highlights farm animals and the sounds they make.

Adams has produced a score of other self-illustrated titles, including adaptations of nursery rhymes such as *Sing a Song of Sixpence,* traditional children's stories such as *The Gingerbread Man* and *There Were Ten in the Bed,* and original stories such as *Mrs. Honey's Hat* and its several sequels, *Mrs. Honey's Glasses, Mrs. Honey's Holiday,* and *Mrs. Honey's Dream.* In addition, she has provided the illustrations for Child's Play's "Pocket Pals" and "Great Pals" series. Now in her eighties, the hardworking Adams is still busy creating children's books that, like her first, contain "bright, clear colours, appealing shapes and attention to detail," qualities that have "made her pictures instantly successful with children," Adey asserted.

Works Cited

Adey, Marianne, "A Conversation with Illustrator, Pam Adams," *Carousel,* Spring, 1999, p. 12.

For More Information See

PERIODICALS

Books for Keeps, September, 1993, p. 6.
Bulletin of the Center for Children's Books, February, 1976, p. 89.
Children's Bookwatch, January, 1994, p. 4.
Horn Book Guide, Fall, 1992, p. 313; Fall, 1994, p. 261.
Publishers Weekly, May 3, 1971, p. 56.

*   *   *

AMOSS, Berthe 1925-

Personal

First name is pronounced Beart (as in "bear"); born September 26, 1925, in New Orleans, LA; daughter of Sumter Davis (a lawyer) and Berthe (Lathrop) Marks; married Walter James Amoss, Jr. (executive vice-president of Lykes Bros. Steamship Co.), December 21, 1946; children: Jim, Bob, Billy, Mark, Thom, John. *Education:* Tulane University of Louisiana, B.A., M.A.; studied art for a total of five years at University of Hawaii, at Kunstschule, Bremen, Germany, and Academie des Beaux Arts, Antwerp, Belgium. *Religion:* Roman Catholic. *Hobbies and other interests:* Amoss speaks French and German.

Addresses

Home—3723 Carondelet St., New Orleans, LA 70115. *Agent*—Harriet Wasserman, Russell & Volkening, Inc., 551 Fifth Avenue, New York, NY 10017.

Career

Writer and illustrator. Tulane University, instructor of children's book writing and illustrating, 1976—. *Exhibitions:* Has participated in group and solo exhibitions; works housed in permanent collections at the University of Minnesota-Minneapolis, the State Library of Louisiana, the University of Southern Mississippi-Hattiesburg, the Howard Tilton Memorial Library at Tulane University, and elsewhere.

Awards, Honors

Runner-up, Edgar Allan Poe Award, 1977, for *The Chalk Cross; The Marvelous Catch of Old Cannibal* was selected for the Child Study Association book list.

Writings

AUTHOR AND ILLUSTRATOR

It's Not Your Birthday, Harper & Row, 1966.
Tom in the Middle, Harper & Row, 1968, reprinted, HarperCollins, 1988.

By the Sea, Parents' Magazine Press, 1969.

The Marvelous Catch of Old Cannibal, Parents' Magazine Press, 1970.

Old Hasdrubal and the Pirates, Scholastic, 1971.

The Big Cry, Bobbs, 1972.

The Very Worst Thing, Scholastic, 1972.

The Great Sea Monster: Or, a Book by You, Scholastic, 1975.

The Chalk Cross (young-adult novel), Seabury, 1976.

The Witch Cat, Preservation Resource Center of New Orleans, 1977.

Secret Lives, Little, Brown, 1979.

The Loup Garou, Pelican, 1979.

Secret Lives (young-adult novel), Little, Brown, 1979.

What Did You Lose, Santa?, Harper & Row, 1987.

The Mockingbird Song, Harper & Row, 1988.

Snow White and the Seven Dwarfs, More than a Card, Inc., 1989.

Rumpelstiltskin, More than a Card, Inc., 1989.

Mother Goose Rhymes, More than a Card, Inc., 1989.

Jack and the Beanstalk, More than a Card, Inc., 1989.

Hansel and Gretel, More than a Card, Inc., 1989.

Cinderella, More than a Card, Inc., 1989.

Noah, More than a Card, Inc., 1989.

Lullaby and Good Night, More than a Card, Inc., 1989.

Little Red Riding Hood, More than a Card, Inc., 1989.

Jonah, More than a Card, Inc., 1989.

David and Goliath, More than a Card, Inc., 1989.

Car Seat Games, More than a Card, Inc., 1989.

Old Hannibal and the Hurricane, Hyperion, 1991.

Lost Magic, Hyperion, 1993.

The Cajun Gingerbread Boy, Hyperion, 1994.

Five Fairytale Princesses: Book and Charm Bracelet, Random House, 1998.

ILLUSTRATOR

Joan L. Nixon, *The Mysterious Prowler,* Harcourt Brace, 1976.

Clement C. Moore, *The Night before Christmas,* More than a Card, Inc., 1989.

Eric Suben, *The Secret of Pirate's Manor,* Andrews and McMeel, 1995.

OTHER; WITH ERIC SUBEN

Writing and Illustrating Children's Books for Publication: Two Perspectives, F & W Publications, 1995.

Ten Steps to Publishing Children's Books: How to Develop, Revise and Sell All Kinds of Books for Children, Writer's Digest Books, 1997.

By the Sea has been made into a motion picture.

Sidelights

Berthe Amoss once told *SATA:* "A picture book is one written and designed for the pre-school child. I think it's safe to say that it is always at least half dependent on its illustrations, and sometimes completely dependent on them. A picture book is not meant to instruct or teach a moral, and woe to the manuscript with a message. They seldom get past the first reader in an editorial office. If they do get published, they quickly gather dust on the child's shelf.

"A picture book is meant to delight a child and to expand his world, a world very different from ours, as any of us who deal with children or remember our own childhood know. I've always loved to draw, and I've always loved books. When I went to college, I studied art and English literature, which was as close as I could stay to the world of picture books."

Years later, married and a mother, Amoss became a writer and illustrator of picture books, including the innovative *The Great Sea Monster: Or, a Book by You.* The book not only tells the story of a boy who goes fishing and gets swallowed by an octopus and rescued by a sea turtle, it also instructs young readers how to tell and illustrate such a story. According to Jean Mercier in *Publishers Weekly,* the book is "an entrancing idea ... and would be a most welcome present for the adventurous child."

Amoss has also written novels for young adults. Set in the New Orleans of the author's childhood, *Secret Lives* tells the story of twelve-year-old Addie's quest to find out the truth about her mother, who died when Addie was only five and who has been made into a saintly model by Addie's elderly aunts. "Addie is a delight with her blunt humor and romantic fantasy into which she keeps trying to fit one, then another of the odd characters who surround her," remarked Dorothy Salisbury Davis in *New York Times Book Review.* Addie's research into her mother's life leaves her with a clearer picture of the real woman and a deeper understanding of herself and those she loves. "*Secret Lives* is filled with the ambiance of New Orleans and is frank and wry and loving in appraising some of its people's beliefs," noted Sara Miller in *School Library Journal.*

Amoss also enjoyed positive critical reception with *The Mockingbird Song,* in which she effectively details Depression-era New Orleans. Young protagonist Lindy has been abandoned by her mother, and is having difficulty adjusting to life with her father's new and pregnant wife. Lindy moves in for an extended visit with an elderly, unmarried neighbor, whose example teaches Lindy about the necessity of making compromises in personal relationships. "The historical background is interesting," noted Ruth K. MacDonald in her review for *School Library Journal,* "but it is certainly secondary to the story of a new family finally finding out how to live as one." *Booklist* contributor Philis Wilson also focused on the relevance of Amoss's story for readers interested in a contemporary story about family relations, and praised the author's "poignantly realistic" tone in depicting Lindy's feelings of rejection and rage and their evolution into "a more mature acceptance of the adults in her world."

With *Lost Magic,* Amoss ventures into the realm of fantasy. Set in medieval England, the book tells the story of Ceridwen, an orphan who possesses magical powers. A wisewoman takes Ceridwen in and teaches her about the healing powers of herbs, and when she saves the life of Lord Robert, he gives her a place to live in his castle. The plague and the machinations of a jealous governess land Ceridwen on a witch's pyre, but she frees herself by taking on the form of a bird. A contributor to *Kirkus Reviews* praised Amoss's "convincingly detailed" portrayal of medieval England, while *Booklist's* Deborah Abbott highlighted "deft characterizations, a taut plot, and absorbing conflicts," along with "fast-paced action," in her positive review of *Lost Magic*.

Works Cited

Abbott, Deborah, review of *Lost Magic, Booklist,* November 1, 1993, p. 514.

Davis, Dorothy Salisbury, review of *Secret Lives, New York Times Book Review,* December 16, 1979, pp. 22-23.

Review of *Lost Magic, Kirkus Reviews,* September 1, 1993, p. 1139.

MacDonald, Ruth K., review of *The Mockingbird Song, School Library Journal,* May, 1988, pp. 94-95.

Mercier, Jean, review of *The Great Sea Monster, Publishers Weekly,* October 27, 1975, p. 53.

Miller, Sara, review of *Secret Lives, School Library Journal,* November, 1979, pp. 72-73.

Wilson, Philis, review of *The Mockingbird Song, Booklist,* April 1, 1988, p. 1338.

For More Information See

PERIODICALS

Bulletin of the Center for Children's Books, February, 1988, p. 109.

Horn Book Guide, Spring, 1993, p. 23; Spring, 1994, p. 72; Fall, 1995, p. 238.

Kirkus Reviews, November 1, 1975, p. 1223.

Publishers Weekly, September, 1991, p. 56; November 1, 1993, p. 81.

Quill & Quire, May 1995, p. 51.

School Library Journal, January, 1976, p. 35; February, 1992, p. 70.

*   *   *

ARCHAMBAULT, John

Personal

Born in Pasadena, CA. *Education:* Attended Columbia Teacher's College; University of California, B.A., 1981; graduate study at University of California, Riverside.

Addresses

Home—5616 Glen Haven Ave., Riverside, CA 92506.

Career

Poet, storyteller, and journalist.

Awards, Honors

Irma Simonton Black Honor Book, Bank Street College of Education, 1985, for *The Ghost-Eye Tree;* Children's Choice, International Reading Association and Chil-

dren's Book Council, 1986, for *The Ghost-Eye Tree,* and 1987, for *Barn Dance!;* Notable Children's Trade Book in the field of social studies, Children's Book Council and National Council on the Social Studies, 1987, for *Knots on a Counting Rope;* Picture Book Honor, *Boston Globe,* 1991, for *Chicka Chicka Boom Boom.*

Writings

FOR CHILDREN

Counting Sheep, illustrated by John Rombola, Henry Holt, 1989.

The Birth of a Whale, illustrated by Janet Skiles, Silver Press (Parsippany, NJ), 1996.

(With David Plummer) *The Fox and the Chicken,* illustrated by Marian Young, Silver Press, 1996.

(With Plummer) *Counting Chickens,* illustrated by Liisa Chauncy Guida, Silver Press, 1996.

Grandmother's Garden, illustrated by Raul Colon, Silver Press, 1997.

(With David Plummer) *I Love the Mountains: A Traditional Song,* pictures by Susan Swan, Silver Press, 1998.

"LITTLE SEASHORE BOOKS" SERIES; WITH BILL MARTIN, JR.

A Harvest of Oysters, Encyclopedia Britannica Educational Corporation, 1982.

The Irritable Alligator, Encyclopedia Britannica Educational Corporation, 1982.

The Loggerhead Turtle Crawls Out of the Sea, Encyclopedia Britannica Educational Corporation, 1982.

The Night-Hunting Lobster, Encyclopedia Britannica Educational Corporation, 1982.

A River of Salmon, Encyclopedia Britannica Educational Corporation, 1982.

The Seafaring Seals, Encyclopedia Britannica Educational Corporation, 1982.

The Silent Wetlands Hold Back the Sea, Encyclopedia Britannica Educational Corporation, 1982.

The Singing Whale, Encyclopedia Britannica Educational Corporation, 1982.

A Skyway of Geese, Encyclopedia Britannica Educational Corporation, 1982.

The Sooty Shearwater Flies over the Sea, Encyclopedia Britannica Educational Corporation, 1982.

WITH BILL MARTIN, JR.

The Ghost-Eye Tree, illustrated by Ted Rand, Holt, 1985.

Barn Dance!, illustrated by Rand, Holt, 1986.

White Dynamite and Curly Kidd, illustrated by Rand, Holt, 1986.

Knots on a Counting Rope (originally published by Bill Martin with illustrations by Joe Smith as part of the "Young Owl Books Social Studies Series," Holt, 1966), illustrated by Rand, Holt, 1987.

Here Are My Hands, illustrated by Rand, Holt, 1987.

Up and Down on the Merry-Go-Round, illustrated by Rand, Holt, 1988.

Listen to the Rain, illustrated by James Endicott, Holt, 1988.

The Magic Pumpkin, illustrated by Robert J. Lee, Holt, 1989.

Chicka Chicka Boom Boom, illustrated by Lois Ehlert, Simon & Schuster, 1989.

(Compilers with Peggy Brogan) *Sounds of the Storyteller,* DLM (Allen, TX), 1991.

Words, illustrated by Lois Ehlert, Little Simon (New York), 1993.

A Beautiful Feast for a Big King Cat, illustrated by Bruce Degen, HarperCollins, 1994.

Chicka Chicka Sticka Sticka: An ABC Sticker Book, illustrated by Lois Ehlert, Simon & Schuster, 1995.

Also author of poetry and educational books.

Adaptations

Three videotapes of Archambault and Martin's poems and stories have been produced by DLM Publishers; *Barn Dance!* and *Knots on a Counting Rope* were featured selections on Public Broadcasting Service (PBS-TV) series, *Reading Rainbow,* 1989.

Sidelights

John Archambault, a children's writer dedicated to making reading comfortable, stimulating, and above all, fun for young readers, was an eager reader and writer himself as a child. His professional writing career began when, as a sophomore in high school, he took a part-time job at the Pasadena *Star,* a local newspaper. His good work was quickly rewarded with a full-time position as a reporter, a job he maintained throughout his high-school years. He carried his involvement in writing and journalism into college as the editor of his campus newspaper. While a graduate student at the University of California at Riverside, Archambault met Dr. Bill Martin, a children's writer and educator who had been working on books and educational techniques for children for many years. In the mid-1980s, the two men began working together on children's picture books designed for new readers aged four and up. Since then, Archambault and Martin have enjoyed a productive and

Five times! Ten times! Fifteen! Twenty!
Now spin once again an' that's a-plenty!
But the fat little pigs whirled 'round 'n 'round,
'Till they got so dizzy that they all fell down.

John Archambault and coauthor Bill Martin, Jr. evoke the lively music and movement of a barn dance in their story of a little boy who discovers the barnyard animals' nighttime revelry. *(From* Barn Dance!, *illustrated by Ted Rand.)*

and **I** and **J**
and tag-along **K**,
all on their way
up the coconut tree.

Chicka chicka boom boom!
Will there be enough room?
Look who's coming!
L M N O P!

When the letters of the alphabet attempt to climb a coconut tree, a spirited race ensues. (From Chicka Chicka Boom Boom, *written by Archambault and Martin and illustrated by Lois Ehlert.*)

successful collaboration. They share a strong common interest in the art of storytelling and create books that are meant to be seen and heard, as well as read. They have also combined their efforts in designing innovative ways to help children discover the sheer joy of reading. *Los Angeles Times Book Review* contributor Kristiana Gregory called Archambault and Martin "a valuable duo with much to offer" young readers.

Ghost-Eye Tree was the first publication written by Archambault and Martin with Ted Rand as illustrator—a trio that would go on to produce several popular juvenile books. *Ghost-Eye Tree* is the story of a boy and his sister sent out by their mother for a pail of milk on a dark, windy night. In order to get to the milkman's farm, the children have to go past an old oak tree that the little boy fears is haunted. On their way back, both the boy and his sister, who has been teasing him for being afraid, see the ghost of the tree and flee home. The story "emphasizes the bonds of love and friendship that develop between a brother and sister as they face their fears together," according to *Washington Post Book World* contributor John Cech. Critics praised *Ghost-Eye Tree* for its imaginatively spooky story, its rhythmic readability, and its effective illustrations. *Ghost-Eye Tree* is "a top-notch hair-raiser," noted a reviewer for the *Bulletin of the Center for Children's Books,* who added that "it's

poetry, too, the kind that reaches out to grab you." *Horn Book* commentator Ann A. Flowers concluded that *Ghost-Eye Tree* is perfect for reading aloud.

In their 1986 book *Barn Dance!,* Archambault, Martin, and Rand again present a child's nighttime adventures. A little boy, lying awake in a sleeping farmhouse, hears the unmistakable pluck of a violin. Following his ears to the barn, he finds a scarecrow playing the fiddle and the farm animals dancing. He joins them and dances until dawn. Read aloud, this book sounds like a square dance. With upbeat words and rhythms—"a hummin' an' a-yeein' an' a-rockin' an' a-sockin,'" or "Let's begin! Grab yourself a partner and jump right in!"—the authors mimic the lively music and dance.

The energy of *Barn Dance!* is more than matched by the spiritedness of the trio's *White Dynamite and Curly Kidd,* the story of a girl watching her rodeo-star father ride White Dynamite, "the meanest bull in the whole United States." Once again, the rhythm and tone of the poetry match the frenzied pace of the rodeo: "Oh! Dad's in the rocker now ... floppin' back and forth! His head's goin' south! Bull's goin' north ... twistin' like a corkscrew straight down the right-away. His middle name's Doomsday! U!S!A!" *Los Angeles Times Book Review* contributor Kristiana Gregory summarized that the story "is rousing as a pep rally and meant to be yelled aloud so GET READY."

Knots on a Counting Rope, the trio's best-seller, scored a resounding success with both readers and critics. It is the story of a blind Indian boy who repeatedly asks his grandfather to tell him the tale of his birth and upbringing. The grandfather tells the boy of two great blue horses that looked upon him when he was a weak newborn baby, giving him strength. The elder also relates how the blind child learned to ride his horse by memorizing trails—and even took part in a horse race. Each time he tells the story, the grandfather ties another knot in his rope, assuring his grandson that when the counting rope is filled with knots, the boy will know the story of his own birth by heart. *Los Angeles Times Book Review* contributor Barbara Karlin noted that the aging grandfather "is telling his grandson that he will not always be there to tell the tale, even though his love for the child will last forever." *Knots on a Counting Rope* reflects the passing on of identity, love, and strength through the spoken word. This "dialogue between generations" observed Richard Peck in *Los Angeles Times Book Review,* demonstrates the power of "the oral tradition, the link best forged by families."

With their later collaborations, Archambault and Martin continue to make reading fun for children by dramatizing familiar experiences in appealing ways. In her *Horn Book* critique of *Up and Down on the Merry-Go-Round,* Ellen Fader found Archambault and Martin to be supremely successful in capturing the motion and joy of riding a carousel. The pair's *Chicka Chicka Boom Boom,* also received enthusiastic reviews. "Rap comes to alphabet books," declared *School Library Journal* critic John Philbrook of the book's "engaging rhyme" and "restless, exciting rhythms." And Mary M. Burns, writing in *Horn Book,* called *Chicka Chicka Boom Boom* "one of the liveliest, jazziest alphabet books on record ... Tongue-tingling, visually stimulating ... Absolutely irresistible. Join in, snap your fingers, listen to the beat, let yourself go—and have fun."

In *A Beautiful Feast for a Big King Cat,* a cat catches a little mouse who has been teasing him. Unable to run to his mother like he did before, the small mouse must save himself. Using his cunning, he entices the feline to dream of a delicious feast, and when the cat closes his eyes to picture the food all laid out before him, the mouse runs to safety. "Archambault and Martin's rambunctious plot and lively, rhymed verse are perfectly complimented by the slapstick in Degen's detailed and faintly Victorian illustrations," noted a *Publishers Weekly* reviewer.

In a solo project, *The Birth of a Whale,* Archambault waxes poetically about the birth of a baby humpback out in deep water. While some information is provided about whales, it is Archambault's verse that illuminates the rhythm and grandeur of the humpback. In her review for *Booklist,* Lauren Peterson noted that the author is "more concerned with capturing the grace and majesty of the magnificent creature than with his presenting informa-

tion." Such is the role of the poet. Peter D. Sieruta, a critic for *Horn Book Guide,* described Archambault's writing as a "gentle prose poem . . . most notable for its graceful, rhythmic writing.

Works Cited

Archambault, John, and Bill Martin, Jr., *Barn Dance!,* Holt, 1986.

Archambault, and Martin, *White Dynamite and Curly Kidd,* Holt, 1986.

Review of *A Beautiful Feast for a Big King Cat, Publishers Weekly,* May 30, 1994, p. 55.

Burns, Mary M., review of *Chicka Chicka Boom Boom, Horn Book,* January-February, 1990, p. 54.

Cech, John, "A Palette of Picture Books," *Washington Post Book World,* November 10, 1985, p. 19.

Fader, Ellen, review of *Up and Down on the Merry-Go-Round, Horn Book,* July-August, 1988, p. 483.

Flowers, Ann A., review of *Ghost-Eye Tree, Horn Book,* January/February, 1986, p. 51.

Review of *Ghost-Eye Tree, Bulletin of the Center for Children's Books,* February, 1986, p. 114.

Gregory, Kristiana, review of *White Dynamite and Curly Kidd, Los Angeles Times Book Review,* June 15, 1986, p. 7.

Karlin, Barbara, review of *Knots on a Counting Rope, Los Angeles Times Book Review,* December 6, 1987, p. 7.

Peck, Richard, "Birds, Deserts, Space Insects and a Navajo Grandfather," *Los Angeles Times Book Review,* March 27, 1988, p. 12.

Peterson, Lauren, review of *The Birth of a Whale, Booklist,* March 15, 1996, p. 1265.

Philbrook, John, review of *Chicka Chicka Boom Boom, School Library Journal,* November, 1989, p. 89.

Sieruta, Peter D. review of *The Birth of a Whale, Horn Book Guide,* Fall, 1996, p. 247.

For More Information See

PERIODICALS

Booklist, July, 1994, p. 1952; March, 14, 1996, p. 1265.
Kirkus Reviews, June 15, 1996, p. 906.
Publishers Weekly, May 30, 1994, p. 55.
School Library Journal, July, 1994, p. 73; March, 1996, p. 184; November, 1996, p. 76.*

*   *   *

AZARIAN, Mary 1940-

Personal

Born December 8, 1940, in Washington, DC; daughter of L. G. (self-employed) and Eleanor (self-employed; maiden name, Hatch) Schneider; married Tomas Azarian (a musician), July 24, 1962; children: Ethan, Jesse, Timothy. *Education:* Smith College, B.A., 1963. *Hobbies and other interests:* Gardening, tournament bridge.

Addresses

Home—258 Gray Rd., Plainfield, VT 05667.

Career

Children's book author and illustrator. One-room school teacher in Walden, VT, 1963-67; freelance printmaker and illustrator, 1967.

Awards, Honors

Parent's Choice Award for Illustration, 1983, for *The Tale of John Barleycorn or, From Barley to Beer: A Traditional English Ballad;* Caldecott Medal, Association for Library Service to Children, 1999, Notable Children's Book, American Library Association, Editor's Choice, *Booklist,* Blue Ribbon, *Bulletin of the Center for Children's Books,* Outstanding Science Trade Book for Children, National Science Teachers Association/Children's Book Council, all for *Snowflake Bentley.*

Writings

AUTHOR AND ILLUSTRATOR

A Farmer's Alphabet (for children), Godine (Boston), 1981.
The Tale of John Barleycorn, or, From Barley to Beer: A Traditional English Ballad (for children), Godine, 1982.
Mary Azarian Address Book, Godine, 1983.

ILLUSTRATOR

Marilyn Kluger, *The Wild Flavor,* Coward, 1973.
John Gardner, *The Art of Living and Other Stories,* Knopf, 1981.
Adelma G. Simmons, *The Caprilands Kitchen Book,* Caprilands Press, 1981.
Lorraine Lee, *The Magic Dulcimer,* Yellow Moon, 1983.
Donald Hall, *The Man Who Lived Alone,* Godine, 1984.
Martin Steingesser, *The Wildman: A Short Fable,* Romulus Editions, Coyote Love Press, 1985.
Marilyn Kluger, *Country Kitchens Remembered,* W. Clement Stone, PMA Communications, 1986.
John Hildebidle, *Stubbornness,* New Myths, 1986.
Wolfgang Mieder, *Talk Less and Say More,* New England Press, 1986.
James Hayford, *Gridley Firing,* New England Press, 1987.
Lisa Carlson, *Caring for Your Own Dead,* Upper Access, 1987.
Wolfgang Mieder, *As Sweet as Apple Cider,* New England Press, 1988.
George Shannon, *Sea Gifts,* Godine, 1989.
Wolfgang Mieder, *Not by Bread Alone,* New England Press, 1990.
Mieder, *Salty Wisdom,* New England Press, 1990.
Lorraine L. Hammond, *Barley Break,* Yellow Moon, 1992.
Kate Barnes, *Where the Deer Were,* Godine, 1994.
C. M. Millen, *A Symphony for the Sheep,* Houghton Mifflin, 1996.
Carol P. Saul, *Barn Cat: A Counting Book,* Little, Brown, 1998.

Jacqueline Briggs Martin, *Snowflake Bentley,* Houghton Mifflin, 1998.
Johanna Hurwitz, *Faraway Summer,* Morrow, 1998.

Sidelights

Artist Mary Azarian, considered an accomplished printmaker, was commissioned by the Vermont Board of Education to design and illustrate a children's alphabet book. The resulting work, *The Farmer's Alphabet,* was published in 1981 to favorable reviews. Heralded by *Village Voice* critic Janice Prindle as the "*sine qua non* of any preschooler's library," Azarian's alphabet book was widely praised for its beautifully carved woodcut illustrations depicting scenes of rural life. A reviewer for *Bulletin of the Center for Children's Books* expressed enthusiastic praise for the design of the book, which features "handsomely detailed and composed prints" in black and white and "deep, rich, red" letters. One *Newsweek* reviewer applauded Azarian for including an "informative" introductory note on woodcut technique. According to John Cech of the *Washington Post Book World,* Azarian's woodcuts are "bold," and have the "grainy, 'primitive' texture of old barn board." Cech noted that Azarian presents a "nostalgic" view of farm life, but Patricia Dooley, a contributor to *School Library Journal,* contended that "Azarian eschews the merely cute or quaint, creating a loving memorial to a way of life."

In *The Tale of John Barleycorn, or, From Barley to Beer,* Azarian adapts Robert Burns's humorous ballad in which the transformation of grain into beer parallels the life of John Barleycorn, beginning with a burial (of the seed in the ground), then growing tall (as a grain), followed by a cruel death (in harvesting and grinding the barley for brewing into beer). "The wry humor of the

Mary Azarian's hand-colored woodcuts provide a cat's-eye-view of the creatures who pass by in Carol P. Saul's rhyming counting book. (From Barn Cat.)

Azarian's illustrations enhance Jacqueline Briggs Martin's biography of Wilson Bentley, the nineteenth-century native of Vermont who photographed snowflakes to study their beauty and uniqueness. (*From* Snowflake Bentley.*)*

ballad ... loses none of its yeasty flavor through time," remarked Anne McKeithen in *School Library Journal*, adding that "artistically the book is a success in every way." Azarian's detailed woodcuts for *The Tale of John Barleycorn* also captured much critical attention. The book contains musical notations for singing the text, and a recipe for making beer at home. "This is woodcut-making of a high order," noted a critic for *Kirkus Reviews*, who concluded that, "as an example of the bookmaking art," *The Tale of John Barleycorn* is "an outright winner."

Azarian's award-winning illustrations also grace the pages of Jacqueline Briggs Martin's *Snowflake Bentley,* a biography of a nineteenth-century Vermont man who became the first person to ever photograph a snowflake. The text for *Snowflake Bentley* called for illustrations celebrating a rural Vermont past, a landscape the illustrator was familiar with from her previous work in picture books. "The bold lines that Azarian achieves through woodcuts give these images [of the Vermont

countryside] the look of folkart," noted Mark I. West in *Five Owls*, "but her subtle use of watercolors adds a level of sophistication. She is especially adept at capturing the wintry interplay of blue and white." The illustrations for *Snowflake Bentley* are woodcuts printed with a nineteenth-century handpress and then colored by hand.

Azarian relied on this same method to produce the illustrations for Carol P. Saul's *Barn Cat: A Counting Book,* which "gives the tried-and-true preschool favorites—animals and counting—a fresh new landscape," according to a contributor to *Kirkus Reviews.* Paul's rhyming text teases the imagination of young audiences by repeatedly asking what the cat could be looking for when one grasshopper, two crickets, three butterflies, and so on, pass within reach of the apparently unmoved feline in the barn. Reviewers noted Azarian's expressive portrayal of the cat, which adds to the tension of the story until it is revealed that what the cat is looking for is the saucer of milk being poured for her in the kitchen. "Azarian's woodcut prints ... are outstanding," exclaimed Lauren Peterson in *Booklist,* while a reviewer for Kirkus Reviews intoned, "Azarian's friendly woodcuts, hand-colored in country-fresh hues, give a novel meaning to summer on the farm."

Works Cited

Review of *Barn Cat: A Counting Book, Kirkus Reviews,* July 1, 1998.

Cech, John, review of *The Farmer's Alphabet, Washington Post Book World,* May 10, 1981, p. 13.

Dooley, Patricia, review of *The Farmer's Alphabet, School Library Journal,* September, 1981, p. 102.

Review of *The Farmer's Alphabet, Bulletin of the Center for Children's Books,* October, 1981, p. 21.

Review of *The Farmer's Alphabet, Newsweek,* December 7, 1981, p. 98.

McKeithen, Anne, review of *The Tale of John Barleycorn, or, From Barley to Beer: A Traditional English Ballad, School Library Journal,* April, 1983, p. 97.

Peterson, Lauren, review of *Barn Cat: A Counting Book, Booklist,* September 15, 1998.

Prindle, Janice, review of *The Farmer's Alphabet, Village Voice,* December 9, 1981, p. 56.

Review of *The Tale of John Barleycorn, or, From Barley to Beer: A Traditional English Ballad, Kirkus Reviews,* December 15, 1982, p. 1335.

West, Mark I., review of *Snowflake Bentley, Five Owls,* March-April, 1999, p. 81.

For More Information See

PERIODICALS

Horn Book, June, 1983, p. 287.
New York Times Book Review, December 1, 1985, p. 39.

B

BAMBARA, Toni Cade 1939-1995
(Toni Cade)

Personal

Surname originally Cade, name legally changed in 1970;
born March 25, 1939, in New York, NY; died of cancer,
December, 1995; daughter of Helen Brent Henderson
Cade; children: Karma (daughter). *Education:* Queens
College (now Queens College of the City University of
New York), B.A., 1959; attended Ecole de Mime
Etienne Decroux (Paris), and Commedia dell'Arte, both
1961, and University of Florence; City College of the
City University of New York, M.A., 1964; attended
New York University and New School for Social
Research. Also attended Katherine Dunham Dance
Studio, Syvilla Fort School of Dance, Clark Center of
Performing Arts, 1958-69, and Studio Museum of
Harlem Film Institute, 1970.

Career

Freelance writer and lecturer. New York State Department of Welfare, social investigator, 1959-61; Department of Psychiatry, Metropolitan Hospital, New York
City, director of recreation, 1961-62; Colony House
Community Center, New York City, program director,
1962-65; English instructor in SEEK Program, City
College of the City University of New York, New York
City, 1965-69, and New Careers Program, Newark, NJ,
1969-74; Livingston College, Rutgers University, New
Brunswick, NJ, assistant professor, 1969-71, associate
professor, 1971-74; visiting professor of African-American studies, Duke University, Durham, NC, 1974, and
Stephens College, Columbia, MO, 1975; Neighborhood
Arts Center, Atlanta, GA, artist-in-residence, 1975-79;
Atlanta University, visiting professor, 1977, research
mentor and instructor, School of Social Work, 1977,
1979; Spelman College, Atlanta, writer-in-residence,
1978-79.

Founder and director of Pamoja Writers Collective,
1976-85. Production artist-in-residence for Neighborhood Arts Center, 1975-79, Stephens College, 1976, and
Spelman College, 1978-79. Production consultant,
WHYY-TV, Philadelphia, PA. Conducted numerous
workshops on writing, self-publishing, and community
organizing for community centers, museums, prisons,
libraries, and universities. Lectured and conducted
literary readings at numerous institutions, including the
Library of Congress, Smithsonian Institute, Afro-American Museum of History and Culture, and other organizations and universities. Humanities consultant to New
Jersey Department of Corrections, 1974, Institute of
Language Arts, New York Institute for Human Services
Training, 1978, and Emory University, 1980. Art

Toni Cade Bambara

consultant to New York State Arts Council, 1974, Georgia State Arts Council, 1976, 1981, National Endowment for the Arts, 1980, and the Black Arts South Conference, 1981. Member of advisory board, Sojourner Productions, *Black Film Review, Essence,* and Black International Cinema (Berlin/Bedford-Stuyvesant). *Member:* National Association of Third World Writers, Screen Writers Guild of America, African-American Film Society, Southern Collective of African American Writers (founding member), Sisters in Support of South African Sisterhood.

Awards, Honors

Peter Pauper Press Journalism Award, *Long Island Star* (NY), 1958; John Golden Award for Fiction, Queens College (now Queens College of the City University of New York), 1959; Theatre of Black Experience Award, 1969, for service; Outstanding Book of the Year, *New York Times,* 1972, for *Tales and Stories for Black Folks;* Rutgers University research fellowship, 1972; Black Child Development Institute Service Award, 1973, for service to Black children; Black Rose Award, *Encore,* 1973, for short story "Gorilla, My Love"; Black Community Award, Livingston College, Rutgers University, 1974, for service to students; award from National Association of Negro Business and Professional Women's Club League, for service to Black women; George Washington Carver Distinguished African American Lecturer Award, Simpson College; Achievement in the Arts award, *Ebony,* Black Arts Award, University of Missouri; National Endowment for the Arts Individual Literature Grant, 1981; American Book Award, 1981, for *The Salt Eaters;* Best Documentary Award, Pennsylvania Association of Broadcasters, and Documentary Award, National Black Programming Consortium, both 1986, both for *The Bombing of Osage;* Langston Hughes Medallion, Langston Hughes Society of City College of New York, 1986; Zora Hurston Award, Morgan State College, 1986; nominated for Black Caucus of the American Library Association Literary Award, 1997, for *Deep Sightings and Rescue Missions: Fiction, Essays, and Conversations.*

Writings

FICTION

Gorilla, My Love (short stories), Random House, 1972.
The Sea Birds Are Still Alive: Collected Stories, Random House, 1977.
The Salt Eaters (novel), Random House, 1980.
If Blessings Come (novel), Random House, 1987.
Raymond's Run (for children), Creative Education (Mankato, MN), 1990.
Those Bones Are Not My Child, Pantheon, 1999.

SCREENPLAYS

Zora, produced by WGBH-TV, 1971.
The Johnson Girls, produced by National Educational Television, 1972.
Transactions, produced by School of Social Work, Atlanta University, 1979.

The Long Night, produced by American Broadcasting Company (ABC), 1981.
Epitaph for Willie, produced by K. Heran Productions, 1982.
Tar Baby (based on Toni Morrison's novel), produced by Sanger/Brooks Film Productions, 1984.
Raymond's Run, produced by Public Broadcasting System (PBS), 1985.
The Bombing of Osage, produced by WHYY-TV, 1986.
Cecil B. Moore: Master Tactician of Direct Action, produced by WHYY-TV, 1987.

OTHER

(Editor and contributor, as Toni Cade) *The Black Woman: An Anthology,* New American Library, 1970.
(Editor and contributor) *Tales and Stories for Black Folks,* Doubleday, 1971.
(With Leah Wise) *Southern Black Utterances Today,* Institute for Southern Studies (Durham, NC), 1975.
(Author of preface) Cecelia Smith, *Cracks,* Select Press, 1980.
(Author of foreword) Cherrie Moraga and Gloria Anzaldua, editors, *This Bridge Called My Back: Writings by Radical Women of Color,* Persephone Press (Watertown, MA), 1981.
(Author of foreword) *The Sanctified Church: Collected Essays by Zora Neale Hurston,* Turtle Island (Berkeley, CA), 1982.
Toni Morrison, editor, *Deep Sightings and Rescue Missions: Fiction, Essays, and Conversations,* Pantheon, 1996.
(Author and narrator with Amiri Buraka, Wesley Brown, and Thulani Davis) *W. E. B. Du Bois: A Biography in Four Voices* (film), produced in association with Scribe Video Center, 1996.

Contributor to numerous books, including: *Black Expression: Essays by and about Black Americans in the Creative Arts,* edited by Gayle Addison, Jr., Weybright, 1969; *Black and White in American Culture,* edited by Jules Chametsky, University of Massachusetts Press, 1970; Ruth Miller, *Backgrounds to Blackamerican Literature,* Chandler Publishing, 1971; *The Writer on Her Work,* edited by Janet Sternburg, Norton, 1980; *On Essays: A Reader for Writers,* edited by Paul H. Connolloy, Harper, 1981; *Women Working,* edited by Florence Howe, Feminist Press, 1982; *Black Women Writers (1950-1980): A Critical Evaluation,* edited by Mari Evans, Doubleday, 1984; *Confirmations,* edited by Baraka and Baraka, Morrow, 1984; *The Black Writer at Work,* edited by Claudia Tate, Howard University Press, 1984. Contributor to *What's Happenin', Somethin' Else,* and *Another Eye* (readers), Scott, Foresman, 1969-70. Contributor of articles and book and film reviews to periodicals, including *Massachusetts Review, Negro Digest, Liberator, Prairie Schooner, Redbook, New York Times, Ms., Callaloo, First World, Audience, Black Works, Umbra,* and *Onyx.* Guest editor of special issue of *Southern Exposure* devoted to new southern black writers and visual artists, summer, 1976.

Bambara's works have been translated into six languages.

Adaptations

Three of Bambara's short stories, "Gorilla, My Love," "Medley," and "Witchbird," were adapted for film. Selections of Bambara's work, read by the author, were recorded on audiocassette.

Sidelights

Before her death in 1995, Toni Cade Bambara was well known as an activist dedicated to expanding the profile of both African-American culture and black women in literature. A professor of English and African-American studies at several universities, she was editor of several anthologies of black literature, and the author of short stories, film scripts, the children's book *Raymond's Run,* and the adult novels *The Salt Eaters* and *If Blessings Come.* Her fiction is infused with the sounds of city streets and the musical inflections of jazz, and her style has been described by critics as both complex and unique. More active as a lecturer than a teacher, Bambara once acknowledged to interviewer Kay Bonetti that her ideal audience was "really the people. The audience that gives me the most feedback tends to be folks I run across in the wash house or on the bus or on a train or just sort of traveling around. People who write letters usually on back of something. And I think it's because their response is straight.... The community that calls me sister or daughter or Mama can make or break me because it's only that group that I'm serving. If that audience is not reached there's almost no point in doing it."

Born in New York City on March 25, 1939, Bambara was raised in Harlem, Bedford-Stuyvesant, and other ethnic urban neighborhoods. Her mother, who had come of age during the flowering of African-American culture known as the Harlem Renaissance, encouraged her daughter's desire for creative expression. Educated in both public and private schools, Bambara credited her mother for much of her success. "She gave me permission to wonder, to dawdle, to daydream ...," the author recalled to interviewer Claudia Tate in *Black Women Writers at Work.* "She thought it was wonderful that I could write things that almost made some kind of sense. She used to walk me over to Seventh Avenue and 125th Street and point out the shop where J. A. Rogers, the historian, was knocking out books. She used to walk me over to the Speaker's Corner to listen to the folks. Of course, if they were talking 'religious stuff,' she'd keep on going to wherever we were going; but if they were talking union or talking race, we'd hang tough on the corner."

Bambara fell in love with writing as a young girl, and completed her first story as a kindergartner. "I began scribbling tales on strips from my daddy's *Daily News,*" she recalled in *Black Women Writers (1950-1980).* "Then, I'd wait by the bedroom door, chewing on a number two pencil, for those white sturdy squares my mama's stockings came wrapped around. I'd fashion two-part, six-block-long sagas to get my classmates to and from P.S. 186." As she advanced in grade-level, she

Bambara paints compelling portraits of a wide range of African-American characters in her collection of fifteen short stories. (Cover illustration by Richard Taddei.)

also soaked up the conversations of people around her—street talk, dinner-table discussions, gossip between friends. Developing an ear for the spoken word, she graduated to writing plays for her classes at school. As she would later note in *Sturdy Black Bridges,* "there was a certain amount of applause that could be gotten if you turned up with the Frederick Douglass play for Negro History Week or the George Washington Carver play for the assembly program. That talent for bailing the English teachers out created stardom, and that became another motive."

Moving frequently with her family, Bambara grew into a very self-reliant young woman. She also developed an independent spirit that would eventually translate into a feminist stance, and had many role models to learn from. "In every neighborhood I lived in there were always two types of women that somehow pulled me and sort of got their wagons in a circle around me," Bambara later told an interviewer in *Sturdy Black Bridges.* "I call them Miss Naomi and Miss Gladys,.... The Miss Naomi types were usually barmaids or life-women, nighttime people with lots of clothes in the closet and a very particular philosophy of life, who would give me advice like, 'When you meet a man, have a birthday, demand a present that's hockable, and be careful.' Stuff like that.... The Miss Naomis usually gave me a great deal of advice about beautification, how to take care of your health and not get too fat. The Miss Gladyses were usually the type that hung out the window in Apartment 1-A leaning on the pillow giving single-action advice on numbers or giving you advice about how to get your homework done or telling you to stay away from those cruising cars that moved through the neighborhood patrolling little girls.... It was those women who had the most influence on the writing."

After graduating from high school, Bambara enrolled at New York City's Queen's College, graduating in 1959 with a B.A. in theater arts and English. Publishing her first short story, "Sweet Town," during her senior year,

TONI CADE BAMBARA

THE SALT EATERS

"A powerful piece of writing."
— Anne Tyler, <u>Washington Post Book World</u>

Two African-American women are brought together when one of them attempts suicide and the other recognizes her friend's fragile state. (Cover illustration by Richard Taddei.)

she also won the Pauper Press Journalism Award from the *Long Island Star*. Moving on to advanced studies, Bambara took graduate courses in modern American fiction at City College in New York City, while also working as a social investigator for the New York State Department of Welfare.

From 1961 to 1963 she traveled to Europe, studying at schools in Italy and France before returning to New York City. In 1964 Bambara received an M.A. in English, enabling her to teach at the college level, and in 1969 she became an assistant professor at Livingston State College of Rutgers University in New Jersey. A year later her daughter Karma was born. During this same time she adopted the surname "Bambara," part of a signature she discovered on a sketchbook in her great-grandmother's trunk. It would be under this name that she would publish her first book, *The Black Woman,* an anthology of poetry, short stories and essays by African-American women that was one of the first books of its kind. Bambara's second anthology, *Tales and Stories for Black Folks,* appeared soon after. The book is divided into two halves; the first half contains short fiction by noted writers like Alice Walker, Pearl Crayton, and Langston Hughes, and the second contains stories by talented students in Bambara's college classes.

In 1972 Bambara's short-story collection, *Gorilla, My Love,* was released. A contributor to *Saturday Review,* praised the stories for their "breezy, engaging style," and counted them "among the best portraits of black life to have appeared in some time." Gale Chevigny also lauded Bambara's debut, noting in her *Village Voice* review that the stories are "lavish in their strokes—there are elaborate illustrations, soaring asides, aggressive sub-plots.... they abound in far-out common sense, exotic home truths." "There are certain kinds of spirits that I'm *very* appreciative of, people who are very tough, but very compassionate," Bambara once commented about the protagonist of the book's title story. "You put me in any neighborhood, in any city, and I will tend to gravitate toward that type. The kid in 'Gorilla' is a kind of person who will survive, and she's triumphant in her survival. Mainly because she's so very human, she cries, her caring is not careless. She certainly is not autobiographical except that there are naturally aspects of my own personality that I very much like that are similar to hers. She's very much like people I like."

During the seventies, Bambara continued writing short fiction, publishing her second short-story collection, *The Sea Birds Are Still Alive,* in 1977. Many of these stories take place in black urban neighborhoods and feature the street talk that frequently peppers Bambara's work, a language that Anne Tyler praised highly in the *Washington Post Book World:* "Everything these people say, you feel, ordinary, real-life people are saying right now on any street corner. It's only that the rest of us didn't realize it was sheer poetry they were speaking."

While serving as artist-in-residence at Spelman College in Atlanta in the late 1970s, Bambara began working on the first of her two novels. "I began the novel *The Salt*

Eaters the way a great many of my writings begin, as a journal entry," the author recalled to Tate. "Several of us had been engaged in trying to organize various sectors of the community—students, writers, psychic adepts, etc.—and I was struck by the fact that our activists ... don't even talk to each other.... The novel, then, came out of a problem-solving impulse—what would it take to bridge the gap, to merge those frames of reference, to fuse those camps? I thought I was just making notes for organizing; I thought I was just exploring my feelings, insights. Next thing I knew, the thing took off and I no longer felt inclined to invest time and energy on the streets."

The Salt Eaters focuses on two African-American women and their relationship with each other. Despite their differences, the women are brought together when one of them attempts to commit suicide, alerting the other to her fragile state and leading to a strong friendship. The novel, which Bambara penned in a dreamy, sometimes poetic, sometimes jivey style, touches on many aspects of mid-twentieth century politics and society, including racism and violence. This focus is characteristic of much of Bambara's work; as John Wideman noted in the *New York Times Book Review,* in both her writing and her lectures, Bambara "emphasizes the necessity for black people to maintain their best traditions, to remain healthy and whole as they struggle for political power. *The Salt Eaters* ... eloquently summarizes and extends [these] abiding concerns." Bambara's second novel, *If Blessings Come,* would continue to reflect this focus.

Combining her background in dance and theater with her writing, Bambara began to work on screenplays and plays in the 1980s, and produced several television documentaries. "My interests have evolved," she explained to Tate of her transition from novelist to scriptwriter. "I no longer have the patience to sit it out in the solitude of my backroom, all by my lonesome self, knocking out books. I'm much more at home with a crew swapping insights, brilliancies, pooling resources, information." The camaraderie of filmmaking proved beneficial to Bambara; in 1986 she won Documentary Awards from the Pennsylvania Association of Broadcasters and the National Black Programming Consortium, both for *The Bombing of Osage,* a drama based on an incident in Philadelphia where lethal force was used by police against a group of black militants.

Working in a variety of genres, Bambara often found herself working on several projects at once. "The actual sit-down work is still weird to me," she admitted to Tate. "I babble along, heading I think in one direction, only to discover myself tugged in another, or sometimes I'm absolutely snatched into an alley. I write in longhand, or what kin and friends call deranged hieroglyphics.... I usually work it over and beat it up and sling it around the room a lot before I get to the type stage. I hate to type—hate, hate—so things get cut mercilessly at that stage. I stick the thing in a drawer or pin it on a board for a while, maybe read it to someone or a group, get some feedback, mull it over, and put it aside. Then, [later], ...

I'll very studiously sit down, edit, type, and send the damn thing out before it drives me crazy."

When asked by Bonetti why she became a writer, Bambara answered: "I'm compelled to write. It's my meditation. Some people have mantras; others go to therapists. Different people have different ways to maintain a balance of sanity. I write because I must. If I didn't I'd probably be homicidal in two weeks. I write because I've got hold of something. If I write I may save somebody else some time—might lift someone's spirits. I don't write because it's a career. If there were no more presses, no more publishing houses, I'd still be writing."

Works Cited

Bambara, Toni Cade, "Salvation Is the Issue," *Black Women Writers (1950-1980): A Critical Evaluation,* edited by Mari Evans, Anchor Books, 1984.

Bonetti, Kay, *The Organizer's Wife: A Reading by and Interview with Toni Cade Bambara* (recording), American Audio Prose Library, 1982.

Chevigny, Gale, review of *Gorilla, My Love, Village Voice,* April 12, 1973, p. 39.

Review of *Gorilla, My Love, Saturday Review,* November 18, 1972.

Guy-Sheftall, Beverly, and others, "Commitment: Toni Cade Bambara Speaks," *Sturdy Black Bridges: Visions of Black Women in Literature,* Anchor Books, 1979.

Tate, Claudia, "Toni Cade Bambara," *Black Women Writers at Work,* Continuum, 1983.

Tyler, Anne, review of *The Salt Eaters, Washington Post Book World,* March 30, 1980, p. 1.

Wideman, John, review of *The Salt Eaters, New York Times Book Review,* June 1, 1980, p. 14.

For More Information See

BOOKS

Black Literature Criticism, Gale, 1990.

Butler-Evans, Elliot, *Race, Gender, and Desire: Narrative Strategies in the Fiction of Toni Cade Bambara, Toni Morrison, and Alice Walker,* Temple University Press, 1989.

Notable Black American Women, Gale, 1992.

Prenshaw, Peggy Whitman, editor, *Women Writers of the Contemporary South,* University Press of Mississippi, 1984.

PERIODICALS

Voice Literary Supplement, October, 1992, p. 24.

Women's Review of Books, July, 1997, p. 31.*

*   *   *

BATEMAN, Teresa 1957-

Personal

Born December 6, 1957 in Moscow, ID; daughter of Donald S. (a financial consultant) and Peggy L. (a homemaker) Bateman. *Education:* Ricks College, Associate of Arts and Sciences, 1978; Brigham Young

Teresa Bateman

University, B.S., 1982; University of Washington, M.A. (Library and Information Science), 1987. *Religion:* Church of Jesus Christ of Latter-Day Saints.

Addresses

Home—2501 57th Ave. NE, Tacoma, WA 98422. *Office*—Brigadoon Elementary School, 3601 SW 336th St., Federal Way, WA 98023. *E-mail*—Teresa-Bateman@fwsd.wednet.edu.

Career

Writer. Federal Way School District, Federal Way, WA, Librarian, 1987-1999. *Member:* Society of Children's Book Writers and Illustrators, Washington Educators Association, Washington Library Media Association.

Awards, Honors

Merit Award, *Society of Children's Book Writers and Illustrators Magazine,* 1993, for "Traveling Tom & the Leprechaun"; "The Alien" was a winner of the *Highlights* Fiction Contest in 1994; Paul A. Witty Short Story Award, 1997, for "Trapped in the Arctic"; Storytelling World Award and Governor's Writers Award, both 1998, both for *The Ring of Truth: An Original Irish Tale.*

Writings

FOR CHILDREN

The Ring of Truth: An Original Irish Tale, illustrated by Omar Rayyan, Holiday House, 1997.
Leprechaun Gold, illustrated by Rosanne Litzinger, Holiday House, 1998.

Regular contributor to *Cricket Magazine;* contributes reviews to the *Puget Sound Council* and *School Library Journal.*

Work in Progress

The Mer-Baby, Harp O' Gold, and a non-fiction book on patriotic symbols, all for Holiday House; *Farm Flu* and *The Princesses Have a Ball,* both for Albert Whitman.

Sidelights

Teresa Bateman told *SATA:* "I was raised in a family of ten children. My mother made a point of reading to us at every opportunity, especially on long car trips. As a result, we are all voracious readers. There are few things that delight me more than a well-written book. Perhaps that's one of the reasons why I decided to write.

"I've always been a storyteller, When I was a teen-ager I had to share a bedroom with a younger sister who always 'ratted me out' to my parents when I stayed up past bedtime, reading. I used to tell her stories about a bear that lived in the closet and liked to eat succulent young things. I, naturally, was too old and stringy . . .

"As the years went by I continued making up stories. Now I tell them to my many nieces and nephews. Eventually I thought it would be fun to write them down and see if they were publishable. I am now the owner of an ENORMOUS stack of rejection letters. (I'm so proud . . .) However, I also have had many things published. I don't let rejection discourage me. I write because I love to write. I'd still write even if none of my stories ever got published. Writing is as much a part of me as breathing. I write each day, without fail. Some days I write a lot. Some days I write a little, but I write EVERY day.

"One of the things I enjoy most is doing research for non-fiction articles and books. To me, research is a blast. I love going to the University of Washington Seseli library and pulling out microfilm, or prowling through stacks of old books. I find the strangest things that way—odd facts that tickle my fancy. Doing the research is often just as much fun as doing the writing! Being a librarian also helps. I'm surrounded by books and children every day. It's a great combination."

Bateman's first book, *The Ring of Truth: An Original Irish Tale,* is the story of Patrick O'Kelly, a peddler who tells impressive tales as a way to keep people buying his wares. Patrick makes the mistake of bragging that he can "spout better blarney" than the king of the leprechauns, which causes the king to become upset and give Patrick

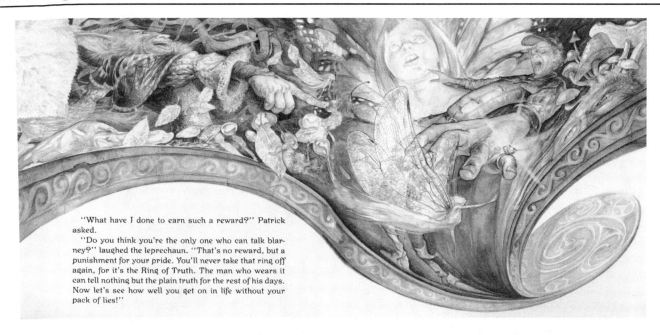

"What have I done to earn such a reward?" Patrick asked.

"Do you think you're the only one who can talk blarney?" laughed the leprechaun. "That's no reward, but a punishment for your pride. You'll never take that ring off again, for it's the Ring of Truth. The man who wears it can tell nothing but the plain truth for the rest of his days. Now let's see how well you get on in life without your pack of lies!"

In Bateman's merry tale, Patrick O'Kelly unexpectedly wins a blarney contest even after the King of the Leprechauns gives Patrick a ring which forces him to tell the truth. (From The Ring of the Truth, *illustrated by Omar Rayyan.)*

a ring which will force him to tell the truth. In a twist, Patrick ends up winning a blarney contest by telling the true story of his meeting with the leprechaun king. A *Kirkus Reviews* critic wrote, "Bateman's first book is a beautifully layered, consistently sprightly take on the notion that truth is stranger than fiction," while a *Publishers Weekly* critic noted, "Epitomizing the best of Irish storytelling, this blithe debut pokes fun at its own blustery genre." Beth Tegart, writing for *School Library Journal,* concluded, "This is a well-crafted tale told with a storyteller's touch; the language flows, and the story satisfies."

Leprechaun Gold is Bateman's story of Donald O'Dell, a kindhearted handyman who rescues a leprechaun from drowning. As a reward, the leprechaun offers Donald gold, but Donald refuses, saying he doesn't need it. The leprechaun, who refuses to take no for an answer, leaves the gold in Donald's pockets, on his doorstep, and in Donald's shoes, but each time Donald returns the gold. The leprechaun ends up tricking the lonely Donald into meeting a similarly lonely beautiful woman with golden hair and a golden heart, ensuring that Donald does receive gold. April Judge, in a review for *Booklist,* declared, "This well-crafted story is told in a robust, lively manner.... a top-notch candidate for reading aloud." A critic for *Kirkus Reviews* stated, "This charming tale has an Irish lilt that would certainly withstand an energetic reading out loud—and not just on St. Patrick's Day."

Bateman commented on her Irish themes to *SATA:* "Many people ask me why I write so many Irish stories. My father says that one of our family lines goes back to Ireland. I've always loved Irish stories, and I enjoy telling them to my students. In fact, during the week of St. Patrick's Day I pick up an Irish accent that follows me around for weeks. It's usually in March that I write my best leprechaun stories.

"Writing is so much a part of me that I cannot imagine my life without it. Most important, however, writing is fun for me. It's often hard work, but it's still a lot of fun."

Works Cited

Judge, April, review of *Leprechaun Gold, Booklist,* August, 1998, p. 2012.

Review of *Leprechaun Gold, Kirkus Reviews,* March 15, 1998, p. 398.

Review of *The Ring of Truth, Kirkus Reviews,* February 1, 1997, p. 218.

Review of *The Ring of Truth, Publishers Weekly,* February 24, 1997, p. 91.

Tegart, Beth, review of *The Ring of Truth, School Library Journal,* May, 1997, p. 92.

For More Information See

PERIODICALS

Bulletin of the Center for Children's Books, May, 1997, p. 313.

Horn Book, July-August, 1998, p. 470.

School Library Journal, June, 1998, p. 94.*

BELLOC, (Joseph) Hilaire (Pierre Sebastien Rene Swanton) 1870-1953 (Joseph Peter Rene Hilaire Belloc; Joseph Pierre Hilaire Belloc)

Personal

Born July 27, 1870, in Le Celle St. Cloud, France; died July 16, 1953, in King's Land, England; son of Louis Swanton Belloc (a lawyer) and Elizabeth Parkes Belloc (a political activist and promoter of women's rights); married Elodie Agnes Hogan, June 16, 1896; children: Louis, Eleanor, Elizabeth, Hilary, Peter. *Education:* Balliol College, Oxford, B.A. (first class), 1895. *Religion:* Roman Catholic.

Career

Author, poet, and essayist. Member of British parliament, 1906-07. Made several lecture tours of the United States with G. K. Chesterton. *Military service:* Joined the French Army, 1891; served in the Eighth Regiment of Artillery at Toul, France.

Awards, Honors

Knight Commander of the Order of St. Gregory the Great, conferred by Pope Pius XI, 1934; honorary degrees from Glasgow and Dublin Universities.

Writings

Verses and Sonnets, Ward & Downey, 1896.
The Bad Child's Book of Beasts, Dutton, 1896.
Syllabus of a Course of Six Lectures on the French Revolution, American Society for the Extension of University Teaching, 1896.
Syllabus of a Course of Six Lectures on the Crusades, American Society for the Extension of University Teaching, 1896.
Syllabus of a Course of Six Lectures on Representative Frenchmen, American Society for the Extension of University Teaching, 1896.
Syllabus of a Course of Six Lectures on Paris, American Society for the Extension of University Teaching, 1897.
More Beasts (For Worse Children), Arnold, 1897.
The Modern Traveller, Arnold, 1898.
Danton: A Study, Nisbet, 1899.
A Moral Alphabet, Arnold, 1899.
Lambkin's Remains (published anonymously), Proprietors of the J. R. C., 1900.
Paris, Arnold, 1900.
Robespierre: A Study, Nisbet, 1901.
The Path to Rome, Allen, 1902.
The Aftermath; or, Gleanings from a Busy Life ... Caliban's Guide to Letters, Duckworth, 1903.
The Great Inquiry (Only Authorized Version) Faithfully Reported by H. B. ... and Ornamented with Sharp Cuts on the Spot by G. K. C., Duckworth, 1903.
Avril: Being Essays on the Poetry of the French Renaissance, Duckworth, 1904.

Hilaire Belloc

Emmanuel Burden, Merchant, of Thames St., in the City of London: A Record of his Lineage, Speculations, Last Days and Death, Methuen, 1904.
The Old Road, Constable, 1904.
Esto Perpetua: Algerian Studies and Impressions, Duckworth, 1906.
Hills and the Sea, Methuen, 1906.
The Historic Thames, Dent, 1907.
Cautionary Tales for Children, Designed for the Admonition of Children between the Ages of Eight and Fourteen Years, Nash, 1908.
An Examination of Socialism, Catholic Truth Society, 1908.
On Nothing and Kindred Spirits, Methuen, 1908.
Mr. Clutterbuck's Election, Nash, 1908.
The Eye-Witness: Being a Series of Descriptions and Sketches in Which It Is Attempted to Reproduce Certain Incidents and Periods in History, as from the Testimony of a Person Present at Each, Nash, 1908.
The Pyrenees, Methuen, 1909.
A Change in the Cabinet, Methuen, 1909.
Marie Antoinette, Methuen, 1909.
On Everything, Methuen, 1909.
On Anything, Constable, 1910.
Pongo and the Bull, Constable, 1910.
On Something, Methuen, 1910.
Verses, Duckworth, 1910.
(With Cecil Chesterton) *The Party System,* Swift, 1911.
First and Last, Methuen, 1911.
The Battle of Blenheim, Swift, 1911.

Malplaquet, Swift, 1911.

Socialism and the Servile State: A Debate between Messrs. Hilaire Belloc and J. Ramsay MacDonald, South West London Federation of the Independent Labour Party, 1911.

Waterloo, Swift, 1912.

The Four Men: A Farrago, Nelson, 1912.

The Green Overcoat, Arrowsmith, 1912.

Tourcoing, Swift, 1912.

Warfare in England, Williams and Norgate, 1912.

This and That and the Other, Methuen, 1912.

The Servile State, Foulis, 1912.

The River of London, Foulis, 1912.

Crecy, Swift, 1912.

The Stane Street: A Monograph, Constable, 1913.

The Book of the Bayeux Tapestry, Presenting the Complete Work in a Series of Colour Fascimiles: The Introduction and Narrative by Hilaire Belloc, Chatto and Windus, 1913.

Poitiers, Rees, 1913.

The History of England from the First Invasion by the Romans to the Accession of King George the Fifth, volume two, Catholic Publication Society of America, 1915.

A General Sketch of the European War, two volumes, Nelson, 1915, 1916, also published as *The Elements of the Great War,* two volumes, Hearst's International Library, 1915, 1916.

High Lights of the French Revolution, Century, 1915.

A Picked Company: Being a Selection from the Writings of H. Belloc, Methuen, 1915.

The Two Maps of Europe and Some Other Aspects of the Great War, Pearson, 1915.

At the Sign of the Lion, and Other Essays from the Books of Hilaire Belloc, Mosher, 1916.

The Second Year of the War, Burrup, Mathieson, and Sprague, 1916.

The Last Days of the French Monarchy: With Many Illustrations from Paintings and Prints, Chapman and Hall, 1916.

Anti-Catholic History: How It Is Written, Catholic Truth Society, 1918.

The Free Press, Allen and Unwin, 1918.

Europe and the Faith, Constable, 1920.

The House of Commons and Monarchy, Allen and Unwin, 1920.

Pascal's "Provincial Letters," Catholic Truth Society, 1921.

The Jews, Constable, 1922.

The Mercy of Allah, Chatto and Windus, 1922.

On, Methuen, 1923.

Sonnets and Verse, Duckworth, 1923; enlarged edition, 1938.

The Contrast, Arrowsmith, 1923.

The Road, C. W. Hobson, 1923.

The Campaign of 1812 and the Retreat from Moscow, Nelson, 1924, also published as *Napoleon's Campaign of 1812 and the Retreat from Moscow,* Harper, 1926.

Economics for Helen, Arrowsmith, 1924, republished as *Economics for Young People: An Explanation of Capital, Labour, Wealth, Money, Production, Exchange, and Business, Domestic and International,* Putnam's, 1925.

The Cruise of the "Nona," Constable, 1925.

A History of England, four volumes, Methuen, 1925-1931.

Mr. Petre: A Novel, Arrowsmith, 1925.

Miniatures of French History, Nelson, 1925.

Short Talks with the Dead and Others, Cayme Press, 1926.

The Emerald of Catherine the Great, Arrowsmith, 1926.

A Companion to Mr. Wells's "Outline of History," Sheed and Ward, 1926.

The Catholic Church and History, Burns, Oates, and Washburn, 1926.

The Highway and Its Vehicles, edited by Geoffrey Holme, The Studio Limited, 1926.

Mr. Belloc Still Objects to Mr. Wells's "Outline of History," Sheed and Ward, 1926.

Mrs. Markham's New History of England: Being an Introduction for Young People to the Current History and Institutions of Our Time, Cayme, 1926.

The Haunted House, Arrowsmith, 1927.

Oliver Cromwell, Benn, 1927.

Towns of Destiny, McBride, 1927, republished as *Many Cities,* Constable, 1928.

James the Second, Faber and Gwyer, 1928.

How the Reformation Happened, Cape, 1928.

But Soft—We are Observed!, Arrowsmith, also published as *Shadowed!,* Harper, 1929.

A Conversation with an Angel and Other Essays, Cape, 1928.

Belinda: A Tale of Affection in Youth and Age, Constable, 1928.

The Chanty of the Nona, Faber and Gwyer, 1928.

Do We Agree? A Debate Between G. K. Chesterton and Bernard Shaw, with Hilaire Belloc in the Chair, Mitchell, 1928.

Survivals and New Arrivals: The Old and New Enemies of the Catholic Church, Sheed and Ward, 1929.

Joan of Arc, Cassell, 1929.

The Missing Masterpiece: A Novel, Arrowsmith, 1929.

Richlieu: A Study, Lippincott, 1929.

Wolsey, Cassell, 1930.

The Man Who Made Gold, Arrowsmith, 1931.

New Cautionary Tales: Verses, Duckworth, 1930.

(With others) *Why I Am and Why I Am Not a Catholic,* Macmillan, 1930.

A Conversation with a Cat and Others, Cassell, 1931.

Essays of a Catholic Layman in England, Sheed and Ward, 1931, also published as *Essays of a Catholic,* Macmillan, 1931.

Cranmer, Cassell, 1931, also published as *Cranmer: Archbishop of Canterbury, 1533-1556,* Lippincott, 1931.

Nine Nines; or, Novenas from a Chinese Litany of Odd Numbers, Blackwell, 1931.

On Translation, Clarendon Press, 1931.

Six British Battles, Arrowsmith, 1931.

Usury, Sheed and Ward, 1931.

An Heroic Poem in Praise of Wine, Davies, 1932.

Ladies and Gentlemen, for Adults Only and Mature Ones at That, Duckworth, 1932.

The Question and the Answer, Bruce, 1932.

Saulieu of the Morvan, Ludowici-Celadon, 1932.

The Postmaster-General, Arrowsmith, 1932.

Napoleon, Cassell, 1932.

The Tactics and Strategy of the Great Duke of Marlborough, Arrowsmith, 1933.

Charles the First, King of England, Cassell, 1933.

William the Conqueror, Davies, 1933.

A Shorter History of England, Harrap, 1934.

Cromwell, Cassell, 1934.

Milton, Cassell, 1935.

The Battle Ground, Cassell, 1936, also published as *The Battleground: Syria and Palestine, the Seedpot of Religion,* Lippincott, 1936.

Characters of the Reformation, Sheed and Ward, 1936.

The Hedge and the Horse, Cassell, 1936.

The County of Sussex: With Six Maps in the Text, Cassell, 1936.

An Essay on the Restoration of Property, Sheed and Ward, 1936.

Selected Essays, compiled by John Edward Dineen, Lippincott, 1936.

The Crusade: The World's Debate, Cassell, 1937, also published as *The Crusades: The World's Debate,* Bruce, 1937.

The Crisis of Our Civilization, Cassell, 1937, also published as *The Crisis of Civilization,* Fordham University Press, 1937.

An Essay on the Nature of Contemporary England, Constable, 1937.

The Issue, Sheed and Ward, 1937.

The Case of Dr. Coulton, Sheed and Ward, 1938.

Stories, Essays, and Poems, Dent, 1938.

The Great Heresies, Sheed and Ward, 1938.

Return to the Baltic, Constable, 1938.

Monarchy: A Study of Louis XIV, Cassell, 1938.

Cautionary Verses: The Collected Humorous Poems, Duckworth, 1939, also published as *Cautionary Verses: Illustrated Album Edition with the Original Pictures,* Knopf, 1941.

On Sailing the Sea: A Collection of the Seagoing Writings of Hilaire Belloc, selected by W. N. Roughead, Methuen, 1939.

The Test Is Poland, [London], 1939.

Charles II: The Last Rally, Harper, 1939, also published as *The Last Rally: A Story of Charles II,* Cassell, 1940.

The Catholic and the War, Burns, Oates, 1940.

On the Place of Gilbert Chesterton in English Letters, Sheed and Ward, 1940.

The Silence of the Sea and Other Essays, Sheed and Ward, 1940.

Places, Sheed and Ward, 1941.

Elizabethan Commentary, Cassell, 1942, also published as *Elizabeth: Creature of Circumstance,* Harper, 1942.

An Alternative: An Article Originally Written During Mr. Belloc's Parliamentary Days, for St. George's Review and Since Revised, Distributist Books, 1947.

Dunction Hill: Unaccompanied Part-song for S.A.T.B., music by David Moule-Evans, B, F. Wood Music, 1947.

Selected Essays, Methuen, 1948.

Hilaire Belloc: An Anthology of His Prose and Verse, selected by Roughead, Lippincott, 1951.

Songs of the South Country, Duckworth, 1951.

World Conflict, Catholic Truth Society, 1951.

The Verse of Hilaire Belloc, edited by Roughead, Nonesuch Press, 1954.

Essays, edited by Anthony Foster, Methuen, 1955.

One Thing and Another: A Miscellany from his Uncollected Essays, edited by Patrick Cahill, Hollis and Carter, 1955.

Collected Verses, Penguin, 1958.

Jim, Who Ran Away from His Nurse, and Was Eaten by a Lion, Little, Brown, 1987.

Matilda Who Told Lies, Dial Books, 1992.

TRANSLATOR

Ferdinand Foch, *The Principles of War,* Holt, 1920.

Ferdinand Foch, *Precepts and Judgements: With a Sketch of the Military Career of Marshal Foch by Major A. Grasset,* Holt, 1920.

Joseph Bedier, *Tristan and Iseult,* Boni, 1930.

Sidelights

Belloc is considered one of the most controversial and accomplished men of letters of early twentieth-century England. An author whose writings continue to draw either the deep admiration or bitter contempt of readers, he was an outspoken proponent of radical social and economic reforms, all grounded in his vision of Europe as a "Catholic society." Although many critics have attacked Belloc's prescriptive polemical works for their tone of truculence and intolerance—and, especially, for recurrent elements of anti-Semitism—they have also joined in praise of his humor and poetic skill, hailing Belloc as the greatest English writer of light verse since Lewis Carroll and Edward Lear.

The son of a wealthy French father and English mother, Belloc was born in La Celle St. Cloud, France, a few days before the Franco-Prussian War broke out. The family fled to England at the news of the French army's collapse, returning after the war's end to discover that the Belloc home had been looted and vandalized by Prussian soldiers. Although the estate was eventually restored and made habitable, the evidence of destruction witnessed by Belloc's parents and later recounted to their children made a deep impression on Hilaire; throughout his life and through the two world wars, he habitually referred to Germany as "Prussia" and considered the "Prussians" a barbaric people worthy only of utter contempt. After the death of Belloc's father in 1872, the family again took up residence in England, where Belloc was raised and received a Catholic education, notably at Cardinal John Henry Newman's Oratory School near Birmingham, where he won many academic prizes and came to the attention of Newman himself. From his numerous travels between England and France, Belloc acquired a deep interest in history, polemics, and world literature. After serving for a year in a French artillery unit (he retained his French citizenship until 1902), Belloc continued his studies at Balliol College, Oxford, where he gained a reputation as a brilliant student, a skilled debater, and an aggressively outspoken champion of Roman Catholicism. Prejudice against Belloc's Catholicism led to his being rejected in his bid for a history fellowship, an experience that intensely embittered him. Through this rejection Belloc came to hate university dons in general, later directing many satiric attacks against them, portraying them as the smug, pretentious defenders of privilege. Years after his disappointment at Oxford, at the age of sixty-six Belloc wrote: "Oxford is for me a shrine, a memory, a tomb, and a poignant possessing grief. All would have been well if they would have received me."

By the mid-1890s Belloc had married and, through the influence of his sister Marie Belloc Lowndes, begun writing for various London newspapers and magazines. His first book, *Verses and Sonnets,* appeared in 1896, followed by *The Bad Child's Book of Beasts,* which satirized moralistic verse for children and proved immensely popular. Illustrated with superb complementary effect by Belloc's friend Basil T. Blackwood, *The Bad Child's Book of Beasts,* according to critics, contains much of the author's best light verse, as do such later collections as *More Beasts (for Worse Children), The Modern Traveller* and *Cautionary Tales for Children.* An impulsive man who seldom lived in any one place for more than a few weeks and whose frequent trips to the continent proved a constant drain on his financial resources, Belloc welcomed the popular success of his verse collections. But, embracing Cardinal Edward Henry Manning's dictum that "all human conflict is ultimately theological," he perceived his primary role as that of polemicist and reformer, whose every work must reflect his desire for Europe's spiritual, social, and political return to its monarchist, Catholic heritage. Belloc's career as an advocate of Catholicism first attracted wide public attention in 1902 with *The Path to Rome,* perhaps his most famous single book, in which he recorded the thoughts and impressions that came to him during a walking trip through France and Italy to Rome. In addition to its infusion of Catholic thought, the work contains what later became acknowledged as typically Bellocian elements: rich, earthy humor; an eye for natural beauty; and a meditative spirit—all of which appear in the author's later travel books, which include *Esto Perpetua, The Four Men,* and *The Cruise of the "Nona."*

The period between the century's turn and the mid-1920s was the time of Belloc's widest fame and influence. Throughout these years Belloc's name and reputation were frequently linked in the public mind with G. K. Chesterton, whom Belloc had met around 1900 when each was a contributor to the radical journal the *Speaker.* In Chesterton, Belloc found a talented illustrator of his books, a friend, and a man who shared and publicly advocated many of his own religious and political views. Anti-industrial and antimodern in much of their advocacy, the two were jointly caricatured in print by George Bernard Shaw as "the Chesterbelloc," an absurd pantomime beast of elephantine appearance and outmoded beliefs. Both, according to Shaw and other adverse critics, had a passion for lost causes. Belloc and Chesterton were "Little Englanders"—opposed to British colonialism and imperialism—whose essays in the *Speaker* had infuriated many Londoners by the authors' opposition to Britain's imperial designs on South Africa and the nation's participation in the Boer War. Each looked to the Middle Ages as an era of

spiritual and material fulfillment when Europe was united in Catholicism and small landowners worked their own, Church-allotted parcels of property, providing for their own individual needs, free from both the wage-slavery that later developed under capitalism and the confiscatory taxation and collectivist policies of state socialism. (Belloc in particular, after serving for several years as a Liberal M.P. in the House of Commons, held a cynical view of the modern British political system, seeing little difference in the methods of the government's Liberal and Conservative ministers, who were often, to his disgust, fellow clubmen and the closest of friends outside the halls of Parliament.) As an alternative both to capitalism and to the Fabian socialism advanced by such contemporaries as Shaw, H. G. Wells, and Beatrice and Sidney Webb, Belloc propounded an economic and political program called Distributism, a system of small landholding which harks back to Europe's pre-Reformation history. This system was outlined in the 1891 Papal Encyclical *Rerum Novarum,* and is fully described in Belloc's controversial essay *The Servile State,* published in 1912. In this work, which attacks both capitalism (which produces the "servile state" of wage-slavery) and socialism, Belloc called for a return to familial self-sufficiency through the widespread restoration of private property; according to his prescription, which has been described by many critics as at best quaint, and at worst ridiculously impractical, every family should own three acres and a cow. "The fundamental position of *The Servile State,*" A. N. Wilson has explained, "is this; that an Irish peasant who earns almost no money but owns his own land, burns his own peat, grows his own potatoes and milks his own cow is a freer creature than a clerk or factory hand who might earn ten times more money, but is compelled to work for someone else, and to live in a rented or leased house, and to be dependent on shopkeepers for his sustenance."

The Chesterbelloc's political ideas were also expounded in the *Eye Witness,* a weekly political and literary journal edited by Belloc, which became one of the most widely read periodicals in pre-war England. Belloc attracted as contributors such distinguished authors as Shaw, Wells, Maurice Baring, and Sir Arthur Quiller-Couch. In addition, he and his subeditor, Cecil Chesterton, involved the *Eye Witness* in a political uproar in 1912 when they uncovered the Marconi Scandal, in which several prominent government officials used confidential information concerning impending international business contracts in order to speculate in the stock of the Marconi Wireless Telegraph Company. Although Belloc continued to contribute articles and occasionally edit the periodical, the Eye Witness eventually passed to Cecil Chesterton's editorship as the New Witness, which, after Cecil's death in World War I, came under his brother's supervision, becoming in 1925 *G. K.'s Weekly,* the principal organ of the Distributist League. By then, Belloc had established himself as a polemicist who could write forceful and convincing essays on nearly any subject, in a prose style marked by clarity and wit. His reputation as a polemicist reached its zenith in 1926 when, in *A Companion to Mr. Wells's "Outline of History,"* he attacked his longtime opponent's popular book as a simpleminded, nonscientific, anti-Catholic document. A war of mutual refutation ensued, fought by both writers in the pages of several books and essays. Ironically, although much of the scientific community now affirms Wells's biological theses as presented in the *Outline,* during the 1920s the preponderance of evidence supported the findings of Belloc, who, in the minds of some observers, bested Wells in their exchange of polemical broadsides.

But his exchange with Wells was Belloc's last major triumph as a man of letters, as throughout the 1920s and 1930s his own ideas were increasingly brushed aside by a public uninterested in seeing Britain return to Catholic values and medieval social structures. Further, in light of the rise to power of Adolf Hitler and Benito Mussolini in Europe, a growing number of readers were offended by Belloc's casual use of anti-Semitic remarks in his works and his view of Mussolini as one of Europe's great warrior-kings reborn. In 1936, with Chesterton ill and near death and with Belloc performing much of the editorial work for *G. K.'s Weekly,* the periodical became one of the very few English journals of opinion to applaud Fascist Italy's one-sided military victory over Abyssinia (Ethiopia)—an editorial position which further tarred Belloc's reputation. Embittered that his opinions were no longer taken seriously and that his creative gifts were diminishing, Belloc spent the last years of his career writing histories and biographies, which have been described by Wilfrid Sheed as "a ream of unsound, unresearched history books blatantly taking the Catholic side of everything." In the early 1940s, after authoring over 150 books, Belloc was forced into retirement by age and a series of strokes. He spent the last ten years of his life in quiet retirement at his longtime home in rural Sussex, King's Land, dying in 1953.

Recent biographical and critical studies have revealed Belloc to be a much more complex and intriguing figure than the predictable, anti-Semitic crank portrayed by critics during his lifetime and the years immediately following. As a man, and particularly as a polemicist, he fought tenaciously to uphold his own conceptions of truth; as Michael H. Markel has described Belloc and his polemical style: "He was never modulated, restrained and understated. When he chose an enemy, he fought completely, with all the weapons he could find. Until the enemy was not only disarmed but conquered, Belloc pressed the attack." He held strong passions and strong hatreds, being at once a monarchist and an ardent admirer of the French Revolution in all its excesses, an insistent Catholic apologist and a man who could refer to Jesus as "a milksop" and the Bible as "a pack of lies," a man who expressed sympathy for Europe's Jews and outrage over the Holocaust, yet sprinkled his correspondence and published works with derisive references to "the Yids." As for this last matter, Belloc's reputation as an anti-Semitic hatemonger rests largely upon his book *The Jews,* published in 1922. In this work, Belloc warned that there existed in post-World War I Europe a "Jewish problem"—tension and mistrust between the Jewish minority and the suspicious, predominantly

Gentile population—and that to ignore this tension would lead to an anti-Semitic persecution such as the world had never seen. But to even acknowledge that such tensions existed was itself considered an act of bigotry, and *The Jews,* then as now, went largely unread, being generally perceived as an anti-Semitic work. Although he admired Mussolini, Belloc detested Hitler, particularly the German's anti-Jewish ravings, and he was outspoken with anger and pity when his prophecy from *The Jews* began to come true within his lifetime. But even though he condemned persecution of Jews, he remained to the last a man who considered Jews "Christ-killers" and shylocks. To Belloc, Jews were altogether too prominent in the world of international finance, maintaining capitalism and industrialism through loans and investments, and thereby extending the "servile state." Capitalism was, to Belloc, itself an outgrowth of Protestantism, which had originated in "Prussia," usurped Church authority during the Middle Ages, given the peasants' Church-allocated land to the wealthy aristocracy, and driven the peasants themselves off the land and into wage-slavery under their new, rich rulers. Among the most scurrilous of Britain's Protestants were university dons, who, according to Belloc, trained the young to embrace the capitalist system, with its inherent need for cheap labor and easily obtained raw materials (hence its need for imperialistic colonialism), the success of which further enriched and entrenched the Jews in their positions of financial power. To replace capitalism and restore the power of Rome as the guiding force in Europe was Belloc's dream, for, as he wrote in his *Europe and the Faith,* "Europe will return to the Faith or she will perish. The Faith is Europe. And Europe is the Faith." A. N. Wilson has written of Belloc: "All his political standpoints sprang from his conviction that the Incarnate Christ had founded a Church, and that it was by divine providence that this Church had been established in the heart of the old Roman Empire. 'The Faith is Europe and Europe is the Faith.' From this conviction sprang, on the one hand his incredibly *naif* notion that Mussolini was a model of ancient imperial virtues; on the other, his detestation of the materialism of capitalists and Bolsheviks, and his yearning for a political system in which the dignity of the poor was recognized; in which they were neither as children in a socialist nursery, nor as cogs in a capitalist machine; but as souls made in God's image and likeness, who in a sane world would lead free and independent lives with property of their own."

While Belloc's political and social views have proven unpopular, critics have highly praised the author's light verse, with W. H. Auden going so far as to state of Belloc that "as a writer of Light Verse, he has few equals and no superiors." In his widely known cautionary verse for children, Belloc assumed the perspective of a ridiculously stuffy and pedantic adult lecturing children on the inevitable catastrophes that result from improper behavior. Among his outstanding verses of this type are *"Maria Who Made Faces and a Deplorable Marriage," "Godolphin Horne, Who Was Cursed with the Sin of Pride, and Became a Bootblack,"* and *"Algernon, Who Played with a Loaded Gun, and, on Missing his Sister,*

Was Reprimanded by His Father." "Unlike Lear and Carroll, whose strategy was to bridge the gulf between adults and children," Markel has written, "Belloc startled his readers by exaggerating that gulf. Belloc's view of children did not look backward to the Victorian nonsense poets, but forward to the films of W. C. Fields." Like his children's verse, Belloc's satiric and noncautionary light verse is characterized by its jaunty, heavily rhythmic cadences and by the author's keen sense of the absurd, as reflected in *"East and West"* and in *"Lines to a Don,"* which skewers a "Remote and ineffectual Don / That dared attack my Chesterton." Garry Wills has written that Belloc's comic verse "is as good as Swift's, as disciplined and as savage, fueled with scorn and hatred for human pettiness, compromise, betrayal." In addition to writing light verse, Belloc also wrote many serious poems and sonnets, which are commonly concerned with the human struggle against the idea of mortality. Of these, *"Heroic Song in Praise of Wine"* and *"The Prophet Lost in the Hills at Evening"* are among the most acclaimed of his poems. "His themes," according to Evelyn Waugh, "are the stuff of common life as he knew it in a warmer age; strenuous male companionship, romantic love of woman, the sea, the seasons, the transience of earthly beauty, the unremitting benevolent watchfulness of Our Lady and the angels, the innocence of childhood, the absurdity of pedantry and ambition, the wickedness and stark danger of power. His diction and prosody are the fruit of classical schooling. He was a Christian Shropshire Lad and, by that enrichment, immeasurably [A. E.] Houseman's superior."

Belloc wrote in every genre except drama, but, according to critics, achieved wide success in but two: poetry and the personal essay. While his novels and polemical writings are considered too tightly bound to obscure issues of the early twentieth century and are little read, his poetry, as well as *The Path to Rome* and *The Four Men,* continue to attract the interest of readers and critics. In addition, Belloc's small corpus of literary criticism is considered highly insightful. But overshadowing his literary accomplishments is the common perception of Belloc as a loud, intolerant bull of a writer whose strongly stated opinions not only tainted the thought of the otherwise genial G. K. Chesterton, but also contributed to the atmosphere of anti-Jewish hatred that culminated in the Holocaust. Some critics have noted the odd fact that while all of Belloc's writings are frequently examined for evidence of anti-Semitism, the works of Shaw, who praised Joseph Stalin's policies during the great purges of the 1930s, and Wells, who in Anticipations (1902) flatly proposed the extermination of any race or group that dared oppose the coming omnicompetent utopian technocracy, are read and critically treated without reference to their authors' excesses. Several critics have explained this discrepancy by pointing out that, in light of the Holocaust, many people today consider anti-Semitism an unforgivable attitude, and that while many moderns have seen newsreel films of Nazi concentration camps, no one has seen so much as a photograph of a Soviet gulag. "Given Belloc's abrasive manner and peculiarities of thought," Robert

Royal has concluded, "it is not surprising that he has failed to attract a larger audience. But many other authors of the same period—Shaw, for example—are still read in spite of their eccentricities. Belloc has clearly been neglected because of his sharp opposition to almost everything that has become part of the liberal modern world. The world will not care to read Belloc, but those who pick up his best books to savor his historical imagination, the overall keenness of his mind, and the simple force of his prose will need no other reason to return to him again and again."

Works Cited

Cahill, Patrick, *The English First Editions of Hilaire Belloc,* privately printed, 1953.

Feske, Victor, *From Belloc to Churchill: Private Scholars, Public Culture, and the Crisis of British Liberalism, 1900-1939,* University of North Carolina Press, 1996.

McCarthy, John P., *Hilaire Belloc: Edwardian Radical,* Liberty Press, 1978.

Morton, J. B., *Hilaire Belloc: A Memoir,* Sheed and Ward, 1955.

Raymond, Las Vergnas, *Chesterton, Belloc, Baring,* Sheed and Ward, 1938.

Speaight, Robert, *Life of Hilaire Belloc,* Ayer, 1957.

For More Information See

PERIODICALS

Horn Book Magazine, May-June, 1987, p. 327; March-April, 1992, p. 215.

National Catholic Reporter, November 19, 1993, p. 31.

New York Review of Books, November 7, 1985, pp. 38-41.

*   *   *

BELLOC, Joseph Peter Rene Hilaire
See BELLOC, (Joseph) Hilaire (Pierre Sebastien Rene Swanton)

*   *   *

BELLOC, Joseph Pierre Hilaire
See BELLOC, (Joseph) Hilaire (Pierre Sebastien Rene Swanton)

*   *   *

BERNARDIN, James (B.) 1966-

Personal

Born June 14, 1966 in Corpus Christy, TX; son of Peter A. (an airline pilot) and Barbara A. (a secretary; maiden name, Wilder) Bernardin; married Lisa Clifton (an administrator), January 1, 1993. *Education:* Cypress College, A.A., 1985; Art Center College of Design, B.F.A., 1991. *Religion:* Presbyterian.

Addresses

Home—738 Main St., Huntington Beach, CA 92648. *Office*—20800 Beach Blvd., Suite 100, Huntington Beach, CA 92648. *Electronic mail*—JimLisaB@aol.com.

Career

Illustrator.

Illustrator

Paul Robert Walker, *Big Men, Big Country: A Collection of American Tall Tales,* Harcourt, 1993.
Dan Elish, *My Christmas Stocking: Stories, Songs, Poems, Recipes, Crafts & Fun for Kids,* Smithmark, 1993.
Geri Keams, *Grandmother Spider Brings the Sun: A Cherokee Story,* Northland, 1995.
Paul Robert Walker (reteller), *Giants! Stories from around the World,* Harcourt, 1995.
Stanton Orser, *Dancing with the Wind,* Rising Moon, 1997.
Lori Walburg, *The Legend of the Candy Cane,* Zondervan, 1997.
Paul Robert Walker, *Little Folk,* Harcourt, 1997.
Nancy Farmer, *Casey Jones's Fireman: The Story of Slim Webb,* Phyllis Fogelman, 1998.
Lori Walburg, *The Legend of the Easter Egg,* Zondervan, 1999.

Sidelights

James Bernardin is an illustrator of books for young people. He has created artwork for a number of books centering on myths and legends, including Paul Robert Walker's *Big Men, Big Country: A Collection of American Tall Tales,* and *Grandmother Spider Brings the Sun: A Cherokee Story* by Geri Keams. Commenting on his work for Walker's *Big Men, Big Country,* a *Publishers Weekly* reviewer asserted: "Bernardin's gouache and pencil illustrations . . . all feature a larger-than-life he-man ready to swagger off the page." *School Library Journal* contributor Ruth K. MacDonald commented on his work in *Giants! Stories from around the World:* "The painterly illustrations . . . are as realistic as they can be, given their subjects. The creatures' gaping, gross features are bold and terrifying, and the perspectives are dizzying."

Works Cited

MacDonald, Ruth K., review of *Giants! Stories from around the World, School Library Journal,* February, 1996, p. 90.
Review of *Big Men, Big Country: A Collection of American Tall Tales, Publishers Weekly,* May 10, 1993, p. 74.

For More Information See

PERIODICALS

Booklist, April 1, 1993, p. 1430.
Booklist, March 15, 1997, p. 1246.
School Library Journal, November, 1995, p. 91.*

James Bernardin's illustrations imaginatively reflect the colossal beings featured in the collection of stories retold by Paul Robert Walker. (From Giants!*)*

BLACKLOCK, Dyan 1951-

Personal

Born in 1951; married, husband's name, David; children: two sons, one daughter.

Career

Writer and children's publisher. Has also worked as an editor, teacher, librarian, shopkeeper, counselor, and children's publisher.

Writings

Comet Vomit and Other Surprising Stories, Allen & Unwin (St. Leonards, Australia), 1995.
The Lighthouse, illustrated by Steven Woolman, Era Publications (Flinders Park, South Australia), 1995.
Call It Love (short stories), Allen & Unwin, 1996.
Crab Bait (short stories), Allen & Unwin, 1996.
Pankration: The Ultimate Game, Allen & Unwin, 1997, Albert Whitman (Morton Grove, IL), 1999.
Nudes and Nikes: Champions and Legends of the First Olympics, Allen & Unwin, 1997.
I Want Earrings!, illustrated by Craig Smith, Omnibus (Norwood, South Australia), 1997.

Sidelights

Dyan Blacklock wrote about how she got the idea for her first book on the publicity Website for her publisher, Allen & Unwin: "My mother read to me, my father and brother told unbelievable, fantastic stories, and S. M. Francis, my teacher, inspired me to write. I decided to write a book when I was eight years old—unfortunately I never finished one until I was forty-two. My husband David was the inspiration—one night he had me in stitches with stories of what it was like to be a fat kid, and Maggot and Mr Little (from Comet Vomit) were the result. I realised that I had a motherlode of stories in all the funny, sad, or silly things that I have come across in my life.

"Most stories have simply tumbled out onto my computer screen in an already-formed state. Sometimes I start with an idea, and by the time the story is finished, I realize it has wandered off in a completely different direction than the one I had in mind. I love writing for that very reason. I am always surprised and pleased (not to mention grateful) at the way my characters take charge of their lives and their stories.

"I love to write. It is the one thing I do that always makes me feel good. Even the editing is pleasurable."

Dyan Blacklock is the author of several collections of short stories for young adults that have been praised for their humor and sensitivity, their realism, and their appeal to both boys and girls, avid and reluctant readers. In her first collection, *Comet Vomit,* the thirteen stories "cover fantasy, fear, and farce; some present serious moments of discovery of such matters as the brevity of human life, ... the capacity to overcome fear, and loyalty to one's home and family," remarked Alan Horsfield in *Magpies.* Horsfield noted that much of the appeal of *Comet Vomit* comes from Blacklock's use of the natural language of her target audience, her fast-paced plots, and satisfying endings. Similar qualities grace *Crab Bait,* another collection of tales for middle-grade readers. According to Russ Merrin, a reviewer for *Magpies,* the stories resonate with "sensitivity, subtlety, humour and poignancy." Individual tales depict the pros and cons of belonging to the popular group at school, family troubles, the comeuppance of a rich girl, or a science-fiction approach to handling a bully. "Dyan Blacklock captures the uncertainty, gullibility and guilelessness of children, while remaining keenly attuned to their thoughts, values, attitudes and mores," Merrin concluded. *School Librarian* contributor Sarah Reed called *Crab Bait* "great for tempting less enthusiastic readers."

Pankration: The Ultimate Game, a novel for young adults, shares with Blacklock's earlier works an ability to inspire enthusiasm in young audiences. Set in ancient Greece, the novel centers on Nic, the pampered son of wealthy parents who is sent away from his Athens home when a plague threatens the city. On board a ship, he meets and is befriended by the ship's captain, an Olympic hopeful training for the pankration event, an especially brutal form of boxing. When pirates attack the ship, young Nic is sold into slavery, escapes, and returns to Athens in time for the games, where he meets up with old enemies as well as old friends and encounters a whole new set of challenges and adventures. In *School Librarian,* critic Jonathan Weir praised *Pankration's* "pacy and involving story," and the author's smooth incorporation of Grecian history. Weir further attested that "the characters and their motivations are never anything short of convincing." *Bulletin of the Center for Children's Books* reviewer Elizabeth Bush stated that though "kid-pleasing adventure-story staples abound" in Blacklock's plot, the author's skill for including historical detail and her avoidance of didacticism raises "the tale beyond simple costume drama." The result is a book that is "about as satisfying as it gets," concluded Bush.

For older adolescents, Blacklock has produced a collection of stories about love and other intensely felt emotions in *Call It Love.* For a younger audience, the

Dyan Blacklock's collection of thirteen stories, told in the natural language of her target audience, combine fast-paced plots and satisfying endings. (Cover illustration by Geoff Kelly.)

author wrote *The Lighthouse,* a picture book about death and grief in which an elderly man loses his wife of many years, grieves the loss of the person who was to him a "lighthouse," and eventually learns to enjoy life again. This "soundly-written story" is also a "sentimental reminiscence," according to Annette Meiklejohn in *Magpies,* but "is saved from becoming maudlin by the author's use of clear and very simple language."

Works Cited

Blacklock, Dyan, author comments at www.allen-un-win.com.au/publicity.

Bush, Elizabeth, review of *Pankration: The Ultimate Game, Bulletin of the Center for Children's Books,* June, 1999, p. 344-45.

Horsfield, Alan, review of *Comet Vomit and Other Surprising Stories, Magpies,* July, 1995, p. 27.

Meiklejohn, Annette, review of *The Lighthouse, Magpies,* September, 1995, p. 27.

Merrin, Russ, review of *Crab Bait, Magpies,* March, 1997, p. 32.

Reed, Sarah, review of *Crab Bait, School Librarian,* spring, 1998, p. 46.

Weir, Jonathan, review of *Pankration: The Ultimate Game, School Librarian,* summer, 1998, pp. 76, 78.

For More Information See

PERIODICALS

Australian Book Review, June, 1995, p. 61.
Kliatt, July, 1997, p. 20.
Magpies, Summer, 1997, p. 42.
School Library Journal, January, 1977, p. 81.

*　　*　　*

Autobiography Feature

Larry Dane Brimner

1949-

The Early Years

He was born a writer. That's what my mother used to tell people about me when I was young. Of course, it wasn't true at all. Like everyone else I was born a baby, and in my case that event took place in 1949 at St. Anthony's Hospital in St. Petersburg, Florida. I was informed of these specifics after I'd started school and explained to a teacher that I wasn't born at all. "My brother," I informed the teacher, "found me under a palm tree and *brought* me home to my family." Although I had the picture to prove it and this had been my parents' explanation to queries about where I'd come from, my parents decided to set the record straight. Whether it accomplished that or not, I am doubtful, because for a long time after I assumed my brother had found me under that palm tree and taken me to St. Anthony's Hospital. There, I was "born" when my parents arrived to get me. I don't remember anything about being born, of course. I'm told I wasn't well, and I accept this since much of my early childhood was spent in hospitals. I do have vivid recollections of sterile hospital operating rooms, tiles glistening white, and of being put under anesthesia. I also can recall frequent instances of waking from whatever the current emergency was to see a blanket-draped mother or father sitting asleep in a chair beside my hospital crib. But these are recollections at some point later in my early life I am sure.

My mother told me the nuns at St. Anthony's were so fearful that I was going to die without being named and, therefore, suffer an everlasting condemnation to some netherworld other than Heaven that they kept pestering her to name me. Not being Catholic, my mother couldn't understand the urgency. The nuns, however, were persistent. Finally, my mother gave in and named me Larry Dane. She never did explain just why it's Larry Dane, for these are not family names, but she often recounted the story of the nun who arrived with paperwork in hand giving my name as "Lawrence Dane." My mother, who was not known for patience with adults or for mincing words, apparently bombarded the poor nun with a barrage of language that left the woman scurrying from the room. Moments later, a dour-looking Mother Superior entered the hospital room, and this time the paperwork reflected my name accurately. I have been Larry Dane ever since and, because I proved the doctors and nuns wrong about my imminent demise, have spent a lifetime explaining to people—school registrars, licensing bureaus, etc.—that I am not a Lawrence.

My father, George Frederick Brimner, was a naval officer and as such was subject to the whims of the navy and government he served. Within a short time after my birth, he was transferred to Key West, Florida; San Juan;

Puerto Rico; and Charleston, South Carolina. Already, the making of a "navy brat" was in the works, for my mother, brother, and I followed him in his work, "home" often being a succession of ever-larger trailers that we could hook up to the car and pull to the next duty station.

By the time I was one year old, however, the trailer was in storage and we were living in naval housing on Kodiak Island, Alaska. Alaska, at this time, was "America's Last Frontier" and not a state. My earliest memories date from this Alaskan adventure: a laundry room that terrified me because a monster lived within it (a water heater that growled and gurgled and breathed fire); being abandoned by my brother in a basement lightwell one winter's day (at the time it seemed deep, although I somehow managed to climb out); long hikes up Old Woman Mountain to a rustic cabin (they must have been even longer for my father because I got to piggyback); and evenings listening to the radio (on those rare occasions there was reception) or reading and telling stories. I would often sit atop my father's shoulders on these evenings, brushing his hair and setting it with my mother's pink curlers. Even today, he maintains I gave him his curly hair (but that doesn't explain mine).

Unlike many families, ours was not large or extended. Perhaps it was a result of a nomadic military life which took us far from my parents' native soil of Birmingham, Alabama, or, as I rather suspect, a family feud, but I didn't meet my father's people until I was well into my forties. His two sisters and a brother are nice people, but I've never been comfortable around strangers. They and their children and their children's children were strangers to me. We met, briefly, and parted strangers still.

The marriage of George Frederick Brimner to Evelyn Abernathy was secret and not welcomed by the bride's parents, Zula and Abbott Hugh Blair. These were not her real parents, but a childless aunt and uncle who took her in, adopted her, and raised her as their own when the Abernathys fell on hard times. This, I understand, was common among families when there were more mouths to feed than there was food to go around or when there was more month left at the end of a paycheck than there were dollars. The exact circumstances of my mother's arrival in the Blair household are unknown to me. All I know for certain is that she was raised a Blair, and this brought with it privileges and responsibilities.

Abbott Hugh Blair was a successful businessman. Born in 1888 in Alton, Illinois, he graduated from college in his midteens and immediately set off on a barge to England. That he shunned the more responsible path of career, marriage, and family for a brief time branded him the black sheep of the family. His older sister, after all, had used her college training to eventually become an author and head curator of the Corning Glass Museum in Corning, New York. She was one of the few Westerners granted an audience with the emperor of Japan prior to World War II and given permission to observe the royal glassmakers at work. His brother became a professor of mathematics and eventually taught in San Diego, California. He, too, was an author—of mathematics textbooks.

Upon his return from England, however, Abbott didn't waste time catching up with the careers of his siblings.

Trained as an engineer, he settled in Birmingham, married, and established the Blair Engineering Corporation. His little engineering firm provided a comfortable life for his wife and her niece, Evelyn, until the Great Depression. Then business boomed. A beneficiary of public works projects meant to stimulate the economy, the firm suddenly had more business than it could handle designing and building roads, bridges, and dams throughout the American South and Southwest. At a time when travel was restricted because of gas shortages, Abbott was crossing the country several times a year on black-market fuel coupons—expanding his business contacts and speculating in California real estate and oil. The oil wells never panned out, and it would be years before any of the real estate ever amounted to more than so much dirt, sand, and rock, but Blair Engineering still provided the Blairs with an early retirement—in California.

It was in this world of privilege that my mother, Evelyn, a kid from the other side of the tracks, found herself living. Abbott and Zula expected her to continue to college after high school and to enter a career in law before settling into a marriage. A career, I'm told they cautioned her, is often more dependable than a marriage. If I read between the lines of family history, then I must speculate that this warning stemmed from the situation that I believe my mother's birth mother found herself in: an abused wife of an alcoholic husband and no training to fend for herself. I can only speculate, for the Abernathys were never discussed in my presence and our paths were never allowed to cross.

The heart, however, does not always heed the wishes of parents or adoptive parents. At some point in high school George met Evelyn, or Evelyn met George. So smitten was he with what one of his sisters described as "a mocha-skinned, exotic beauty" that he transferred across town to Birmingham's then prestigious Ensley High School just so he could carry her books to class. But times and circumstances worked against him. He was forced to leave school to help support his mother and younger siblings. In whatever free time he had available, however, he continued to court my mother, and they secretly married seven months shy of her high school graduation in 1937. Of necessity, the marriage was secret: married women were not allowed to attend school, and Abbott had a quick temper.

My parents never discussed in detail any family reaction to their marriage, although they made it clear that Abbott and Zula thought they both were throwing away their futures. The marriage was an action that Evelyn and George took responsibility for and, as far as Abbott and Zula were concerned, they would claim its consequences as well. They withheld their support, financial and otherwise. If there was a scene, no one ever informed me of it.

The newlyweds apparently didn't care that the Blairs were not forthcoming with their blessings. Upon Evelyn's graduation, George enlisted in the navy; and although his military salary was meager, it proved ample enough to support his young wife. Or perhaps it was the adventure of new assignments and travel that sustained them. Whatever it was, this odd coupling worked. By the time my brother, Donald Wayne, was born in San Pedro, California, in 1939, whatever riff may have existed between my parents and Abbott and Zula had been smoothed over. Abbott's diaries,

"The proof! Big brother Wayne brings Larry home supposedly after finding him under a palm tree," 1949.

which I read after his death in the 1970s, recall extended car and rail trips to visit the Brimners at various duty assignments during this time. They also record the trust funds which he set up to benefit the young military family and which would eventually help me as a young teacher get over the shock of that first full-time teaching contract (salary: $7,800 for the year).

My mother mentioned once that Abbott had confided in her that he had misjudged George. Indeed, he had. With my mother's encouragement and nudging, George advanced rapidly through the ranks, completed his high school equivalency, and continued his education. My mother, who was ambitious for them both, eventually fulfilled all those expectations that Abbott and Zula had for her.

This, then, became the family I would know: father, mother, brother, and Abbott and Zula Blair, whom I knew as my mother's parents and whom both my brother and I called PaPa and Mamaw.

The assignment in Alaska lasted for several years, and I consider myself fortunate to have spent my earliest years there where television was nonexistent and radio reception only sporadic. Books filled our evening hours. My parents read to me, and not just children's books. They acquainted me with Twain and Hemingway and Steinbeck and Fitzgerald and were always patient with their explanations, of which I'm sure there must have been many. Then something magical happened: my mother taught me to read. By the time I was four, I could decipher very basic sentences, and it filled me with such enthusiasm for reading that my excitement was hard to contain. I wanted to read

everything. Alas, even Hemingway's simple writing style contained sentences loaded with many more than the basic words I knew, so I contented myself with simple stories— some from the published children's books in our family library, like *Goldilocks and the Three Bears*, and some that I would make up myself. The writer inside me was born.

I recall Alaska with absolute fondness. My mother, always up to a dare, posed knee-deep in snow in a swimsuit just to have the photo to send to friends "back home." My brother, ten years my senior, became an inseparable friend. Even if he did try to ditch me in a lightwell from time to time, he usually allowed me to tag along with his friends and included me in some way in whatever activities were going on. I'm sure it helped that we were island-bound and that there was a limited number of other playmates for him. (The combined junior and senior high school enrollment numbered fewer than a dozen.) Our house seemed always bursting with people. Half of my father's crewmates, many of whom would become lifelong family friends, seemed to call our house home in their off-duty hours. Naval assignments, however, are seldom permanent.

The School Years

Just after my fourth birthday, we started packing again—at least my mother and father did. This time my father had received transfer orders to Pearl Harbor, Hawaii. At the time, PaPa and Mamaw were living in San Diego, California. Both military and public housing in Hawaii were in high demand and short supply during those post-World War II days. There was adequate housing for my father in Officers' Quarters but nothing available for the family. So the decision was made that my mother, brother, and I would join PaPa and Mamaw in California. My father would go to Hawaii alone, and we would join him when suitable housing was found.

No one knew at the time, but the decision to ship my parents' furniture and belongings to California and not to Hawaii saved the government all kinds of money because just two short months after arriving in Hawaii, my father received new orders again. Whoever in the navy was responsible for deciding these things determined that my father was needed to command a ship based in San Diego.

At first, home in San Diego was a green Vagabond trailer, the biggest the industry made at the time. Twin beds at the back served as a bedroom that my brother and I shared. A fold-out sofa bed at the front was both living room and, at night, my parents' bedroom. A kitchen and water closet occupied the midportion of the trailer. The water closet was strictly that—a toilet. Bathing was done in the kitchen sink in bad weather or in the trailer park's bathhouse in good weather. Fortunately, "it never rains in California," or so the song says, and this meant that just about every evening the Brimner clan, towels thrown over our shoulders and bath gear in hand, would trek to El Capitan Trailer Park's bathhouse to cleanse away the day's grime.

Although we did not live at the El Capitan Trailer Park for long, I recall it as a fun place to be. Located in El Cajon, a rural community about twenty-five miles east of my grandparents' house in San Diego, it meant I could see PaPa and Mamaw on a regular basis. There was also a child in the park, the manager's grandson, who was just a year or two older than me. For somebody whose sole playmate until then had been his big brother, this was a novel experience for me. I can't remember his name now, but I do know that this youngster and I climbed in the apple orchard next door and got in trouble for eating—okay, stealing—apples. We got in trouble for climbing inside the fenced-off area for the park's giant propane tank. But it wasn't all trouble.

While living there, I got my first two-wheeler—a red one with red, white, and blue streamers that jetted out from the handlebars when I rode fast. One day my father gave in to my begging him to remove the bike's training wheels. He took me to a flat dirt lot near the park and ran along beside me, providing balance where precious little existed. Before I knew it, I was flying. And just as suddenly, I realized my father was no longer balancing me. I came up from the crash sobbing and crying, and my father gave me his standard warning in such situations: "You'd better stop that right now, or I'll give you something to cry about." Then he pointed out that I'd really ridden all by myself, without training wheels, and I could do it again if I tried. I did, and from then on a bicycle opened up new worlds for me to explore.

I also learned how to swim in the park's pool. What a daring boy I was to jump from poolside into the deep end where my mother or father waited to retrieve me! Could the diving board be far off?

For some reason, three particular things stand out in my mind during this time. My parents took up square dancing, and my fourteen-year-old brother was often recruited to be my baby-sitter. On one occasion, my

brother's girlfriend, Judy—a girl from the park who would several years later become his first wife—was visiting, and I was acting like a brat and refusing to go to bed so they could be alone. To embarrass me, he pulled down my pajamas, exposing all of my four-year-old boyhood. It wasn't just a quick glimpse either. He held me in front of Judy for what seemed an eternity. Thoroughly embarrassed after that, I went to bed quietly and never mentioned the incident to a soul (until now).

Another thing was television. Bobbie and Blackie, the people in the silver trailer next door, got a television. Every evening as they were sitting down to dinner, they'd tune in *Howdy Doody* just so I could sit on their step and watch it through the screen door. I was fascinated. Even so, television was black and white compared to books. Reading continued to rank up there with favorite things to do, and my fondest title from that period in my life was *The House That Jack Built*. I sometimes wonder if my interest in restoring and building houses doesn't stem from that book.

Then there was school. Enrollment at El Cajon's Meridian Elementary School weaned me from home. Well, it did as much as it does any young child. Kindergarten was nap time on small carpets which we brought from home to soften the cold, hard, tile floor. It was an old wooden rowboat docked in a sandbox and from which I acquired more than a few splinters as my classmates and I acted out sea battles. Today, such a "toy" would raise the hackles of every child-safety agency known to exist. It was also chicks that we hatched from eggs. I suppose you could say that kindergarten instilled in me a sense of adventure and a love of animal life. I'm always willing to try something new, and my pets throughout the years have included the usual cats and dogs, along with rabbits, chickens, and a goat. My mother drew the line with the goat, however. When I asked for a cow and horse, she said, "Absolutely not!"

From kindergarten to third grade I attended three different schools. This isn't unusual for a military kid, but these transfers were the result of only one move. My

Larry with his parents and brother, Wayne, in Florida, 1949.

parents decided that they wanted to settle in El Cajon, which at the time had a population of only 4,000 to 5,000 people. I mention this because this same town now has well over 100,000 people living in it. Anyway, in 1955, they built a three-bedroom, two-bathroom, ranch-style house on Marline Avenue, and that would be my home until I reached adulthood. Naturally, I was excited about the move; I'd have a bedroom of my very own! There was also room for animals.

My brother, however, did not share the excitement. He was in high school and had his own circle of friends, most of whom lived in or near El Capitan Trailer Park. Then, of course, there was Judy—now about three miles away. It must have seemed like half a world away to a teenaged Wayne because I recall that he seemed to be in a perpetual angry mood after we moved into the house. Even the party my parents threw for him on our backyard patio to celebrate his sixteenth birthday didn't seem to make him truly happy.

After high school, my brother enlisted in the air force. Although he has never said this, I think part of the reason he enlisted instead of going on to college was because of his unhappiness at the house on Marline Avenue. Ever the writer, though, I wrote him a letter even before he'd left explaining how much he was missed.

During Wayne's basic training, I wrote him every week, and sometimes more often than that. To this day, I can recall one letter's brevity:

> Dear Wayne,
> Since I had nothing to do I thought I would write.
> Since I have nothing to say I guess I will close.
> Love,
> Larry

Wayne has said my letters to him got him through basic training and his assignment to Turkey, but I was just doing what a writer has to do. This, I'm sure, was why my mother professed I'd been born a writer.

The first school I attended after the move to Marline Avenue was Bostonia Elementary. I had the same teacher for first and second grades and, sadly, learned the truth about Santa Claus. Fortunately, there were still the Easter Bunny and Tooth Fairy, so I wasn't a child completely without fantasies. By the time I was ready for third grade, a new school—Naranca Elementary—had opened just one and one-half blocks away from where I lived, and I completed my elementary education there. Although it had no library or cafeteria, Naranca had many wonderful, dedicated teachers and Mrs. Culbertson (my fourth-grade nemesis whom I would later feature in *Cory Coleman, Grade 2*).

Today, I'm an avid gardener. I think I can trace this back to a plot of ground on Marline Avenue that my parents gave me. It was mine to do with as I pleased, a section of the backyard. It had its own picket fence, its own grassy area, and its own flowers and vegetables. It was a simple gift, and I doubt my parents ever realized just how important it was to me. I not only took solace in my garden when childhood worries got the better of me, but also great pride when the flowers and vegetables I'd planted did well. It was a great responsibility and since I knew nothing about

plants and gardening when my parents entrusted the little plot of land to me, it forced me to find out more. I did this with weekly bicycle trips to the El Cajon Public Library, where I was probably the only youngster to check out gardening books meant for adults. (Okay, there were the requisite Hardy Boys mysteries, as well.) By the time I was ten, my father was carting me to the local garden center every weekend where I'd spend my allowance on seeds and plants.

Having my own plot of ground to garden did something else that, certainly, no one planned. It connected me to that house and property and made it mine in a way that nothing else could have. After my mother passed away in 1988 and we decided to sell it, I was the one who had the most trouble letting go. I don't think my brother cared one way or the other. My father looked at the house as a good investment. I, however, found myself drawn to that little corner where I'd spent so much time digging in the dirt and to the lath-house that sheltered my tropical plants from El Cajon's frost and scorching heat, and I wept.

The only real deficiency to the house on Marline Avenue was that there were no kids even close to my age nearby. There were one or two kids my brother's age and one or two kids much younger than me, but that was it. In part, this was because it was a rural area. I imagine that children today who live in rural areas have the same problem. Neighbors are far-flung, and the gap between playmates one's own age can be even farther. But we'd always been an insular family, so it wasn't the end of the world.

In those early years on Marline Avenue, my parents "imported" a friend for me. At the time, kids could get into

With his maternal grandparents, Abbott and Zula Blair, and brother Wayne, 1949.

On a spring holiday in White Sands, New Mexico, 1951.

a noon matinee for a quarter. Jan Boyles, the daughter of a family friend, and I would spend our Saturdays at the movies. One Saturday her mother would drive us to the theater and the next my mother would drive us. Jan, who was two or three years older, was my first real sweetheart. I even carved her name into my bedside table and encircled it with a heart. Imagine how crushed I was to meet her again as an adult and to realize she had absolutely no recollection of our Saturdays together! Love is the cruelest season.

Eventually, a few couples with children close to my age did move into the area. Cintra Clark, or "Cindy" as we called her, was a year ahead of me in school and two years ahead of me in age. We were playmates for a while, but it was a turbulent relationship. Cindy was a temper tantrum waiting to explode. On the day it did explode, she threw a butcher knife at me. As luck would have it, the knife glanced off a tree in the Clark's orchard and pierced my foot. Had it not been for that tree, I'd have been history! Our relationship cooled after that.

Ronnie Nielsen's parents bought the house next door. Although he was closer to my brother's age than to mine, I attended Lutheran church with him because my parents thought it would be healthy to expose me to religions other than our own—our own being Southern Baptist and Jewish. On our way home from Sunday school, we walked through a field with a large eucalyptus tree. Ronnie, who was much taller than me, dared me to climb it with him. I suppose in this regard I'm somewhat like my mother: always up to a dare. Ronnie gave me a boost, and before I knew it, I was sitting in the Y of two branches much higher up than I ever should have been. About then, Ronnie's expression turned to fright and he shouted, "There's a werewolf coming!" I

had no idea what a werewolf was, but I knew it must have been bad because Ronnie was screaming and running toward home. Undiluted panic and fear set in, and I jumped. The air whooshed out of me and pain stung every part of my body, but I forced myself to follow at lightning speed in Ronnie's footsteps. By the time we reached our homes, Ronnie was laughing himself silly and I was hysterical. After that, Ronnie and I seldom played, and it concluded my experimentation with the Lutheran denomination.

Mine was a typical childhood filled with summer camping trips and music lessons. Every summer, we'd load our camping gear into the station wagon and set off for Yosemite National Park for six weeks at a time. Camp was always set up at the Wawona Campground, just inside the south gate to the park. PaPa, a widower by then, would join us by taking lodging at the nearby Wawona Hotel. Together as a family, we'd hike the trails and swim and float in the brisk Merced River. We'd fish, although I was more interested in watching the fish swim between my legs in that crystal clear water than in catching them.

PaPa influenced me greatly, especially during those summer trips. He was never without a book, and he always had some interesting fact to share about something he'd read. On one trail he began smelling the conifer trees. I sniffed, too. Did you know that the bark of certain types of conifers smells just like vanilla? He'd read that, and for much of that trip grandfather and grandson had their noses pressed up against the bark of pine trees. Even today, I can't resist the temptation to smell the bark of a pine tree. And when it smells like vanilla, summers of long ago flood my memory.

I inherited the music lessons and trombone from Wayne after he joined the air force. It wasn't a welcomed bequest. I wanted to study piano, but trombone it would be. I was so small that to reach seventh position on the trombone's slide, I had to use my foot! But I was a diligent student. I figured that if I stuck with it and nagged enough, my parents would eventually break down and buy me the grand piano I wanted.

Early one Christmas morning about three years into trombone lessons I went into the living room and spied the partially unwrapped keyboard behind the tree. (Okay, I helped to expose it!) Clearly, it wasn't a grand piano, but the fragment of keyboard I saw filled me with joy. When my parents came out, they encouraged me to open this special gift first. What I found was an organ. An organ! I was disappointed big time and refused to ever touch it just to make my point. I stopped playing trombone after that, too, and thus ended my musical career.

The greatest thing happened when I was in fifth grade. A family built and moved into a house about a block away from my own. This was not just any family either. It was a Catholic family, and it consisted of a dozen kids. Michael Kearney was only a month or two older than me and in exactly the same grade and classroom. We became instant best friends and often spent our time playing school. He was the principal. I was the teacher. His younger brothers and sisters were our students. For two years, I practically lived at the Kearney house. As junior high approached, however, things changed. Michael and I would not be going to junior high together. He would be going to a

Catholic junior high like his older sister. Without the bond of school, Michael and I drifted apart.

I am not certain when Orman moved into the neighborhood. Three years ahead of me in school, he did not associate with Michael and me—except to terrorize us. Orman was a fiery kid built like a boxer, and I learned early on not to cross him. He had a fierce right hook and knew how to place a kick where it hurt the most. It didn't matter to Orman whether you were male or female, if you crossed him you took your punishment. Everyone avoided him—even a lot of the adults. Yet, with Michael destined for Catholic school and no one else in the neighborhood even remotely close to my own age, Orman and I shared a brief friendship that summer before I entered junior high. It was a strange friendship, for it was not based on hobbies or sports or interests in common that I'd shared with my other friends. It was based on sex. Wiser than I about the facts of life (I was still under the impression that babies were found under palm trees), Orman taught me to masturbate and to satisfy him sexually. These were thoroughly enjoyable activities. Although psychologists tell us this is often how it is among boys, older ones taking younger ones under a sort of tutelage, I knew not to discuss our activities, even without being told, and never did. Even so, I am grateful to Orman for that summer's lessons; when my parents explained the facts of life to me three years later—long after I'd reached puberty—they supplied scant details and abundant myths. But "school" was in short session that summer. Another family moved into the neighborhood, and Orman stopped our weekly assignations in the tree house behind his house to buddy-up with the new boy on the block.

Seventh grade came at a time when miniskirts were invading this country from England. So was long hair. It was deemed such a serious problem that many thought the moral decay of the country was going to come in the form of short skirts (on girls) and long hair (on boys). School administrators seemed to concur. It was a common and weekly practice for the principal to line the girls up in the school auditorium. Once there, they had to kneel on the floor, and the principal, yardstick in hand, would measure the distance between the floor and their hemlines. The ideal was a skirt that touched the floor. Those girls dressed in skirts that did not meet that ideal were sent home to change. Although routine, these inspections were not regular; a student could never predict on which day of the week they might fall.

Boys, too, were inspected, lined up like so many cadets in basic training. The principal would walk behind. If your hair hung over your collar at the back, it was too long. The shower room in physical education class always revealed who would be getting a haircut after school, for the individual always bore the tell-tale signs of "swats"—a rectangular red welt across the buttocks from the principal's paddle.

Junior high was not a happy time for me. Seventh grade was confusing, at best, and there was no strong connection with any of the teachers as there had been in elementary school. At this point, school became something I just wanted to get through. Then in eighth grade my father suffered a near-fatal heart attack. This caused a strain on my mother that was formidable and was worsened by the accusation that my father's mother hurled. When informed of my father's condition, his mother, Ruth Montgomery, said it was my mother's fault for pushing him too hard to succeed.

Although my father recovered, the next several months were difficult. My mother felt that Ruth's accusation was inappropriate and that my father should say as much. When my father didn't broach the subject with Ruth in subsequent telephone conversations, my mother felt betrayed and fell into a depression manifested by excessive drinking and threats of suicide. For months, she kept a loaded handgun in her room and divorce was a frequent topic of discussion. During most of eighth grade I didn't know if I was going to come home from school to find my mother or my mother's corpse, my father or my father's corpse. I tried discussing my fears and concerns with my brother, who was by then married to his second wife, Pat, and it was the first time he let me down. "It's your problem," I remember him saying. "I don't live there anymore." Somehow the Brimners survived intact as a family, although we would never be as close-knit as once we were.

It was 1963, and I lurched into my high school years at El Cajon Valley High School. I neither liked nor disliked high school. In part, I suppose I felt the rift between my parents was my fault, and so I strived to succeed, thinking this might make things the same again. This left little time for the usual socialization that is typical in high school. Oh, I never missed a school dance and was involved in activities—student government and boys' federation, a community service organization—but I was always on the fringes. It seemed I knew a lot of people, but I had no close

Larry, striking out on his own through Alaskan snow, 1953.

friends.

My freshman year was marked by an accident in wrestling, my opponent slicing my left eye with his fingernail. Amid boos and catcalls, I immediately went limp just to end the match. The coach checked my eye and said it was nothing. I was sent on to my next class. The fact was that my eye was filled with blood and I could not keep it open. That afternoon I went home and lay down in my room. After an hour or so, I still could not open my eye without severe pain, so I told my mother I thought there might be something wrong. She took one look and rushed me to an ophthalmologist. He confirmed that the eye itself had sustained a ragged, deep gash and prescribed treatment and medication.

That wrestling match ended my experience in school-sponsored physical education. In fifth grade I had been diagnosed with amblyopia of the right eye. This is when a perfectly healthy eye fails to learn how to see. In essence, I was (and still am) blind in my right eye. I relied (and still do) on my left eye for sight. With my left eye bandaged after the wrestling accident, I was out of commission for several weeks. I found the experience an inconvenience. My parents found it frightening. What if I were one hundred percent blind one hundred percent of the time? My parents requested that I be exempted from physical education. The school district, citing a state law that mandated that every youngster had to be enrolled in physical education, said I'd have to risk it and be more careful next time. This was not the response my mother wanted to hear, and she was a woman long accustomed to hearing what she wanted. She dusted off her law books and filed suit against the coach for practicing medicine without a license (diagnosis of condition) and against the school district as his employer. The case was settled without going to trial, and I never saw the inside of a gymnasium for the next four years—except to attend school dances.

Lest I become a couch potato, my parents enrolled me in a private gym. There, I lifted weights, swam, and—best of all—ice-skated. I could lose myself on the ice as I now do roller-skating or riding my mountain bike.

Not having physical education at school was a blessing. It meant I had a free period to do something else, and I chose—*chose*, since no one at school was willing to tangle with my mother again—a special studies program that allowed me to read and report on books of my own selection. As far as I was concerned, it was a great use of time. Until then, the junior high coaches I'd had were mostly out-of-shape baby-sitters with no more ability to teach than single-celled amoebas. Kids who arrived in a physical education class with no prior knowledge of the rules of baseball, football, wrestling, or basketball were simply out of luck. My father was not sports-minded, so I had always been one of those out-of-luck kids trying to figure out what was meant by a "first down" or a "safety." The coaches at the high school level seemed to be no different. (I trust things are not this way today.) An hour a day spent reading and writing seemed far more productive to me.

My high school teachers were neither good nor bad. Many were retired from the military and simply filling up their days while adding to their retirement. Others were clearly bored housewives. Very few seemed to be educators because of a special desire to teach or a love of their subject

Larry with his brother, Wayne, on the day before Wayne left for basic training with the U.S. Air Force, 1957.

or children. A Spanish teacher stands out, not for any outstanding ability to teach—although I would rank him as one of the better teachers I had at El Cajon Valley High School—but more for throwing an overly ripe banana at a female student. It burst open on her blouse, and he thought it was great sport. Another teacher weighed our creative writing journals on a scale and gave us grades accordingly. That unpleasant experience almost ended my writing career prematurely, for although my journal contained nothing but positive feedback it was not massively thick. (I'm a slow writer who prefers to nurture each word, each sentence, before going to the next!)

In three years I had accumulated enough school credits to graduate, but my parents assured me that senior years were special, that they were not to be missed. So, although I longed to escape to college, I remained. About the only special thing I recall of my senior year was graduating eleventh in my class and being singled out as an "honor graduate." It was the first time I could recall that academic achievement was elevated to the level of athletic attainment.

I graduated from El Cajon Valley High School, class of 1967, on a Thursday in June and began at San Diego State College the very next Monday.

I thrived in the college setting. Academic discussions, however silly they seem to me now, were stimulating. College offered so much more than I'd ever been exposed

Uncle Larry with newborn Steven Hugh Brimner, 1964.

to—most of all a wider selection of books. I read, and as I took interest in a new topic, I would change my major. I must have changed majors as often as the weather changed. For a brief while I was interested in architecture (*The House That Jack Built* again), then history, then philosophy, then landscape architecture (a natural for a long-time gardener), and, finally, literature.

As much as I enjoyed it, the study of literature, I discovered, was elitist. Although I loved American literature and really wished to study it, at the time it wasn't considered "real" literature. For that, one had to study British literature. I complied and took my degree in 1971—all the while a closet reader of American literature.

The late 1960s and early 1970s were turbulent times in American history. Marchers protesting the war in Vietnam filled every college campus, and San Diego State College was no different. In spite of having classes disrupted because of bomb threats and student strikes, I somehow managed to skate through college oblivious to most of the protests. To be sure, I did not condone the war, but I was also a product of a military family. It was only later that I realized a great deal of history was being made while I had my nose stuck in a volume of Victorian British literature.

What I remember most about my college years—aside from the abundance of books and those deep, academic discussions—were the friendships I made, the closest I'd known until then. Ironically, my closest friend, Norvin Vernon, was himself a military veteran, although he had

served in Germany and not Vietnam. There was a significant difference in our ages, since I began college straight out of high school at the age of eighteen. Norvin completed a tour in the military first. But age had never been a topic of discussion.

One evening, however, Norvin and a couple of our other buddies—college juniors all—decided we'd visit a few of San Diego's abundant striptease clubs. Age was suddenly a consideration—a big consideration. I was included in this expedition, but I was well aware that November—when I'd be "legal"—was still several months away. Nobody realized that I was not only younger than anyone else in our little group, I was a lot younger. I remember sitting in the backseat of Norvin's beige Thunderbird wondering how I was going to explain that I wasn't old enough to get into any of the clubs they were considering. As we pulled into the parking lot of Les Girls, I finally blurted out my confession. Three heads spun in my direction and, in unison, they asked, "How old are you anyway?" I winced and confessed. Even so, we tried to get in, but the bouncer—or whatever you call the brutes who check identification at the doors of sleazy nightclubs—did not buy my story about being from out of town and having forgotten my wallet. "Come back when you're out of diapers," he barked.

My friends were sports about it; we went to a movie instead. On my twenty-first birthday—well, that's another story.

Having a degree in British literature, with a minor in physical geography, doesn't really qualify one to do much. My fascination with literature never waned long enough for me to consider how I might actually use this academic knowledge to secure a career. Today, I would probably be knocking on publishing doors. At the time, the thought never occurred to me.

I suggested to my family that I thought I'd like to write, but my father pulled me aside. "Real people," he said, "don't become writers. Real people get a job."

Right ... a job. Teaching was one of those career choices I noodled with when I was a youngster playing with the Kearney offspring. Of course, I'd also thought it would be fun to be a garbage collector at one time, too. Imagine the treasures one could find in other people's garbage. My parents and grandfather lobbied against both. Garbage collecting wasn't exactly a suit-and-tie sort of job, and it smelled. Okay, I was convinced that I wasn't cut out to be a garbage collector. But what about teaching?

PaPa maintained that people with a talent pursued it; teaching was for those without talent. My parents feared that teaching, although honorable, was not highly respected (read "not highly paid"). Echoing a PaPa of long ago, they suggested I study law, with an eye toward holding political office. I knew lawyers; heck, I was surrounded by lawyers. I knew politicians; they were my parents' friends. I didn't want to be either. Teaching, and my profound interest in young people and their well-being, won out. I went into teaching.

The Teaching Years

My first few years in teaching were rocky ones. I'd graduated *cum laude* and had received special recognition for my student teaching—Outstanding Student Teacher of the Year. Supervising teachers and advisers all told me I'd have no difficulty finding a job. The Vietnam years, however, had swelled enrollment in the nation's colleges— to a number larger than at any time before or since— because college exempted one from military service. A good many of these college-educated folk went into teaching. Contrary to the predictions of my supervising teachers and advisers, a teaching job was not immediately forthcoming. Teaching jobs were just plain scarce, and I seemed to be either the wrong ethnicity or gender for the few that were available.

So my first jobs were temporary. They included a first-grade class, which I loved. Unfortunately, the thinking of the time (and this is still largely true) was that men did not belong at the primary level. As soon as a female first-grade teacher was found, I was moved to a combination fourth-, fifth-, and sixth-grade class. This was not an ideal situation, but we—the forty-five students and I—made the best of it.

The next year I was assigned to seventh-grade English. There is a special place in heaven for good, dedicated seventh-grade teachers. The fact is there are very few good, dedicated seventh-grade teachers because most individuals are driven crazy by the hormone-activated behaviors of seventh graders. I knew two weeks into that assignment that I would study law or go into politics before making a career of it.

Finally, a full-time, tenure-track position opened up, but I was emotionally hard-pressed to deal with it. It wasn't in one of the premier school districts where I'd been assured I'd land a job. It was in Barstow, California—a mere speck in the desert, a fuel-stop on the Los Angeles to Las Vegas highway. And it was anything but a dream position. Hired in October, I was already the fourth teacher that year to be put on trial. The other three had been driven from the position by the very high school students they had been charged to teach. By November, I'd accepted another temporary high school position in Carlsbad, California, this time filling in for a woman on maternity leave.

Those first three to five years after student teaching were the most traumatic I'd ever faced. My self-esteem plummeted. My self-doubt soared. I was an emotional wreck.

I accepted another full-time, tenure-track position in El Centro, California—also a speck in the desert. And after a somewhat bumpy start—it took a while to figure out the hierarchy of small-town politics—I settled into teaching high school composition (something, at last, that my background qualified me to do). I also settled onto a therapist's couch. It took some work and some time, but I finally came to realize that I wasn't a failed teacher just because I was not teaching in a prestigious school system. Once I came to that realization, I loved every minute of my job.

I never planned to remain in El Centro for the ten years I did. It was my plan to move about the country and the world teaching. But it's a funny thing about teaching: the more experience you gain, the less attractive you are to other school districts. This is because in teaching, experience equates to position on the salary schedule. To school administrators, the most attractive teaching candidate is anyone with the most minimal qualifications. By default, I remained in El Centro.

If I did not plan to remain in El Centro, I also did not plan to remain in teaching for a lifetime. One consideration for this decision was that I did not want to become the cliche found on every campus I've ever visited: that ineffective teacher counting the days, hours, and seconds until retirement and a *real* life. I cared about children too much to do that to them. The other factor was my closet desire to be a self-sustaining writer, even though I knew the odds against that happening were formidable. I can see now that this harks back to PaPa's words: people with a talent pursue it. I wanted to find out if I, indeed, had any writing talent worth pursuing.

My interest in writing has been life-long, as you've surmised by now. I had been told that I showed some talent with the written word, this by Dr. Paul Anderson, a children's literature professor with whom I'd studied at San Diego State College.

It was Dr. Anderson who had encouraged me to write and publish. He was familiar mostly with my poetry. When he suggested that I submit it for publication, I demurred. Always a shy person, I wasn't sure I wanted the public at large reading my work, especially not that highly personal writing called poetry. So Dr. Anderson did something that changed my life forever: he submitted my work for me.

When my poetry later appeared in a couple of literary journals—"The Business Lunch" in *Voices International* and another that has long since faded from memory—he shared them with me. "Look at the table of contents," I recall him saying. There was my byline! I was flooded with emotions—happiness, excitement, pride. (Fortunately, anger was not one of the emotions I felt or the outcome may have been different.) Dr. Anderson made me promise that

One of Larry's endless gardening projects: a wall garden, which became the basis for a gardening article published in 1983.

Buddy, the dog that eventually inspired **If Dogs Had Wings.**

I'd continue to write for publication because he said I had something to say, a gift—a *talent*.

While teaching, I kept my promise to Dr. Anderson, writing for various publications—*Sunset* magazine, *San Diego Home-Garden* magazine, the *Seattle Post-Intelligencer*, the *California Highway Patrolman*, *Flower and Garden*, among others. My topics ranged from travel to history to humor to cooking. It was while finishing work on a graduate degree in writing at San Diego State that I became interested in writing for children. It seemed a natural calling as I had spent years either being a child or teaching children. I also knew that in my spare time, I was drawn to the crispness and pacing of contemporary children's literature—in books like *Corduroy*, *Island of the Blue Dolphins*, and Sid Fleischman's "McBroom" series. These are stories without one unnecessary word in them, and that is the sort of story I wished to write.

In 1984, I decided to take a leap of faith. The little success I'd had writing for newspapers and magazines was the encouragement I needed—at least editors did not laugh themselves comatose when I submitted a proposal or article. I applied for and received a leave of absence, the first my school district had given in ten years because they'd discovered teachers who were granted leaves rarely returned to the classroom.

I returned to Central Union High School, but not until fifteen years later and not as a teacher, but as a guest lecturer on writing. Yet, I didn't exactly close the door to teaching immediately either.

An odd thing happened after my leave of absence was approved. A professor in San Diego State's School of Education took ill, and he recommended me to temporarily take over his classes. Since I had never taught at the college level before, I accepted the challenge. It left me with plenty of time to write and, perhaps best of all, provided me with a financial cushion just in case there was need. That August of 1984, just as classes were about to commence, I sold my first children's book, *BMX Freestyle* (which was published in 1987). Between the sale of that first book and its publication, three other books sold: *Footbagging*, *Karate*, and *Country Bear's Good Neighbor*. My career in children's books had been launched, but I would continue to teach at San Diego State until 1992.

The Writing Years

Being a reader does not necessarily mean that one can write. Neither is it true that just because one has experienced a childhood one is qualified to write for children. Although I was attempting to write for children, my efforts were being met with scores upon scores of rejections—enough eventually to fill three large cardboard boxes.

To find out more about the specifics of writing for children, I enrolled in a writing course taught by middle-grade novelist Ron Roy. This was followed by another taught by picture book writer Joan Chase Bowden. I came to understand the concept of conflict, that unharried lives do not make for interesting fiction. It became clear to me why point of view is so critical to children's fiction. And suddenly, the rejections began to turn into acceptances, with a short easy-read story called "Boo!" being the first to find print in *Turtle* magazine. This was followed by other children's stories in *Humpty Dumpty's* magazine, *Listen*, and *Jack and Jill*. Book publication, however, remained elusive, and this was my goal.

Every August, as a special treat, I gave myself the gift of registration to the national conference of the Society of Children's Book Writers (SCBW). Today this organization is called the Society of Children's Book Writers and Illustrators (SCBWI). I would attend the lectures and soak up tips and suggestions. I would submit my latest picture book manuscript for critique by a published professional and carefully take notes when we met for consultation. Best of all, I would meet other people like myself—people with a serious interest in writing for children.

Through SCBW, I was encouraged and nurtured by professional writers such as Eve Bunting, Sue Alexander, Audrey Wood, and Caroline Arnold. A chance meeting with James Edward Marshall led to him taking me under his wing for a couple of years, Jim offering long-distance advice on the manuscripts I was writing. These were people whose books I studied and admired. They were the giants in a field I wished to join!

Every year one speaker or another would discuss the merits of writing nonfiction for children. I enjoyed nonfiction, but for some reason I did not see myself as a nonfiction writer. The nonfiction newspaper and magazine work I did was temporary. My goal was to write and publish picture books and middle-grade novels. So, although I listened attentively and took notes, I was more interested in hearing what Eve Bunting or Audrey Wood had to say about writing the picture book. Then one year it clicked: I spent a good portion of my school day explaining nonfiction topics to my students in terms they could understand. I was, in everything but print, a children's nonfiction writer. And I went home from the 1984 SCBW conference thinking about this fact.

It was shortly after that August conference that I witnessed a few neighborhood teens performing stunts on their bicycles in my driveway. Their younger brothers and sisters were trying to emulate them. It dawned on me then that, by God, what they were doing was nonfiction! I raced outside and began to "research" a book idea; more than a few of the youngsters were surprised I wasn't threatening to call their parents!

I knew from the SCBW conferences that the correct protocol for nonfiction book topics was to send publishers a query letter to describe the proposed book and ask if they would be interested in seeing a completed manuscript. I sent my first query letter for *BMX Freestyle* to the late Ann Troy of Clarion Books. She responded with what I have come to call a "positive rejection" letter. She said the idea was viable and exciting. But, she went on to explain that sports books did not do well on the Clarion list. Even so, she encouraged me to find the right publisher because "this is going to be a terrific book on somebody's list."

To find the right publisher, I went to the children's room of the San Diego Public Library. There in the middle of the sports section, I sat on the floor and stacked the books according to the publisher. Once this was complete, I looked them over and decided that what I had in mind best fit those books published by Franklin Watts, Inc.

I had met the editorial director of Franklin Watts through the SCBW conferences, so I went home and sent him a one-page query letter. At most, I expected Frank Sloan to invite me to send him a manuscript when I'd completed it. Instead, he called three weeks later to say that he wanted to contract the book. I remember him saying, "The big question is will you be able to accept my terms?" The fact that he was offering any terms at all was the fulfillment of a dream, but I remained calm. We discussed the terms, and he said I could get back to him once I'd had a chance to consider them. Without skipping a beat, I said, "Your terms sound quite fair to me. I think we can go ahead and contract the book." My first book "deal" was complete. The fact is I was damned worried I was hallucinating and wanted that contract as confirmation that the conversation had been real. Years later, Frank told me I'd been so calm when he called that he was certain I'd published several books and simply hadn't mentioned them in my query letter. He wasn't around for the shouts of jubilation after I'd put down the receiver or the calls to family members and friends. The book went on to be named a "Children's Choice" by the International Reading Association.

When Grolier Publishing, the parent company of Franklin Watts, decided it was going to launch a fiction imprint called Orchard Books, Frank encouraged me to submit some of my picture book manuscripts to Orchard's editorial director, Sandra Jordan. I did, and each of the first three manuscripts was rejected within six weeks of mailing. Someone long ago once told me that a failed person is one who gave up too soon. So I submitted a fourth picture book manuscript to Sandra and after ten weeks, became cautiously optimistic. Then twelve weeks after mailing off the fourth manuscript I received a phone call from Sandra. "I'd like to discuss *Country Bear's Good Neighbor*," she said,

and my goal to write and publish a picture book, although not yet a printed and bound reality, was on its way.

I'm fifty now and celebrating the publication of my fiftieth book, *The Official M&M's Brand Chocolate Candies Book of the Millennium*. It is really my fifty-second published book, among the nearly eighty I have sold. The two other books released simultaneously are *The NAMES Project* and *Butterflies and Moths*. To designate a book about time as my fiftieth published book, though, somehow seems more fitting given its publication during my fiftieth year when we are on the eve of a new century and the brink of a new millennium.

Throughout my writing career, I have been blessed with supportive friends and family. My writers' group—Kathleen Krull, Jean Ferris, and Sheila Cole—is always there for me with advice and a chuckle. Other writer friends—Judy Enderle, Stephanie Gordon, Sue Alexander, Helen Foster James, Pamela Munoz Ryan, and Sneed B. Collard III—"talk" contracts, promotion, and the general business of writing with me via E-mail. My mother, proud as a newly crowned grandparent, paraded *Footbagging* around with her just as she had photographs of my nephew. It was a book I dedicated to her and my father, and I was able to give it to her just a short two months before she passed away unexpectedly. And in spite of his admonition about real people and writing, my father now always introduces me as "my son, the writer." He has come to understand that writing is a job for some real people, just as I'm sure my grandfather would have come to understand that teaching is the talent of some people. Writing is simply an extension of my teaching.

Although I was not born a writer, as once my mother liked to claim, I am one now. And when I see a book I have

On a pair of fast-flying rollerskates.

Signing books with writer Judith Ross Enderle at a teachers' conference, 1993.

written on a shelf at a library or bookstore or in a child's hands, it feels so good it hurts.

Writings

FOR CHILDREN; NONFICTION

BMX Freestyle, Watts, 1987.
Footbagging, Watts, 1988.
Karate, Watts, 1988.
Snowboarding, Watts, 1989.
Animals That Hibernate, Watts, 1991.
A Migrant Family, photographs by Larry Dane Brimner, Lerner, 1992.
Unusual Friendships: Symbiosis in the Animal World, Watts, 1993.
Rolling ... In-line!, Watts, 1994.
Bobsledding and the Luge, Children's Press, 1997.
E-mail, Children's Press, 1997.
Figure Skating, Children's Press, 1997.
Mountain Biking, Watts, 1997.
Rock Climbing, Watts, 1997.
Skiing, Children's Press, 1997.

Speedskating, Children's Press, 1997.
Surfing, Watts, 1997.
The Winter Olympics, Children's Press, 1997.
The World Wide Web, Children's Press, 1997.
Earth, Children's Press, 1998.
Mars, Children's Press, 1998.
Mercury, Children's Press, 1998.
Venus, Children's Press, 1998.
Bees, Children's Press, 1999.
Butterflies and Moths, Children's Press, 1999.
Cockroaches, Children's Press, 1999.
Flies, Children's Press, 1999.
Jupiter, Children's Press, 1999.
The NAMES Project, Children's Press, 1999.
Neptune, Children's Press, 1999.
The Official M&M's Brand Chocolate Candies Book of the Millennium, illustrated by Karen Pellaton, Charlesbridge (Waterstown, Mass.), 1999.
Pluto, Children's Press, 1999.
Praying Mantises, Children's Press, 1999.
Saturn, Children's Press, 1999.
Uranus, Children's Press, 1999.
Angel Island, Children's Press, 2000.

FICTION

Country Bear's Good Neighbor, illustrated by Ruth Tietjen Councell, Orchard, 1988.

Cory Coleman, Grade 2, illustrated by Karen Ritz, Holt, 1990.

Country Bear's Surprise, illustrated by Ruth Tietjen Councell, Orchard, 1991.

Max and Felix, illustrated by Les Gray, Bell Books, 1993.

Elliot Fry's Goodbye, illustrated by Eugenie Fernandes, Boyds Mills Press, 1994.

Merry Christmas, Old Armadillo, illustrated by Dominic Catalano, Boyds Mills Press, 1995.

Brave Mary, illustrated by Marilyn Mets, Children's Press, 1996.

Firehouse Sal, illustrated by Ethel Gold, Children's Press, 1996.

If Dogs Had Wings, illustrated by Chris L. Demarest, Boyds Mills Press, 1996.

Polar Mammals, Children's Press, 1996.

How Many Ants?, illustrated by Joan Cottle, Children's Press, 1997.

Aggie and Will, illustrated by Rebecca McKillip Thornburgh, Children's Press, 1998.

Dinosaurs Dance, illustrated by Patrick Girouard, Children's Press, 1998.

Lightning Liz, illustrated by Brian Floca, Children's Press, 1998.

Nana's Hog, illustrated by Susan Miller, Children's Press, 1998.

What Good Is a Tree? Illustrated by Leo Landry, Children's Press, 1998.

Cowboy Up!, illustrated by Susan Miller, Children's Press, 1999.

Raindrops, illustrated by David J. Brooks, Children's Press, 1999.

A Cat on Wheels, Boyds Mills Press, 2000.

FOR YOUNG ADULTS; NONFICTION

Voices from the Camps: Internment of Japanese Americans during World War II, Watts, 1994.

Being Different: Lambda Youths Speak Out, Watts, 1995.

(Compiler and editor) *Letters to Our Children: Lesbian and Gay Adults Speak to the New Generation,* Watts, 1997.

BROOKS, Bruce 1950-

Personal

Born September 23, 1950, in Washington, DC; son of Donald D. Brooks and Lelia Colleen Collins; married Penelope Winslow, June 17, 1978; children: Alexander. *Education:* University of North Carolina at Chapel Hill, B.A., 1972; University of Iowa, M.F.A, 1982. *Politics:* "Certainly." *Religion:* "Lapsed Baptist." *Hobbies and other interests:* Music, nature study, sports, reading.

Addresses

Home and office—11208 Legato Way, Silver Spring, MD 20901.

Career

Writer. Has worked variously as a letterpress printer, newspaper and magazine reporter, and teacher.

Awards, Honors

Best Books, *School Library Journal,* and Notable Books, *New York Times,* both 1984, Newbery Honor, American Library Association (ALA), and *Boston Globe-Horn Book* Award, both 1985, and Notable Books, ALA, all for *The Moves Make the Man;* Best Books, *School Library Journal,* and Best Books for Young Adults, ALA, both 1986, Fanfare Honor List, *Horn Book,* and teacher's choice, National Council of Teachers of English, both 1987, young adult choice, International Reading Association, 1988, and Best Books for Young Adults of the 1980s, ALA/*Booklist,* all for *Midnight Hour Encores;* Best Books for Young Adults, ALA, young adult editor's choice, ALA/*Booklist,* Best Books, *School Library Journal,* and Notable Children's Trade Book in the Field of Social Studies, National Council for the Social Studies/Children's Book Council, all for *No Kidding;* Notable Books, ALA, and Best Books, *School Library Journal,* both for *Everywhere;* Best Books for Young Adults, ALA, 1990, for *On the Wing: The Life of Birds from Feathers to Flight;* Best Books for Young Adults, ALA, 1992, for *Predator!;* John Burroughs Award, 1992, for *Nature By Design;* Newbery Honor Book, Notable Books, and Best Books for Young Adults, all ALA, and Fanfare book, *Horn Book,* all 1993, all for *What Hearts.*

Writings

FOR YOUNG ADULTS

FICTION

The Moves Make the Man, Harper, 1984.
Midnight Hour Encores, Harper, 1986.
No Kidding, Harper, 1989.
What Hearts, HarperCollins, 1992.
Asylum for Nightface, HarperCollins, 1996.
Vanishing, HarperCollins, 1999.

"THE WOLFBAY WINGS" SERIES

Woodsie, HarperCollins, 1997.

Zip, HarperCollins, 1997.
Cody, HarperCollins, 1997.
Boot, HarperCollins, 1998.
Prince, HarperCollins, 1998.
Shark, HarperCollins, 1998.
Billy, HarperCollins, 1998.
Dooby, HarperCollins, 1998.
Reed, HarperCollins, 1998.
Subtle, HarperCollins, 1999.
Barry, HarperCollins, 1999.
Woodsie, Again, HarperCollins, 1999.

NONFICTION

On the Wing: The Life of Birds from Feathers to Flight,
Scribner, 1989.
Predator!, Farrar, Straus, 1991.
Nature by Design, Farrar, Straus, 1991.
Making Sense: Animal Perception and Communication,
Farrar, Straus, 1993.
(Editor) *The Red Wasteland: A Personal Selection of
Writings about Nature for Young Readers,* Holt, 1998.

FOR CHILDREN

FICTION

Everywhere, Harper, 1990.
Each a Piece, illustrated by Elena Pavlov, HarperCollins,
1996.

NONFICTION

Boys Will Be, Holt, 1993.
(With Glenn Rivers) *Those Who Love the Game,* Holt,
1994.
NBA by Numbers, Scholastic, 1997.

Author of introductions to reprinted sports fiction of
John R. Tunis, including *The Kid from Tomkinsville,
Rookie of the Year, World Series,* and *Keystone Kids.*
Brooks's work has been translated into German.

Sidelights

Two-time Newbery Honor book winner Bruce Brooks is
an author of nonfiction, novels, and stories for both YA
and younger readers. Called "an outstandingly perceptive writer," by a critic for *Kirkus Reviews,* Brooks has
blended interests in sports and in nature to create a
diverse body of work for readers of a wide range of ages.
A graduate of the prestigious University of Iowa writing
program, Brooks put his prodigious talents to work in
his first novel, *The Moves Make the Man,* an interracial
tale of hoops and hopes, to create an impressive debut;
the book won a Newbery Honor and a *Boston Globe-
Horn Book* Award. Since that 1984 novel, Brooks has
gone on to pen some thirty books in genres from serious
fiction to series fiction, from picture books to detailed
accounts of the lives of birds.

In his fiction, Brooks often deals with outsider themes,
placing his young protagonists in the crosshairs of adult
incompetence—victims of a broken home or of alcoholic
abuse. In this respect, Brooks writes out of his own
personal experience. Even in his "Wolfbay Wings"
series about a high-school hockey team, Brooks man-

Bruce Brooks

ages to invest his prose with depth, both in characterization and in ideas. As Michael Cart put it in *St. James
Guide to Young Adult Writers,* "Bruce Brooks is that
rarity in the world of books for young readers—a
novelist of ideas. But he is also a rare stylist whose
writer's razzle always dazzles thanks to his uncanny ear
for voice and his powerful imagery and unforgettable
simile and metaphor."

Brooks was born on September 23, 1950, in Washington, DC, but spent much of his childhood in North
Carolina, where he moved after the divorce of his
parents when he was six years old. The child of a
divided family, Brooks shuttled back and forth between
parents, learning to adapt to different surroundings in the
process. At his father's in Washington, DC, he was part
of a "smaller, urban-oriented family" as he once told
Authors and Artists for Young Adults (AAYA), while in
North Carolina he belonged to a "larger Southern clan."
Moving back and forth, he felt he never had the chance
to develop close friendships with his peers; he was
always the new kid, learning to grab friendship fast
when he could. He developed fast-talking, story-telling
skills to this end.

"Belonging to both worlds but not belonging completely
to either was really an experience that made me an
observer and a student of social situations," Brooks told
AAYA. "[I]t made me learn how to apply myself to
people and activities and to figure out how to belong,
after figuring out which natural parts of me belonged
and which did not." But such chameleon-like skills also
had their cost. "I could never really relax and just say,

'Ah, this is me, I'm among my peers.' I was never among my peers. I was always somewhat different from everyone else. I was always the Yankee kid in the South, and when I went back to the North I was always the Southern kid. It led me to simply be very watchful." It also led to an early love of books and reading, constants in an otherwise ever-changing world.

Brooks attended college at the University of North Carolina at Chapel Hill, graduating in 1972. He had long harbored the notion of becoming a writer, but upon graduation, he quickly understood the realities of simply making a living. Working variously as a letterpress printer and journalist, Brooks used the hours before and after work to hone his writing skills. Then in the late 1970s he attended the Iowa Writer's Workshop, an experience that not only trained him in the technique of writing, but that also afforded him two years to simply write. "I went there very aggressive intellectually," Brooks told Christine McDonnell of *Horn Book,* "and came out very ambitious and increasingly confident. I used the workshop to boost my feeling that anything is possible. The only things I want to do are books that are unique and different."

Like so many authors for young adults, Brooks never intended to write for a niche audience. The fact that his first novel had teenage protagonists was enough to prompt editors to advise Brooks to send it to the children's divisions of their houses. "I've never written *for* kids," Brooks told Leonard S. Marcus in a *Publishers Weekly* interview. Instead, as he put it, he writes for "intelligent people. I write *about* kids because my own childhood is still something that I am very much wondering about." Overcoming initial surprise over his YA audience, Brooks quickly came to prize this readership. "They don't just read a book," Brooks told Marcus, "they *use* it. And reading matters so much to the kids themselves that it's enthralling to have them respond to my books."

Brooks's first novel was *The Moves Make the Man,* set against the historical background of the 1950s school desegregation in the South. Brooks's own childhood spent moving between the South and the North gave him an eyewitness perspective from which to view the budding interracial friendship between two boys, Jerome and Bix. The boys discover that their racial differences prove less important than their common personality traits. Both loners, they frequent a secluded basketball court where Jerome teaches Bix how to play the game. Through this activity, Jerome learns about his new friend's unfortunate domestic situation. Bix's confidence and happiness has eroded since his mother suffered a nervous breakdown and entered the hospital. In addition, his stepfather refuses to take Bix to see her. Determined to visit his mother, Bix proposes a deal to his stepfather. If Bix beats him at a game of one-on-one, they will go to the hospital. Although Bix wins and invites Jerome along for the ensuing trip, the reunion is not what Bix had expected and he runs away from home, leaving Jerome alone to sort out the jarring events.

The Moves Make the Man earned enthusiastic critical response; it was named a Newbery honor book and won a *Boston Globe-Horn Book* Award. Writing in the *New York Times,* Mel Watkins declared that "we get one of the most charming, witty protagonists you're likely to encounter" in this "excellent novel about values and the way people relate to each other." Robert E. Unsworth noted in *School Library Journal* that this first novel was more than just a sports story. "The sport is merely the vehicle for delivering a serious story of friendship and madness," Unsworth wrote. "The description of the basketball action is simply excellent, but all the writing is top rank. Brooks is, indeed, a major new talent in the YA field." *Booklist's* Denise M. Wilms pointed to "savvy monologue," while Allan A. Cuseo in *Voice of Youth Advocates* commented on the "fast hilarious prose" and *Horn Book's* Nancy Hammond enjoyed the "breezy, irreverent first-person narration." It seemed there was something for everyone in Brooks's first novel.

Yet Brooks confessed that such praise was not as heady as might be expected for a first-time novelist. At the times the awards were bestowed, the author explained to *AAYA,* "I hadn't written a word of fiction in three years. I'd been working out the story on my second book, *Midnight Hour Encores,* for three years mentally, but I had not written anything because I was too busy earning a living and I had a new child. So when the awards came, I felt like a hypocrite. Here everybody was saying 'Oh, brilliant new writer' and I didn't *feel* like a *writer.*" Nonetheless, Brooks's success afforded him new career opportunities; he decided to quit his job and write full-time.

Brooks's next, and equally successful, venture was *Midnight Hour Encores,* a story narrated by Sibilance (Sib for short), a sixteen-year-old musical prodigy. Sib, whose parents separated after her birth, lives with her father, Taxi, in Washington DC, and has never met her mother. The self-absorbed Sib, one of the top-ranked cello players in the world, is wrapped up in her practices, competitions, and concerts, and is preparing to attend the prestigious Juilliard School of Music in New York City. While searching for a mentor after her cello teacher dies, Sib discovers that a brilliant but reclusive player may accept a teaching post at a new music school in California. Under the guise of visiting her mother, who also lives in the state, Sib travels to California to audition for the institution. Taxi drives her there, afraid all the while that his daughter will leave him. Sib initially considers Taxi's fears unfounded, but after an enjoyable and educational stay with her mother, she gradually becomes aware of what her father means to her. *Midnight Hour Encores* ends as Sib decides what school to attend and, consequently, which parent to live with.

Midnight Hour Encores was favorably received by critics. Deeming the work "another terrific book" from Brooks, *Washington Post Book World* contributor Katherine Paterson acknowledged the welcome complexity of the novel. "This is a book the reader will have to fool around with, poke into, and tell in his own accents," Paterson insisted. Although several reviews of the book focused on the novel's coming-of-age slant, Brooks remarked in *AAYA* that "to me *Midnight Hour Encores* is about being a father. I wrote that book in the year after my son was born. The most important thing in my life was being a father.... My curiosity about the future—of what you get when you invest certain things in the very early days of your child's life—inspired my imagination to come up with those characters and that story."

Brooks's 1989 literary enterprise, *No Kidding,* again tackles a sophisticated topic. Set in twenty-first century Washington DC, *No Kidding* presents a bleak environment in which alcoholics compose the majority of the population. Society is overwhelmed by this problem and schools have curriculum geared specifically toward alcoholics' offspring, more commonly referred to as AOs. The fourteen-year-old protagonist, an AO named Sam, has been forced to assume adult-level responsibility in his fatherless home. He previously committed his mother to a rehabilitation program and placed his younger brother, Ollie, with foster parents. Now that his mother's stint is completed, Sam must decide whether to reunite the family. Complicating Sam's decision is the knowledge that his mother may revert to her old behavior and that Ollie, who is unaware of her alcoholism, may experience emotional problems. At book's end, however, Sam's mother manipulates events to generate the outcome, giving Sam the chance to assume the role of a child once again. Elizabeth S. Watson, reviewing the novel in *Horn Book,* remarked that "Brooks is a fine writer."

In 1990 Brooks published a short novel titled *Everywhere.* In this book, a nameless young protagonist frets about his beloved grandfather, who has suffered a heart attack and is near death. As the boy keeps a vigil, a local nurse arrives with her nephew, Dooley, who suggests killing an animal in a soul-switching ceremony to save the grandfather. During the course of the story, the boy ponders his grandfather's fate, his own mortality, and the ethics of taking one life to save another. Recognizing *Everywhere* for both its accessibility and complex issue, *Horn Book* contributor Nancy Vasilakis dubbed the work a "masterly novella" and added that "Brooks's precise use of language is a tour de force." Carolyn Phelan noted in a *Booklist* review of this novel for younger readers that the "magnetic force of Brooks's graceful prose seems to increase right to the end, drawing readers further into the hearts of his characters and into the mystery of the human heart."

Brooks won a second Newbery Honor for his 1992 *What Hearts,* a volume of four short stories all dealing with crucial events in the life of young Asa. Asa experiences the breakup of his home at age seven, when his mother takes him to live with a stepfather, Dave; he falls in love at age twelve; and experiences a rivalry with his stepfather until finally mother and son leave Dave behind to find a new life. "The book defies category and asks much of the reader," observed Vasilakis in *Horn*

Book. "As with an important truth, its meaning comes slowly and stays forever." Eric Kraft noted in the *New York Times Book Review* that Brooks "writes with great respect for his audience, a respect that shows in the richness and subtlety of expression throughout *What Hearts* and in the complexity of the characters' emotions and their attempts to make sense of themselves and their lives." *Kirkus Reviews* declared that the book was a "brilliant demonstration that childhood's battles are less important than what one brings to them."

Brooks continued his unique and thoughtful approach to literature for young adults with 1996's *Asylum for Nightface* and the 1999 *Vanishing.* In the former novel, Brooks delves into "philosophical and theological questions rarely raised in children's literature," according to Deborah Stevenson in *Bulletin of the Center for Children's Books.* Zim, short for Zimmerman (named after Bob Dylan) is fourteen and religious—a cipher to his fun-loving parents. But when they suddenly acquire a religion on a vacation and hope to use Zim as a poster child for their cult, he takes it into his own hands to escape becoming "his parents' holy relic," as Stevenson put it. Incorporating a sub-plot about a local card shop and the display of artwork there, Brooks, "a brilliant and original writer," fashioned an "intriguing" book for young readers "hungry for philosophical challenges," according to Stevenson. Michael Cart, writing in *Booklist,* felt that despite some structural problems there were still "many moments of Brooks's signature brilliance here, and since he has tackled a difficult subject with passion, the novel is sure to provoke heated—and welcome—discussion."

Vanishing is the story of two eleven-year-olds sharing a hospital room. Rex is dying of cancer while Alice is floating in a hallucinatory world as a result of a self-imposed hunger strike to avoid being sent home to her alcoholic mother and bitter stepfather. Both youngsters are "vanishing" in a sense, but it is Rex—"a fiery outspoken boy who rages against his terminal illness with all his energy," according to Grace Anne A. DeCandido in *Booklist*—who is truly alive. Ultimately it is Rex who brings Alice back to the world of the living; she is too weak to visit him before he dies unless she eats. A critic for *Horn Book* called the novel a "trenchant and powerful fable," while a *Kirkus Reviews* contributor commented that Brooks "deftly fills in a complex background, peopled by adults who have failed his protagonist in various ways, and, without forcing an agenda onto events, presents Alice with reasons to take up her life again ..."

Brooks has also turned his fictional hand to series writing, with his "Wolfbay Wings" hockey books. Each book in the series, which is geared for readers between nine and twelve, focuses on a different member of the squad, from new member Dixon Woods, AKA Woodsie, to the rude goalie, Zip, to team captain and coach's son, Cody. Readers also meet Boot, the right wing, Prince, the sole black player on the team, Shark, the weak link on the team, and Billy with the sports dad from hell, among other players. Reviewing the first in the series,

Woodsie, a *Kirkus Reviews* commentator noted that Brooks's "knowledge and love of the sport, in all its thrilling complexity, and his respect for his audience and athletes, comes through on every page," while "[w]it and intelligence run as undercurrents to the game." Reviewing the second book, *Zip,* a reviewer for *Horn Book Guide* commented that "the well-individuated protagonists relate their experience in loosely structured plots that contain hockey tips, comic riffs, schoolboy vulgarity, and lots of action on the ice." In a review of *Shark,* the sixth in the series, a critic for *Kirkus Reviews* called the "Wolfbay Wings" series "thoughtful though action-oriented," noting the "intelligence that informs the book is every bit as sharp as the action …"

Brooks is also the author of several nonfiction works, including the nature and wildlife books *On the Wing: The Life of Birds from Feathers to Flight, Predator!, Nature by Design,* and *Making Sense: Animal Perception and Communication;* and a book of essays on boyhood and fatherly concerns, *Boys Will Be.* In a *Publishers Weekly* interview with Leonard Marcus, the author commented that he wrote *On the Wing* because "by explaining why [birds] have the equipment they do … we can begin to understand their behavior while still enjoying that wonderful sense of difference." Brooks added two more works about facets of animal life to his corpus with his 1991 publications *Predator!* and *Nature by Design.* Reviewers admired the colorful photographs in both books and praised the author for his grasp of his subjects and for injecting humor into the narratives. A third book in the "Knowing Nature" series was *Making Sense,* a book "[p]acked with surprising examples," according to Roger Sutton in *Bulletin of the Center for Children's Books,* with "a vibrantly synthesizing approach."

Reviewing Brooks's *Boys Will Be,* Hazel Rochman noted in *Booklist* that this "thoughtful celebration of growing up male now" was "[p]art parenting book for fathers, part self-help book for boys …" Brooks tackles subjects from sports to the wearing of baseball caps to dangerous friends in these essays which a *Kirkus Reviews* contributor characterized as a "funny, thoughtful miscellany." Additionally, Brooks has penned a rhyming picture book, illustrated by Elena Pavlov, *Each a Piece,* described as a "valentine of a picture book" by a critic for *Kirkus Reviews.*

With each of his literary endeavors Brooks has shown his versatility. The opportunity for variety pleases the author, who concluded in *AAYA:* "One of the nice things about being a writer is also the biggest challenge about being a writer: you're always going to be a beginner as soon as you finish something. You wrap up one book and immediately you are a rookie again because you've never written your next book." Respect for the reader is a hallmark of Brooks's literary production. "I leave my books open-ended on purpose," Brooks explained to *AAYA,* "because I want my readers to continue to think about the characters. I want the characters to come to life in the imagination of the readers."

Works Cited

Authors & Artists for Young Adults, Volume 8, Gale, 1992, pp. 17-24.

Review of *Boys Will Be, Kirkus Reviews,* October 1, 1993, p. 1270.

Cart, Michael, review of *Asylum for Nightface, Booklist,* June 1, 1996, p. 1696.

Cart, entry on Bruce Brooks in *St. James Guide to Young Adult Writers,* edited by Tom Pendergast and Sara Pendergast, St. James Press, 1999, pp. 102-04.

Cuseo, Allan A., review of *The Moves Make the Man, Voice of Youth Advocates,* February, 1983, p. 322.

DeCandido, Grace Anne A., review of *Vanishing, Booklist,* May 15, 1999.

Review of *Each a Piece, Kirkus Reviews,* September 15, 1998, p. 1381.

Hammond, Nancy C. review of *The Moves Make the Man, Horn Book,* March-April, 1985, p. 185.

Kraft, Eric, "Thrown Out at Home," *New York Times Book Review,* November 9, 1992, p. 40.

Marcus, Leonard, interview with Brooks for *Publishers Weekly,* July 29, 1990, pp. 214-215.

McDonnell, Christine, "New Voices, New Visions: Bruce Brooks," *Horn Book,* March-April, 1987, pp. 188-190.

Paterson, Katherine, "Heart Strings and Other Attachments," *Washington Post Book World,* November 9, 1986, p. 17.

Phelan, Carolyn, review of *Everywhere, Booklist,* October 15, 1990, p. 441.

Rochman, Hazel, review of *Boys Will Be, Booklist,* December 1, 1993, p. 687.

Review of *Shark, Kirkus Reviews,* April 1, 1998.

Stevenson, Deborah, review of *Asylum for Nightface, Bulletin of the Center for Children's Books,* June, 1996, p. 328.

Sutton, Roger, review of *Making Sense, Bulletin of the Center for Children's Books,* June, 1994, pp. 148-49.

Unsworth, Robert E., review of *The Moves Make the Man, School Library Journal,* December, 1984, p. 103.

Review of *Vanishing, Horn Book,* May-June, 1999.

Review of *Vanishing, Kirkus Reviews,* June 1, 1999.

Vasilakis, Nancy, review of *Everywhere, Horn Book,* January, 1991, pp. 72-73.

Vasilakis, review of *What Hearts, Horn Book,* January-February, 1993, p. 89.

Watkins, Mel, "A Trickster and His Upright Friend," *New York Times Book Review,* November 11, 1984, p. 54.

Watson, Elizabeth S., review of *No Kidding, Horn Book,* July, 1989, p. 486.

Review of *What Hearts, Kirkus Reviews,* October 15, 1992, p. 1307.

Wilms, Denise M., review of *The Moves Make the Man, Booklist,* February 1, 1985, pp. 782-83.

Review of *Woodsie, Kirkus Reviews,* October 1, 1997.

Review of *Zip, Horn Book Guide,* Spring, 1998, p. 68.

For More Information See

BOOKS

Children's Books and Their Creators, edited by Anita Silvey, Houghton, 1995.

Children's Literature Review, Volume 25, Gale, 1991, pp. 16-26.

PERIODICALS

Publishers Weekly, September 27, 1993, p. 65; May 1, 1995, p. 60; June 3, 1996, p. 84; October 26, 1998.
School Library Journal, June, 1996, p. 150; June, 1998, p. 143; July, 1998, p. 92; September, 1998, p. 120; October, 1998, p. 87.*

—*Sketch by J. Sydney Jones*

*   *   *

BROOKS, Charlotte K(endrick) 1918-1998

OBITUARY NOTICE—See index for *SATA* sketch: Born June 5, 1918, in Washington, DC; died of a heart attack on December 7, 1998. English teacher and author. Charlotte Kendrick Brooks was in charge of the Washington DC public school system English department. She also authored books on teaching English. Brooks received a college education which culminated in a Ph.D. from Walden University in Florida. She worked as an English teacher for twenty years in the Washington DC area school system. In 1961, Brooks was promoted to assistant director of the English department for that school system. During her career she also received a grant to study British schools, and served as an adjunct lecturer at American University. In addition to serving as a textbook editor, Brooks authored books that addressed learning issues for the disadvantaged, including *They Can Learn English* (1972) and *Language Arts for the Black Learner* (1985) and also books exploring black history, including, *Remembering: Stories and Poems about the Brooks and Kendrick Families* (1994).

OBITUARIES AND OTHER SOURCES:

PERIODICALS

Washington Post, December 11, 1998, p. G11.

*   *   *

BYRD, Robert (John) 1942-

Personal

Born January 11, 1942, in Atlantic City, NJ; son of Robert and Phoebe Byrd; married; children: Robby, Jennifer. *Education:* Attended Trenton Junior College, 1963; Philadelphia Museum College of Art, B.F.A., 1966.

Addresses

Home—409 Warwick Rd., Haddonfield, NJ 08033.

Career

Illustrator and author. Philadelphia College of Art, Philadelphia, PA, instructor in illustrating, 1976-77; Moore College of Art, Philadelphia, instructor in illustrating, 1977—. *Exhibitions:* Numerous shows, including Society of Illustrators, New York, NY, 1971-77; Graphis Press, Zurich, Switzerland, 1974-77; Philadelphia Art Alliance, Philadelphia, 1974; Bologna Children's Book Fair, Bologna, Italy, 1975; and Rosenfeld Gallery, Philadelphia, 1982. Work held in permanent collections of the Free Library of Philadelphia and Philadelphia College of Art. *Military service:* U.S. Navy, 1961-62. *Member:* Graphic Artists Guild, Philadelphia Children's Reading Round Table, Philadelphia College of Art Alumni Association.

Awards, Honors

Children's Book Showcase, Children's Book Council, 1975, for *The Pinchpenny Mouse;* Citation of Merit, Society of Illustrators, 1976; *The Gondolier of Venice* and *The Detective of London* were both Junior Literary Guild selections.

Writings

AUTHOR AND ILLUSTRATOR

Marcella Was Bored, Dutton, 1985.
(Reteller) *The Bear and the Bird King,* Dutton, 1994.
(Reteller) *Finn MacCoul and His Fearless Wife: A Giant of a Tale from Ireland,* Dutton, 1999.

ILLUSTRATOR

Jack Stokes, adaptor, *Wiley and the Hairy Man,* Macrae Smith Co. (Philadelphia, PA), 1970.
I. G. Edmonds, adaptor, *The Possible Impossibles of Ikkyu the Wise,* Macrae Smith Co., 1971.
Vicki Cobb, *Heat,* F. Watts, 1973.
Robert Kraus, *Poor Mister Splinterfitz!,* Springfellow Books, 1973.
Ida Scheib, revised by Carole E. Welker, *The First Book of Food,* revised edition, F. Watts, 1974.
Robert Kraus, *The Pinchpenny Mouse,* Windmill Books (New York), 1974.
Kraus, *Rebecca Hatpin,* Windmill Books, 1974.
Kraus, *The Gondolier of Venice,* Windmill Books, 1976.
Robert Kraus and Bruce Kraus, *The Detective of London,* Windmill Books, 1978.
Susan Saunders, *Charles Rat's Picnic,* Dutton, 1983.
Stephanie Calmenson, selector and reteller, *The Children's Aesop,* Doubleday Book and Music Club, 1988.
Riki Levinson, reteller, *The Emperor's New Clothes,* Dutton Children's Books, 1991.
Kathleen Kain, *All about How Things Are Made: With Inspector McQ,* World Book (Chicago, IL), 1992.
Marilyn Jager Adams, *The Market,* Open Court, 1995.
Kathleen Kain, *Inspector McQ Presents All About How Things Are Made,* World Book, 1995.
Paula Fox, *The Little Swineherd and Other Tales,* Dutton, 1996.

Sidelights

Robert Byrd once told *SATA:* "To me, illustrating means making pictures. That is all I really ever wanted to do with my 'ability.' I always drew as a child, but oddly enough never thought of it as a profession, or what you did when you grew up . . . .

"I could always draw, but I never took art courses in high school. After a stint in the Navy I went to Trenton Junior College for a year, trying to 'find myself' academically and otherwise. I did well in the art courses and switched to the Philadelphia Museum School of Art. I wanted to be an illustrator from the very beginning of my studies there.

"Out of all my creative work, illustrating children's books gives me the greatest satisfaction. It is my 'fine art.' It keeps me going aesthetically. The books have a permanence and a quality of something meaningful. I have complete freedom working with [author] Robert Kraus and this is of the greatest importance to me."

Robert Byrd illustrated numerous picture books written by others before he attempted the dual role of author-illustrator. His first solo project was *Marcella Was Bored,* in which a cat, bored with her usual activities, runs away from home, where she quickly discovers that the sympathy and attention she receives from her family are what she really wants after all. A reviewer for *Growing Point* noted that in this telling of a familiar story, the cat stands in for the usual portrait of a dissatisfied teenager, and the humor of the incongruities resulting from the switch from human to cat might shed new light on "an all too familiar family situation." *School Library Journal* contributor Lorraine Douglas dubbed Byrd's illustrations "charming" and declared: "Filled with details, these gently colored scenes are filled with activity and portray Marcella as a childlike and expressive feline."

For his next solo effort, Byrd retold the Brothers Grimm tale *The Bear and the Bird King.* This little-known fable highlights how easily and how foolishly wars get started. *School Library Journal* critic Linda Boyles described Byrd's successful adaptation as "an easy narrative" with "bright watercolor washes [that] are filled with humor and movement" and "complement the text." Other reviewers found Byrd's busy illustrations equally enjoy-able, as they set the story in the eighteenth century, with birds in frock coats, top hats, and bustled costumes. A reviewer for *Publishers Weekly* noted the "verve and humor that infuse" Byrd's retelling and "are reflected and multiplied in wonderfully detailed artwork."

Byrd adapted a Celtic myth in *Finn MacCoul and His Fearless Wife.* The giant Finn and his wife Oonagh possess magical powers that they use to outsmart their enemy, the bully Cucullin, whose loss of a golden finger means the end of his power. Karen Morgan, a critic for *Booklist,* praised Byrd for his creative partnering of text and illustration. The story, filled with historical and cultural details, attracts children because of its combination of humor and suspense. A contributor to *Kirkus Reviews* lauded the illustrations as "elegant" and filled with historical detail. They "not only spur interest in the proceedings [of the plot] but convey a palpable sense of the Celtic past," according to the critic.

Works Cited

Review of *The Bear and the Bird King, Publishers Weekly,* December 13, 1993, p. 69.

Boyles, Linda, review of *The Bear and the Bird King, School Library Journal,* May, 1994, p. 108.

Douglas, Lorraine, review of *Marcella Was Bored, School Library Journal,* January, 1986, p. 55.

Review of *Finn MacCoul and His Fearless Wife: A Giant of a Tale from Ireland, Kirkus Reviews,* December 15, 1998.

Review of *Marcella Was Bored, Growing Point,* May, 1987, p. 4806.

Morgan, Karen a review of *Finn MacCoul and His Fearless Wife: A Giant of a Tale from Ireland, Booklist,* January 1, 1999.

For More Information See

PERIODICALS

Booklist, January 1, 1999.
Horn Book Guide, Fall, 1994, p. 340.
Kirkus Reviews, January 1, 1994, p. 67.*

C

CADE, Toni
See BAMBARA, Toni Cade

*   *   *

CONLY, Jane Leslie 1948-

Personal

Born in 1948 in Virginia; daughter of Robert Leslie (a writer and editor) and Sally (a writer and editor; maiden name, McCaslin) Conly; married Peter Dwyer (a public-interest attorney and social worker); children: Eliza, Will. *Education:* Degree from Smith College, 1971; Johns Hopkins University, graduate of Writing Seminars Program, 1974. *Hobbies and other interests:* Gardening, cooking, reading, fishing, "working on a dilapidated log cabin that we own on Muddy Creek in southern Pennsylvania."

Addresses

Home—Baltimore, MD. *Office*—c/o Henry Holt & Co., 115 West 18th St., New York, NY 10011.

Career

Writer. Has also worked as a director of a community center, a camp director, and a mortgage counselor. *Member:* Children's Book Guild (Washington, DC).

Awards, Honors

Notable Trade Book in the Field of Social Studies, National Council for the Social Studies/Children's Book Council, 1986, and Children's Choice, International Reading Association (IRA), 1987, both for *Racso and the Rats of NIMH;* Children's Choice, IRA, 1990, for *R-T, Margaret, and the Rats of NIMH;* Newbery Honor Book, Notable Children's Books, and Best Books for Young Adults, all American Library Association, all 1994, all for *Crazy Lady!*

Jane Leslie Conly

Writings

Racso and the Rats of NIMH, illustrated by Leonard Lubin, Harper & Row, 1986.
R-T, Margaret, and the Rats of NIMH, illustrated by Lubin, Harper & Row, 1990.
Crazy Lady!, HarperCollins, 1993.
Trout Summer, H. Holt, 1995.
While No One Was Watching, H. Holt, 1998.
What Happened on Planet Kid, H. Holt, 1999.

Sidelights

The daughter of two writers, Jane Leslie Conly has had no shortage of models for her own literary career. Her father was a staff member of *National Geographic* who wrote under the pen name Robert C. O'Brien; he won the Newbery Medal in 1972 for his children's classic *Mrs. Frisby and the Rats of NIMH.* Not only did Conly assist him with his final novel, *Z for Zachariah,* but she based her first books on characters and situations from her father's most popular novel. In *Racso and the Rats of NIMH* and *R-T, Margaret, and the Rats of NIMH,* Conly continues the story of the super-intelligent rats whose escape from the city and establishment of a farm at Thorn Valley was at the core of *Mrs. Frisby and the Rats of NIMH.* "Conly appeals to a young-adult audience through her ability to inject humor and lively action into the adventures and challenges of the younger NIMH generation," Richard D. Seiter asserted in *St. James Guide to Young Adult Writers.* Since those first books, Conly has broadened the subjects of her novels to focus on the lives of children living in difficult circumstances. In works such as the Newbery Honor Book *Crazy Lady!,* the author has been praised for her vivid characterizations and realistic portrayals of life's problems.

Conly was born in 1948, the second of four children. While both her parents worked as writers and editors, the family lived in the country. "Most of my childhood was spent on a small farm adjacent to the Potomac River near Leesburg, Virginia," the author once commented to *SATA.* "We children had a cow, several horses, a sheep, and chickens to care for, as well as dogs and cats. We worked in my mother's large garden and also cut wood. Our chores had to be done, but otherwise we were almost completely unsupervised by today's standards. I especially enjoyed fishing in the river and nearby ponds."

While the outdoor life provided lots of entertainment for the children, Conly also enjoyed more academic pursuits. "Both my parents were writers and editors, and I wrote stories from first grade on," the author remarked. "My father ... taught me to try to give my writing the cadence of spoken conversation, and to eliminate unnecessary description. (I am still working on this.) My mother taught me that good characters are the most important element in fiction." The family moved from the country to Washington, DC while Conly was a teenager, and she attended high school there. Upon graduation, she entered Smith College, and completed her degree in 1971.

Conly graduated from the Writing Seminars Program at Johns Hopkins University in 1974, and turned her hand to literary pursuits. As she told *SATA,* "I finished my father's young-adult novel, *Z for Zachariah.* (He had asked me to finish it when he realized he was going to die from heart failure.) My mother edited this book, and it was published in 1975." While the book was successful, it produced mixed emotions for Conly. Not only was it connected to her father's early death—he was only fifty-five when he died of heart disease—but

the actual process was rather lonely. As a result, the author noted on a Children's Book Guild Website, "I decided then that I didn't want to be a writer because I didn't enjoy being alone so much of the day." She changed her mind, however, after the birth of her first child, Eliza. Having children around the house made for a less solitary writing environment, and she published her first novel, *Racso and the Rats of NIMH,* in 1986.

In what a critic for *Bulletin of the Center for Children's Books* described as "short, fast-paced chapters [that] make this an excellent classroom read-aloud," *Racso and the Rats of NIMH* presents the story of the friendship of Timothy, a field mouse walking back to the school at Thorn Valley after summer vacation, and Racso, the city-slicker rat he meets on the way. Racso wants to learn how to read, and dreams of performing heroic deeds, but the wise rats at Thorn Valley consider cooperation and living in harmony higher goals than conventional heroism. Like many reviewers, *Horn Book's* Ann A. Flowers compared Conly's book to her father's, observing that the sequel "is cleverly and gracefully built upon both the philosophy of self-suffi-

In Conly's first-person narrative, seventh-grader Vernon Dibbs moves from ridicule to kindness in his treatment of his neighbor and her mentally impaired son. (Cover illustration by Vince Natale.)

Two siblings forge a summer friendship with a cantankerous old man who brings them to an appreciation of the ecosystem of the Leanna River.

ciency and the details of the plot of its predecessor." Similarly, *Booklist* critic Ilene Cooper noted that "Conly does a superb job of imbuing her animals with the originality of character and wry wit they displayed in the earlier book."

Racso gets the opportunity to learn what true heroism is not long after reaching Thorn Valley, when it is discovered that humans plan to flood the valley in order to construct a resort area for vacationers. The rats pool their resources and devise a complicated plan to reprogram the computer that controls the flood gates, but in the culmination of a subplot, Racso's father, one of the original rats of NIMH, appears to save the day. Though most reviewers applauded Conly's sequel to her father's classic children's book, some compared the work of father and daughter and found the latter lacking. Yvonne A. Frey noted in *School Library Journal:* "Conly's novel lacks the light touch of O'Brien's work, as well as the richness of character development and description." Sarah Hayes similarly observed in the *Times Literary Supplement* that "Robert O'Brien never forgot how the world might look and feel to a rat. His daughter's story, with its love interest and teenage

preoccupations, superimposes a human way of life on to the rat world and blurs the distinction between animal and man." However, many critics commented favorably on what Margery Fisher described in *Growing Point* as the book's "affectionate, shrewd humour, racy action, a background of mountain, river, and underground tunnels, the emotional force of friendships and rivalries ... [and] a consistently rhythmical, rich prose style." *Racso and the Rats of NIMH* is "another potential classic to set beside its forerunner," concluded the critic, "a second story which, like the first, deserves to last for many generations to come."

Conly followed her initial success with *R-T, Margaret, and the Rats of NIMH,* another sequel to her father's Newbery-winning classic. In this work, two unhappy children become separated from their parents while camping in Thorn Valley and are taken in by the community of rats. Due to their height, the children are able to easily accomplish tasks impossible or very time-consuming for the rats, and in this way both learn self-respect. When Margaret and Artie—known as R-T by the rats—return home, the secret of the rats' existence soon leaks out, but the children manage to save the rats from those who would return them to the laboratory from which they escaped. Reviewers debated Conly's inclusion of human characters in the fantasy world of the earlier books. *Bulletin of the Center for Children's Books* reviewer Roger Sutton, for instance, wrote that "the book is fast-moving and easy to read, but the addition of human characters renders the fantasy less convincing." Others, like *School Library Journal* contributor Susan M. Harding, were not troubled by this twist: "This new adventure about the rats of NIMH does not disappoint. The characters are full and rich, and Margaret's change ... is gradual and believable." As Alice M. Johns concluded in *Voice of Youth Advocates:* "This sensitive, modern fairy tale is a good choice for leisure reading."

Conly's Newbery Honor book, *Crazy Lady!,* is a departure from her earlier works in that it is a realistic story about humans. The book centers on Vernon Dibbs, who feels lost in the seventh grade: too old to play games with little kids, and too young to get a job. He begins to hang around street-corners with other young teenagers, stealing from the local stores and harassing Maxine, the neighborhood "crazy lady," and her mentally impaired son, Ronald. When his bad grades threaten to keep Vernon in the seventh grade for another year, he gets help from a retired teacher, who requests as payment that he run errands for Maxine and Ronald. Vernon quickly becomes emotionally involved with the family and even raises money to buy Ronald shoes so that he can run in the Special Olympics. But despite his best efforts, Vernon cannot help the family when the state decides that Maxine, who is an alcoholic, is an unfit mother. His grief over the loss of his new friends brings him closer to his own family, and together they finally mourn for Vernon's mother, who died three years earlier.

Crazy Lady! was warmly received by critics like *Horn Book* reviewer Nancy Vasilakis, who focused on the book's believable, three-dimensional characters: "Vernon's instinctive ability to connect with Ronald has an authentic ring to it, as does the narrative's first-person voice and its description of the dilapidated but cohesive urban neighborhood." "Vernon's story is an interesting and involving one," *School Library Journal* contributor Alice Casey Smith wrote, "that reveals the enormous capacity of teens for both cruelty and compassion." Hazel Rochman similarly praised the novel in *Booklist*: "Growing out of a tangle of love and laughter and grief, this story transcends formula. Right up until the very last line, the drama is in the characters, their sadness and their surprise." In 1993 Conly was recognized by the Newbery Award committee with an Honor Book citation, a "worthy" distinction in the eyes of Richard D. Seiter, who explained in *St. James Guide to Young Adult Writers* that "Vern's point of view gives authenticity, immediacy, and readability to the plot without being preachy."

In the 1995 novel *Trout Summer,* two siblings forge a similar friendship with an older outsider. After their father leaves the family, Shana and Cody move with their mother from a rural Virginia town to a Maryland suburb. Unhappy with the change, the children jump at the chance to spend the summer at an old cabin near the Leanna River. There they meet a crotchety old man named Henry, who claims to be a ranger. He teaches Cody and Shana about the river's ecosystem, as well as his belief that "you can't trust people." Nevertheless, he comes to depend on the children, who end up trying to rescue him after a trip down the rapids ends in injury. In a *Bulletin of the Center for Children's Books* featured review, Deborah Stevenson praised Conly's evocation of the river environment, noting that it "never bogs down the story ... but allows readers to understand and share Henry's, and, eventually, Shana's, feeling for the Leanna." *School Library Journal* contributor Joel Shoemaker similarly hailed the "quirky character" of Henry and added that as in her previous book, "Conly succeeds in telling a good story while demonstrating the value of knowing and learning from someone who most people call 'crazy.'" "Major and minor characterizations in this quietly affirming novel are revealing and especially well drawn," wrote *Horn Book's* Nancy Vasilakis, "and the intelligent, probing first-person voice lifts it a notch above the typical survival story." As Mary Hedge concluded in *Voice of Youth Advocates:* "The general theme of dealing with changes in life makes this an important book in today's world."

With her 1998 novel *While No One Was Watching,* the author "once again explores vivid characters living on the fringe of society," as a *Publishers Weekly* critic described it. Siblings Earl, Angela, and Frankie Foster are living with their Aunt Lula while their father is away earning money to buy the family a house. Aunt Lula proves to be a poor caretaker, however, as her drinking problem escalates and the children are left mostly to themselves. Oldest brother Earl falls in with his scheming eighteen-year-old cousin, Wayne, who uses him to help steal bicycles. When seven-year-old Frankie kidnaps a pet rabbit while tagging along on one of these escapades, it sets two well-off children on their trail. The way in which the resulting encounter affects both rich and poor children makes for an interesting conclusion. The novel is told from the viewpoints of the three Foster children, creating "a riveting immediacy and a wistful sense of irony," according to the *Publishers Weekly* reviewer. *School Library Journal* contributor Cindy Darling Codell similarly praised the author's portrayal of the siblings, and stated that while the upper-class characters were "flat and stereotypical" at times, "Conly is at her best when depicting the working poor in their struggle for survival." Deborah Stevenson believed that Conly "astutely depicts" the clash of these two worlds, and concluded in her *Bulletin of the Center for Children's Books* review: "The cultural contrast and the eventual benefit of the relationship to both sides of the track is an interesting and unusual exploration."

Although she was once reluctant to make writing her career, Conly has become a consistent author of quality novels for young adults. Since the birth of her son in 1985, the author once related, "most of my 'free' time has been spent writing. There are some aspects of writing that I really enjoy, and some that I don't like. However, I've noticed that if I don't write a certain amount each week, I lose my overall sense of contentment."

Works Cited

Codell, Cindy Darling, review of *While No One Was Watching, School Library Journal,* July, 1998, p. 92.

Conly, Jane Leslie, comments on Children's Book Guild Website at http://www.childrensbookguild.org/conly.html.

Cooper, Ilene, review of *Racso and the Rats of NIMH, Booklist,* June 1, 1986, p. 1458.

Fisher, Margery, review of *Racso and the Rats of NIMH, Growing Point,* November, 1986, pp. 4696-97.

Flowers, Ann A., review of *Racso and the Rats of NIMH, Horn Book,* September, 1986, pp. 588-89.

Frey, Yvonne A., review of *Racso and the Rats of NIMH, School Library Journal,* April, 1986, p. 85.

Harding, Susan M., review of *R-T, Margaret, and the Rats of NIMH, School Library Journal,* June, 1990, p. 118.

Hayes, Sarah, "Following On," *Times Literary Supplement,* September 19, 1986, p. 1042.

Hedge, Mary, review of *Trout Summer, Voice of Youth Advocates,* February, 1996, p. 369.

Johns, Alice M., review of *R-T, Margaret, and the Rats of NIMH, Voice of Youth Advocates,* December, 1990, p. 295.

Review of *Racso and the Rats of NIMH, Bulletin of the Center for Children's Books,* June, 1986, pp. 182-83.

Rochman, Hazel, review of *Crazy Lady!, Booklist,* May 15, 1993, p. 1691.

Seiter, Richard D., entry on Conly *St. James Guide to Young Adult Writers,* St. James Press, 1999, pp. 185-86.

Shoemaker, Joel, review of *Trout Summer, School Library Journal,* December, 1995, p. 102.

Smith, Alice Casey, review of *Crazy Lady!, School Library Journal,* April, 1993, pp. 117-18.

Stevenson, Deborah, review of *Trout Summer, Bulletin of the Center for Children's Books,* January, 1996, pp. 153-54.

Stevenson, review of *While No One Was Watching, Bulletin of the Center for Children's Books,* September, 1998, p. 11.

Sutton, Roger, review of *R-T, Margaret, and the Rats of NIMH, Bulletin of the Center for Children's Books,* June, 1990, p. 235.

Vasilakis, Nancy, review of *Crazy Lady!, Horn Book,* July-August, 1993, p. 465.

Vasilakis, review of *Trout Summer, Horn Book,* March-April, 1996, p. 195.

Review of *While No One Was Watching, Publishers Weekly,* April 20, 1998, p. 68.

For More Information See

PERIODICALS

Booklist, March, 15, 1996, p. 1289.
Kirkus Reviews, May 1, 1993, p. 595.
Teaching and Learning Literature, May-June, 1997, pp. 29-32.
Voice of Youth Advocates, June, 1993, p. 87.*

—*Sketch by Diane Telgen*

D

DeCANDIDO, Keith R. A.

Personal

Born in New York, NY; son of Robert (a librarian) and GraceAnne (a writer and editor; maiden name, Andreassi) DeCandido; married Marina Frants (a writer), May 2, 1992. *Education:* Attended Fordham University. *Hobbies and other interests:* Virtual baseball.

Addresses

Home—New York City. *Office*—21 West 100th St., New York, NY 10025-4842. *E-mail*—krad@ix.netcom.com.

Career

Library Journal, assistant editor, 1990-93; Byron Preiss Visual Publications and Multimedia Company, New York, NY, associate editor, then editor, of science fiction, fantasy, and horror, 1993—; *Chronic Rift* (talk show), New York, co-host and producer, 1990-94; Albe-Shiloh (editorial and writing service company), New York, NY, founder, 1998. Editorial director of Marvel novels. Percussionist for musical group "Don't Quit Your Day Job Players." Actor and voice-over actor.

Writings

FOR YOUNG ADULTS

(With Jose R. Nieto) *Spider-Man: Venom's Wrath,* Boulevard/BPMC (New York City), 1998.
(With Christopher Golden and Nancy Holder) *Buffy the Vampire Slayer: The Watcher's Guide,* Pocket Books, 1998.
Buffy: The Vampire Slayer: The Xander Years, Pocket Books, 1999.
Young Hercules: Cheiron's Warriors, Archway, 1999.
Young Hercules: The Ares Alliance, Archway, in press.

EDITOR

(With Byron Preiss and John Gregory Betancourt) *The Ultimate Alien,* illustrated by Christopher H. Bing, Dell, 1995.
(Editor with Preiss and Betancourt) *The Ultimate Dragon,* illustrated by Lars Hokanson and Frances Cichetti, Dell, 1995.
(Editor with Laura Anne Gilman) *OtherWere: Stories of Transformation,* Ace Books, 1996.
(Editor with Byron Preiss and Robert Silverberg) *Virtual Unrealities: The Short Fiction of Alfred Bester,* Vintage, 1997.
(Editor with Josepha Sherman) *Urban Nightmares* (short stories), Baen Books (New York City), 1997.

Author of numerous comic-book episodes for *Marvel Comics.* Short stories published in numerous anthologies, including "United We Fall," in *Doctor Who: Decalog 3: Consequences,* edited by Andy Lane and Justin Richards, Virgin, 1996; "Arms and the Man," in *Untold Stories of Spider-Man,* edited by Stan Lee and Kurt Busiek, Boulevard/BPMC, 1997; "Playing it Safe," in *The Ultimate Hulk,* edited by Lee and Peter David, Boulevard/BPMC, 1998; and "Diary of a False Man," in *Legends of the X-Men,* edited by Lee, Boulevard/BPMC, 1999. Frequent contributor of reviews, interviews, and articles to periodicals, including *Publishers Weekly, Library Journal, Wilson Library Journal,* and *Creem.*

Sidelights

Keith R. A. DeCandido is a prolific writer of science fiction. According to his Website, DeCandido's parents, both involved in literary interests, groomed their son as a writer with "a steady diet of Robert A. Heinlein, Ursula K. Le Guin, J. R. R. Tolkien, and P. G. Wodehouse, which corrupted him for life—not only instilling in him a great love of science fiction, fantasy, and silly British humor, but also likely being responsible for his pretentious insistence on using both his middle initials all the time."

Works Cited

SFF Net, www.sff.net/people/frantsdecandido (May 1999).*

*   *   *

DUNBAR, Joyce 1944-

Personal

Born January 6, 1944, in Scunthorpe, England; daughter of Russell (a steel worker) and Marjorie (a homemaker; maiden name, Reed) Miles; married James Dunbar-Brunton (an illustrator), January 27, 1972; children: Ben, Polly. *Education:* Goldsmiths College, London University, B.A. (with honors). *Hobbies and other interests:* Gardening, walking, theatre, art, building, traveling.

Addresses

Agent—Rosemary Sandberg, 6 Bayley Street, London, WC1B 3HB, England.

Career

Writer. English teacher, 1968-1989; employed in the drama department at the college at Stratford-on-Avon; teaches occasional courses in creative writing, including workshops for deaf playwrights at the Unicorn Theatre; visits numerous schools and literature festivals. Facilitator in creative writing on Greek Island of Skyros, 1998 and 2000. Member of judging panel for Mother Goose Award, 1996-1999. *Member:* Society of Authors, Norfolk Contemporary Art Society, East Anglian Society of Authors.

Awards, Honors

Guardian Children's Fiction Award runner-up, 1986, for *Mundo and the Weather-Child; A Bun for Barney* was shortlisted for Parents' Best Books for Babies Award, 1987; *Software Superslug* was listed on Smarties' Guide to Children's Reading, 1991; Best Books, *Publishers Weekly,* 1996, and Pick of the Lists, American Booksellers Association, both for *This is the Star;* Editor's Choice, *Bookseller,* 1998, and Best Books, *Child Education,* 1999, both for *Before I Go to Sleep.*

Writings

FOR CHILDREN

Mundo and the Weather-Child, Heinemann, 1985.

A Bun for Barney, illustrated by Emilie Boon, Orchard Books (London), 1987, published in the U.S. as *A Cake for Barney,* Orchard Books (New York), 1988.

The Raggy Taggy Toys, illustrated by P. J. Lynch, Orchard Books, 1987.

Tomatoes and Potatoes, illustrated by Lynn Breeze, Ginn, 1988.

Billy and the Brolly Boy, illustrated by Nick Ward, Ginn, 1988.

One Frosty Friday Morning, illustrated by John Dyke, Ginn, 1989.

Joanna and the Bean-Bag Beastie, illustrated by Francis Blake, Ginn, 1989.

I Wish I Liked Rice Pudding, illustrated by Carol Thompson, Simon & Schuster, 1989.

Ten Little Mice, illustrated by Maria Majewska, Harcourt, 1990.

Five Mice and the Moon, illustrated by James Mayhew, Orchard Books, 1990.

Lollopy, illustrated by Susan Varley, Anderson Press, 1991.

Four Fierce Kittens, illustrated by Jakki Wood, Orchard Books, 1991.

Can Do, illustrated by Carol Thompson, Simon & Schuster, 1992.

Mouse and Mole, illustrated by James Mayhew, Transworld, 1993.

Mouse and Mole Have a Party, illustrated by Mayhew, Transworld, 1993.

The Spring Rabbit, illustrated by Susan Varley, Anderson Press, 1993.

Seven Sillies, illustrated by Chris Downing, Anderson Press, 1993.

(Editor) *My First Read Aloud Story Book,* illustrated by Colin and Moira Maclean, Kingfisher Books, 1993.

Brown Bear, Snow Bear, Candlewick Press, 1994.

The Wishing Fish Tree, Ginn, 1994.

Little Eight John, illustrated by Rhian Nest-James, Ginn, 1994.

Oops-a-Daisy: And Other Tales for Toddlers, Candlewick Press, 1995.

Joyce Dunbar's cumulative-verse text describes the birth of Jesus for a picture-book audience. (Cover illustration by Gary Blythe.)

Panda and Gander had a big bowl of fruit to share.

Panda took a pear. Gander took a pomegranate. "I like pears." said Panda.

"And I like pomegranates," said Gander.

Greedy Panda consumes a whole bowl of fruit while Gander judiciously limits his appetite in Dunbar's humorous picture book. (From The Bowl of Fruit, *written by Dunbar and illustrated by Helen Craig.)*

Happy Days for Mouse and Mole, illustrated by James Mayhew, Picture Corgi, 1996.
A Very Special Mouse and Mole, illustrated by Mayhew, Picture Corgi, 1996.
Freddie the Frog, illustrated by Dennis Hockerman, 1996.
Indigo and the Whale, illustrated by Geoffrey Patterson, BridgeWater Books, 1996.
This Is the Star, illustrated by Gary Blythe, Harcourt, 1996.
Hansel and Gretel, illustrated by Ian Penney, Hove, 1997.
The Selfish Snail, illustrated by Hannah Giffard, Hamish Hamilton, 1997.
If You Want to Be A Cat, illustrated by Allan Curless, Hove, 1997.
Baby Bird, illustrated by Russell Ayto, Candlewick Press, 1998.
Tell Me Something Happy Before I Go to Sleep, illustrated by Debi Gliori, Harcourt, 1998.
Pomegranate Seeds, Candlewick Press, 1998.
The Secret Friend, illustrated by Helen Craig, Candlewick Press, 1998.
Gander's Pond, illustrated by Craig, Candlewick Press, 1998.
Tutti Frutti, illustrated by Craig, Walker, 1999.
Panda's New Toy, illustrated by Craig, Candlewick Press, 1999.
The Bowl of Fruit, illustrated by Craig, Candlewick Press, 1999.
The Pig Who Wished, illustrated by Selina Young, DK Publishers, 1999.
Eggday, illustrated by Jane Cabrera, Holiday House, 1999.
The Sand Children, illustrated by Mark Edwards, Crocodile Books, 1999.
The Very Small, illustrated by Debi Gliori, Transworld, 2000.
The Ups and Downs of Mouse and Mole, Transworld, 2000.
Hip-Dip-Dip with Mouse and Mole, Transworld, 2000.

This is the Star has been translated into ten languages, including Zulu and Hebrew.

FOR CHILDREN; ILLUSTRATED BY JAMES DUNBAR

Jugg, Scolar Press, 1980.
The Magic Rose Bough, Hodder & Stoughton, 1984.
Software Superslug, Macdonald, 1987.
Mouse Mad Madeline, Hamish Hamilton, 1988.
Software Superslug and the Great Computer Stupor, Simon & Schuster, 1989.
Ollie Oddbin's Skylark, Heinemann, 1989.
Software Superslug and the Nutty Novelty Knitting, Simon & Schuster, 1990.
The Scarecrow, Collins Educational, 1991.
Giant Jim and Tiny Tim, Collins Educational, 1991.
I Want a Blue Banana, Houghton, 1991.
Why Is the Sky Up?, Houghton, 1991.
Doodlecloud, Longman, 1994.
Doodledragon, Longman, 1994.
Doodlemaze, Longman, 1994.
Doodling Daniel, Longman, 1994.

Also author of many stories for children's educational series. Contributor of stories to anthologies, including "The Wishing Fish Clock," in *Tobie and the Face Merchant,* edited by Julia Eccleshare, Collins, 1991; "The Fly," in *The Trick of the Tale,* edited by Eccleshare, Viking, 1991; "The Way Out," in *Bedtime Stories for the Very Young,* edited by Sally Grindley, Kingfisher, 1991; and "Hilda Mathilda," in Fairy Tales, edited by Grindley, Little, Brown, 1993. Stories have been broadcast on the BBC Radio show *Listening Corner,* including "Jim Sparrow," 1982, "Sally and the Magic Rattle," 1983, "Doomuch and Doolittle," 1983, and "Shapes and Sounds," 1983 and 1984. *A Bun for Barney* was made into an interactive video game by the Multimedia Corporation of the BBC, 1990.

Adaptations

A Bun for Barney was adapted into a musical play and performed by the Royal Shakespeare Company for their children's Christmas Pantomime, 1988 and 1989; *Software Superslug* was adapted into a musical play performed at the Angel Road School, Norwich, England, 1990. *Mouse and Mole* has been produced in a twenty-six part animated series by Grasshopper Productions, with animation by Alison de Vere and featuring the voices of Alan Bennett and Richard Briers. First shown on B.B.C. 1, April, 1997.

Sidelights

Joyce Dunbar once told *SATA:* "I'd been writing for some time before a strange combination of circumstances turned me into a writer for children: First, I found myself married to an illustrator. A barrister by training, he used to draw a character called Jugg who was his alter-ego. I liked this character so much that I thought he should have a story. *Jugg* became our first book. Secondly, my children. Writing children's stories was a way of entering into and sharing their world. Third, desperation. The house was falling down round

This is the frog that

When a baby bird attempts to fly, he meets several animals who witness his progress. (*From* Baby Bird, *written by Dunbar and illustrated by Russell Ayto.*)

my ears and I needed to do something to cheer myself up."

A reviewer for *Junior Bookshelf* further explained that Dunbar suffers from a genetic disorder called sensory neural deafness, and that writing *Mundo and the Weather-Child* was her way of helping her son accept his own subsequent loss of hearing. "What was started as a therapeutic exercise emerges as a delicate work of fantasy which explores the difficult world of those childhood days when the border between the real and the imaginary has not yet been drawn," the critic explained. Told through the voice of a seven-year-old, the story "makes for powerful narration."

A Bun for Barney is a fanciful story for a younger preschool audience. In her *Growing Point* review, Margery Fisher noted that the fantasy—about a bear with a sweet roll who succumbs to other animals' demands for a taste—comes alive through "the use of alliteration" that "gives the text a flavour of its own." In a *School Library Journal* review, Lee Bock added that the surprise ending "is also a satisfying one for children because Barney learns to stand up for himself."

Lollopy, on the other hand, offers a reassuring story for youngsters learning about separation and reunion, and how to reconcile fantasy with reality. Liza Bliss commented in *School Library Journal* that the simple and direct text about a little girl who ventures into the forest with a stuffed rabbit, Lollopy, as her only companion, "leaves readers enough space for their own reactions and emotions."

Smudge, another rabbit, appears as the protagonist in *The Spring Rabbit.* Smudge, too impatient to wait until spring for a brother or sister, immediately starts looking for a sibling, but in all the wrong places. *Booklist* reviewer Mary Harris Veeder commented that "the prose is tender and [the] illustrations are wondrous depictions of gentle woodland life," and concluded that this "bunny book" would stand out among all the others in the marketplace. Another book for very young children, *Oops-a-Daisy: And Other Tales for Toddlers,* portrays situations common to this age group. *Booklist's* Hazel Rochman noted that "toddlers will recognize the situations [all about learning to play with others], and will be delighted to find that there are books about the games they play."

Although the majority of Dunbar's books are best suited for children of preschool or primary-school age, two titles stand out for their appeal to older audiences. *Indigo and the Whale* and *This Is the Star* address complex themes with engaging simplicity. Of *Indigo and the Whale,* a story of one boy's painful, yet rewarding saga of self-discovery, Elizabeth Baynton-Clarke wrote in *School Librarian:* "The storyline is lively, fantastic, surreal in places, and all through sings praises in support of the individual." Critical praise also followed *This Is the Star,* Dunbar's rendition of the Nativity story written in rhyming cumulative text. A reviewer in *Publishers Weekly* asserted that Dunbar's "sophisticated vocabulary and phrasing guard against the singsong rhythm that so frequently governs cumulative verse," while a *Kirkus Reviews* critic declared that text and illustrations "do full justice both to the glory and to the simple humanity of the Christmas story."

Other books of note for toddlers is *Baby Bird,* a story that *Booklist* reviewer Helen Rosenberg claimed will inspire children to "cheer Baby Bird as he lifts himself into the sky" after the other animals dared to make fun of his attempts. *The Bowl of Fruit, Panda's New Toy, Tutti Frutti* and *The Secret Friend* are about the friendship between Panda and Gander. Elizabeth Bush, reviewing the Panda series in *Bulletin of the Center for Children's Books,* predicted that children will energetically respond to the books because "they will know the rules [of sharing and jealousy told in the books] and be more than happy to inform Panda of them along the way." Vivian French, writing in *Guardian Education,* declared of *Tutti Frutti:* "Everything—and I mean everything—about this book is a total delight: the look, the feel, the format; even the colour...." Concluding the work a "lovely, lovely book," French asserted that it is "enormous fun to read aloud."

In her interview with *SATA,* Dunbar shared her reflections about writing: "The great thing about writing is that it makes almost every experience worthwhile because you can make a story out of it. The other great thing is that you can live two lives at once: one in the so-called 'real' world (which is never quite what we ordered), and one inside your head, which you can order in whatever way you like.

"I used to be a teacher and loved it, but deafness put an end to that career. I'm glad in a way, because it gave me a very strong motive to survive the early difficult stages of writing, when you are very unsure of yourself, and can't believe that anyone will want to read what you write, never mind publish it!"

Works Cited

Baynton-Clarke, Elizabeth, review of *Indigo and the Whale, School Librarian,* August, 1996, pp. 98-99.

Bliss, Liza, review of *Lollopy, School Library Journal,* August, 1992, p. 135.

Bock, Lee, review of *A Cake for Barney, School Library Journal,* May, 1988, p. 83.

Bush, Elizabeth, review of *The Bowl of Fruit, Bulletin of the Center for Children's Books,* June, 1999, pp. 349-350.

Bush, review of *Panda's New Toy, Bulletin of the Center for Children's Books,* June, 1999, pp. 349-350.

Bush, review of *The Secret Friend, Bulletin of the Center for Children's Books,* June, 1999, pp. 349-350.

Fisher, Margery, review of *A Bun for Barney, Growing Point,* January, 1988, p. 4921.

French, Vivian, review of *Tutti Frutti, Guardian Education.*

Review of *Mundo and the Weather-Child, Junior Bookshelf,* February, 1986, p. 32.

Rochman, Hazel, review of *Oops-a-Daisy: And Other Tales for Toddlers,* September 1, 1995, p. 84.

Rosenberg, Helen, review of *Baby Bird, Booklist,* June 1, 1998, p. 1778.

Review of *This Is the Star, Kirkus Reviews,* October 1, 1996, p. 1476.

Review of *This Is the Star, Publishers Weekly,* September, 30, 1996, p. 88.

Veeder, Mary Harris, review of *The Spring Rabbit, Booklist,* April 15, 1994, p. 1538.

For More Information See

PERIODICALS

Booklist, February 15, 1988, p. 1000; April 15, 1990, p. 1628.

Books For Keeps, May, 1994, p. 11.

Junior Bookshelf, April, 1994, pp. 48-49.

Publishers Weekly, October 4, 1991, p. 86; August 14, 1995, p. 82.

School Librarian, November, 1991, p. 139; May, 1993, p. 54.

School Library Journal, May, 1994, p. 91; August, 1996, p. 121.

Sunday Telegraph, December 1, 1996, p. 13.

E

ECKLAR, Julia (Marie) 1964-

Personal

Born March 14, 1964, in Greenville, OH; daughter of William T. and Constance Mary (Huffman) Ecklar. *Education:* Attended University of Dayton and University of Pittsburgh. *Politics:* Democrat. *Hobbies and other interests:* Music, animal husbandry, horseback riding, Native-American bead crafts, softball.

Addresses

Office—322 Mall Blvd., Ste. 141, Monroeville, PA 15146.

Career

Worked variously as a secretary and data processor; freelance writer, 1987—. *Member:* Science Fiction Writers of America, Pennwriters.

Awards, Honors

John W. Campbell Award, World Science Fiction Society, 1991.

Writings

Star Trek: The Kobayashi Maru, Pocket Books, 1989.
Ice Trap (Star Trek, No. 60), Pocket Books, 1992.
Regenesis, Ace, 1995.

Contributor of novellas to magazines, including *Analog Science Fiction/Science Fact,* and the *Magazine of Fantasy and Science Fiction.*

Adaptations

The Kobayashi Maru was adapted for audiocassette.

Sidelights

Author Julia Ecklar has long been interested in science. After growing up on farms in Ohio and Kentucky, she studied physics, biology, and computer science at several universities. Her interest in science and the desire to tell a good story led her to write two science-fiction novels and a number of speculative short stories, which have been published in leading genre magazines. "Julia tries to show that women and men are capable of the entire range of human activities and aspirations," wrote Jay Kay Klein in *Analog Science Fiction/Science Fact.* "It's this truth that she wants to bring to her fiction."

Ecklar's debut novel, *The Kobayashi Maru,* is part of the Star Trek series, based on the perennially popular television show. In her novel, Ecklar strands the main leaders of the starship *Enterprise* on a space shuttle. Because they believe that they are in a hopeless situation, the crew members discuss their performances on a Starfleet Academy test that presented them with a no-win scenario. Though true Star Trek fans need little coaxing to read new episodes, reviewer A. C. P. of *Kliatt* predicted that *The Kobayashi Maru,* which "is an easy read," would be "especially interesting" to younger YA readers. "While the novel has a slow start and lacks an initial reader's hook, the revelations about the characters' experiences at the academy more than make up for these deficiencies with humor, pathos, and courage," enthused *Wilson Library Bulletin's* Gene LaFaille.

Ecklar's *Regenesis,* a collection of four short novels, deals with a place of her own design—an organization called Noah's Ark that seeds Earth's endangered species on other planets. Rahel Tovin, the organization's troubleshooter, travels from planet to planet, overcoming a host of challenges involving the animals. Critics offered qualified praise. In *Science Fiction Chronicle,* Don D'Ammassa judged the stories to be "all good ones" but faulted Tovin's sharp disposition. Likewise, Avila Lamb, writing in *Kliatt,* described *Regenesis* as "exciting and thought-provoking"; yet she bemoaned the main character's frequent use of profanity.

Works Cited

D'Ammassa, Don, review of *Regenesis, Science Fiction Chronicle,* July, 1995, p. 36.

Klein, Jay Kay, "Biolog" feature on Ecklar, *Analog Science Fiction/Science Fact,* September, 1991, p. 71.

LaFaille, Gene, review of *Star Trek: The Kobayashi Maru, Wilson Library Bulletin,* May, 1990, pp. 107, 133.

Lamb, Avila, review of *Regenesis, Kliatt,* September, 1995, p. 20.

Review of *Star Trek: The Kobayashi Maru, Kliatt,* April, 1990, pp. 24-26.

For More Information See

PERIODICALS

Booklist, November 1, 1990, p. 554.

BookWatch, February, 1991, p. 8.

Science Fiction Chronicle, June, 1990, p. 38; October, 1990, p. 34.*

*   *   *

EDENS, Cooper 1945-

Personal

Born Gary Drager on September 25, 1945, in Washington, D.C.; son of Otto (an electrical engineer) and Garnet (Cooper) Drager; married Louise Arnold, March 3, 1979; children: David, Emily. *Education:* University of Washington, B.A., 1970. *Politics:* "Universalist." *Religion:* "Universalist."

Addresses

Home—4204 NE 11th Ave. #15, Seattle, WA 98105. *Agent*—C/o Green Tiger Press, 1061 India St., San Diego, CA 92101.

Career

Author and illustrator, 1978—. Participant in programs of the Children's Museum of the Museum of Seattle, WA. *Exhibitions:* Foster-White Gallery, Seattle, WA, 1970—.

Awards, Honors

Children's Critic Award from the Bologna International Children's Book Fair, 1980, for *The Starcleaner Reunion;* American nominee for the Golden Apple Award from the Czechoslovakian government (Prague), 1983, for *Caretakers of Wonder.*

Writings

AUTHOR AND ILLUSTRATOR; PUBLISHED BY GREEN TIGER PRESS, UNLESS OTHERWISE NOTED

If You're Afraid of the Dark, Remember the Night Rainbow, 1978, 2nd edition, 1984, reprinted, 1991.

The Starcleaner Reunion, 1979.

Caretakers of Wonder, 1980, reprinted, 1991.

With Secret Friends, 1981, reprinted, 1992.

Inevitable Papers, 1982.

Nineteen Hats, Ten Teacups, an Empty Birdcage and the Art of Longing, 1986, reprinted, 1992.

(With others) *Paradise of Ads,* 1987.

Now Is the Moon's Eyebrow, 1987.

Hugh's Hues, 1988.

The Little World, Blue Lantern Books, 1994.

If You're Still Afraid of the Dark, Add One More Star to the Night, Simon & Schuster, 1998.

FOR CHILDREN

Emily and the Shadow Shop, illustrated by Patrick Dowers, Green Tiger, 1982.

A Phenomenal Alphabet Book, illustrated by Joyce Eide, 1982.

The Prince of the Rabbits, illustrated by Felix Meroux, Green Tiger, 1984.

Santa Cows, illustrated by Daniel Lane, Green Tiger, 1991.

The Story Cloud, illustrated by Kenneth LeRoy Grant, Green Tiger, 1991.

A Present for Rose, illustrated by Molly Hashimoto, Sasquatch Books, 1993.

Shawnee Bill's Enchanted Five-Ride Carousel, illustrated by Daniel Lane, Green Tiger, 1994.

Santa Cow Island, illustrated by Daniel Lane, Green Tiger, 1994.

How Many Bears?, illustrated by Marjett Schille, Atheneum, 1994.

The Wonderful Counting Clock, illustrated by Kathleen Kimball, Simon & Schuster, 1995.

Santa Cow Studios, illustrated by Daniel Lane, Simon & Schuster, 1995.

Nicholi, illustrated by A. Scott Banfill, Simon & Schuster, 1996.

(With Alexandra Day) *The Christmas We Moved to the Barn,* illustrated by Alexandra Day, Harper Collins, 1997.

(With Alexandra Day) *Taffy's Family,* HarperCollins, 1997.

(With Harold Darling and Richard Kehl) *Invisible Art,* Blue Lantern Studio, 1999.

(With Daniel Lane) *The Animal Mall,* illustrated by Edward Miller, Dial, 2000.

ILLUSTRATOR

Alexandra Day, *Helping the Sun,* Green Tiger, 1987.

Alexandra Day, *Helping the Flowers and Trees,* Green Tiger, 1987.

Alexandra Day, *Helping the Night,* Green Tiger, 1987.

Alexandra Day, *Helping the Animals,* Green Tiger, 1987.

OTHER

(With Alexandra Day and Welleran Poltarnees) *Children from the Golden Age, 1880-1930,* Green Tiger, 1987.

(Selector) *The Glorious Mother Goose,* illustrated by various artists, Atheneum, 1988, reprinted, 1998.

(Compiler) Lewis Carroll, *Alice's Adventures in Wonderland: The Ultimate Illustrated Edition,* Bantam Books, 1989.

(Selector and arranger of illustrations) *Beauty and the Beast,* Green Tiger, 1989.

In Cooper Edens's magical self-illustrated picture book, fantastic events take place in the middle of a seemingly uneventful night. (From Caretakers of Wonder.)

(Selector) *The Glorious ABC,* illustrated by various artists, Atheneum, 1990.

(Conceiver) *Day and Night and Other Dreams,* Green Tiger, 1990.

(Selector and arranger of illustrations) *Hansel and Gretel,* illustrated by various artists, Green Tiger, 1990.

(Compiler with Harold Darling) *Favorite Fairy Tales,* Chronicle Books, 1991.

(Conceiver, compiler, and arranger) *The Three Princesses,* Bantam Books, 1991.

(Selector and arranger of illustrations) *Jack and the Beanstalk,* illustrated by various artists, Green Tiger, 1990.

(Selector and arranger of illustrations) *Goldilocks and the Three Bears,* illustrated by various artists, Green Tiger, 1989.

(Selector and arranger of illustrations) *Little Red Riding Hood,* illustrated by various artists, Green Tiger, 1989.

(With Alexandra Day and Welleran Poltarnees) *An ABC of Fashionable Animals,* Green Tiger, 1991.

(Compiler with Richard Kehl) *The Flower Shop,* Blue Lantern Books, 1992.

(Compiler with Richard Kehl) *The Heart Shop,* Blue Lantern Books, 1992.

(Compiler with Harold Darling), Clement Moore, *The Night before Christmas,* Chronicle Books, 1998.

How Many Bears? has been translated into Spanish.

Sidelights

Cooper Edens once told *SATA* interviewer Rachel Koenig about his childhood, growing up in Washington State on Lake Washington: "A huge highway separated me from prospective playmates who might otherwise have come to visit. Consequently, I spent many hours alone by the lake, daydreaming. I would imagine the island in the lake to be a pirate ship, or another world altogether. It seems to me that many artists are, or were in childhood, enchanted by bodies of water—the sea, a lake, a creek or a pond. This was certainly true for me. I had a rowboat which I repainted again and again; first it was a giraffe, then a zebra, then . . . .

"I tended to miss quite a bit of school. I don't remember whether this was for some legitimate reason, or simply because I didn't want to go. My earliest 'textbooks' were coloring books which I would color in peculiar ways, changing the words as I went along. I cut up and reorganized comic strips from the newspaper, superimposing, say, Felix the Cat into the alien world of another comic strip character.

"On very hot days I would invite friends to watch me draw on the walls of my tent, listening to nonsensical recitations of my own stories. I guess my storytelling actually began in those strange tent proceedings. I also wrote songs. My art work began by coloring over other people's drawings. My uncle campaigned for mayor and when he lost the election, I inherited all of his posters. I colored them, and then began to design my own, inspired by such television shows as 'Hopalong Cassidy.' In fourth grade, when my attendance in school became more regular, I was put in charge of the bulletin board, changing it for each holiday and season. It could be said in relation to my work today that I am *still* doing the bulletin board!

"My confidence grew out of these coloring book and bulletin board escapades. I considered myself master of color. In junior high school, I was regarded the 'art guy,' who was always hanging out in the 'art room.' Philosophically I hold that everyone comes into the world with something great to share. The first authority figure we encounter, be it parent or teacher, encourages or stifles the gift. Our early creativity is fragile and can be easily crushed. As luck had it, I was encouraged in school."

Edens continued: "When I began to exhibit my work, I noted that some of the characters in my paintings tended to recur. One day I randomly laid the paintings on the floor and began to lace the images together with titles. I wrote a story around the paintings, which became *The Starcleaner Reunion.* So my first book was about tying images together with words. Since then, however, I write the story first and then illustrate it.

"My original Starcleaners, as I was to discover, were oversized for standard publishing practice. I put these giant cardboard figures in a suitcase—the combined weight of which was over two hundred pounds—and carried them to New York in the middle of the summer, sweating profusely as I made the rounds of New York publishers. I had visions of publishers occupying grand rooms, where all of an illustrator's art work was hung on white, spotlighted gallery walls. In fact, the offices of these prominent people were often smaller than my suitcase! I often set up my gigantic Starcleaners on top of someone's bologna sandwich. Everyone responded favorably to my work, but felt that it was too expensive to reproduce. This was in 1978, before four-color printing was feasible for large publishers.

"Several editors suggested that I contact Green Tiger Press, which had a reputation for being eccentric. I went to Green Tiger, and they were willing to invest in my work, although they published my second book, *If You're Afraid of the Dark, Remember the Night Rainbow,* first. *Night Rainbow* was a song I had many times attempted to have recorded. I submitted the song as a text and Green Tiger okayed it, but they didn't know that I could draw. They had already submitted the book to several well-known illustrators, but liked my work and decided to accept my illustrations. Green Tiger put up the money to make four-color separation and we came out with a soft-cover first edition, which was very unusual because there weren't many soft-covered children's books. An advantage is that they can be easily mailed as gifts and are, therefore, sold in gift shops. *Night Rainbow* was often the only book sold in such shops. These outside markets helped get 200,000 copies of the book sold because it never had to compete with other children's books."

"With *The Starcleaner Reunion* I couldn't draw mouths. As a result, all the men sport mustaches. This inability got me into other kinds of trouble. I've been asked why there aren't any women in *Starcleaner*. It isn't because I think women can't clean stars, it's simply because women don't have mustaches! Now that I've learned how to paint mouths, I'd like to update it and add many women.

"I think about writing in terms of meter, and I have noticed that when *Night Rainbow* is read out loud it sings. I don't rhyme intentionally, but I consider my books melodic. I hear melodies as I write. I suppose one could say my meter, my phonetic or in-line rhyming, has its origins in the melodies of Buddy Holly and the Beatles."

Edens's general philosophical approach to children's literature is a departure from traditional precepts. "*Alice in Wonderland, Peter Pan, The Wizard of Oz,* and Sendak's *Where the Wild Things Are* are the classic big four stories in my opinion, and they all work in a similar way. Essentially these stories transport us to the world of dreams from which we must return. In essence these books are saying, 'You must be home for dinner.' They present a dualistic vision: there is a dream world, and there is a real world to which you must return. I'm trying to break the dualism of the classic tale. My stories embrace the philosophy that these two worlds exist simultaneously—the real world is a dream and the dream world is real. Because of this, there are no classic quests in my books. I don't have people going away to the dream world and returning to reality. In *Caretakers of Wonder,* for example, the characters are real people doing such surreal things as balancing rainbows or mending clouds. My characters are in a real world doing dream things or in a dream doing real things. It isn't a voyage through a door to some strange and secret place. After all, the only real secret is that when you're awake you're in a dream and when you are asleep you're in reality.

"*Starcleaner Reunion* presents an alternate version of the Creation Story. The book does not suggest that the Bible is wrong, nor does it suggest that Buddha is wrong. It says that everyone is capable of making up their own version of the way the world came to be. No one really knows the mystery. The fact that no one knows makes it

At an annual snow-sculpting event, a stranger appears and carves a sleigh and team of reindeer that magically come to life. (*From* Nicholi, *written by Edens and illustrated by A. Scott Banfill.*)

SANTA COWS

By Cooper Edens • Illustrated by Daniel Lane

In Edens's spoof of Clement Clarke Moore's famous yuletide poem, a modern family's microwaved Christmas dinner is followed by a visit from a herd of cows bearing decorations and equipment for a game of baseball. (Cover illustration by Daniel Lane.)

beautiful, because it ultimately allows everyone to know. If there were but one answer, the world would be very dull. I want everyone to feel that he's 'in on it.'

"People have sent me their own version of my books. Children in Colombia who were learning English for the first time sent me their response to *Night Rainbow*. 'What if the tomato doesn't ripen? Get a new universe ...' were some of their solutions. Many schools use *Caretakers of Wonder* to teach children about ecology. This feels good because it means I'm not sending a completed work into the world, but a catalyst. I want my readers to have the necessary room for a *creative* response to my work."

Stars and hearts are recurring images in Edens's artwork. "When I read Carl Jung I realized how very few symbols there are in the world, and how strong the symbols *star* and *heart* really are. They're symbolically odd because a heart doesn't really look like the organ, and a star doesn't look like an astronomical star. I wondered one day, 'What if stars and hearts were really the same thing?' And that is what *The Starcleaner Reunion* is about."

"The symbol of a heart/star embodies both the infinite and the individual. I'm trying to break up dualities and scale; I believe that's the function of art. It's about getting more room to breathe. It's about fighting stagnation. It isn't the verb, it's the loving. It's not what you love, it's *that* you love. It's not the art, it's that you're painting. I believe in the verb, and that's why I make books."

Poet W. S. Merwin and painter Henri Matisse are Edens's heroes. "A rather strange combination, but I respond to them from both my sense of words and my sense of visuals. Their work has given me confidence and kinship. Matisse's cutouts—a series of pieces he did when he was very ill and could no longer paint—were inspiring. He resorted to scissors, as did I in *Inevitable Papers*. I often wonder what would have become of me had I not run across Merwin's poems and the paintings of Matisse—perhaps I would still be drawing Hopalong Cassidy!"

Edens offers the following encouragement to young artists: "The hardest step is to admit that you want to do it. But the second you start, something will come back to you—call it God or nature or mystery. I'm a witness to the fact that if you participate you will be joined by some other energy or spirit or friend; then, you're instantly a team, a couplement, and once this happens, everything is easy. When people submit their books to me I always say, 'The one thing that separates you from most people is that you *want* to do it; the minute you want to do it, you're a very select person.' There aren't that many people who consistently work at something, who consistently show up.

"Another lesson is that at first, perhaps only one of ten paintings you make will be good. But one will always be better than the other nine. So you throw away nine and the next day, maybe two of ten will work. Pretty soon half of what you make will be good. You learn that sometimes things come out instantly and sometimes they have to be fixed.

"There is craft involved in any art. You'll have to know the brushes and paints eventually. But there are victories before you learn the right brush. You can make a lot of spills and still find a reason to show up again. After all, you're with friends. As a philosopher once said, 'The planet exists because life needs it.' It isn't the earth that makes life possible, it's life that makes the earth what it is. That's the way it is with art. It exists because you want it to."

Following his early, whimsical, self-illustrated books, Edens wrote a number of humorous picture books for children, including *Santa Cows,* a spoof of the Santa Claus myth. Edens's story is "a preposterous yarn that plays havoc with Clement Clarke Moore's famous Christmas rhyme and attacks our fast-food, video-driven culture," Stephanie Zvirin wrote in *Booklist.* In *Santa Cows,* the nine members of the modern family at the center of Edens's story are enjoying their microwaved Christmas dinners when they are visited by a herd of cows bearing decorations for the house and equipment for a Christmas day game of baseball. The result is a "wacky fantasy," according to a reviewer for *Publishers Weekly,* that "will leave readers who appreciate its irreverent humor wanting more." Daniel Lane, the illustrator for *Santa Cows,* teamed up with Edens again for *Shawnee Bill's Enchanted Five-Ride Carousel.* In this story, Shawnee Bill, "summertime's answer to Saint Nick," according to a reviewer for *Publishers Weekly,* provides a special ride on the carousel's animals, now freed from the carousel, for the nearby town's babies, who cavort through fields of wildflowers on the backs of the fantastical animals come alive. The critic for *Publishers Weekly* dubbed Edens's story "sweet as a taffy apple."

For *Nicholi,* Edens returned to the theme of Christmas with the story of an annual snow-sculpting event at which a stranger appears, carving out a sleigh and a team of reindeer that magically come to life. Nicholi then offers the townspeople a ride on the sleigh, where they sail over the earth and meet up with the other ice sculptures in the show. "Edens's first-person text bespeaks genuine childlike exhilaration," contended a reviewer for *Publishers Weekly,* and contributes much of the enjoyment to be gleaned from this "brightly wrapped holiday fantasy."

Edens has also created a series of books celebrating the history of children's book illustration. In these books, Edens reprints one version of a classic children's story, such as *Hansel and Gretel, Little Red Riding Hood,* or *Beauty and the Beast,* along with illustrations from a number of artists who have adapted the tales since the nineteenth century. In *The Three Princesses: Cinderella, Sleeping Beauty, Snow White,* Edens does the same for three traditional tales about princesses. The great asset of this work "for anyone interested in the history of book illustration," attested Michael Dirda in the *Washington Post Book World,* is Edens's selection of more than 150 illustrations from artists of the past. As a "sampler" in the history of children's book illustration, *The Three Princesses* is "tantalizing," Dirda concluded, and should inspire readers to seek out the original books Edens drew upon as his sources.

Works Cited

Dirda, Michael, review of *The Three Princesses, Washington Post Book World,* January 12, 1992, p. 8.

Review of *Nicholi, Publishers Weekly,* October 6, 1997, p. 55.

Review of *Santa Cows, Publishers Weekly,* September 20, 1991, p. 133.

Review of *Shawnee Bill's Enchanted Five-Ride Carousel, Publishers Weekly,* May 30, 1994, p. 54.

Zvirin, Stephanie, review of *Santa Cows, Booklist,* November 1, 1991, p. 531.

For More Information See

PERIODICALS

Kirkus Reviews, September 1, 1997, p. 1387.

Newsweek, November, 1979, p. 64; December 5, 1983, p. 111.

School Library Journal, October, 1979, p. 138.*

* * *

EIDSON, Thomas 1944-

Personal

Born in 1944, in Kansas.

Addresses

Agent—c/o Dutton, Penguin USA, 375 Hudson St., New York, NY 10014.

Career

Hill & Knowlton (public relations firm), president and chief executive officer. *Military service:* Served in U.S. Army.

Awards, Honors

W. H. Smith Thumping Good Read citation, 1995, for *St. Agnes' Stand.*

Writings

St. Agnes' Stand, Putnam, 1994.
The Last Ride, Putnam, 1995.
All God's Children, M. Joseph (London), 1996, Dutton, 1997.
Hannah's Gift, M. Joseph, 1998.

Adaptations

St. Agnes' Stand was adapted for the screen by Larry McMurtry as *The Standoff,* Universal.

Sidelights

Public-relations professional and novelist Thomas Eidson is known for writing western fiction emphasizing moral questions and rugged living conditions in a 19th-century Kansas setting. As a child Eidson heard stories about homesteading life directly from his grandparents, who had been among the first to settle the American West. Eidson has attributed the heightened quality of such storytelling to the fact that it was an important form of entertainment in a land of isolation. Eidson, too, was raised on his parents' farm, and he worked on a Texas ranch as a young man, competing in horse shows and rodeos.

In his debut novel, *St. Agnes' Stand,* Eidson tells the story of a man on the run. Nat Swanson has just killed a Texas cowboy and, injured in the leg, is having a hard time fleeing to California. On his way west he meets up with a wagon under attack by Apaches that contains several nuns and orphans. Swanson kills an Apache and ends up helping the stranded group, despite the heat and limited food and water. A nun named St. Agnes provides a contrast to the gruff Swanson; she is absolutely sure that Swanson is a savior sent from God. According to *Times Literary Supplement* contributor John Melmoth, *St. Agnes' Stand* effectively portrays the grittiness of the true West with such details as people being slowly baked to death, eyes being gouged out, and other natural and human dangers. But the novelist is over his head, in Melmoth's opinion, when Eidson concentrates on the supernatural and the "mystery of life." A *Publishers Weekly* reviewer called Eidson's prose "taut, spare, visual, and reminiscent of Larry McMurtry."

Eidson continued his study of human spirituality in *The Last Ride,* which contrasts Christian and Native-American beliefs in the American West. Maggie, a devout Christian, is infuriated when her dying father returns home to make amends before he dies. Her father, once married to an Indian, has adopted Native-American beliefs, while Maggie, the victim of Apache raids, harbors a deep resentment toward Native Americans. When Maggie's eldest daughter is kidnapped by a Native-American witch, Maggie is forced to join her father in search of the girl. The father employs Native-American magic to help locate the captor, and Maggie gains an appreciation of another spiritual paradigm. A *Publishers Weekly* contributor found the premise of the story ineffective and termed *The Last Ride* a "hackneyed effort."

In Eidson's third western, *All God's Children,* a lone Quaker woman named Pearl Eddy tries to sustain her belief in nonviolence in a town full of Methodists, even though she has roused the ire of her neighbors. Pearl has offered sanctuary in her home to both a black man on the run from lynching and a Japanese family suffering the indignities of racism. Despite some difficulties, Eddy's house guests eventually become allies. Though one reviewer found the story contrived and predictable, a *Publishers Weekly* contributor called *All God's Children* a "powerfully visual tale filled with the timeless virtues of courage and loyalty."

Hannah's Gift is the story of an injured sheriff who awakens to find himself miraculously cured of a gunshot chest wound due to the care of Hannah, a beautiful and mysterious woman. While the sheriff searches for the truth about what happened, he comes to believe that Hannah has powers akin to the Virgin Mary. *Times Literary Supplement* reviewer Andrew M. Brown found the sheriff's character unrealistically sentimental for a man of his day and age, but praised Hannah's development and deemed the novel well done despite the intrusion of an occasional cliche.

Works Cited

Review of *All God's Children, Publishers Weekly,* May 5, 1997, p. 197.
Brown, Andrew M., review of *Hannah's Gift, Times Literary Supplement,* May 29, 1998, p. 27.
Review of *The Last Ride, Publishers Weekly,* January 23, 1995, p. 59.
Melmoth, John, review of *St. Agnes' Stand, Times Literary Supplement,* July 1, 1994, p. 20.
Review of *St. Agnes' Stand, Publishers Weekly,* March 7, 1994, p. 56.

For More Information See

PERIODICALS

Quill and Quire, April, 1994, p. 6.
Roundup, July, 1995, p. 23.
School Library Journal, July, 1994, p. 128; January, 1998, p. 136.
Times Literary Supplement, July 1, 1994, p. 20.*

F

FIENBERG, Anna 1956-

Personal

Born November 23, 1956, in Canterbury, England. *Hobbies and other interests:* Reading and traveling.

Addresses

Office—c/o Allen & Unwin Pty. Ltd., 9 Atchison Street, St. Leonards, New South Wales 2065, Australia.

Career

Writer. *School Magazine,* New South Wales, 1980-90 (editor, 1988-90); national book club consultant; lecturer on creative writing.

Anna Fienberg

Awards, Honors

Book of the Year for younger readers, Children's Book Council of Australia, 1992, for *The Magnificent Nose and Other Marvels;* Alan Marshall Prize for Children's Literature, Victorian Premier's Literary awards, 1993; shortlist, New South Wales Premier's Prize, 1995, for *Power to Burn*; shortlist, Children's Book of the Year Award, Children's Book Council of Australia, for both *Wiggy and Boa* and *Tashi.*

Writings

FOR CHILDREN; FICTION

Billy Bear and the Wild Winter, illustrated by Astra Lacis, Angus & Robertson (New South Wales, Australia), 1988.

The Champion, seven volumes (includes *Con the Whiz Kid, Marisa's Party, My Goldie, Stefano's Nonna, A Teddy for Louise, Please, Teresa Trouble,* and *Tien Tells Minh*), illustrated by Felicity Meyer, Traffic Authority of New South Wales (Sydney, Australia), 1988.

Wiggy and Boa, illustrated by Ann James, Dent (Melbourne, Australia), 1988, Houghton (Boston, MA), 1990, as *Pirate Trouble for Wiggy and Boa,* Allen & Unwin (New South Wales, Australia), 1996.

The 9 Lives of Balthazar, illustrated by Donna Gynell, Houghton (Victoria, Australia), 1989.

The Magnificent Nose and Other Marvels, illustrated by Kim Gamble, Allen & Unwin, 1991.

Ariel, Zed and the Secret of Life, illustrated by Gamble, Allen & Unwin, 1992.

The Hottest Boy Who Ever Lived, illustrated by Gamble, Allen & Unwin, 1993, Whitman (Morton Grove, IL), 1995.

Madeline the Mermaid: And Other Fishy Tales, illustrated by Ann James, Allen & Unwin, 1995.

Power to Burn, Allen & Unwin, 1995.

(With mother, Barbara Fienberg) *Tashi,* illustrated by Kim Gamble, Allen & Unwin, 1995.

(With B. Fienberg) *Tashi and the Giants,* illustrated by Gamble, Allen & Unwin, 1995.

Dead Sailors Don't Bite, illustrated by Ann James, Allen & Unwin, 1996.

(With B. Fienberg) *Tashi and the Ghosts,* illustrated by Kim Gamble, Allen & Unwin, 1996.

(With B. Fienberg) *Tashi and the Genie,* illustrated by Gamble, Allen & Unwin, 1997.

The Doll's Secret, Australia Post (Melbourne), 1997.

(With B. Fienberg) *Tashi and the Baba Yaga,* illustrated by Kim Gamble, Allen & Unwin, 1998.

Minton Goes Flying, illustrated by Gamble, Allen & Unwin, 1998.

Minton Goes Sailing, illustrated by Gamble, Allen & Unwin, 1998.

Minton Goes Driving, illustrated by Gamble, Allen & Unwin, 1999.

Tashi and the Demons, illustrated by Gamble, Allen & Unwin, 1999.

OTHER

Eddie, Jacaranda Wiley (Queensland, Australia), 1988.

(Reteller) *The World of May Gibbs* (includes "Snugglepot and Cuddlepie," "Snugglepot and Cuddlepie at Sea," "Snugglepot and Cuddlepie Meet Little Obelia," "Cuddlepie Goes to the Dentist," "Snugglepot and Cuddlepie and the Banksia Men," and "Snugglepot and Cuddlepie Go Home"), illustrated by Vicky Kitanov, HarperCollins (New South Wales, Australia), 1997.

Borrowed Light (young-adult novel), Allen & Unwin, 1999.

Sidelights

Australian picture-book author Anna Fienberg got her start in the field of children's literature while working as an editor at *School Magazine* in her native Australia. After reading over one thousand children's books for review purposes, she decided that she was expert enough to begin writing her own stories for young children. *Billy Bear and the Wild Winter,* which was published in 1988, would be the first of many popular books Fienberg has written, featuring what Kerry White described in *St. James Guide to Children's Writers* as "resourceful children who develop their special talents in worlds where almost anything is possible." In 1999 Fienberg expanded her writing into a new genre. Her first young-adult novel, *Borrowed Light,* examines life and love from a more mature teenage perspective.

Born in England in 1956, Fienberg moved with her family to Australia when she was three years old. Five years later, the imaginative young girl could proudly announce that she was an author, having written her first complete story, an energetic tale that recounted the escapades of talking dolphins spouting ten-cent words. Other stories quickly followed, leading to a college degree in English and a job as an editor at a magazine-publishing company.

The Magnificent Nose and Other Marvels is a collection of stories that focus on the whimsical worlds captured in daydreams. In each of Fienberg's tales the main character is a young person with a unique talent that in his or her daydreams becomes a source of power—like

Ferdinand Feedlebenz, a curious young lad whose fascination with warts, moles, and bumps causes him to find a way to cure people of all manner of misshapenness. Praising the sense of humor that runs throughout *The Magnificent Nose,* *Horn Book* contributor Karen Jameyson noted that a "magical feeling drifts pleasantly from page to page" throughout the entire volume.

The Hottest Boy Who Ever Lived, another picture-book offering by Fienberg, isn't the story of a adolescent dream date; instead, the story finds Hector heating up everything around him, making it difficult to find anything other than cold-blooded, reptilian companionship as a result. Hector lives alone in a jungle near a steamy volcano until one day when he is washed out to sea. Ultimately running aground in more northern climes, where Hector melts the icebergs in his path, he meets Gilda, a young Viking girl who can appreciate the heat this strange boy throws off, and the two become friends. A pleasant tale that emphasizes friendship and overcoming differences, *The Hottest Boy Who Ever Lived* was praised by *Magpies* reviewer John Murray as "a happy tale of friendship found and loneliness defeated, with characters that complement one another in the most direct way."

Characters embodying opposites are also featured in *Wiggy and Boa.* Here Fienberg introduces Boadicea Bolderack, or Boa, a young teen who is constantly cajoled as to the virtues of tidiness by her grandfather, a retired sea captain whose stories of his seafaring past fuel her imagination. Wishful thinking about the days of old ends in chaos as Boa finds she has summoned forth several of her grandfather's coarse, unruly, pirate-looking crew. Harboring ill will toward the captain who stranded them on a deserted island, the pirates plot

Hector is lonely until he meets a Viking teen who welcomes the heat the boy throws off in Fienberg's pleasant tale of friendship and mutual appreciation. (Cover illustration by Kim Gamble.)

'Ooah, did you run away home?' asked Jack.
'Not me,' said Tashi. 'I took my buckets and
climbed up the mountain and there, sitting at
the mouth of the cave, was the biggest dragon
I'd ever seen.'

'Have you seen many?' asked Jack.
'I've seen a few in my time,' said Tashi. 'But not
so close. And *this* dragon made me very cross.'

Fienberg and her mother developed the character of Tashi, whose outlandish tall tales are related to his gullible, awestruck best friend Jack in **Tashi,** *written by Anna Fienberg and Barbara Fienberg and illustrated by Kim Gamble.*

revenge, and it is up to Boa and pal Wiggy—an expert in confusion and chaos of all sorts—to come up with a solution to the dilemma. *Horn Book* contributor Ellen Fader described *Wiggy and Boa* as "a robust tale ... told with great energy and rollicking good humor," while in *School Library Journal,* reviewer Ruth Smith maintained that Fienberg's book was an entertaining combination of "an Aikenesque sense of melodrama [and] ... Roald Dahl's appetite for the grotesque." *Dead Sailors Don't Bite* continues the salty pirate escapades, as the loss of their favorite possessions—a bunch of marbles—causes the still-surly pirate crew to kidnap the thief: an unwitting teacher. With no grown-ups in sight, the collective smarts of Boa and Wiggy must set things right.

The "Tashi" stories, which were praised by *Magpies* contributor Russ Merrin as "a gentle, imaginative, and highly enjoyable fantasy," began with a chat between Fienberg and her mother. Barbara Fienberg admitted that when she was a child she used to tell some amazing stories to entertain her friends. Brainstorming about a character like that—someone who told outlandish tall tales and was believed—the two women developed the character of Tashi, along with Tashi's best friend, the

somewhat gullible and totally awestruck Jack. Tashi debuted in a self-titled picture book in 1995, and immediately mesmerized readers with his story of arriving in his new town on the back of a swan, having only barely escaped death at the hands of a horrid warlord in his own, far-off country. His further quasi-adventures are recounted in a series of books, among them *Tashi and the Ghosts* and *Tashi and the Baba Yaga.*

In 1999 Fienberg penned her first novel for young-adult readers, *Borrowed Light.* Featuring sixteen-year-old Callisto May, the novel focuses on unwanted pregnancy and the inner and outer turmoil it causes in Callisto's life, as her boyfriend becomes unavailable, her parents distance themselves, and friends don't quite know how to deal with this major shift in their relationship.

Works Cited

Fader, Ellen, review of *Wiggy and Boa, Horn Book,* July-August, 1990, p. 454.

Jameyson, Karen, "News from Down Under," *Horn Book,* July-August, 1992, pp. 497-500.

Merrin, Russ, review of *Tashi, Magpies,* May, 1995, p. 31.

Murray, John, review of *The Hottest Boy Who Ever Lived, Magpies,* November, 1993, p. 29.

Smith, Ruth, review of *Wiggy and Boa, School Library Journal,* May, 1990, pp. 104-05.

White, Kerry, essay on Fienberg in *St. James Guide to Children's Writers,* St. James Press, 1999, pp. 366-67.

For More Information See

PERIODICALS

Horn Book, July-August, 1993, pp. 496-98; March-April, 1994, pp. 242-43.

Magpies, November, 1991, p. 30.

ON-LINE

Author's Web site at http://www.allen-unwin.com.au/publicity/anna.htm (June 7, 1999).

* * *

FRASIER, Debra 1953-

Personal

Born April 3, 1953, in Vero Beach, FL; daughter of George (stepfather; in marine sales) and Mildred (an artist; maiden name, Carter) Bunnell; married James V. Henkel (an artist/photographer), March 17, 1984; children: Calla Virginia Frasier-Henkel. *Education:* Florida State University, B.S., 1976; attended Penland School of Crafts, 1976-81, and Humphrey Institute, University of Minnesota, 1988-89.

Addresses

Home—45 Barton Ave. SE, Minneapolis, MN 55414. *Office*—Harcourt, Inc., 525 B St., No. 1900, San Diego, CA 92101. *Agent*—Virginia Knowlton, Curtis Brown, Ltd., 10 Astor Pl., New York, NY 10003.

Career

Author and illustrator. Director of visual-arts department for Project CAST, Tallahassee, FL, 1974-75; participant in various national "Artist-in-Education" programs, 1976—; artist-in-residence, Penland School, 1981-83; sculptor, projects for cities in the U.S., 1981-86; sculptor-in-residence, American Cultural Center and Cite des Arts, Paris, France, 1986-87; artist-in-residence, Department of Community Services, City of St. Paul, MN, 1989. Lecturer at numerous conferences and workshops, including International Reading Association, National Council of Teachers of English, American Library Association, and universities. *Exhibitions:* Has exhibited her works in solo and group shows in the U.S. and Europe, including "Salmon Run" in Alaska, "Windwalk: A Wind/Poem Environment" in Minnesota and Pennsylvania, "Windwalls" in New York, "Windtent" and "Window" in North Carolina, and "Layered Windows" in Switzerland. *Member:* Society of Children's Book Writers and Illustrators.

Awards, Honors

National Endowment for the Arts project grant, 1980; Parents' Choice Illustrators Award and American Graphics Society honor list citation, both 1991, both for *On the Day You Were Born;* Pick of the Lists, American Booksellers, Minnesota Book Award, and SEBA award, children's book category, all 1999, all for *Out of the Ocean;* Carnegie Medal for Best Children's Video, American Library Association, 1997, for *On the Day You Were Born.*

Writings

AUTHOR AND ILLUSTRATOR

On the Day You Were Born, Harcourt, 1991.
Out of the Ocean, Harcourt, 1997.
Miss Alaineus: A Vocabulary Disaster, Harcourt, 2000.

ILLUSTRATOR

William Stafford, *The Animal That Drank Up Sound,* Harcourt, 1992.
Kim R. Stafford, *We Got Here Together,* Harcourt, 1994.

On the Day You Were Born has been translated into Spanish, Japanese, and Portuguese.

Debra Frasier

Adaptations

A Quest and *The Late Great American Picnic,* both by Dan Bailey Films, document two of Frasier's outdoor collaborative pageants. *On the Day You Were Born* has been adapted as an animated video for the "Notes Alive!" series, with music composed by Steve Heitzeg and performed by the Minnesota Symphony Orchestra.

Frasier collaborated with In the Heart of the Beast Puppet and Mask Theatre in producing *On the Day You Were Born,* which toured the United States in 1992. She also designed a Braille edition of *On the Day You Were Born,* where each visual illustration has a tactile counterpart.

Work in Progress

Several picture books and longer texts.

Sidelights

Debra Frasier was born and raised in Vero Beach, Florida, where her family has lived since her great grandfather helped to lay out the streets in 1911. "Vero Beach faces the Atlantic Ocean," Frasier once told *SATA,* "and I grew up looking out at the great curved line made where the ocean meets the sky. Summers were my favorite time and often my brother and I would crawl into bed with our bathing suits hidden under our pajamas so we did not have to waste time changing for the beach the following morning! Swimming and walking the beaches were our daytime pastimes, along with collecting shells, drawing with mangrove seeds, and building sand castles and forts out of driftwood. Around fourth grade I discovered books, and began reading with a passion. I remember keeping a flashlight under my pillow so I could creep into the bathroom to read at night."

"I loved art from the beginning," says Frasier. "My mother is an artist and she was always collecting shells and bits of surf-worn glass to glue into collaged pictures. She also painted on driftwood and taught me how to paint canvas when I was about twelve." Frasier nurtured her love of art and eventually received her college degree in textiles. "I studied batik, an ancient wax resist process, with the idea of designing for interiors. But, upon graduation, I gave a final party that changed my life—I staged a giant puppet show in my backyard, drafting all of my neighbors into an improvised version of the story of Persephone. I loved making the characters and figuring out the staging, and that led to years of building large, outdoor puppet pageants." Her outdoor pageants have integrated fabrics, words, and even wind; her sixty-foot puppets have danced on a North Carolina mountaintop, and an exhibit called "Windwalk" led viewers through an outdoor trail lined with thousands of strips of cloth blowing in the breeze, interspersed with quotes about the wind.

Frasier has devoted a great deal of time to introducing art to children in the classroom through various "Artist-

Frasier combines collages of photographs and cut-paper shapes with a poetic text in her picture book about the wonder and joy of her childhood experiences beach-combing with her mother. (From Out of the Ocean.*)*

in-Education" programs in Minneapolis and elsewhere. One of her programs, titled "Walk Around the World," integrates art, storytelling, and academic material into a unified curriculum "where art plays a major part in the learning process rather than its usual minor role," she told *SATA.* Students are asked to use factual information *and* their imagination to understand how people in other countries live. The experience is "aimed at tolerance," Frasier told Mike Steele, a *Star Tribune: Newspaper of the Twin Cities* reviewer. "The geography, architecture, languages [we study] are different from [the children's] experience. Instead of being afraid of that, they learn to enjoy the differences."

A desire to explore the ways that children understand the world gave Frasier the idea of writing a book, but experiencing a difficult pregnancy provided the special motivation that she needed. "I hoped my baby would be born safe and sound, and, while I was hospitalized, I began the notes for the book, *On the Day You Were Born.* I wanted to write about all the things that would welcome my child if she could just get here. I started making notes of things that defied boundaries, that were everywhere and could be counted on to welcome all children. After my daughter was born, I began writing those notes into a manuscript. All of the illustrations were made with cut paper. I was influenced by the work of Matisse and the clear, clean shapes in Japanese textiles."

The best-selling *On the Day You Were Born* is "exceptionally simple and marvelously deep. It's simply a welcome to the world and to each reader's place in it," said Steele. The poetic text describes the welcome that the sun, the trees, the moon, and other natural forces extend to every newborn child. The illustrations are bold paper cutouts vividly portraying that welcome, and depict children of all colors dancing in the natural world. Michele Landsberg, writing in *Entertainment Weekly,* declared that the award-winning book "will make each child feel linked to planet Earth in a thrillingly personal way."

In addition to contributing illustrations to picture books by other authors, Frasier has also produced *Out of the Ocean,* a self-illustrated picture book celebrating her childhood experience of beachcombing with her mother. "As in *On the Day You Were Born,* the layout is inventive and effective, whether cradling the text or propelling readers on to the next page," remarked Liza Bliss in *School Library Journal.* Frasier combines collages of photographs and cut-paper shapes with a poetic text emphasizing the wonder and joy of collecting the ocean's sights and sounds as well as more material delights such as sea glass and the proverbial message in a bottle. The book concludes with a journal offering factual details about some of the objects depicted in the story. "Debra Frasier ... has made a kind of mixed-media naturalist's diary of the beach in front of her house. It's very low-tech and quite endearing," attested Penelope Green in the *New York Times Book Review. Out of the Ocean* was likewise recognized by other reviewers as a moving tribute to the spiritual solace to be gained from an awareness of the natural world. "The value of this treasure hunter's appreciation is in the notion that real 'treasure' is in the looking," observed a contributor to *Kirkus Reviews.*

In *Miss Alaineus: A Vocabulary Disaster,* the main character, Sage, mis-hears and misunderstands one of her vocabulary words. Her error leads to a humbling catastrophe in front of the entire class. This "outrageous and touching story of loving—and mistaking—our glorious language," grew out of Frasier's desire to make a story about a mistake carrying someone to a new place. "My daughter confessed to me one night when she was nine years old that she had just figured out that miscellaneous was not a person ... Miss Alaineus! I couldn't stop thinking about that marvelous mistake!"

Works Cited

Bliss, Liza, review of *Out of the Ocean, School Library Journal,* August, 1998, p. 139.

Green, Penelope, review of *Out of the Ocean, New York Times Book Review,* July 19, 1998, p. 24.

Landsberg, Michele, "Happy Birthdays," *Entertainment Weekly,* April 5, 1991, pp. 72-73.

Review of *Out of the Ocean, Kirkus Reviews,* March 1, 1998, p. 337.

Steele, Mike, "In Book and Play, Debra Frasier Celebrates Life," *Star Tribune: Newspaper of the Twin Cities,* March 17, 1991, pp. 1, 7F.

For More Information See

PERIODICALS

Emergency Librarian, March, 1993, p. 18.

Five Owls, March-April, 1991.

Publishers Weekly, February 15, 1991; March 22, 1991; February 16, 1998, p. 209; May 17, 1999, p. 24.

Reading Teacher, December, 1991.

School Library Journal, June, 1991.

Star Tribune: Newspaper of the Twin Cities, April 21, 1991.

St. Paul Pioneer Press, March 16, 1991.

Twin Cities Reader, March 20, 1991.

G

GALLO, Donald R. 1938-

Personal

Born June 1, 1938, in Paterson, NJ; son of Sergio and Thelma Mae (maiden name, Lowe) Gallo; married Christie Jo Bott (an English teacher), February 14, 1997; children: Brian, Chris Perrett (stepdaughter). *Education:* Hope College, B.A., 1960; Oberlin College, M.A.T., 1961; Syracuse University, Ph.D., 1968. *Hobbies and other interests:* Travel, gardening, photography.

Addresses

Home—34540 Sherbrook Park Drive, Solon, OH 44139. *E-mail*—GalloDon@aol.com.

Career

Educator, writer, and editor. English teacher, Bedford Junior High School, Westport, CT, 1961-65; research associate, Syracuse University, 1965-67; assistant and associate professor of education, University of Colorado, 1968-72; reading specialist, Golden Junior High School, Colorado, 1972-73; professor of English, Central Connecticut State University, 1973-97; visiting faculty member, Wesleyan University, 1983; adjunct instructor, Cleveland State University, 1997-98. Has also served on the executive board or committee of numerous educational organizations, including NCTE and ALAN (president, 1986-87). *Member:* Authors Guild, Society of Children's Book Writers and Illustrators, National Council of Teachers of English, Assembly on Literature for Adolescents, National Council of Teachers of English, International Reading Association, Conference on English Education, Ohio Council of Teachers of English Language Arts.

Awards, Honors

Best Books for Young Adults 1966-1986 and Best Books for Young Adults, 1985, American Library Association (ALA), Best Books, *School Library Jour-*

Donald R. Gallo

nal, 1985, and nominee, Colorado Blue Spruce Award, 1988, all for *Sixteen: Short Stories by Outstanding Writers for Young Adults;* Best Books for Young Adults, ALA, Pick of the Lists, American Booksellers, and Books for the Teen Age, New York Public Library, all 1988, all for *Visions: Short Stories by Outstanding Writers for Young Adults;* Books for the Teen Age, New

York Public Library, 1990, for *Connections: Short Stories by Outstanding Writers for Young Adults;* Best Books for Young Adults, ALA, 1991, for *Speaking for Ourselves: Autobiographical Sketches of Notable Authors of Books for Young Adults;* Books for the Teen Age, New York Public Library, 1991, for *Center Stage: One-Act Plays for Teenage Readers and Actors;* Junior Library Guild selection, Pick of the Lists, American Booksellers, and Books for the Teen Age, New York Public Library, both 1993, YALSA Humor Book list, selection for *The Year's Best Fantasy and Horror,* and Texas Lone Star Reading List selection, 1994-95, all for *Short Circuits: Thirteen Shocking Stories by Outstanding Writers for Young Adults;* Best Anthology/Collection, *VOYA,* 1993, Books for the Teen Age, New York Public Library, and Pick of the Lists, American Booksellers, all for *Join In: Multiethnic Short Stories by Outstanding Writers for Young Adults;* Best Books for Young Adults and Quick Pick, ALA, 1998, for *No Easy Answers: Short Stories about Teenagers Making Tough Choices.*

Awarded life membership in the Connecticut Council of Teachers of English for "Exceptional Contributions to the Council," 1983; recipient of the Distinguished Service Award from the Connecticut Council of Teachers of English, 1989; recipient of the ALAN Award from the Assembly on Literature for Adolescents of the National Council of Teachers of English for "outstanding contributions to the field of adolescent literature," 1992; recipient of Certificate of Merit from the Catholic Library Association, 1995.

Writings

EDITOR; FOR YOUNG ADULTS

Sixteen: Short Stories by Outstanding Writers for Young Adults, Delacorte, 1984.

Books for You: A Booklist for Senior High Students, National Council for Teachers of English, 1985.

Visions: Short Stories by Outstanding Writers for Young Adults, Delacorte, 1987.

Connections: Short Stories by Outstanding Writers for Young Adults, Delacorte, 1989.

Speaking for Ourselves: Autobiographical Sketches of Notable Authors of Books for Young Adults, National Council of Teachers of English, 1990.

Center Stage: One-Act Plays for Teenage Readers and Actors, HarperCollins, 1990.

Short Circuits: Thirteen Shocking Stories by Outstanding Writers for Young Adults, Delacorte, 1992.

Speaking for Ourselves, Too—More Autobiographical Sketches of Notable Authors of Books for Young Adults, National Council of Teachers of English, 1993.

Within Reach: Ten Stories, HarperCollins, 1993.

Join In: Multiethnic Short Stories by Outstanding Writers for Young Adults, Delacorte, 1993.

Ultimate Sports: Short Stories by Outstanding Writers for Young Adults, Delacorte, 1995.

No Easy Answers: Short Stories about Teenagers Making Tough Choices, Delacorte, 1997.

Time Capsule: Short Stories About Teenagers Throughout the Twentieth Century, Delacorte, 1999.

NONFICTION; FOR ADULTS

Reading Rate and Comprehension: 1970-1971 Assessment, National Assessment of Education Progress, 1972.

Recipes, Wrappers, Reasoning and Rate: A Digest of the First Reading Assessment, National Assessment of Educational Progress, 1974.

Presenting Richard Peck, Twayne, 1989.

Authors' Insights: Turning Teenagers into Readers and Writers, Boynton/Cook-Heinemann, 1992.

(With Sarah K. Herz) *From Hinton to Hamlet: Building Bridges between Young Adult Literature and the Classics,* Greenwood, 1996.

Also served as editor for the *Connecticut English Journal,* and as author and consultant for anthologies and textbooks, including *Heath Middle Level Literature Program* and *Bookmark Reading Program.* His works have been translated into French and Italian.

Gallo's collection brings together short stories by some of the best-known writers of adolescent fiction.

Adaptations

Sixteen and *Visions* have been adapted for audiocassette by Listening Library; *No Easy Answers* has been adapted for audiocassette by Recorded Books.

Work in Progress

Editing a collection of short stories about conformity, popularity, and acceptance; writing two picture books and several informational books for younger readers, including one about walls and another about the history of popular foods and snacks.

Sidelights

Dubbed the "Godfather of YA short stories" by Chris Crowe in the *English Journal,* Don Gallo has edited numerous award-winning anthologies dealing with themes from the moral development of teenagers to athletics and multiculturalism. His groundbreaking *Sixteen* inaugurated Gallo's interest in YA short story collections as well as the popular use of that format for younger readers. The book gathered the writings of well-known authors such as Robert Cormier and Richard Peck and ultimately found a place on the ALA Best of the Best Books for Young Adults published between 1966 and 1986. In books such as *Visions, Connections, Short Circuits, Join In, Ultimate Sports,* and *No Easy Answers,* Gallo has continued this winning formula of collecting the shorter writings of popular YA novelists and writers to present engaging anthologies.

Born in Paterson, New Jersey, in 1938, Gallo was one of those reluctant readers at whom his anthologies are in part targeted. He found more enjoyment in outdoor activities than in reading; sports and scouting were his main interests. As Gallo told *Something about the Author (SATA),* "I did not read anything that was not required of me in school.... I almost never sat down to read for what we call 'pleasure.' Reading was too boring for me." Gallo became an Eagle Scout and was named Outstanding Scout in his council while in high school. He also played football and ran track. "For parents and teachers who agonize over their inability to get their otherwise bright and successful teenagers to read, I provide hope," Gallo quipped. In spite of terrible spelling skills and a limited vocabulary in high school, he went on to college and it was there he finally discovered the joys of reading.

Hemingway's *The Old Man and the Sea,* a tedious exercise in high school, suddenly came to life for him in college. "I fell in love with Hemingway's writing and his macho image. I was in that skiff with Santiago; I struggled beside him to land that magnificent fish; I raged at the sharks that attacked the marlin lashed to the boat; and I fell into bed exhausted with the old man in the end, knowing that even though we may have been beaten, we would never be defeated. Literature had finally come alive for me." He read Steinbeck, Camus, Zola, Dostoyevsky, and other standard-bearers of Western literature, and as he did so his writing also improved.

Gallo edited this volume of stories centering on characters of diverse ethnic backgrounds, living in America and sharing common experiences.

When an essay on e e cummings earned him an A and also won $25 for a school essay contest, Gallo was converted. "Although my spelling was still quite poor, my writing career began at that point," Gallo told *SATA.*

Involved in religious issues and training from his teenage years, Gallo intended to attend a seminary after graduating from college; instead he went to Oberlin College where he earned a masters and a teaching certificate. Thereafter he took a teaching position in Westport, Connecticut, "one of the nation's best school systems back in the 1960s." In a sense, he received on the job training not only in teaching, but also in writing, for he edited a newsletter for the local education association, served as advisor to the school's literary magazine, and also kept one step ahead of his precocious students, daughters and sons of famous writers, editors, broadcast journalists, and company executives.

Married for the first time, Gallo and his wife returned to graduate school, where he earned his doctorate. Thereafter the couple found jobs in Colorado, but Gallo's interest in literature never waned. During his doctoral studies, a quiet revolution in publishing was taking place with the arrival of a new and gritty literature aimed at the YA audience and led by such writers as S. E. Hinton and Robert Lipsyte. "Although I focused a great deal of my scholarly activities on the teaching of developmental reading skills and writing skills in secondary schools at that time, I slowly began to shift my attention to books for teenagers," Gallo told *SATA*. "I continued to read YA books voraciously and to survey students about their reading interests and habits." Moving on to a position at Central Connecticut State University, Gallo observed teenage students, tracking their reading habits and how they reacted to various books. Serving on various reading and education committees and editing professional journals, Gallo met many of the shining lights of YA literature.

Slowly Gallo began to discover a black hole in reading for young people. As he told *SATA*, "while most schools required students to read short stories, there were only a handful of books of short stories written by young adult novelists. Those collections had each been written by a single author." Anthologies at that time were constructed largely of stories reprinted from adult magazines. "Why weren't there any collections of good short stories about teenagers that were written by people whose novels were being read by teenagers?" Gallo asked himself. He set about to provide not so much an answer as a solution. Parlaying his wealth of knowledge about YA subjects with his acquaintanceship with a wide variety of YA novelists, Gallo solicited manuscripts for a story collection. He brought people like Robert Cormier on board, whose story, "In the Heat," had never before been published. After two years of cajoling and editing, Gallo had a book in hand, *Sixteen: Short Stories by Outstanding Writers for Young Adults*. "That collections is now viewed as a milestone in young adult literature," Gallo told *SATA*.

Sixteen proved such a success that Gallo decided to continue with the idea of story collections. *Visions* came next, followed by *Connections* in 1989. "The procedures were the same for these volumes as for the first one: I sent letters to as many as forty-five authors, starting with the most famous people in the field, inviting them to write a story for my next book." Some, such as Judy Blume and Paula Danziger, did not feel comfortable in the short story format; others did not have the time. But for each collection he would end up with about twenty-five manuscripts from which he would cull anywhere from a dozen to sixteen of the best for the collection. Gallo brought together authors such as Richard Peck, Norma Fox Mazer, and Walter Dean Meyers for his second collection. Reviewing *Visions*, Lola H. Teubert noted in *Voice of Youth Advocates* that "these stories capture your attention continually, as each plot is timely and exciting. Whether you prefer science fiction, fantasy, living in the fast lane or current teen social problems you can take your pick from this lovely reading." A reviewer for *Kliatt* concluded that "Reluctant readers will be good candidates for this collection, because the

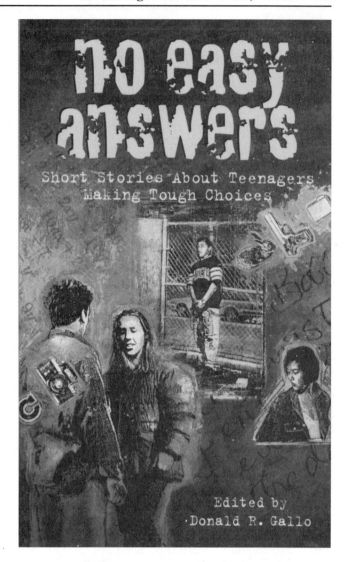

Teenagers face moral dilemmas and deal with the consequences of their decisions in one of Gallo's most recent anthologies. (Cover illustration by Alan Mazetti.)

stories are brief, and an interest in the authors may result in further reading." Gallo enlisted Colby Rodowsky, Alden R. Carter, M. E. Kerr, and Ouida Sebestyen among others for *Connections*, a collection "[i]nfused with warmth and discerning respect for young adults and their concerns," and containing "both elegant and humorous treats," according to *Kirkus Reviews*.

While these first collections were non-thematic, Gallo decided to narrow the focus with his fourth collection, *Short Circuits*. With this and following volumes, he has established books built around specific subject matter. The stories in *Short Circuits* deal with horror and the supernatural. *Kirkus Reviews* described the collection succinctly: "From both sides of the Atlantic, thirteen horror stories featuring teenagers giving good accounts of themselves in scary situations." The reviewer went on to note that Gallo prefaced each story with "a practiced teaser and appends intriguing comments about the author's life and writing." Christy Tyson noted in *Voice of Youth Advocates* that, like other Gallo collections,

Short Circuits "is a fine collection indeed.... Gallo ... has managed to pull together some truly terrifying stories that will satisfy even the most demanding horror fan." Joan Lowery Nixon, Joan Aiken, Robert Westall, Ellen Conford, and Jane McFann are among the YA writers included in this volume. *Booklist*'s Chris Sherman concluded that *Short Circuits* was "sure to be as popular as Gallo's other story collections."

Something of a departure for Gallo was the collection targeted at middle grade readers, *Within Reach,* ten tales focusing on kids who take risks. *Publishers Weekly* felt that "reluctant readers are especially likely to appreciate the accessibility of the stories' themes, conflicts and down-to-earth language." Additionally, Gallo has edited two editions of *Speaking for Ourselves,* collections of autobiographical essays from notable YA authors, as well as a volume for Twayne publishers on the YA author Richard Peck.

Returning to story anthologies, Gallo delivered his editorial treatment to sports with *Ultimate Sports,* including stories from such notables as Robert Lipsyte and Chris Crutcher, while multiculturalism formed the heart of *Join In,* an exploration of multiethnic experiences. Gallo included writers of color as well as white authors for these stories about teenagers of various ethnic backgrounds. *Kirkus Reviews* noted that "Gallo opens with an essay on whether authors can or should write about cultures other than their own and appends a thumbnail biography to each story." The same reviewer concluded that the collection was "[d]iverse, thought-provoking, and consistently well-written."

Gallo takes his editing responsibilities seriously. "My first reading of any story is for appreciation," he told *SATA.* "The next couple of readings are to confirm the general structure of the story and to note any places that don't make perfect sense. Along the way I fix mechanical errors I notice: misspellings, improper use of punctuation, subject-verb agreement, etc.... Because I have experienced what it feels like to have editors change pieces of my writing without my permission ... I never change anything in anyone's writing (except for mechanical errors) without the writer's approval.... One of the most rewarding parts of my job is having the opportunity to read a brand new story that no one besides the author has ever seen ... And when my attention is grabbed on the first page, I know this is going to be a great story."

A further theme-driven collection, *No Easy Answers,* focuses on teenagers facing moral dilemmas and dealing with the consequences of their decisions. Gallo gathered a diverse group of authors for the task, including Ron Koertge, Rita Williams-Garcia, Monica Hughes, and Graham Salisbury, to write "thought-provoking stories about such topics as peer pressure, computer blackmail, academic cheating, drug use, gang violence, and unwanted pregnancy," as Gallo described the volume to *SATA.* Roxy Ekstrom praised the collection in *Voice of Youth Advocates,* noting that "Gallo knows well his YA audience." Ekstrom went on to laud Gallo's editorial

abilities in all his collections. "From *Sixteen* to *Short Circuits* with stops between and beyond, he has shown his mastery at soliciting attention-grabbing short stories from the cream of the crop among YA authors." For Gallo, the self-confessed reluctant reader, this is sweet praise.

Works Cited

Review of *Connections: Short Stories by Outstanding Writers for Young Adults, Kirkus Reviews,* December 1, 1989, p. 1747.

Crowe, Chris, interview with Donald R. Gallo, *English Journal,* March, 1997.

Ekstrom, Roxy, review of *No Easy Answers: Short Stories about Teenagers Making Tough Choices, Voice of Youth Advocates,* October, 1997, p. 246.

Review of *Join In: Multiethnic Short Stories by Outstanding Writers for Young Adults, Kirkus Reviews,* December 1, 1993, p. 1522.

Sherman, Chris, review of *Short Circuits: Thirteen Shocking Stories by Outstanding Writers for Young Adults, Booklist,* December 1, 1992, p. 659.

Review of *Short Circuits: Thirteen Shocking Stories by Outstanding Writers for Young Adults, Kirkus Reviews,* November 15, 1992, p. 1442.

Teubert, Lola H., review of *Visions: Short Stories by Outstanding Writers for Young Adults, Voice of Youth Advocates,* February, 1988, p. 284.

Tyson, Christy, review of *Short Circuits: Thirteen Shocking Stories by Outstanding Writers for Young Adults, Voice of Youth Advocates,* October, 1992, p. 243.

Review of *Visions: Short Stories by Outstanding Writers for Young Adults, Kliatt,* January, 1989, p. 31.

Review of *Within Reach: Ten Stories, Publishers Weekly,* June 28, 1993, p. 78.

For More Information See

BOOKS

Who's Who in America, 54th edition, Marquis Who's Who, 1999.

PERIODICALS

Booklist, November 1, 1989, p. 534; December 15, 1989, p. 826; June 1, 1990, p. 1888; December 1, 1990, p. 730; January 15, 1994, p. 918; April 1, 1996, p. 1386; March 15, 1998, p. 1218; September 15, 1999.

Bulletin of the Center for Children's Books, December, 1989, p. 83; September, 1990, p. 8; November, 1993, pp. 79-80; January, 1998, p. 159.

Horn Book, May-June, 1990, pp. 352-53.

New York Times Book Review, November 15, 1987, p. 37.

School Library Journal, December, 1989, p. 124; May, 1990, p. 50; August, 1993, p. 163; October, 1995, p. 152; December, 1997, p. 124.

—Sketch by J. Sydney Jones

GALLOWAY, Priscilla 1930-
(Anne Peebles)

Personal

Born July 22, 1930, in Montreal, Quebec, Canada; daughter of Allon (an economist) and Noeline (a social worker and printmaker; maiden name, Bruce) Peebles; married Bev Galloway, September 17, 1949 (died October 25, 1985); married Howard Collum, October 9, 1994; children: Noel, Walt, Glenn. *Education:* Queen's University, B.A., 1951; University of Toronto, M.A., 1959, Ph.D., 1977.

Addresses

Home and office—12 Didrickson Dr., North York, Ontario, Canada M2P 1J6.

Career

Writer. English teacher in public schools in Toronto, Ontario, 1954-1956; Board of Education for the City of North York, North York, Ontario, 1956-1986, first as English teacher, then as reading and language-arts consultant. Scholar-in-residence at Queen's University, Kingston, Ontario, 1978; instructor at University of Toronto, 1979-93, University of British Columbia, summer, 1980, Christchurch Teachers College, Christchurch, New Zealand, 1985-1986, and Acadia University, 1991; writer-in-residence in the libraries of Cobalt, Haileybury, and New Liskeard, northern Ontario, 1987-1988; member of Council of Queens University. *Member:* International Board on Books for Young People, PEN Canada, Canadian Children's Book Centre, The Writers' Union of Canada, Canadian Society of Children's Authors, Illustrators, and Performers.

Awards, Honors

Teacher of the Year, Ontario Council of Teachers of English, 1976; Marty Memorial Scholarship for Doctoral Study, Queen's University, 1976-77; book of choice, Canadian Children's Book Centre, 1996, for *Aleta and the Queen: A Tale of Ancient Greece, Atalanta, the Fastest Runner in the World,* and *Truly Grim Tales;* Best Books for Young Adults and Quick Picks for Young Adults, American Library Association, and Young Adult Book Award finalist, Canadian Library Association, all 1996, all for *Truly Grim Tales;* book of choice, Canadian Children's Book Centre, 1997, Mr. Christie's Book Awards finalist, Christie Brown & Co., 1998, and Red Cedar Book Award finalist, 1999-2000, all for *Daedalus and the Minotaur;* book of choice, Canadian Children's Book Centre, 1998, and Books for the Teen Age, New York Public Library, 1999, both for *Snake Dreamer.*

Writings

FOR CHILDREN

Good Times, Bad Times, Mummy and Me, illustrated by Lissa Calvert, Women's Press, 1980.
When You Were Little and I Was Big, illustrated by Heather Collins, Annick Press, 1984.
Jennifer Has Two Daddies, illustrated by Ana Auml, Women's Press, 1985.
Seal Is Lost, illustrated by Karen Patkau, Annick Press, 1988.
Atalanta, the Fastest Runner in the World, illustrated by Normand Cousineau, Annick Press, 1995.
Aleta and the Queen: A Tale of Ancient Greece, illustrated by Normand Cousineau, Annick Press, 1995.
Truly Grim Tales, Delacorte, 1995.
Daedalus and the Minotaur, illustrated by Norman Cousineau, Annick Press, 1997.
Snake Dreamer, Delacorte Press, 1998.
Young Reader's Emily, Bantam Books, 1998.
My Hero Hercules, Annick Press, 1999.

TRANSLATOR OF "ANNA, PAUL AND TOMMYCAT" SERIES; ALL BY NICOLE GIRARD AND PAUL DANHEUX

Anna, Paul and Tommycat Say Hello, Lorimer, 1987.
Looking for Tommycat, Lorimer, 1987.
Where Is Tommycat?, Lorimer, 1988.
A Letter from the Moon, Lorimer, 1988.
Tommycat Comes Back at Last, Lorimer, 1988.
Tommycat Is Gone Again, Lorimer, 1988.

Priscilla Galloway

FOR ADULTS; NONFICTION

Sexism and the Senior English Literature Curriculum in Ontario Secondary Schools (Ph.D. thesis), University of Toronto, 1977.

What's Wrong With High School English?: It's Sexist, UnCanadian, Outdated, Ontario Institute for Studies in Education Press, 1980.

(Compiler and editor) *Timely and Timeless: Contemporary Prose* (and teachers' guide), Clarke, Irwin, 1983.

(Contributor) *Still Running: Personal Stories by Queen's Women to Celebrate the Fiftieth Anniversary of the Marty Memorial Scholarship,* edited by Joy Parr, Queen's Alumnae Association, 1987.

(Editor) *The Tri-Town Writers' Anthology,* Cobalt Public Library, 1988.

(Adaptor) *Emily of New Moon,* Delacorte, 1998.

(Compiler and contributor) *Too Young To Fight: Memories from Our Youth During WW II,* Stoddart Kids, 1999.

Also author of more than twenty teaching guides and student activities for *Books about You* kits published by Annick Educational. Contributor of stories, poems, and articles to newspapers, education journals, and popular magazines, including *Chatelaine, Canadian Forum, Waves,* and *Atlantis.* Both *Aleta and the Queen: A Tale of Ancient Greece* and *Atalanta, the Fastest Runner in the World* have been translated into French and Spanish. Galloway sometimes writes under the pseudonym Anne Peebles.

Sidelights

Priscilla Galloway was born in Montreal and spent her childhood in western Canada, learning to swim in the icy waters of the Pacific Ocean. She moved to Central Canada with her family during World War II, attending secondary school in Ottawa. "I began writing poetry almost as soon as I could form words on a page," she once told *SATA.* "My father had literary ambitions for me. When I came home at age fourteen, thrilled with my first summer job offer as half-time sales clerk in a shoe store, Dad was indignant at this proposed waste of my time. He matched the shoe store's offer of seven dollars per week, paying me to spend the same amount of time at home, writing. My first paid publication was a story in a Sunday School paper when I was twelve; it earned three dollars.

"When I began undergraduate studies in 1947, universities were full of men (and some women) back from war, often many years in the armed forces or in prisoner of war camps. I was a very naive civilian, just turned seventeen. I began my apprenticeship in journalism on the university paper, where I had the library beat. Ours was a professional paper, edited by men with years of pre-war and wartime experience. Because I had to support myself, I was not able to continue this unpaid work after my first year, and the journalism dream began to fade.

"I married and had a baby before completing my undergraduate degree, taking my final courses extramur-

ally. Journalism was abandoned, and I began a thirty-one year career in education.

"From the beginning, however, I wrote articles for other teachers. I also wrote poetry with my students. I worked with associations of English teachers and began to know the important people in the academic literary establishment in Canada.... I wrote short stories, and made sales to two of the three most prestigious markets in Canada: the Canadian Broadcasting Corporation's literary program, *Anthology,* and *Chatelaine.*"

Galloway's first two books were published within a month of each other: *Good Times, Bad Times, Mummy and Me,* a children's picture book; and *What's Wrong with High School English?: It's Sexist, UnCanadian, Outdated,* based on her doctoral research. *When You Were Little and I Was Big* followed soon after. A reviewer for *Canadian Children's Literature* commented that the story's somewhat demanding content was

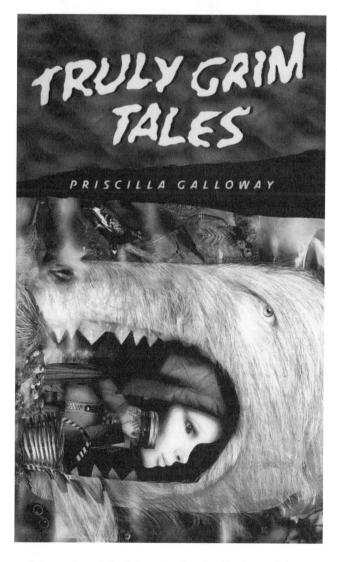

Interpreting eight fairy tales by the Brothers Grimm, Charles Perrault, and Hans Christian Andersen, Galloway recasts the villians into more sympathetic roles. (Cover illustration by Janet Woolley.)

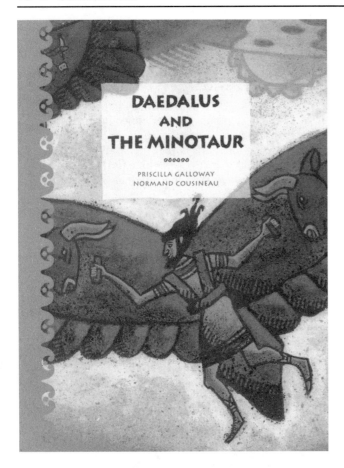

The story of Daedalus, who must invent a labyrinth by command of the malevolent King and Queen of Crete, is retold with suspense and vitality by Galloway. (Cover illustration by Normand Cousineau.)

softened by the author's "inferred sub-text [that] reveals the warmth uniting mother and daughter as they play.... their closeness is a positive affirmation of strength."

Galloway has a penchant for retelling fairy tales and putting ancient myths in context with the modern world. In *Truly Grim Tales,* she recast villainous characters into more sympathetic roles. Mary Jo Drungil, writing for *School Library Journal,* declared the author's job of "getting inside of the characters 'masterful'; the concept of 'two sides to every story' is illustrated with some excellent examples.... The addition of unusual details, such as the sci-fi setting for "The Good Mother" ... underscores the uniqueness of this volume." In her review for The *Bulletin of the Center for Children's Books,* Deborah Stevenson noted: "The interpretations are provocative and ingenious throughout, managing to add magic to the originals rather than allowing the new layers to diminish them."

Snake Dreamer is based on the Greek Gorgon myth of Medusa, whose power to change people to stone can be activated only by reconnecting her severed head and body. Galloway's heroine, Dusa, suffers from incapacitating dreams about snakes and seeks out the "help doctors" in Greece who believe she has the power to communicate with Medusa, their dead sister. Jennifer Fakolt, reviewing the title for *School Library Journal,* praised the combined "elements of fantasy and thriller" and called the Galloway's effort "an intriguing expansion of a classical tale into contemporary times, a thought-provoking meeting of myth and modern science." In a *Bulletin of the Center for Children's Books* review, Deborah Stevenson added that "The book makes its clues obvious enough for non-classicists to get the drift."

Delving again into Greek mythology, Galloway reinterprets the story of Daedalus and his son, Icarus, in *Daedalus and the Minotaur.* Philippa Sheppard assessed the book for *Quill & Quire,* concluding that by "abandoning the traditional image of the Minotaur for that of a mute and deformed child, born with a huge head and lopsided eyes," Galloway actually makes the "story more suitable for, and appealing to, young readers." Lesley Mitchell voiced a similar opinion in *School Librarian,* saying the book is written "in a style which creates suspense and intrigue while at the same time bringing out the human side of the characters and their situations."

The author concluded her comments to *SATA* by summing up her view of life: "Life is rich and full. As I write this, I have many books in print. Larger projects are forming in my mind and notebooks are filling. Is a novel next? Or two?"

Works Cited

Drungil, Mary Jo, review of *Truly Grim Tales, School Library Journal,* September, 1995, p. 218.

Fakolt, Jennifer A., review of *Snake Dreamer, School Library Journal,* July, 1998, p. 95.

Mitchell, Lesley, review of *Daedalus and the Minotaur, School Librarian,* Summer, 1999, pp. 80, 89.

Sheppard, Philippa, review of *Daedalus and the Minotaur, Quill & Quire,* February, 1998, p. 51.

Stevenson, Deborah, review of *Snake Dreamer, Bulletin of the Center for Children's Books,* May, 1998, p. 321.

Stevenson, review of *Truly Grim Tales, Bulletin of the Center for Children's Books,* January, 1996, p. 158.

Review of *When You Were Little and I Was Big, Canadian Children's Literature,* 1986, pp. 70-74.

For More Information See

PERIODICALS

Booklist, March 15, 1996, p. 1294; January 1, 1998, p. 802; June 1, 1998, p. 1746.

Books in Canada, Fall 1999.

Canadian Children's Literature, Summer, 1996, pp. 85-87; Spring, 1999, pp. 51-52.

Forever Young, September 1999, p. 2.

The Globe and Mail, November 6, 1999, p. D8.

Horn Book, January-February, 1996, p. 78.

Kirkus Reviews, May 15, 1998, p. 737.

Publishers Weekly, September 11, 1995, p. 86.

Resource Links, August 1997, pp. 247-50.

School Library Journal, January, 1996, p. 118; February, 1998, p. 115.*

* * *

GELLMAN, Marc

Personal

Born in Wisconsin; married; has children. *Education:* University of Wisconsin, B.A.; Northwestern University, doctorate with dissertation (medical ethics). *Religion:* Jewish.

Addresses

Office—Temple Beth Torah, 35 Bagatelle Rd., Melville, NY 11747.

Career

Reform rabbi and author of children's books. Beth Torah Synagogue, Melville, NY, rabbi; *The God Squad* (syndicated interfaith program), Faith & Values/VISN cable network, co-host, with Monsignor Thomas Hartman. Has made regular appearances with Monsignor Hartman on ABC's *Good Morning America* and on Don Imus's radio talk show *Imus in the Morning.* Also served on the faculty of Northwestern University and Hebrew Union College and as chair of the Medical Ethics Committee, UJA/Federation. *Member:* New York Board of Rabbis (served as president), World Union for Progressive Judaism.

Awards, Honors

(With Thomas Hartman) Christopher Award, 1991, for *Where Does God Live?*

Writings

FOR CHILDREN

Does God Have a Big Toe? Stories about Stories in the Bible, paintings by Oscar de Mejo, Harper & Row (New York City), 1989.

(With Thomas Hartman) *Where Does God Live?,* illustrated by William Zdinak, Triumph Books (New York City), 1991.

(With Hartman) *How Do You Spell God? Answers to the Big Questions from Around the World,* illustrated by Jos. A. Smith, foreword by the Dalai Lama, Morrow (New York City), 1995.

God's Mailbox: More Stories about Stories in the Bible, illustrated by Debbie Tilley, Morrow (New York City), 1996.

"Always Wear Clean Underwear!": And Other Ways Parents Say "I Love You," illustrated by Debbie Tilley, Morrow (New York City), 1997.

Contributor of a *midrash* (a story that elaborates on a story in the Hebrew Bible) to *Rosh ha-Shanah & Yom Kippur,* by Joel Lurie Grishaver, Torah Aura Productions (Los Angeles), 1987.

OTHER

Editor of journal of the New York Board of Rabbis. Contributor of book reviews to periodicals.

Sidelights

Rabbi Marc Gellman is the author and co-author of children's books that address religious and moral themes. Gellman is also known, along with Catholic priest Monsignor Thomas Hartman, as part of a duo that writer Jim Brosseua, in an article for *Town & Country,* called "the Siskel and Ebert of spirituality." Together Hartman and Gellman host *The God Squad,* a cable television show appearing on the Faith & Values/VISN network that addresses issues relating to religion. The pair have also been regulars on ABC's *Good Morning America,* as well as on radio.

Gellman's first book, *Does God Have a Big Toe?* (1989), is a collection of lighthearted stories inspired by the Jewish tradition of the midrash, a story that elaborates on a tale in the Hebrew Bible. One of Gellman's midrashim, for example, explains that God invented the Sabbath (the day of rest) because the animals in the Garden of Eden were complaining that Adam was always giving them lists of things to do. *Booklist's* Ilene Cooper wrote that Gellman's "quirky, often humorous ... stories will get children thinking about the Bible ... in a new way." Patricia Dooley, writing in *School Library Journal,* praised the "qualities of joy, spirituality, playfulness, and reflection" found in the stories. Although she expressed concern about how the book is structured, and commented that the book's coverage of the early events of the Hebrew Bible (Adam through Noah) is stronger than its coverage of later events (Abraham through Joshua), she also declared that each story, taken on its own, offers "a thoughtful and funny antidote to the idea that reverence can only be solemn." A reviewer in *Horn Book* observed that Gellman tells his stories "[w]ith affection and humor founded on deep respect and study." Both this reviewer and Dooley also thought that Oscar de Mejo's paintings were a fitting accompaniment to the text.

God's Mailbox: More Stories About Stories in the Bible (1996) is Gellman's second collection of *midrashim.* A reviewer in *Publishers Weekly* wrote that the book opens up "whole new perspectives" on familiar Bible stories. *School Library Journal* contributor Patricia Pearl Dole noted Gellman's use of "a thoroughly modern vocabulary, a completely informal style, and plenty of sly humor" as devices for making his stories accessible to his readers. She added that Gellman refrains from "trivializing the sacred" by having each tale clearly convey an "appropriate ... message" and by sticking with the essential biblical characters and events. Less enthusiastically, Elizabeth Bush of the *Bulletin of the Center for Children's Books* called *God's Mailbox* "somewhat sugary," though she admitted that it does provide "food for thought and nourishment for the soul."

In addition to appearing on television together, Gellman and Hartman teamed up to write several books, including *How Do You Spell God?* (1995), a work directed at teenagers with the intent of providing basic information on the world's major religions. A reviewer in *Publishers Weekly* praised the authors for their "great facility in discussing potentially thorny subjects." *Booklist's* Ilene Cooper observed that the pair had made the right choice in organizing the book thematically rather than giving each religion a chapter of its own. Cooper also declared that the book offers "a wealth of facts as well as thought-provoking ideas," and concluded that *How Do You Spell God?* performs a useful service by prompting children to think about "a sorely neglected subject."

"Always Wear Clean Underwear!": and Other Ways Parents Say "I Love You" (1997) attempts to explain the reasoning behind "clean your plate," "because I say so," and thirty other parental expressions of advice and instruction that children often find burdensome or baffling. *School Library Journal* contributor Jerry D. Flack called the book a "warm, witty, and instructive primer for children about the whys and wherefores of parenting." *Booklist's* Stephanie Zvirin praised Gellman for his "down-to-earth," humorous approach and for showing children how parental commands exist within a larger moral context.

Works Cited

Brosseua, Jim, "The Meaning of Marriage," *Town & Country,* February, 1999, p. 126.

Bush, Elizabeth, review of *God's Mailbox, Bulletin of the Center for Children's Books,* May, 1996, p. 301.

Cooper, Ilene, review of *Does God Have a Big Toe?, Booklist,* October 15, 1989, p. 457.

Cooper, Ilene, review of *How Do You Spell God?, Booklist,* June 1 and 15, 1995, p. 1743.

Review of *Does God Have a Big Toe?, Horn Book,* March-April, 1990, p. 219.

Dole, Patricia Pearl, review of *God's Mailbox: More Stories about Stories in the Bible, School Library Journal,* March, 1996, p. 196.

Dooley, Patricia, review of *Does God Have a Big Toe?, School Library Journal,* December, 1989, pp. 107-08.

Flack, Jerry D., review of *"Always Wear Clean Underwear!": and Other Ways Parents Say "I Love You," School Library Journal,* November, 1997, p. 127.

Review of *God's Mailbox: More Stories about Stories in the Bible, Publishers Weekly,* April 8, 1996, p. 62.

Review of *How Do You Spell God, Publishers Weekly,* June 19, 1995, p. 62.

Zvirin, Stephanie, review of *"Always Wear Clean Underwear!": and Other Ways Parents Say "I Love You," Booklist,* October 1, 1997, pp. 321-22.

For More Information See

PERIODICALS

Booklist, September 1, 1995, p. 60.
Children's Book Review Service, February, 1990, p. 76.
Kirkus Reviews, February 1, 1996, p. 226.
New York Times Book Review, June 4, 1995, p. 25.
Publishers Weekly, August 18, 1997, p. 94.
School Library Journal, June, 1991, p. 45; June, 1994, p. 52; May, 1995, p. 126.
Voice of Youth Advocates, April, 1990, p. 48; October, 1995, p. 248.*

*   *   *

GRAHAM, Ian 1953-
(James Young, a pseudonym)

Personal

Born September 9, 1953, in Belfast, Northern Ireland; *Education:* City University, London, B.S. (applied physics), 1975, graduate diploma (journalism), 1978. *Hobbies and other interests:* Keeping fish, growing bonsai trees, crosswords, photography, lateral thinking, coin collecting, banknote collecting, special-issue stamp collecting, watching too much television.

Addresses

Home—Ash Vale, England. *Electronic mail*—iangraham@msn.com.

Career

Freelance writer and editor, 1982—. Argus Specialist Publications, editorial positions, including assistant editor of *Electronics Today International,* then deputy editor, *Which Video,* 1978-82. Consultant editor, *Space Voyager* (magazine), 1983-84, and *Micro Challenge* (magazine), 1985. *Member:* American Institute of Aeronautics & Astronautics, Authors' Lending & Copyright Society, British Association for the Advancement of Science, British Interplanetary Society, Institute of Journalist, Society of Authors, Farnborough Air Sciences Association, Mensa.

Writings

NONFICTION

Computer & Video Games, Usborne (London, England), 1982.

(With Lynn Myring) *Information Revolution,* Usborne, 1983.

The Inside Story: Computer, Collins (London, England), 1983, illustrated by Denis Bishop et al., Gloucester Press (New York), 1983.

(With Helen Varley) *The Personal Computer Yearbook,* Pan (London, England), 1983, published in the U. S. as *The Home Computer Handbook: The Foremost Guide to the New Home Technology,* Simon & Schuster, 1984.

(Editor) *Choose Your Own Video: A Guide to Buying the Best Video System for Your Money,* Dorling Kindersley (London, England), 1983, Barron's Educational (New York), 1983.

Step-by-Step Programming for the Sinclair Spectrum, two volumes, Dorling Kindersley, 1984.

Step-by-Step Programming for the Sinclair Spectrum Plus, two volumes, Dorling Kindersley, 1984.

Step-by-Step Programming for the BBC Micro, two volumes, Dorling Kindersley, 1984.

Step-by-Step Programming for the Acorn Electron, two volumes, Dorling Kindersley, 1984.

Inventions, Wayland Publishing, 1986, published as *Topics: Inventions,* Bookwright Press (New York, NY), 1987.

How to Look after Your Home Computer, Editorial Gustavo Gili, 1986.

(With Douglas Garr) *The Video Maker's Handbook,* Octopus (London, England), 1986, published in the U.S. as *The Home Video Makers' Handbook,* St. Martin's, 1986.

Science Frontiers: Communications, Macdonald, 1988, Hampstead (New York), 1989.

Science Frontiers: Transportation, Macdonald, 1988, Hampstead, 1989.

Engineers at Work: Attack Submarine, Gloucester Press, 1989.

Engineers at Work: Salvage at Sea, Gloucester Press, 1990.

Our Solar System, Two-Can Publishing (London, England), 1990, Scholastic (New York, NY), 1991.

The Universe, Two-Can Publishing, 1990.

Space Travel, Two-Can Publishing, 1990.

Stars & Galaxies, Two-Can Publishing, 1990.

Facing the Future: Communications, Evans Bros. (London, England), 1991, Raintree Steck-Vaughn (Austin, TX), 1991.

Concorde, Pan, 1991.

Be an Expert: Astronomer, Gloucester Press, 1991.

Facing the Future: Space Science, Evans Bros., 1992, Raintree Steck-Vaughn, 1993.

Skyscrapers, Pan, 1992.

Channel Tunnel, Pan, 1992.

Facing the Future: Transport, Evans Bros., 1992, published in the U.S. as *Facing the Future: Transportation,* Raintree Steck-Vaughn, 1993.

The Big Book of Flight, Hamlyn, 1993.

How Things Work: Cars, Bikes, Trains, and Other Land Machines, Kingfisher (New York), 1993.

How Things Work: Boats, Ships, Submarines, and Other Floating Machines, Kingfisher, 1993.

101 Questions and Answers: How Things Work, Hamlyn, 1993, Facts on File (New York), 1995.

Pointers: Cars, Simon & Schuster (Hemel Hempstead, England), 1993, illustrated by Mick Gillah, Raintree Steck-Vaughn, 1994.

Pointers: Spacecraft, Simon & Schuster, 1994, illustrated by Roger Stewart, Raintree Steck-Vaughn, 1995.

101 Questions and Answers: Transport, Hamlyn, 1994.

Transport by Design, Simon & Schuster, 1995, published in the U.S. as *Transport: How it Works,* Sterling, 1995.

How It Goes: Racing Cars, Barron's Educational, 1995.

How It Goes: Boats, Barron's Educational, 1995.

Supercutaways: Aircraft & Spacecraft, Colour Library Books (Godalming, England), 1995.

Visual Reality: Aircraft, Vineyard Books, 1995.

Discoveries: How Things Work, Allen & Unwin, 1996, Time-Life Books (Alexandria, VA), 1996.

(With Paul Sterry) *Questions & Answers Book of Facts,* Vineyard Books, 1996, published in the U.S. as *Questions & Answers Book of Science Facts,* Facts on File, 1997.

Worldwise: Photography & Film, illustrated by Nicholas Hewetson, F. Watts, 1997.

Collect-a-Classic: Ford Mustang, Templar Communications, 1997.

Collect-a-Classic: Chevrolet Corvette, Templar Communications, 1997.

Spaceflight, Disney Corporation, 1997.

Worldwise: Motorcycles, F. Watts, 1998.

The Best Book of Spaceships, Kingfisher, 1998.

Computers & Communications, Horus Editions, 1998.

Energy, Motion & Machines, Miles Kelly Publishing, 1998.

The Best Book of the Moon, Kingfisher, 1999.

In Control: How to Fly a Boeing 747, Walker, 1999.

Investigations: Space, Anness Publishing, 1999.

Future Tech: Space, Belitha Press (London, England), 1999.

Future Tech: Transport, Belitha Press, 1999.

"HOW IT WORKS" SERIES

Submarines, Gloucester Press, 1989.

Helicopters, illustrated by Aziz Khan, Gloucester Press, 1989.

Space Shuttles, Gloucester Press, 1989.

Combat Aircraft, Gloucester Press, 1989.

Racing Cars, Gloucester Press, 1990.

Battle Tanks, illustrated by Aziz Khan, Gloucester Press, 1990.

Trucks, illustrated by Khan, Gloucester Press, 1990.

Television and Video, illustrated by Alex Pang and Ian Moores, Gloucester Press, 1991.

Cameras, Gloucester Press, 1991.

Lasers and Holograms, Gloucester Press, 1991.

Telescopes, Gloucester Press, 1991.

Computers, Gloucester Press, 1992.

"SCIENCE SPOTLIGHT" SERIES

Crime-Fighting, Evans Bros., 1993, Raintree Steck-Vaughn, 1995.

Fighting Disease, Evans Bros., 1994, Raintree Steck-Vaughn, 1995.

Fakes and Forgeries, Evans Bros., 1994, Raintree Steck-Vaughn, 1995.

Astronomy, Evans Bros., 1994, Raintree Steck-Vaughn, 1995.

Sport, Evans Bros., 1994, published in the U.S. as *Sports,* Raintree Steck-Vaughn, 1995.

Stage and Screen, Evans Bros., 1995, Raintree Steck-Vaughn, 1995.

"BUILT FOR SPEED" SERIES

Aircraft, Belitha Press, 1997, illustrated by Tom Connell, Raintree Steck-Vaughn, 1999.

Boats, Belitha Press, 1997, illustrated by Tom Connell, Raintree Steck-Vaughn, 1999.

Cars, Belitha Press, 1997, illustrated by Tom Connell, Raintree Steck-Vaughn, 1999.

Motorcycles, Belitha Press, 1997, illustrated by Tom Connell, Raintree Steck-Vaughn, 1999.

"SKY FLIES" SERIES

Modern Passenger Aircraft, Hawkswell Associates, 1997.

History of Flying Machines, Hawkswell Associates, 1997.

Record Breakers, Hawkswell Associates, 1997.

At the Controls, Hawkswell Associates, 1997.
At the Airport, Hawkswell Associates, 1997.
Fighters & Bombers, Hawkswell Associates, 1997.

"ENERGY FOREVER?" SERIES

Water Power, Lionheart, 1997, Raintree Steck-Vaughn, 1999.
Solar Power, Lionheart, 1998, Raintree Steck-Vaughn, 1999.
Wind Power, Wayland, 1998, Raintree Steck-Vaughn, 1999.
Fossil Fuels, Wayland, 1998, Raintree Steck-Vaughn, 1999.
Nuclear Power, Wayland, 1999, Raintree Steck-Vaughn, 1999.
Geothermal and Bio Power, Wayland, 1999, as *Geothermal and Bio-Energy,* Raintree Steck-Vaughn, 1999.

"COMMUNICATIONS" SERIES

Books and Newspapers, Evans Bros., 1999.
Photography and Film, Evans Bros., 1999.
Radio and TV, Evans Bros., 1999.
Global Networks, Evans Bros., 1999.

Contributor to periodicals, including *Wallace & Grommit's Techno Quest, Air World International, What Video, Gold, Movies, Autocar, Space Voyager, Choice, Complete Traveller, Everyday Electronics, Electronics Australia, What Hi-Fi, High Fidelity, Fishkeeping Answers, Practical Fishkeeping, Hobby Electronics, Computing Today,* and *Video Today.* Contributor to reference books, including *Kingfisher Children's Science Encyclopedia,* Kingfisher, 1991; and *Kingfisher Children's Encyclopedia,* 1998.

Also author of books under pseudonym James Young.

Work in Progress

A fictionalized account of day-to-day life amid guerilla warfare in Belfast during the "Troubles" of the 1970s.

Sidelights

Prolific nonfiction writer Ian Graham shares his expertise and enthusiasm on a number of topics with young readers, specializing in the ever-changing areas of science and technology. Among his more than one hundred titles are *How Things Work: Boats, Ships, Submarines, and Other Floating Machines, Energy Forever?: Geothermal and Bio Power,* and the "Communications" series of books, which includes titles such as *Radio and TV* and *Photography and Film.* "In general, I find it impossible NOT to write," the Irish-born Graham admitted to *SATA.* "I am always either writing commissioned books, or writing articles for a major international CAD software company, or penning poetry (usually nonsense rhymes for children)."

Born in 1953, Graham pursued a bachelor of science degree, before indulging in his other interest—writing—and earning an advanced degree in journalism. He worked in various editorial positions for Argus Special-

ist Publications, a trade-magazine publisher, before breaking out into a career as a freelance writer and editor in 1982. Since then, Graham has produced, on average, four or more books a year. While most of his books are written under his own name, he has used the pseudonym James Young on a few occasions.

As a way to inform elementary-aged young people about their ever-changing world, Graham has written a number of books on computers and related technology. In 1983's *The Inside Story: Computer,* he discusses everything from microchips to mainframes, showing both how computers are manufactured and how they impact society. Other books by Graham that reflect the growing importance of computers in modern life are several programming manuals and his 1986 work, *How to Look after Your Home Computer.*

In *Transportation,* one volume in the "Science Frontiers" series, Graham reviews the new ways in which people and things are getting from one place to another. Against a backdrop of photographs and other illustrations, he explains improvements in transportation that

Ian Graham's **Fakes and Forgeries** *looks at the process whereby works of art are dated and authenticated to protect the investment of private collectors and museums.*

we now benefit from, as well as those, such as solar power, that are still in the planning stages, and looks at trends in technology within the transportation industry, such as a focus on improving the design of aircraft wings. Praising *Transportation* as well as the other books in the "Science Frontiers" series, *Booklist* contributor Beth Herbert noted that the books' "international approach will be especially welcome to technologically curious youngsters, who will appreciate the well-researched texts." "A vast amount of information is available to browsers," added Sylvia S. Marantz in her review of the series for *School Library Journal,* "while researchers have both glossary and index." Another title by Graham in the "Science Frontiers" series is *Communications.*

Graham has also contributed volumes on a wide range of subjects to the "Science Spotlight" series released by Texas-based publisher Raintree Steck-Vaughn. Not only science, but entertainment and social life also come in for scrutiny, in titles like *Sports, Fighting Disease, Stage and Screen,* and *Fakes and Forgeries.* In *Fighting Disease,* Graham focuses on ailments such as coronary disease and other problems that plague many modern adults and discusses the advances that make these illnesses less of a threat than they may have been in previous years. *Fakes and Forgeries* looks at the process whereby works of art are dated and authenticated prior to changing hands, to ensure that private collectors and museums are getting what they are paying for. Among the topics Graham includes are the Shroud of Turin, UFO sightings, the Loch Ness monster, and crop circles. And in *Sports,* training techniques used by modern athletes are explained, and the scientific principles involved in different sporting events are also discussed. While *School Library Journal* reviewer Ann M. Burlingame remarked that students seeking detailed information would "need to use additional sources," other reviewers found Graham's coverage to be adequate. Praising the series as a whole, an *Appraisal* contributor concluded that these books "[discuss] in an eminently readable fashion, a large number of sophisticated scientific techniques and concepts," and judged the series "well worth the time and effort for readers."

Graham was living in Belfast during the worst years of "The Troubles," a period characterized by numerous random acts of street violence in which many people were killed, that had its roots in a centuries-old conflict between the Irish and the English. "For many years, I was unable to write anything about it," Graham explained to *SATA,* "but I have now finally got round to putting my experiences down on paper. I am writing a fictionalized account of what it was like trying to live a normal day-to-day life in the middle of a guerilla war. Half of the story deals with the Troubles and their effect on ordinary families like mine, while the other half of the story deals with my father's death and my mother's Alzheimer's Disease. I would love to find a U.S. publisher for this book and, ultimately, see it made into a film—I can dream!"

Works Cited

Burlingame, Ann M., review of *Science Spotlight: Fakes and Forgeries, School Library Journal,* July, 1995, p. 86.

Herbert, Beth, review of *Science Frontiers: Transportation, Booklist,* June 1, 1989, p. 1720.

Marantz, Sylvia S., review of *Science Frontiers: Communications* and *Science Frontiers: Transportation, School Library Journal,* September, 1989, p. 259.

Review of "Science Spotlight" series, *Appraisal,* autumn, 1995, pp. 88-89.

For More Information See

PERIODICALS

School Librarian, December, 1983, pp. 367-68; May, 1994, p. 65; summer, 1998, p. 92.

School Library Journal, January, 1984, p. 76.*

H

HANSEN, Mark Victor

Personal

Married Patty Hansen (a chief financial officer); children: two daughters.

Addresses

Agent—c/o Health Communications, Inc., 3201 SW 15th St., Deerfield Beach, FL 33442.

Career

Motivational speaker and author of inspirational books. *Member*: National Speakers Association.

Writings

Future Diary, edited by Patty Hansen, Keith Terry, Carol Foreman Brockfield, M. V. Hansen Publishing Co. (Newport Beach, CA), 1983.
(With Gregory J. P. Godek) *1001 Ways to Be Romantic,* Casablanca Press, 1995.
(With Joe D. Batten) *The Master Motivator: Secrets of Inspiring Leadership,* Health Communications, 1995.
(Editor with Canfield) *A Fifth Portion of Chicken Soup for the Soul: 101 More Stories to Open the Heart and Rekindle the Spirit,* Health Communications, 1998.
(With Jim Paluch) *Leaving A Legacy,* JP Horizons, 1998.
(With Lisa McCourt and Jack Canfield), *Chicken Soup for Little Souls: The Best Night Out with Dad* (children's book), illustrated by Bert Dodson, Health Communications, 1998.
(With Jack Canfield) *Chicken Soup for the Unsinkable Soul: Stories of Triumphing Over Life's Obstacles,* Health Communications, 1999.
(Editor with Canfield) *A 6th Bowl of Chicken Soup for the Soul: More Stories to Open the Heart and Rekindle the Spirit,* Health Communications, 1999.

COMPILER AND CONTRIBUTOR

Chicken Soup for the Soul: 101 Stories to Open the Heart & Rekindle the Spirit, edited by Jack Canfield, Health Communications, 1993.
A 2nd Helping of Chicken Soup for the Soul: 101 More Stories to Open the Heart and Rekindle the Spirit, edited by Jack Canfield, Health Communications, 1995.
(With Canfield and Diana von Welanetz Wentworth) *Chicken Soup for the Soul Cookbook: 101 Stories with Recipes from the Heart,* Health Communications, 1995.
Jack Canfield, *The Aladdin Factor,* Berkley Books (New York City), 1995.
A 3rd Helping of Chicken Soup for the Soul: 101 More Stories to Open the Heart and Rekindle the Spirit, edited by Jack Canfield, Health Communications, 1996.
(With Barbara Nichols and Patty Hansen) *Out of the Blue: Delight Comes into Our Lives,* HarperCollins (New York City), 1996.
(With Canfield and Patty Hansen) *Condensed Chicken Soup for the Soul,* Health Communications, 1996.
(With Canfield and Barry Spilchuk) *A Cup of Chicken Soup for the Soul: Stories to Open the Heart and Rekindle the Spirit,* Health Communications, 1996.
(With Hanoch McCarty and Meladee McCarty) *A 4th Course of Chicken Soup for the Soul: 101 Stories to Open the Heart and Rekindle the Spirits,* edited by Jack Canfield, Health Communications, 1997.
(With Canfield and Kimberly Kirberger) *Chicken Soup for the Teenage Soul: 101 Stories of Life, Love, and Learning,* Health Communications, 1997.
(With Jack Canfield and Lisa McCourt): *The Chicken Soup for Little Souls Goodness Gorillas,* (children's book) illustrated by Pat Grant Porter, Health Communications, 1997.
(With Jack Canfield, Jennifer Read Hawthorne, and Marci Shimoff) *Chicken Soup for the Mother's Soul,* Health Communications, 1997.
(With Canfield and Ron Camacho) *Chicken Soup for the Country Soul: Stories Served Up Country Style and*

82

Straight from the Heart, Health Communications, 1998.

(With Canfield and Kirberger) *Chicken Soup for the Teenage Soul II: 101 More Stories of Life, Love, and Learning,* Health Communications, 1998.

(With Canfield and Kirberger) *Chicken Soup for the Teenage Soul: Journal,* Health Communications, 1998.

Hansen and his colleagues compiled many more inspirational books, covering topics such as: pet lovers, the surviving soul, the college soul, books for couples, and even golfers.

Sidelights

A modern publishing success story started in 1989 when Mark Victor Hansen and Jack Canfield, two motivational speakers who had met at a holistic-health conference in California, decided to put together some of the inspirational stories they had collected through their travels and careers and compile them into a book. As Canfield told Andrew Ferguson in *Time,* "*Chicken Soup for the Soul* came about because someone in a seminar said to me one day, 'You know that story about the dog that you told? Is that in a book somewhere?' . . . After hearing this month after month, I finally went, 'Someone's trying to tell me to put these stories in a book.' It became a divine obsession."

But that obsession did not initially inspire any of thirty-three publishers whom Canfield and Hansen approached with the book. Even their agent quit after the thirty-third rejection. Finally, in 1993, they got the attention of a small Florida publisher, who estimated that the book might sell 20,000 copies. In fact, adding together the original book and all of its permutations published thus far, it sold more than 28 million copies by mid-1998. Ferguson, who wrote about the *Chicken Soup* phenomenon, suggested a new title: "Chicken Soup for the Souls of Thirty-Three Publishers Who Really, Really Screwed Up."

The *Chicken Soup* series of books is built around the notion of compiling real life stories, aphorisms, poems, quotations, fables, essays, anecdotes, jokes, illustrations, and letters, organized under headings like "On Love," "Learning to Love Yourself," "Live Your Dream," and "A Matter of Attitude." Hansen told Ferguson, "Our books go heart to heart, soul to soul, to the core being of a person." He explained the incredible success of the books by noting that: "Our stories are so little, so bite-sized, that they don't intimidate people . . . . People can read them in the bathroom. They ignite the spirit." In the original *Chicken Soup* book, the authors advise their readers not to "hurry through this book. Take your time. Enjoy it. Savor it." They also advise that "reading a book like this is a little like sitting down to eat a meal of all desserts. It may be "too rich" to be absorbed in just one sitting.

Given the original *Chicken Soup for the Soul*'s phenomenal success, it is no surprise that many critics felt the book's appeal. Writing for the *English Journal,* Gena

Lengel extolled its virtues: "With simple vocabulary and short (one, two, or three-page) selections, the authors offer the reader an experience that is gentle on the mind and soothing to the soul . . . . [The book] is just a nice, warm, compassionate, colloquial adventure in feeling good. Like homemade chicken soup for the body remedy, I tried *Chicken Soup for the Soul,* and it made me feel better."

Within two years of the publication of the original *Chicken Soup* book, Canfield and Hansen had teamed up with cookbook writer Diana von Welanetz Wentworth to produce the *Chicken Soup for the Soul Cookbook,* which combined one-hundred-and-one inspirational anecdotes with related soul-satisfying recipes for dishes like creamed corn, baked beans, pot roast and chocolate cinnamon rolls. Chapter titles include "Mom's Kitchen," "Men in the Kitchen," and "Love, Romance, and Marriage." Reviewers predicted enormous popularity for the book, based on the sales for the original collection.

Recently Canfield and Hansen, among others, have been contributing to a children's series called "Chicken Soup for Little Souls"; a book cowritten by Canfield and Hansen called *The Best Night Out with Dad* tells the story of young Danny's night out at the circus with his father. Waiting in line, they discover that another boy and his father cannot afford tickets, and Danny and his dad give theirs up and go instead to a basketball game. According to Nancy Menaldi-Scanlan in *School Library Journal,* the stories in the series are meant to inspire "generosity and unexpected kindness."

Works Cited

PERIODICALS

English Journal, October, 1995, pp. 127-128.
School Library Journal, January, 1998, p. 80.

For More Information See

PERIODICALS

Library Journal, October 15, 1995, p. 83.
Publishers Weekly, April 29, 1996, p. 63; September 18, 1995, pp. 127-128; March 3, 1997, p. 58.
Time, June 8, 1998, p. 62.*

*   *   *

HAWKINS, Colin 1945-

Personal

Born 1945, in England; married Jacqui (a writer and illustrator), 1968; children: Finbar, Sally. *Education:* Blackpool Art School.

Addresses

Home—London, England.

Career

Author and illustrator. *Daily Express,* London, reportage illustrator, 1971; teacher at Medway and Norwich, England, Art Schools.

Writings

AND ILLUSTRATOR; WITH WIFE, JACQUI HAWKINS

Witches (also see below), Granada (London, England), 1981, Silver Burdett (Morristown, NJ), 1985.

It's a Fact and It's Very Funny, ITV Books (London, England), 1982.

How to Look after Your Cat, Evans (London, England), 1982.

(With Enid Von Bluoton) *Vampires* (also see below), Granada, 1982, Silver Burdett, 1985.

Spooks (also see below), Granada, 1983, Silver Burdett, 1985.

What's the Time, Mr. Wolf?, Heinemann (London, England), 1983, as *What Time Is It, Mr. Wolf?,* Putnam (New York, NY), 1983.

Adding Animals, Pepper (London, England), 1983, Putnam, 1983.

Pat the Cat, Pepper, 1983, Putnam, 1983.

Baby Boo!, Pepper, 1983, published in the U.S. as *Boo! Who?,* Holt, 1983.

Take Away Monsters, Piccadilly (London, England), 1984, Putnam, 1984.

The Monsters Go on a Picnic, Beanstalk, 1984.

The Monsters Visit Granny, Beanstalk, 1984.

The Granny Book, Granada, 1984.

Snap! Snap!, Heinemann, 1984, Putnam, 1984.

Mig the Pig, Piccadilly, 1984, Putnam, 1984.

Old Mother Hubbard, Piccadilly, 1984, Putnam, 1985.

I'm Not Sleepy, Walker (London, England), 1985, published in the U.S. as *I'm Not Sleepy!,* Crown, 1986.

Where's My Mummy?, Walker, 1985, published in the U.S. as *Where's My Mommy?,* Crown, 1986.

Hush Now, Baby Bear, Random House, 1985.

My First Book, Viking, 1985.

'Round the Garden, Viking, 1985.

This Little Pig, Viking, 1985.

Jen the Hen, Piccadilly, 1985, Putnam, 1985.

Incy Wincy Spider, Viking, 1985.

Shriek! A Compendium of Witches, Vampires and Spooks (includes *Witches, Vampires,* and *Spooks*), Granada, 1985, expanded as *The Monster Book of Witches, Vampires, Spooks, and Monsters)* (includes *Witches, Vampires, Spooks,* and *Monsters),* Collins (London, England), 1997.

Mr. Wolf's Week, Heinemann, 1985.

This Little Pig, Viking, 1985.

The Elephant, Viking, 1985.

Zoo Animals, Methuen (London, England), 1985, expanded as *Zoo Animals; Park Animals,* Macmillan, 1990.

Dip, Dip, Dip, Little, Brown, 1986.

One Finger, One Thumb, Little, Brown, 1986.

Oops-a-Daisy, Little, Brown, 1986.

Farmyard Sounds, Crown (New York, NY), 1986, Walker, 1990.

Where's Bear?, Little, Brown, 1986.

Tog the Dog, Piccadilly, 1986, Putnam, 1986.

Jungle Sounds, Crown, 1986, Walker, 1990.

Max and the Magic Word, Viking, 1986.

Busy ABC, Viking, 1987.

The Wizard's Cat, Walker, 1987, Warner (New York, NY), 1987.

Pirates, Collins, 1987.

Terrible, Terrible Tiger, Walker, 1987, Warner, 1987.

(Reteller) *I Know an Old Lady Who Swallowed a Fly,* Methuen, 1987, published in the U.S. as *There Was an Old Lady Who Swallowed a Fly,* Putnam, 1987.

Mr. Wolf's Birthday Surprise, Heinemann, 1987.

Here's a Happy Elephant, Walker, 1987, Warner, 1988.

Here's a Happy Pig, Walker, 1988, Warner, 1988.

Zug the Bug, Piccadilly, 1988, Putnam, 1988.

This Old Car: A Counting Book, Orchard, 1988, published in the U.S. as *How Many Are in This Old Car?: A Counting Book,* Putnam, 1988.

Cosmic Cat and the Pink Planet, Collins, 1988.

Cosmic Cat and the Space Spider, Collins, 1988.

Crocodile Creek, Collins, 1988, published in the U.S. as *Crocodile Creek: The Cry in the Night,* Doubleday, 1989.

Pets, Macmillan, 1989.

I Spy: The Lift-the-Flap ABC Book, Walker, 1989, Little, Brown, 1989.

Noah Built an Ark One Day, Methuen, 1989, Putnam, 1989.

Mr. Bear's Plane, Orchard, 1989.

The House That Jack Built, Piccadilly, 1990, Putnam, 1990.

When I Was One, Viking, 1990.

Knock! Knock!, Walker, 1990, Simon & Schuster (New York, NY), 1991.

How to Look after Your Dog, Walker, 1991.

Old MacDonald Had a Farm, Methuen, 1991, Putnam, 1991.

Monsters, Collins, 1991.

The Numberlies, eleven volumes, Bodley Head (London, England), 1991.

Max and the School Dinners, Viking, 1992.

Hey Diddle Diddle, Walker, 1992, published in the U.S. as *Hey Diddle Diddle: Five Fingerwiggle Nursery Rhymes,* Candlewick Press, 1992.

Humpty Dumpty, Walker, 1992, published in the U.S. as *Humpty Dumpty: Five Fingerwiggle Nursery Rhymes,* Candlewick Press, 1992.

Meet Zero, Bodley Head, 1992.

Come for a Ride on the Ghost Train, Walker, 1993, Candlewick Press, 1993.

Colin and Jacqui Hawkins' Word Book, Simon & Schuster (Hemel Hempstead, England), 1994.

Grannies, Granada, 1994.

School, Collins, 1994.

Ghosts, Reader's Digest, 1994.

Pirate Ship: A Pop-up Adventure, HarperCollins (London, England), 1994, Cobblehill (New York, NY), 1994.

Foxy and the Spots, HarperCollins, 1995.

Foxy Goes to Bed, HarperCollins, 1995.

Foxy in the Kitchen, HarperCollins, 1995.

Foxy Loses His Tail, HarperCollins, 1995.

How to Look after Your Hamster, Walker, 1995.

How to Look after Your Rabbit, Walker, 1995.

Foxy Plays Hide and Seek, HarperCollins, 1996.

Here's a Happy Kitten, Candlewick Press, 1996.

Here's a Happy Puppy, Candlewick Press, 1996.

Aliens, Collins, 1996.
Foxy and His Naughty Little Sister, Collins, 1997.
Mr. Wolf's Sticker Ticker Time, Heinemann, 1997.
Whose House?, Barron's, 1998.
Foxy and Friends Go Racing, Collins, 1998.
An ABC Picture Gallery, Butterworth-Heinemann, 1999.
Daft Dog, HarperCollins, 1999.
Greedy Goat, HarperCollins, 1999.

Illustrator

Peter Eldin, *The Armada TV Quiz Book,* Armada Books (London, England), 1976.
(With Brian Robins) James Webster, *Webster's English Workbook,* four volumes, Nelson (Sunbury-on-Thames, England), 1976.
John M. Hughes, *Sounds in Sentences,* four volumes, Nelson, 1977.
Christopher Maynard, *Father Christmas and His Friends,* W. H. Allen (London, England), 1979.
Stewart Cowley, *The Social Climbing Cat: How to Catch the Right Owner,* Simon & Schuster (New York, NY), 1981.
Tony Bradman, *See You Later, Alligator,* Methuen, 1986, Dial (New York, NY), 1986.

Adaptations

The "Foxy" stories have been adapted as a British television series, 1999.

Sidelights

Together with wife, Jacqui Hawkins, author and illustrator Colin Hawkins has created a wide array of unique picture books that appeal to both youngsters and their parents. Often saturating their work with a sense of humor that borders on the impish, the Hawkinses have seduced a legion of young fans with tales of foxes, bears, pigs, and other creatures engaged in all manner of activity. With titles like *Greedy Goat, Daft Dog,* and *Boo! Who?,* books by the Hawkinses have been translated into several languages, and have also found their way onto television. The *Foxy* stories, which are based on the exploits of the couple's own two children, were developed into an animated series airing in Great Britain in the late 1990s. A *Books for Keeps* contributor noted that the "combination of zany illustration with the ability to pinpoint absurdity is a potent mix" used to excellent effect in Colin and Jacqui Hawkins's many books.

Although Colin and Jacqui spent many holidays during their childhood at their family's farms, which were only a mile apart, they did not formally meet until they were in their mid-teens, and were married in 1968. Both had a background in the graphic arts, and at the time of their marriage Colin worked as an illustrator for London's *Daily Express* newspaper. When the newspaper went through some hard times a few years later, he lost his job and became a freelance illustrator. In the mid-1970s, after their first child was born, the couple began to assemble ideas for children's picture books. With Colin's flair for cartoon drawings and Jacqui's graphic

sense and dogged persistence, they put together a collection of drawings that they collectively titled *Witches.* The proposed book didn't get an immediate response from publishers, so the Hawkinses started another project, and then another. *Witches* eventually attracted the attention of not one publisher, but four, and upon its release in 1981, the Hawkinses' career took off.

Most of the Hawkinses' picture-book creations involve their audience in a learning activity, but with so much fun surrounding the lesson, no one is any the wiser. In *What's the Time, Mr. Wolf,* children are taught the basic techniques of telling time through the antics of a scruffy wolf. Mr. Wolf makes a return engagement in *Mr. Wolf's Week,* as the vagaries of weather are explained. As *Books for Keeps* contributor Liz Waterland described it, an "ungainly wolf blunders his way through the days of the week.... Dressing for the extraordinary changes of climate he encounters." In addition to providing an introductory lesson in vocabulary, the book "encourage[s children] to memorise ... details ... and to connect cause and effect—weather and appropriate clothing," added a *Junior Bookshelf* reviewer.

Basic math and reading concepts are introduced to the preschool set through such works as *Adding Animals,* a lift-the-flap book that uses animals to teach counting skills. Praising the book's brightly colored drawings for bringing "an energetic, fun-filled appearance" to a simple math lesson, *Booklist* contributor Denise M. Wilms noted that while "mathematics is the point," learning basic sums is transformed into something fun through the couple's colorful concoction. In *Max and the Magic Word,* good manners are taught through the experience of Max the dog. Max's requests are ignored because he doesn't follow them with "please" and "thank you." *School Library Journal* contributor Anne Wirkkala praised the book's artwork, noting that Max "is particularly expressive as he becomes more and more frustrated."

Pat the Cat coaches beginning readers in sound-alike words with the help of an obviously overfed feline. Amid illustrations in shades of yellow, orange, and blue are words like "fat", "bat", "cat", "mat", and "sat", with appropriate stress placed on the changing consonant sounds. In her appraisal for *Booklist,* Denise M. Wilms concluded that *Pat the Cat* was "fun, and a painless way to absorb some phonics and a sight vocabulary." Sight vocabulary is also taught in a series of books geared toward toddlers and consisting of titles including *This Little Pig, Incy Wincy Spider,* and *The Elephant.* First published in the mid-1980s and re-released in both the United States and England, these titles "have stood the test of time delightfully" due to illustrations that *Books for Keeps* reviewer Roy Blatchford called "witty" and "animated."

While many of the Hawkinses' books have a serious purpose at their core, others are just plain fun. In the lift-the-flap book *Boo! Who?,* someone or something is hiding out of sight in each picture, and perceptive youngsters can try to guess who or what with the clues

W hose palace is this
with its towers and flags?
Who's the fine lady no longer in rags?
Who are the guests having fun at the Ball?
Look inside and you'll see them all
—well, nearly all.

Rhyming text and visual clues lead readers to the identity of the folklore characters associated with each home depicted in Colin Hawkins's Whose House?, *illustrated by his wife, Jacqui.*

provided by the book's creators. "The hiders are all different from what the reader expects …," noted a *Publishers Weekly* contributor, "a ploy that should keep little ones giggling." The couple also put their unique slant on a traditional nursery rhyme in *Old Mother Hubbard,* a "romp" that a *Publishers Weekly* contributor noted "stands out among countless variations" with its lift-the-flap format and silly verses. And school gets the full comic treatment in the Hawkinses' aptly titled *School,* as jokes and riddles abound while readers meet a "veritable gallery of school stereotypes from bullies, toadies and goody goodies to the all-seeing teacher with eyes in the back of his head," according to Julie Blaisdale in *School Librarian.*

In each of their picture-book projects, the Hawkinses work together as a team, blending their styles to create an indivisible whole. As Colin noted in an interview with Stephanie Nettell in *Books for Keeps:* "People see the final book, but before that you have lots of roughs, overdrawings, talking, working out working out words." Jacqui loves the beginning stages of their joint projects: "the planning and roughs, going down different routes to solve a problem," as she explained to Nettell. While Colin's illustration predominate in most of their books, in 1998's *Whose House?* Jacqui's art takes center stage. "For ever and ever I've seen these beautiful rough … [sketches] coming through," Colin explained of Jacqui's contribution to the story's initial design, but he noted that she always requested that he add his own "slight edge" to them. After enough encouragement from her husband, *Whose House?* finally made it from roughs to published book with Jacqui's finely detailed artwork intact.

The popularity of the Hawkinses' books in both their native England and elsewhere—their works are pub-

lished worldwide and have been translated into several different languages—have made them almost an industry unto themselves. But, in addition to the availability of a wide range of titles and the high exposure their works receive in bookstores, the reason for the couple's success can be traced to their attitude regarding their craft, and the spirit of fun with which they approach each project. "Their whole philosophy is to make books *fun,*" explained Nettell; "regardless of educational fashions, this, they believe, is the only way to get kids reading."

Works Cited

Blaisdale, Julie, review of *School, School Librarian,* November, 1994, p. 151.

Blatchford, Roy, review of *This Little Pig, Incy Wincy Spider,* and *The Elephant, Books for Keeps,* March, 1998, p. 18.

Review of *Boo! Who?, Publishers Weekly,* February 3, 1984, p. 402.

Review of *Max and the Magic Word, Books for Keeps,* July, 1988, p. 6.

Review of *Mr. Wolf's Week, Junior Bookshelf,* April, 1986, p. 64.

Nettell, Stephanie, interview in *Books for Keeps,* May, 1999, pp. 12-13.

Review of *Old Mother Hubbard, Publishers Weekly,* March 22, 1985, pp. 59-60.

Waterland, Liz, review of *Mr. Wolf's Week, Books for Keeps,* January, 1988, p. 16.

Wilms, Denise M., review of *Adding Animals, Booklist,* September, 1983, p. 85.

Wilms, review of *Pat the Cat, Booklist,* August, 1983, p. 1465.

Wirkkala, Anne, review of *Max and the Magic Word, School Library Journal,* April, 1987, p. 83.

For More Information See

PERIODICALS

Books for Keeps, January, 1992, p. 7.
Junior Bookshelf,, 1995, p. 36; June, 1995, p. 99.
School Librarian, August, 1995, p. 103.

*   *   *

HAWKINS, Jacqui

Personal

Born in England; married Colin Hawkins (a writer and illustrator), 1968; children: Finbar, Sally. *Education:* Goldsmiths College.

Addresses

Home—London, England.

Career

Author and illustrator.

Writings

AND ILLUSTRATOR; WITH HUSBAND, COLIN HAWKINS

Witches (also see below), Granada (London, England), 1981, Silver Burdett (Morristown, NJ), 1985.
It's a Fact and It's Very Funny, ITV Books (London, England), 1982.
How to Look after Your Cat, Evans (London, England), 1982.
(With Enid Von Bluoton) *Vampires* (also see below), Granada, 1982, Silver Burdett, 1985.
Spooks (also see below), Granada, 1983, Silver Burdett, 1985.
What's the Time, Mr. Wolf?, Heinemann (London, England), 1983, as *What Time Is It, Mr. Wolf?,* Putnam (New York, NY), 1983.
Adding Animals, Pepper (London, England), 1983, Putnam, 1983.
Pat the Cat, Pepper, 1983, Putnam, 1983.
Baby Boo!, Pepper, 1983, published in the U.S. as *Boo! Who?,* Holt, 1983.
Take Away Monsters, Piccadilly (London, England), 1984, Putnam, 1984.
The Monsters Go on a Picnic, Beanstalk, 1984.
The Monsters Visit Granny, Beanstalk, 1984.
The Granny Book, Granada, 1984.
Snap! Snap!, Heinemann, 1984, Putnam, 1984.
Mig the Pig, Piccadilly, 1984, Putnam, 1984.
Old Mother Hubbard, Piccadilly, 1984, Putnam, 1985.
I'm Not Sleepy, Walker (London, England), 1985, published in the U.S. as *I'm Not Sleepy!,* Crown, 1986.
Where's My Mummy?, Walker, 1985, published in the U.S. as *Where's My Mommy?,* Crown, 1986.
Hush Now, Baby Bear, Random House, 1985.
My First Book, Viking, 1985.
'Round the Garden, Viking, 1985.
This Little Pig, Viking, 1985.

Jen the Hen, Piccadilly, 1985, Putnam, 1985.
Incy Wincy Spider, Viking, 1985.
Shriek! A Compendium of Witches, Vampires and Spooks (includes *Witches, Vampires,* and *Spooks*), Granada, 1985, expanded as *The Monster Book of Witches, Vampires, Spooks, and Monsters)* (includes *Witches, Vampires, Spooks,* and *Monsters),* Collins (London, England), 1997.
Mr. Wolf's Week, Heinemann, 1985.
This Little Pig, Viking, 1985.
The Elephant, Viking, 1985.
Zoo Animals, Methuen (London, England), 1985, expanded as *Zoo Animals; Park Animals,* Macmillan, 1990.
Dip, Dip, Dip, Little, Brown, 1986.
One Finger, One Thumb, Little, Brown, 1986.
Oops-a-Daisy, Little, Brown, 1986.
Farmyard Sounds, Crown (New York, NY), 1986, Walker, 1990.
Where's Bear?, Little, Brown, 1986.
Tog the Dog, Piccadilly, 1986, Putnam, 1986.
Jungle Sounds, Crown, 1986, Walker, 1990.
Max and the Magic Word, Viking, 1986.
Busy ABC, Viking, 1987.
The Wizard's Cat, Walker, 1987, Warner (New York, NY), 1987.
Pirates, Collins, 1987.
Terrible, Terrible Tiger, Walker, 1987, Warner, 1987.
(Reteller) *I Know an Old Lady Who Swallowed a Fly,* Methuen, 1987, published in the U.S. as *There Was an Old Lady Who Swallowed a Fly,* Putnam, 1987.
Mr. Wolf's Birthday Surprise, Heinemann, 1987.
Here's a Happy Elephant, Walker, 1987, Warner, 1988.
Here's a Happy Pig, Walker, 1988, Warner, 1988.
Zug the Bug, Piccadilly, 1988, Putnam, 1988.
This Old Car: A Counting Book, Orchard, 1988, published in the U.S. as *How Many Are in This Old Car?: A Counting Book,* Putnam, 1988.
Cosmic Cat and the Pink Planet, Collins, 1988.
Cosmic Cat and the Space Spider, Collins, 1988.
Crocodile Creek, Collins, 1988, published in the U.S. as *Crocodile Creek: The Cry in the Night,* Doubleday, 1989.
Pets, Macmillan, 1989.
I Spy: The Lift-the-Flap ABC Book, Walker, 1989, Little, Brown, 1989.
Noah Built an Ark One Day, Methuen, 1989, Putnam, 1989.
Mr. Bear's Plane, Orchard, 1989.
The House That Jack Built, Piccadilly, 1990, Putnam, 1990.
When I Was One, Viking, 1990.
Knock! Knock!, Walker, 1990, Simon & Schuster (New York, NY), 1991.
How to Look after Your Dog, Walker, 1991.
Old MacDonald Had a Farm, Methuen, 1991, Putnam, 1991.
Monsters, Collins, 1991.
The Numberlies, eleven volumes, Bodley Head (London, England), 1991.
Max and the School Dinners, Viking, 1992.
Hey Diddle Diddle, Walker, 1992, published in the U.S. as *Hey Diddle Diddle: Five Fingerwiggle Nursery Rhymes,* Candlewick Press, 1992.

Humpty Dumpty, Walker, 1992, published in the U.S. as *Humpty Dumpty: Five Fingerwiggle Nursery Rhymes,* Candlewick Press, 1992.

Meet Zero, Bodley Head, 1992.

Come for a Ride on the Ghost Train, Walker, 1993, Candlewick Press, 1993.

Colin and Jacqui Hawkins' Word Book, Simon & Schuster (Hemel Hempstead, England), 1994.

Grannies, Granada, 1994.

School, Collins, 1994.

Ghosts, Reader's Digest, 1994.

Pirate Ship: A Pop-up Adventure, HarperCollins (London, England), 1994, Cobblehill (New York, NY), 1994.

Foxy and the Spots, HarperCollins, 1995.

Foxy Goes to Bed, HarperCollins, 1995.

Foxy in the Kitchen, HarperCollins, 1995.

Foxy Loses His Tail, HarperCollins, 1995.

How to Look after Your Hamster, Walker, 1995.

How to Look after Your Rabbit, Walker, 1995.

Foxy Plays Hide and Seek, HarperCollins, 1996.

Here's a Happy Kitten, Candlewick Press, 1996.

Here's a Happy Puppy, Candlewick Press, 1996.

Aliens, Collins, 1996.

Foxy and His Naughty Little Sister, Collins, 1997.

Mr. Wolf's Sticker Ticker Time, Heinemann, 1997.

Whose House?, Barron's, 1998.

Foxy and Friends Go Racing, Collins, 1998.

An ABC Picture Gallery, Butterworth-Heinemann, 1999.

Daft Dog, HarperCollins, 1999.

Greedy Goat, HarperCollins, 1999.

Adaptations

The "Foxy" stories were adapted as a British television series, 1999.

Sidelights

In league with her husband, author and illustrator Colin Hawkins, Jacqui Hawkins is part of the popular children's book-writing team that has created such popular works as *Tog the Dog, Terrible, Terrible Tiger,* and *Foxy and Friends Go Racing.* Featuring engaging animal characters, an offbeat sense of fun, and engaging texts, these and many other titles have proved popular with the picture-book set in both Hawkinses' native England as well as in the United States and many other countries. In addition to their constant presence on bookstore shelves, the Hawkinses and their comic vision have also made their way to British television in the form of a weekly series featuring the character "Foxy," the main character in such books as *Foxy in the Kitchen, Foxy Plays Hide and Seek,* and *Foxy and His Little Sister.*

After forming a friendship during their teen years, Colin and Jacqui fell in love and were married in 1968. One of the things cementing their long relationship has been their common interests in art and writing, which they have combined in their successful career as picture-book authors. A few years after their first child, Finbar, was born, the Hawkinses began coming up with ideas for story books, and decided to approach several publishers

with their proposals in the form of "roughs": words accompanied by sketchy drawings. Despite little initial interest, they persisted, and their first book, *Witches,* was purchased by Granada in 1981. That book would be the start of something big—within a decade the prolific Hawkins duo could boast authorship of more than sixty titles. Interestingly, on many of their earliest books, Jacqui did not have her name on the title page; in *Witches,* for example, the book was credited to "Colin Hawkins and an old witch." This would change after a few titles, and after Colin demanded that his wife receive equal billing from publishers who incorrectly considered her only a minor contributor to each volume. As Colin recalled to *Books for Keeps* interviewer Stephanie Nettell, [one] publisher said, "'Well, we can't put every little housewife's name on all the books.' Well, without *this* little housewife, the book wouldn't be here!"

Among the many titles issuing from the creative minds of the Hawkinses are *Adding Animals,* a brightly colored lift-the-flap book that *Booklist* contributor Denise M. Wilms noted transforms basic math into something fun. In their *Pat the Cat,* designed for beginning readers, words like "fat", "bat", "cat", "mat", and "sat" tell the story of a plump kitty, a "fun, and ... painless way to absorb some phonics and a sight vocabulary," according to Wilms. First published in the mid-1980s and re-released in both the United States and England, the books *This Little Pig, Incy Wincy Spider,* and *The Elephant* "have stood the test of time delightfully," according to *Books for Keeps* reviewer Roy Blatchford.

For more information on Jacqui Hawkins, please see the entry on Colin Hawkins in this volume.

Works Cited

Blatchford, Roy, review of *This Little Pig, Incy Wincy Spider,* and *The Elephant, Books for Keeps,* March, 1998, p. 18.

Nettell, Stephanie, interview in *Books for Keeps,* May, 1999, pp. 12-13.

Wilms, Denise M., review of *Adding Animals, Booklist,* September, 1983, p. 85.

Wilms, Denise M., review of *Pat the Cat, Booklist,* August, 1983, p. 1465.

For More Information See

PERIODICALS

Books for Keeps, January, 1992, p. 7.

Junior Bookshelf, February, 1995, p. 36; June, 1995, p. 99.

School Librarian, August, 1995, p. 103.

*   *   *

HELLER, Ruth M. 1924-

Personal

Born April 2, 1924, in Winnipeg, Manitoba, Canada; daughter of Henry (a merchant) and Leah (a homemaker; maiden name, Serkau) Rosenblat; married Henry Heller, December 22, 1951 (died, 1965); married Richard Gross (an investment broker), March 21, 1987; children: Paul Garson, Philip Heller. *Education:* University of California, Berkeley, B.A., 1946; attended California College of Arts and Crafts, 1963-65. *Politics:* Democrat. *Religion:* Jewish. *Hobbies and other interests:* Tennis, swimming, cooking.

Addresses

Home—999 Green St., San Francisco, CA 94133.
Office—150 Lombard St., San Francisco, CA 94111.

Career

Mount Zion Hospital, San Francisco, CA, medical secretary, 1949-53; free-lance designer and illustrator, 1967-; writer, 1981—. Art consultant for Physicians Art Service, 1975-76. *Member:* Artists in Print, National Women's Book Association, Authors Guild, Society of Children's Book Writers, San Francisco Society of Illustrators, New York Society of Illustrators, Guild of Natural Science Illustrators (honorary member).

Awards, Honors

Honorable mention, New York Academy of Science's Children's Book Award competition, 1983, for *Chickens Aren't the Only Ones;* illustrations from *Animals Born Alive and Well* were exhibited at the Bologna International Children's Book Fair, 1983.

Writings

SELF-ILLUSTRATED CHILDREN'S BOOKS

Chickens Aren't the Only Ones, Grosset, 1981.
Animals Born Alive and Well, Grosset, 1982.
The Reason for a Flower, Grosset, 1983.
Plants That Never Ever Bloom, Grosset, 1984.
Natural Camouflage of Animals, Grosset, 1985.
A Cache of Jewels and Other Collective Nouns, Grosset, 1987.
Kites Sail High: A Book about Verbs, Grosset, 1988.
Many Luscious Lollipops: A Book about Adjectives, Grosset, 1989.
Merry-Go-Round: A Book about Nouns, Grosset, 1990.
Up, Up and Away: A Book about Adverbs, Grosset, 1991.
Behind the Mask: A Book about Prepositions, Grosset, 1995.
Color, Color, Color, Color, Putnam & Grosset, 1995.
Mine, All Mine: A Book about Pronouns, Grosset, 1997.
Fantastic! Wow! and Unreal!: A Book about Interjections and Conjunctions, Grosset, 1998.

"HOW TO HIDE" SERIES; ALL SELF-ILLUSTRATED

How To Hide a Polar Bear and Other Mammals, Grosset, 1985.
How to Hide a Butterfly and Other Insects, Grosset, 1985.
How to Hide an Octopus and Other Sea Creatures, Grosset, 1985.
How to Hide a Crocodile and Other Reptiles, Grosset, 1986.
How to Hide a Whip-Poor-Will and Other Birds, Grosset, 1986.
How to Hide a Grey Tree Frog and Other Amphibians, Grosset, 1986.

Illustrator

Color and Puzzle, Troubador Press, 1968.
Color and Stitch, Troubador Press, 1971.
Maze Craze, Troubador Press, 1971.
The Butterfly Coloring Book, Price, Stern, 1971.
The Butterfly Coloring Book, Number 2, Price, Stern, 1972.
The Tropical Fish Coloring Book, Price, Stern, 1972.
The World's Largest Maze, Series Number 1, Price, Stern, 1972.
The Endangered Species Coloring Book, Price, Stern, 1973.
The Oriental Rug Coloring Book, Price, Stern, 1973.
The Shell Coloring Book, Price, Stern, 1973.
The Tropical Bird Coloring Book, Price, Stern, 1974.
The World's Largest Maze, Series Number 2, Price, Stern, 1974.
Color Puzzles, Golden Press, 1974.
Designs for Coloring, Grosset, 1976.
More Designs for Coloring, Grosset, 1976.
Designs for Coloring 3, Grosset, 1977.
Designs for Coloring 4, Grosset, 1977.
Opt-Iddle, Golden Press, 1977.
Chroma-Schema, Golden Press, 1977.
Designs for Coloring 5, Grosset, 1978.
Designs for Coloring 6, Grosset, 1978.
Designs for Coloring 7: Sea Shells, Grosset, 1978.
Designs for Coloring 8: Alphabet and Numbers, Grosset, 1978.
Designs for Coloring 9: Birds, Grosset, 1979.
Designs for Coloring 10: Butterflies and Moths, Grosset, 1979.
Animal Designs for Coloring 11: Cats, Grosset, 1979.
Animal Designs for Coloring 12: Owls, Grosset, 1979.
Deluxe Designs for Coloring I, Grosset, 1981.
Deluxe Designs for Coloring II, Grosset, 1981.
Miriam Schlein, *Purim,* Behrman House, 1982.
Shirley Climo, *King of the Birds,* Harper, 1987.
Climo, *The Egyptian Cinderella,* Crowell, 1989.
The Hebrew Alphabet, by Helen Ducoff, Putnam, 1991.
More Geometrics, Putnam Publishing, 1991
Dalia Hardof Renberg (adapter) *King Solomon and the Bee,* HarperCollins, 1994.
Rosalind Creasy, *Blue Potatoes, Orange Tomatoes: How to Grow a Rainbow Garden,* Sierra Club (San Francisco), 1994.

Also author of *Fine Lines,* photographed by Michael Emery for Richard C. Owen. Illustrator of "Ponder Posters," for Creative Playthings; "Puzzle Posters" and *Aftermath I-IV,* for Creative Publications; a "Barbie Talk" graphic puzzle for Mattel; and *Contact Lenses* for Physicians Art Service.

Heller's illustrations have been exhibited at Pasadena Art and Cal Expo, Sacramento, 1968; Master Eagle Gallery, 1985 and 1986; and Palo Alto Cultural Center, 1985.

Sidelights

Ruth Heller once told *SATA:* "I began my career designing wrapping paper, cocktail napkins, kites, mugs, greeting cards, posters, and then coloring books. While researching at Steinhart Aquarium for a coloring book on tropical fish, I became intrigued with a strange looking shape floating in one of the tanks, and found that it was the egg sac of a dogfish shark. This led me to read about other egg-laying (oviparous) animals. My reading stimulated visions of colors and shapes and compositions. In addition to this visual wealth, I felt I had found enough information to convince me that I wanted to write and illustrate a book. *Chickens Aren't the Only Ones* is the title I chose.

"It proved to be successful enough to warrant a sequel which I called *Animals Born Alive and Well.* As seeds (in the plant kingdom) are comparable to eggs, I titled the third book in the series, *The Reason for a Flower,* and the fourth, *Plants That Never Ever Bloom.* I also have a series of six science books for very young children. The subject of these is camouflage. The titles include *How to Hide a Butterfly and Other Insects, How to Hide an Octopus and Other Sea Creatures,* and *How to Hide a Polar Bear and Other Mammals.* My science background is minimal, so I must depend on meticulous research and professional approval.

"I find writing in rhyme enjoyable and think it is an easy way for the reader or listener to remember new facts and vocabulary. I try to be succinct, to decide what it is I wish to say, to say it simply and directly allowing the illustration to convey as much information as possible. I am delighted to find that my books appeal to teachers and librarians as well as to the public. There is never a lack of ideas. As I am working on one project, ideas for others keep arising. Creativity begets creativity."

'Creative' best describes Heller's self-illustrated books on parts of speech. Reviewers extol her ability to take these dry subjects and imbue them with color both textually and pictorially. *Many Luscious Lollipops: A Book about Adjectives* motivated Zena Sutherland, a critic for *Bulletin of the Center for Childrens Books,* to write, "there is great diversity and technical brilliance in the art work, and the text has rhyme, rhythm, humor, and a very clear presentation." Carolyn Phelan, in her review for *Booklist* described the illustrations in *Merry-Go-Round,* a book on nouns, as "lush, exuberant full-color artwork [that] will grab kids' attention, even if they're sitting in the back of the classroom." Writing for *Bulletin of the Center for Childrens Books,* Deborah Stevenson pointed out that *Up, Up and Away: A Book about Adverbs,* "doesn't limit itself to old standards," rather, Stevenson concluded, "this eye-catching book explains its perplexing subject well and clearly, and more memorably than could any grammar textbook."

After vigorously tackling parts of speech in a colorful manner that would interest young readers, Heller takes up the subject of 'color' itself. She covers different media for producing color and then goes on to describe color printing. A reviewer for *Publishers Weekly* claimed Heller "leaves no color-producing instrument unexplored," and Deborah Stevenson writing once again for *Bulletin of the Center for Childrens Books,* declared *Color* "one of the neatest and most effective explanations of color printing for kids."

Works Cited

Review of *Color, Publishers Weekly,* February 6, 1995, p. 85.

Stevenson, Deborah, review of *Color, Bulletin of the Center for Childrens Books,* June, 1995, p. 347.

Stevenson, Deborah, review of *Up, Up and Away: A Book about Adverbs, Bulletin of the Center for Childrens Books,* January, 1992, p. 128.

Sutherland, Zena, review of *Many Luscious Lollipops: A Book about Adjectives, Bulletin of the Center for Childrens Books,* November, 1989, pp. 58-59.

For More Information See

PERIODICALS

Booklist, January 1, 1991, p. 933; December, 1995, p. 706; September, 1, 1996, p. 121;

Kirkus Reviews, November 15, 1989, p. 1670, November 15, 1990, p. 1608.

Publishers Weekly, October 16, 1981, p. 79; November 10, 1989, p. 60; January 20, 1992, p. 66.

School Library Journal, January, 1990, p. 95; February, 1992, p. 82; May, 1995, p. 99; January, 1997, p. 102; February, 1998, p. 100.*

*   *   *

HELMER, Marilyn

Personal

Born in St. Johns, Newfoundland, Canada. *Hobbies and other interests:* Reading, collecting.

Addresses

Home—3191 Heathfield Dr., Burlington, ON, L7M 1E1, Canada. *Electronic-mail*—helmerg@mail.mohawkc.on.ca.

Career

Author of books for children and young adults. *Member:* Canadian Society of Children's Authors, Illustrators and Performers (CANSCAIP), Burlington Storytellers' Guild.

Awards, Honors

Second prize, *Children's Writer* science article writing contest, 1997; Toronto IODE Book Award, 1998, for *Fog Cat;* Best Children's Book for Children Seven Years and Younger, Mr. Christie's Book Award, 1999, for *Fog Cat;* numerous prizes in adult short story contests.

Writings

The Boy, the Dollar and the Wonderful Hat, Stoddard Kids (Toronto, ON), 1992.
Boathouse Treasure, ITP Nelson (Toronto, ON), 1998.
Fog Cat, Kids Can Press (Toronto, ON), 1998.
Mr. McGratt and the Ornery Cat, Kids Can Press, 1999.

Contributor of articles, stories and poems to juvenile periodicals and anthologies, including *Cricket, Spider, Chickadee, Children's Playmate, Humpty Dumpty, Hopscotch, Children's Digest,* and *Jack and Jill.*

Work in Progress

A series of ten books of retold fairy tales titled "Once Upon a Time Tales" for Kids Can Press.

Sidelights

In addition to publishing short stories and poems for children in juvenile magazines, Marilyn Helmer is the author of two picture books: *The Boy, the Dollar and the Wonderful Hat* and *Fog Cat.* In her first picture book, Helmer tells the story of a young boy, Benno, who goes to the fair with his father. When his father gives him a dollar, he tells Benno to choose carefully between riding

FOG CAT

MARILYN HELMER
PAUL MOMBOURQUETTE

In Marilyn Helmer's picture book about the patient nurturing of relationships, young Hannah spends months persuading a stray cat to stay with her and her grandfather. (Cover illustration by Paul Mombourquette.)

on the midway, buying treats or souvenirs, or taking a pony ride. Instead, Benno buys a hat and with his hat manages to get a little of everything the fair has to offer. Reviewers found much to like about the picture book. Children "will be tickled by Helmer's plot," predicted *Quill & Quire* critic Janet McNaughton, who also commended Helmer's "lively" writing. Kay Kerman, writing in *Canadian Materials,* "highly recommend[ed]" the work, declaring, "this book is a fine example of how children can be creative problem solvers." "Helmer's moving celebration of a young child's ingenuity and resourcefulness is narrated with economy and precision," remarked Ajay Heble in *Canadian Children's Literature.* "The Boy, The Dollar and the Wonderful Hat* is genuinely a wonderful book," he concluded.

Helmer's second picture book, *Fog Cat,* revolves around a young girl, Hannah, who lives alone with her grandfather in a fishing village on the eastern seaboard. When Hannah discovers a stray cat living on the beach, she tries to make it her pet. Commenting on the "spirited, lyrical prose" and "sensitive, unsentimental story," Annette Goldsmith in *Quill & Quire* deemed Helmer's *Fog Cat* a "beautifully produced, thoroughly engaging picture book."

Helmer once commented: "My primary motivation for writing is the desire to share my love of books with other people, especially children. I remember the joy of being read to as a child and the thrill of getting my first library card. Walking into the children's department, seeing that huge collection of books and anticipating the wonderful adventures that waited for me between the covers was the beginning of a lifelong love of reading.

"Of my many interests, the two which have had the most significant influence on my life are reading and collecting. As well as being avid readers, my parents were collectors and I followed suit. Be it stamps, coins, trading cards, buttons or sea shells, if it can be collected, I have likely collected it at one time or another. These two interests came together to launch my writing career. As a teenager, I began collecting old souvenir spoons and postcards. Curiosity about their origin and the events and people they commemorate prompted me to do some research. Years later, my first published writing was a series of articles on antiques. When my children were born, it was natural for me to share my love of books with them. To my delight they enjoyed being read to as much as I enjoyed reading to them. I rediscovered old friends I hadn't read in years and my children introduced me to new ones. And I discovered something else—I wanted to be a writer and I wanted to write for children.

"I write on such a wide variety of topics that it is difficult to pinpoint a general inspiration. I write articles because I enjoy doing research, poetry because I love the rhythm of words and retellings of traditional tales because I am impressed by their longevity. Pinpointing my inspiration for my books is a little easier. My love of the sea and cats was the inspiration for *Fog Cat.* My enthusiasm for antiques and intriguing old buildings and a similar childhood experience resulted in *Boathouse*

Treasure. A combination of the fascination of a country fair and a child's ingenuity led to *The Boy, the Dollar, and the Wonderful Hat.* My book *Mr. McGratt and the Ornery Cat* was inspired by my own twenty-year-old very ornery feline."

Works Cited

Goldsmith, Annette, review of *Fog Cat, Quill & Quire,* September, 1998, p. 66.

Heble, Ajay, review of *The Boy, The Dollar and the Wonderful Hat, Canadian Children's Literature,* summer, 1997, pp. 64-68.

Kay Kerman, review of *The Boy, the Dollar and the Wonderful Hat, Canadian Materials,* October, 1992, p. 262.

McNaughton, Janet, review of *The Boy, the Dollar and the Wonderful Hat, Quill & Quire,* August, 1992, p. 24.*

*   *   *

HILL, Pamela Smith 1954-

Personal

Born March 24, 1954, in Springfield, MO; daughter of Dennis R. (a retired minister and printer) and Carolyn (a homemaker; maiden name, Clark) Smith; married Richard Lowell Hill (a wildlife biologist), June 18, 1979; children: Emily Melinda. *Education:* Attended Southwest Missouri State University, 1972-1974; University of South Dakota, B.A., 1976, M.A., 1983; *Politics:* Democrat. *Hobbies and other interests:* Gardening, reading and Middle Eastern tribal dance.

Addresses

Home—2570 S.W. Crestdale Drive, Portland, OR 97225. *Office*—Washington State University, 14204 N.E. Salmon Creek Ave., Vancouver, WA 98686. *Agent*—Emilie Jacobson, Curtis Brown LTD, Ten Astor Place, New York, NY 10003. *Electronic mail*—hillpam@teleport.com

Career

Washington State University, Vancouver, WA, Director of Professional Writing and lecturer, 1996-. Southwest Missouri State University, Springfield, editor of *The Southwest Standard,* 1973; *The Springfield Leader & Press,* Springfield, MO, staff writer, 1974; *The Sioux City Journal,* Sioux City, IA, special correspondent, 1974-1977; Sioux City Center for Women, Sioux City, IA, public relations coordinator, 1976; South Dakota Department of Social Services, Pierre, SD, editor, 1977-1978; South Dakota Division of Tourism, Pierre, SD, public information specialist, 1978-1981; Free-lance journalist, 1977-1990; Teledyne Water Pik, Fort Collins, CO, creative supervisor and marketing communications manager, 1983-1988. Colorado State University Department of Technical Journalism, Fort Collins, lecturer, 1986, 1989-1990; University of Colorado School of Journalism, Boulder, visiting professor, 1988-1990.

Microware Distributors, Portland, OR, sales promotion manager, 1991. AVIA Group International, Portland, OR, marketing communications director, 1991-1993. University of Portland Department of Communications Studies, Portland, OR, lecturer, 1991-1995; Children's book writer, 1994-; Portland State University School of Business Administration, Portland, OR, lecturer, 1997-1998. *Member:* Authors Guild, Society of Children's Book Writers, Willamette Writers.

Awards, Honors

Heartland Regional Emmy, 1992; Oregon Literary Fellowship in Young Readers, 1995, for *A Voice from the Border;* Kay Snow Contest Juvenile Fiction Winner, 1996; Junior Library Guild Selection, 1996, for *Ghost Horses;* Spur Finalist in Juvenile Fiction, Western Writers of America, 1996, for *Ghost Horses.* Books for the Teen Age, New York Public Library; Shaara Nominee, United States Civil War Center; Best Children's Books of the Year, Banks Street College; finalist, Oregon Book Award, all 1999, all for *A Voice from the Border.*

Writings

Ghost Horses, Holiday House, 1996.
A Voice from the Border, Holiday House, 1998.

Pamela Smith Hill

Sidelights

Pamela Smith Hill told *SATA:* "I grew up in Springfield, Missouri, on a steady diet of Bible stories and old television Westerns. Maybe that's why I like to write about the past. Or maybe it was Jo March in *Little Women.* She was a tomboy and a bookworm—just like me. But somehow she managed to become a writer. And almost from the very beginning, that's what I wanted to be, too.

"My first real job was as a newspaper staff writer on an old-fashioned society page. I wrote about weddings and Girl Scout jamborees and old ladies who carved little statues out of gourds. Then I moved to South Dakota, where the job market for society page writers was pretty slim. So I began a career in advertising and public relations. Over the next twenty years, I wrote about everything from Mount Rushmore to Water Piks, Navajo rugs to basketball shoes. Along the way I lived in Kansas, Colorado, and Oregon.

"Then in 1994, I left the corporate world behind and started writing books for young adults. *Ghost Horses* was published two years later. That first book and my latest, *A Voice from the Border,* explore the lives of two young women, coming of age in the nineteenth century."

Ghost Horses is the story of sixteen-year-old Tabitha Fortune, the daughter of a preacher who believes that a woman should serve her husband and God. When a paleontological expedition comes to the area to find dinosaur bones, Tabitha disguises herself as a boy to fool her father and the equally sexist Professor Parker, the leader of the excavation. Tabitha reveals herself at the end of the novel, only to join another excavation group, this time headed by a woman. In a review for *Booklist,* critic Frances Bradburn stated: "This multilayered first novel is fast paced and intriguing, one that will quickly become an easy, word-of-mouth sell." Elizabeth Bush, writing for *The Bulletin of the Center for Children's Books,* noted that "Hill provides some refreshing twists to the stock girl-in-disguise plot ... Tabitha herself is a credible heroine whose determination to strike out on her own will win her some fans."

Hill's second novel, *A Voice from the Border,* describes the tangle of relationships that existed in Missouri during the Civil War. Margaret "Reeves" O'Neill is a fifteen-year-old girl who is growing up during this time. Both her father and the young man Reeves likes are lost in the war, and Reeves must deal with her feelings of betrayal: not only does her father not release the family slaves as he promised, but the wife of a Union general staying at the family's home steals all of Reeves's writings. A critic for *Kirkus Reviews* described *A Voice from the Border* as "an engrossing novel, thoroughly researched, despite the modern sensibility that pervades it." In *School Library Journal,* contributor Bruce Anne Shook commented that "the author does a good job of describing the complexities of the relationships among Union loyalists, secessionists, slaves, and slave owners."

Hill told *SATA:* "In *Ghost Horses,* Tabitha Fortune has to become someone else to pursue her dream of searching for dinosaur bones in the Badlands of South Dakota. Margaret Reeves O'Neill, in *A Voice from the Border,* struggles to become a writer as the world around her descends into the hopeless violence of the American Civil War. What binds these two books together is the theme of following your heart, learning to understand yourself and finding your place in the world. Perhaps I'm haunted by this theme because it's taken me so long to find my own way.

"I continue to write young adult fiction, but I also teach a variety of writing classes as the Professional Writing Program Director at Washington State University in Vancouver. My husband and I live in Portland, Oregon, with Kate and Bess, our flat-coated retrievers. Our daughter is studying mathematics at Bryn Mawr College.

"So like Jo March, I've at last become an 'American authoress.' But it's taken much, much longer than I ever imagined all those years ago when I first read *Little Women.*"

Works Cited

Bradburn, Frances, review of *Ghost Horses, Booklist,* April 15, 1996, p. 1434.
Bush, Elizabeth, review of *Ghost Horses, The Bulletin of the Center for Children's Books,* September, 1996, p. 15.
Review of *A Voice from the Border, Kirkus Reviews,* June 15, 1998, p. 895.
Shook, Bruce Anne, review of *A Voice from the Border, School Library Journal,* September, 1998, pp. 203-04.

For More Information See

PERIODICALS

The Bulletin of the Center for Children's Books, September, 1998, p. 16.
Kirkus Reviews, December 15, 1995, pp. 1770-771.
School Library Journal, March, 1996, p. 196.
Voice of Youth Advocates, October, 1996, p. 210.

*   *   *

HONEY, Elizabeth 1947-

Personal

Married to a graphic designer; children: two. *Education:* Attended Swinburne Art School. *Hobbies and other interests:* Reading, music, movies, theater.

Addresses

Home—Melbourne, Australia.

Career

Author and illustrator of poetry, picture books, and novels for middle-grade readers.

Awards, Honors

Young Australian's Best Book Award, fiction for young readers, 1986, for *The Twenty-Seventh Annual African Hippopotamus Race;* Australian Children's Book of the Year Award, Children's Book Council of Australia, 1997, for *Not a Nibble;* named Honour Books, Children's Book Council of Australia, for *The Cherry Dress* and *45 & 47 Stella Street and Everything That Happened.*

Writings

AUTHOR AND ILLUSTRATOR

What's the Time, Mr. Wolf? (picture book), Macmillan, 1988.
Festivals, Ideas from around the World, Allen & Unwin, 1988.
Princess Beatrice and the Rotten Robber (picture book), Puffin, 1990.
Honey Sandwich (poems), Allen & Unwin, 1993.
The Cherry Dress, Allen & Unwin, 1993.
The Book of Little Books, Allen & Unwin, 1994.
45 & 47 Stella Street and Everything That Happened (juvenile novel), Allen & Unwin, 1995.
Not a Nibble! (picture book), Allen & Unwin, 1996.
What Do You Think, Feezal? (juvenile novel), Allen & Unwin, 1997.
Mongrel Doggerel, Allen & Unwin, 1998.
Fiddleback (sequel to *45 & 47 Stella Street*), Allen & Unwin, 1998.

ILLUSTRATOR

Morris Lurie, *The Twenty-Seventh Annual African Hippopotamus Race,* Penguin, 1977.
Michael Dugan, *Melissa's Ghost,* Dent, 1986.
Dream Time: New Stories by Sixteen Award-Winning Authors, edited by Toss Gascoigne, Jo Goodman, and Margot Tyrrell, Houghton Mifflin, 1991.
Christobel Mattingley, *No Gun for Asmir,* Puffin, 1993.
Christobel Mattingley, *Asmir in Vienna,* Puffin, 1995.

Also illustrator of *S.C.A.B.,* by Manny Clarke, 1975; *Puzzles Galore!,* by Meryl Brown Tobin, 1978; *Snakes Alive!,* by Maureen Stewart, 1978; *So What's New?,* by Bettina Bird, 1978; *Gone Children,* by Phyllis Harry, 1978; *Gino and Dan,* by Carolyn Marrone, 1979; *Us Three Kids,* by Bettina Bird, 1979; *Call It Quits,* by Bettina Bird, 1979; *Fame and Misfortune,* by John Jones, 1979; *Feel, Value, Act,* by Laurie Brady, 1979; *Growing Things: Nature Study Ideas for the Primary School,* by Brian McKinlay, 1979; *Mexican Beans,* by L. M. Napier, 1980; *All Change at the Station,* by Susan Burke, 1980; *Barney, Boofer, and the Cricket Bat,* by Judith Worthy, 1980; *More Puzzles Galore!,* by Meryl Brown Tobin, 1980; *Themes through the Year,* by Cathy Hope, 1981; *The Tucker Book,* by Jessie Apted, 1981; *Salt River Times,* by William Mayne, 1982; *Flora's*

Treasures, by Ted Greenwood, 1982; *Brave with Ben,* by Christobel Mattingley, 1982; *History Alive: Introducing Children to History around Them,* by Brian McKinlay, 1983; *Boilover at Breakfast Creek,* by Roger Vaughan Carr, 1986; *The Prize,* by Helen Higgs, 1986; *I Don't Want to Know: Towards a Healthy Adolescence,* by Ted Greenwood, 1986; *Outdoors for Kids,* by Brian McKinlay, 1987; *Energy for Kids,* by Gilbert Tippett, 1987; *Trees for Kids,* by Ian Edwards, 1988; *Oh No! Not Again,* by Linda Allen, 1989; *Asmir in Vienna,* by Christobel Mattingley, 1995.

OTHER

Don't Pat the Wombat!, illustrated by William Clarke, Allen & Unwin, 1996.

Sidelights

Elizabeth Honey grew up on a farm near Wonthaggi in Australia, where her favorite activities were reading books, showing off, drawing, and preparing for a career as a trapeze artist, according to the publicity website for her publisher, Allen & Unwin. After art school, Honey traveled through Europe, South America, and the United States, and then embarked on a career illustrating and eventually writing books for children. Her advice to aspiring authors is "Get stuck into your plot early on. Don't waffle on for pages then have all the action in the last couple of paragraphs." Honey's own books include award-winning collections of poetry, picture books, and young adult novels which are lauded by critics for the author's uncanny ability to capture the essence of childhood through language and image. For children themselves, "it is the wacky humour and exuberant action that make Elizabeth Honey's novels immensely popular," according to *Magpies* reviewer Kevin Steinberger.

Honey's self-illustrated picture books include *Princess Beatrice and the Rotten Robber,* about a young girl

They tried their luck from the bridge again.
Dad caught two bream.
Alex caught a mullet.

'Hey, Susie! There's something
on your line,' yelled Alex.
Quickly Susie reeled in, but it was
only a fish cut out of seaweed.
'*Alex!*' growled Dad.
'It's not funny,' said Susie.

Elizabeth Honey's self-illustrated picture book, **Not a Nibble!,** *tells of a family vacation almost ruined by little Susie's failure to catch a single fish.*

whose love of dress-up and wearing jewelry leads to her kidnaping by the Rotten Robber, and, surprisingly, to lots of trouble for the kidnapper. The result is a "jolly romp of a book," according to Judith Sharman in *Books for Keeps.* Honey's picture book *Not a Nibble!* tells of a family vacation almost ruined by the fact that little Susie fails to catch a single fish, until the last day when she catches a glimpse of a mother whale with its young. Honey's watercolor illustrations ably convey the beauty of bright summer days spent by the sea, contended Alicen Geddes Ward in *School Librarian,* who added: "*Not a Nibble!* is a book which totally captures for me the spirit of childhood holidays and the cherished days of family life."

Honey's novels for the middle grades feature strong, outspoken child characters who get involved in zany, action-packed adventures. In *45 & 47 Stella Street and Everything That Happened,* twelve-year-old Henni and her friends are upset by the arrival of a wealthy, and secretive, new family on Stella Street, and begin to spy on the people they call "the Phonies" in order to uncover the origins of their aloof, and sometimes mean-spirited, behavior. Honey's young characters and their parents "burst from these pages, full of an infectious joy in one another and in their shared lives," attested GraceAnne A. DeCandido in *Booklist.* The story, which is told in the form of Henni's journal, augmented by notes from the Phonies' threatening lawyers and other clues to the mystery, is a testament to the enthusiasm of its narrator for her tale begins on the book's cover and continues on to the title page before moving on into the book proper. American critics noted that while Honey's narrative does contain some Australian vernacular unlikely to be familiar to audiences in the United States, "it doesn't make the book any less delightful," Lucy Rafael contended in *School Library Journal.* The gang from Stella Street go camping with a heavily pregnant adult in *Fiddle-back,* a sequel to *45 & 47 Stella Street and Everything That Happened,* and find more adventures than they bargained for.

In *Don't Pat the Wombat,* illustrated with photos taken by the author's son, William Clarke, a character known as Exclamation Mark tells the story of a week spent at an Australian school camp under the direction of a bullying teacher. "The interaction between teachers, pupils, loners and oddballs is vividly brought out and the dialogue is totally credible," attested Valerie Caless in *School Librarian.* Honey brings to life another pre-teen protagonist in *What Do You Think, Feezal?,* in which nine-year-old Bean finds a way to interpret the nefarious goings-on around her by reading Honey's picture book, *Princess Beatrice and the Rotten Robber.* *Magpies* reviewer Kevin Steinberger lauded the author's insight into the "worldview and vernacular of the preteens" she depicts, and concluded that "[Honey's] young fans will certainly be delighted with her latest novel."

Similarly, in a review of Honey's collection of poetry for children, *Mongrel Doggerel,* Steinberger stated in *Magpies:* "Elizabeth Honey knows children well. She has the happy knack of being able to convincingly

Twelve-year-old Henni and her friends decide to unearth the origins of the wealthy, secretive, and arrogant new family on Stella Street. (Cover illustration by Honey.)

perceive the world through their senses and unfettered imagination." Humor is the point of the poems collected here and in the preceding volume, *Honey Sandwich,* in which a messy room, the daily cleaning of one's ears, a condescending teacher, playing doctor, and getting hurt form the author's subjects. Critics noted that while Honey's verses are indeed "doggerel," their sense of fun would make them appealing to children and would serve as an inviting introduction to the world of more traditional poetry. In his review of *Honey Sandwich* in *Magpies,* critic John Murray concluded: "The verses may not be all that memorable as literature, but they are fun."

Works Cited

Caless, Valerie, review of *Don't Pat the Wombat!, School Librarian,* November, 1997, p. 191.

DeCandido, GraceAnne A., review of *45 & 47 Stella Street, and Everything That Happened, Booklist,* June 1, 1998, p. 1766.

Murray, John, review of *Honey Sandwich, Magpies,* November, 1993, p. 40.

Rafael, Lucy, review of *45 & 47 Stella Street, and Everything That Happened, School Library Journal,* September, 1998, p. 204.

Sharman, Judith, review of *Princess Beatrice and the Rotten Robber, Books for Keeps,* January, 1991, p. 7.

Steinberger, Kevin, review of *Mongrel Doggerel, Magpies,* July, 1998, p. 19.

Steinberger, Kevin, review of *What Do You Think, Feezal?, Magpies,* March, 1998, p. 33.

Ward, Alicen Geddes, review of *Not a Nibble!, School Librarian,* summer, 1998, p. 74.*

* * *

HULME, Joy N. 1922-

Addresses

Home and office—15941 Viewfield, Monte Sereno, CA 95030.

Career

Writer. Has worked at a variety of jobs, including newspaper circulation manager and self-employed floral designer. *Member:* Society of Children's Book Writers and Illustrators (corresponding secretary, 1989-92; board of directors, NorCal chapter, 1991—).

Awards, Honors

Writing award, *Ensign* (magazine), 1978; Outstanding Science Trade Book citation, 1991, and Children's Choice citation, 1992, both for *Sea Squares;* also recipient of California Writers' Contest award.

Writings

The Illustrated Story of President Lorenzo Snow, illustrated by B. Keith Christensen, Eagle Systems (Provo, UT), 1982.

The Illustrated Story of President George Albert Smith, illustrated by B. Keith Christensen, Eagle Systems, 1982.

The Illustrated Story of President David O. McKay, illustrated by B. Keith Christensen, Eagle Systems, 1982.

A Stable in Bethlehem, illustrated by J. Ellen Dolce, Western (Racine, WI), 1989.

The Other Side of the Door, Deseret Books (Salt Lake City, UT), 1990.

Sea Squares, illustrated by Carol Schwartz, Hyperion, 1991.

Climbing the Rainbow (sequel to *The Other Side of the Door*), Deseret Books, 1992.

What If?: Just Wondering Poems, illustrated by Valeri Gorbachev, Boyds Mills, 1993.

Counting by Kangaroos, illustrated by Betsy Scheld, Scientific American Books (New York), 1995.

Sea Sums, illustrated by Carol Schwartz, Hyperion, 1996.

(With Donna W. Guthrie) How to Write, Recite, and Delight in All Kinds of *Poetry,* Millbrook, 1996.

Eerie Feary Feeling: A Hairy Scary Pop Up Book, Orchard, 1998.

The Whistling and Whittling Brigade, Hyperion, 1999.

Bubble Trouble, illustrated by Mike Cressy, Children's Press, 1999.

(With Donna Guthrie) *Supermarket Math,* Millbrook, 2000.

Through the Open Door, HarperCollins, 2000.

Also contributor to periodicals, including *Better Homes and Gardens, Good Housekeeping,* and *Sunset Magazine.*

Sidelights

Joy N. Hulme draws on a wide variety of writing experience to create picture books that are both instructive and fun. Hulme began her career as a contributor to magazines, selling stories, poems, articles, and Christmas crafts to both adult and children's periodicals. For many years, however, the author's dreams of publishing a children's book were frustrated by repeated rejections. Eventually, Hulme became part of a San Francisco Bay-area writers' group that included Patricia Polacco and

TOAD

Old toad sits like a lumpy gray stone
Scarcely moving a muscle or bone,
Till quick as a zip
With a lickety flick
Of his stickety tongue
He snatches a snack
And sucks it back.

In a collection of twenty-nine poems about animals, Joy N. Hulme poses questions about nature and answers them with wit and accuracy. (From What If?, *illustrated by Valeri Gorbachev.)*

Elisa Klevin. "This was my biggest breakthrough," Hulme once told *SATA*. "I was exposed to many opportunities to learn from and be encouraged by other writers and illustrators." Through this association, Hulme found her first agent, who gave the author "just what I needed to absorb the rejection and heartbreak and resubmit my books instead of stashing them away to mildew in a drawer."

Hulme's first major children's book was *A Stable in Bethlehem.* Since it first appeared in 1989, this counting book has become a Christmas favorite. Hulme followed *Stable* with *The Other Side of the Door* and *Climbing the Rainbow,* middle-grade historical books about a young girl who rises above a disability; and *Sea Squares,* which combines three of her loves—"math, biology, and wonderful words." In this picture book, the author introduces young children to the concepts of multiplication and square numbers through rhyming scenarios featuring creatures from the ocean. Hulme relied upon a similar format in *Sea Sums,* in which the concepts of addition and subtraction are introduced in rhymes detailing the antics of other sea animals. Critics noted that both of these books attempt to fill a striking need for math-concept books for early readers. *Booklist* reviewer Carolyn Phelan praised the abundance of information about coral reefs and their inhabitants, along with the visual and verbal reinforcement of the numerical concepts introduced, all of which make *Sea Sums* "a useful supplement to science and math units."

In *Counting by Kangaroos* Hulme once again uses nature to teach math. She encourages children to count by twos, threes, and so forth, by picturing groups of Australian marsupials as they fly out of the pouches of three kangaroos. The text is composed of "verse lively as a jump rope rhyme," according to Suzy Schmidt in *Horn Book.* Hulme's poetry collection, *What If?: Just Wondering Poems,* was described by a reviewer for *Publishers Weekly* as a "cheery collection of 29 poems about animals." In this book, Hulme begins with "childlike questions" about nature, and proceeds with "wry speculations about animals," in language that is "simple and conversational," explained Lee Bock in *School Library Journal.* The result is a book that is "thoughtful and quietly humorous," Bock contended, also noting its appeal for both pre-readers and those more advanced. For middle-graders who want to write their own poetry, Hulme prepared *How to Write, Recite, and Delight in All Kinds of Poetry* with co-author Donna W. Guthrie. Using examples written by children, the authors introduce the basic concepts of rhyme, rhythm, and repetition, and then proceed to the various forms of poetry, including free verse and haiku. *School Library Journal* critic Jean Pollock praised the "open, appealing, and approachable format" used in this work, and the applicability of the examples to a variety of age groups.

In describing her career, Hulme observed: "Life as an *author* is much different from life as a *writer!* At last my efforts have been validated.... At an age when most people have retired, my career is just beginning. My part-time-everything life, resulting from a wide range of interests and knowledge, and my child-like fascination with the ingenious intricacy and beauty of nature, is proving very valuable to me as an author of children's books. It is always my goal to encourage the creative awareness that is inborn in youngsters and to keep it alive in them forever.

"No life is long enough to run out of fresh surprises if we watch out for them.... I like to be accurate about facts, fanciful about fiction, and to combine truth and imagination—to make learning as much fun for others as it is for me by creating in a light-hearted manner.... It is my aim that a child of any age can become a little better in some way as a result of reading what I have written."

Works Cited

Bock, Lee, review of *What If?: Just Wondering Poems, School Library Journal,* August, 1993, p. 158.

Phelan, Carolyn, review of *Sea Sums, Booklist,* December 1, 1996, p. 662.

Pollock, Jean, review of *How to Write, Recite, and Delight in All Kinds of Poetry, School Library Journal,* December, 1996, p. 130.

Schmidt, Suzy, review of *Counting by Kangaroos, Horn Book,* July-December, 1995, p. 31.

Review of *What If?: Just Wondering Poems, Publishers Weekly,* June 21, 1993, p. 104.

For More Information See

PERIODICALS

Booklist, December 1, 1991, p. 701.

BookWorld, October 11, 1998, p. 11.

Horn Book, July-December, 1996, p. 148.

School Library Journal, January, 1992, p. 103; February, 1996, p. 85; December, 1996, p. 114.

I–J

IGUS, Toyomi 1953-

Personal

Born October 10, 1953, in Iowa City, IA; daughter of Will (an attorney) and Kazumi (a homemaker; maiden name, Tamori) Gibson; married Darrow Igus (an actor); children: Kazumi, Kenji. *Education:* Barnard College, B.A., 1974. *Politics:* Liberal Democrat.

Addresses

Office—P.O. Box 10421, Marina Del Rey, CA 90295.

Career

Writer. *L.A. Style,* Los Angeles, CA, associate managing editor, 1986-89; University of California at Los Angeles Center for Afro-American Studies Publications, managing editor, 1990—. *Member:* American Black Book Writers Association, Society of Scholarly Publishing.

Awards, Honors

The illustrations for Igus's *I See the Rhythm,* received the Coretta Scott King Award in 1999.

Writings

JUVENILE

(With Veronica Freeman Ellis, Diane Patrick, and Valerie Wilson Wesley; and editor) *Great Women in the Struggle: An Introduction for Young Readers,* Book of Black Heroes, Volume 2, Just Us Books (Orange, NJ), 1992.

When I Was Little, illustrated by Higgins Bond, Just Us Books, 1992.

Two Mrs. Gibsons, illustrated by Daryl Wells, Children's Book Press (San Francisco, CA), 1996.

Going Back Home, illustrated by Michele Wood, Children's Book Press, 1996.

I See the Rhythm, illustrated by Michele Wood, Children's Book Press, 1998.

FOR ADULTS

(Editor with Charles Roland) *Life in a Day of Black L.A.: The Way We See It: L.A.'s Black Photographers Present a New Perspective on Their City,* photographs by Nathaniel Belamy [et al], Center for Afro-American Studies, University of California (Los Angeles), 1992.

Contributor of articles and reviews to the *American Black Book Writers Association Journal.* Co-author of several plays and screenplays, including *Zeke: History of Blacks in the Movies. American Black Book Writers Association Journal,* executive editor, 1986-1992.

Sidelights

It was not until the birth of her daughter, Kazumi, and her son, Kenji, that Igus was motivated to write books for children. The first to be published was a project that Igus coordinated, edited, and co-wrote, *Great Women in the Struggle,* volume two in the "Book of Black Heroes" series published by Just Us Books. This reference work spotlights more than eighty historical and contemporary women of African descent, offering biographical information and photos of subjects; a chronology of black history appears in an appendix. In the picture book *When I Was Little,* published in 1992, a little boy visits his grandfather and imagines life without televisions, VCRs, and video games, and learns that the need for love and sharing is one thing that will not change with time. A reviewer for *Publishers Weekly* spoke of the author's heartwarming depiction of relationship, writing: "Igus's comfortable story unwinds through a gentle and credible conversation between an African American boy and his grandfather." *Booklist* critic Ilene Cooper urged teachers to "use this for history or genealogy units; it opens the door for discussion."

For her next picture book, *Two Mrs. Gibsons,* Igus drew directly from her own childhood experience. On alternating pages, the author relates a young girl's differing experiences with her Japanese mother and her African-American grandmother. "The story is a loving mood piece," noted John Philbrook in *School Library Journal,* praising the author's "simple, affecting prose [which] speaks directly to the heart." A reviewer for *Kirkus Reviews* concurred with this positive assessment of Igus's accomplishment, adding that *Two Mrs. Gibsons* works equally well as a loving memoir and as "an understated tribute to the ability of people from widely different cultures to live together."

Reviewers were enthusiastic about Igus's *I See the Rhythm*, which a contributor to *Kirkus Reviews* called "a stunning history of African-American music." Igus presents a wide range of music, from that heard on the African continent five hundred years ago, to that associated with the slave trade and work on the plantations of the American South, to blues, ragtime, jazz, gospel, funk, rap, and hip hop, using descriptive poetry to reflect the rhythms and language of the music itself. In addition, *I See the Rhythm* sports a timeline of African-American history that a critic in *Kirkus Reviews* dubbed "terrific," noting that it "roots the whole book in a broader context."

Works Cited

Cooper, Ilene, review of *When I Was Little, Booklist,* March 1, 1993, p. 1236.

Review of *I See the Rhythm, Kirkus Reviews,* April 15, 1998, p. 582.

Philbrook, John, review of *Two Mrs. Gibsons, School Library Journal,* October, 1996, pp. 98-99.

Review of *When I Was Little, Publishers Weekly,* January 4, 1993, p. 73.

Review of *Two Mrs. Gibsons, Kirkus Reviews,* March 15, 1996, p. 448.

For More Information See

PERIODICALS

Booklist, February 15, 1998, p. 1003.
Horn Book, fall, 1992, p. 331.
Horn Book Guide, fall, 1996, p. 261; Fall, 1998, p. 399.
School Library Journal, August, 1992, p. 166; August, 1993, p. 146; June, 1998, p. 400.*

* * *

JONES, Constance 1961-

Personal

Born in 1961. *Education:* City University of New York; studied women's history at the doctoral level.

Addresses

Home—New York City. *Office*—c/o Lisa Milberg, Facts on File, Inc., 11 Penn Plaza, 15th Floor, New York, NY 10001.

Career

Writer.

Writings

(With Derris L. Raper and Jon J. Sbrega) *The American Experience: Documents and Notes,* Kendall/Hunt Publishing Company (Dubuque, IA), 1985.

(With The Philip Leif Group) *The 220 Best Franchises to Buy; The Sourcebook for Evaluating the Best Franchise Opportunities,* Bantam, 1987.

Beat the MBAs to the Top!: A Guide to Over 500 Courses Most Valuable to Business People on their Way Up, Addison-Wesley (Reading, MA), 1987.

Karen Horney, Chelsea House (New York City), 1989.

Pasta, H.P. Books (Los Angeles), 1990, enlarged as *Pasta: Sauces and Fillings for All Shapes and Sizes,* Fairfax (New York City), 1993.

(With Derris L. Rapper) *A Goodly Heritage: The Episcopal Diocese of Southern Virginia,* Pictorial Heritage Publishing Company (Norfolk, VA), 1992.

Africa, 1500-1900, Facts on File (New York City), 1993.

The European Conquest of North America, Facts on File, 1995.

Constance Jones's informational volume details the European settlement of the North-American continent and the impact of exploration on the indigenous people.

Trailblazers: The Men and Women Who Forged the West, MetroBooks (New York City), 1995.

Sexual Harassment, Facts on File, 1996.

R.I.P: The Complete Book of Death and Dying, Harpercollins, 1997.

(Editor) *The Love of Friends: An Anthology of Gay and Lesbian Correspondence with Friends and Lovers,* Simon & Schuster, 1997.

1001 Things Everyone Should Know about Women's History, Doubleday, 1998.

In addition, Constance Jones has edited, ghostwritten, or contributed to many more titles.

Sidelights

According to contributor Pat Royal in *School Library Journal,* Constance Jones's *Africa 1500-1900* fills a gap in history collections and was deemed to be accessible even to "reluctant high school readers." Royal commented on the attractive layout of the book, which includes maps and historical photographs, as well as the inclusion of a chronology and a suggested reading list. The book, which details African history, doesn't make the mistake of assuming that white settlement was the only important event in the continent's history, according to a *Kirkus Reviews* contributor. Instead, *Africa* covers many interesting aspects of that continent's history and culture, including kingdoms, city-states, and the slave trade. Economic factors are considered in the recap of Africa's history, including their impact on and contribution to the decline in slave trading. *Booklist* critic Hazel Rochman commented on an interesting chapter that takes a close look at the impact of slavery on family and clan life, as well as on Africa's agriculture.

The European Conquest of North America details the settlement of the North American continent and its impact upon the indigenous people already living there. Jones takes an objective look at the havoc placed on Native American culture after Europeans landed, including exposure to diseases such as smallpox, according to *Booklist* contributor Ann O'Malley. Jones also, however, notes some of the good that came from European settlement, such as exchange of products and adoption of cultural practices. Victoria Yablonsky of *Voice of Youth Advocates* praised the "abundance of factual material," including the book's substantial chronology, bibliography, and index. Though the reviewer concluded that covering the subject is hardly possible in one book, she calls the work "a good introduction to an important era in world history."

Works Cited

Review of *Africa 1500-1900, Kirkus Reviews,* February 15, 1993, p. 228.

O'Malley, Ann, review of *The European Conquest of North America, Booklist,* May 1, 1995, p. 1559.

Rochman, Hazel, review of *Africa 1500-1900, Booklist,* March 1, 1993, p. 1221.

Royal, Pat, review of *Africa 1500-1900, School Library Journal,* October, 1993, p. 170.

Yablonsky, Victoria, review of *The European Conquest of North America, Voice of Youth Advocates,* August, 1995, p. 183.

For More Information See

PERIODICALS

Children's BookWatch, September, 1995, p. 5.*

K–L

KNIGHT, Brenda 1958-

Personal

Female. Born in 1958.

Addresses

Agent—c/o Groundwood Books, 585 Bloor St., W. Second Floor, Toronto, Ontario, M6G 1K5, Canada.

Career

Child psychologist in Vancouver, British Columbia, Canada; writer.

Writings

Runaway's Chance, (juvenile novel), Faber, 1973.
(Compiler) Dennis Foon, editor, *Am I the Only One?,* Groundwood Books, 1985.
Women of the Beat Generation: The Writers, Artists, and Muses at the Heart of a Revolution, Conari Press, 1996.

Sidelights

Brenda Knight is a child psychologist specializing in runaways and victims of abuse. Among her writings is *Runaway's Chance,* a novel for juveniles. It is the story of Paolo, an Italian boy who flees his stepfather, the owner of a squalid bar, and determines to head for London, England, where he hopes to find work as a waiter. In his travels, Paolo befriends an eccentric woman searching for her lost brother. Together they travel to London.

Knight also served as the compiler for editor Dennis Foon's volume *Am I the Only One?,* a collection of various writings produced by children who had been sexually abused. Knight described *Am I the Only One?,* in Diane Turbide's *Quill & Quire* article, as "a book about pain and people's anger," and she contended:

"There is nothing in the book that is sensational or exploitative."

Works Cited

Turbide, Diane, review of *Am I the Only One?, Quill & Quire,* October, 1985, p. 16.

For More Information See

PERIODICALS

Library Journal, October 1, 1996, p. 102.
Publishers Weekly, September 16, 1996, p. 77.
Times Literary Supplement, June 15, 1973, p. 684.*

*   *   *

KNIGHT, Kathryn Lasky
See LASKY, Kathryn

*   *   *

LANKFORD, Mary D. 1932-

Personal

Born December 7, 1932, in Denton, TX; divorced, 1983; married John Briley, 1994; children: four. *Education:* University of North Texas, B.A., 1952; Texas Woman's University, M.L.S., 1982; graduate study at Eastern New Mexico State University. *Hobbies and other interests:* Gardening, travel, piano, reading.

Addresses

Home—110 White Sands, Austin, TX 78734. *Office*—Texas Education Agency, 1701 North Congress Ave., Austin, TX 78701-1494. *E-mail*—mlankf2191@ aol.com.

Career

Author and librarian. Elementary-school librarian in Dover, DE, 1962-63; Walker Air Force Base, Roswell, NM, media services librarian, 1965-66; Irving Independent School District, Irving, TX, director of library and media services, 1966-1996; Texas Education Agency, Austin, TX, assistant director of library services, 1999—. Adjunct professor, University of North Texas and Texas Woman's University, School of Library and Information Studies. Member of selection committee, Elementary School Library Collection, Brodart Foundation, 1977—; member of Teacher Education Advisory Committee, University of Dallas, 1980-88; member of advisory committee, University of North Texas, School of Library Science, 1981-83; chair, advisory committee, Texas Woman's University, School of Library and Information Studies, 1984-91. *Member:* American Library Association, Texas Library Association.

Awards, Honors

Texas Association of School Librarians distinguished library service award for school administrators, 1984; University of North Texas School of Library and Information Science distinguished alumnus award, 1984; Texas Library Association distinguished service award, 1985; inducted into University of North Texas School of Library and Information Science Hall of Fame, 1989; Media Program of the Year Award, American Association of School Librarians, 1991; University of North Texas distinguished alumni award, 1992.

Writings

FOR CHILDREN

Is It Dark? Is It Light?, illustrated by Stacey Schuett, Knopf, 1991.
Hopscotch Around the World, illustrated by Karen Milone, Morrow, 1992.
The Quinceanera: A Latina's Journey to Womanhood, illustrated by Jesse Herrera, Millbrook Press, 1994.
Christmas around the World, Morrow, 1995.
Jacks around the World, illustrated by Karen Dugan, Morrow, 1996.
Dominoes Around the World, illustrated by Dugan, Morrow, 1998.
Birthdays Around the World, Morrow, 2000.

FOR ADULTS

Successful Field Trips, ABC-CLIO, 1992.
Films for Learning, Thinking, and Doing, Libraries Unlimited, Inc., 1992.

Contributor to *School Library Journal, Texas School Business, Texas Library Journal, Booklist, Five Owls Magazine,* and other publications. Member of editorial advisory board, *Booklist,* 1979-83, and *Book Links,* 1993; consultant, *Children's Catalog,* 15th edition, H. W. Wilson, 1986. Newsletter editor, Texas Association of School Library Administrators, 1985-87.

Mary D. Lankford

Sidelights

"Books and writing have been a part of my life since childhood," Mary D. Lankford once told *SATA.* "My decision to become a librarian was made in the fourth grade. I loved the librarian; I loved the way the library smelled (she used lacquer on the books); I loved to read; and I knew I would be happy doing something with books and reading.

"*Is It Dark? Is It Light?* is the result of an idea I got while driving. The road looked as if it could drive into a full moon. As clouds moved across the moon, it began to look square, not round. I started playing with opposites about the moon, putting some of those words on a post-it note on my steering wheel." The result was a "cleverly conceived and executed picture book," according to a reviewer in *Publishers Weekly,* in which information about the moon is combined with an introduction to the concept of opposites. "This concept/puzzle book glows with clues from the first page on," remarked Roger Sutton in *Bulletin of the Center for Children's Books,* noting that "the hushed tone of Lankford's simple questions" are appropriately echoed in the book's illustrations.

Lankford has published several books on childhood games "around the world" that have been lauded for their natural multiculturalism. "*Hopscotch Around the World* was a result of curiosity," the author told *SATA.*

"I read that this game was etched in the Forum in Rome, and was considered one of the oldest games. I began checking the indexes of game books, looking for the word 'hopscotch'. I made copies of these games. I then started interviewing people about how they played hopscotch in their state or country." This research resulted in the discovery of nineteen variations on the game originating from sixteen countries. Each game is presented in a general way, and then with detailed instructions for a modernized version, accompanied by a map showing the location of the country of origin and a few facts about its culture. *School Library Journal* contributor Janie Schomberg called *Hopscotch around the World* both "enjoyable and informative," adding that "the book has varied and creative uses." A critic for *Kirkus Reviews* likewise described Lankford's work as "a good multicultural resource for elementary schools and children's collections."

Lankford employed the same format for *Christmas around the World,* a picture book which compares the holiday celebrations of twelve different cultures. The book concludes with detailed instructions for craft activities, a bibliography, a pronunciation guide, and what Lauren Peterson called in *Booklist* "an interesting selection of Christmas superstitions." The result is both "informative" and "useful," according to a reviewer in *Horn Book.* Reviewers similarly welcomed Lankford's *Jacks around the World,* which employs the same format as her earlier books on hopscotch and Christmas to highlight the historic game of jacks and its variations in fourteen cultures. Critics again emphasized the usefulness of this approach to teachers wishing to emphasize multiculturalism in the classroom. "The subject is manageable, and the presentation encourages readers to try each new version," added a critic for *Horn Book.*

Lankford is also the author of *Quinceanera: A Latina's Journey to Womanhood,* a photo-essay that offers an indepth look at the traditional rite of passage celebrated by Mexican Americans when a girl reaches her fifteenth birthday. Critics, including Ann Welton of *School Library Journal,* described Lankford's text as "straightforward and informative," incorporating the history of this ceremony which is likened to the Jewish bar mitzvah and the Navajo *kinaalda.* "This will be particularly welcome as the only children's book on this important ceremony," averred a contributor to *Kirkus Reviews.*

Works Cited

Review of *Christmas Around the World, Horn Book,* Spring, 1996, p. 81.

Review of *Hopscotch around the World, Kirkus Reviews,* February 15, 1992, p. 257.

Review of *Is It Dark? Is It Light?, Publishers Weekly,* June 28, 1991, p. 100.

Review of *Jacks around the World, Horn Book,* September, 1996, p. 617.

Peterson, Lauren, review of *Christmas Around the World, Booklist,* September 15, 1995, p. 171.

Review of *Quinceanera: A Latina's Journey to Womanhood, Kirkus Reviews,* February 15, 1994, p. 229.

Schomberg, Janie, review of *Hopscotch around the World, School Library Journal,* April, 1992, p. 138.

Sutton, Roger, review of *Is It Dark? Is It Light?, Bulletin of the Center for Children's Books,* September, 1991, p. 14.

Welton, Ann, review of *Quinceanera: A Latina's Journey to Womanhood, School Library Journal,* April, 1994, p. 140.

For More Information See

PERIODICALS

Booklist, July, 1996, p. 1823; March 15, 1998, p. 1238.

Publishers Weekly, May 27, 1996, p. 81; March 30, 1998, p. 84.

School Library Journal, October, 1995, p. 39; April, 1998, p. 118.

*   *   *

LASKY, Kathryn 1944-
(Kathryn Lasky Knight)

Personal

Born June 24, 1944, in Indianapolis, IN; daughter of Marven (a wine bottler) and Hortense (a social worker) Lasky; married Christopher G. Knight (a photographer and filmmaker), May 30, 1971; children: Maxwell, Meribah. *Education:* University of Michigan, B.A., 1966; Wheelock College, M.A., 1977. *Religion:* Jewish. *Hobbies and other interests:* Sailing, skiing, hiking, reading, movies.

Addresses

Home—7 Scott St., Cambridge, MA 02138. *Agent*—Jed Mattes, 175 West 73rd St., New York, NY; also represented by Jane Chelius.

Career

Writer.

Awards, Honors

Boston Globe-Horn Book Award, 1981, for *The Weaver's Gift;* Notable Books, American Library Association (ALA), 1981, for *The Night Journey* and *The Weaver's Gift;* National Jewish Book Award, Jewish Welfare Board Book Council, and Sydney Taylor Book Award, Association of Jewish Libraries, both 1982, both for *The Night Journey;* notable book, *New York Times,* and Best Books for Young Adults, ALA, both 1983, both for *Beyond the Divide;* Newbery Honor Book, and Notable Books, both ALA, both 1984, and both for *Sugaring Time;* Best Books for Young Adults, ALA, 1984, for *Prank;* Notable Books, ALA, 1985, for *Puppeteer;* Best Books for Young Adults, ALA, 1986, for *Pageant;* "Youth-to-Youth Books: A List for Imagination and

Survival" citation, Pratt Library's Young Adult Advisory Board, 1988, for *The Bone Wars;* Golden Trilobite Award, Paleontological Society, 1990, for *Traces of Life: The Origins of Humankind;* Parenting Reading Magic Award, 1990, for *Dinosaur Dig;* Edgar Award nominee for Best Juvenile Mystery, 1992, for *Double Trouble Squared;* Sequoyah Young Adult Book Award, 1994, for *Beyond the Burning Time;* National Jewish Book Award and Notable Books, ALA, both 1997, both for *Marven of the Great North Woods;* John Burroughs Award for Outstanding Nature Book for Children, and Editor's Choice, *Cricket* magazine, both 1998, both for *The Most Beautiful Roof in the World: Exploring the Rainforest Canopy;* Western Heritage Award, National Cowboy Hall of Fame, and Edgar Award nominee, both 1999, both for *Alice Rose and Sam.* In 1986, Lasky won the *Washington Post*/Children's Book Guild Nonfiction Award for her body of work; she is also the recipient of several child-selected awards.

Writings

FOR CHILDREN; AS KATHRYN LASKY

(With Lucy Floyd) *Agatha's Alphabet,* Rand McNally, 1975.
I Have Four Names for My Grandfather, illustrated with photographs by husband, Christopher G. Knight, Little, Brown, 1976.
Tugboats Never Sleep, illustrated with photographs by Knight, Little, Brown, 1977.
Tall Ships, illustrated with photographs by Knight, Scribner, 1978.
My Island Grandma, illustrated by Emily McCully, Warne, 1979, illustrated by Amy Schwartz, Morrow, 1993.
The Weaver's Gift, illustrated with photographs by Christopher G. Knight, Warne, 1981.
Dollmaker: The Eyelight and the Shadow, illustrated with photographs by Knight, Scribner, 1981.
The Night Journey, illustrated by Trina Schart Hyman, Warne, 1981.
Jem's Island, illustrated by Ronald Himler, Scribner, 1982.
Sugaring Time, illustrated with photographs by Christopher G. Knight, Macmillan, 1983.
Beyond the Divide, Macmillan, 1983.
A Baby for Max (in the words of son, Maxwell B. Knight), illustrated with photographs by Christopher G. Knight, Scribner, 1984.
Prank, Macmillan, 1984.
Home Free, Macmillan, 1985.
Puppeteer, illustrated with photographs by Christopher G. Knight, Macmillan, 1985.
Pageant, Four Winds Press (New York City), 1986.
Sea Swan, illustrated by Catherine Stock, Macmillan, 1988.
The Bone Wars, Morrow, 1988.
Traces of Life: The Origins of Humankind, illustrated by Whitney Powell, Morrow, 1989.
Dinosaur Dig, illustrated with photographs by Christopher G. Knight, Morrow, 1990.
Fourth of July Bear, illustrated by Helen Cogancherry, Morrow, 1991.

Kathryn Lasky

Surtsey: The Newest Place on Earth, illustrated with photographs by Christopher G. Knight and Sigurdur Thoraisson, Hyperion, 1992.
Think Like an Eagle: At Work with a Wildlife Photographer, illustrated with photographs by Knight and Jack Swedberg, Little, Brown, 1992.
I Have an Aunt on Marlborough Street, illustrated by Susan Guevara, Macmillan, 1992.
The Solo, illustrated by Bobette McCarthy, Macmillan, 1993.
The Tantrum, illustrated by McCarthy, Macmillan, 1993.
Monarchs, illustrated with photographs by Christopher G. Knight, Harcourt, 1993.
(With daughter Meribah Knight) *Searching for Laura Ingalls: A Reader's Journey,* illustrated with photographs by Knight, Macmillan, 1993.
Lunch Bunnies, illustrated by Marylin Hafner, Little, Brown, 1993.
Memoirs of a Bookbat, Harcourt, 1994.
Beyond the Burning Time, Blue Sky Press/Scholastic, 1994.
Cloud Eyes, illustrated by Barry Moser, Harcourt, 1994.
The Librarian Who Measured the Earth, illustrated by Kevin Hawkes, Little, Brown, 1994.
Days of the Dead, illustrated by Christopher G. Knight, Hyperion, 1994.
Pond Year, illustrated by Mike Bostok, Candlewick, 1995.
She's Wearing a Dead Bird on Her Head! illustrated by David Catrow, Hyperion, 1995.
The Gates of the Wind, illustrated by Janet Stevens, Harcourt, 1995.
A Journey to the New World: The Diary of Remember Patience Whipple, Mayflower, 1620, Scholastic, 1996.

True North: A Novel of the Underground Railroad, Blue Sky Press/Scholastic, 1996.

A Brilliant Streak: The Making of Mark Twain, illustrated by Barry Moser, Harcourt, 1996.

The Most Beautiful Roof in the World: Exploring the Rainforest Canopy, illustrated with photographs by Christopher G. Knight, Harcourt, 1997.

Marven of the Great North Woods, illustrated by Kevin Hawkes, Harcourt, 1997.

Hercules: The Man, the Myth, the Hero, illustrated by Mark Hess, Hyperion, 1997.

Grace the Pirate, illustrated by Karen Lee Schmidt, Hyperion, 1997.

Shadows in the Dawn: The Lemurs of Madagascar, illustrated with photographs by Christopher G. Knight, Harcourt, 1998.

Dreams in the Golden Country: The Diary of Zipporah Feldman, a Jewish Immigrant Girl, Scholastic, 1998.

Sophie and Rose, illustrated by Wendy Anderson Helperin, Candlewick, 1998.

Alice Rose and Sam, Hyperion, 1998.

Show and Tell Bunnies, illustrated by Marylin Hafner, Candlewick, 1998.

The Emperor's Old Clothes, illustrated by David Catrow, Harcourt, 1999.

Star Split, Hyperion, 1999.

Elizabeth I, Red Rose of the House of Tudor, Scholastic, 1999.

Vision of Beauty: The Story of Sarah Breedlove Walker, illustrated by Nneka Bennett, Candlewick, 2000.

"STARBUCK FAMILY" SERIES; MIDDLE-GRADE FICTION

Double Trouble Squared, Harcourt, 1991.
Shadows in the Water, Harcourt, 1992.
A Voice in the Wind, Harcourt, 1993.

FOR ADULTS; AS KATHRYN LASKY KNIGHT, EXCEPT AS NOTED; FICTION, EXCEPT AS NOTED

Atlantic Circle (nonfiction), illustrated with photographs by Christopher G. Knight, Norton, 1985.

Trace Elements, Thorndike Press (Thorndike, ME)/Norton, 1986.

The Widow of Oz, Norton, 1989.

Mortal Words, Simon & Schuster, 1990.

Mumbo Jumbo, Simon & Schuster, 1991.

Dark Swan, St. Martin's Press, 1994.

(Under pseudonym E. L. Swann) *Night Gardening,* Hyperion, 1998.

Contributor to periodicals, including the *Horn Book Magazine,* the *New York Times Book Review,* and *Sail.*

Adaptations

Sugaring Time was adapted as a filmstrip by Random House/Miller-Brody, 1984, for audiocassette, 1986, and for videocassette, 1988.

Work in Progress

Mommy, I Love Your Hands, for Hyperion; *Early Man,* for Morrow; *Lulu's Dinosaur,* for Morrow.

Sidelights

Called "a remarkably versatile writer" by *Booklist*'s Ilene Cooper, Kathryn Lasky is an American author of fiction, nonfiction, and picture books who is noted for her success in several genres. A prolific writer, she is the creator of contemporary fiction, historical fiction, informational books, and picture books that incorporate both fictional and nonfictional elements. Lasky aims her work at an audience ranging from preschool- to high school-age readers, but most often addresses her books to middle graders and older teenage readers; she is also the author of fiction and nonfiction for adults. Lasky's books range from humorous picture books and light middle-grade fiction to extensively researched informational books and thought-provoking novels for young adults on such serious subjects as slavery, censorship, and anti-Semitism. In her nonfiction, the author characteristically explores science, nature, and arts and crafts as well as both familiar and unfamiliar aspects of world and American history. Lasky's nonfiction encompasses a wide range of subjects, including the origin of humankind, the gathering of maple sugar, the life cycle of the monarch butterfly, the story of American sailing ships, and the wonders of the Belize rainforest. In addition, Lasky has written biographies of ancient and contemporary scientists and such well-known figures as Queen Elizabeth I and Mark Twain. In her fiction, Lasky usually features strong-willed, free-thinking female protagonists whose experiences, often centered around historical, ethnic, or moral issues, strengthen the character's independence and self-reliance; several of her novels reflect the author's Jewish heritage. Lasky is the creator of the "Starbuck Family" series, a popular trilogy of mystery/adventure stories for middle-graders about a family with two sets of twins who communicate telepathically and become involved in cases set in London, Florida, and New Mexico. In addition, Lasky is the reteller of the legends of Hercules and Robin Hood and has written several books—both fiction and nonfiction—based on her own experiences and those of her family. Lasky often collaborates on her books with her husband, photographer Christopher G. Knight.

Lasky is praised for exploring topics not often covered in books for the young and for explaining them in an accessible, enjoyable manner. She is also acknowledged for her well-developed characterizations—both in her fiction and nonfiction—and for her narrative skill, and noted for providing young readers with strong storylines, even in her informational books. Lasky favors clear, concise language with vivid imagery that is often called poetic; writing in *Booklist,* Ilene Cooper stated, "Few authors are as eloquent as Lasky." She is considered a writer of unusual, effective books that reveal their author's enthusiasm for her subjects. In an essay in *Twentieth-Century Young Adult Writers,* Linda Garrett commented that Lasky "has made and continues to make an impact on young-adult literature. Her well-researched books provide a thorough, accurate picture of whatever theme is being presented. Her use of lyrical language captures the moods as well as facts leaving the reader with [in Lasky's words] 'a sense of joy—indeed

Will Meribah find what she's looking for?

BEYOND *the* DIVIDE

KATHRYN LASKY

Set in the mid-1800s, Lasky's novel outlines the journey of fourteen-year-old Meribah Simon, an Amish girl who travels with her father from Pennsylvania to California by wagon train during the Gold Rush. (Cover illustration by Ben Stahl.)

celebration' of the world in which they live." Carol Hurst of *Carol Hurst's Children's Literature Newsletter* added, "I'm always impressed when an author can move from one genre to another with competence, but Kathy Lasky does so with such ease and skill that I am more than impressed, I'm awed."

Born in Indianapolis, Indiana, Lasky is the descendant of a family who escaped from czarist Russia to avoid religious persecution; their exodus forms the basis of her novel *The Night Journey.* Lasky is the daughter of social worker Hortense Lasky and Marven Lasky, a wine bottler whose boyhood experience of being sent to a logging camp in the Minnesota woods is recounted by his daughter in the picture book *Marven of the Great North Woods.* Lasky was a storyteller from an early age; she once told *Contemporary Authors New Revision Series* (*CANR*), "When I was growing up, I was always thinking up stories—whether I wrote them down or not

didn't seem to matter. I was a compulsive story-maker. I was fiercely private about these early stories—never really sharing them with anybody. I always wanted to be a writer, but on the other hand it seemed to lack a certain legitimacy as a profession. It was enjoyable, not reliable, and you were your own boss. This all seemed funny. It was only when I began to share my writing with my parents (and much later my husband) and sensed their responsiveness that I began to think that it was OK to want to be a writer." As a child, Lasky was labeled a reluctant reader. "The truth is," she stated on her Website, "I didn't really like the kind of books they had you reading at school—the 'See Dick, See Jane' books. So I made a voluntary withdrawal from reading in school. But I loved the books my mom was reading to me, books like *Peter Pan* and *The Wonderful Wizard of Oz.*" Lasky first realized that she could become a writer when she was about ten years old. She and her family, which also included an older sister, were driving at night in their convertible. The top was down and, Lasky recalled on her Website, "The sky looked so interesting—you couldn't see the stars because of these woolly clouds. And I said it looked like a sheepback sky. My mom turned around and said, 'Kathryn, you should be a writer.' When my mom said that, I thought, 'Wow, maybe I will be.'"

Although Lasky is well respected as an author of informational books, she claims that as a young reader she was not a fan of the genre. She stated on her Website, "I didn't like nonfiction as a kid—the nonfiction books were really dry back then. But then I realized that you can make the characters in nonfiction as fascinating as those in fiction." In an article in *Horn Book,* Lasky described how she employed her research techniques as a seventh-grader in writing a report on the Pleistocene Age due the next morning. "First," the author recalled, "I went to the dictionary and looked up a definition. Webster really had a knack for providing material for desperate seventh-graders. Then I would proceed to the *World Book Encyclopedia.* If I was feeling very scholarly, I would persevere and take on the Mount Everest of research—*Encyclopedia Brittanica.*" If she chose to use the latter, Lasky would "silently curse the idiot who had set his mind to collecting all this information in the first place." Mostly, though, Lasky would move to the final step in her research: "Bursting into my sister's room, I would fling myself on her bed and in anguish cry, 'Quick, I need a first sentence about the Pleistocene Age!' Sometimes I would get one from her and sometimes she'd tell me to get out." As a last resort, Lasky would go to her mother, who would "toss off opening sentences like a comedy writer searching for one-liners. Like all seventh-graders, I considered the quality of my mother's thoughts stupid, boring, and embarrassing. I would roll my eyes and groan and wish that Ozzie and Harriet were my real parents."

Lasky attended a private all-girls school in Indianapolis, which she felt did not particularly suit her; later, she would draw on her experiences in the autobiographical novel *Pageant,* a humorous coming-of-age story about Sarah Benjamin, a Jewish teenager in a Christian girls' school who learns what she really wants from life. After finishing high school, Lasky attended the University of Michigan as an English major; after receiving her degree, she became a teacher and began writing seriously in her spare time. In 1971, Lasky married Christopher Knight, whose youthful experiences kayaking and camping with his father and grandfather form the basis for the novel *Jem's Island.* The couple have two children: Max, whose desire for a baby sister inspired the photo-essay *A Baby for Max,* and Meribah, who shares her name with the title character of the young-adult novel *Beyond the Divide* and who collaborated with her mother on *Searching for Laura Ingalls,* the story of her family's journey to the settings of the "Little House" books by Laura Ingalls Wilder.

In 1975, Lasky published her first book for children, the colorful concept book *Agatha's Alphabet.* Her second work, *I Have Four Names for My Grandfather,* was published the following year. A picture book, *Four Names* depicts Tom and his grandfather fishing, planting flowers, and looking at a train, among other activities; Tom concludes that although his grandfather has four names—Poppy, Pop, Grandpa, and Gramps—he is always the same grandfather to him. The first of Lasky's books to be illustrated by her husband, *Four Names* also introduces one of the author's major themes: intergenerational bonding. Barbara S. Wertheimer of *Children's Book Review Service* noted "the sensitivity and depth of feeling within the text," while Andd Ward of *School Library Journal* said that the strength of the book "lies in the compatibility of the text with the abundant photographs." In 1977, Lasky received her master's degree in English from Wheelock College. Her first work to win a major award is *The Weaver's Gift,* a photo-essay that won the *Boston Globe-Horn Book* Award for juvenile nonfiction in 1982. In this book, Lasky and Knight spotlight weaver Carolyn Frye, a Vermont woman who raises sheep and converts their wool to finished products; the author and photographer document Frye's hard work and artistry while demonstrating how sheared wool becomes a child's blanket. Writing in *Interracial Books for Children,* Jan M. Goodman stated that *The Weaver's Gift* "is a rare find," adding that the text is "extremely well-written and factual and shows deep appreciation and respect for a woman and her trade." A critic for *Kirkus Reviews* noted, "In recent years there have been other juvenile introductions to this basic sequence, but they are dull or feeble in comparison."

In 1981, Lasky published *The Night Journey,* a young-adult novel that is highly respected as a work of Jewish literature. Based on a true story, the novel outlines how a nine-year-old girl orchestrates her family's escape from religious persecution in czarist Russia. The girl grows up to become Nana Sachie, great-grandmother to thirteen-year-old Rachel, who learns this piece of family history during their afternoons together; Sachie finishes the tale, which is filled with excitement, shortly before her death. Calling *The Night Journey* "[a] story to cherish," Ilene Cooper of *Booklist* noted that it "has so many aspects that each person will come away with his own idea of

what makes the book memorable." Peter Kennerley of the *School Librarian* concluded, "I believe this to be a satisfying novel, if not without blemish, and I recommend it strongly." *Sugaring Time,* a photo-essay also illustrated by Knight, was named a Newbery honor book in 1984. The volume outlines the activities of the Lacey family during the month of March, the period they call "sugaring time," on their Vermont farm. Lasky and Knight portray the hard work—and the pleasure—involved in turning maple sugar into maple syrup while providing young readers with a sense of the seasons and the value of the earth. Alice Naylor of *Language Arts* called Lasky's text "a model of good exposition," while Martha T. Kane of *Appraisal: Science Books for Young People* said, "You can almost hear the crunch of snow beneath the horses' feet, the sweet maple sap dripping into the buckets, and the roar of the fire in the sugarhouse.... Kathryn Lasky involves *all* the reader's senses in her memorable description of the collection and processing of maple sap in a small sugarbush in Vermont."

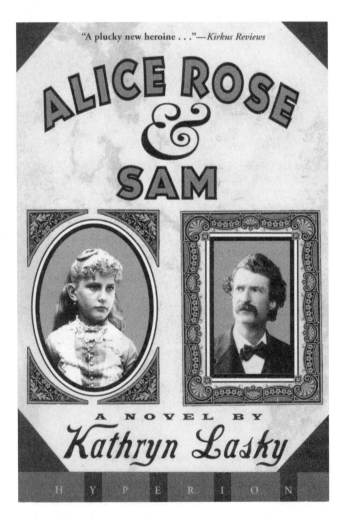

Twelve-year-old Alice Rose, a newspaperman's daughter, joins forces with reporter Samuel Clemens to solve a murder and expose a plot by a group of Confederate vigilantes.

Lasky's heartwarming picture book recounts her father's boyhood experience of life at a logging camp in the Minnesota woods. (From Marven of the Great North Woods, *illustrated by Kevin Hawkes.)*

One of Lasky's most critically acclaimed novels for young adults is *Beyond the Divide.* Set in the mid-1800s, the story outlines the journey of fourteen-year-old Meribah Simon, an Amish girl who travels with her father from Pennsylvania to California by wagon train during the Gold Rush. Meribah's trek to California is an ordeal: her father dies after one of his wounds becomes infected; a friend is raped and commits suicide; and Meribah—left alone—struggles to survive in the wilderness. Rescued by a group of Yahi Indians, Meribah learns to understand them and to appreciate their lifestyle; at the end of the novel, she decides to go back to a fertile valley she had seen from the wagon train and make a life for herself. Calling *Beyond the Divide* an "elegantly written tour de force," Ilene Cooper commented that Lasky has written a "quintessential pioneer story, a piece so textured and rich that readers will remember it long after they've put it down." Dick Abrahamson of *English Journal* called *Beyond the Divide* "one of the finest historical novels I've read in a long time. It certainly ought to be considered for the Newbery Award." Writing in *Language Arts,* M. Jean Greenlaw concluded that the major strength of the book is that it "is a magnificent story. The westward movement is an integral part of American history and nature, and this book is the most gripping account of that time I have ever read," Linda Garrett of *Twentieth-Century Children's Writers* added that the novel "is so realistic it would be easy to believe that *Beyond the Divide* is directly from a diary of a young girl going West."

In 1989, Lasky published *Traces of Life: The Origins of Humankind,* an informational book that outlines the history of evolution. In this work, the author, who has had a longtime interest in paleontology, attempts to determine the moment at which humanity as we know it began to exist. She discusses evolution and the science of paleoanthropology while presenting biographical information about several notable scientists. *Voice of Youth Advocates* contributor Shirley A. Bathgate said that Lasky "combines research and creativity in yet another excellent book"; the critic concluded, "Younger young-adult readers will find the book both easy and fun to read." *Traces of Life* received the Golden Trilobite Award from the Paleontological Society in 1990. Lasky received consistently favorable reviews for *Monarchs,* an informational book that describes the cycle of the migrating monarch butterfly. In recreating the monarch's journey from Maine to Mexico, Lasky and Christopher Knight blend scientific facts with information about adults and children involved with preserving the monarch and its environment. Susan Oliver of *School Library Journal* noted that *Monarchs* "strikes a perfect balance between science and humanity"; the critic added that "the diversity of the people who care about conserving the beauty and mystery of nature makes it a truly compelling book." Betsy Hearne of *Bulletin of the Center for Children's Books* concluded that Lasky "has trimmed her prose for an action-packed nature narrative that crosses cultural as well as geographic boundaries."

In 1994, Lasky published *The Librarian Who Measured the Earth,* an informational picture book about Eratosthenes, the Greek scholar who became the head librarian of the famous library in Alexandria, Egypt, and was the first person to determine and document the size of the earth. Using a technique that she calls "responsible imagining," Lasky combines existing information about Eratosthenes and his times with what Joanne Schott of *Quill and Quire* called "some reasonable assumptions" about her subject's early life and personality. Schott called *The Librarian Who Measured the Earth* a "beautiful picture-book biography" in which "Eratosthenes comes across as an individual rather than just another name from the history books." Anne Lundin of the *Five Owls* posed the question: "How many counting books count in a whole language program? After a while, the numbers themselves are pretty familiar, and the challenge is to find a book that explores mathematics and geography from a more human scale, as a quest to answer the mysteries of life. Here it is." Describing herself as "a rather nonnumerate soul and a naturalist," Lundin concluded, "For someone like me, [this book] shakes the sky. I am proud to associate with the librarian Eratosthenes, who goads me to ask my own questions."

One of Lasky's most well-received picture-book biographies is *Marven of the Great North Woods,* a vignette from her father's childhood. As a ten-year-old, Marven Lasky was sent to a logging camp in the Minnesota north woods to avoid the influenza epidemic that had hit Duluth in 1918. At first, Marven finds this new world to be foreign—for example, there was no kosher food at the camp—but he adjusts to his situation and forms warm friendships with the lumberjacks, especially Jean Louis, a French-Canadian who is the biggest man in the camp. Calling *Marven of the Great North Woods* a story of "courage inspired by familial affection and the unexpected kindness of strangers," a critic in *Publishers Weekly* predicted, "Thanks to Lasky's considerable command of language and narrative detail, readers will linger over" the descriptions in the book. Roger Sutton of *Horn Book* called *Marven of the Great North Woods* "both invigorating and cozy" and noted that the text, though long for a picture book, is "fully eventful." In her newsletter, Carol Hurst concluded that Lasky "makes the extraordinary adventure possible and [Kevin Hawkes's] paintings combine with her writing to show wonder and tenderness." *Marven of the Great North Woods* won the National Jewish Book Award in 1997.

Lasky has a particular fascination with American author Samuel Langhorne Clemens, who wrote as Mark Twain: the subject of the picture book biography *A Brilliant Streak: The Making of Mark Twain,* he also appears as a major character in *Alice Rose and Sam,* a story for middle-graders. In *A Brilliant Streak,* Lasky recounts Clemens's life until he takes on his famous pseudonym at the age of thirty. The author details Twain's Missouri childhood and his experiences as a steamboat pilot, prospector, and reporter as well as a humorist and social commentator; in addition, Lasky provides a sense of how Twain's life and personality are reflected in his works. Stephanie Zvirin of *Booklist* predicted that after reading *A Brilliant Streak,* "Children will definitely want to find out more about Clemens . . . ," while a critic in *Kirkus Reviews* concluded that Twain's "successes are the source of one colorful anecdote after another, which Lasky taps and twirls into an engaging narrative that glimmers with its own brand of brilliance." Set in Virginia City, Nevada, during the 1860s, *Alice Rose and Sam* describes how twelve-year-old Alice Rose, a newspaperman's daughter, joins forces with reporter Samuel Clemens to solve a murder and expose a plot by a group of Confederate vigilantes called the Society of Seven. "Ultimately," noted Jennifer A. Fakolt of *School*

Library Journal, Alice Rose and Clemens "end up teaching one another valuable lessons about life and truth." Calling the book an "open-throttled page-turner," a critic for *Kirkus Reviews* concluded that fans of Karen Cushman's *The Ballad of Lucy Whipple* and Kathleen Karr's *Oh, Those Harper Girls!* "have a plucky new heroine to admire," while a reviewer for *Publishers Weekly* called *Alice Rose and Sam* a "view of American history teeming with adventure and local color." *Alice Rose and Sam* won the Western Heritage Award and was nominated for an Edgar Award in 1999.

Lasky once told *SATA,* "I write directly from my own experiences." In an article for the *Horn Book Magazine* on writing nonfiction, she stated that as a writer she searches "for the story among the truths, the facts, the lies, and the realities . . . . I have always tried hard to listen, smell, and touch the place that I write about— especially if I am lucky enough to be there." She continued, "I have a fascination with the inexact and the unexplainable. I try to do as little explaining as possible, but I try to present my subject in some way so it will not lose what I have found to be or suspect to be its sacred dimension." The author concluded, "In my books I am not concerned with messages, and I really do not care if readers remember a single fact. What I do hope is that they come away with a sense of joy—indeed celebration—about something they have sensed in the world in which they live." Regarding her fiction, much of which reflects her extensive research, Lasky stated on her Website, "I want young readers to come away with a sense of joy about life. I want to draw them into a world where they're really going to connect with the characters." In another article for the *Horn Book,* Lasky claimed, "I can't stand doing the same thing twice. I don't want to change just for the sake of change. But the whole point of being an artist is to be able to get up every morning and reinvent the world."

Works Cited

Abrahamson, Dick, "To Start the New Year Off Right," *English Journal,* January, 1984, pp. 87-89.

Review of *Alice Rose and Sam, Kirkus Reviews,* March 1, 1998, p. 341.

Review of *Alice Rose and Sam, Publishers Weekly,* February 16, 1998, p. 212.

Bathgate, Shirley A., review of *Traces of Life: The Origin of Humankind, Voice of Youth Advocates,* June, 1990, pp. 126-27.

Review of *A Brilliant Streak: The Making of Mark Twain, Kirkus Reviews,* April 1, 1998, p. 497.

Cooper, Ilene, review of *Beyond the Divide, Booklist,* July, 1983, p. 1402.

Cooper, review of *Jem's Island, Booklist,* November 15, 1982, p. 446.

Cooper, review of *Home Free, Booklist,* January 15, 1986, pp. 758-59.

Cooper, review of *The Night Journey, Booklist,* November 15, 1981, pp. 439-40.

Fakolt, Jennifer A., review of *Alice Rose and Sam, School Library Journal,* May, 1998, p. 145.

Garrett, Linda, entry on Lasky in *Twentieth-Century Young Adult Writers,* edited by Laura Standley Berger, Gale, 1994, pp. 371-73.

Goodman, Jan M., review of *The Weaver's Gift, Interracial Books for Children Bulletin,* Vol. 12, nos. 4 and 5, 1981, p. 38.

Greenlaw, M. Jean, review of *Beyond the Divide, Language Arts,* January, 1984, pp. 70-71.

Hearne, Betsy, review of *Monarchs, Bulletin of the Center for Children's Books,* November, 1993, pp. 88-89.

Hurst, Carol, with Rebecca Otis, "Featured Author: Kathryn Lasky," *Carol Hurst's Children's Literature Newsletter,* winter, 1999, p. 4.

Jameyson, Karen, review of *Sugaring Time, Horn Book,* June, 1983, p. 323.

Kane, Martha T., review of *Sugaring Time, Appraisal: Science Books for Young People,* winter, 1984, pp. 34-35.

Kennerley, Peter, review of *The Night Journey, School Librarian,* June, 1983, p. 144.

Landis, Anne, review of *The Librarian Who Measured the Earth, Five Owls,* February, 1995, pp. 61-62.

Lasky, Kathryn, commentary in *Contemporary Authors New Revision Series,* Volume 11, Gale, 1984, p. 320.

Lasky, "Creativity in a Boom Industry," *Horn Book,* November-December, 1991, pp. 705-11.

Lasky, "Reflections on Nonfiction," *Horn Book Magazine,* September-October, 1985, pp. 527-32.

Lasky, "More about Kathryn Lasky (Knight)," *Kathryn Lasky's Home Page,* http://www.xensei.com/users/newfilm/more.htm.

Review of *Marven of the Great North Woods, Publishers Weekly,* October 6, 1997, p. 83.

Naylor, Alice, review of *Sugaring Time, Language Arts,* September, 1984, p. 543.

Oliver, Susan, review of *Monarchs, School Library Journal,* September, 1993, p. 244.

Schott, Joanne, "The One Who...," *Quill and Quire,* October, 1994, p. 46.

Sutton, Roger, review of *Marven of the Great North Woods, Horn Book,* November-December, 1997, p. 670.

Ward, Andd, review of *I Have Four Names for My Grandfather, School Library Journal,* November, 1976, p. 48.

Review of *The Weaver's Gift, Kirkus Reviews,* March 1, 1981, p. 286.

Wertheimer, Barbara S., review of *I Have Four Names for My Grandfather, Children's Book Review Service,* November, 1976, p. 22.

Zvirin, Stephanie, review of *A Brilliant Streak: The Making of Mark Twain, Booklist,* April, 1998, p. 1317.

For More Information See

BOOKS

Children's Books and Their Creators, edited by Anita Silvey, Houghton Mifflin, 1995.

Children's Literature Review, Volume 11, Gale, 1986, pp. 112-22.

Holtze, Sally Holmes, editor, *Sixth Book of Junior Authors and Illustrators,* Wilson, 1989, pp. 160-61.

PERIODICALS

Booklist, October 1, 1991, pp. 246-47; November 1, 1994, p. 494.

Emergency Librarian, November-December, 1996, pp. 65-68.

Los Angeles Times Book Review, March 25, 1990, p. 8.

Publishers Weekly, February 23, 1990, pp. 126+.

School Librarian's Workshop, April, 1995, pp. 4-5.

Washington Post Book World, July 8, 1990, p. 10.

—*Sketch by Gerard J. Senick*

* * *

LASKY KNIGHT, Kathryn
See Kathryn Lasky

* * *

LAXDAL, Vivienne 1962-

Personal

Born April 23, 1962, in Marathon, Ontario, Canada; daughter of Paul Chevrier (a French teacher) and Tamara Atkinson (an equestrian trainer; maiden name, Karbach); married Larry Laxdal (a designer), October 13, 1984; children: Ryan Alexander, William Paul. *Education:* Attended the University of Victoria and the Banff School of Fine Arts.

Addresses

Home—RR#2, Box 206, Masham, Quebec J0X 2W0. *Agent*—c/o Centaur Theatre Company, 453 St. Francois Xavier, Montreal, QC H1A 1A1, Canada. *Electronic-mail*—laxdal@msn.com.

Career

Playwright and actor, premiering often in Ottawa by the Great Canadian Theatre Company and the National Arts Centre; Centaur Theatre (Montreal), Canadian Stage Company (Toronto), Odyssey Theatre (Ottawa), resident playwright. *Member:* Playwrights Union of Canada, Writers Guild of Canada, Canadian Actors Equity Association.

Awards, Honors

Canadian National Playwriting Competition, first prize, 1990, for *Karla and Grif;* Canadian Author's Association, Air Canada Award, 1991; CBC Radio Ottawa Drama Competition, winner, 1994, for *Frog in a Hot Pot;* Ottawa Valley Book Festival Playwriting Award, for *Cyber:flwomb.*

Writings

PLAYS

Blood-Brother, Step-Sister (juvenile), 1986, produced in Canada at The Great Canadian Theatre Company, 1986, Playwrights Union of Canada, 1990.

(With Barbara Lysnes) *A Quantum Leap,* produced at the Great Canadian Theatre Company, 1987.

Goose Spit, produced at the Great Canadian Theatre Company, 1988.

Ruby and the Rock, produced in Canada at Green Thumb Theatre, 1991.

Karla and Grif, produced in Canada at the National Arts Centre, 1991, published by Playwrights in Canada Press, 1999.

Personal Convictions, produced at the National Arts Centre, 1991.

Angel's Goose, CBC Radio, 1992.

(With Jean Marc Dalpe) *National CAPITALe Nationale,* produced at the National Arts Centre, 1993.

Cyber:flwomb, produced at the National Arts Centre, 1994, published in *Prerogatives: Contemporary Plays by Women,* Blizzard Press, 1998.

The Family Canoe, CBC Radio, 1995.

These Girls, produced at the Pressed for Time Theatre, 1999.

Also creates own performance pieces, including *The Mother Beat, Ratiocination,* and *Iron Maids.*

Work in Progress

A play about sisters and their kidneys called *The Spirit of Giving.*

Sidelights

Award-winning Canadian playwright Vivienne Laxdal has seen her works mounted at theaters in Quebec and Ontario. Among her plays are *Blood-Brother, Step-Sister,* about a blended family, and *Cyber:flwomb,* about a failed in vitro fertilization. *Blood-Brother, Step-Sister,* written for children, revolves around the activities of three children—two from one family, one from another—who form a new family as a result of divorce. At first the children quarrel, but eventually they come to an understanding and acceptance of their new roles. Bernie Warren, writing in *Canadian Children's Literature* found the characters to be "very warm and human." Warren concluded that children will likely identify with the "issues [which] are raised in an accessible and non-patronising" manner.

In *Cyber:flwomb,* which was published in 1998 in the collection *Contemporary Plays by Women,* Laxdal depicts the deranged psychological condition of Oneida, an infertile woman who desperately wants to conceive a child. In her paranoia, Oneida believes that her attempt at in vitro fertilization failed because the government controls who is able to bear children in order to ensure that only "perfect" children are born. Calling the work a "moving portrait of loss," Kevin Burns in *Quill & Quire*

remarked, "Laxdal flips effortlessly between well-observed comedy and tough emotional drama."

Laxdal once commented: "I approach playwriting the same way I approach road kill: I don't want to look, but I can't help it. I have to see how much of the 'viscera' is exposed."

Works Cited

Burns, Kevin Burns, review of *Cyber:flwomb, Quill & Quire,* September, 1998, p. 62.

Warren, Bernie, review of *Blood-Brother, Step-Sister, Canadian Children's Literature,* volume 57-58, 1990, pp. 86-88.

For More Information See

PERIODICALS

Ottawa Citizen, November 13, 1994, p. B6.*

*   *   *

LESTER, Julius (Bernard) 1939-

Personal

Born January 27, 1939, in St. Louis, MO; son of W. D. (a minister) and Julia (Smith) Lester; married Joan Steinau (a researcher), 1962 (divorced, 1970); married Alida Carolyn Fechner, March 21, 1979; children: (first marriage) Jody Simone, Malcolm Coltrane; (second marriage) Elena Milad (stepdaughter), David Julius. *Education:* Fisk University, B.A., 1960.

Addresses

Home—600 Station Rd., Amherst, MA 01002. *Office*—University of Massachusetts, Amherst, MA 01002.

Career

Professional musician and singer in the 1960s, recorded with Vanguard Records; Newport Folk Festival, Newport, RI, director, 1966-68; WBAI-FM, New York City, producer and host of live radio show, 1968-75; WNET-TV, New York City, host of live television program "Free Time," 1971-73; University of Massachusetts—Amherst, professor of Afro-American studies, 1971-88, professor of Near Eastern and Judaic Studies, 1982—, acting director and associate director of Institute for Advanced Studies in Humanities, 1982-84. Lecturer, New School for Social Research, New York City, 1968-70; writer in residence, Vanderbilt University, 1985.

Awards, Honors

Newbery Honor Book citation, 1969, and Lewis Carroll Shelf Award, 1970, both for *To Be a Slave;* Lewis Carroll Shelf Award, 1972, and National Book Award finalist, 1973, both for *The Long Journey Home: Stories from Black History;* Lewis Carroll Shelf Award, 1973, for *The Knee-High Man and Other Tales;* honorable mention, Coretta Scott King Award, 1983, for *This Strange New Feeling,* and 1988, for *Tales of Uncle Remus: The Adventures of Brer Rabbit;* Parents' Choice Story Book award, 1987, for *The Tales of Uncle Remus,* and 1990, for *Further Tales of Uncle Remus;* Reading Magic Award, 1988, for *More Tales of Uncle Remus;* *Boston Globe-Horn Book* award, 1995, for *John Henry.* Distinguished Teacher's Award, 1983-84; Faculty Fellowship Award for Distinguished Research and Scholarship, 1985; National Professor of the Year Silver Medal Award, Council for Advancement and Support of Education, 1985; Massachusetts State Professor of the Year and Gold Medal Award for National Professor of the Year, both from Council for Advancement and Support of Education, both 1986; Distinguished Faculty Lecturer, 1986-87.

Writings

(With Pete Seeger) *The 12-String Guitar as Played by Leadbelly: An Instructional Manual,* Oak, 1965.

The Angry Children of Malcolm X, Southern Student Organizing Committee, 1966.

(Editor with Mary Varela) *Our Folk Tales: High John, The Conqueror, and Other Afro-American Tales,* illustrated by Jennifer Lawson, privately printed, 1967.

(Editor with Varela) Fanny Lou Hamer, *To Praise Our Bridges: An Autobiography,* KIPCO, 1967.

The Mud of Vietnam: Photographs and Poems, Folklore Press, 1967.

Look Out Whitey! Black Power's Gon' Get Your Mama!, Dial, 1968.

To Be a Slave, illustrated by Tom Feelings, Dial, 1969, 1998.

Black Folktales, illustrated by Feelings, Baron, 1969, Grove Press, 1992.

Search for the New Land: History as Subjective Experience, Dial, 1969.

Revolutionary Notes, Baron, 1969.

(Editor) *The Seventh Son: The Thoughts and Writings of W. E. B. DuBois,* two volumes, Random House, 1971.

(Compiler with Rae Pace Alexander) *Young and Black in America,* Random House, 1971.

The Long Journey Home: Stories from Black History, Dial, 1972.

The Knee-High Man and Other Tales, illustrated by Ralph Pinto, Dial, 1972.

Two Love Stories, Dial, 1972.

(Editor) Stanley Couch, *Ain't No Ambulances for No Nigguhs Tonight* (poems), Baron, 1972.

(With David Gahr) *Who I Am* (photopoems), Dial, 1974.

All Is Well: An Autobiography, Morrow, 1976.

This Strange New Feeling (short stories), Dial, 1982, published in England as *A Taste of Freedom: Three Stories from Black History,* Longman, 1983.

Do Lord Remember Me (adult novel), Holt, 1984.

The Tales of Uncle Remus: The Adventures of Brer Rabbit, illustrated by Jerry Pinkney, Dial, 1987.

More Tales of Uncle Remus: Further Adventures of Brer Rabbit, His Friends, Enemies, and Others, illustrated by Pinkney, Dial, 1988.

Lovesong: Becoming a Jew (autobiographical), Holt, 1988.

Julius Lester

How Many Spots Does a Leopard Have? and Other Tales, illustrated by David Shannon, Scholastic, 1990.

Further Tales of Uncle Remus: The Misadventures of Brer Rabbit, Brer Fox, Wolf, the Doodang, and Other Creatures, illustrated by Pinkney, Dial, 1990.

Falling Pieces of the Broken Sky, Arcade, 1990.

The Last Tales of Uncle Remus, illustrated by Pinkney, Dial, 1994.

John Henry, illustrated by Pinkney, Dial, 1994.

The Man Who Knew Too Much: A Moral Tale from the Baila of Zambia, illustrated by Leonard Jenkins, Clarion, 1994.

And All Our Wounds Forgiven, Arcade, 1994.

Othello: A Novel, Scholastic, 1995.

Sam and the Tigers: A New Retelling of Little Black Sambo, illustrated by Pinkney, Dial, 1996.

How Butterflies Came to Be, Scholastic, 1997.

What a Truly Cool World, illustrated by Joe Cepeda, Scholastic, 1998.

Black Cowboy, Wild Horses: A True Story, illustrated by Pinkney, Dial, 1998.

From Slave Ship to Freedom Road, illustrated by Rod Brown, Dial, 1998.

When the Beginning Began: Stories about God, the Creatures, and Us, illustrated by Emily Lisker, 1998.

Uncle Remus, Tales from the Briar Patch (reprinting of *The Tales of Uncle Remus, More Tales of Uncle Remus, Further Tales of Uncle Remus,* and *The Last Tales of Uncle Remus*), illustrated by Pinkney, Phyllis Fogelman Books, 1999.

Shining, illustrated by Terea Shaffer, Harcourt Brace, 2000.

Pharaoh's Daughter, Harcourt Brace, 2000.

The Autobiography of God, Arcade, 2000.

Contributor of essays and reviews to numerous magazines and newspapers, including *New York Times Book Review, New York Times, Nation, Katallagete, Democracy,* and *Village Voice.* Associate editor, *Sing Out,* 1964-70; contributing editor, *Broadside of New York,* 1964-70.

Lester's works have been translated into seven languages.

Sidelights

With his 1970 proclamation that African Americans "no longer (and never did) need whites to interpret our lives or our culture," Julius Lester threw down the gauntlet to children's literature and what this black writer, radio personality, educator, and folksinger saw as a literary establishment out of touch with the times. "Whites can only give a white interpretation of blacks," Lester went on to write in an exchange of letters in the *New York Times Book Review* with George Woods, children's book editor of the *Times.* Such an interpretation, Lester felt, "tells us a lot about whites, but nothing about blacks. But the way it generally turns out is that the white perception of blacks becomes accepted as the thing itself, as black reality.... Could you take seriously a history of Jews written by an Arab?" Lester also once noted in *Publishers Weekly* that too much of children's literature was out of touch with the times and with the needs of children. "In a world in which a child can be dead from an overdose of heroin at age twelve, Snow White is not only inadequate, it is in danger of being vulgar."

Lester has spent his professional life rectifying these perceived inadequacies: in fiction, biography, and the retelling of black folktales, Lester has presented the black experience in America as slave and freeman alike. Lester's award-winning list of books are an attempted palliative and as such have helped an entire generation of black youth to approach their culture through their own language and psyche. While Lester's creed of black writers for black readers has set off heated debate, the effect on the ground has been to encourage the development of African-American voices. In books such as *To Be a Slave, Long Journey Home, This Strange Feeling,* and in his many retellings of Uncle Remus stories, Lester has helped to preserve the history of black Americans, often focusing on black experience in the rural Deep South, especially during slavery and the Reconstruction period after the Civil War. Throughout, he has been acclaimed for his blend of realistic detail, dialogue, and storytelling—all contributing to important historical knowledge about African Americans. Quoted in *Twentieth-Century Children's Writers,* Lester upholds history as "the lives of people more than ... the recording of politics and wars," and describes his work as an effort "to explore and illumine the lives of ordinary men and women, who are history." Moreover, his work aims to illuminate themes central to black history, such as oppression and racism. His ultimate goal, noted Eric Foner and Naomi Lewis in the *New York Review of*

Books, is to provide readers with "a sense of history which will help shape their lives and politics."

Lester's early years were spent in the segregated South of the 1940s and 1950s. He was born in 1939 in St. Louis, Missouri, the son of a Methodist minister from whom, as Lester stated in *Fourth Book of Junior Authors and Illustrators,* he "absorbed so much of Southern rural black traditions, particularly music and stories." At the age of two he moved with his family to Kansas City, Kansas, and as a teenager lived in Nashville, Tennessee, spending summers at his grandmother's farm in rural Arkansas. While Lester's memories of the South were not, as he stated in *Fourth Book,* "wholly negative, despite segregation and discrimination," he was profoundly influenced by what he described in *Horn Book* as the South's atmosphere of "deathly spiritual violence." In addition to its "many restrictions on where [blacks] could live, eat, go to school, and go after dark," the segregated South was a dangerous place where there existed "the constant threat of physical death if you looked at a white man in what he considered the wrong way or if he didn't like your attitude."

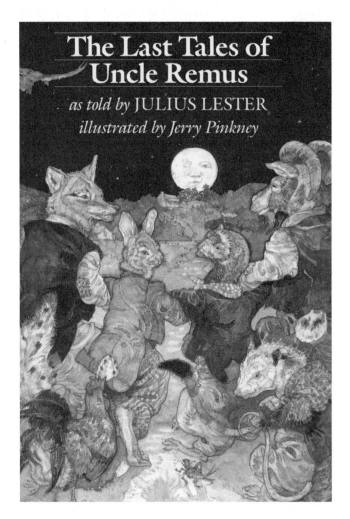

Lester rewrote the African-American trickster tales, recreating the stories in a contemporary idiom without losing the bite of the originals. (Cover illustration by Jerry Pinkney.)

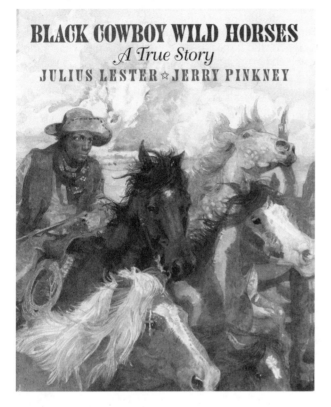

In **Black Cowboy Wild Horses,** *Lester turned his historian's eye to the story of Bob Lemmons, one of many unheralded slaves who became cowboys and helped settle the West.* (Cover illustration by Jerry Pinkney.)

Lester's early artistic interests were with music, yet he also had aspirations to become a writer. In books he found an outlet from the daily realities of racism, and at a young age became an avid reader despite limited access to libraries. Confined to the books supplied by the mobile reading van, Lester cut his teeth on westerns and mysteries and soon turned to adult books that his minister father had on his shelves. One influential early book was *Thirteen Against the Odds,* a collection of biographical sketches of African Americans who beat the odds and succeeded in white culture. Lester was particularly struck by the tale of W. E. B. DuBois, and would later come to write his own studies on the man.

Lester graduated in 1960 from Nashville's Fisk University with a degree in English and became politically active in the Civil Rights struggle to desegregate the South and bring about social change. In the mid-1960s he joined the Student Non-Violent Coordinating Committee (SNCC), at a time when the group advocated that blacks assume a more militant stance to fight racism. He became head of the SNCC's photo department and traveled to North Vietnam during the Vietnam War to document the effects of U.S. bombing missions. During the same period, he pursued his music interests and played the guitar and banjo at civil rights rallies. Lester went on to record two albums and performed with such folksingers as Pete Seeger, Phil Ochs, and Judy Collins. His interests in black folk music led to the writing of his

first book, *The 12-String Guitar as Played by Leadbelly: An Instructional Manual,* which he co-authored with Seeger in 1965. He then wrote a number of adult books on political themes, including *The Angry Children of Malcolm X* (1966), *Look Out Whitey, Black Power's Gon' Get Your Mama!* (1968), and a book of photographs and poems entitled *The Mud of Vietnam* (1967).

In the late 1960s Lester moved to New York City, where he was the only African-American announcer at WBAI-Radio, a noncommercial station featuring alternative programming. Continuing his varied involvement in black politics, Lester followed the advice of an editor at Dial Press who suggested he branch out into writing children's books. In 1969, he published two books which came to mark his future success as a writer for young people. *To Be a Slave,* a collection of six stories based on historical fact, evolved from an oral history of slaves Lester was compiling. Runner-up for the Newbery Medal, *To Be a Slave* was acclaimed for its contributions to African-American history. "Aside from the fact that these are tremendously moving documents in themselves," wrote *Black Like Me* author John Howard Griffin in the *New York Times Book Review,* "they help to destroy the delusion that black men did not suffer as another man would in similar circumstances, a delusion that lies at the base of much racism today." Reviewing the title in *Bulletin of the Center for Children's Books,* Zena Sutherland described *To Be a Slave* as "moving and explicit," a documentation of slavery from "capture to auction, from servitude to freedom." Evelyn Geller remarked in *School Library Journal* that Lester's book "quietly lays bare the shame of American history while making slavery, suffering, and resistance part of [a] black child's heritage."

Also in 1969, Lester published his widely praised *Black Folktales,* recasting various human and animal characters from African legends and slave narratives. "Although these tales have been told before, in most of them Lester brings a fresh street-talk language ... and thus breathes new life into them," wrote John A. Williams in the *New York Times Book Review.* "It is a tribute to the universality of these tales—and Lester's ability to see it—that we are thus presented with old truths dressed for today."

During the 1970s and 1980s, Lester followed with a number of similarly acclaimed books that showed his overlapping interests in African-American history, folklore, and political themes. *The Knee-High Man and Other Tales* (1972) compiles six black folktales, including those of the famous Brer Rabbit, and brings together humorous, satirical sketches with political overtones. In the story "The Farmer and the Snake," for example, as Ethel Richard noted in the *New York Times Book Review,* "the lesson is that kindness will not change the nature of a thing—in this case, the nature of a poisonous snake to bite." With such books as *Long Journey Home* (1972), *Two Love Stories* (1972), and *This Strange New Feeling* (1982), Lester continued to explore black heritage by writing fiction rooted in African-American experience. *Long Journey Home,* a finalist for the

National Book Award, was drawn from actual events of everyday blacks during the post-Civil War Reconstruction period. "Abandoning familiar biographical territory," wrote William Loren Katz in *Book World,* "Lester seeks out the lives of footnote people, ordinary men and women who might appear only in a Brady Civil War photograph or a neglected manuscript at the Library of Congress. His tales ... are explorations of the human condition in adversity."

In addition to writing for young readers, Lester has also continued with books for adults, including his 1985 novel *Do Lord Remember Me* and his two-volume compilation *The Seventh Son,* which brings together the writings of the early black political activist W. E. B. DuBois. He has also authored two autobiographies, *All Is Well* and *Love Song,* the latter which recounts his conversion in the late 1980s to Judaism. In addition to his writing career, Lester has served as a professor since the early 1970s at the University of Massachusetts in Amherst, first as a professor of Afro-American studies, and then as a professor of Near Eastern and Judaic studies. Writing for children, however, has been a particularly rewarding area to explore aspects of his African-American heritage. "Children's literature is the one place where you can tell a story," he told Barry List in *Publishers Weekly.* "Just, straight, tell a story, and have it received as narrative without any literary garbage. I've done a fair amount of historically based fiction that would be derided as adult literature because it's not 'sophisticated.' I'm just telling a story about people's lives. In children's literature, I can do that."

Lester has continued to do so with vigor in the 1990s. His four compilations of Uncle Remus tales have taken that stock figure out of the Uncle Tom orbit and made the language accessible for today's youth. Originally compiled by the newspaperman Joel Chandler Harris between 1876 and 1918 and written in an approximation of the black dialect of the original tellers, the Brer Rabbit tales of the Uncle Remus stories have deep African roots. Folklorists have long noted similarities between the quick-witted rabbit and Anansi, the spider trickster of West Africa or Wakaima, the hare trickster of the West Coast of Africa. Lester managed to recreate these tales in a contemporary idiom without losing the bite of the original.

In *The Tales of Uncle Remus, More Tales of Uncle Remus, Further Tales of Uncle Remus,* and *The Last Tales of Uncle Remus,* Lester goes to the heart of the tales without eviscerating them. Irene Babsky, reviewing *The Tales of Uncle Remus* in *School Librarian,* noted that "the writing is a masterly combination of black oral storytelling techniques blended with a clear, direct writing style." Reviewing the second collection, *More Tales of Uncle Remus,* Mary M. Burns observed in *Horn Book* that "either of the two volumes of the Uncle Remus tales would be a major contribution to folklore for children in recent years; together they outdistance all challengers." *Kirkus Reviews* dubbed the entire four-volume production "a landmark retelling," while Betsy Hearne concluded in a review of *The Last Tales of Uncle Remus* in *Bulletin of the Center for Children's Books* that "respect is a key word here. That's what Lester shows for the largest body of African-American folklore collected in this country. You can't get any more respectful of a cultural tradition than recharging the elements that helped it survive and that affirm its kinship with other peoples of the world."

More folktales are served up in *How Many Spots Does a Leopard Have? And Other Tales,* a collection of ten African stories and two with traditional Jewish roots. Intended for children of all ages, "the stories in this collection are as rich, various, and intriguing as the titles," according to Susan Perren in *Quill & Quire.* Another African folktale, this one detailing the first murder, informs *The Man Who Knew Too Much,* a "poetic version," according to *Booklist's* Hazel Rochman. "Readers will trust this book," concluded Rochman. In *Sam and the Tigers,* Lester takes on the possibly contentious Little Black Sambo tale, and with the author's sensitive retelling readers can, according to Rayma Turton in *Magpies,* "enjoy this new version for what it is—a joyous romp with a true storyteller's pattern." Turton concluded that "no storyteller can afford to be without this book."

Retellings of a different sort are contained in Lester's award-winning writings *John Henry, Othello: A Novel,* and *Black Cowboy, Wild Horses.* Working with his long-time illustrator, Jerry Pinkney, Lester took on the legendary steel-drivin' man in *John Henry,* a tall tale that "bursts to life," according to Elizabeth Bush in *Bulletin of the Center for Children's Books.* Jack Zipes commented in the *New York Times Book Review* that "Lester's eloquent prose ... incorporates light, humorous remarks and sayings," and the book as a whole suggests "that we still have a lot to learn from folk heroes, even if they may not have existed." With *Othello,* Lester moved to Shakespeare for a retelling, resettling the Moor in London and making race a more central theme to the action. In the process he created "a wonderful achievement," according to Margaret Cole in *School Library Journal,* which "is a must for all libraries." In *Black Cowboy, Wild Horses,* Lester turned his historian's eye to the true story of Bob Lemmons, one of many unheralded slaves who became cowboys and as such helped build the West. Working again with Pinkney, Lester created a picture book "rich with simile and metaphor," according to *Booklist's* Michael Cart. "A spirit of freedom pervades the pages of this picture book," noted a reviewer for *Publishers Weekly.* "Notable for the light it sheds on a fascinating slice of Americana, this book is essential for anyone interested in the Wild West."

Another historical picture book of note is Lester's 1998 *From Slave Ship to Freedom Road,* in which he returned to his familiar themes of tracing the history and effects of slavery in America. Working with illustrator Rob Brown, Lester put into the picture book format the entire two-hundred-fifty-years of black history in America from the arrival of the first slave ships to Emancipation. "This is a powerful book, and it is an important one," commented Shirley Wilton in *School Library Journal.* Lester's powerful imagination has also fueled no less than a retelling of the Creation story, from a black point of view, in *What a Truly Cool World,* and other musings on Genesis in *When the Beginning Began.* This latter title was intended as "storytelling, not theology," according to Kathleen Beck in *Voice of Youth Advocates,* "and readers approaching it in that spirit will have a wonderful time."

Though entertainment is not what Lester sets out to do with his works, his infectious storyteller's idiom accomplishes that task as well. But his larger purpose is to educate. In his early books Lester set about such a purpose quite directly: his historical sketches and historical fiction provided readers with an inside view of the African-American experience. Much of his later work has been purposive, as well, though with books such as *John Henry,* he has attempted something new. "What children need are not role models but heroes and heroines," Lester told an audience of the New England Library Association in a speech reprinted in *Horn Book.* "A hero is one who is larger than life. Because he or she is superhuman, we are inspired to expand the boundaries of what we had thought was possible. We are inspired to attempt the impossible, and in the attempt, we become more wholly human.... The task of the hero and heroine belongs to us all. That task is to live with such exuberance that what it is to be human will be expanded until the asphyxiating concepts of race and gender will be rendered meaningless, and then we will be able to see the rainbow around the shoulders of each and every one of us, the rainbow that has been there all the while."

Works Cited

Babsky, Irene, review of *The Tales of Uncle Remus, School Librarian,* May, 1988, p. 72.

Beck, Kathleen, review of *When the Beginning Began, Voice of Youth Advocates,* June, 1999, p. 194.

Review of *Black Cowboy, Wild Horses, Publishers Weekly,* April 6, 1998, p. 77.

Burns, Mary M., review of *More Tales of Uncle Remus, Horn Book,* September-October, 1988, pp. 639-40.

Bush, Elizabeth, review of *John Henry, Bulletin of the Center for Children's Books,* October, 1994, p. 54.

Cart, Michael, review of *Black Cowboy, Wild Horses, Booklist,* May 1, 1998, p. 1522.

Cole, Margaret, review of *Othello, School Library Journal,* April, 1995, p. 154.

Foner, Eric, and Naomi Lewis, review of *Long Journey Home: Stories from Black History, New York Review of Books,* April 20, 1972, pp. 41-42.

Geller, Evelyn, "Julius Lester: Newbery Runner-Up," *School Library Journal,* May, 1969.

Griffin, John Howard, review of *To Be a Slave, New York Times Book Review,* November 3, 1968, p. 7.

Hearne, Betsy, review of *The Last Tales of Uncle Remus, Bulletin of the Center for Children's Books,* February, 1994, pp. 179-80.

Katz, William Loren, review of *Long Journey Home, Book World,* September 3, 1972, p. 9.

Review of *The Last Tales of Uncle Remus, Kirkus Reviews,* January 1, 1994, p. 70.

Lester, Julius, "The Kinds of Books We Give Our Children: Whose Nonsense?," *Publishers Weekly,* February 23, 1970, pp. 86-88.

Lester, Julius, "Black and White: An Exchange," *New York Times Book Review,* May 24, 1970, pp. 1, 34, 36, 38.

Lester, Julius, article in *Fourth Book of Junior Authors and Illustrators,* edited by Doris De Montreville and Elizabeth D. Crawford, H. W. Wilson, 1978, pp. 223-24.

Lester, Julius, "The Beechwood Staff," *Horn Book,* March-April, 1984, pp. 161-69.

Lester, Julius, "John Henry," *Horn Book,* January-February, 1996, pp. 28-31.

List, Barry, "Julius Lester," *Publishers Weekly,* February 12, 1988, pp. 67-68.

MacCann, Donnarae, "Julius Lester," *Twentieth-Century Children's Writers,* 3rd edition, edited by Tracy Chevalier, St. James Press, 1989, pp. 575-76.

Perren, Susan, review of *How Many Spots Does a Leopard Have? And Other Tales, Quill & Quire,* December, 1989, p. 24.

Richard, Ethel, review of *The Knee-High Man, and Other Tales, New York Times Book Review,* February 4, 1973, p. 8.

Rochman, Hazel, review of *The Man Who Knew Too Much, Booklist,* October 14, 1994, p. 4342.

Sutherland, Zena, review of *To Be a Slave, Bulletin of the Center for Children's Books,* April, 1969, pp. 129-30.

Turton, Rayma, review of *Sam and the Tigers, Magpies,* March, 1997, p. 27.

Williams, John A., review of *Black Folktales, New York Times Book Review,* November 9, 1969, pp. 10, 12.

Wilton, Shirley, review of *From Slave Ship to Freedom Road, School Library Journal,* February, 1998, pp. 119-20.

Zipes, Jack, "Power Rangers of Yore," *New York Times Book Review,* November 13, 1994, p. 30.

For More Information See

BOOKS

Children's Literature Review, Gale, Volume 2, 1976, Volume 41, 1997.

Lester, Julius, *Lovesong: Becoming a Jew,* Holt, 1988.

St. James Guide to Young Adult Writers, edited by Tom Pendergast and Sara Pendergast, St. James Press, 1999.

PERIODICALS

Booklist, November 1, 1995, p. 494; June 1, 1996, p. 1727; January, 1997, p. 768; February 15, 1998, p. 1009.

Bulletin of the Center for Children's Books, February, 1998, p. 212; May, 1998, p. 327.

Horn Book, September-October, 1996, p. 536; July-August, 1998, p. 477.

Kirkus Reviews, November 15, 1997, p. 1709; May 1, 1998, p. 661.

Kliatt, May, 1998, p. 14.

New York Times Book Review, November 19, 1996, p. 34.

Publishers Weekly, December 1, 1997, p. 54.

School Library Journal, November, 1997, p. 41; June 1998, p. 113; August, 1998, p. 43.

Voice of Youth Advocates, April, 1998, p. 43.*

—*Sketch by J. Sydney Jones*

*   *   *

LEVY, Barrie

Personal

Education: Received M.S.W.

Addresses

Home—California. *Agent*—c/o Seal Press, 3131 Western Ave., Ste 410, Seattle, WA 98121.

Career

Therapist, consultant, and nonfiction author.

Writings

NONFICTION

Skills for Violence-Free Relationships: Curriculum for Young People, Ages 13-18, The Coalition (Santa Monica, CA), 1984.
(Editor) *Dating Violence: Young Women in Danger,* Seal Press (Seattle, WA), 1991.
In Love and in Danger: A Teen's Guide to Breaking Free of Abusive Relationships, Seal Press, 1993.
(With Patricia Occhiuzzo Giggans) *What Parents Need to Know about Dating Violence,* Seal Press, 1995.
(With Giggans) *50 Ways to a Safer World,* Seal Press, 1997.

Sidelights

Barrie Levy is the author of several books on the physical, emotional, and sexual violence that sometimes occurs in dating. She addresses the subject for teens and parents as well as for social workers and other professionals. Drawing on cases from her own work as a therapist, Levy has illustrated the kinds of violence that are experienced by an estimated one-third of all young women, with the goal of arresting a pattern of domestic violence.

As editor of *Dating Violence: Young Women in Danger,* Levy presents research and first-person accounts for professionals who seek to intervene in abusive relationships. In her next book, *In Love and in Danger: A Teen's Guide to Breaking Free of Abusive Relationships,* she seeks to advise young women directly, with chapters that focus on identifying abusive relationships and that offer ways to initiate change. The book also invites the reader to participate by answering questions and writing about their feelings. *Voice of Youth Advocates* reviewer Suzanne Manczuk judged *In Love and in Danger* to be "one of the few nonfiction titles that speaks specifically to teens [on the subject], in teen language, and very movingly." Levy covers similar issues for parents in *What Parents Need to Know about Dating Violence*

(1995). Identifying abuse, coping methods, a safety plan, and ways to help children are included in the discussion. *Voice of Youth Advocates's* Sarah A. Hudson called the book "an eye-opening and helpful resource," while Carol R. Nelson deemed it "[i]nsightful and very readable," in *Library Journal.*

Works Cited

Hudson, Sarah A., review of *What Parents Need to Know about Dating Violence, Voice of Youth Advocates,* December, 1995, p. 336.
Manczuk, Suzanne, review of *In Love and in Danger, Voice of Youth Advocates,* August, 1993, p. 179.
Nelson, Carol R., review of *What Parents Need to Know about Dating Violence, Library Journal,* June 1, 1995, p. 150.

PERIODICALS

Booklist, August, 1993, pp. 2045-46.
Library Journal, April 15, 1991, p. 114.
Publishers Weekly, February 22, 1991, p. 216.
Wilson Library Bulletin, November, 1993, pp. 76-77.*

*   *   *

LODGE, Jo 1966-

Personal

Born April 4, 1966 in Surrey, England; daughter of Bernard (an illustrator) and Maureen (an illustrator; maiden name Rottey) Lodge; married Robert Eager (an education advisor), October 7, 1995; children: Ben, Louis. *Education:* Kingston Polytechnic, Surrey, England, B.A., 1985, B.A. and Honors Degree, 1988.

Addresses

Home—Hilva, The Street, Poynings, Brighton BN45 7AQ, England.

Career

Author and illustrator. Artwork Apparel, knitwear designer, 1989-1992; worked as a freelance knitwear designer for Next, Marks and Spencer, Saks Fifth Avenue, Scotch House, Hennes, Harvey Nichols, and Elle Magazine, 1992-94.

Writings

FOR CHILDREN

If You're Happy and You Know It, Barrons (Hauppauge, NY), 1996.
This Is the Way We Pull a Face, Bodley Head, 1996, published in the U.S. as *This Is the Way We Make a Face,* Barrons, 1996.
Patch Bakes a Cake, Campell Books, 1996.
Patch Grows Flowers, Campbell Books, 1996.
Patch Goes on Holiday, Campbell Books, 1996, published in the U.S. as *Patch Takes a Vacation,* Red Wagon (San Diego, CA), 1997.

Young readers can pull the tabs and help Patch the dog enjoy his vacation in Jo Lodge's self-illustrated board book. (*From* Patch Takes a Vacation.)

Patch Goes to the Park, Campbell Books, 1996.

Patch and His Favorite Things, Harcourt, 1996.

Patch in the Garden, Harcourt, 1996.

Patch's House, Campbell Books, 1997, published in the U.S. as *Play and Count in Patch's House,* Harcourt, 1997.

Going to Bed with Rabbit, Bodley Head, 1997, published in the U.S. as *Can You Do What Rabbit Can Do? In the Evening,* Barrons, 1997.

Getting Up with Dog, Bodley Head, 1997, published in the U.S. as *Can You Do What Dog Can Do? In the Morning,* Barrons, 1997.

Busy Farm Carousel, Campbell Books, 1998.

Hide and Seek with Duck, Barrons, 1998.

Pass the Parcel with Pig, Barrons, 1998.

Playschool, Campbell Books, 1999.

Rainbows Are Best, Bodley Head, 1999.

Bedtime Is Best, Bodley Head, 1999.

(As illustrator) *Busy Preschool: An Interactive Book With Pull Out Tabs,* edited by Toby Sherry, Dial, 1999.

Busy Farm: A Counting Book With Pull-Out Tabs, edited by Phyllis Fogelman, Dial, 1999.

Work in Progress

Going Shopping, a Carousel Book for Macmillan.

Sidelights

Jo Lodge told *SATA:* "Although I originally trained in fashion design, I have always been interested in children's books. Having both parents in the same business has been a big influence and also a great help. During a quiet period in the knitwear business, I put together some ideas and took them along to show Rod Campbell of Campbell Books. He was very interested but obviously I had much to learn. Rod kindly taught me all I know

about paper engineering, which I have found invaluable. It has been a great advantage for me to be able to do my own paper engineering.

"I am married to Rob Eager who is an education advisor for the Royal Society for the Prevention of Cruelty to Animals. We have two boys, Ben (four years) and Louis (one year). I get many of my ideas from reading, playing, and making things with the boys. Juggling my career with raising two young children takes up most of my time, but when I get the opportunity I do enjoy walking in the countryside."

For More Information See

PERIODICALS

Publishers Weekly, September 23, 1996, p. 78; September 23, 1996, p. 78; March 24, 1997, p. 85; September 29, 1997, p. 91.

*   *   *

LOGSTON, Anne 1962-

Personal

Born February 15, 1962, in Indianapolis, IN; married husband, Paul. *Education:* University of Indianapolis, Associate's degree (computer science), B.A. (English), 1984. *Hobbies and other interests:* Growing and/or cooking strange and spicy things, and I am an avid collector of anything about vampires.

Addresses

Agent—c/o Ace Books, 200 Madison Ave., New York, NY 10016.

Career

Writer. Has worked as a legal secretary.

Writings

Shadow, Ace Books (New York City), 1991.
Shadow Dance, Ace Books, 1992.
Shadow Hunt, Ace Books, 1992.
Greendaughter, Ace Books, 1993.
Dagger's Edge, Ace Books, 1994.
Dagger's Point, Ace Books, 1995.
Wild Blood, Ace Books, 1995.
Guardian's Key, Ace Books, 1996.
Firewalk, Ace Books, 1997.
Waterdance, Penguin (New York City), 1999.
Exile, Ace Books, 1999.

Work in Progress

"I am currently contracted with Berkley (Ace) for two more novels—a 'next generation' to *Firewalk,* which I'm due to turn in shortly, and a 'next generation' to *Guardian's Key.*"

Sidelights

Anne Logston has gained much success as a science fiction writer, in particular for her "Shadow" series, which depicts the adventures of a five-hundred-year-old elf. Many reviewers maintained that what distinguishes Logston's books from others in the genre is the strength and abundance of Logston's female characters.

Logston's first book, *Shadow,* introduces its title character, an ancient and mischievous elf wandering into a town ruled equally by elves and humans. Shadow herself is often cited as one of the most engaging aspects of the book. *Locus* contributor Carolyn Cushman wrote that Shadow is "unquestionably a good guy," while Stacey M. Conrad of *Kliatt* deemed the title character to be "spunky and afraid of very little." Concluding her review of *Shadow,* Cushman noted that "Logston has a definite knack with the elements that make medieval fantasies so popular."

Logston continues her chronicle of Shadow and her elfin world in other books, including *Greendaughter, Shadow Dance, Shadow Hunt, Dagger's Edge, Dagger's Point,* and *Wild Blood.* Reviewing *Shadow Hunt* in *Science Fiction Chronicle,* Don D'Ammassa praised the novel's depiction of the relationship between the two female protagonists, Shadow and Blade, "which evolves nicely as their adventures continue."

Logston also finds success in the energy of her stories. *Greendaughter* is "a fast-paced book with interesting characters, sometimes confusing," yet "never boring," said Judith H. Silverman, writing in *Kliatt.* In a later issue of *Kliatt,* Silverman observed that Logston's *Dagger's Edge* "is a good story, fast-moving and clever." *Voice of Youth Advocates* contributor Linda Palter noted that Logston's "writing is fluid and colorful."

Deirdre B. Root, praised *Wild Blood* in *Kliatt,* noting how "the two cultures, elven and human, are interesting and well described and the plot is never predictable." Again contributing to *Locus,* Carolyn Cushman lauded Logston's books about the two cultures, stating that the novels constitute a "consistently entertaining series."

For more information, see Logston's homepage on the World Wide Web at http://home.att.net/~logston.

Works Cited

D'Ammassa, Don, review of *Shadow Hunt, Science Fiction Chronicle,* June, 1992, p. 33.
Conrad, Stacey M., review of *Shadow, Kliatt,* January, 1992, p. 18.
Cushman, Carolyn, review of *Shadow, Locus,* August, 1991, pp. 27, 55.
Cushman, Carolyn, review of *Dagger's Point, Locus,* December, 1994, p. 29.
Palter, Linda, review of *Dagger's Edge, Voice of Youth Advocates,* August, 1994, p. 158.
Root, Deirdre B., review of *Wild Blood, Kliatt,* November, 1995, p. 17.
Silverman, Judith H., review of *Dagger's Edge, Kliatt,* July, 1994, p. 16.
Silverman, Judith H., review of *Greendaughter, Kliatt,* September, 1993, p. 18.

For More Information See

PERIODICALS

Kliatt, May, 1995, p. 16.
Locus, January, 1993, pp. 31; July, 1993, p. 50; April, 1994, p. 29.
Voice of Youth Advocates, June, 1992, p. 111.*

*   *   *

LOGUE, Mary 1952-

Personal

Born April 16, 1952; daughter of Robert P. (an auditor) and Ruthmary (Leirwin) Logue.

Addresses

Office—c/o Mid-List Press, 4324 12th Avenue S., Minneapolis, MN, 55407-3218. *Agent*—Jennifer Flanney, Flanney Literary, 1140 Widefield Ct., Napervielle, IL 60563 (for children's and young adult); Jane Chelius, 548 Second St., Brooklyn, NY 11215 (for adult).

Career

Poet, mystery novelist, editor, and author of children's books.

Awards, Honors

First Book of Poetry award, Mid-List Press, for *Discriminating Evidence.*

Writings

FOR CHILDREN; FICTION

The Missing Statue of Minnehaha, illustrated by Duane Krych, Child's World (Mankato, MN), 1993.
The Haunting of Hunter House, illustrated by Krych, Child's World, 1993.
Dancing with an Alien, HarperCollins, 2000.

FOR CHILDREN; NONFICTION

Forgiveness: The Story of Mahatma Gandhi, Child's World (Plymouth, MN), 1996.
Elizabeth Barrett Browning: Love, Child's World, 1996.
Trust: The Story of Helen Keller, Child's World, 1999.
Imagination: The Story of Walt Disney, Child's World, in press.

FOR ADULTS

(Editor) *The Thief of Sadness/NorHaven Poetry Collective,* illustrated by Marion Pinski et al., PLS Press (St. Paul, MN), 1979.
(Editor with Lawrence Sutin) *Believing Everything: An Anthology of New Writing,* illustrated by Lynn Weaver, Holy Cow! Press (Minneapolis, MN), 1980.
Red Lake of the Heart (mystery), Dell, 1987.
Discriminating Evidence (poetry), Mid-List Press (Denver, CO), 1990.
Still Explosion: A Laura Malloy Mystery (novel), Seal Press (Seattle, WA), 1993.
Halfway Home: A Granddaughter's Biography, Minnesota Historical Society (St. Paul, MN), 1996.
Settling: Poems, Mid-List Press (Minneapolis, MN), 1997.
Blood Country: A Clare Watkins Mystery, Walker & Co., 1999.

Sidelights

The versatile Mary Logue has established a multidimensional presence in the literary world as poet, editor of poetry anthologies, author of mystery novels for adults, and author of children's books that include nonfiction and mystery fiction. Her first publications were achieved by anthologies that she edited or co-edited. In 1979, she brought together *The Thief of Sadness,* an anthology of the NorHaven Poetry Collective in the Twin Cities area, which brought to light several new voices of mentally challenged women authors in that region. A second anthology came one year later, *Believing Everything: An Anthology of New Writing,* on which Logue worked with Lawrence Sutin. As a poet herself, Logue has authored two volumes of verse, *Discriminating Evidence,* which won a First Book of Poetry award from Mid-List Press, and *Settling,* a 1997 offering from the same publishing house. Except for the fact that Mid-List Press was located in Denver when *Discriminating Evidence* was published, all the aforementioned titles were brought out by Minnesota houses, Mid-List having moved to Minneapolis in the

Mary Logue

interim. Indeed, the same can be said of all of Logue's other books, with the exception of her adult mystery novels, *Red Lake of the Heart,* issued in 1987 by Dell of New York City, and *Still Explosion,* which was published by Seattle's Seal Press in 1993.

Still Explosion features as its detective-narrator a female journalist named Laura Malloy, who works for the *Twin Cities Times.* Only moments after Malloy has arrived at an abortion clinic to interview the director, a bomb goes off in the clinic, killing a young man who had been escorting his girlfriend to get an abortion. The young man himself is suspected of being the bomber, but Laura, doubting that story, investigates others as well. Suspects include the hard-line leader of an anti-abortion organization, his wife, his lesbian ex-wife, and the girlfriend and brother of the dead man. In the course of her protagonist's investigation, Logue finds opportunities to sketch in a brief history of abortion and of the controversy surrounding that procedure. The plot, which includes the depositing of a dead fetus on the doorstep of the bombing victim's girlfriend, builds to what Marie Kuda, a *Booklist* reviewer, called "an explosive ending."

A *Publishers Weekly* reviewer commented that Laura Malloy's investigation is "carefully constructed" so that neither Laura nor the reader can "ascertain the balance of personal and political causes behind Bobby's [the bombing's victim] death." Assessing the novel's own political stance as "emphatically pro-choice," the *Publishers Weekly* critic predicted that readers' degree of satisfaction with the book would depend largely on the extent to which they shared that outlook. A reviewer for

Library Journal, however, recommended library purchase of the volume because of its "workable prose, plot, and issue."

Among Logue's books for children are biographies of historical figures, including Victorian British poet Elizabeth Barrett Browning, Mohandas Karamchand (Mahatma) Gandhi, Helen Keller, and animator Walt Disney. Logue has also written two children's mysteries featuring a young heroine named Barb. In *The Haunting of Hunter House,* Barb glimpses a light in a vacant house and investigates the phenomenon along with two of her cousins, Burr and Smidgen. In *The Missing Statue of Minnehaha,* the setting is a summer retreat named Camp Minnehaha where Barb and Burr are junior counselors. The pair investigate the disappearance of a statuette which is the prize in the camp's annual contest.

Logue is also the author of *Halfway Home: A Granddaughter's Biography,* which the Minnesota Historical Society Press issued in 1996. It deals with the life of Logue's grandmother, Mae McNally Kirwin (1894-1961), who lived in Chokio, Minnesota, for much of her life; it is also, in the nature of things, a study of family and social life in Minnesota during the earlier part of the twentieth century.

Works Cited

Kuda, Marie, review of *Still Explosion, Booklist,* April 1, 1993, p. 1415.

Review of *Still Explosion, Library Journal,* April 1, 1993, p. 135.

Review of *Still Explosion, Publishers Weekly,* April 5, 1993, p. 68.

For More Information See

PERIODICALS

Booklist, October 1, 1999, p. 346.
Horn Book Guide, January-June, 1993, p. 301.
Kirkus Reviews, March 15, 1993, p. 335.

ON-LINE

Minnesota Center for the Book, http://www.mnbooks.org.

*   *   *

LOTTRIDGE, Celia Barker 1936-

Personal

Born April 1, 1936, in Iowa City, IA; daughter of a professor and a teacher; married a serviceman (divorced); children: one son. *Education:* Stanford University, B.A., 1957; Columbia University, M.L.S., 1959; University of Toronto, B.Ed, 1975.

Addresses

Home—42 Vermont Ave., Toronto, Ontario M6G 1X9, Canada.

Career

Writer and storyteller. Children's librarian in San Diego, CA; lower-school librarian at Dalton School, New York City; librarian in Rhode Island, 1965-72; Toronto School Board, teacher-librarian. Children's Book Store, Toronto, book buyer, 1977-90. Regina Public Library, Regina, Saskatchewan, Canada, writer-in-residence, 1991; Parent-Child Mother Goose program, director. Member of founding board, Storyteller's School of Toronto.

Awards, Honors

Mr. Christie's award in English illustration, 1989, and second runner-up, Amelia Frances Howard-Gibbon award, and Elizabeth Mrazik-Cleaver award, both 1990, all for *The Name of the Tree;* Book of the Year, Canadian Library Association, 1993, for *Ticket to Curlew.*

Writings

Gerasim and the Lion, illustrated by Joanne Page, Bright Star Bookstores (Erin, Ontario, Canada), 1979.

(With Ariadna Ochrymovych) *The Juggler,* North Winds Press (Richmond Hill, ON), 1985.

(With Susan Horner) *Prairie Dogs,* Grolier, (Toronto, ON), 1985, published with *Bighorn Sheep,* by Bill Ivy, Grolier, 1985.

(With Susan Horner) *Mice,* Grolier, 1986.

One Watermelon Seed, illustrated by Karen Patkau, Oxford University Press (Toronto, ON), 1986.

(Reteller) *The Name of the Tree: A Bantu Tale,* illustrated by Ian Wallace, Douglas & McIntyre (Toronto, ON), 1989, M. K. McElderry Books (New York, NY), 1990.

(Compiler with Alison Dickie) *Mythic Voices: Reflections in Mythology* (textbook with teacher's guide), Nelson Canada (Scarborough, ON), 1990.

Ten Small Tales, illustrated by Joanne Fitzgerald, M. K. McElderry Books, 1990, Douglas & McIntyre, 1993.

(Editor) *The American Children's Treasury,* Key Porter (Toronto, ON), 1991.

Ticket to Curlew, illustrated by Wendy Wolsak-Frith, Douglas & McIntyre, 1992, published in the U.S. as *Ticket to Canada,* Silver Burdett, 1996.

Something Might Be Hiding, illustrated by Paul Zwolak, Douglas & McIntyre, 1994.

The Wind Wagon, illustrated by Daniel Clifford, Douglas & McIntyre, 1995, Silver Burdett Press, 1995.

(Compiler) *Letters to the Wind: Classic Stories and Poems for Children,* Key Porter, 1995.

Wings to Fly, illustrations by Mary Jane Gerber, Douglas & McIntyre, 1997.

(Adaptor) Sandra Carpenter-Davis, compiler, *Bounce Me, Tickle Me, Hug Me: Lap Rhymes and Play Rhymes from around the World,* Parent-Child Mother Goose Program (Toronto, ON), 1997.

(Reteller) *Music for the Tsar of the Sea: A Russian Wonder Tale,* Groundwood Books (Toronto, ON), 1998.

Several of Lottridge's books have been translated into French and published in braille editions.

Adaptations

The Juggler was adapted as a sound recording, CNIB (Toronto, ON), 1987; *Mythic Voices* was adapted as a sound recording, Alberta Education (Edmonton, Alberta, Canada), 1992; *Ticket to Curlew* was adapted as a sound recording, Library Services Branch of British Columbia (Vancouver, BC), 1994.

Sidelights

Born in the United States in the state of Iowa, Celia Barker Lottridge writes novels that reflect her adopted country of Canada, where she settled permanently as an adult. Among the works she has published for children are the picture books *One Watermelon Seed* and *The Name of the Tree,* and the juvenile novel *The Wind Wagon.* She has also written longer novels *Ticket to Curlew* and *Wings to Fly* that recount life in rural Canada at the turn of the twentieth century. "Lottridge is particularly adept at evoking time and place," noted Jennifer Sullivan in *Canadian Review of Materials.* Sullivan also praised *Wings to Fly* for the inclusion of "independent and resourceful women."

Born in Iowa City in 1936, Lottridge and her family moved frequently due to her father's transient career as a college professor, and by the age of twelve she could count seven towns in the United States that she had, at one time or another, called home. "One thing [the moves] did was turn me into an avid reader," Lottridge later recalled to Dave Jenkinson in *Canadian Review of Materials.* "I gave up really working at making friends when I was going on ten, but books were always there, so reading, and the people in books, were very important to me." While explaining that her family's constant moves prevented her from maintaining close friendships

with other children her age, Lottridge also noted that it broadened her perspective on people and places.

After graduating from high school, Lottridge attended Stanford University and graduated with a degree in modern European history in 1957. Two years later, she earned her master of library science degree at Columbia University. Married to a man in the U.S. Navy, she soon found herself on the road again—this time in San Diego, where she got a job as a children's librarian before transferring to a library position in a private school in New York City when her husband's career brought the couple back to the East Coast. Lottridge and her husband eventually divorced in the early 1970s, leaving her with the decision of where she and her six-year-old son should permanently settle. A visit to her brother in Toronto helped her on this score, and mother and son soon found themselves living in a new country.

In Toronto, Lottridge added some more qualifications to her resume by becoming an accredited teacher-librarian. She worked for the Toronto School Board before being laid off after only a year due to downsizing. But her background in books gave her an easy in at a local bookstore, and Lottridge was quickly promoted to book buyer. After a few years she began to combine her work at the store with storytelling and writing. Her first published work, *Gerasim and the Lion,* was released in 1979.

Lottridge began a serious commitment to writing for children during the mid-1980s, several years after helping to form the Storyteller's School of Toronto to promote storytelling in the city's schools. Among her first works were several nature books, including *Mice* and *Prairie Dogs,* as well as adaptations of foreign-language folk tales into fluid narrations that would be

10　They picked ten watermelons, big and green.　　　　And twenty pumpkins, glowing orange.　**20**

In her counting book for young children, Celia Barker Lottridge follows two youngsters through the process of planting a garden and harvesting the crop. (From One Watermelon Seed, *illustrated by Karen Patkau.)*

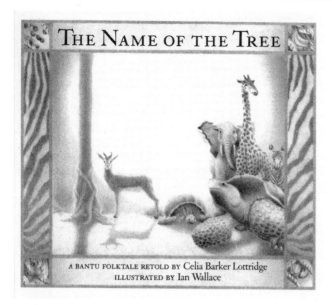

Lottridge retells a Bantu folktale in which several animals attempt to acquire the juicy fruit of an inaccessible tree during a drought. (Cover illustration by Ian Wallace.)

enjoyable to English-speaking readers. Several of these works, undertaken to supplement her income as a single parent, were published under a pseudonym. *The Name of the Tree* would be the first book where, as the author later recalled in her interview, "I just said, 'I'll write this book myself.'" The story, which had its seeds in a tale she recalled from her own childhood, focuses on Africa during a time when a lack of rain causes animals to search for a new source of water. Full of much-needed liquid, the fruit of a tall tree would suffice, but it could only be had if the animals formally request the tree to release its fruit. To do this they must learn the tree's name.

Quill & Quire contributor Michele Landsberg had lavish praise for *The Name of the Tree,* declaring: "Lottridge's subtlety and skill as a storyteller reverberate on every page of this flowing narrative; its artful simplicity and freshness make it a joy to read aloud." Landsberg further commended Lottridge's use of language, noting that she "tells the story with delectable rhythm, just the right amount of repetition, gentle suspense, and deftly underplayed humor."

Other books for young children that have their basis in spoken stories are *Something Must Be Hiding,* about moving to a new town and coping with feelings of not fitting in, and *Ten Small Tales,* a collection of folk tales Lottridge adapted from those told to youngsters during her storytelling program. "I'm mainly interested in putting into print stories that aren't already easily available and usually ones that I've told a lot so that I have a real feeling for the story," Lottridge explained in her interview. *Ten Small Tales* includes several lesser-known folktales such as a Malaysian tiger story and a Khanti fairy tale of a mouse sailing in a walnut shell—

which *Horn Book* critic Sarah Ellis noted would be "welcome in a world that contains too many lush editions of 'Goldilocks.'"

Like many of her works, *Ten Small Tales* demonstrates Lottridge's knack for storytelling. Julie Corsaro declared in her *Booklist* appraisal of the collection that "Lottridge knows what little ones like in their folklore: simple and direct storylines, rhythmic rhyme and repetition ... plenty of action, and a reassuring ending." And according to a commentator for *Kirkus Reviews,* Lottridge's "fresh, simple renditions are beautifully paced and full of the kind of nuanced repetitions that build suspense and invite participation."

During 1991, Lottridge had the opportunity to expand her career as a writer when she was awarded a one-year stint as writer-in-residence at the public library in Regina, Saskatchewan. "Getting that writer-in-residence position probably made more difference to my writing than almost anything else," the author recalled in her interview. "It enabled me to expand and move on." Indeed, it was during that time that Lottridge began what

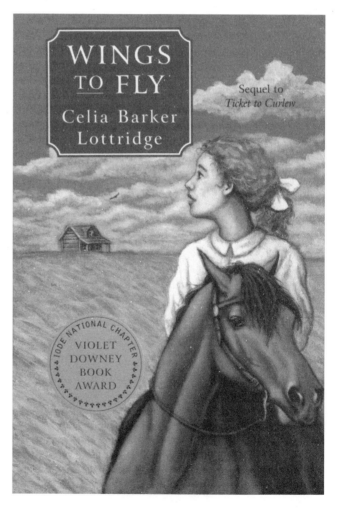

Set in 1918, Lottridge's novel follows twelve-year-old Josie's attempts to adjust to lonely life on the prairie and her fascination with the exploits of a daring female pilot. (Cover illustration by Mary Jane Gerber.)

would become her award-winning novel, *Ticket to Curlew.* The book, which was published for U.S. children as *Ticket to Canada,* tells the story of Sam Ferrier, a pre-teen growing up in the Alberta prairie around the turn of the twentieth century. Based on Lottridge's father's memories of seven of his teen years spent on an Alberta farm, the novel brings to life an era where things moved at a much slower pace, where changes occurred less frequently. "For children," Lottridge noted in her interview, "I think that what brings historical fiction alive is a character in the book they feel akin to or have empathy with. Then they can experience the historical part of it. They're not just reading it as: 'Well this happened here back then.' "

Lottridge would follow *Ticket to Curlew* with *Wings to Fly,* published in 1997. In this novel, which takes place in 1918, Lottridge follows Sam's younger sister, twelve-year-old Josie, as she tries to adjust to the lonely life on the prairie. When a British couple named Mr. and Mrs. Graham move into a nearby sod house, Josie's hopes of finding a friend rise when she discovers that the Grahams have a daughter, Margaret, who is Josie's age. Unfortunately, Margaret seems less than friendly, leaving Josie hurt and confused, until her imagination is captured by the exploits of a daring female pilot. "In *Wings to Fly,* the rigors of prairie life are made real," Jennifer Sullivan declared in *Canadian Review of Materials,* "from the influenza epidemic and winter storms that ravage the small community, to the patriarchal society that confines women to the home." The critic also praised the novel for depicting the coming-of-age of its young protagonist and for "painting an interesting picture of a society on the verge of reform" following World War I. *Quill & Quire* reviewer Barbara Greenwood averred that with *Wings to Fly,* readers "will gain a multi-layered sense of Canadian society in 1918." Greenwood also called Lottridge's story "appealing" and "well-written" and her characters "fully developed," concluding that "the situations ... will keep readers turning the pages."

Continuing to share her imagination and talents as a storyteller with children in Canada, Lottridge also has plans for more books, including several short chapter books for beginning readers as well as a third novel, again based on the exploits of the Ferrier family. "I have a lot of ideas," she admitted. "I still have more ideas than time."

Works Cited

Corsaro, Julie, review of *Ten Small Tales, Booklist,* March 15, 1994, p. 1368.

Ellis, Sarah, review of *Ten Small Tales, Horn Book,* January-February, 1994, pp. 112-14.

Greenwood, Barbara, review of *Wings to Fly, Quill & Quire,* June, 1997, p. 66.

Jenkinson, Dave, "CM Magazine Profile: Celia Lottridge," in *Canadian Review of Materials* online, http://www.umanitoba.ca/cm/profiles/lottridge.html (June 4, 1999).

Landsberg, Michele, review of *The Name of the Tree, Quill & Quire,* October, 1989, p. 13.

Sullivan, Jennifer, review of *Wings to Fly, Canadian Review of Materials* online, http://www.umanitoba.ca/cm/vol4/no1/wingstofly.html (January 16, 1998).

Review of *Ten Small Tales, Kirkus Reviews,* April 1, 1994, pp. 481-82.

For More Information See

PERIODICALS

Booklist, February 1, 1996, p. 932; August, 1996, p. 1908; January 1, 1999, p. 882.

Canadian Book Review Annual, 1997, p. 516.

Canadian Children's Literature, vol. 47 (1987), p. 96; spring 1996, p. 45.

Canadian Review of Materials, January, 1988, p. 7; November, 1994, p. 208.

Five Owls, May-June, 1990, p. 85.

Horn Book, March, 1990, p. 85; January, 1994, p. 112.

Junior Bookshelf, August, 1987, p. 164.

Quill and Quire, July, 1980, p. 57; December, 1985, p. 27; June, 1986, p. 28; October, 1993, p. 37; June, 1995, p. 58.

Publishers Weekly, February 28, 1994, p. 88.

School Librarian, May, 1988, p. 53.

School Library Journal, March, 1990, p. 209; June, 1994, p. 122; June, 1996, p. 104; August, 1995, p. 125.

Times Educational Supplement, August 21, 1987, p. 17.

*   *   *

LURIE, Alison 1926-

Personal

Born September 3, 1926, in Chicago, IL; daughter of Harry (a social-work executive) and Bernice (maiden name, Stewart) Lurie; married Jonathan Peale Bishop (a professor), September 10, 1948 (divorced, 1985); married Edward Hower (a writer), May 10, 1996; children: John, Jeremy, Joshua. *Education:* Radcliffe College, A.B., 1947.

Addresses

Office—Department of English, Cornell University, Ithaca, NY 14853.

Career

Author. Cornell University, Ithaca, NY, lecturer, 1969-73, associate professor, 1973-76, professor of English, 1976—, Frederic J. Whiton Professor of American Literature, 1989—. Has also worked as a ghostwriter and librarian.

Awards, Honors

Yaddo Foundation Fellow, 1963, 1964, 1966; Guggenheim grant, 1965-66; Rockefeller Foundation grant, 1967-68; New York State Cultural Council Foundation grant, 1972-73; American Academy of Arts and Letters

Alison Lurie

award in literature, 1978; American Book Award nomination in fiction, 1984, nomination for best work of fiction, National Book Critics Circle Award, 1984, and Pulitzer Prize in fiction, 1985, all for *Foreign Affairs;* runner-up, Children's Literature Association Excellence in Criticism, for "E. Nesbit: Riding the Wave of the Future"; Radcliffe College Alumnae Recognition Award, 1987; Prix Femina Etranger, 1989.

Writings

FOR CHILDREN

The Heavenly Zoo, illustrated by Monika Beisner, Farrar, Straus, 1980.
Clever Gretchen and Other Forgotten Folk Tales, illustrated by Margot Tomes, Crowell, 1980.
Fabulous Beasts, illustrated by Monika Beisner, Farrar, Straus, 1981.
The Black Geese: A Baba Yaga Story from Russia, illustrated by Jessica Souhami, DK Publishers, 1999.

NOVELS

Love and Friendship, Macmillan, 1962, Holt, 1997.
The Nowhere City, Coward, 1965, Holt, 1997.
Imaginary Friends, Coward, 1967, Holt, 1998.
Real People, Random House, 1969, Holt, 1998.
The War between the Tates, Random House, 1974.
Only Children, Random House, 1979.

Foreign Affairs, Random House, 1984.
The Truth about Lorin Jones, Little, Brown, 1988.
The Last Resort, Holt, 1998.

OTHER

V. R. Lang: A Memoir, privately printed, 1959.
V. R. Lang: Poems and Plays, Random House, 1974.
The Language of Clothes (nonfiction), Random House, 1981, Bloomsbury, 1992.
Don't Tell the Grown-Ups: Subversive Children's Literature (nonfiction), Little, Brown, 1990.
(Editor) *The Oxford Book of Modern Fairy Tales,* Oxford Univesity Press, 1993.
Women and Ghosts (short stories), Doubleday, 1994.
(Editor) *American Fairy Tales,* Hyperion, 1998.
(Editor) Frances Hodgson Burnett, *The Secret Garden,* Penguin Books, 1999.

Also editor, with Justin G. Schiller, of "Classics of Children's Literature, 1631-1932" series, Garland Publishing, and author of preface to *American Fairy Tales,* Frances Hodgson Burnett's *The Secret Garden,* and of an abridgement of James M. Barrie's *Peter Pan.* Contributor of articles and reviews to periodicals, including *New York Review of Books, New York Times Book Review, New Statesman,* and *New Review.*

Adaptations

Imaginary Friends, The War between the Tates, and *Foreign Affairs* were adapted for television.

Sidelights

Alison Lurie is an award-winning author of novels and nonfiction for adults who has also turned her hand to children's books. Known for her comedy and social satire as a novelist, Lurie brings these same traits to play in such works as *The Heavenly Zoo, Clever Gretchen and Other Forgotten Folk Tales, Fabulous Beasts,* and *The Black Geese,* books specifically written for the juvenile audience. Many reviewers also recommend some of her adult titles for YA readers, in particular her Pulitzer Prize-winning novel, *Foreign Affairs,* a book which has as one of its major themes a discussion of children's literature. Lurie, herself a professor of English with a specialty in children's literature, has interesting things to say about the genre. In her 1990 nonfiction work, *Don't Tell the Grown-Ups,* Lurie examines the subversive nature of some of the more powerful books written for young readers. "I think we should ... take children's literature seriously," Lurie wrote, "because it is sometimes subversive; because its values are not always those of the conventional adult world.... The great subversive works of children's literature suggest that there are other views of human life besides those of the shopping mall and the corporation. They mock current assumptions and express the imaginative, unconventional, noncommercial view of the world in its simplest and purest form...."

Born in Chicago, Illinois, Lurie grew up in Westchester, New York, where the family moved just before Lurie started school. It is no matter of serendipity that Lurie later went into academe and that her adult writings generally have an academic setting and theme. Both parents encouraged an intellectual outlook; her father was a sociology professor who became a welfare administrator, and her mother was at one time a journalist. Lacking in coordination and sports ability as a child, Lurie turned naturally to books and the imagination. "I was encouraged to be creative past the usual age because I didn't have much else going for me," Lurie once noted in an article for the *New York Times Book Review.* "I was a skinny, plain, odd-looking little girl." From an early age, Lurie reveled in making up stories and poems.

As a teenager, her favorite authors were Charles Dickens, Jane Austen, and E. Nesbit. While attending college at Radcliffe, Lurie sold three poems and a short story, launching her professional writing career. At Radcliffe too, she met a different kind of people than those she had encountered in Westchester, and began to feel accepted for whom she was. Male attention also finally came her way, though Lurie, like most Radcliffe

Lurie outlines the habits and characteristics of strange birds and beasts, including the unicorn, griffin, and others, all thought to inhabit the earth at one time. (Cover illustration by Monika Beisner.)

students, felt a poor country cousin to the men of Harvard with whom the college was affiliated at the time. But there were still distinct advantages to such an affiliation, not the least of which were the shared professors. Lurie studied everything from folktales to cartography during her four years, and received a fine education in literature for someone determined to become a writer. During her senior year she attended the fiction seminar held by Albert Guerard at Harvard; among other class members were Alice Adams, John Hawkes, and Robert Crichton.

Upon graduation in 1947, Lurie worked as a manuscript reader at Oxford University Press, then in 1948 she married Jonathan Peale Bishop, whom she had met at college. Over the next ten years, Lurie twice tried to abandon writing and settle into being the perfect 1950s housewife, making children, home, and husband her only priorities. Twice she failed in this. Unpublished manuscripts piled up alongside her children's diapers. "I passed in public as a normal woman, wife and mother," she wrote in the *New York Times Book Review,* "but inside I was still peculiar, skewed, maybe even wicked or crazy." She still wanted most of all to be a professional writer.

In 1959 she privately printed a monograph on the writer V. R. Lang; in 1962 her first novel, *Love and Friendship,* was published by Macmillan. Throughout the 1960s she was awarded various fellowships to help with her writing; in 1969 she joined the faculty of Cornell University. By this time she had published four adult novels, all of them well-received and dealing with many of the same characters from one book to the next. Each book was a comedy of manners about people in academe, many of them located at Convers College in New England or at Corinth College in upstate New York, which seems to be a stand-in for Lurie's own Cornell University. Love and friendship in marriage is a theme explored in Lurie's first novel, and also in one of her most popular novels, *The War between the Tates,* in which a seemingly perfect academic couple has their marriage rocked when the husband, Brian, impregnates one of his students. The Tates' relationship is beset by the antics of rebellious teenage children and by Brian's sense of failure in his career as middle age approaches. His affair forces the Tates to look at themselves with new eyes, and attempt to find some peace in their marriage. Set amidst the social unrest of the late 1960s, the novel also offers an ironic glimpse of the days of student rebellion, nascent feminism, the drug culture, and religious cults. Doris Grumbach, reviewing the novel in *Washington Post Book World,* noted that Lurie "has taken a set of ordinary characters, or at least not exceptional ones, submitted them to the strains and battles of time, sex, legal alliances, generation gaps, politics and work: all the ingredients of a popular novel. But her sensibility and talent are so superior that she has given us an artistic work, which every one will read because it is 'common' to us all, but which some will perceive to have the crafted look and feel of a first-rate work."

The Black Geese
A Baba Yaga Story from Russia

Retold by Alison Lurie
Illustrated by Jessica Souhami

Aided by her black geese, Elena sets out to rescue her little brother, who has been kidnaped by the witch Baba Yaga in Lurie's retelling of the Russian folktale. (Cover illustration by Jessica Souhami and Paul McAlinden.)

Only Children, another adult novel, reprises these same themes, but this time views them through the eyes of two eight-year-old girls. Set on a Depression-era farm on one Fourth of July, the novel brings to the fore Lurie's own interests in children's literature and in gender discrimination. Characters in Lurie's Pulitzer Prize novel *Foreign Affairs* include fifty-four-year-old Vinnie Miner, female professor of English with a specialty in children's literature; a Southern businessman whom she meets on a trans-Atlantic flight; a young American faculty member at a London university; and an aristocratic English television actress. The story centers on Vinnie, who, while on sabbatical leave in London, learns far more about love than she does about the folk-rhymes of schoolchildren. Some reviewers found elements of fairy tale in the novel, especially in the unlikely romance between the educated Vinnie and the retired waste-disposal engineer, Chuck Mumpson. The recipient of prestigious awards and nominations, *Foreign Affairs* brought Lurie's name to the attention of literary America. Among a long list of other reasons why young adults should read the novel, Margaret Meek of *School Librarian* included its high literary quality. "Above all," Meek wrote, "to encounter this skilled narration and really fine-honed surface text is to discover the modern

novel before leaving school and surrendering to the blatantly banal."

Though she has continued to write adult novels, Lurie has also devoted time to children's literature. The theme of feminism so often examined in her novels also finds a treatment in one of Lurie's first books for young readers, *Clever Gretchen and Other Forgotten Folk Tales,* in which Lurie presents women in a positive light. A reviewer for *The Junior Bookshelf* noted that all the stories "show women in the dominant roles: quick-witted, shrewd, adventurous, enduring." Lurie brought together some little known and other popular tales for her collection, including "Clever Gretchen," "Manka and the Judge," "The Black Geese," "Mizilca," "The Baker's Daughter," and many more tales from Grimm, Afanase, Ashbjornsen, and Jacobs. Margery Fisher, reviewing the book in *Growing Point,* called it a "fashionable collection ... retold in a fluent colloquial style suitable for reading aloud or story-telling."

Other early children's works from Lurie include *The Heavenly Zoo* and *Fabulous Beasts,* both catalogues of animals, celestial and mythical. The former title looks at the stories behind sixteen constellations and how they got their names, according to stories from ancient Greece, Babylon, Egypt, Sumeria, the Balkans, Norway, Indonesia, and the Bible. Lurie teamed up with British illustrator Monika Beisner on *The Heavenly Zoo* as well as on *Fabulous Beasts,* a look at the habits and characteristics of strange birds and beasts, including the unicorn, griffin, phoenix, and basilisk, all thought at one time to inhabit various regions of the earth. A reviewer for *School Library Journal* felt that "Beisner and Lurie have produced a fabulous beast themselves," while a *Publishers Weekly* contributor noted that "Beisner's fabulous paintings in glorious colors illustrate Lurie's splendid tales of mythical animals, creatures immortalized in legends kept alive in remote parts of the globe."

In 1993 Lurie turned an editorial hand to *The Oxford Book of Modern Fairy Tales,* a "delightful volume," according to *School Library Journal* critic Cathy Chauvette, "full of old favorites and some priceless new gems." Chauvette concluded that the collection "is first rate." Donna L. Scanlon observed in *Kliatt* that "[f]orty tales spanning 150 years make up this celebration of the literary fairy tale," and that "Lurie's insightful and lucid introduction unifies the collection and should not be skipped." *Booklist's* Ray Olson dubbed the collection "a winner." Another such winner is the picture-book retelling of a Baba Yaga tale, *The Black Geese.* Again, a strong female protagonist is at the heart of this Russian folktale in which the witch Baba Yaga, aided by her black geese, makes off with Elena's little brother while their parents are away. Elena sets out to rescue the child, enlisting the aid of a fish, a squirrel, and a mouse, and is able to bring her brother home just before the return of her parents. "Here's one well-known novelist for adults who can summon exactly the right voice for a tale for the youngest children: clean, clear, flowing easily and directly from one thought to the next," commented *Horn Book* reviewer Joanna Rudge Long, who concluded that the book was "a winner of a story." *Booklist* critic Ellen Mandel declared that Lurie's retelling was a "standout for storytelling as for one-on-one sharing."

Interviewed by Larry Van Dyne of the *Chronicle Review of Higher Education,* Lurie outlined why she enjoys writing for children and why she is involved in the academic pursuit of children's literature: "Children— almost like foreigners—sometimes see things because they don't have a stake in everything being respectable or correct. They're not affected by the grown-up reasons for doing things. Adults go to a political speech and see a man discussing this issue and that issue. Children go to the same speech and think: 'There's a man standing up in front of all these other people shouting and waving his arms.'" In her study of children's literature, *Don't Tell the Grown-Ups,* Lurie gives further oblique reasons for her interest in children's literatre: "There exists in our world an unusual, partly savage tribe, ancient and widely distributed, yet until recently little studied by anthropologists or historians. All of us were at one time members of this tribe; we knew its customs, manners, and rituals, its folklore and sacred texts. I refer, of course, to children."

Works Cited

Chauvette, Cathy, review of *The Oxford Book of Modern Fairy Tales, School Library Journal,* May, 1994, p. 146.

Review of *Clever Gretchen and Other Forgotten Folk Tales, Junior Bookshelf,* June, 1990, pp. 87-88.

Review of *Fabulous Beasts, Publishers Weekly,* November 27, 1981, p. 87.

Review of *Fabulous Beasts, School Library Journal,* January, 1982, p. 79.

Fisher, Margery, review of *Clever Gretchen and Other Forgotten Folk Tales, Growing Point,* July, 1990, p. 5362.

Grumbach, Doris, review of *The War between the Tates, Washington Post Book World,* August 1, 1974, p. 1.

Long, Joanna Rudge, review of *The Black Geese: A Baba Yaga Story from Russia, Horn Book,* May-June, 1999, pp. 343-44.

Lurie, Alison, *Don't Tell the Grown-Ups: Subversive Children's Literature,* Little, Brown, 1990, pp. ix, x.

Lurie, "Nobody Asked Me to Write a Novel," *New York Times Book Review,* June 6, 1982.

Don't Tell the Grown-Ups

The Subversive Power of Children's Literature

"ILLUMINATING...A THOROUGHLY ABSORBING BOOK." —Rosellen Brown, *New York Times Book Review*

ALISON LURIE

Lurie's study examines the subversive nature of some of the more powerful works for children. (Cover photo by Arthur Tess.)

Mandel, Ellen, review of *The Black Geese: A Baba Yaga Story from Russia, Booklist,* June 1, 1999.

Meek, Margaret, review of *Foreign Affairs, School Librarian,* September, 1985, p. 284.

Olson, Ray, review of *The Oxford Book of Modern Fairy Tales, Booklist,* May 1, 1993, p. 1572.

Scanlon, Donna L., review of *The Oxford Book of Modern Fairy Tales, Kliatt,* January, 1995, pp. 16-17.

Van Dyne, Larry, "Exploring the Worlds of Novelist Alison Lurie," *Chronicle Review of Higher Education,* April 30, 1979.

For More Information See

BOOKS

Contemporary Literary Criticism, Volume 39, Gale, 1986.

Costa, Richard Hauer, *Alison Lurie,* Twayne, 1992.

Great Women Writers, edited by Frank N. Magill, Holt, 1994.

PERIODICALS

Booklist, March 15, 1980, p. 1060; July 15, 1980, p. 1676; June 1, 1983, p. 1283; March 15, 1990, p. 1411.

Horn Book, March-April, 1980, p. 180; March-April, 1982, p. 182; May-June, 1990, p. 364.

Los Angeles Times Book Review, October 3, 1993, p. 1.

New York Times Book Review, March 11, 1990, p. 13; July 26, 1998, p. 28.

School Library Journal, June, 1999, p. 118.

Times Educational Supplement, June 8, 1990, p. B10; August 27, 1993, p. 17.

—*Sketch by J. Sydney Jones*

M

MARUKI, Toshi 1912-

Personal

Born Toshi Akamatsu in Chippubetsu, Hokkaido, Japan, in 1912; married Iri Maruki (an artist), in 1941. *Education:* Joshi Bijutsu Art College, Tokyo, completed four-year course of study in Western art.

Career

Artist, author. Substitute teacher, Ichikawa Elementary School, Chiba, Japan, in the early 1930s; private tutor, 1937; began exhibiting her art work in 1938. *Exhibitions:* Include solo shows and exhibition of paintings done with husband Iri Maruki throughout the world.

Awards, Honors

Sekai Heiwa Bunka Sho World Peace and Culture Prize, World Peace Council, 1953, for the Hiroshima Panels; Jane Addams Children's Book Award from the Jane Addams Peace Association, 1983, Mildred L. Batchelder Award, American Library Association, 1983, Ehon Nippon Taisho, the Japan Picture Book Grand Prize, Honor Book, *Boston Globe-Horn Book* Awards, 1983, and Notable Book, American Library Association, 1982, all for *Hiroshima No Pika;* honorary doctoral degree in fine arts from Massachusetts College of Art in Boston, 1988.

Writings

Hiroshima No Pika (self-illustrated picture book), Lothrop, Lee & Shepard, 1980.
(With Iri Maruki) *Genbaku no zu: Kyodo seisaku Maruki Iri, Maruki Toshi* (title means "The Hiroshima Panels: Joint Works of Iri Maruki and Toshi Maruki), 1972, revised edition, Hatsubaimoto Komine Shoten (Tokyo), 1983.
(With Iri Maruki) *The Hiroshima Murals: The Art of Iri Maruki and Toshi Maruki,* edited by John W. Dower and John Junkerman, Kodansha International, 1985.

OTHER

(Illustrator) Haruko Shogenji, *The Rainbow Deer: A Story from the Uji Miscellany,* translated by Ann Herring, Gakken (Tokyo), 1973.

Sidelights

Toshi Maruki is a Japanese artist whose best-known works express and extend her lifelong commitment to total nuclear disarmament. Maruki knew from early childhood that she wanted to be an artist and studied the western style of painting at the Joshi Bijutsu Art College in Tokyo in the 1930s. The early influence of Gauguin took her to the islands of the South Pacific and she returned to Tokyo with the intention of earning enough money to buy one of the region's tiny islands. She showed her work in solo exhibitions in Tokyo and joined the Bijutsu Bunka Kyokai Art Association. In 1941, she married fellow artist Iri Maruki, with whom she would work, travel, and be politically active, within and without the Japanese Communist Party from which they were expelled in 1964. When the United States dropped an atomic bomb on Hiroshima in 1945, Maruki and her husband traveled there to help the victims, staying with her husband's family. The horrifying experience of living in the devastated city, amongst piles of dead bodies and continuing radioactive fallout, was pivotal for the Marukis. Together they created the Hiroshima Panels which, since their completion in 1955, have been exhibited all over the world, and in 1967 were installed in the Maruki Gallery for the Hiroshima Panels in Higashimatsuyama, Saitama, Japan. Maruki began to paint using the tools of the traditional Japanese artist, and traveled to Europe in the 1970s to research a series of sketches entitled Auschwitz, which were exhibited at the Nagai Gallery in 1977. Other artistic subjects taken up in ensuing years include the battle of Okinawa, the atomic holocaust at Nagasaki, and the mercury poisoning of citizens in Minamata from industrial waste.

Maruki is best known in the United States for *Hiroshima No Pika,* a picture book rendition of the events at Hiroshima just before, during, and after the atomic bomb was dropped. Using a simple, third-person narrative and powerful, expressionistic illustrations, Maruki reenacts one family's true-life experiences on and after August 6, 1945. The story centers on seven-year-old Mii and her parents, who are eating breakfast when the bomb hits. Mii's mother rescues her father from the firestorm and the three escape to an island before returning to the bombed out city. Mii's father dies from radiation poisoning and Mii stops growing because of the radiation. Years later, her mother continues to find shards of glass that had been imbedded in her scalp during the blast and are gradually working their way back to the surface. By relating graphic, troubling details in a calm, even tone, Maruki gives the reader an intimate knowledge of the tragedy and destruction that resulted from the bomb and its fallout. "The balance of small examples—a swallow hopping by because its wings are too burnt to fly—with historical description of a city laid waste is perfectly maintained," explained Betsy Hearne in *Booklist*.

Reviewers debated the age of the book's intended audience and the context in which children should be exposed to *Hiroshima No Pika*. For some, Maruki's text, which ends with the positive assertion that such a tragedy will never again happen if an atomic bomb is never dropped again, is not explicitly hopeful enough to reassure younger readers. Other reviewers contend that Maruki's non-representational style of painting and inclusion of hard-to-imagine statistics in the text regarding the size of the explosion and the amount of devastation it wrought would distance older children in particular, allowing them to imagine Hiroshima as a myth about a faraway place and time rather than a modern reality. However, still other observers contend that in *Hiroshima No Pika* Maruki gives her readers an accurate picture of historical interest and personal import in a manner both poignant and compelling. "This is a painful book," remarked Hearne, adding: "It is also an extremely important book that should be bought and discussed with children in homes, schools, and libraries." *Children's Literature Association Quarterly* contributor Hamida Bosmajian similarly addressed this issue: "I contend that if such literary works are shared within a context where youngsters can voice their concerns and where adults are ready to engage in dialogue rather than diatribe, rationalization, and assuagement, they cannot but be therapeutic. They define and thereby set limits to the anxieties of young readers."

Works Cited

Bosmajian, Hamida, "Nightmares of History—the Outer Limits of Children's Literature," in *Children's Literature Association Quarterly,* winter, 1983, pp. 20-22.
Hearne, Betsy, review of *Hiroshima No Pika, Booklist,* October 1, 1982, p. 201.

For More Information See

BOOKS

Children's Literature Review, Volume 19, Gale, 1990, pp. 132-35.

Sixth Book of Junior Authors and Illustrators, Wilson, 1989, pp. 189-91.

PERIODICALS

New York Times Book Review, October 10, 1982, p. 24.
School Library Journal, August, 1982, p. 119.
Times Educational Supplement, January 13, 1984, p. 37.*

*   *   *

MARX, Patricia Windschill 1948- (Trish Marx)

Personal

Born April 24, 1948, in St. Paul, MN; daughter of Erwin "Red" (a CPA) and Jean (an artist; maiden name, Simser) Windschill; married Owen C. Marx (an attorney), August 1, 1971; children: Patrick Cox, Molly Simser, Annie Windschill. *Education:* College of St. Catherine, B.A., (journalism), 1970; Washington Montessori Institute, Montessori Education Degree, 1971; University of Minnesota, M.A., (journalism and mass communication), 1990. *Politics:* "I try—but I am really apolitical." *Religion:* "Catholic but endorse all religions."

Addresses

Home—129 E. 69th St., #6C, New York, NY 10021. *Office*—New York Society Library. *E-mail*—PMarx 34351@aol.com.

Patricia Windschill Marx

Career

Author and editor. Condrell School, Bethesda, MD, Montessori teacher, 1972-73; Montessori Foundation of Minnesota, St. Paul, MN, teacher, 1973-74; United Nations Montessori School, New York, NY, 1974-75; Lucas-Evans Books (book packager), New York, NY, editor, 1993-94; Simon & Schuster, Parsippany, NJ, editorial assistant, 1997-99; MacMillan Reference USA, New York City, copyeditor, 1998-99; Scholastic, Inc., New York City, project job writer, 1999.

Participant in the Learning Readers division of the New York City School Volunteer Program; Oral History Association of Minnesota (panel member); New Media Repertory Company (board member); Birthday Club (co-founder); guest lecturer. *Member:* Author's Guild, PEN, New York Society Library.

Awards, Honors

Notable Children's Book in the Field of Social Studies, National Council for Social Studies-Children's Book Council, for *Echoes of the Second World War.*

Writings

Echoes of the Second World War, Macdonald, 1989.

Hanna's Cold Winter, illustrated by Barbara Knutson, Carolrhoda Books, 1993.

(With Dorita Beh-Eger) *I Heal: The Story of the Children of Chernobyl in Cuba,* illustrated by Cindy Karp, Lerner Publications, 1996.

(With Sandra Joseph Nunez) *And Justice for All: The Legal Rights of Young People,* Millbrook, 1997.

A Beautiful Obsession: The Life and Times of Jeannette Rankin, Lerner Publications, 2000.

One Boy From Kosovo, illustrated by Cindy Karp, Harper-Collins, 2000.

Work in Progress

More picture books based on true events; some nonfiction about children of war.

Sidelights

Patricia Windschill Marx told *SATA:* "I signed my first book contract on my fortieth birthday. I had sent off a manuscript to five publishers not knowing that simultaneous submissions were not the way to an editor's heart. What did I know? I was an excited 'author' with an idea that put fire in my belly. In a week, I had heard from two publishers—MacDonald Books and Macmillan. I had first answered the call from MacDonald, so I happily went with them. Boy, was this easy! And on my fortieth birthday, holding a crystal glass full of champagne in one hand and a pen in the other, I signed the contract. I was sitting on my bed, in my bedroom in Chelsea, London, looking out onto a walled garden, the view I had looked at while writing the book. I had a new career, or a career to be exact. I knew what I wanted to do for the rest of my life.

"That was ten years and five books ago. Some were exciting to research and easier to write. Others took years and still are not written properly—and not yet published. When people take aptitude tests and are told they are wonderful writers and that would be a great profession for them, they should step back and take another test—how good are they at accepting rejections? ... because every author, even really prolific authors, gets rejections. It is part of the package, and one that I had to learn after too many years in the business. Also, when experiencing those first moments of organizing and researching and trying for that first sentence (because once the right one comes, you are on your way), and the drops of blood are emerging on your forehead as you sit in front of the blank screen on your computer, there's often a little voice that says, 'You idiot! What makes you think you can pull this off? Who are you kidding?' In heartfelt writing conversations with fellow—that is, female-writer-friends—I find that female writers have that voice, and have to struggle through it, tell it to shut up, or somehow put it in a locked box until the writing is well underway. I don't think male writers have the voice, at least not the ones I know. They seem to have more of a straight line to the computer keys. Maybe this is called esteem, or confidence, or growing up male in America, and bravo for them. I am truly happy for them. I wish no one the Idiot voice. I wish most of all that the present generation of strong women growing up will share this confidence with their male counterparts in our society.

"I know, too, that writing is therapy. Whatever turmoil is going on in one's life, whatever craziness, whatever the self-inflicted or other-inflicted chaos from life in our day is occurring, taking pen to paper, or fingers to keys, is a true and glorious escape. It becomes a need, like breathing and eating. It seeps into thoughts and dreams. You find yourself waking at 3:00 in the morning and reaching for the ever-present pad (that, too, is a discipline) by your bed, and in the dark, jotting down an idea that grows into a sentence, then ends up a paragraph or two. And maybe a book, down the line. If I don't wake up enough to write that first word, I always regret it in the morning; I know that THAT would have been the Newbery winner.

"And you meet the nicest, the very nicest, people as a writer. Other writers are caring and gentle and supportive and sharing with ideas and time and encouragement. They share their horror stories, and make them sound funny and educational. Many editors still write long and helpful rejection letters. Some take their writers to elegant clubs for lunch, others to the pub down the road, still others into their homes. They always, always want to talk about things of the heart. When my first editor, who had worked on two of my books, decided she was really a poet and went back to school, I was in the mental fetal position for months. She is now editing my sixth book as a freelancer for the publisher, and it is much better because of her. Perhaps it was good for me, too, that she left publishing as a full-time pursuit. I had to take stock, rely on myself, branch out, find other ways and places to go. I did.

Soon we would reach the zoo. The balloon men and ice cream ladies lined the street in front of the entrance. "Hurry, hurry," one of them would shout. "It is feeding time for Hanna."

In Marx's true-life picture book story, the inhabitants of Budapest rally to save the hippos in their zoo one particularly harsh winter during World War II. (From Hanna's Cold Winter, *illustrated by Barbara Knutson.)*

"Right now I am between books. I just sent my last one off after changing it according to editorial comments. I find there is always a depression after sending a book off for me. What should be, and is for a day or two, elation that I don't have to commune any longer with that subject, turns to depression over NOT having a work-in-progress. I worry, I fret, I clean my refrigerator. Then someone sends me a clipping that I put aside, then take a glance at, then mentally gage the angle, the work, the research, the money, the possible publisher. Often, I put it aside again, to be found months later and again pondered over. But as often, whatever the stimulus—a clipping, a poem, a story told or overheard, a child asking a question—I listen to the voice that begins to speak within me—not the Idiot voice, but the voice of possibility, the voice of creativity, the voice of belief in MY idea, and I act upon it. I am, again, writing."

Trish Marx writes nonfiction books for children, often depicting how real children acted or survived in actual situations. In *Hanna's Cold Winter,* for example, "a curious true incident is incorporated into a pleasant glimpse of a Budapest family during WWII," as a critic for *Kirkus Reviews* explained. Marx tells the story of Tibor, who lives with his family in Budapest, Hungary, during World War II. The privations suffered by people during the war take a back seat to the possibility that the hippos in the nearby zoo may starve when shipments of hay are halted during a particularly harsh winter. Tibor's father gets the idea to feed Hanna and the other hippos

the family's straw mat and straw slippers, and when that succeeds, Tibor and the other children begin a campaign to collect straw hats, mats, and slippers from other concerned citizens in wartime Budapest. Marx's narrative "has a ring of authenticity," noted *Five Owls* contributor Kathie Krieger Cerra, who further praised *Hanna's Cold Winter* as "a simply told story in which something happens that really matters to children."

Marx again highlights the survival skills of children in *Echoes of the Second World War,* which portrays the international range of the war through the experiences of six children. In relating the stories of a girl who joined the French Resistance, a German Jewish boy who was sent to live in London, and a British boy who spent the war in a prison camp in the Philippines, Marx intertwines quotes from interviews with each of her subjects as adults with background information about the war as it was conducted in each context. "The blend of personal anecdote and factual account brings the war into immediate focus," contended Betsy Hearne in *Bulletin of the Center for Children's Books.*

Children as survivors of catastrophe are also the subject of *I Heal: The Story of the Children of Chernobyl in Cuba,* in which Marx relates the story of the thousands of Russian children who traveled to Cuba to receive medical care for the cancers suffered as a result of exposure to radiation from the meltdown of the nuclear reactor in Chernobyl. Twelve-year-old Elena narrates the story, which only lightly touches on the realities of surgery, chemotherapy, and other forms of treatment undergone by the children in the resort town of Tarara, Cuba, during their stay there, instead emphasizing the beauty of the tropical locale and the fun they have playing there. "Her story is heartwarming and at times poignant," remarked Elizabeth Talbot in *School Library Journal. Booklist* reviewer Julie Corsaro suggested teachers introduce *I Heal* alongside Toshi Maruki's tale of the dropping of the atomic bomb on Hiroshima in *Hiroshima No Pika,* and concluded: "It is hard to imagine any young reader not being moved by these stories."

Works Cited

Cerra, Kathie Krieger, review of *Hanna's Cold Winter, Five Owls,* March-April, 1994, p. 88.
Corsaro, Julie, review of *I Heal: The Story of the Children of Chernobyl in Cuba, Booklist,* December 1, 1996, p. 651.
Review of *Hanna's Cold Winter, Kirkus Reviews,* July 1, 1993, p. 864.
Hearne, Betsy, review of *Echoes of the Second World War, Bulletin of the Center for Children's Books,* May, 1994, p. 295.
Talbot, Elizabeth, review of *I Heal: The Story of the Children of Chernobyl in Cuba, School Library Journal,* October, 1996, p. 136.

For More Information See

PERIODICALS

Kirkus Reviews, February 15, 1994, p. 230.
School Library Journal, November, 1993, p. 86.

*   *   *

MARX, Trish
See Marx, Patricia Windschill

*   *   *

MASTERS, Anthony 1940-
(Richard Tate)

Personal

Born in 1940 in Esher, Surrey, England; son of Ronald Richard and Margery (Pitt) Masters; married Robina Farbrother (an editor). *Education:* Attended King's College School, Wimbledon, England, 1953-1957. *Religion:* Church of England.

Addresses

Home—Whitewood Cottage, Swiffe Lane, Broad Oak, Sussex, England. *Agent*—Michael Sissors, A.D. Peters,10 Buckingham St. London WC2N 6BU, England.

Career

Journalist, 1958-1959; book salesman, 1959-1960; production assistant, 1960-1964; writer, 1964—; University of Reading, lecturer, Language in Education, present.

Awards, Honors

John Llewellyn Rhys Memorial Prize, 1967, for *The Sea Horse; Streetwise,* short-listed for the Carnegie Prize.

Writings

JUVENILE LITERATURE

Napoleon, Longman, 1981; McGraw-Hill, 1981.
(Selector) *True Stories,* pictures by Chris Molan, Kingfisher, 1994.
(Selector) *Heroic Stories,* illustrated by Chris Molan, Kingfisher, 1994.
True Survival Stories, Sterling, 1997.

JUVENILE FICTION

The Sea Horse, Atheneum, 1966; illustrated by James Mayhew, Hemel Hempstead: Macdonald Young, 1995.
The Return of Murphy's Mob, Puffin, 1983.
Murphy & Co., Puffin, 1983.
Badger, Methuen, 1986.
Streetwise, Methuen, 1987.
Dream Palace, Methuen, 1988.
Leave It Out Arthur!, Sphere, 1988.
Cat Burglars, Teens Mandarin, 1989.
All the Fun of the Fair, Teens Mandarin, 1989.
Frog, Blackie, 1989.
Mel's Run, Methuen, 1989.
Nobody's Child, Hippo, 1989.
Nightmare in New York, Teens, 1990.
Siege, Teens, 1990.
African Queen, Teens Mandarin, 1990.
Playing with Fire, Blackie, 1990.
Travellers' Tales, Blackie, 1990.
Shellshock, Methuen, 1990.
Sad Song of the Whale, Scholastic, 1990.
Battle for the Badgers, Scholastic, 1990.
The Seventh Stream, Mammoth, 1990.
Spirit of the Condor, illustrated by Pauline Hazelwood, Scholastic, 1991.
Gorilla Mountain, illustrated by Pauline Hazelwood, Scholastic, 1991.
Traffic, Simon & Schuster, 1991.
Vanishing Point, illustrated by Richard Jones, Hippo Books, 1991.
Klondyker, Simon & Schuster, 1991; published in the U.S. as *A Watching Silence,* Simon & Schuster, 1992.
Tunnel Terror, Red Fox, 1992.
Crab, Yearling, 1992.
The Transformation of Jennifer Howard, Methuen, 1992.
The Roost, illustrated by Lynne Willey, Blackie Children's, 1993.
Spinner, Blackie Children's, 1993.
Horror Stories to Tell in the Dark, Puffin, 1994.
White Out, Bantam, 1994.
Vampire Stories to Tell in the Dark, Puffin, 1995.
Ivy, illustrated by Ian Miller, Ginn, 1995.

Twister, Macmillan Children's Books, 1995.

Waternsnake, illustrated by Stephen Player, Ginn, 1995.

Raven, The First Bird of Prey, Puffin, 1995.

Roadkill: The Beginning, Bloomsbury, 1995.

The Ghost Bus, illustrated by Alan Marks, Hemel Hempstead: Macdonald Young, 1996.

Werewolf Stories to Tell in the Dark, Puffin, 1996.

Ghost Stories to Tell in the Dark, Puffin, 1996.

The Mystery of Captain Keene's Treasure, Hove: Macdonald Young, 1996.

Ghost Blades, illustrated by Chris Price, Ginn, 1997.

Enemy Fire, Watts, 1997.

Extreme Survival, Watts, 1997.

Held to Ransom, Watts, 1997.

The Men, Constable, 1997.

Greek Myths and Legends, illustrated by Andrew Skilleter, Hove: Macdonald Young, 1999.

The Haunted Surfboard, illustrated by Peter Dennis, A. & C. Black, 1999.

Tod in Biker City, Barrington Stoke, 1999.

Myths and Legends, illustrated by Andrew Skilleter, Hove: Macdonald Young, 1999.

Roman Myths and Legends, illustrated by Andrew Skilleter, Peter Bedrick Books, 2000.

Serpent Mound, Simon & Schuster Children's, 2000.

"MINDER" SERIES; BASED ON TELEVISION SERIES BY LEON GRIFFITHS

Minder, Sphere, 1984.

Minder—Back Again, Sphere, 1984.

Minder—Yet Again!, Sphere, 1985.

"THE MARLOW HOUSE MYSTERIES" SERIES

The Mystery of Bloodhound Island, Hove: Macdonald Young, 1996.

The Mystery of the White Knuckle Ride, Hove: Macdonald Young Books, 1996.

The Mystery of the Shadow Caves, Hove: Macdonald Young Books, 1996.

"IMPACT HORROR" SERIES

Lights Out, illustrated by Stephen Player, Ginn, 1997.

"POLICE DOG" SERIES

The Taking of Doug Fox, Bloomsbury, 1997.

"DANGER ZONE" SERIES

Ocean Tomb, Watts, 1997.

"GHOSTHUNTERS" SERIES

Haunted School, Orchard, 1996.

Poltergeist, Orchard, 1996.

Possessed, Orchard, 1997.

Dancing with the Dead, Orchard, 1998.

"TREMORS" SERIES

The Haunted Lighthouse, illustrated by Alan Marks, Hove: Macdonald Young, 1997.

Phantoms in the Fog, illustrated by Alan Marks, Hove: Macdonald Young, 1998.

The Curse of the Ghost Horse, illustrated by Alan Marks, Hove: Macdonald Young, 1999.

"GRAFFIX" SERIES

Biker, illustrated by Gary Rees, A. & C. Black, 1997.

Hero, illustrated by Peter Dennis, A. & C. Black, 1999.

"LITERACY WORLD" SERIES

Cal's Log, illustrated by Mark Oldroyd, Heinemann, 1999.

"WEIRD WORLD" SERIES

Cloning Me, Cloning You, Bloomsbury, 1997.

Black Rot, Bloomsbury, 1998.

"TEACH YOURSELF" SERIES

(Reviser), David James, *Letter Writing Skills,* Second Edition, N T C/Contemporary Publishing Company, 1998.

FOR ADULTS

A Pocketful of Rye, Secker & Warburg, 1964.

A Literary Lion, Secker & Warburg, 1968.

Conquering Heroes, M. Joseph, 1969.

Rousseau's First & Second Discourses, St. Martin's Press, 1969.

Dreams about H. M. the Queen and Other Members of the Royal Family, Blond & Briggs, 1972.

The Natural History of the Vampire, Putnam, 1972.

The Summer that Bled: The Biography of Hannah Senesh, St. Martin's Press, 1972.

Bakunin: The Father of Anarchism, Sidgwick & Jackson, 1974.

Cries of Terror, Arrow books, 1976.

Bedlam, M. Joseph, 1977.

The Devil's Dominion: The Complete Story of Hell and Satanism in the Modern World, Putnam, 1978.

Doing a Runner, Bloomsbury, 1997.

The Dark Side of the Brain, Bloomsbury, 1997.

Day of the Dead, Orchard, 1998.

Temper, Temper, Bloomsbury, 1998.

Dark Tower, Orchard, 1998.

Phantoms in the Fog, Llandysul: Gwasg Gomer, 1998.

The Good and Faithful Servant, Constable, 1998.

Rosa Lewis: An Exceptional Edwardian, Weidenfeld and Nicolson, 1977, St. Martin's Press, 1978.

Inside Marbled Halls: Life Above and Below Stairs in the Hyde Park Hotel, Sidgwick & Jackson, 1979.

Mind Map, illustrated by Boris Weltman, Methuen, 1980.

Nancy Astor: A Biography, McGraw-Hill, 1981.

The Man Who Was M: The Life of Maxwell Knight, Blackwell, 1984.

Red Ice, with Nicholas Barker, St. Martin's Press, 1986.

Literary Agents: The Novelist as Spy, Blackwell, 1987.

The Song of the Dead, Hippo, 1990.

Murder Is a Long Time Coming, Constable, 1991.

Dead Man at the Door, Viking, 1992.

Confessional, Constable, 1993.

Hell on Earth, Bantam Books, 1993.

Raven, Viking, 1993.

(With Philip Falle) *The Newall Murders* (nonfiction), Constable, 1994.

The Confessional, St. Martin's Press, 1994.

Death's Door, Constable, 1995.

Bullies Don't Hurt, Viking, 1995.

Beginning, Bloomsbury, 1995.

Deadly Games, Orchard, 1996.

I Want Him Dead, Constable, 1996.
Wicked, Orchard Books, 1997.

Masters also wrote the novel *Tenko,* based on the BBC-TV series created by Lavinia Warner and scripted by Jill Hyem, Anne Valery, and Paul Wheeler, British Broadcasting Corporation, 1981.

UNDER PSEUDONYM RICHARD TATE

The Donor, Constable, 1970.
The Dead Travel Fast, Sphere, 1972.
The Emperor on Ice, Constable, 1974.
Birds of a Bloodied Feather, Constable, 1974.
Terminal Agreement, Fantail, 1994.

EDITOR

The Jesus File, Dobson, 1975.
The Wind on the Heath, Dobson, 1975.
Taking Root: A Multicultural Anthology, Teens, 1989.

OTHER

The Best of the First Ten Years of the Samoyed Quarterly, Donald R. Hoflin, 1995.
The Play of Personality in the Restoration Theatre, Boydell & Brewer, 1992.

Sidelights

Anthony Masters is a writer both prolific and eclectic. Under the pseudonym Richard Tate, he has written several paperback thrillers. As Anthony Masters, he has explored subjects as serious as England's Queen, as fantastic as the vampire, and as compelling as the life of the man upon whom Ian Fleming based his "M" character for the James Bond books. In addition, Masters's numerous fictional works for adult and juvenile audiences have won critical acclaim.

Masters has a solid reputation as a biographer. *Nancy Astor, A Biography* chronicles the life of the British House of Commons's first elected female representative (and wife of the wealthy Waldorf Astor). In the *New York Times,* Enid Nemy described Nancy Astor as "one of the most fascinating and powerful women of her time." Nemy labeled Masters's portrayal of this complex woman as "scholarly," noting, "he paints ... a vivid and poignant portrait" of Astor's life. In the *Washington Post Book World,* Eve Auchincloss described Nancy Astor as "thoroughly capable and entertaining." Nemy added in her conclusion: "There is an era portrayed here, as well as an individual."

"Espionage addicts should relish Masters's *The Man Who Was M: The Life of Maxwell Knight,*" declared Curtis Carroll Davis in the *New York Times Book Review.* The biography of the man Ian Fleming used as a model for the fictional character "M" in the James Bond books, the take has an appeal that goes beyond its link to popular fiction, according to critics. In the words of William French in the *Toronto Globe & Mail,* "Knight's story can stand on its own; in fact, it's so bizarre that if Fleming had modelled M faithfully on Knight, he would have had a credibility problem."

In *The Man Who Was M, Times Literary Supplement* contributor T. J. Binyon noted Masters displays an astute observation of "the connection between sensational literature and the world of espionage" in the lives of Knight, his companion, and his colleagues, many of whom dabbled in writing thrillers. This is a theme Masters takes up again in *Literary Agents: The Novelist as Spy,* an exploration of the real life espionage experiences of some popular spy novelists.

Masters's first novel, *The Sea Horse,* describes a fantasy that takes place within the highly realistic setting of a coastal town preparing for a storm. In a review for *Books for Keeps,* Gill Roberts wrote that "Jamie's magical encounter with a sea horse" is "inspired" in its depiction of the sea's power and danger. Roberts also commented on "the intensity of Jamie's emotions" when rescued by the sea horse.

Although known primarily for adult fiction, Masters also writes for children. According to George Hunt's article about the author and his work in *Books for Keeps,* Masters's first children's book, *Badger,* "is typical of subsequent novels in its ability to ... combine a social issues theme with a concern for the complex tensions with a specific family." The story depicts one family's involvement with the brutal sport of badger-baiting. While the father and son capture wild badgers and pit them against terriers trained in the game, Jenny and her sensitive cousin try to bring the bloodshed to a halt. According to Adele Geras in *New Statesman,* Masters's descriptions are "convincing" in their portrayal of the "vileness of such practices." *Badger* explores the cruelty humans can inflict, and it does so with subtlety, in the opinion of Maureen McCulloch, writing for the *Times Literary Supplement.* She asserted: "Anthony Masters deals with powerful and complex emotions in understated, plain prose." A reviewer for *Junior Bookshelf* opined: "Everyone in this story has a valid point of view, and the drama grows out of real conflicts.... it is the human characters who dominate the scene and haunt the memory after the book is finished."

Streetwise, Masters's second novel for children, sets forth another family dilemma—this time amid police corruption and racial prejudice. A policeman's son examines the circumstances of his father's violent death, and learns more than anticipated. A reviewer for *Junior Bookshelf* commented: "There is action and excitement aplenty ... in this rather bleak story set in the suburban wastelands where violence seems to be a way of life. It is the stuff of countless TV programs...."

Travellers' Tale unveils the lives of gypsies, or Romany travelers. Masters describes a family's unconventional lifestyle, moving from place to place in a trailer, and the impact a disapproving society has on the family, particularly the children. A critic writing for *Junior Bookshelf* noted Masters "has written a strong novel which, if it presents social problems, is concerned with people, Travellers and others, and the irreconcilable differences which face them."

Masters has a talent for depicting extremely real settings for his novels. This sense of place comes alive in The Isle of Wight for *Dead Man at the Door,* a novel about newcomers to an insular island community who ignore the locals' superstitions. Renya Spratt called this story of "unleashed dangerous and vengeful supernatural powers, a chilling and fast moving" tale in her *Magpies* review.

The multitalented author is equally adept at creating "sharply drawn characters" and revealing their "emotional turmoil" according to a reviewer in *Junior Bookshelf* of *The Transformation of Jennifer Howard.* Masters depicts eighteen-year-old Jennifer's angst as she lives through one tumultuous event after another—her brother dies from AIDS, her parents' marriage is dissolving, she is assaulted, and then falls in love with a boy from an entirely different background. Peter Hollindale commented in *School Librarian* that: "This is a 'casebook' novel of family crisis and emotional upheaval," which takes Jennifer from being a "gifted, loved, and confident" teen to the depths of despair and back again.

The difficult subject of autism is tackled in a mystery entitled, *Spinner.* A *Junior Bookshelf* reviewer noted that Masters has made "an intractable subject interesting to young readers by embodying into it an exciting thriller." The reviewer continued, "Gary [an autistic child] is the star of the story," but Jane, who becomes involved in his determination to find his father "realizes that she has something to learn from him, and comes a good second in the credits."

Based on his interview with Masters, Hunt commented: "These books deal with troubling, realistic crises, but they are written with the same engaging straightforwardness as his purely recreational collections of fantasies and entertainments."

A Watching Silence exemplifies the latter. In a story of mystery and adventure set in the Shetland Islands, an American boy accidentally finds part of a cache of antiquities stolen from a local museum. Deborah Stevenson, in her review for *Bulletin of the Center for Children's Books,* said that "Masters successfully evokes the spookiness of an abandoned village at the edge of the sea." Cynthia Brown, writing in *Voice of Youth Advocates (VOYA),* opined: "Greed and obsession abound and Martin is caught in the middle.... By the end of the third page, the reader is hooked and wants to know more."

Masters shifted from mystery adventure to science fantasy adventure in two novels, *The Dark Side of the Brain* and *Cloning Me, Cloning You.* Julia Wright, reviewing the titles for *School Librarian,* said: "Both books use topical themes which are successfully woven into storylines." The first illustrates how being able to read other people's minds and having X-ray vision impacts the friendship of two boys, while *Cloning Me, Cloning You* relies on computer technology to create a plot for the "takeover of the world."

In his article for *Books for Keeps,* Hunt referred to Masters's ability to attract the interest of teenage boys, which has, in the author's words, "brought him to the attention of publishers seeking ... the 'Holy grail of young male readership.'" Masters added, "As a writer you need to get totally involved with what children feel and think, and exactly what they want to read.... I see an important part of my job as answering the challenge of kids who say, 'I bet you're going to bore me.'"

Works Cited

Auchincloss, Eve, review of *Nancy Astor, A Biography, Washington Post Book World,* May 31, 1981, p. 8.

Review of *Badger, Junior Bookshelf,* October, 1986, pp. 197-98.

Brown, Cynthia, review of *A Watching Silence, Voice of Youth Advocates,* February, 1993, p. 340.

Davis, Curtis Carroll, review of *The Man Who Was M, New York Times Book Review,* May 26, 1985, p. 15.

French, William, review of *The Man Who Was M, Toronto Globe & Mail,* February 2, 1985.

Geras, Adele, review of *Badger, New Statesman,* October 10, 1986, p. 30.

Hollindale, Peter, review of *The Transformation of Jennifer Howard, School Librarian,* November, 1992, p. 159.

Hunt, George, "Authorgraph No. 108," *Books for Keeps,* January, 1998, pp. 12-13.

McCulloch, Maureen, review of *Badger, Times Literary Supplement,* October 3, 1986, p. 1119.

Nemy, Enid, review of *Nancy Astor, A Biography, New York Times,* August 26, 1981.

Roberts, Gill, review of *The Sea Horse, Books for Keeps,* November, 1995, p. 11.

Review of *Spinner, Junior Bookshelf,* April, 1994, p. 73.

Spratt, Renya, review of *Dead Man at the Door, Magpies,* November, 1992, p. 33.

Stevenson, Deborah, review of *A Watching Silence, Bulletin of the Center for Children's Books,* November, 1992, p. 81.

Review of *Streetwise, Junior Bookshelf,* February, 1988, p. 50.

Review of *The Transformation of Jennifer Howard, Bookshelf,* October, 1992, pp. 218-19.

Review of *Travellers' Tales, Junior Bookshelf,* February, 1991, pp. 34-35.

Wright, Julia, review of *Cloning Me, Cloning You, School Librarian,* summer, 1998, p. 102.

Wright, Julia, review of *The Dark Side of the Brain, School Librarian,* summer, 1998, p. 102.

For More Information See

PERIODICALS

Books for Keeps, May, 1990, p. 14; July, 1990, p. 16; September, 1991, p. 13; January, 1994, p. 9; September, 1997, p. 25.

Growing Point, January 15, 1987, p. 4698.

Junior Bookshelf, August, 1990, pp. 189-190; December, 1990, p. 280; December, 1991, pp. 265-66.

School Librarian, February, 1991, p. 24; May, 1991, p. 74.*

Autobiography Feature

Carol Matas

1949-

MY STORY

When I was young I never dreamed of becoming a writer, but I always knew I was a reader. It was absolutely my favorite thing to do. Naturally it all began with my parents reading to me, which they did a lot. But it wasn't long before I was reading on my own. I remember the best part of my day would be coming home for lunch from school, hurrying to my room after eating, and lying down on my bed to read my book. I had many favorite books when I was young, but the first ones I remember were the Oz series by L. Frank Baum. Dorothy, a girl only a little older than me, was the heroine. She was always brave, had a charming sense of humor, and always thought about justice—she always helped those in need. Her adventures took her to places that simply delighted me. How did the author *think* of such things? For example one of my favorite books in the series was *Ozma of Oz.* Dorothy finds herself in the land of the Wheelers after being tossed into the ocean during a terrible storm. She is hungry. She spies some trees and goes to investigate.

> One was quite full of square paper boxes, which grew in clusters on all the limbs, and upon the biggest and ripest boxes the word "lunch" could be read, in neat raised letters. . . . The leaves of the trees were all paper napkins. . . .

Dorothy sits down to eat.

> Inside she found, nicely wrapped in white papers, a ham sandwich, a piece of sponge-cake, a pickle, a slice of new cheese and an apple. Each thing had a separate stem, and so had to be picked off the side of the box. . . .

Each book was full of such gems. One of my other favorite books was *The Secret Garden.* And in grade five, I read every single Nancy Drew mystery that had been written. In grade ten I remember the principal coming into our geography class to scold us for not paying attention. He noticed that I had a paperback hidden behind my geography book. He strode over, grabbed the book, and said, "This is what I mean! Reading novels when you should be studying geography!" But then he noticed that the book was *War and Peace* by Leo Tolstoy, a classic. "Well," he huffed, turning red, "you *still* shouldn't be reading books in class,

but if you *have* to you could read something like this." My problem was once I started a book I couldn't put it down, no matter what.

Around that time I was bitten by the theatre bug, and I began to take acting classes. It wasn't long before I decided I wanted to be an actor. I still loved reading though, and when I went away to university I took a degree in English, spending all my extra time acting in university productions. I loved it, but I also loved studying Shakespeare and reading all those great authors. When I graduated I moved to London, England, for two years to follow my dream and to go to acting school. I then moved to Toronto and began working as a professional actor. I was pretty good, I think, and I got quite a lot of work, but still, as with all actors, I did have times when I was out of work. I hung around with a group of actors who happened to be writing in their spare time.

They used to share their stories. I remember one day hearing a story, a fantasy, and thinking it was delightful. I thought I'd like to try to do that. So I went home and sat down at my kitchen table with a sheet of paper. But what to write? I looked at the flowered teapot sitting in front of me. I thought, what if the teapot were magic? What if there were a brother and sister, home alone, fighting? What if they tumbled into the kitchen, knocked against the teapot, and *shrank*! I stared at the table, which was beside the window, filled with plants. What if they ended up on the plant table and met the various plants, and what if the plants had personalities which matched their names, such as Professor Ivy, the scary Spider Plant, etc.

I read this story to my friends a few days later. They liked it! I had so much fun writing it that I decided to write another. This too was a fantasy. The first story I wrote was five pages long. The second was ten. The third was twenty. They kept getting longer and longer. For a couple of years I did this strictly as a hobby, never even considering publication.

It wasn't until I had to take a break from acting because I was pregnant with my first child that I decided to try writing my first full-length book. That was the summer of 1977. This book was also a fantasy. It was the story of a rich boy and a poor boy who decided to switch places, a little like the *Prince and the Pauper,* by Mark Twain. I loved writing it.

I must say that during all those years I didn't think of myself as writing for children. I was writing stories that happened to have young people as the lead characters.

When I finished this book, for the first time I thought of showing it to someone. I sent it to the National Film Board of Canada, hoping they would make it into a movie. They didn't, but the letter I got was full of encouragement. It said I should continue to write, that I obviously had talent, and that Canada needed more good writers for children. Was that what I was doing? I didn't even realize I was writing for children. I thought I was writing fantasy for all ages.

I began to think about this business of writing for children. The next book would be *specifically* for young people. I got my inspiration one day glancing out a window in our apartment in Montreal. My husband, daughter, and I had moved there in 1978. A huge black moving van was parked on the residential street. Well, that wasn't unusual. However, when it was still there the next day I began to wonder. What was it still doing there? A moving van never stays longer than it takes to load. Whom did it belong to? By the third day my imagination began to run wild. It was ominous looking, wasn't it? Perhaps there were bad people hiding in it. Kidnappers! They were waiting for unsuspecting children to walk by them, spiriting them off into the van. But why? I had been reading a lot recently about nuclear war and the danger we were in on this planet. It occurred to me—what if the kidnappers were from the future? They would need children because a nuclear war had killed all the children and the human race was in danger of dying out. So children were being stolen from our present into the future by people (deformed from radiation sickness) using a time machine. A twelve-year-old girl, Rebecca (the name of my little girl), from Winnipeg (living in the same house I grew up in), would be the main character. Looking out the window early one morning she sees a boy from her class being kidnapped. She runs to tell her parents, but they think she's been dreaming. The police agree. And apparently his father doesn't care and thinks he's just run away, again. Rebecca never liked this boy, but she knows what she saw and she feels she must do *something*. So she follows another child whom she sees being pulled into a van—and she ends up in the future.

I was very fortunate to be able to ask a close friend of my husband's to read the manuscript for me. His name is George Szanto. He was a professor of communications at McGill University. He began to tutor me. He critiqued that manuscript over and over, and I did draft after draft. Really, George trained me in the way I write today. I still write a first draft quickly but then do numerous drafts afterwards. I began to send out the manuscript, but it was rejected time after time. Then I got the idea for my second book. My husband and I had gone to a movie, *Apocalypse Now,* based on the Joseph Conrad book *Heart of Darkness*. In it a man who thinks he is sane is really quite insane. It made me think of all the dictators of the world—men who surely didn't think of themselves as crazy but men who *were* crazy. At the same time I had been reading a lot about genetic engineering and had just seen a long special on it on TV. So I decided to write about a dictator who controlled the world through genetic engineering. This book became *The D.N.A. Dimension*.

I feel I should include here something about my career paths. Before I became pregnant I had always intended to return to the stage. However, after Rebecca was born something odd happened. Every time I tried to go back to work she got sick. It was as if she had a different plan for me, and it was not to be an actor.

Eventually I gave up trying to find acting work and stayed home to take care of her. But I still needed some intellectual stimulation. So, I turned to my writing. It was during this time that I wrote my first two science fiction books, the ones I have just described. I would get a neighbor who was a high school student to come over every day at 3:30 p.m. She would stay until 5:30, either taking Rebecca to the park or staying right there in the apartment. I was always aware of how little time I had, and I'd sit down and write like crazy. I didn't think about my story during the day—I seemed to have the ability to concentrate on Rebecca and then when it was time to write I'd tune into the story. (I can't do that anymore—now when I'm writing I think about the story all the time.) I sometimes wonder if that's part of the reason my writing style is so fast-paced—I only had those two hours a day.

I began to send out manuscripts to publishers and received one rejection after another. In fact I believe *The Fusion Factor,* my book about a kidnapped child, must have gotten at least twenty rejections. When Rebecca was a little older, I began to think about returning to acting. However, just then I submitted the short story to a Canadian publisher and it was accepted. Now I felt I was a writer. Actually the story was never published but being accepted at that moment made a huge difference to me and was probably the turning point in my career.

Then came the idea for my third science fiction book, *Zanu.* The lead character was still Rebecca, and this time she would go into a future run by big business. As I wrote I continued to send out my other books. I'd joined CAN-SCAIP (Canadian Society of Children's Authors, Illustrators and Performers). The newsletter always included a marketing section. I'd noticed that Gage Publishing was looking for manuscripts so I sent them *The D.N.A. Dimension* and *The Fusion Factor.* And, miracle of miracles, I received a letter in the mail, only three months after my son Sam was born, saying that *The D.N.A. Dimension* had been accepted for publication. They also agreed to publish the other Rebecca books at a later date. Naturally, I was thrilled.

It was at this time that we moved from Montreal to Winnipeg. I lost my mentor, George Szanto, but was excited about moving to the city where my family still lived. In the fall of 1982, just after we had moved, my first book was published. I had been using the name Carol Matas Brask, but when we moved to Winnipeg, the city I had grown up in, I thought people would remember my maiden name, Matas, so I dropped the Brask and stuck with Matas. I suppose having your first book published is the greatest thrill imaginable. Although I continued to do some acting for a number of years, writing became my profession.

My husband had gotten a job at the University of Winnipeg teaching theatre. I'd quickly met his colleagues and other professors who had offices on the same floor. One of them was a professor of children's literature, Perry Nodelman. I asked if he would mind reading one of my

Carol Matas by her house, 1997.

books—I had started on the new Rebecca title about time travel. He graciously agreed and provided me with a fantastic critique.

It is impossible to tell your life story in a straight line. Now it's time for me to backtrack to Montreal. In Montreal my husband worked at the Jewish community center running the theatre that was part of the center. At one point an exhibit about the Holocaust came through. He began to tell me stories of what had happened to his father when Germany invaded Denmark in 1942. My husband is from Denmark, and his mother and father were just twelve years old when Denmark was invaded. They had never told me anything about the war and neither had my husband until the exhibits jogged his memory. Then he began to tell the most amazing stories. My father-in-law had started out with small pranks against the Germans, such as filling the gas tanks of their trucks with sugar so they couldn't run. If caught, these small pranks could have gotten them killed. By the time he was fifteen years old my father-in-law was a full-fledged member of the resistance. In fact, one of the stories my husband told me concerned the time that my father-in-law was the most frightened. His mother had been making his bed one morning when she felt something lumpy under the mattress. She picked up the mattress only to find two handguns and a machine gun. Apparently she almost killed him. He was certainly more afraid of *her* than he was of the Germans. The funny thing was, his father was also in the resistance, but he did not know about his father and his father did not know about him. Every night after dinner they would listen to the BBC radio broadcasts. Birthday greetings and other messages would be code for the resistance groups telling them where to meet. He would make an excuse, saying for instance he was going to a friend's house to do homework, and he would leave. His father would do the same—except he would have a different excuse. It was important that neither of them knew

about the other in case one of them got caught. All resistance cells were kept small in case someone was captured—should this happen they would be tortured and inevitably would give away the other members of their cell. Therefore the fewer people in a cell the better. The rule once captured was to try to hold out under torture for twenty-four hours and then tell everything. If your cell were small enough it would be quickly noticed that you were missing. The others would then have time to go into hiding, or as they called it, to go underground.

As my husband told the stories about his father and grandfather during the war I decided that I would like to write a book about a boy in the Danish resistance. Although I was still working on my science fiction books I began to read and think about Denmark in World War II. That was when a friend gave my husband a book called *Rescue in Denmark.* It was about the rescue of the Danish Jews. This was a story I had never heard before. It described how the Danish people had managed to rescue almost all of their Jewish population from the Nazis during the Second World War. I was shocked. How was it that I had never heard this story before? After all, I am Jewish, I went to Hebrew school, I went to university, and I thought I was educated. I had been taught about the Holocaust and about the six million who had been murdered. And yet nobody had taught me about this country that had managed to save its entire Jewish population. How could this be? I knew I had to write about it.

My science fiction books were all on different topics (in *The D.N.A. Dimension,* the idea of a ruler who *thinks* he is sane and doing everything for the best who is really insane; in *Me, Myself and I,* the question of whether a Utopia is possible; and in *Zanu,* deception and illusion—Rebecca when she first arrives in that world likes all the wrong people and wrong things because they appear beautiful and orderly, and only later discovers who the truly "good" people are), but they all had one theme in common: *one person can make a difference.* In each book Rebecca discovers that even her smallest actions have an effect on the future. When I read about the rescue in Denmark I felt I would still be writing on the same theme—except in this case one entire country made a difference. But never forget that one country was made up of individuals making individual choices. So when I finished my final book in the science fiction series, *Me, Myself and I,* I decided to write the book about Denmark, called *Lisa.* It never occurred to me that I was now writing historical fiction. I simply wanted to tell a good story, an important story that happened to be set in the past.

Just after *The D.N.A. Dimension* was published in 1982 I was given some bad news. Although Gage had agreed to publish *The Fusion Factor* and *Zanu,* their publishing program called the Jean-Pac, so titled because the covers all had a denim look and the books were meant to fit in the back pocket of your jeans, was discontinued. Gage informed me that they would not, after all, publish the next two books. I tried to find a publisher for years, but had no luck. I received one rejection notice after another. I was beginning to think that I should give up all together when something very strange happened. My cousin had gone to see a psychic whom he thought was very good. I decided to

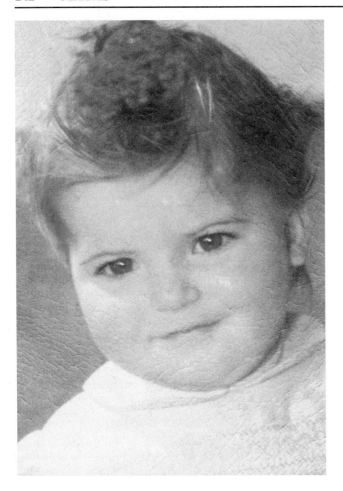

Carol, about age one.

go. The psychic gave me a reading and I can't remember much of what he said now. But I do remember one thing. As is often the case, he asked me if I had any questions. I explained that I was a writer and that I was unable to find a publisher. I asked him if my books would ever be published.

"Yes," he answered, "and within the year. They will be published by a publisher in Saskatoon."

Well, that was certainly specific, but I didn't know any publishers in Saskatoon. I didn't even know if Saskatoon *had* publishers. About a week later I got a phone call from the awards officer at the Manitoba Arts Council. I had submitted my two books as background for a small writing grant—perhaps to start work on *Lisa,* I can't remember.

"Carol," she said, "one of the members on a different jury is a publisher from Saskatoon. I thought your books might be perfect for her. Can I show them to her?"

I screamed. I blurted out the whole thing about the psychic. I suppose she thought I was a little crazy. She gave the manuscripts to Carolyn Heath at Fifth House Press in Saskatoon. And not long afterwards Carolyn offered me a contract for all three books, two to come out in 1986, the final one to come out in 1987. I have been to many psychics since then but never once have I received a reading as specific or as accurate as that one!

I began to research *Lisa* and did most of the research for that book in Winnipeg. The first thing I did was go to the Danish Club with my husband for a war memorial.

Resistance fighters stood and one by one told their stories. It was a gold mine for an author. I introduced myself to many of them afterwards and made appointments for interviews. Many of the incidents in *Lisa* and *Jesper* are based on stories I was told in these interviews, including the last scene of *Lisa.*

I had so much material after a while that I simply couldn't write the book. I remember one day we were at a good friend's apartment—Amatzia Huni, who was an Israeli living in Winnipeg with his wife, Etti. Amatzia had been a filmmaker in Israel. He suggested that I write from a first-person perspective in order to narrow the material down—after all, that way I only had to include what my character experienced firsthand.

I tried it and I wrote that book in three weeks. It simply poured out of me, often surprising me along the way. For instance I had not planned for Lisa to throw up on the German soldiers in the streetcar. But I had established that she had a "funny" stomach, so when put under stress, throwing up simply appeared. As in my previous books I didn't begin with an outline. Basically, I had a rough idea of how it would begin and how it would end. Then when I wrote the first draft I created the rest. *Lisa*'s theme, of course, was that one person could make a difference.

I ran into an interesting problem when I began to send the book out. It was taken almost immediately by one of the best publishers in Canada at that time, Lester and Orpen Dennys. Louise Dennys called me one day to say that one of the top writers in Canada had agreed to edit *Lisa* but only if I did a major rewrite. "No child will read a book like this," apparently was the writer's comment. What was wrong? Well, I had no texture in the book, no details of how things looked, or smelled, or tasted. Also, I didn't describe my character's thinking; I simply had dialogue and action to describe the character.

"That's my older sister Susan in the middle and my younger brother John on the other side."

Looking back on it now I think that my early theatre training has had a huge influence on all of my writing. I write with what is known as "subtext" in the theatre. In other words, the character may say one thing but is thinking another. Unlike many authors, though, I do not describe the character's thoughts. The readers must deduce their thoughts by their words and by their actions. For instance when Lisa kills a German soldier she doesn't think about it—but she does throw up, *showing* how horrible the act of killing is for her. And she wouldn't have had *time* to *think* about the act—that wouldn't be realistic. (Some adult readers are upset by this, but children never are.)

So I had to decide—do I listen to one of the top writers in Canada and change my style? Perry urged me not to. He was convinced the book worked very well as it was, and he encouraged me to stick to my guns and not allow it to be changed in any major way. I told Louise and she acquiesced. In fact it took three more editors before she could find someone who basically agreed to simply copyedit the manuscript and leave it mostly intact.

When it was published it came out to only fair reviews in Canada. And for all the reasons this editor had mentioned. However it was then bought by Macmillan in the United States, and one day I was told that the *New York Times* would be running a review. When I read it I remember literally jumping up and down. I had never hoped to be reviewed by the *Times*—but to get a rave review! The reviewer compared *Lisa's War* (*Lisa*) to *Number the Stars* by Lois Lowry and said *Lisa's War* was a far superior book. (Of course as I write this *Lisa's War* is out of print in the United Stated and *Number the Stars* is a Newbery Award Book which will *never* go out of print.)

Canadians, as is always the way here, are impressed by a Canadian who "makes it" in the United States. Everyone in Canada seemed to forget that it had received lukewarm reviews here, but when the sequel, *Jesper,* came out all the reviews referred to *Lisa* as my "brilliant" book, etc., which apparently it had become, in retrospect. *Jesper* (called *Code Name Kris,* or *Kris's War* in the United States) received rave notices from almost all the Canadian papers and did well in the United States as well.

Jesper is about belief. The lead character Jesper has a best friend, Frederik, who becomes a Nazi. The two characters interweave throughout the story, and we see that Frederik believes in what he is doing just as Jesper does. Is one better than the other then? Jesper wonders this, the book asks this, but it, I think, says yes, there *is* a big difference. Frederik and the Nazis, after all, kill in order to control others. Jesper kills in order to be free.

After writing these two books I became interested in writing other historicals. I had written about my husband's family, and I began to think of writing about my own family. My grandfather had escaped from the Russian army then traveled across land to England. There he saw my grandmother at a theatre but had no way to meet her. The next night he went on a blind date—and it was she. They immigrated to Winnipeg at the turn of the century. My mother's parents emigrated from Rumania, also at the turn of the century.

One night I went to a local synagogue to hear a speech by Chaim Potok. At the end of the talk someone asked him

Carol, about ten years old.

a question about the Kapos in the concentration camps in World War II. Mr. Potok answered that that had not been the only time Jews had treated Jews badly. He cited the era of Tsar Nicholas II when the tsar tried to forcibly convert Jews by conscripting them into the army—especially very young Jews. Because the quotas for the army were so hard to fill, often there weren't enough Jews in any one village to comply. A practice was begun by local communities— they hired a kidnapper to kidnap Jewish boys so the quotas would be met, otherwise the leaders of the community would have been taken.

As soon as I heard him talk about this I knew I had to write about it. True, it was earlier Russian history than I had imagined writing about, but the moral conundrum and ethical questions it raised were immediately evident to me. I still believe that *Sworn Enemies* is one of my best books, although it is now out of print in the United States. It was difficult to research in that it was the first book where I couldn't interview people and I had to find all my material from books. One day I counted how many books I had on the floor around my desk—fifty!

In *Sworn Enemies,* I asked the question "Is it possible to live a moral life in an immoral universe?" The two lead characters, Aaron and Zev, are both religious, Aaron a scholar, Zev a poor boy who has little capacity to learn. When Zev is asked to be a kidnapper by the leaders of the community he sees nothing wrong because he views everything in stark realities—including his religion, which cannot be questioned. Is he the "good" one because he will never stray from his faith? Or is Aaron who questions everything? For me it is Aaron, who does *not* have the answers, who is the hero of the book, not the fanatic Zev.

It was while I was finishing *Sworn Enemies,* working with my editor Beverly Horowitz at Bantam Doubleday Dell who was, by the way, a terrific editor, that my agent (at the time), Amy Berkower, called to ask if I'd be interested in writing a book for a new Holocaust Centre to

Carol in April 1955.

open in Washington, D.C., called the United States Holocaust Memorial Museum. Apparently the museum had approached Beverly and asked her to recommend an author—she recommended me. Some problems then ensued, and for some reason the museum and Bantam could not come to an understanding. The project was moved to Scholastic who had just bought *Lisa's War* and *Code Name Kris* for paperback publication. They seemed happy to have me remain on the project.

And then began the most difficult project of my writing career. It was March when Amy called, March of 1992. The museum was due to open in the spring of 1993. They needed the book in three months, and I had already committed to a long speaking tour in April. They flew me to Washington where I met those in charge. I assumed they would give me all kinds of material, but in fact they simply told me this: We are having an exhibit called Daniel's Story. We want a book to complement the exhibit so children who have been through it can go to the bookstore and read about what it might have been like for a real boy. Our character is an everyboy. Yours must be an individual story. We want you to use the same name, Daniel; he must live in Germany, be sent to the Lodz Ghetto, Auschwitz, then Buchenwald. He must live. The rest is up to you. (Since the publication there has been constant confusion about my book—is it based on the exhibit or is the exhibit based on my book? Americans almost universally assume the former, Canadians the latter. Neither is true. They are two completely separate entities, but complementary.) I was then sent home.

Unlike my other historicals I had no time to organize interviews so I did all my research from books and videos. There is really an amazing amount of material on video—for instance there was a film shot of the Lodz Ghetto so I was able to see exactly what it looked like then. I read history books, and I also read as many memoirs and diaries

as I could—many of which were found after the war, the writer not having survived. I cried every day.

Although I *had* written two books set in World War II, they were not Holocaust books in the strict sense. One was about the *rescue* of the Jews, the other about the resistance. I had *never* considered writing about the Holocaust—I'd felt it was a topic only to be tackled by those who had been through it. But when the museum asked I never considered saying no. It was a great responsibility, but I felt that with them behind me I could tackle it. I had no idea how it would change my life. More about that a little later.

I had to change my usual way of writing, which was to research first, spend time thinking, and then write. In this case I began to write as I was still researching—continuing to read at night while I wrote during the day. I felt that I was on the right track when one day I wrote a scene (the one where Daniel is close to death from typhus and his mother heals him in a dream) and that night *after* writing it I read almost the same story in a book called *Hasidic Tales of the Holocaust.*

Finally by the end of July I had written three drafts (as usual Perry Nodelman had read at least one draft and given me a critique, something he does before I ever send it off to the publisher) and sent it off.

And then out of the blue I received a twenty-page fax (in small type) from the museum's resident scholar listing all the "mistakes" in the book. I was truly beside myself. Luckily my oldest, dearest friend, Morri Mostow, was in town and she calmed me down so I was able to tackle this fax. The first thing I did was call the museum and go over every note explaining where I had gotten the material. It turned out that their scholar didn't like the historian I was using—Martin Gilbert—saying his was secondary source

"I think this is from a trip to Israel in 1968."

"My daughter Rebecca and me, probably in 1979."

work while the museum worked strictly from primary sources. (Only years later was I told that many historians disagree with the museum's historian and prefer Gilbert.)

Then there were specific disagreements. For instance the museum was uncomfortable with a scene I had written when Daniel's aunt is attacked for being a Jew on the streets of Frankfurt. This attack happened *before* Kristalnacht, which according to my research was accurate. However they wanted my readers to think of Kristalnacht (the night of the broken glass when the brown shirts attacked Jewish shops and broke their windows, burned, looted, and beat up Jews) as the beginning of the violence. I loved the scene and didn't want to lose it, and besides I knew that my research was correct. Perry came up with the compromise. He suggested making the scene a bad nightmare Daniel has before Kristalnacht actually happened. The museum was happy with that.

Another note here: because I was dealing with the museum, Scholastic, and Daniel Weiss, the packager who had put the deal together, we had decided I should only have one contact—my editor at Daniel Weiss—so I didn't have three different people telling me what to do. This was resolutely stuck to except for the one conversation about the fax. It was for the best, but sometimes it would have helped if I could have fought things out directly with the museum.

Another problem the museum had was the scene where Daniel dressed up in a Hitler Youth uniform. They felt it was immoral for a Jewish boy to do such a thing, but I had read about exactly this happening in one of the memoirs and I thought it worked. I wouldn't back down on that, but I did put in a scene where Daniel himself decides to put it away, not wanting to wear the uniform of such brutality, even if it meant less freedom for himself.

Another fight didn't end so happily. They insisted I take out all references to the Jewish Police in the ghetto. I felt they were being revisionist, not wanting me to discuss the fact that Jews worked with the Nazis either to gain privileges for themselves and their families, or because they felt they could enforce the rules in a more humane way than the Nazis. I rewrote those scenes over and over, but each time they came back with a "no," take it all out. On this they refused to budge. I did finally take out most of my references. It wasn't until the museum opened and I was able to speak to Susan Morgenstern at the museum directly (remember this had all gone through my editor) that she told me the reason they didn't want the police included was not because they were trying to deny it happened but because they felt the Jewish Police were as bad as the Nazis—not something I could have dealt with in such a short book. I still disagree with that decision, but it was the only thing (and we are talking about a few paragraphs) that I really never felt comfortable with.

Finally all the big and small changes were made and the book was done. Scholastic was so pleased they decided to do a limited run in hardcover. When the reviews came out, unfortunately they reviewed the book as if it were no more than a novelization of the exhibit. Scholastic's publicity department was partly to blame because they basically said that was what the book was in all their press releases. It was only years later when I met the Scholastic publicity head in person that I was able to convince him of his mistake. (I had tried, my agent had tried, but they just didn't seem to understand!) It didn't matter though. The book had been review proof. It is now on the curriculum of many school districts (including all of Illinois, I believe) and continues to sell strongly all over North America, far exceeding the small expectation of a book to be sold in the museum bookstore.

I mentioned earlier that this book changed my life. Let me go into that in more detail. When I was a child I learned about the Holocaust, became so distraught and upset at the cruelty, that it was probably the beginning of my loss of faith. After all, if there was a God, how could God permit such cruelty? From then on I basically tried to avoid the topic, doing no reading on it, avoiding anything about it because it was too upsetting. When asked if I would write this book I can't really say why I agreed so quickly—it never felt like a decision. I simply would never have said no to such an offer. But once into the material I had to confront all the cruelty I had been avoiding all my life. It was then that I became so depressed I decided that the world, the human race, didn't deserve to exist as we were capable of too much evil. But in the middle of this terrible depression I suddenly realized something else. Who was I to make such a judgement? Wasn't it similar to the judgement the Nazis had made about the Jews—the Jews didn't deserve to exist? I had to accept that the world *is*. And as is, it is populated with human beings, each one of whom is capable of good or evil. I would have to accept that.

The key scene of *Daniel's Story* is when Erika expresses this view to Daniel and Rosa. And then she tells them that they do have choices—the choice to choose love or hate. And I believe that to be true. No matter what, we can always choose—even during the Holocaust those whose free choice had been completely taken away, those who were brutally murdered, could choose whether to die in love or hate. And so many had love in their hearts (not for their enemies, that is *not* the Jewish way) but for their families. The Nazis could not destroy that.

I suppose that was the beginning of my return to some kind of faith and to a belief in God—not an old man looking down on us God, but God as Creator, as One. I now read a lot of Jewish spirituality, Rabbi David Cooper, Lawrence Kushner, and in a slightly different vein, the Dalai Lama! So strange that writing about the worst of humankind could return my faith.

At this point in this essay I'd like to stop going over each and every book and write a little about my writing process in general. I have developed a particular way of working. First comes the idea—a story and along with the story an issue, ethical or moral, that I want to explore. I start to think about it, live with it. Characters begin to form in my mind. If it is an historical, I begin my research and reading and do my interviews. When I really settle down to work it probably takes three months to do most of my intensive research. I then write the first draft, which takes perhaps three or four weeks. I give it to Perry to read. He reads it, we meet, he gives me his thoughts—often a very detailed critique. I rewrite the book, which takes another three or four weeks. Then I send it off to the publisher.

Over the years I've had a number of different publishers because I write so many different kinds of books—I've never been able to find one publisher who wanted to publish all my different books. One wants my historicals, one prefers fantasies, and another likes the contemporary fiction. The closest I have ever come to a publisher who is open to all sorts of different books is my present Canadian publisher, Scholastic Canada. They are definitely the most flexible of any publisher I've dealt with—something I credit almost completely to my editor there, Diane Kerner.

At any rate my editor or, as is often the case, my editors—one in the United States and one in Canada—will

Carol with her father, about 1982. "He passed away in 1986."

Sam as a baby.

give me their critiques. They can consist of many small things or, as in the case of *In My Enemy's House,* the addition of three more chapters! David Gale, my editor at Simon and Schuster, felt *The Garden* started too slowly, so chapter three became chapter one, to start the story off with more punch. Some editors make fewer suggestions, some make very detailed suggestions. The only editor I had a really hard time working with was the editor of *Jesper,* in Canada. She had previously only worked on nonfiction books, and she demanded changes, almost sentence by sentence. To make matters worse, if she didn't like what I'd written, she would rewrite it herself! It is one thing to say to an author, "This doesn't work, change it." But when you discover half your manuscript rewritten, it is a nightmare. I was young then (as a writer) and I acquiesced far too much, although I also fought her over practically everything. Now I would simply send back the manuscript and demand a different editor. In fact, there are some sentences in that book that are not mine at all—or I don't *feel* they are mine, she interfered so much. Other than that experience my editors have been wonderful to work with—Beverly Horowitz, who edited *Sworn Enemies* and *The Burning Time;* Barbara Berson, who edited *The Race, The Freak,* and *Telling*; David Gale, who edited *After the War, The Garden, Greater Than Angels, In My Enemy's House,* the entire "Mind" series, and continues as my editor at the time of this writing; Diane Kerner, who published all of the same books as David and had her editorial input as well as editing *Cloning Miranda* and *The Lost Locket*; and Peter Atwood, who edited the Canadian edition of *Of Two Minds,* which was published first. Since I have published twenty-five books at this time, there are more editors I have worked with, but these are the pivotal ones.

So, I finish the third draft and send it back to my editor. There is always a fourth draft. This is mostly little things—details that are not clear, sentences not working, etc. For instance I rewrote the scene in *The Garden* when Ruth shoots the Arab soldiers at least ten times before David felt it was clear enough. Finally, it is time for the copyedit. This is the part I like the least. Grammar, small inconsistencies. . . . I had one copy editor (they are different for each book) who was a comma maniac. She put commas in every single sentence I'd written. I couldn't simply take them out without considering each one. A week later and with the biggest headache of my life, the manuscript was practically back to the way it looked before she'd done the copyedit. Commas are very important. I like to leave them out at times, though, to give the feeling of real thought, to keep a certain rhythm.

Finally, there is the last draft or the galleys, or page proofs. This is the way the book will look when it goes into print, so it is important to try to catch any typos. Actually, I'm not very good at that—most writers aren't. We are too familiar with the material. That is why the publisher hires a totally separate person to copyedit—someone who's never seen the manuscript before and will see the little mistakes.

During this time there is work on the title and the cover. I'm not very good at titles and often my titles have been thought up by my editor, or a friend—sometimes Perry. Usually the title I like the publisher hates, thinking it won't sell the book. Covers are another issue. The publisher is supposed to send you a rough draft of the cover and is supposed to consult you. I find that often I don't see it until it is a finished copy and too late to make any changes. I have a couple of favorite covers and a couple I hate. Most are OK. *In My Enemy's House* is a favorite. *The Burning Time* and *The Race* are my least favorite. I also loved *Of Two Minds,* the Simon and Schuster version.

This entire process usually takes two years from the beginning to the end when the book comes out. Because of the way I work, however, I don't only produce one book every two years. Usually I produce two books every year.

"My mother and I," August 1997.

"From left: my husband, Per Brask, my stepson, Justin Brask, my father in law, Olaf Brask, and my mother in law, Inge Brask," Tivoli, Copenhagen, 1998.

This is because I like to work—and while a manuscript may be sitting with my editors, for instance, I can be working on a draft of another title.

I'd like to talk a little, here, about my collaboration with Perry Nodelman. We have written four books together to date. It all started when I gave him a first draft of a fantasy I'd written. As usual he gave me his critique, I went away, did some rewriting, came back, and he reread it. He told me I hadn't done anything he'd suggested—which mainly was to expand the male character, Coren. I told him I couldn't, and if he thought it was so easy then he should do it himself! He said fine, he would! And so began our collaboration. He did draft two. I did a third one. He did a fourth. We went on like that for years until we felt it was good enough to send out to publishers. A local publisher, Bain and Cox, was starting a new fiction line and decided to take it. One winter day, at thirty-five degrees below zero, Perry, Peter Atwood, the publisher and the editor of Bain and Cox, and I met at the University of Winnipeg for an editorial session. A tire on my car had burst from the cold just as I arrived for the meeting and so we were stuck there for hours waiting for the Canadian Automobile Association repair truck. We sat in Perry's office as Peter put his finger on what wasn't working—and then Perry and I started brainstorming. By the time the afternoon was over we'd completely restructured the novel. Perry up until then had been writing the character of Coren, I'd been doing Lenora. After that we stopped taking a character each but continued to alternate drafts, never actually writing together. After each draft we would discuss what needed to be done next and whoever's turn it was would go and do the work.

In fact we've worked that way ever since. We brainstorm the outline, then I do the first draft, he does the second, etc. It's a lot of fun working together because you don't have half the pressure of working alone—well, in fact, you have half. If you get stuck there's always someone

Carol Matas with her co-author and friend, Perry Nodelman.

to call. And I always enjoy our brainstorming sessions, which usually take place on the phone.

As well as my collaboration with Perry I've also collaborated with my husband, Per Brask. He has been a huge support to me throughout my writing career. When I write a first draft, I read whatever I've written that day to him, every night. He doesn't criticize much, he just tells me that he wants to know what happens next, and that really helps me keep up my momentum. We decided to adapt my book *Lisa* for the theatre. He is a professor of theatre and teaches play writing. He is also a playwright. I think he did more of the writing in this case than I did, but both our names are on the play. It had very successful runs across Canada and may be done soon in Israel. We also adapted *Jesper* together, and on my own I did an adaptation of *Sworn Enemies,* called *The Escape,* that was produced in Winnipeg.

My book *The Primrose Path* is the title I'd like to end this article on. I consider it one of my best books. It is not, however, one of my best-sellers, for the reasons that it has quietly been taken off the shelves (or never put there) by most Jewish libraries and it could never find an American publisher. It is about an Orthodox Jewish rabbi who molests children. Publishers were afraid to publish it,

afraid they would be accused of being anti-Semitic. As for me, I got a lot of advice—most of it to change the rabbi to a priest! Jews didn't want anyone thinking they could be or do bad. But what does that say? Doesn't it say that we Jews are *better* than everyone else, not having both good and bad? Doesn't it say to any Jewish children who may have been abused—keep quiet, it doesn't happen to Jews? The other thing that really upset me about this was the adult assumption that children should be "kept" innocent. The first problem with that is that they are *not* innocent. They have encountered the school bully, a mean friend, even a cruel parent. The second thing is that this so-called innocence is really ignorance, and ignorance is *not* bliss. Knowledge is power. And children *must* be empowered. When I look back at most of my books the central character is not the one who has the answers. She is the one who asks the questions. But she must also make decisions, decisions that will matter to her and to those around her. And pretending the world is different than it is, is no help to young people. They need help dealing with reality. They also deserve to have fun and enjoy themselves.

At this point in time my twenty-sixth book is on the way. I have just finished a second draft of my book on the Civil War and am waiting, anxiously, to hear from my editors. I hope to continue doing what I'm doing as long as I can—because I love it. There's really no other reason. And as long as I have a story to tell and a question to ask, I hope I'll continue to write books that young people like to read.

Which brings me to my last point. Since writing my first word my goal has always been to tell a good story and, like my hero, L. Frank Baum, delight my readers. Many of my books are considered controversial because I deal with topics I think young people are concerned about, even if they are things adults don't like to deal with. I know I write about heavy topics. But more important is the fact that I write so that whoever is reading won't want to put the book down—they'll want to read after lights out, or after they've been called for dinner. And when they are finished they'll be a little sorry, because they had fun. Few people these days seem to talk about the pleasure of reading, but that is the main reason I write. Even when choosing a topic, I always choose one that hasn't been done before, thinking what fun it'll be for the reader to read on a topic they've never encountered before.

So happy reading.

Writings

FOR YOUNG ADULTS; FICTION

The D.N.A. Dimension, Gage Publishing (Toronto), 1982.
The Fusion Factor, Fifth House (Saskatoon), 1986, published as *It's Up to Us,* Stoddard, 1991.
Zanu, Fifth House, 1986.
Me, Myself and I, Fifth House, 1987.
Lisa, Lester & Orpen Dennys (Toronto), 1987, published in the U.S. as *Lisa's War,* Scribner, 1989.

Jesper, Lester & Orpen Dennys, 1989, published in the U.S. as *Code Name Kris,* Scribner, 1990.

The Race, HarperCollins, 1991.

Sworn Enemies, Bantam, 1993.

Daniel's Story, Scholastic, 1993.

The Burning Time, Bantam, 1994.

The Primrose Path, Bain & Cox, 1995.

After the War, Simon & Schuster, 1996.

The Freak, Key Porter (Toronto), 1997.

The Garden, Simon & Schuster, 1997.

Greater Than Angels, Simon & Schuster, 1998.

Telling, Key Porter, 1998.

In My Enemy's House, Simon and Schuster, 1999.

Cloning Miranda, Scholastic (Canada), 1999.

"MIND" SERIES; WITH PERRY NODELMAN

Of Two Minds, Bain & Cox (Winnipeg), 1994, Simon & Schuster, 1995.

More Minds, Simon & Schuster, 1996.

Out of Their Minds, Simon and Schuster, 1998.

Meeting of Minds, Simon and Schuster, 1999.

FOR CHILDREN; FICTION

Adventure in Legoland, Scholastic, 1991.

Safari Adventure in Legoland, Scholastic, 1993.

The Lost Locket, illustrated by Susan Gardos, Scholastic, 1994.

OTHER

Several of Matas's novels have been translated into Danish, French, Swedish, Spanish, Dutch and Turkish. *Lisa* was adapted for a play with Per Brask, Prairie Theater Exchange, 1991; Geordie Productions, Montreal, 1994; and Golden Horse Shoe, Toronto, 1994. *Sworn Enemies* was adapted for a play from the book for adult audiences, was read at Jewish Repertory Theater, New York, 1994, and was also read at the Barbra Streisand New Play Festival in Los Angeles in 1997. *The Escape* was produced by the Winnipeg Jewish Theater, 1993, as a young adult play. *Telling* was adapted for a radio play, CBC Manitoba, October 1994. *Jesper* was adapted for a play with Per Brask.

McDONALD, Meme 1954-

Personal

Born July 19, 1954 in St. George, Australia; daughter of Kevin and Pat McDonald.

Addresses

Agent—Jenny Darling & Associates, P.O. Box 235, Richmond, Victoria 3121, Australia.

Career

Writer and photographer. Worked as a theater performer and director.

Awards, Honors

New South Wales State Literary Award for Nonfiction and Braille and Talking Book Award, both 1993, both for *Put Your Whole Self In;* Wilderness Society Environmental Award Shortlist, 1997, for *The Way of the Birds;* Special Commendation at the 1998 Human Rights Awards, and shortlisted for Book of the Year, Children's Book Council of Australia, 1998, both for *Maybe Tomorrow;* Book of the Year, Children's Book Council of Australia, 1999, for *My Girragundji.*

Writings

FOR CHILDREN

The Way of the Birds: A Child and a Curlew Travel Across the World, illustrated by Shane Nagle, Allen & Unwin, 1996.

(With Boori (Monty) Pryor) *My Girragundji,* with photographs by McDonald, Allen & Unwin, 1998.

(With Boori (Monty) Pryor) *The Binna Binna Man,* with photographs by McDonald, Allen & Unwin, 1999.

OTHER

Put Your Whole Self In, Penguin, 1992.

(With Boori (Monty) Pryor) *Maybe Tomorrow,* illustrated by Lilian Fourmile, with photographs by McDonald, Penguin, 1998.

Adaptations

The Way of the Birds was animated for broadcast television and international distribution, Daro Film Distribution, 1999.

Sidelights

Meme McDonald told *SATA:* "Growing up in the bush, I have always related very strongly to the land. I remember wondering about the spirits you could feel all around. Working with the Wurundjeri, the people indigenous to where I now live in Melbourne, and writing books with Boori [Pryor] and being part of his family, fills that vacuum, giving me a new and richer understanding of belonging in this country."

Meme McDonald

Although Meme McDonald lived in Australia, she knew little of the Aboriginal culture as a child. As she began to listen to others' stories, the basis for her writing began to grow. She worked with a theater group that performed outdoors, telling epic stories with large visual images, dance, music, pyrotechnics, and casts of hundreds. While working with the Wurundjeri people, she met Boori Pryor. They have since collaborated on three books.

"All my books have been written in collaboration with other people," McDonald continued, "the women at the baths, bird-lovers, Boori [Pryor] and his family, and also agents, editors, publishers, and friends offering opinions. This is a very important aspect of writing for me. I also like to write for many different age groups. It is the idea that dictates the form of the story."

Maybe Tomorrow, written in collaboration with Boori Pryor, is an autobiographical account of Pryor's struggle with discrimination and tragedy as an Aborigine in Australia, and his attempts to reconcile his Aboriginal heritage with the "white man's world" through mutual respect and understanding. Critics have praised the book as intimate and honest—*Magpies* critic Kevin Steinberger wrote, "*Maybe Tomorrow* deserves a wide audience—as young as twelve-years-old—not just for Pryor's positive mission but equally for the easy

storytelling of his memoirs of childhood and growing up black in a white man's world."

Works Cited

Steinberger, Kevin, review of *Maybe Tomorrow, Magpies,* March 1998, p. 41.

*   *   *

McKIE, Robin

Personal

Male.

Addresses

Office— *Observer,* London, England. *Agent*—c/o Henry Holt and Co., 115 West Eighteenth St., New York, NY 10011.

Career

Writer and editor. Science editor of the *Observer,* London, England.

Writings

NONFICTION; FOR CHILDREN

Lasers, illustrations by Paul Cooper, Elsa Godfrey, and Rob Shone, Franklin Watts (New York City), 1983.
Technology: Science at Work, Franklin Watts (New York City), 1984.
Nuclear Power, illustrations by Mike Saunders and others, Gloucester Press (New York City), 1985.
Solar Power, Gloucester Press (New York City), 1985.
Robots, Franklin Watts (New York City), 1986.
Energy, Hampstead Press (New York City), 1989.

FOR ADULTS

Panic: The Story of AIDS, Thorsons, 1986.
(With Nigel Hawkes, Geoffrey Lean, David Leigh, Peter Pringle, and Andrew Wilson) *Chernobyl: The End of the Nuclear Dream,* Vintage Books (New York City), 1987.
The Genetic Jigsaw: The Story of the New Genetics, Oxford University Press (New York City), 1988.
(With Walter Bodmer) *The Book of Man: The Human Genome Project and the Quest to Discover Our Genetic Heritage,* Little, Brown (London), 1994, Scribner (New York City), 1995.
(With Christopher Stringer) *African Exodus: The Origins of Modern Humanity,* Holt/John Macrae (New York City), 1997.

Contributor to periodicals, including *World.*

Sidelights

Robin McKie is a writer and science editor of the *Observer* in London, England. McKie has published books on subjects ranging from human origin to acquired immune deficiency syndrome (AIDS) and has produced many science volumes for children. Noteworthy among McKie's works is *African Exodus: The Origins of Modern Humanity,* which was written with Christopher Stringer. *African Exodus* challenges the notion that humans evolved in multiple regions approximately two million years ago; rather, it argues that the human race developed in Africa and began migrating throughout the remainder of the world approximately one hundred thousand years ago. In the book, McKie and Stringer contend that the remarkable genetic similarities among various races are of greater importance than the racial differences revealed in other studies. Despite its unconventional approach to the theory of human evolution, *African Exodus* received widely positive reviews, in particular for its authors' ability to make complex anthropological information comprehendible to readers. A reviewer for *Publishers Weekly* called *African Exodus* "intellectually potent yet eminently accessible."

McKie has also written about genetics in such works as *The Genetic Jigsaw: The Story of the New Genetics* and—with Walter Bodmer—*The Book of Man: The Human Genome Project and the Quest to Discover Our Genetic Heritage.* In addition, McKie has published *Panic: The Story of AIDS.*

McKie has also produced many science volumes for young readers. These writings for children include *Energy,* which considers alternatives to petroleum and nuclear power; *Lasers; Technology: Science at Work,* which addresses subjects such as energy generation, computer design, and space exploration; *Nuclear Power,* which explains both fission and fusion and provides arguments both for and against nuclear energy; *Solar Power;* and *Robots.* McKie's books for children have been highly praised for their deft handling of the material and inclusion of glossaries, photographs, and diagrams designed to further facilitate children's understanding of complex subjects.

Works Cited

Review of African Exodus, *Publishers Weekly,* June 9, 1997, p. 33.

For More Information See

PERIODICALS

Booklist, July, 1997, p. 1785.
Growing Point, September, 1985, p. 4500.
Junior Bookshelf, December, 1983, p. 246.
Library Journal, June 15, 1997, p. 78.
School Library Journal, March, 1986, p. 158; September, 1989, p. 259.*

MITCHISON, Naomi Margaret (Haldane) 1897-1999

OBITUARY NOTICE—See index for *SATA* sketch: Born November 1, 1897, in Edinburgh, Scotland; died January 11, 1999, in Mull of Kintyre, Argyll, Scotland. Political activist and author. Throughout Mitchison's long life she was perhaps equally well known for her occasionally shocking personal life as for her astonishingly busy writing life. The author of thousands of magazine articles as well as books of biography, fiction, philosophy, short stories, memoirs, plays, poems, and histories, Mitchison will likely be remembered as one of the century's first feminists. She was born to a privileged background and educated at Oxford but was prevented from following in the footsteps of her scientist father by the conventions of her class and gender. She married in 1916 and began publishing in 1923, causing a sensation by her treatment of such taboo subjects as incest, abortion, rape, and infanticide in her work, elements that often brought her up against censors and hesitant publishers. In the 1920s, she and her husband agreed to conduct an open marriage and, in the 1930s, she helped establish the first birth control clinics in London. Mitchison was known for her passions: it is said that she physically assaulted an objectionable dinner guest or two in her time, and her strong political opinions inspired her to run, if unsuccessfully, for parliament in the 1930s. Her 1931 novel *The Corn King and the Spring Queen* examines sexual and cultural conflicts in ancient Greece, and she considered her 1935 novel *We Have Been Warned,* a tale of seduction, rape, and abortion, a contemporary history of her own generation. Among other notable works may be included two classic science fiction novels, *Travel Light,* published in 1952, and *Memoirs of a Spacewoman,* which appeared in 1962. She wrote numerous works for children, such as *Nix-Nought-Nothing: Four Plays for Children,* published in 1928, and *The Far Harbour: A Novel for Girls and Boys,* published in 1957. Her *Outline for Boys and Girls and Their Parents,* which was published in 1932, was long considered an invaluable guide for politically progressive parenting. A son introduced her to James Watson, whose groundbreaking work on DNA, published in *The Double Helix,* which is dedicated to her, she helped edit. In the 1960s, she became honorary mother to the chief of a tribe in Botswana, where she travelled several times while in her nineties. Her interest in Africa also inspired several books, including *African Heroes* in 1968, and in 1973, *Sunrise Tomorrow: A Story of Botswana* and *A Life for Africa: The Story of Bram Fischer.* Though her husband was a baron, Mitchison refused to be addressed by her title, as she once refused to accept the Order of the British Empire; she did accept a Companion of the British Empire appointment in 1985, however.

OBITUARIES AND OTHER SOURCES:

PERIODICALS

London Times, January 13, 1999.
Los Angeles Times, January 13, 1999, p. A12.

New York Times, January 16, 1999, p. C17.

* * *

MULFORD, Philippa Greene 1948-

Personal

Born May 29, 1948, in New York, NY; daughter of Philip Murray (a radio station owner) and Constance (an author of books for young people; maiden name, Clarke) Greene; married Andrews S. Kennedy, January 9, 1971 (divorced); married R. Edward Mulford (a businessman), September 29, 1978; stepchildren: Nicholas, Leslie. *Education:* Skidmore College, B.A., 1971. *Hobbies and other interests:* "My interests include tennis, water and snow skiing, and my two stepchildren who keep me on my toes. I am also an avid bluefisherwoman (meaning I fish blues off of Chappaquiddick Island where we have a house)."

Addresses

Home and office—Rural Delivery 1, Box 14, Norton Ave., Clinton, NY 13323. *Agent*—Marilyn Marlow, Curtis Brown, Ltd., 575 Madison Ave., New York, NY 10022.

Career

Steuben Glass, New York, NY, sales clerk and customer relations; *Clinton Courier* (weekly newspaper), Clinton, NY, feature writer, 1971-73; Central New York Community Arts Council, Inc., Utica, NY, executive director, 1971-78; full-time writer, 1978-. Consultant to the New York State Council on the Arts, 1973-79. *Member:* New York State Council on the Arts (Arts Service Organization Panel, 1976-78).

Writings

If It's Not Funny, Why Am I Laughing? (young adult novel), Delacorte, 1982.
The World Is My Eggshell (young adult novel), Delacorte, 1986.
Everything I Hoped For (young adult novel), Avon, 1990.
Making Room for Katherine (young adult novel), Simon & Schuster, 1994.
Keys to Successful Stepmothering, Barron's Educational Series, 1996.
Emily Smiley Takes a Shot, Tor, 1998.
The Holly Sisters on Their Own (young adult novel), Marshall Cavendish, 1998.
Emily Smiley Sings the Blues, Tor, 1998.

Sidelights

Philippa Mulford once told *SATA:* "Having a mother who wrote for as long as I can remember is probably the main reason I became a writer. My brother, Shep Greene, has also published a young adult novel, *The Boy Who Drank Too Much,* and that really spurred me on. Talk about sibling rivalry—I know quite a lot about it

coming from a family of five children. You'll probably be seeing more books over the years from Greenes, as my two sisters and younger brother have to keep up with me *and* Shep now. I like to laugh and make other people laugh, and the teenage years are chock-full of reasons to laugh (rather than cry)."

Philippa Greene Mulford's young adult novels are often considered light reading for their focus on the humorous aspects of adolescent romance and family life. Realistically rendered dialogue and a tendency to pack numerous incidents into quick-moving plots complete the picture of novels guaranteed to appeal in particular to adolescent girls. In her first book, *If It's Not Funny, Why Am I Laughing?*, Mulford introduces Mimi Canfield and her best friend, Tuna McElliott, fifteen-year-old girls concerned with losing their virginity and how to relate to members of the opposite sex. When the winner of the "Virgin Pool" meets tragedy at a school picnic, Mimi gains the courage to voice her doubts about the irresponsible expression of sexuality among some of her classmates in the school newspaper. "The author's first book, told in an 'oh my, why is all this happening to me' style, should win her some fans among teenage girls," predicted Frances Friedman in *Voice of Youth Advocates.* The friendship between Mimi and Tuna takes center stage again in Mulford's *Everything I Hoped For,* in which the girls, now sixteen and seventeen, plan a cross-country trip to Arizona during summer vacation, and Mimi's glamorous but irresponsible mother asks Mimi to come live with her. The girls continue to struggle in their relationships with boys, and Mimi must decide whether she wants to be swept up in Tuna's grand plans for summer vacation, and which parent she wants to live with. As in reviews of *If It's Not Funny, Why Am I Laughing?*, critics praised Mulford's grasp of adolescent concerns and their ways of talking about and dealing with them in *Everything I Hoped For.*

In *The World Is My Eggshell,* sixteen-year-old Abbey struggles to create a self-confident identity in a new town after the death of her father. Overshadowed by a seemingly perfect twin, Abbey struggles with school, sports, and boys, aided by her helpful sibling, "with hilarious results," according to Janet Bryan in *School Library Journal.* Crediting Mulford with realistic dialogue and an eye for what teenagers really care about, Bryan also praised the author for her "wonderful picture of family life." A contributor to *Kirkus Reviews* called *The World Is My Eggshell* "intelligent and perceptive," adding that "humor, strong characterization and a lively style distinguish this duckling-to-swan story."

Abbey and her siblings' grief over the loss of their father plays a more central part in the sequel to *The World Is My Eggshell.* In *Making Room for Katherine,* the family is struggling to deal with their loss when they must face the fact that their mother is dating again, and then Katherine, a sophisticated thirteen-year-old cousin who has been living in Paris with her divorced mother, comes to stay, bringing her own share of problems. As reviewers noted in the earlier books, Mulford's "dialogue is witty and realistic" in *Making Room for*

Katherine, according to Connie Tyrrell Burns in *School Library Journal. Booklist* reviewer Jeanne Triner called this "a crisply paced light read that should work especially well with junior-high and reluctant readers."

Works Cited

Bryan, Janet, review of *The World Is My Eggshell, School Library Journal,* May, 1986, pp. 106-7.

Burns, Connie Tyrrell, review of *Making Room for Katherine, School Library Journal,* May, 1994, p. 131.

Friedman, Frances, review of *If It's Not Funny, Why Am I Laughing?, Voice of Youth Advocates,* April, 1983, p. 40.

Triner, Jeanne, review of *Making Room for Katherine, Booklist,* April 15, 1994, p. 1526.

Review of *The World Is My Eggshell, Kirkus Reviews,* March 1, 1986, pp. 391-92.

For More Information See

PERIODICALS

Kliatt, April, 1991, p. 12.
Voice of Youth Advocates, June, 1991, pp. 99-100.*

*   *   *

MUMY, Bill 1954-

Personal

Surname pronounced "*Moo*-mee"; born Charles William Mumy, Jr., February 1, 1954, in San Gabriel, CA; son of Charles William (a cattle rancher) and Muriel Gertrude (Gould) Mumy; married Eileen Joy Davis (a childbirth instructor), October 9, 1986; children: Seth, Liliana. *Education:* Attended Santa Monica City College, CA, 1972-73. *Politics:* Democrat. *Hobbies and other interests:* Comic book collecting, racquetball, swimming, sketching.

Addresses

Agent—Richard Sindell and Associates, 8271 Melrose Avenue, Suite 202, Los Angeles, CA 90046.

Career

Actor, writer, and recording artist. Artist, writer, and producer, *Zabagabee* (video), 1987; creator, with Peter David, *Space Cases* (television series), Nickelodeon, 1996-97. Has performed in or done voice-overs for numerous commercials. Author of musical score for episodes of *The Universe and I* (television series), Public Broadcast System (PBS). Performed with America (rock band), c. 1970s, and with the bands Bill Mumy & the Igloos and the Jenerators. Recording artist on albums, including *Bill Mumy 'BB',* 1980; America's *View from the Ground,* Capitol, 1982, and *Encore: More Greatest Hits,* 1991; as a choir member for *Which One of Us Is Me,* by Jay Gruska, Rhino, 1984; Barnes & Barnes' *Loozanteen,* Rhino, 1991, and *Yeah: The Essential Barnes & Barnes,* Varese Serabande, 1999; *The Dino-*

saur Album (for children), Kid Rhino, 1993; *The Yogi Bear Environmental Album: This Land is Your Land* (for children), Kid Rhino/Hanna Barbera, 1993; the Jenerators' *The Jenerators,* Asil Records, 1994, and *Hitting the Silk,* Wildcat Records, 1998; Seduction of the Innocent's *Golden Age,* 1990; (with Sarah Taylor) *I've Got Some Presents for Santa,* Rhino Records, 1994; and (with the Be Five) *Trying to Forget,* Renaissance Records, 1998.

Actor in television series, including *Matty's Funday Funnies* (animated), ABC, 1959-61; Will Robinson, *Lost in Space,* CBS, 1965-68; *The Two of Us* (pilot), CBS, 1966; Nick Butler, *The Rockford Files* (pilot), NBC, 1974; Weaver, *Sunshine,* NBC, 1974-75; Larry, *Archie* (pilot), ABC, 1976; host, *Inside Space,* 1992-97; Lennier, *Babylon 5,* syndicated, 1994—; and Will Robinson, *Space Family Robinson.* Also appeared as a guest on episodic television, including (debut) *Romper Room; The Twilight Zone,* CBS, 1960, 1961, 1963; *Alfred Hitchcock Presents,* NBC, 1961, 1962, 1975, 1985; *Wagon Train,* NBC, 1962; *Bewitched,* ABC, 1964, 1965; *I Dream of Jeannie,* NBC, 1965; *The Munsters,* CBS, 1965; *The Rockford Files,* NBC, 1975; *Matlock,* NBC, 1986, 1988; *The Flash,* CBS, 1991; *Animaniacs,* Fox, 1993; *Space Ghost Coast to Coast,* Cartoon Network, 1994; *Space Cases,* Nickelodeon, 1996; *The Weird Al Show,* CBS, 1997; *Lancer,* CBS; *Here Come the Brides,* ABC; *Riverboat,* NBC; *Have Gun, Will Travel,* CBS; *The Adventures of Ozzie and Harriet,* ABC; *Ben Casey,* ABC; *Playhouse 90,* CBS; *The Red Skelton Show; The Tennessee Ernie Ford Show; The Loretta Young Show; Dr. Kildare; Me and Mom;* and *Superboy.* Actor in television movies, including *Sunshine,* CBS, 1973, and *Sunshine Christmas,* NBC, 1977.

Actor in films, including *Tammy, Tell Me True,* Universal, 1961; *Sammy the Way-out Seal,* 1962; *Palm Springs Weekend,* Warner Brothers, 1963; *A Ticklish Affair,* Metro-Goldwyn-Mayer, 1963; *A Child Is Waiting,* United Artists, 1963; *Dear Brigitte,* Twentieth Century-Fox, 1965; *Rascal,* Buena Vista, 1969; *Bless the Beasts and Children,* Columbia, 1971: *Papillon,* Allied Artists, 1973; *Sunshine Part II,* 1976; *Twilight Zone—The Movie,* Warner Brothers, 1983; *Hard to Hold,* Universal, 1983; *Captain America,* Columbia, 1992; *Double Trouble,* Motion Picture Corporation of America, 1992; *Three Wishes,* Savoy Pictures, 1995; and *The Wizard of Bagdad. Member:* Academy Motion Picture Arts and Sciences, American Society of Composers, Authors, and Publishers, Screen Actors Guild, American Federation of Musicians, American Federation of Television and Radio Artists.

Awards, Honors

Emmy nomination, for music composition, 1992, for *Disney's Adventures in Wonderland.*

Writings

COMIC BOOKS

(With Miguel Ferrer) *Comet Man,* drawn by Kelley Jones, Marvel Comics, 1987.

(With Ferrer) *The Dreamwalker* (graphic novel), drawn by Gray Morrow, Marvel Comics, 1989.

The Hulk, drawn by Marshall Rogers, Marvel Comics, 1989.

(With Ferrer) *Trypto the Acid Dog,* drawn by Steve Leialoha, Renegade Press, 1989.

Spider Man, drawn by Aaron Lopresti, Marvel Comics, 1990.

Wonder Man, drawn by Brian Murray, Marvel Comics, 1990.

Star Trek (three-issue series), DC Comics, 1990.

Iron Man, drawn by Steve Leialoha, Marvel Comics, 1991.

Lost in Space (four-issue series), drawn by Michael Dutkiewicz, Innovation Comics, 1991-93.

(With Peter David), *The Spectre,* drawn by Steve Ditko, DC Comics, 1998.

Also contributor to comic book series, including "Star Trek," "The Comet Man 2"; "She Hulk"; "The Trainer"; author of "Aquaman," number 44, 1998.

LYRICIST

Bill Mumy, BB, 1980.
Dying to be Heard, Renaissance, 1997.

Author of lyrics for *Kiss My Boo Boo,* Infinite Visions. Composer of more than one hundred songs for episodes of *Disney's Adventures in Wonderland* television program, Disney Channel, 1992.

OTHER

(With Peter David; and composer of music) *Space Cases* (television series), Nickelodeon, 1996-97.

Author, illustrator, and producer of *Zabagabee* (video), 1987.

Work in Progress

A CD-ROM *Lost in Space* story.

Sidelights

In 1995, thirty years after CBS-TV launched its family science-fiction series *Lost in Space, People* magazine ran a profile of the show's former stars, all of whom had kept in touch with one another over the decades. The premise of *Lost in Space,* of course, is contained in its title, and only a little more elaboration serves to give the whole story behind the show: a modern-day Swiss Family Robinson—the Robinsons, as a matter of fact—are sent into space aboard the *Jupiter II,* headed for the Alpha Centauri star cluster. The family includes a father and mother, as well as a teenaged daughter, Judy, and a younger daughter, Penny. Their ship is piloted by the intrepid Don West. But the most memorable characters from the show are the evil Dr. Zachary Smith, who stows away on their craft and causes them to get lost in space; the Robinsons' son Will, who continually succumbs to Dr. Smith's wily attempts at subterfuge; and Will's robot, who utters the most famous line of the show: "Danger, Will Robinson!"

Bill Mumy, who had played the part of Will as an eleven-year-old, told the *People* interviewer that fans of the series still came up to him in public and—much to his chagrin—uttered the infamous warning. It was particularly ironic, given the fact that Mumy had immersed himself in other projects to an extent greater than almost any of his fellow stars on the series. Beginning his acting career at the age of six, Mumy went on to play the alien Lennier on the syndicated television series *Babylon 5,* and has been featured in numerous television series and motion pictures. Aside from *Lost in Space* and *Babylon 5,* his notable television appearances include an unforgettable role on *Twilight Zone* in 1961 as Anthony, a boy with sinister and mysterious powers over others.

In addition to his acting career, Mumy has authored several comic books, and performed guitar as a recording artist. He has received critical praise for his musicianship—Mumy plays guitar, bass, keyboards, banjo, mandolin, percussion, and sings—and has performed both with the rock band America and with fellow musician Robert Haimer as part of Barnes & Barnes. As Barnes & Barnes Mumy and Haimer have recorded a number of albums for both Rhino and CBS Records, and released a feature-length video called *Zabagabee,* for which Mumy authored the script. Mumy had also released a solo album, *Dying to Be Heard* (1998), for which he wrote and performed all the music. With members of the *Babylon 5* cast, he formed the Be Five and released an album called *Trying to Forget.* His other recording projects included several children's releases such as *The Yogi Bear Environmental Album, The Dinosaur Album,* and *Kiss My Boo Boo.* Another CD, on which he performed with Sarah Taylor, was definitely *not* for children: *I've Got Some Presents for Santa,* a sexy novelty Christmas recording.

It was Mumy's music career that led him into comic book writing. With Miguel Ferrer, who played Alfred on the series *Twin Peaks* in the early 1990s, Mumy had formed the Jenerators, a rock band that recorded two CDS. Teaming with Ferrer, he authored several comic books for Marvel Comics, including *The Comet Man,* and the graphic novel *The Dreamwalker* in 1989. Mumy has published comics with Dark Horse Comics, DC Comics, and Pocket Books, and has contributed to several popular comic book series, among them "Star Trek" "Aquaman," and "The Spectre."

With regard to Mumy's *Lost in Space* comic book, according to a contributor to *USA Today,* Mumy had been "skeptical" about the project at first, simply because he had long tried to bring it to fruition but had been stymied by licensing issues. And though he had planned "a one-shot finale," when comic publisher Innovation turned *Lost in Space* into a multi-issue set that sold between 25,000 and 40,000 copies per issue, he was not displeased. "I had grave reservations about going back to *Lost in Space,*" Mumy told *USA Today.* "On the other hand, I felt very protective about the characters. I thought that this way I could keep my eyes on them and keep them moving in the right direction."

Yet another Mumy project was *Space Cases,* a show on the Nickelodeon cable network that he created with Peter David. Walt Belcher of the *Tampa Tribune* described the series, which Mumy co-wrote and for which he composed the music, as "a cross between 'Lost in Space' and 'Star Trek.' It's about a crew of teen space cadets, some of them aliens, who were on a training mission when they got lost in space. Now they have to work together to get out of jams." Mumy told Belcher: "The beauty of working in science fiction is you can let your imagination run wild. But I wanted to do a show that had humor in it. So, we write the show the same way we write the comic books—for ourselves. We want it to be fun." Another feature of the show is its use of titles that refer to rock songs: "We Gotta Get out of This Place," "Nowhere Man," and "Forever Young." "It's an inside joke," Mumy said.

In 1998, with the release of the film version of *Lost in Space,* Mumy revealed that years earlier, he had written his own *Lost in Space* script, which would now serve as a basis for a CD-ROM. The story behind the script was painful for Mumy, as he indicated in a *New York Times* article. He had written the screenplay, called *The Epilogue,* and in 1980 submitted it to Irwin Allen, creator of *Lost in Space,* for his approval. But by then Allen had gone on to other things, developing a reputation for disaster films such as *The Towering Inferno.* "He was really rude," Mumy recalled. "He was making feature films, and the last words he said were, 'If at any future time I want to do "Lost in Space," it will be because I want to, not you.'" Mumy planned to re-work the story, which finds the cast marooned for years with no hope of returning to Earth, for CD-ROM. As the story progresses, the Robinsons discover a means to return to Earth, and they do so—but only after they run into trouble with aliens, a conflict from which not everyone will survive. According to the *New York Times,* "Mumy won't say who" dies. But he did express his purpose in writing the script: "I wanted to bring them home."

Works Cited

Belcher, Walt, "Billy Mumy Makes a Case for Space," *Tampa Tribune,* March 16, 1996, p. 1.
"Danger! Your Script Will Not Be Optioned!" *New York Times,* March 22, 1998, p. 19.
"Mumy's Trip Back to Space," *USA Today,* June 10, 1992, p. 4D.

For More Information See

BOOKS

Contemporary Theatre, Film, and Television, Volume 18, Gale (Detroit), 1998.

PERIODICALS

Orange County Register, October 16, 1997, p. E1.
People, June 3, 1991, p. 46; July 17, 1995, pp. 46-47.
Publishers Weekly, October 18, 1993, p. 28.
Tampa Tribune, November 7, 1995, p. 3.
USA Today, February 28, 1996, p. 3D.

OTHER

The Official Bill Mumy Web Site, http://www.billmumy.com (January 5, 1999).*

P–R

*   *   *

PRYOR, Boori (Monty) 1950-

Personal

Born July 12, 1950 in Townsville, North Queensland, Australia; son of Monty and Dot Pryor.

Addresses

Agent—Jenny Darling & Associates, P.O. Box 235, Richmond, Victoria 3121, Australia.

Career

Performer, storyteller, and writer. Has worked in various industries, including education, film, television, modeling, sports, and music.

Awards, Honors

Award from the National Aboriginal and Islander Observance Committee, 1993, for the promotion of indigenous culture; Special Commendation at the 1998 Human Rights Awards, and shortlisted for Book of the Year, Children's Book Council of Australia, 1998, both for *Maybe Tomorrow;* Book of the Year, Children's Book Council of Australia, 1999, for *My Girragundji.*

Writings

(With Meme McDonald) *Maybe Tomorrow,* illustrated by Lilian Fourmile, with photographs by McDonald, Penguin, 1998.
(With McDonald) *My Girragundji* (for children), with photographs by McDonald, Allen & Unwin, 1998.

Boori Pryor

(With McDonald) *The Binna Binna Man,* (for children), with photographs by McDonald, Allen & Unwin, 1999.

Sidelights

Boori Pryor told *SATA:* "I've written a lot of poetry over the years. I always thought I was too busy to sit down and write a book. That's why it worked well writing *Maybe Tomorrow, My Girragundji,* and *The Binna*

Binna Man with Meme [McDonald]. It is like we are both looking through the same window but with different eyes, with different points of view. We combine our strengths—my storytelling and her writing—so that what is created is better than either of us could do on our own."

Pryor has collaborated with Meme McDonald on three books, *Maybe Tomorrow, My Girragundji,* and *The Binna Binna Man.* The two met in Melbourne where they were both working for the Wurundjeri, the people indigenous to the Melbourne area.

Maybe Tomorrow is an autobiographical account of Pryor's struggle with discrimination and tragedy as an Aborigine in Australia, and his attempts to reconcile his Aboriginal heritage with the "white man's world" through mutual respect and understanding. Critics have praised the book as intimate and honest. Kevin Steinberger, a critic for *Magpies,* wrote, "*Maybe Tomorrow* deserves a wide audience—as young as twelve-years-old—not just for Pryor's positive mission but equally for the easy storytelling of his memoirs of childhood and growing up black in a white man's world."

Pryor went on to tell *SATA:* "For Aboriginal people, storytelling is a large part of our lives. Because of my love of stories as a child, I found myself being a storyteller as an adult. I learned to be the story as I told it, so that people would go on the journey with me. They could taste the saltwater and see the teeth of the giant crocodile shining in the sun, creating their own images through watching and listening."

Pryor sees himself as one of the many who are creating links between Aboriginal culture and other cultures within Australia and across the world, He travels extensively throughout the year to perform for school students and adult groups throughout Australia and Europe.

Works Cited

Steinberger, Kevin, review of *Maybe Tomorrow, Magpies,* March 1998, p. 41.

*   *   *

RADLEY, Gail 1951-

Personal

Born May 21, 1951, in Boston, MA; daughter of Earl Adrian (a government employee) and Bernice Howell (a social worker) Radley; married Joseph Killeen (director of a community corrections center), July 23, 1975; children: Anthony, Jana. *Education:* Mary Baldwin College, B.A, 1989; Stetson University, M.A. 1994. *Politics:* "Not aligned." *Religion:* Baha'i.

Gail Radley

Addresses

Home—875 Church St., DeLand, FL 32724. *Electronic mail*—gradley@stetson.edu.

Career

Lecturer, Stetson University, 1993-present. *Member:* Florida College English Association (FCEA), Society of Children's Book Writers and Illustrators (SCBWI).

Writings

PICTURE BOOKS

The Night Stella Hid the Stars, illustrated by John Wallner, Crown, 1978.
Zahra's Search, illustrated by Winifred Barnum Newman, Baha'i, 1982.
The Spinner's Gift: A Tale, illustrated by Paige Miglio, North-South Books, 1994.
A Feast of ABCs, George Ronald Publisher, 1996.
The Flute Player and the Lazy One, George Ronald, 1999.

PRETEEN NOVELS

Nothing Stays the Same Forever, Crown, 1981.
CF in His Corner, Four Winds, 1984.
The Golden Days, Macmillan, 1991.
Odd Man Out, Macmillan, 1995.
Dear Gabby, Things Are Getting out of Hand, Avon Books, 1998.
Kyle Jeffries, Pilgrim, George Ronald Publisher, forthcoming.

YOUNG ADULT

The World Turned Inside Out, Crown, 1982.
Second Birth, (nonfiction) Baha'i (Great Britain), 1984.
The Quest, Nine Pines, 1993.

"VANISHING FROM" SERIES

Waterways, illustrated by Jean Sherlock, Lerner, 1998.
Deserts and Plains, illustrated by Jean Sherlock, Lerner, 1999.
Forests and Jungles, illustrated by Jean Sherlock, Lerner, forthcoming.
Skies, illustrated by Jean Sherlock, Lerner, forthcoming.
Grasslands and Deserts, illustrated by Jean Sherlock, Lerner, forthcoming.

OTHER

Special Strengths (short story collection), Bellwood, 1984.
(Selector) *Rainy Day Rhymes* (juvenile poetry anthology), Houghton Mifflin, 1992.
Treasure Chest: A Workbook About Baha'u'llah (juvenile workbook), Wing and a Prayer, 1992.

Has contributed book reviews, feature stories, and a children's column to numerous publications including the *Carroll County Evening Sun,* the *Mecklenberg Sun, Florida Times Union, The Writer,* and the *ALAN Review.*

Adaptations

A film based on *The Golden Days* entitled *First of May* starring Julie Harris, Charles Nelson Reilly, Joe DiMaggio, and Mickey Rooney, S.H.O. Entertainment, 1999.

Sidelights

In an interview with *SATA,* Radley spoke about her source of inspiration for writing: "Two constants in my life have been writing and the Baha'i Faith. Since age eight or nine I have been interested in writing as a profession. At age fifteen I was introduced to and became a member of the Baha'i Faith.

"*The Writings of My Faith* have provided me with themes of hope and promise and have strengthened a sense of order and purpose in the world. I hope to provide readers with a sense of kinship with others, a belief that feelings can be viewed honestly and solutions found."

Radley's writing career began with *The Night Stella Hid the Stars,* a children's book steeped in fantasy. Denise M. Wilms's *Booklist* review acknowledged the young author's "imaginative text that renders the coming of night in warmly theatrical fantasy conventions . . . ." The author found her voice, however, in writing about the troubling issues that teens often confront. Among Radley's first in this genre, *Nothing Stays the Same Forever* explores a twelve-year-old's feelings of anger and resentment toward her widowed father when he starts dating seriously. Mary Hamilton, in her review in *Voice of Youth Advocates (VOYA)* observed that "it describes accurately feelings adolescent children have toward death and the subsequent feelings of loneliness

that death brings." In *School Library Journal,* Karen Harris noted that the story "realistically explores the conflict of a preteen who feels threatened by the proposed changes in her family."

Another difficult subject Radley tackles is teen suicide. In what *Booklist's* Ilene Cooper called a "powerful story," *The World Turned Inside Out* reveals a brother's feelings of guilt, inadequacy, and resentment over his dead sibling. Karen Harris commented in *School Library Journal* about some of the story's lessons, "that compassion needs to moderate judgment; and that some problems do not have satisfactory solutions."

According to Jody McCoy in *VOYA,* "*The Golden Days* offers both problems and solutions for middle schoolers who want realistic stories that aren't too grim." The problem, experienced by two unlikely friends—a teenager and an elderly woman, is finding a place where one feels welcome and "at home." Deborah Abbott noted in a *Booklist* review that: "This realistic, intergenerational narrative cuts through the issues of abandonment and the yearning for family to culminate in an upbeat resolution."

Radley has a talent for turning negatives into positives. *Rainy Day Rhymes* is a case in point. Radley brings together poems by noted writers such as Rachel Field, Robert Louis Stevenson, and Dorothy Aldis. Amy Nunley praised the book in *School Library Journal,* saying that the "seventeen short poems convey an appreciation and a mostly humorous attitude toward that inevitable gift of nature that ruins the picnics and pool parties of life."

Few people have escaped feeling 'left out' at one time or another. *Odd Man Out* examines that predicament from two points of view—being the new kid in town and being a mentally disabled person coping in society. Sixth-grade twins Kit and Jordy have always had each other, but when they move to a small Missouri town Kit takes an interest in eighth-grader Davis Jenkins, and also in befriending Oakley, a mentally disabled man. At first Jordy wants nothing to do with Oakley, but stands by him when Oakley is threatened. Rebecca O'Connell applauded the author's point that "it's far more satisfying to be loyal and kind than 'in'" in her *School Library Journal* review.

The author told *SATA,* "I'm primarily interested in novels for older children which deal with the real and difficult issues they may face. Preteens are on the verge of a new awakening. They are trying to make sense of the world, to understand it, often while wading through some tough problems. They need to know that they are not alone, that there are answers."

Works Cited

Abbott, Deborah, review of *The Golden Days, Booklist,* April 1, 1991, p. 1568.
Cooper, Ilene, review of *The World Turned Inside Out, Booklist,* March 15, 1983, pp. 971-72.

Hamilton, Mary M., review of *Nothing Stays the Same Forever, Voice of Youth Advocates,* February, 1982, p. 37.

Harris, Karen, review of *Nothing Stays the Same Forever, School Library Journal,* January, 1982, p. 80.

Harris, Karen, review of *The World Turned Inside Out, School Library Journal,* May, 1983, p. 85.

McCoy, Jody, review of *The Golden Days, Voice of Youth Advocates,* June, 1991, p. 100.

Nunley, Amy, review of *Rainy Day Rhymes, School Library Journal,* June, 1992, p. 110.

O'Connell, Rebecca, review of *Odd Man Out, School Library Journal,* June, 1995, p. 113.

Wilms, Denise M., review of *The Night Stella Hid the Stars, Booklist,* December 15, 1978, p. 689.

For More Information See

PERIODICALS

Booklist, August, 1995, p. 1947.

Bulletin of the Center for Children's Books, June, 1982, p. 196.

Kirkus Reviews, May 15, 1991, p. 675; February 1, 1992, p. 189; June 1, 1995, p. 785.

Publisher's Weekly, December 17, 1982, p. 75.

Voice of Youth Advocates, August, 1995, p. 323.

*   *   *

REED-JONES, Carol 1955-

Personal

Born February 22, 1955, in Los Angeles, CA; daughter of Gilbert (an engineer) and Hazel May (a stenographer) Jones; married Steve Reed; children: one son. *Education:* University of British Columbia, B.Mus., 1983; Western Washington University, teaching certificate, 1984, M.Mus., 1996. *Politics:* Democrat. *Religion:* Christian Science. *Hobbies and other interests:* Reading, writing, hiking, back packing, cross country skiing, wool feltmaking, singing.

Addresses

Home—P.O. Box 29292, Bellingham, WA 98228. *Electronic mail*—carolrj@nas.com.

Career

Writer. Music teacher in La Conner, WA, 1984-85; Music teacher in Soap Lake, WA, 1985-86; Music teacher in Bellingham, WA, 1994-. Substitute teacher in Bellingham, WA, 1987-91. *Member:* Society of Children's Book Writers and Illustrators, American Orff-Schulwerk Association, Environmental Educators Association of Washington, Children's Center for Environmental Literature, Mensa.

Awards, Honors

Nora Black Memorial Scholarship, 1983, for potential in lyric vocal composition. Annual Best Children's Book List, *Science Books and Films,* 1995, for *Tree in the Ancient Forest.* Benjamin Franklin Award for Best Children's Picture Book, Publishers Marketing Association, 1996, for *Tree in the Ancient Forest.*

Writings

FOR CHILDREN

The Tree in the Ancient Forest, illustrated by Christopher Canyon, Dawn Publications, 1995.

The poem "Winter Wraps" has been included in *Once Upon Ice and Other Frozen Poems,* edited by Jane Yolen, Boyds Mills Press, 1997.

FOR ADULTS

Green Weddings that Don't Cost the Earth, Paper Crane Press, 1996.

Work in Progress

Salmon Stream, for Dawn Publications (spring, 2001); *Hildegard of Bingen: A Renaissance Woman in the Middle Ages* (a biography); *Longtail of the Forest,* and *Medieval Women Writers.*

Sidelights

Carol Reed-Jones told *SATA:* "I've always loved reading and writing. I wrote my first 'for fun' story when I was

Carol Reed-Jones

eight; it was about a talking pumpkin who finds buried pirate treasure with the help of animal friends. When I was twelve, I started a newspaper for the children in my neighborhood and called it *The Neighborhood News.* There wasn't much news in it, just brief articles on things like Komodo dragons and the story of Robin Hood, and connect-the-dot puzzles for the youngest kids. It didn't last more than a few issues, because I was the only contributor, but I had fun.

"Fun is a major factor in whatever I do. My first published story was a humorous essay I sent to the Home Forum page of the *Christian Science Monitor* in 1985. I stayed up late one night to finish it and type it up, laughing out loud at the silly things I'd written. Other fun things I've done: raft down the Colorado River when I was fourteen; play the drums, in a very mediocre way, in a bagpipe band; and sing each summer in the chorus of our local music festival. School author visits, where I do poetry workshops, are fun for me, and so is music teaching, my other job.

"When I write, I try to keep a notebook at hand for any ideas that come to me, even if it's only 'write a story about . . . .' If my notebook isn't near, I use whatever is handy—grocery receipts, scraps of paper in my pockets, old ticket stubs. Then I write it into my notebook, and later into my computer. I never throw any of my ideas away—all ideas are valuable. When I revise something I've entered into my computer, I make a copy of it, and only revise the copy, not the original. Only then do I feel free to change sentences and move paragraphs around.

"All of my life, I've had lots of interests, some of them extremely short-lived. When I was a teenager, I became fascinated with Belgian horses, researching them and seriously considering acquiring one. That passion lasted exactly one day. My latest interest is wool feltmaking. I go through life acquiring unusual bits of knowledge, and know that eventually I'll use them somewhere. *The Tree in the Ancient Forest* came about because I went to a slide presentation on old-growth forests and learned something new. The interdependence between trees, truffles, and truffle-eating rodents was news to me and I thought, 'there's a story here.' I began working on it, trying to make it rhyme, which didn't work at all. I put it aside for a year and a half, and one day realized that I could structure it like the cumulative nursery rhyme 'this is the house that Jack built.' As a writer, I get to discover new and exciting things, do further research on them, and write books and articles based on my discoveries. I can't imagine a better job."

For More Information See

PERIODICALS

Booklist, July, 1995, p. 1881.
Children's Bookwatch, July, 1995, p. 8.
School Library Journal, September, 1995, p. 196.
Science Books and Films, December, 1995, p. 268; January-February, 1996, p. 4.

ROUNDS, Glen (Harold) 1906-

Personal

Born April 4, 1906, in a sod house near Wall, SD; son of William E. (a rancher) and Janet I. (Barber) Rounds; married Mary Lucas, December, 1928 (divorced, 1937); married Margaret Olmsted, January, 1938 (died December, 1968); married Elizabeth Anne High, 1989; children: William E. II. *Education:* Attended Kansas City Art Institute, 1926-27, and Art Student's League, 1930-31.

Addresses

Home—Box 763, Southern Pines, NC 28387.

Career

Author and illustrator, 1936—. Worked previously as mule skinner, cowboy, sign painter, railroad section hand, baker, carnival medicine man, and textile designer. *Military service:* U.S. Army, 1941-45, served in coast artillery and infantry; became staff sergeant. *Member:* Authors Guild.

Awards, Honors

Picture book honor, Spring Book Festival, 1942, for *Whitey's First Roundup;* Lewis Carroll Shelf Award, 1958, for *Ol' Paul, the Mighty Logger,* 1960, for *Blind Colt,* 1969, for *Wild Horses of the Red Desert,* 1973, for *Stolen Pony,* 1976, for *The Day the Circus Came to Lone Tree,* and 1978, for *Mr. Yowder and the Giant Bull Snake;* juvenile award, American Association of University Women, 1961, for *Beaver Business: An Almanac,* 1967, for *The Snake Tree,* 1976, for *Mr. Yowder and the Lion Roar Capsules,* and 1983, for *Wild Appaloosa;* New Jersey Institute of Technology Award, 1963, for *Firefly,* 1972, for *A Twister of Twists, a Tangler of Tongues,* and 1977, for *Kickle Snifters and Other Fearsome Critters;* Boys Club Junior Book Award, 1965, for *Rain in the Woods and Other Small Matters;* Aurianne Award, 1966, for *Big Blue Island;* Kerlan Award, University of Minnesota, 1980; North Carolina Award for Literature, 1981; *Parents' Choice* award, 1984, for *The Morning the Sun Refused to Rise: An Original Paul Bunyan Tale,* and 1985, for *Washday on Noah's Ark: A Story of Noah's Ark.*

Writings

AUTHOR AND ILLUSTRATOR

Ol' Paul, the Mighty Logger, Holiday House, 1936, revised edition, 1949.
Lumbercamp, Holiday House, 1937, published as *The Whistle Punk of Camp 15,* 1959.
Paydirt, Holiday House, 1938.
The Blind Colt (excerpts contained in *Whitey's Sunday Horse*), Holiday House, 1941.
Whitey's First Roundup, Grosset, 1942.
Whitey's Sunday Horse, Grosset, 1943.

Glen Rounds

Whitey Looks for a Job, Grosset, 1944.

Whitey and Jinglebob, Grosset, 1946.

Stolen Pony (sequel to *The Blind Colt*), Holiday House, 1948, revised edition, 1969.

Rodeo: Bulls, Broncos, and Buckaroos, Holiday House, 1949.

Whitey and the Rustlers (also see below), Holiday House, 1951.

Hunted Horses, Holiday House, 1951.

Whitey and the Blizzard (also see below), Holiday House, 1952.

Buffalo Harvest, Holiday House, 1952.

Lone Muskrat, Holiday House, 1953.

Whitey Takes a Trip, Holiday House, 1954.

Whitey Ropes and Rides, Holiday House, 1956.

Swamp Life: An Almanac, Prentice-Hall, 1957.

Wildlife at Your Doorstep: An Illustrated Almanac, Prentice-Hall, 1958.

Whitey and the Wild Horse, Holiday House, 1958.

Beaver Business: An Almanac, Prentice-Hall, 1960.

Wild Orphan, Holiday House, 1961.

Whitey and the Colt Killer, Holiday House, 1962.

Whitey's New Saddle (contains *Whitey and the Rustlers* and *Whitey and the Blizzard*), Holiday House, 1963.

Rain in the Woods and Other Small Matters, World, 1964.

The Snake Tree, World, 1966.

The Treeless Plains, Holiday House, 1967.

The Prairie Schooners, Holiday House, 1968.

Wild Horses of the Red Desert, Holiday House, 1969.

Once We Had a Horse, Holiday House, 1971.

The Cowboy Trade, Holiday House, 1972.

The Day the Circus Came to Lone Tree, Holiday House, 1973.

Mr. Yowder and the Lion Roar Capsules, Holiday House, 1976.

The Beaver: How He Works, Holiday House, 1976.

Mr. Yowder and the Steamboat, Holiday House, 1977.

Mr. Yowder and the Giant Bull Snake, Holiday House, 1978.

Mr. Yowder, the Peripatetic Sign Painter: Three Tall Tales, Holiday House, 1980.

Blind Outlaw, Holiday House, 1980.

Mr. Yowder and the Train Robbers, Holiday House, 1981.

Wild Appaloosa, Holiday House, 1983.

Mr. Yowder and the Windwagon, Holiday House, 1983.

The Morning the Sun Refused to Rise: An Original Paul Bunyan Tale, Holiday House, 1984.

Washday on Noah's Ark: A Story of Noah's Ark, Holiday House, 1985.

Old MacDonald Had a Farm, Holiday House, 1989.

I Know an Old Lady Who Swallowed a Fly, Holiday House, 1990.

Cowboys, Holiday House, 1991.

Three Little Pigs and the Big Bad Wolf, Holiday House, 1992.

(Reteller) *Three Billy Goats Gruff,* Holiday House, 1993.

Sod Houses on the Great Plains, Holiday House, 1995.

Beavers, Holiday House, 1999.

Rounds's works have been translated into Spanish, Dutch, Danish, and German.

ILLUSTRATOR

Irma S. Black, *Flipper, a Sea Lion,* Holiday House, 1940.

Walter Blair, *Tall Tale America,* Coward, 1944.

Frank O'Rourke, *"E" Company,* Simon & Schuster, 1945.

Martha Hardy, *Tatoosh,* Macmillan, 1947.

Wheaton P. Webb, *Uncle Swithin's Inventions,* Holiday House, 1947.

Aesop's Fables, Lippincott, 1949.

Vance Randolph, *We Always Lie to Strangers,* Columbia University Press, 1951.

Randolph, *Who Blowed up the Church House?,* Columbia University Press, 1952.

Sarah R. Riedman, *Grass, Our Greatest Crop,* Thomas Nelson, 1952.

Jim Kjelgaard, *Haunt Fox,* Holiday House, 1954.

Paul Hyde Bonner, *Those Glorious Mornings,* Scribner, 1954.

Vance Randolph, *The Devil's Pretty Daughter,* Columbia University Press, 1955.

Paul M. Sears, *Firefly,* Holiday House, 1956.

Vance Randolph, *The Talking Turtle,* Columbia University Press, 1957.

Randolph, *Sticks in the Knapsack,* Columbia University Press, 1958.

Elizabeth Seeman, *In the Arms of the Mountain,* Crown, 1961.

Wilson Gage, *A Wild Goose Tale,* World, 1961.

Gage, *Dan and the Miranda,* World, 1962.

Gage, *Big Blue Island,* World, 1964.

Adrien Stoutenburg, *The Crocodile's Mouth,* Viking, 1966.

Richard Chase, editor, *Billy Boy,* Golden Gate, 1966.

Maria Leach, *How the People Sang the Mountains Up,* Viking, 1967.

Gladys Conklin, *Lucky Ladybugs,* Holiday House, 1968.

A. Stoutenburg, *American Tall Tale Animals,* Viking, 1968.

John Greenway, *Folklore of the Great West,* American West, 1969.

Rebecca Caudill and James Ayars, *Contrary Jenkins,* Holt, 1969.

Austin Fife and Alta Fife, *Ballads of the Great West,* American West, 1970.

Wilson Gage, *Mike's Toads,* World, 1970.

Alexander L. Crosby, *Go Find Hanka!,* Golden Gate, 1970.

Ida Chittum, *Farmer Hoo and the Baboons,* Delacorte, 1971.

Alvin Schwartz, editor, *A Twister of Twists, a Tangler of Tongues,* Lippincott, 1972.

Gladys Conklin, *Tarantula, the Giant Spider,* Holiday House, 1972.

Sandra S. Sivulich, *I'm Going on a Bear Hunt,* Dutton, 1973.

Alvin Schwartz, *Tomfoolery: Trickery and Foolery with Words,* Lippincott, 1973.

Schwartz, editor, *Witcracks,* Lippincott, 1973.

Schwartz, editor, *Cross Your Fingers, Spit in Your Hat: Superstitions and Other Beliefs,* Lippincott, 1974.

Alvin Schwartz, *Whoppers, Tall Tales and Other Lies,* Lippincott, 1975.

Mark Taylor, *Jennie Jenkins,* Little, Brown, 1975.

Betty Baker, *Three Fools and a Horse,* Macmillan, 1975.

Berniece Freschet, *Lizard Lying in the Sun,* Scribner, 1975.

Wilson Gage, *Squash Pie,* Morrow, 1976.

Alvin Schwartz, editor, *Kickle Snifters and Other Fearsome Critters,* Lippincott, 1976.

Robbie Branscum, *Toby, Granny and George,* Doubleday, 1976.

Branscum, *The Saving of P.S.,* Doubleday, 1976.

Berniece Freschet, *The Happy Dromedary,* Scribner, 1977.

Freschet, *Little Black Bear Goes for a Walk,* Scribner, 1977.

Wilson Gage, *Down in the Boondocks,* Morrow, 1977.

Gladys Conklin, *Praying Mantis,* Holiday House, 1978.

Theo Gilchrest, *Halfway up the Mountain,* Lippincott, 1978.

Berniece Freschet, *Elephant and Friends,* Scribner, 1978.

Mary Blount Christian, *The Lucky Man,* Macmillan, 1979.

Judith St. George, *The Amazing Voyage of the New Orleans,* Putnam, 1979.

Jim Aylesworth, *Hush Up!,* Holt, 1980.

Jane Yolen, *Uncle Lemon's Spring,* Dutton, 1981.

Jim Aylesworth, *Shenandoah Noah,* Holt, 1985.

Jill Wright, *The Old Woman and the Willy Nilly Man,* Putnam, 1987.

Jim Aylesworth, *Hanna's Hog,* Atheneum, 1988.

David Adler, *Wild Bill Hickok and Other Old West Riddles,* Holiday House, 1988.

Eric A. Kimmel, *Charlie Drives the Stage,* Holiday House, 1989.

Jill Wright, *The Old Woman and the Jar of Umms,* Putnam, 1989.

Eric A. Kimmel, *Four Dollars and Fifty Cents,* Holiday House, 1990.

EDITOR AND ILLUSTRATOR

Andy Adams, *Trail Drive* (based on Adams's *Log of a Cowboy*), Holiday House, 1965.

George F. Ruxton, *Mountain Men,* Holiday House, 1966.

Boll Weevil, Golden Gate, 1967.

Casey Jones, Golden Gate, 1968.

The Strawberry Roan, Golden Gate, 1970.

Glen Rounds's self-illustrated picture book portrays life on the prairie in spare text and expressive black-and-white drawings.

Sweet Betsy from Pike, Golden Gate, 1973.

Also author of radio scripts for "School of the Air," Columbia Broadcasting System (CBS), 1938-39. Contributor to *Treasury of American Folklore,* edited by Benjamin Botkin, Crown, 1944, and *Subtreasury of American Humor,* edited by E. B. White and Katherine S. White, Modern Library, 1948. Contributor to *Story Parade.*

Adaptations

Whitey's First Roundup was adapted for broadcast by the British Broadcasting Corporation (BBC), 1960; several of Rounds's books have been recorded on audiocassette.

Sidelights

Author/illustrator Glen Rounds is known for works that tell adventure-filled stories of the West or expand upon popular American tall tales. Classified as a juvenile author because of his direct writing style and clear, often humorous brush-line drawings, Rounds insists that his works are meant for all age groups.

Born in 1906, Rounds grew up on ranches in South Dakota and Montana, learning to draw the animals and workers that shared his environment. As an adult, he wandered through the western United States, taking odd jobs to support himself. His travels, although filled with adventure and material for storytelling, did not satisfy Rounds. He was determined to make his living as an artist.

Eventually, Rounds traveled to New York, hoping to sell his pictures. When he was broke, Rounds visited editors near lunch time, using his storytelling ability to pique their interest, then wrangled a lunch invitation to continue the tale. Vernon Ives, a founding member of Holiday House, which published Rounds's first book, shared his initial impression of Rounds with Russell Freedman in a *Horn Book* article: "He was a young, footloose westerner with a discerning eye, a quick, sketchy style of drawing that had enormous vitality, and a tongue even more facile than his brush."

Rounds considered himself an artist and believed that stories should be told, instead of written, until editors convinced him that the best way to get his drawings published would be to write a story to go with them. Heeding their advice, Rounds, using unorthodox compilation methods, wrote and illustrated *Ol' Paul, the Mighty Logger* in 1936. The author revealed to Freedman in *Horn Book* that instead of researching Paul Bunyan tales, "I made them up as I went along."

Rounds has produced a slew of western adventures in his long career. The title character of his "Whitey" series is a cowboy. The books earned Rounds commendation from a *Saturday Review* contributor for their "economy of words and distinctive black-and-white drawings." His picture of prairie life in *The Treeless Plains* is "authentic to the last detail and salted with wry but realistic humor," recalled Hal Borland in the *New York Times Book Review.* For more than fifty years, Rounds has

continued his streak of successful books, but his career nearly came to an end in 1989, when the onset of severe arthritis made it impossible to continue drawing with his right hand. "A problem," he admits. But "rather than take up horse-shoeing," he spent a summer learning how to draw left-handed, and since then has continued to illustrate full-color picture books, drawing with his left hand only. In his 1991 publication, *Cowboys,* Rounds describes an average workday for a ranch hand, augmenting the text with "lively, rough-hewn sketches," according to Diane Roback of *Publishers Weekly.*

When illustrating books by other authors, Rounds favors tall tales. He gravitates toward stories that display tongue-in-cheek humor, such as John Greenway's *Folklore of the Great West,* Alvin Schwartz's *Whoppers, Tall Tales and Other Lies,* and Jill Wright's *The Old Woman and the Willy Nilly Man.* Rounds supplies these tales with his trademark brush-line drawings and provides the realistic, animated artwork that has earned him years of recognition.

With *Sod Houses on the Great Plains,* Rounds's tongue-in-cheek humor filters down through his text and pictures. This picture book gives a detailed look at life on the plains, where families built sod houses because no trees grew on the land. Primitive life and uncomfortable living conditions were commonly known on the plains, but Rounds's mix of humor and simple, earthy drawings engaged young readers and critics alike. In a review for *Bulletin of the Center for Children's Books,* Elizabeth Bush pointed out Rounds's humor in a scene where a snake falls through the roof and lands on the table in front of the woman of the house. Rounds says in his understated manner, "Uninvited wildlife was another housekeeping problem." Susannah Price indicated in her review for *School Library Journal* that "details left out in the author's text find a place in the story's illustra-

A COWBOY'S FIRST CHORE AFTER BREAKFAST IS TO CATCH AND SADDLE A HORSE~

A ranch hand's average workday is detailed in Rounds's unromanticized picture-book portrayal. (*From* Cowboys, *written and illustrated by Rounds.*)

tions." *Five Owls* critic Kathie Krieger Cerra also described the complementary relationship between Rounds's words and pictures, noting how the "words provide authentic information in an inviting style, and the pictures show action and humor that engage children in a graphic subtext."

Brevity of lines, in text and drawings, describes *Beaver,* Rounds's book on the animal and its habitat. In this nonfiction piece about the long-toothed animal, Rounds effectively uses a minimum of words. Joanna Rudge Long pointed out in a review for *Horn Book* that "the text, outlining the beaver's daily habits and modus vivendi, is a model of how to convey a wealth of information in just a few clear, well-phrased statements." Long likens Rounds's illustrative style to the beaver's method of constructing a habitat, "aimless when taken stick by stick or line by line but wonderfully effective in sum." In her review for *Bulletin of the Center for Children's Books,* Janice M. Del Negro called it an "easy introduction to the natural sciences."

Works Cited

Borland, Hal, review of *The Treeless Plains, New York Times Book Review,* May 14, 1967, p. 30.

Bush, Elizabeth, *Sod Houses on the Great Plains, Bulletin of the Center for Children's Books,* March, 1995, p. 248.

Cerra, Kathie Krieger, review of *Sod Houses on the Great Plains, Five Owls,* March-April, 1995, p. 86.

Del Negro, Janice M., review of *Beaver, Bulletin of the Center for Children's Books,* June, 1999, p. 363.

Freedman, Russell, "Glen Rounds and Holiday House," *Horn Book,* March-April, 1985, pp. 222-25.

Long, Joanna Rudge, review of *Beaver, Horn Book,* May-June, 1999, pp. 352-53.

Price, Susannah, *Sod Houses on the Great Plains, School Library Journal,* March, 1995, p. 200.

Roback, Diane, review of *Cowboys, Publishers Weekly,* May 3, 1991, p. 71.

Review of *Whitey and the Wild Horse, Saturday Review,* May 10, 1958, p. 41.

For More Information See

PERIODICALS

Booklist, January 15, 1992, p. 943; December 15, 1995, p. 706; September 1, 1996, p. 121.

Publishers Weekly, October 5, 1992, p. 63; February 6, 1995, p. 85.

School Library Journal, May, 1995, p. 99; January, 1997, p. 102; February, 1998, p. 100.

*   *   *

RYLANT, Cynthia 1954-

Personal

Surname is pronounced "rye-*lunt*"; born June 6, 1954, in Hopewell, VA; daughter of John Tune (an army sergeant) and Leatrel (a nurse; maiden name, Rylant) Smith; twice married and divorced; children (first marriage): Nathaniel; companion of Dav Pilkey (an author/illustrator). *Education:* Morris Harvey College (now University of Charleston), WV, B.A., 1975; Marshall University, Huntington, WV, M.A., 1976; Kent State University, Kent, OH, M.L.S., 1982. *Politics:* Democrat. *Religion:* "Christian, no denomination." *Hobbies and other interests:* Pets, reading, quilt making, going to movies, watching television, and eating chocolate brownies.

Addresses

Home—Eugene, OR.

Career

Writer, educator, librarian. Marshall University, Huntington, WV, part-time English instructor, 1979-80; Akron Public Library, Akron, OH, children's librarian, 1983; University of Akron, Akron, part-time English lecturer, 1983-84; Northeast Ohio Universities College of Medicine, Rootstown, OH, part-time lecturer, 1991—.

Awards, Honors

Booklist reviewer's choice, 1982, American Book Award nomination, American Library Association (ALA) notable book, and Reading Rainbow selection, 1983, and English Speaking Union Book-across-the-Sea Ambassador of Honor Award, 1984, all for *When I Was Young in the Mountains; School Library Journal* best book of 1984, National Council for Social Studies best book, and ALA notable book, 1984, and Society of Midland Authors best children's book, 1985, all for *Waiting to Waltz ... a Childhood;* Children's Book of the Year, Child Study Association of America, and *Horn Book* honor book, 1985, for *The Relatives Came;* Children's Book of the Year, Child Study Association of America, 1985, for *A Blue-Eyed Daisy; School Library Journal* best book citation, 1985, for *Every Living Thing;* Parents' Choice Award, 1986, Newbery Medal honor book, ALA, and *Horn Book* honor book, 1987, all for *A Fine White Dust;* ALA best book for young adults citation, 1988, for *A Kindness;* Ohioana Award, 1990, for *But I'll Be Back Again;* Parents' Choice Award (picture book) and *Boston Globe/Horn Book* honor book for nonfiction, 1991, and Ohioana Award, 1992, for *Appalachia: The Voices of Sleeping Birds; Boston Globe-Horn Book* Award for children's fiction, Reading Magic Award, and Parents' Choice Award, 1992, and John Newbery Medal and Hungry Mind Award, 1993, for *Missing May;* ALA best book for young adults citation, for *A Couple of Kooks and Other Stories about Love; School Library Journal* best book of the year citation, for *Children of Christmas.* Several of Rylant's "Henry and Mudge" books have received child-selected awards, including the Garden State Children's Book Award, Children's Services Section of the New Jersey Library Association, and the Children's Choice Award, Association of Booksellers for Children. In 1983, *When I Was Young in the Mountains* was named a Caldecott

Honor Book for its illustrations by Diane Goode. *The Relatives Came* was named a *New York Times* best illustrated book, 1985, and a Caldecott Medal honor book, 1986, for its illustrations by Stephen Gammell.

Writings

FOR CHILDREN; PICTURE BOOKS AND EARLY FICTION, EXCEPT AS NOTED

When I Was Young in the Mountains, illustrated by Diane Goode, Dutton, 1982.

Miss Maggie, illustrated by Thomas DiGrazia, Dutton, 1983.

This Year's Garden, illustrated by Mary Szilagyi, Bradbury (New York), 1984.

The Relatives Came, illustrated by Stephen Gammell, Bradbury, 1985.

Night in the Country, illustrated by Szilagyi, Bradbury, 1986.

Birthday Presents, illustrated by Sucie Stevenson, Orchard Books (New York), 1987.

All I See, illustrated by Peter Catalanotto, Orchard Books, 1988.

Mr. Griggs' Work, illustrated by Julie Downing, Orchard Books, 1989.

An Angel for Solomon Singer, illustrated by Catalanotto, Orchard Books, 1992.

Best Wishes (autobiographical picture book), photographs by Carlo Ontal, Richard C. Owen (Katonah, NY), 1992.

The Dreamer, illustrated by Barry Moser, Blue Sky Press (New York), 1993.

(Self-illustrated) *Dog Heaven,* Blue Sky Press, 1995.

Gooseberry Park, illustrated by Arthur Howard, Harcourt (San Diego), 1995.

The Van Gogh Café (middle-grade fiction), Harcourt, 1995.

The Bookshop Dog, Blue Sky Press, 1996.

The Whales, Blue Sky Press, 1996.

The Old Woman Who Named Things, illustrated by Kathryn Brown, Harcourt, 1996.

(Self-illustrated) *Cat Heaven,* Blue Sky Press, 1997.

An Everyday Book, Simon & Schuster, 1997.

Silver Packages: An Appalachian Christmas Story, illustrated by Chris K. Soenpiet, Orchard Books, 1997 (story taken from *Children of Christmas: Stories for the Season,* see below).

Bear Day, illustrated by Jennifer Selby, Harcourt, 1998.

Tulip Sees America, illustrated by Lisa Desimini, Blue Sky Press, 1998.

The Bird House, illustrated by Moser, Blue Sky Press, 1998.

Scarecrow, illustrated by Lauren Stringer, Harcourt, 1998.

The Heavenly Village, Blue Sky Press, 1999.

The Cookie-Store Cat, Blue Sky Press, 1999.

Bunny Bungalow, illustrated by Nancy Hayashi, Harcourt, 1999.

The Troublesome Turtle, Greenwillow (New York), 1999.

Puzzling Possum, Greenwillow, 1999.

Let's Go Home: The Wonderful Things about a House, illustrated by Wendy Anderson Halperin, Simon & Schuster, 2000.

Little Whistle, illustrated by Tim Bowers, Harcourt, 2000.

In November, illustrated by Jill Kastner, Harcourt, 2000.

Thimbleberry Stories, illustrated by Maggie Kneen, Harcourt, 2000.

The Ticky-Tacky Doll, illustrated by Harvey Stevenson, Harcourt, 2000.

"HENRY AND MUDGE" SERIES; BEGINNING READERS, ILLUSTRATED BY SUCIE STEVENSON, EXCEPT AS NOTED

Henry and Mudge: The First Book of Their Adventures, illustrated by James Stevenson, Macmillan, 1987.

Henry and Mudge in Puddle Trouble: The Second Book of Their Adventures, illustrated by James Stevenson, Macmillan, 1987.

Henry and Mudge in the Green Time: The Third Book of Their Adventures, Macmillan, 1987.

Henry and Mudge under the Yellow Moon: The Fourth Book of Their Adventures, Macmillan, 1987.

Henry and Mudge in the Sparkle Days: The Fifth Book of Their Adventures, Macmillan, 1988.

Henry and Mudge and the Forever Sea: The Sixth Book of Their Adventures, Macmillan, 1989.

Henry and Mudge Get the Cold Shivers: The Seventh Book of Their Adventures, Macmillan, 1989.

Henry and Mudge and the Happy Cat: The Eighth Book of Their Adventures, Macmillan, 1990.

Henry and Mudge and the Bedtime Thumps: The Ninth Book of Their Adventures, Macmillan, 1991.

Henry and Mudge Take the Big Test: The Tenth Book of Their Adventures, Macmillan, 1991.

Henry and Mudge and the Long Weekend: The Eleventh Book of Their Adventures, Macmillan, 1992.

Henry and Mudge and the Wild Wind: The Twelfth Book of Their Adventures, Macmillan, 1992.

Henry and Mudge and the Careful Cousin: The Thirteenth Book of Their Adventures, Macmillan, 1994.

Henry and Mudge and the Best Day of All: The Fourteenth Book of Their Adventures, Bradbury Press, 1995.

Henry and Mudge in the Family Trees: The Fifteenth Book of Their Adventures, Simon & Schuster, 1997.

Henry and Mudge and the Sneaky Crackers: The Sixteenth Book of Their Adventures, Simon & Schuster, 1998.

Henry and Mudge and the Starry Night: The Seventeenth Book of Their Adventures, Simon & Schuster, 1998.

Henry and Mudge and Annie's Good Move: The Eighteenth Book of Their Adventures, Simon & Schuster, 1998.

Henry and Mudge and Annie's Perfect Pet: The Nineteenth Book of Their Adventures, Simon & Schuster, 1999.

Henry and Mudge and the Funny Lunch: The Twentieth Book of Their Adventures, Simon & Schuster, 1999.

Henry and Mudge and the Tall Tree House: The Twenty-First Book of Their Adventures, Simon & Schuster, 1999.

Henry and Mudge and Mrs. Hopper's House: The Twenty-Second Book of Their Adventures, Simon & Schuster, 1999.

Henry and Mudge and the Great Grandpas: The Twenty-Third Book of Their Adventures, Simon & Schuster, 1999.

Henry and Mudge and a Very Special Merry Christmas: The Twenty-Fourth Book of Their Adventures, Simon & Schuster, 1999.

Henry and Mudge and the Snowman Plan: The Twenty-Fifth Book of Their Adventures, Simon & Schuster, 1999.

Henry and Mudge and the Wild Goose Chase: The Twenty-Sixth Book of Their Adventures, Simon & Schuster, 1999.

Henry and Mudge and the Big Sleepover: The Twenty-Seventh Book of Their Adventures, Simon & Schuster, 1999.

Henry and Mudge and the Tumbling Trip: The Twenty-Eighth Book of Their Adventures, Simon & Schuster, 1999.

"THE EVERYDAY BOOKS" SERIES; SELF-ILLUSTRATED BOARD BOOKS

The Everyday Pets, Macmillan, 1993.
The Everyday Children, Macmillan, 1993.
The Everyday Garden, Macmillan, 1993.
The Everyday House, Macmillan, 1993.
The Everyday School, Macmillan, 1993.
The Everyday Town, Macmillan, 1993.

"MR. PUTTER AND TABBY" SERIES; BEGINNING READERS, ILLUSTRATED BY ARTHUR HOWARD

Mr. Putter and Tabby Walk the Dog, Harcourt, 1994.
Mr. Putter and Tabby Pour the Tea, Harcourt, 1994.
Mr. Putter and Tabby Bake the Cake, Harcourt, 1994.
Mr. Putter and Tabby Pick the Pears, Harcourt, 1995.
Mr. Putter and Tabby Fly the Plane, Harcourt, 1997.
Mr. Putter and Tabby Row the Boat, Harcourt, 1997.
Mr. Putter and Tabby Toot the Horn, Harcourt, 1998.
Mr. Putter and Tabby Take the Train, Harcourt, 1998.
Mr. Putter and Tabby Paint the Porch, Harcourt, 2000.

"THE BLUE HILL MEADOWS" SERIES; MIDDLE-GRADE FICTION, ILLUSTRATED BY ELLEN BEIER

The Blue Hill Meadows, Harcourt, 1997.
The Blue Hill Meadows and the Much-Loved Dog, Harcourt, 1997.

"POPPLETON" SERIES; BEGINNING READERS, ILLUSTRATED BY MARK TEAGUE

Poppleton, Blue Sky Press, 1997.
Poppleton and Friends, Blue Sky Press, 1997.
Poppleton Everyday, Blue Sky Press, 1998.
Poppleton Forever, Blue Sky Press, 1998.
Poppleton in Fall, Blue Sky Press, 1999.
Poppleton in Spring, Blue Sky Press, 1999.

"THE COBBLE STREET COUSINS" SERIES; MIDDLE-GRADE FICTION, ILLUSTRATED BY WENDY ANDERSON HALPERIN

The Cobble Street Cousins: In Aunt Lucy's Kitchen, Simon & Schuster, 1998.
The Cobble Street Cousins: A Little Shopping, Simon & Schuster, 1998.
The Cobble Street Cousins: Some Good News, Simon & Schuster, 1999.
The Cobble Street Cousins: Special Gifts (also published as *The Cobble Street Cousins: Winter Gifts*), Simon & Schuster, 1999.
The Cobble Street Cousins: Spring Deliveries, Simon & Schuster, 1999.

FOR YOUNG ADULTS; NOVELS AND SHORT STORIES

A Blue-Eyed Daisy (young adult novel), Bradbury, 1985 (published in England as *Some Year For Ellie,* illustrated by Kate Rogers, Viking Kestrel, 1986).
Every Living Thing (short stories), illustrated by S. D. Schindler, Bradbury, 1985.
A Fine White Dust (young adult novel), Bradbury, 1986.
Children of Christmas: Stories for the Season (short stories), illustrated by Schindler, Orchard Books, 1987 (published in England as *Silver Packages and Other Stories,* 1987).
A Kindness (young adult novel), Orchard Books, 1988.
A Couple of Kooks: And Other Stories about Love (short stories), Orchard Books, 1990.
Missing May (young adult novel), Orchard Books, 1992.
I Had Seen Castles (young adult novel), Harcourt Brace, 1993.
The Islander: A Novel (young adult novel), DK Ink (New York), 1998.

FOR YOUNG ADULTS; POETRY

Waiting to Waltz ... a Childhood, illustrated by Gammell, Bradbury, 1984.
Soda Jerk, illustrated by Catalanotto, Orchard Books, 1990.
Something Permanent, photographs by Walker Evans, Harcourt, 1994.

FOR YOUNG ADULTS; NONFICTION

But I'll Be Back Again: An Album (autobiography), Orchard Books, 1989.
Appalachia: The Voices of Sleeping Birds (nonfiction), illustrated by Barry Moser, Harcourt, 1991.
Margaret, Frank, and Andy: Three Writers' Stories (biography), Harcourt, 1996 (also issued as individual volumes *A Story of Margaret Wise Brown, A Story of L. Frank Baum, A Story of E. B. White*).
Bless Us All: A Child's Yearbook of Blessings, Simon & Schuster, 1998.
Give Me Grace: A Child's Daybook of Prayers, Simon & Schuster, 1999.

Some of Rylant's "Henry and Mudge" books have been translated into Spanish and published in Braille. Her papers are housed in Special Collections at Kent State University, Kent, OH.

Adaptations

When I Was Young in the Mountains, 1983, *This Year's Garden,* 1983, and *The Relatives Came,* 1986, were adapted as filmstrips by Random House. *When I Was Young in the Mountains* and *The Relatives Came* were released on audio cassette by SRA McGraw-Hill, 1985. *This Year's Garden* was released on audio cassette by SRA McGraw-Hill, 1987. *Henry and Mudge in the Green Time* was released on audio cassette by SRA McGraw-Hill, 1988. *Children of Christmas* and *Every Living Thing* were released as book and audio versions in 1993. *Missing May* was released on audio cassette by BDD Audio Publishing, 1996. *Henry and Mudge: The First Book, Henry and Mudge and the Bedtime Thumps, Henry and Mudge Take the Big Test,* and *Henry and Mudge and the Happy Cat* were released on audio cassette by Recorded Books, Inc., 1997. *Missing May* was released on audio cassette by Recorded Books, Inc., 1997. *The Children of Christmas* and *Every Living Thing* were released on audio cassette by Chivers North America, 1997. *A Fine White Dust* was released on audio cassette by Recorded Books, Inc., 1997. *Henry and Mudge in Puddle Trouble* and *Henry and Mudge under the Yellow Moon* were released on audio cassette by Live Oak Media, 1998. Several of Rylant's books are available on film through American School Publishers. She is also the subject of the video *Meet the Author: Cynthia Rylant,* 1990.

Work in Progress

Little Whistle's Dinner Party, for Harcourt; *Little Whistle's Medicine,* for Harcourt.

Sidelights

An author of fiction, nonfiction, and poetry for children and young adults as well as an author and author/ illustrator of picture books for children, Rylant is recognized as a gifted writer who has contributed memorably to several genres of juvenile literature. A prolific author who often bases her works on her own background, especially on her childhood in the West Virginia mountains, she is the creator of contemporary novels and historical fiction for young adults, middle-grade fiction and fantasy, lyrical prose poems, beginning readers, collections of short stories, volumes of poetry and verse, books of prayers and blessings, two autobiographies, and a biography of three well-known children's writers; several volumes of the author's fiction and picture books are published in series, including the popular "Henry and Mudge" easy readers about a small boy and his very large dog. Rylant is perhaps most well known as a novelist. Characteristically, she portrays introspective, compassionate young people who live in rural settings or in small towns and who tend to be set apart from their peers. Her young male and female protagonists meet the challenges in their lives with the help of their families and friends as well as acquaintances from their communities. The author is often noted for stressing the importance of family and community in her works. Praised for her sensitivity toward young people and understanding of their feelings, Rylant is also acknowledged for her rounded characterizations of adults, especially the elderly, and for exploring themes such as religion and death that are not often addressed in children's literature. Rylant often focuses on relationships between the old and the young and between people and animals. In addition, she underscores her works with such themes as the act of creation, both by God and by human artists; the transforming power of love; the importance of all living things; and the need to let go.

As a literary stylist, Rylant favors prose that is both lyrical and direct. Her straightforward style is often felt to have a disarming simplicity that balances the emotional intensity of her themes. Lauded for her characterizations and ability to provide a strong sense of place, she is recognized as a keen observer of human nature as well as a sincere and elegant writer. The author began illustrating some of her picture books in the early 1990s and has developed a folk-art style that is usually thought to complement her texts nicely. She has also worked with a number of outstanding illustrators, such as Peter Catalanotto, Barry Moser, James and Sucie Stevenson, and Walker Evans. Two of her books have been honored by the Caldecott Medal committee for their illustrations by Diane Goode and Stephen Gammell, respectively. Rylant is seen as the creator of works that are consistently varied, well-crafted, perceptive, and affirming. Writing in *Children's Books and Their Creators,* Eden K. Edwards said that the author "demonstrates an inimitable ability to evoke the strongest of emotions from the simplest of words.... In her work, Rylant gives depth and dignity to a litany of quiet characters and sagaciously reflects on some of life's most confusing mysteries." Miriam Lang Budin of *School Library Journal* noted that readers "have come to expect resonant, deeply felt work from Rylant," while Hollis Lowery-Moore of *St. James Guide to Young Adult Writers* concluded: "All of Rylant's stories, including her picture story books marketed for younger readers, create memorable characters and places and provide teens with a window on the world."

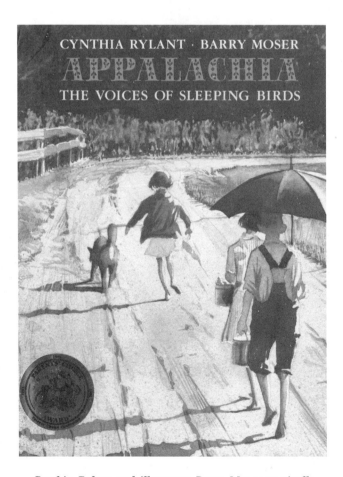

Cynthia Rylant and illustrator Barry Moser poetically evoke the spirit of Appalachia in a picture-book tribute to the land and its people.

Many of Rylant's works are rooted in her own experience, especially in the memories and images of her childhood and youth. Born in Hopewell, West Virginia, Rylant spent her first four years in Illinois, where she lived with her father John Tune Smith, a sergeant in the U. S. Army who had fought in the Korean War, and her mother Leatrel Rylant Smith. According to his daughter in *Children's Books and Their Creators (CBATC),* John Tune Smith "longed to be an artist, a musician, a star. But like many with strong artistic streaks, he managed only to be a sad alcoholic, whose wonderful imagination could not save him from the knowledge of his own failure, his unworthiness." Smith had contracted hepatitis while in Korea, a situation that weakened his condition. Writing in her autobiography *But I'll Be Back Again: An Album (BIBBA),* Rylant said, "I felt a lot of unhappiness when I was with my parents in those very early years. I think I believed that if I were really really good then I would make them happy and they wouldn't fight . . . . No one ever told me when I was little that my parents' battles were not my fault. I am certain I must have felt they were, and I believe I grew up with this big feeling inside that said: 'Whenever anyone who is with you is unhappy, it is your fault.' I didn't know, growing up, that I didn't have to make people happy." When she was four, Rylant's parents separated, and she went to live with her mother's parents in the Appalachian mining town of Coal Ridge, West Virginia. Rylant never saw her father again. He died in a veteran's hospital in Florida when she was thirteen. Rylant wrote in *BIBBA,* "I did not have a chance to know him or to say goodbye to him, and that is all the loss I needed to become a writer."

After a few months with her parents, Leatrel Smith left to go away to nursing school. She would be away for nearly four years. Although her mother wrote regularly and visited a few times a year, "it was," Rylant wrote in *BIBBA,* "not enough for a little girl. I believe that deep down I felt I just had not been good enough to make her want to stay." Happily, though, her grandparents and extended family provided a positive, nurturing environment. The author noted in *BIBBA* that it was in her grandmother's "love and safety, and the kind presence of my grandfather, that I managed to survive the loss of my dear parents." She commented in *Something about the Author Autobiography Series (SAAS)* that "my grandparents became my parents." Quiet, gentle people, Rylant's grandparents raised six children without much income. After her grandfather, a coal miner, was disabled during a slate fall in a mine, the family lived by her grandparents' wits and on food supplied by the government. Rylant wrote in *SAAS:* "My memories of those four years are so keen." Living in a four-room house without running water or indoor plumbing, Rylant learned about the joys of country life and the kindness of the townspeople. She summarized her years in Coal Ridge in *BIBBA:* "My years with my grandparents were good ones, and while I waited for both my father and my mother to come back, I had big stacks of pancakes and hot cocoa, hot dogs and chickens, teaberry leaves and honeysuckle, and aunts and cousins to sleep with at night and hug until someone could return for me."

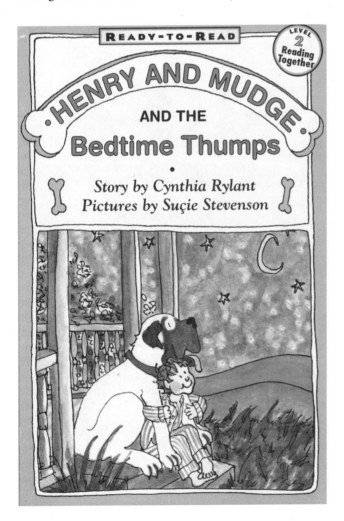

Rylant's popular duo takes a trip to Grandmother's house in the country and Henry frets when Mudge is made to sleep outside. (Cover illustration by Sucie Stevenson.)

When Rylant was eight, her mother finished school and came back for her. They moved to Beaver, a town near Coal Ridge, and settled in a three-room apartment with running water, an indoor bathroom, and a television set. Rylant noted in *SAAS,* "I felt rich." When she was nine, Rylant sat transfixed as the Beatles performed on *The Ed Sullivan Show;* she wrote in *SAAS,* "[I]t turned me and the rest of the world upside down." Rylant fell in love with Beatles bassist Paul McCartney. She wrote in *SAAS,* "The Beatles gave me a childhood of sweetest anticipation. Our country was falling apart with war and riots and assassinations but the Beatles gave me shelter from these things in their music and in the dreams they caused me to dream." She added in *But I'll Be Back Again,* the title of which is taken from the song "I'll Be Back" by the Beatles, "I think that in a lot of ways Paul McCartney became for me my lost father . . . . Paul and the Beatles became more for me than just rock 'n' roll heroes. They became something for me to know, a dream I could see . . . ." Rylant concluded, "I felt I knew them better than the father I could not find and the mother who did not speak of him."

During her early years, Rylant did not read many books. Not only that, she wrote in *SAAS,* "I did not *see* many books." There were no libraries or bookstores in Beaver, so adults got paperbacks from the drug stores and children read comic books. Rylant read hundreds of comics. She mused in *SAAS,* "I guess most people assume that future famous authors are supposed to be reading fat hardbound books and writing poetry by age ten. But all I wanted to do was read *Archie* and play the Beatles." When she was in junior high, the New Orleans Symphony Orchestra stopped in Beaver. As with the Beatles, Rylant was bowled over by the music that the symphony played. She wrote in *BIBBA:* "The New Orleans Symphony was for me like a visit from God Himself, so full of awe and humility was I." She added, "watching the conductor and his beautiful orchestra, I felt something in me that wanted more than I had.... I wanted to be someone else, and that turned out to be the worst curse and the best gift of my life. I would finish out my childhood forgetting who I really was and what I really thought, and I would listen to other people and repeat their ideas instead of finding my own. That was the curse. The gift was that I would be willing to try to write books when I grew up." She added in *SAAS:* "It wasn't an obvious talent, it wasn't piles of poems or short stories which were the hints in my childhood that I might be a writer someday. The clues were much more subtle and had something to do with the way I grieved over stray animals, the heroes I chose (a presidential candidate, a symphony orchestra conductor), and the love I had of solitude. It is called sensitivity, this quality which sets creative people apart.... [I]f they possess only a little-more-than-reasonable amount, they can see into things more deeply than other people and can write or paint or sing what they saw in a way that moves people profoundly."

In junior high, Rylant stated in *SAAS,* "I had the time of my life." She was, as she noted in her essay, "completely boy-crazy.... I believe I drove my mother out of her mind." High school was more difficult. When she was thirteen, Rylant lost her father, who had planned to come to visit her before he suddenly passed away. She was also deeply affected by the death of Robert Kennedy, the senator whom she had met when he came to West Virginia as part of his presidential campaign. Rylant also fell in love with a boy from school whom she planned to marry. When he dropped her for another girl, she was devastated. When Rylant took him back, the boy did the same thing a year later. Since Rylant had focused so intently on her relationship, she did not have anyone else to turn to for companionship. She wrote in *SAAS,* "[P]robably no one would have guessed in a million years how lonely I was. I was head majorette, a school queen, always the president of this or that. But those things could not give me what I lacked—one true friend." At the end of her senior year, Rylant dumped her erstwhile boyfriend. With the help of the Veterans Administration, she became a student at Morris Harvey College, now the University of Charleston.

Rylant initially thought that she would be a nurse like her mother. However, after taking her first college English class, she switched her major to English. She noted in *SAAS,* "I heard and read stories I had never heard or read before, and I was in love with words." As a college student, Rylant did well academically. "But the real achievement for me," she wrote in her essay, "was more personal. I began to think for myself, to throw off some of the RULES OF LIFE that had been drummed into me in my small town, and my mind began to grow and blossom.... I became really alive." She became editor of the campus newspaper and enjoyed the variety of personalities that the college included. "I liked college so much that when I finished I didn't want to stop being a student," Rylant noted in *SAAS.* She wrote in her essay that her first year of graduate school at Marshall University in Huntington, West Virginia, was "without a doubt the happiest year of my life.... I loved literature so much and every day all I had to do was attend class and listen to it and talk about it and write about it. Like a chocolate lover at a Hershey's factory, I was completely content." After receiving her master's degree in 1976, Rylant got married to a young man who taught classical guitar and was learning to be a carpenter. She also got a job at the public library in Huntington, working in the children's room. Rylant began reading the books that she was supposed to be shelving and discovered a brand new world. She wrote in *SAAS,* "I was enchanted. I read children's books all night long.... And I knew, with a certainty like I'd never had about anything before, that I wanted to write children's books. And I believed I would be good at it. I wasn't afraid of it."

Rylant bought a copy of *The Writer's Market,* a book containing the addresses of publishers, and started writing. She was particularly influenced by Donald Hall's poetic picture book *The Ox-Cart Man* and Randall Jarrell's lyrical novella *The Animal Family.* Writing in *SAAS,* she called these works "perfect little pieces of art. And that's what I wanted to make." Shortly after she started writing, Rylant and her husband had a son, Nathaniel, whom they named after Nathaniel Hawthorne, one of Rylant's favorite authors. Rylant managed to keep writing; six months after the birth of her son, she wrote the words "when I was young in the mountains." She said in *SAAS,* "I don't know where they came from. I guess from the twenty-four years I had lived. From all the fine books I had read. From angels." In an hour, she had finished her first book. Without revising it, she sent it to E. P. Dutton publishers in New York. The company published *When I Was Young in the Mountains* in 1982.

A picture book that poetically describes the years that Rylant spent with her grandparents in Appalachia, *When I Was Young in the Mountains* is a collection of vignettes about the busy, joyous life of her small community—the title phrase introduces each memory. The book was favorably received by critics and received a Caldecott Award honor book designation for its illustrations by Diane Goode. A reviewer in *Publishers Weekly* stated that the author's debut "proves she knows precisely how to tell a story that brings the reader into the special world of her recollecting.... These are memories of a way of living that will entrance readers

He walks

in His garden

with a good black book

and a kitty

asleep on His head.

A multiethnic God provides a perfect environment for cats in Rylant's portrayal of feline hereafter. (From Cat Heaven, *written and illustrated by Rylant.*)

and broaden their outlook." Writing in *Bulletin of the Center for Children's Books,* Zena Sutherland noted that *When I Was Young in the Mountains* "is given appeal by the warmth and contentment that emerge from an account of daily satisfaction and small, occasional joys, described with appropriate simplicity." Leigh Dean of *Children's Book Review Service* commented: "There was something effortless, simple, and pure about [the book's] first-person narrative language.... It came, unadulterated, from the heart." After the success of her first book, Rylant realized, as she noted in *SAAS,* that she had "a gold mine of stories stored up in my head. Memories I could use to make books. I wrote and wrote, sold book after book, most of them true or partly true. All of them realistic. And most coming as quick and pure as that first book came." *Waiting to Waltz: A Childhood* is a collection of thirty autobiographical poems in free verse published in 1984 that outlines the author's reminiscences of the next stage of her life—growing up in Beaver, West Virginia. In this work, Rylant portrays the happy and sad times she felt—such as, in an example of the latter category, the death of her father—while offering incisive portraits of the townspeople. A reviewer in *Publishers Weekly* wrote that everyone in Beaver "becomes as real to the reader as

they are to Rylant," while Ethel R. Twichell of *Horn Book* predicted that the poems "will gently pluck a long-forgotten memory or awaken a shared experience." Writing in *School Library Journal,* Margaret C. Howell stated: "These are not easy poems, but rather a quiet yet moving internalization of growing up. As such, they are a fine example for introspective readers of how poetry expresses intense feelings...."

Rylant's marriage to her first husband ended after a few years. She was also married briefly to a college professor. She worked as a part-time English teacher at Marshall University for a year, then relocated to Kent, Ohio. Rylant received her library science degree from Kent State University in 1982 and worked at the Akron Public Library as a children's librarian and at the University of Akron as a part-time English teacher the next year. In 1985, Rylant published her first novel, *A Blue-Eyed Daisy* (British edition as *Some Year for Ellie*). The story describes a year in the life of Ellie Farley, an eleven-year-old girl who lives in the hills of West Virginia. Ellie recounts several memorable moments that occur over the course of her eleventh year, such as getting kissed at her first co-ed party and attending the funeral of a classmate. Throughout the narrative, Ellie deepens her relationship with her father, Okey, a former miner who lost his job in an accident. A reviewer in *Publishers Weekly* said of *A Blue-Eyed Daisy:* "No reader will be able to resist Ellie or her kith and kin. Their ability to live life and endure ills is the core of an exquisite novel, written with love." Katherine Bruner of *School Library Journal* added that Rylant's "low-key, evocative style . . . is the shining quality which sets this book apart. Through her understatedly elegant prose, readers come to know a beautiful person, easy to read about, but hard to forget." In 1986, Rylant published one of her most well-received books, the young adult novel *A Fine White Dust.* In this work, Pete, a seventh-grader who lives in the rural South, becomes a born-again Christian after being converted by the charismatic Preacher Man, James W. Carson. When Carson offers Pete the chance to go with him as his disciple, the boy decides, after much soul-searching, to leave his parents and his best friend, Rufus. Carson, who is viewed by Pete as God in the flesh, runs off with Darlene, a young woman who works at the town soda fountain. Although Pete feels betrayed, he comes through his experience with an unshaken faith in God and a more realistic view of human nature. A critic in *Kirkus Reviews* stated: "Rylant has explored a theme vital to many young people but rare in children's books." Writing in *School Library Journal,* Julie Cummins noted: "Few books have explored young people's fascination with God and their soul. . . . Like Peter, this story has soul." Calling the novel "an achingly resonant portrayal of a naive youth," Denise M. Wilms of *Booklist* concluded that *A Fine White Dust* is "poignant and perceptive, with almost all of the characters subtly drawn." *A Fine White Dust* was designated as a Newbery Medal honor book in 1987.

In 1987, Rylant published *Henry and Mudge: The First Book of Their Adventures,* a story that she based on her son and a dog that she knew. In this book, Henry, an only child, receives a pet, Mudge, a three-foot tall dog that appears to be a cross between a Saint Bernard and a Great Dane. Henry and Mudge form a deep attachment to each other. The tension comes when Mudge is lost, but happiness is restored when he is found again. Rylant presents lots of humorous details, such as Mudge's drooling and love of dirty socks, in prose that is designed for beginning readers. Reviewing *Henry and Mudge* and the second volume of the series, *Henry and Mudge in Puddle Trouble,* a critic in *Kirkus Reviews* called the author's language "easy to read but vividly evocative" and concluded: "Warm, loving, and gently philosophical, these stories about an only child and his closest companion deserve a place in every library collection." Rylant has written approximately thirty volumes about Henry and Mudge. In *Henry and Mudge and the Happy Cat,* she describes the arrival of a scraggly kitty to Henry's home. Mudge and the cat form an immediate bond, and he is heartbroken when the cat's owner comes and takes it away; however, Mudge is pleased with the owner's gift of thirty huge bones. Writing in *School Library Journal,* Trev Jones said that the story "sparkles with good humor and affection," while Betsy Hearne of *Bulletin of the Center for*

Children's Books stated: "It's hard to keep a series fresh, especially at the easy-to-read level, but this may be the best Henry and Mudge book since the first two." In her review of *Henry and Mudge and the Happy Cat,* Susan Perren of *Quill & Quire* called the series "enough to make a grown-up weep—Oh that early readers could have been this much fun back then!"

In *Henry and Mudge and the Bedtime Thumps,* the pair take a trip to Grandmother's house in the country. When Mudge is deemed too large for the small home and is made to sleep outside, Henry is afraid both for Mudge and for himself. However, when Mudge finds a spot under a large table on the porch, both he and Henry curl up happily and fall sleep. Writing in *Horn Book,* Elizabeth S. Watson said, "the delectable duo are back, and once again the author has developed a fresh, warm, imaginative, and yet absolutely realistic tale for the beginning reader." A critic in *Kirkus Reviews* wrote: "As always, Rylant's telling is affectionately humorous and the conclusion is a realistic, humorous surprise. Still tops." Nancy Seiner of *School Library Journal* queried: "Will this lovable duo ever run out of opportunities for good times and good feelings? Not as long as there are childhood joys and fears to be remembered and recorded by this talented author-artist team [illustrations are by Sucie Stevenson]." Seiner concluded by trumpeting: "Bravo Henry and Mudge. May they go on forever!"

In 1989, Rylant published *But I'll Be Back Again: An Album,* an autobiography for young adults. Describing her childhood and early adolescence and referencing the people and places that appear in her works, Rylant prefaces each section of her autobiography—which deals candidly with important events in her life—with appropriate song lyrics by the Beatles. Denise Wilms of *Booklist* wrote: "Autobiographies are hard to come by; this one will be quite accessible to readers." Betsy Hearne called *But I'll Be Back Again* "well written and revealing" and "[h]onest and [h]eartfelt," while Amy Kellman of *School Library Journal* concluded: "Don't let older readers be put off by the format: the text is sophisticated and will ring true for them. Reluctant readers, on the other hand, may be moved to pick up the book. Neither group will be disappointed." Another of the author's well-received forays into nonfiction is *Appalachia: The Voices of Sleeping Birds,* a picture book for older readers which poetically evokes the spirit of Appalachia in a tribute to the land and its people. Rylant describes the living conditions, hard work, customs, activities, and personalities of the Appalachian people in lyrical prose. Illustrated with realistic paintings by artist Barry Moser who, like Rylant, has roots in Appalachia, the book is generally considered an excellent marriage of text and picture. Barbara Chatton of *School Library Journal* noted that it should "encourage original writing or art as it reveals how illustrations and words can interact, how prose can illuminate a painting, and how simple paintings can bring power to prose." A critic in *Kirkus Reviews,* noting the author's "carefully pitched, melodious voice," concluded that *Appalachia: The Voices of Sleeping Birds* is "a special book for creative sharing." A reviewer in *Publishers Weekly*

A charming orphaned cat becomes the mascot of a cookie store in Rylant's engaging self-illustrated picture book. (Cover illustration by Rylant.)

stated, "Neither story nor factual treatise, the text offers pure nostalgia—a skillfully structured essay that appears, deceptively, to meander like a dusty country lane and underscores the warmth, generosity of spirit and steadfastness" of the Appalachian people.

With *Missing May,* a novel for young adults published in 1992, Rylant created what is perhaps her most highly acclaimed book. The story outlines how twelve-year-old Summer, who came to stay with her Aunt May and Uncle Ob in West Virginia after the death of her mother six years before, attempts to save her uncle from despair after the death of his beloved wife. In the midst of his mourning, Ob senses May's presence. Looking for an interpreter, Ob and Summer settle on Cletus, an unusual boy from Summer's class who once had a near-death experience and is, according to Caroline S. McKinney of *Voice of Youth Advocates (VOYA),* "as full of the energy for living as Ob is with the numbness of grieving." Through his suggestion, the trio go to Charleston to find a medium at the Spiritualist Church. The trip becomes a quest for each of them. The group reaches Charleston to find that the medium has died. Rather than sinking deeper into despair, Ob decides to take the children to the State Capitol. At the end of the novel, Summer realizes that Ob chooses to go on with his life because he cannot bear to say goodbye to her. McKinney conclud-

ed, "*Missing May* will be passed around by many of us who love beautiful words. It will speak in that warm, flowing West Virginia tongue to young people and old." Betsy Hearne of *Bulletin of the Center for Children's Books* noted: "Strong nuances of despair and hope create a suspense that forcefully replaces action and that will touch readers to tears." Writing in *Booklist,* Ilene Cooper referred to the "sheer pleasure of Rylant's writing," adding that "[d]eath, pain, and grief are the topics at hand, but they're written about with humor, grit, and love. Rylant makes us aware of the possibilities of life, even in the midst of tragedy. There is a freshness here that feels like a cool breeze." *Missing May* received the Newbery Medal in 1993.

In 1991, Rylant became a part-time lecturer at Northeast Ohio Universities College of Medicine, a position that she continues to hold. Two years later, she created "The Everyday Books," a series of board books for very young children. In these volumes, Rylant introduces her audience to literature by centering on subjects familiar to them, such as their homes and pets. The first of Rylant's works to include her own illustrations, "The Everyday Books" feature the artist's child-appealing collages. In 1995, Rylant published another self-illustrated title, *Dog Heaven.* This picture book portrays the author/illustrator's idea of what dogs experience in the afterlife, such as fields to run in, plenty of angel children to pet them, and appetizing cat-shaped biscuits to eat. It ends with the concept that dogs will be at Heaven's Door to greet old friends. The book is illustrated in bright acrylics that blend naive forms with unusual colors. According to a critic in *Kirkus Reviews,* the illustrations are "infused with simple doggy joy." The critic concluded by calling *Dog Heaven* "[p]ure, tender, lyrical without being over earnest, and deeply felt." Joy Fleishhacker of *School Library Journal* observed: "The reassuring story may comfort a child after the loss of a pet, but this pleasant, imaginary paradise will have a broader appeal to all animal lovers." Roger Sutton of *Bulletin of the Center for Children's Books* noted that Rylant maintains "a plain, conversational tone that resists gooeyness.... [T]he paintings allow viewers to imagine their own pets at play in the fields of the Lord." In 1997, Rylant produced a companion volume, *Cat Heaven.* Writing in rhyme, Rylant describes a heaven full of trees and clouds to perch on, soft angel laps to sit on, lots of toys to play with, and full dishes of food to eat. The author portrays God as a cat-lover who walks around Heaven with a cat asleep on His head and lets the felines lie on His bed. Full of cutout stars and broad sweeps of color, the illustrations depict a multiethnic God whose skin changes periodically from pink to brown to beige. A critic in *Kirkus Reviews* called *Cat Heaven* "[e]very bit as rich in eye-dimming sentiment as *Dog Heaven*"; the critic added that the book "will kindle sighs even from the feline-indifferent." Writing in *Bulletin of the Center for Children's Books,* Pat Mathews concluded: "Cats pretty much divide people into two categories—lovers and haters—so don't expect felinophobes to be crazy about this book. Kids will love it, though, and cat owners will get all misty-eyed."

Rylant has also provided the pictures for several of her other works, such as *The Whales,* a picture book published in 1996 which portrays the great beasts of the sea in lyrical prose and rich paintings done with acrylics and natural sea sponges, and a set of companion volumes, *The Bookstore Dog* and *The Cookie-Store Cat.* Published in 1996 and 1998 respectively, these picture books describe how a dog brings a couple together and how an orphaned cat becomes the mascot of a cookie store. Rylant illustrates these tales with double-page spreads in bold colors that are surrounded by decorative borders.

Rylant wrote in her second autobiography, the picture book *Best Wishes:* "Sometimes your best wishes really do come true. When I was a little girl I used to wish for a pretty house with a big picture window, a faithful dog who loved me, cats, and a chance to do something important . . . . I did a lot of wishing for a lot of things. And when I was grown, I got many of those things. I got the house with the window, the faithful dog, the cats. And I also did something important: I became a writer." In an essay in *CBATC,* Rylant wrote about some of the sources for her works. Her father "left me his flair for storytelling, his magic. And I often feel that he protects me now, trying to earn some redemption. And perhaps still trying, stubbornly, to entertain." Rylant described her mother as a wonderful letter writer who "has read more serious literature than anyone I know. She loves beautiful writing and perhaps, given a life lived any-where except coal camps and hospitals, she might have found her own incomparable voice, and we could have been graced with another Harper Lee or Eudora Welty. She never had the faith, though, the confidence, to try. Somehow, she planted these in me instead. My grand-mother blessed me with the sound of her beautiful wisdoms at the kitchen table . . . . My grandfather, a careful listener, chose his words just as carefully. He taught me discretion." The author concluded, "I still want to be that really good writer. That E. B. White. That James Agee. I am still hoping to be that good. Maybe my father, with wings and inspiration, is listening." In an interview with Anita Silvey of *Horn Book,* Rylant commented that writing "has given me a sense of self-worth that I didn't have my whole childhood. I am really proud of that. The [books] have carried me through some troubled times and have made me feel that I am worthy of having a place on this earth." In her essay in *SAAS,* Rylant concluded, "I will write, because I have to earn my way and because it seems to be what God put me here to do. I hope one day to write a great book, a magnificent book, which people will buy for those they love best, which they will place in someone else's hands and say: 'Before you do anything else, *you must read this.'*" Writing in *SBJAI,* Rylant concluded, "I'm grateful that I'll be leaving something important and beautiful on the earth for other people, something honest for them to read."

Works Cited

Review of *Appalachia: The Voices of Sleeping Birds, Kirkus Reviews,* March 1, 1991, p. 322.

Review of *Appalachia: The Voices of Sleeping Birds, Publishers Weekly,* March 1, 1991, p. 74.

Review of *A Blue-Eyed Daisy, Publishers Weekly,* March 8, 1985, p. 91.

Bruner, Katherine, review of *A Blue-Eyed Daisy, School Library Journal,* April, 1985, p. 92.

Budin, Miriam Lang, review of *Bear Day, School Library Journal,* January, 1999, pp. 101-02.

Review of *Cat Heaven, Kirkus Reviews,* July 1, 1997. p. 1035.

Chatton, Barbara, review of *Appalachia: The Voices of Sleeping Birds, School Library Journal,* April, 1991, p. 137.

Cooper, Ilene, "The Other Side of Good-bye," *Booklist,* February 15, 1992, p. 1105.

Cummins, Julie, review of *A Fine White Dust, School Library Journal,* September, 1986, p. 138.

Dean, Leigh, review of *Waiting to Waltz: A Childhood, Children's Book Review Service,* November, 1984, p. 32.

Review of *Dog Heaven, Kirkus Reviews,* July 1, 1995, p. 951.

Edwards, Eden K., essay in *Children's Books and Their Creators,* edited by Anita Silvey, Houghton Mifflin, 1995, pp. 566, 568.

Review of *A Fine White Dust, Kirkus Reviews,* July 1, 1986, pp. 1023-24.

Fleishhacker, Joy, review of *Dog Heaven, School Library Journal,* October, 1995, p. 115.

Hearne, Betsy, review of *But I'll Be Back Again: An Album, Bulletin of the Center for Children's Books,* July-August, 1989, p. 283.

Hearne, review of *Henry and Mudge and the Happy Cat, Bulletin of the Center for Children's Books,* October, 1990, pp. 43-44.

Hearne, review of *Missing May, Bulletin of the Center for Children's Books,* March, 1992, p. 192.

Review of *Henry and Mudge* and *Henry and Mudge in Puddle Trouble, Kirkus Reviews,* February 15, 1987, p. 300.

Review of *Henry and Mudge and the Bedtime Thumps, Kirkus Reviews,* February 1, 1991, p. 184.

Howell, Margaret C., review of *Waiting to Waltz: A Childhood, School Library Journal,* November, 1984, p. 138.

Jones, Trev, review of *Henry and Mudge and the Happy Cat, School Library Journal,* August, 1990, p. 134.

Kellman, Amy, review of *But I'll Be Back Again: An Album, School Library Journal,* July, 1989, p. 97.

Lowery-Moore, Hollis, essay in *St. James Guide to Young Adult Writers,* edited by Tom and Sara Pendergast, St. James Press, 1999, pp. 731-33.

Mathews, Pat, review of *Cat Heaven, Bulletin of the Center for Children's Books,* November, 1997. p. 100.

McKinney, Caroline S., review of *Missing May, Voice of Youth Advocates (VOYA),* April, 1992, pp. 35-36.

Perren, Susan, review of *Henry and Mudge and the Happy Cat, Quill & Quire,* December, 1990, p. 19.

Rylant, Cynthia, *Best Wishes,* Richard C. Owen, 1992, pp. 5-7.

Rylant, *But I'll Be Back Again: An Album,* Beech Tree Books/Orchard Books, 1993, pp. 16-17, 19-20, 26-27, 43-44.

Rylant, essay in *Children's Books and Their Creators,* edited by Anita Silvey, Houghton Mifflin, 1995, p. 567.

Rylant, essay in *Sixth Book of Junior Authors and Illustrators,* edited by Sally Holmes Holtze, Wilson, 1989, pp. 255-56.

Rylant, Cynthia, entry in *Something about the Author Autobiography Series,* Volume 13, Gale, 1991, pp. 155-163.

Seiner, Nancy, review of *Henry and Mudge and the Bedtime Thumps, School Library Journal,* April, 1991, p. 101.

Silvey, Anita, "An Interview with Cynthia Rylant," *Horn Book,* November-December, 1987, pp. 695-703.

Sutherland, Zena, review of *When I Was Young in the Mountains, Bulletin of the Center for Children's Books,* April, 1982, p. 157.

Sutton, Roger, review of *Dog Heaven, Bulletin of the Center for Children's Books,* October, 1995, pp. 66-67.

Twichell, Ethel R., review of *Waiting to Waltz: A Childhood, Horn Book Magazine,* January-February, 1985, p. 64.

Review of *Waiting to Waltz: A Childhood, Publishers Weekly,* August 17, 1984, p. 60.

Watson, Elizabeth S., review of *Henry and Mudge and the Bedtime Thumps, Horn Book,* May-June, 1991, pp. 328-29.

Review of *When I Was Young in the Mountains, Publishers Weekly,* March 19, 1982, pp. 70-71.

Wilms, Denise M., review of *A Fine White Dust, Booklist,* September 1, 1986, p. 67.

Wilms, review of *But I'll Be Back Again: An Album, Booklist,* May 15, 1989, p. 1655.

For More Information See

BOOKS

Authors & Artists for Young Adults, Volume 10, Gale, 1993, pp. 163-68.

Children's Literature Review, Volume 15, Gale, 1988, pp. 167-174.

St. James Guide to Children's Writers, 5th edition, Gale, 1999.

PERIODICALS

Booklist, June 1, 1993, pp. 1993-94; September 1, 1997, p. 135.

Horn Book, March-April, 1992, p. 206.

Instructor, April, 1994, p. 60.

New York Times Book Review, June 30, 1990, p. 24; January 26, 1993, p. C-16.

Publishers Weekly, July 27, 1990, p. 128; March 1, 1991; February 3, 1992, p. 82; July 21, 1997, p. 178.

School Library Journal, March, 1992, pp. 241-42; May, 1993, p. 26.

—Sketch by Gerard J. Senick

S–T

SCHAER, Brigitte 1958-

Personal

Born February 1, 1958, in Zurich, Switzerland; daughter of Willi (an engineer) and Lisa (Schmiedl) Schaer. *Education:* Gymnasium Hohe Promenade, B.A., 1977; University of Zurich, study of German literature and linguistics, 1977-84. Vocal training, 1972-84.

Addresses

Home—Badenerstrasse 531, 8048 Zurich, Switzerland.

Brigitte Schaer

Career

Writer, 1988—. German literature instructor for a college in Zurich, 1984-88; vocal instructor, 1988—; experimental jazz vocalist, 1988—. Invited to the Solothurner Literature Congress, 1991. Has read for more than three-hundred schools at home and abroad. *Member:* Gruppe Olten (writers' association), Autillus (Association for writers of books for children of Switzerland).

Awards, Honors

Swiss Children's Book Award (Schweizer Jugendliteraturpreis), 1993, for *Das geht doch nicht!;* "Schnabelsteher"-Preis, Association of North German Children's Book Stores and Kinderbuchpreis, Nordrhein-Westfallen, both 1997, and International Board on Books for Children (IBBY) Honor List, 1998, all for *Monsterbesuch!; Die rote Zora* award for children's and youth media, Federal Office for the Education of Men and Women, 1999, for both *Das geht doch nicht!* and *Das Haus auf dem Huegel.*

Writings

FOR CHILDREN AND YOUNG ADULTS

Das Schubladenkind (stories), Nagel & Kimche, 1988.
Das geht noch nicht!, illustrated by Jacky Gleich, Carl Hanser, Munich Vienna, 1995.
Monsterbesuch!, illustrated by Jacky Gleich, Carl Hanser, Munich Vienna, 1996.
Das Haus auf dem Huegel (stories), illustrated by Jacky Gleich, Carl Hanser, Munich Vienna, 1998.
Die blinde Fee, illustrated by Julia Gukova, Nord-Sued, 1998, translation by J. Alison James published as *The Blind Fairy,* North-South Books, 1998.

OTHER

Auf dem hohen Seil (stories for adults), eFeF Publishers, Zurich, 1991.
Liebesbriefe sind keine Rechnungen (stories for adults), Carl Hanser, Munich Vienna, 1998.

Contributor to many highly regarded anthologies and to literary magazines. Children's stories and stories for young adults have appeared in such publications as *Jahrbücher der Kinderliteratur* (Yearbook of Children's Literature), *Der Bunte Hund, Daumesdick, der neue Märchenschatz, Texte dagegen* (all published by Beltz & Gelberg publishers, Weinheim).

Adaptations

Schaer's works have also been adapted for radio and television programs. *Das geht doch nicht!* and *Monsterbesuch!* have been adapted for the theater.

Work in Progress

The Kidnapping of the Earth, a novel for children.

Sidelights

Brigitte Schaer is a Swiss author of children's books. She has written the award-winning *Das geht doch nicht!* and *Monsterbesuch!*, both of which have been adapted for the theater. The first of her books to be translated into English is *The Blind Fairy.*

In addition to her writing, Schaer is a jazz vocalist who has performed concerts of improvisational music and experimental jazz in many countries. She has worked on multi-media projects in the area of dance, theater, video, film, and performance art. She also released the recording *Vocal Flight to Beirut,* a daring album on the border of jazz, chanson, rap, pop, and oriental tradition. The recording was made in Beirut, Lebanon, with Arabic guest musicians.

Schaer told *SATA:* "It was always my dream to write a beautiful book for children, and I really did it. As a child, I told my own stories to my sisters and my brother. Before sleeping, we would lay in the darkness of our beds, our eyes closed, and they listened to my stories. They were a way for us to go on voyages together, and to get over the barriers of space, time and reality, all because of imagination.

"I have a wonderful experience writing stories. Every time I want to write another story, I sit in front of my computer, waiting like a cat in front of a mouse-hole until I get the strong feeling that soon the adventure will begin.

"Writing for children gives me the possibility to prolong my childhood forever, and never to lose the childlike heart-full of hope, curiosity and sympathy."

*   *   *

SILVERMAN, Erica 1955-

Personal

Born May 21, 1955, in Brooklyn, NY; daughter of Harold (in sales) and Gloria (Phillips) Silverman.

Education: Attended State University of New York, Albany; University of California, Los Angeles, B.A. (magna cum laude), 1982. *Politics:* Democrat. *Religion:* Jewish. *Hobbies and other interests:* Psychology, politics, wildlife, ecology, social history.

Addresses

Office—c/o Publicity Director, Macmillan Publishing Co., 866 3rd Ave., New York, NY 10022.

Career

Freelance writer, 1982—. Teacher of English as second language, Los Angeles, CA, 1982—. Manuscript consultant and speaker. *Member:* Society of Children's Book Writers and Illustrators, National Association for the Preservation and Perpetuation of Storytelling, Sierra Club, Southern California Council on Literature for Children and Young People.

Awards, Honors

North Carolina Children's Book Award Nomination, "Books for Children," Library of Congress, 1992, Children's Choice, Children's Book Council, Children's Choice, International Reading Association, 1993, all for *Big Pumpkin.*

Writings

Warm in Winter, illustrated by M. Deraney, Macmillan, 1989.

On Grandma's Roof, illustrated by Deborah Kogan Ray, Macmillan, 1990.

Big Pumpkin, illustrated by S. D. Schindler, Macmillan, 1992.

Mrs. Peachtree and the Eighth Avenue Cat, illustrated by Ellen Beier, Macmillan, 1994.

Don't Fidget a Feather, illustrated by Schindler, Macmillan, 1994.

Fixing the Crack of Dawn, illustrated by Sandra Spiedel, Bridgewater Books, 1994.

Mrs. Peachtree's Bicycle, illustrated by Beier, Macmillan, 1996.

Gittel's Hands, illustrated by Deborah Nourse Lattimore, BridgeWater Books, 1996.

The Halloween House, illustrated by Jon Agee, Farrar Straus Giroux, 1997.

On the Morn of Mayfest, illustrated by Marla Frazee, Simon & Schuster, 1998.

Railel's Riddle, illustrated by Susan Gaber, Farrar Straus Giroux, 1999.

Follow the Leader, illustrated by G. Brian Karas, Farrar Straus Giroux, 2000.

Contributor of stories to periodicals, including *Scholastic Scope* and *Schofar.*

Sidelights

"As an only child, I spent a lot of time in pretend worlds, talking to imaginary animals and people," Erica Silver-

A witch learns the value of cooperation when she tries to move her immense pumpkin by herself in Erica Silverman's humorous Halloween picture book. (From Big Pumpkin, *illustrated by S. D. Schindler.)*

man once told *SATA.* "Now, many years later, when I am working on a story, I feel the same sense of total absorption as I create a world, fill it with characters and watch and listen to them interact.

"Mother Goose rhymes gave me my first awareness of the pleasure of language. My father had a big reel-to-reel tape recorder. Together we recited Mother Goose rhymes onto tape. As I grew older, our reciting material changed to include all kinds of poems and stories. Those hours of reciting onto tape nurtured in me a love for the sounds and rhythms of language."

In Silverman's first book, *Warm in Winter,* Rabbit tells her friend Badger that the best experience of warmth comes in winter. Badger finds this difficult to believe on a sunny, summer day. However, Badger learns the truth of Rabbit's claim when she visits Rabbit during the winter's first snow. After Badger travels through the blustery storm and is offered a seat next to the fire, she

agrees warmth is best appreciated during winter. Commenting on the relationship between Badger and Rabbit in a *Booklist* review, Julie Corsaro called *Warm in Winter* an "affectionate tale of friendship." In a *School Library Journal* review, Marianne Pilla found the "narration descriptive," and also complemented the witty conversations between Rabbit and Badger.

Silverman once described her work to *SATA:* "Without consciously deciding on it, my books seem to touch on the need to be connected; my characters seem to be concerned with the question of needing others and being needed.... In *Warm in Winter,* a lonely Badger must confront a blizzard in order to find the warmth of friendship."

Silverman's second book, *On Grandma's Roof,* follows a young girl and her grandmother through the day's single activity: hanging laundry out to dry. Emily and her grandmother take a picnic basket along with the laundry, and spend the day on the roof of the grandmother's apartment building, where the chore is transformed into an expression of the loving relationship between the two. Mary M. Burns, writing in *Horn Book,* described the combination of text and illustrations as "superb," and went on to praise the "childlike celebration of life and love" as particularly suited for its intended audience. The story "vibrates with the delight the characters feel in each other," noted Virginia Opocensky in a *School Library Journal* review.

"My grandmother started me on the road to reading before I was in school," Silverman told *SATA.* "She took me to the public library on 23rd street in Manhattan, up the endless staircase to the children's room and let me pick out books to take home. I particularly loved folk tales. One of my favorites was an East European folk tale called 'The Turnip.' Years later, I walked into a library and heard a librarian reading 'The Turnip' to a group of children. I started wondering how I could adapt it in order to tell my own story."

In Silverman's *Big Pumpkin,* based on "The Turnip," a witch grows a pumpkin too large to move. After encounters with a cast of Halloween characters, none of whom can move the pumpkin either, a little bat suggests that they all work together to move the pumpkin. "It is only by working together that the boastful characters can finally have their pumpkin pie," Silverman commented for *SATA.* A *Publishers Weekly* reviewer felt that the dialogue created "a pleasantly sinister mood that stops just short of being scary," while in the *School Library Journal* Elizabeth Hanson called the book "rousing good fun for the Halloween season and far beyond."

"I didn't set out to write stories about teamwork or interdependence," Silverman concluded for *SATA.* "That would have resulted in an essay rather than a picture book. I generally start with a setting, the voices of characters, and an unidentified mood or feeling that I am trying to bring into focus. Part of the fun of starting a new book is finding out something new about myself along the way."

Critics repeatedly describe Silverman as a good storyteller. Susan Scheps called *Gittel's Hands* "a charming tale . . . told in the careful words of a storyteller, with a bit of repetition thrown in for good measure," in her review for *School Library Journal. Booklist* contributor Ellen Mandel remarked that *Gittel* has "much to occupy the eyes as well as the hearts of story lovers" and holds a "satisfying conclusion." *Gittel's Hands* portrays the dilemma a young girl faces when her father brags about her sewing and cooking talents to a man who holds the father's debts. When Gittel is forced by the man into an impossible claim upon her handy talents in order to repay her father's debts, Gittel unwittingly saves herself with an act of kindness to a stranger.

Silverman not only tells a good tale in *Mrs. Peachtree's Bicycle,* she offers her readers other ways to view people and their behavior by calling into question narrow patterns of thinking. According to a critic for *Kirkus Reviews,* "Silverman's story makes statements against sexism, ageism, and mindless adherence to convention." It's the turn of the century, and Mrs. Peachtree, white-haired and female to boot, takes on the established way of doing things with a show of open determination to ride a bicycle in order to make delivering food an easier job for herself. Silverman doesn't use heavy-handedness to tell her story but rather a "light, breezy tone throughout" claimed the *Kirkus Reviews'* critic. "Kids will relate to the intrepid, grandmotherly Mrs. Peachtree" predicted Carolyn Noah, a reviewer for *School Library Journal.*

Children love a fine-told Halloween tale and with *The Halloween House.* Silverman offers them a humorous tale of two convicts who seek shelter in a deserted house but find they are not alone on Halloween night. Susan Dove Lempke declared in *Booklist* that Silverman's *The Halloween House* is a "very funny story" and predicted it would be a "story-hour hit all year round." At the center of the story are two escaped convicts who seek shelter in an abandoned house and become the target of numerous creatures who make it their business to scare the living daylights out of these two criminals. And scare them they do, right out of the house and back to their prison cell where they find safety in "home sweet home."

Works Cited

Review of *Big Pumpkin, Publishers Weekly,* July 20, 1992, p. 248.

Burns, Mary M., review of *On Grandma's Roof, Horn Book,* July, 1990, p. 448.

Corsaro, Julie, review of *Warm in Winter, Booklist,* December 1, 1989.

Hanson, Elizabeth, review of *Big Pumpkin, School Library Journal,* September, 1992, p. 211.

Lempke, Susan Dove, review of *The Halloween House, Booklist,* September 1, 1997, p. 141.

Mandel, Ellen, review of *Gittel's Hands, Booklist,* May 15, 1996, p. 1594.

Review of *Mrs. Peachtree's Bicycle, Kirkus Reviews,* May 1, 1996, p. 693.

Noah, Carolyn, review of *Mrs. Peachtree's Bicycle, School Library Journal,* July, 1996, pp. 72-73.

Opocensky, Virginia, review of *On Grandma's Roof, School Library Journal,* March, 1990, p. 201.

Pilla, Marianne, review of *Warm in Winter, School Library Journal,* October, 1989, p. 1332.

Scheps, Susan, review of *Gittel's Hands, School Library Journal,* June, 1996, pp. 109-10.

For More Information See

PERIODICALS

Booklist, March 1, 1990, p. 1349; April 1, 1995, p. 1409; May 15, 1996, p. 1594.

Kirkus Reviews, March, 15, 1996, p. 452.

Los Angeles Times Book Review, April, 14, 1996, p. 10; July 7, 1996, p. 11.

School Library Journal, January, 1995, p. 93; November, 1994, p. 90.*

Zilpha Keatley Snyder

1927-

When I look back to the beginning, at least as far back as memory will take me, I see most vividly animals and games and books. People are there, too, my mother and father and older sister, but in those earliest memories they are much less distinct. I don't know what this says about my priorities at the time, but there it is.

There were lots of animals. Although my father worked for Shell Oil, he had grown up on cattle ranches, and by dream and desire he was always a rancher. So we lived in the country where he had room for a garden and as many animals as possible. Among my earliest acquaintances were cows, goats, ducks, chickens, rabbits, dogs, cats and, a little later on, horses. I can recall in some detail the day we acquired a collie puppy and a young kitten. I was three years old. The kitten was nominally mine and from the mysterious depths of a three-year-old's mind I produced a name—Maryland. I can remember some of the ensuing argument—no one else thought it was a sensible name, but I can't remember the reason for my choice. Neither the kitten nor I had ever been to Maryland, nor had either of us, as far as I know, ancestors from there. But Maryland she was, and she and her offspring play a prominent part in many of my early memories.

And then there were games. Some were secret, some less so, and most of them grew out of a compulsion to endow everything animal, vegetable and mineral with human characteristics. I suspect that all very young children are naturally given to anthropomorphism, but with me it must have been almost a full-time occupation. Not only animals, but also trees, plants, toys, and many other inanimate objects had personalities, and sometimes complicated life histories. Often these creatures seemed to have been in need of a helping hand. I built leafy shelters for homeless insects, doctored ailing toys, and every morning I saved Orphan Annie from drowning.

Glazed on the bottom of my cereal bowl, Orphan Annie was daily threatened by a sea of milk and gummy oatmeal. It was necessary for me to eat the disgusting mess quickly to save her from drowning. But once her face was uncovered, and the milk dammed behind a dike of oatmeal, my duty was done. My mother may have wondered why I began so eagerly and then left that thick dam of oatmeal around the center of the bowl.

Other inhabitants of my world of secret games were not so helpless, or so innocuous. Knives and hammers could be intentionally cruel; wagons and roller skates and all their ilk were often sneakily vindictive; and at the foot of my bed there lived a permanent settlement of little black demons with pitchforks just waiting for me to carelessly straighten out my legs. But I fooled them. For years I slept curled in a ball.

There were many other demons, most of whom haunted closets and the dark corners of rooms. Although they really frightened me, I don't think I would have wanted to be talked out of them. They were *my* demons, and we had a working relationship.

Books and reading must have had a beginning somewhere, but it is beyond memory. I seemed to have been born reading. Actually my mother claimed I taught myself after eavesdropping on lessons she was giving my older sister. Then one day when she was sick and I was four years old, I offered to read to her. When I proceeded to do so she thought I had memorized the book until she began to ask me individual words. Later when I became, briefly, a kind of neighborhood oddity—I had not yet been to school and I could read the newspaper and was sometimes called into neighbors' homes to demonstrate to skeptical guests—my mother claimed to have had nothing to do with it. Actually I think she used two methods which are almost certain to produce an early reader. First of all, she read to us—a lot. And then, when I tried to horn in on my sister's reading lessons, she told me I was too young—a challenge that no self-respecting four-year-old is going to take lying down.

Of course the games and the reading merged. Little Orphan Annie and the demons were soon joined by the likes of Heidi, Dorothy and Dr. Dolittle, not to mention some of the more intriguing characters I met in the pages of a very fat book called *Hurlbut's Story of the Bible*. My favorites were the ones whose lives included episodes that played well, such as Noah, Daniel and Jonah. Jonah, in particular, was a role that adapted well when one had, as I often did, tonsillitis. Being forced to stay in bed was less of a handicap when the scene being enacted took place in a whale's stomach.

But something should be said about the real people who were an important part of those early years. My father, William Solon Keatley, was a tall slow-moving man, the memory of whose kindness, patient devotion and unfailing

Zilpha (right) with her parents, Dessa J. and William S. Keatley, and her sister, Elisabeth, about 1930.

sense of humor is, to me, proof that it is possible to surmount the effects of an appalling childhood.

The first child of John William Keatley, a young Englishman who immigrated to America in the 1870's, and Zilpha Johnson his Nebraskan bride—my father's first few years of life were happy ones. But when he was five years old his mother died. Putting my father and his two younger brothers in an orphanage, my grandfather went to California, promising to send for the boys as soon as he was able. But for some reason the summons to a new life never came. The orphanage, losing patience, allowed the two younger boys to be adopted. But by then my father was too old to interest adoptive parents, and old enough to be of temporary interest to various people, some of them relatives of his mother, who needed an extra ranch hand. Forced to do a man's work at the age of eight, often beaten, punished by being sent out mittenless in freezing weather, so that his frozen hands very nearly had to be amputated, he survived to become a gentle man with crooked hands, who loved people almost as much as he loved horses, and who treated both with unfailing kindness.

As a young man he worked as a cowboy, in the days when many ranges were still unfenced; and in later years he told wonderful stories about bronco-busting, roundups and stampedes and above all HORSES. He sometimes said that he might forget a man but never a horse, and I'm sure it was true. As a child I knew all his horses through his stories including Old Washboard who had an iron mouth and a penchant for hunting wild horses and who, on spotting a herd of wild ones, took off, completely ignoring the desires of his helpless rider who willy-nilly accompanied him on a mad chase, leaping gullies and plunging down almost vertical cliffs with wild abandon. Fearing that someday Old Washboard would tackle a cliff he couldn't handle—"the only horse that ever scared me spitless," my father would say—he chickened out and sold him to a gullible passerby; just as innumerable owners had surely done before.

It was not until my father was in his forties and the owner of a small horse ranch in Wyoming that he was contacted by his father. Warmly received by his father's second family in California, he decided to relocate there. And it was there that he met Dessa Jepson, a thirty-five-year-old spinster schoolteacher, a cousin of his stepmother.

The Jepsons were Quakers. They had lived for many generations in Maine, the first Jepson arriving there in 1720, but in the 1870s several branches of the family moved west. My mother was born in California, the youngest of six children. Several years younger than her nearest sibling, she was born when her parents were middle-aged, and on the death of her mother she became her father's housekeeper and companion.

I never knew my grandfather, Isaiah Clarkson Jepson, but he must have been a complicated and determined man. A farmer who had tried photography and teaching and who loved poetry, he doted on Dessa, his youngest daughter, and effectively discouraged her early suitors. She became a schoolteacher, attending UCLA when it was still Los Angeles Normal School, and devoted herself to teaching and to her father. His death when she was in her early thirties left her rudderless and she suffered what she later referred to as a nervous breakdown. On recovering she returned to work and was teaching in Yorba Linda, California, when she met my father. It was a romance right out of Zane Grey—the bachelor rancher meets the lonely schoolteacher.

My parents were living in Lemoore, California, when my older sister, Elisabeth, and I were born, my father having accepted what he thought of as a temporary job until he could get back to ranching. But the Depression deepened and, to support his growing family, he continued at a job he hated. It was after he was transferred to Ventura, California, that my younger sister, Ruth, was born.

Like my father, my mother was a storyteller. Like his, her stories were true accounts of past events. Mother's childhood was always very close to her and she had a tremendous memory for detail. She made the people and events of rural California at the turn of the century as real to me as were those of my own childhood in the 1930s.

So I came by my storytelling instincts honestly but, as it soon became apparent, their acquisition was all that was honest about them. It wasn't exactly that I was a liar. I

"Princess" Zilpha in the wagon, about 1933.

don't think I told any more of the usual lies of childhood—those meant to get you out of trouble or get someone else into it—than most children. It was just that when I had something to tell I had an irresistible urge to make it worth telling, and without the rich and rather lengthy past that my parents had to draw on, I was forced to rely on the one commodity of which I had an adequate supply—imagination. Sometimes when I began an account of something I had heard or witnessed my mother would sigh deeply and say, "Just tell it. Don't embroider it."

At the age of eight I became, in my own eyes at least, a writer. I sometimes say that I decided on a writing career as soon as it dawned on me that there were people whose life's work consisted of making up stories. Up until then my tendency to "make things up" was one of the things that came to mind when I repeated that phrase about "trespasses" in our nightly prayers. The idea that there were people who were paid, even praised, for such activities was intriguing. I began as most children do with poems and very short stories, and I was fortunate to have a fourth-grade teacher who took an interest in what I was doing. She collected my works, typed them, and bound them into a book. I loved it—and her.

This early opus, while showing no great originality of thought or unique turns of phrase, does seem to exhibit a certain feeling for the rhythm and flow of words. The following excerpt owed its subject matter to a "social studies project" on China.

The Water Buffalo

Did you ever see a water buffalo,
Slowly around a rice field go,
Dragging a plow at every step?
To plow a rice field takes lots of pep,
So when the buffalo's work is done
He goes down to the river to have some fun.
He wallows down where the mud is deep,
And shuts his eyes and goes to sleep.

My memories of my first five years of school are pleasant ones. I was a good student, although my abilities were decidedly lopsided. I could memorize a poem in a flash, but the result of multiplying seven times eight eluded me for months, until my mother printed this slippery bit of information on a card and pinned it to the wall in front of the kitchen sink where I was forced to stare at it every evening while doing the dishes. It worked, I guess. I'm not sure whether my hatred of doing dishes spilled over onto the multiplication tables or vice versa, but I'm still not particularly fond of either.

Although there were times when I would have gladly traded my proficiency in reading and writing for a little skill at something that really mattered to my contemporaries such as running races or catching fly balls, I had few problems in the small country schools I attended until the end of sixth grade. But then came the seventh grade in the big city of Ventura. Too young for my grade, having been advanced by a first grade teacher who didn't know what to do with me while she was teaching reading, and further handicapped by being raised by a mother who hadn't really

Zilpha at Whittier College, about 1947.

faced up to the twentieth century, I was suddenly a terrible misfit. Still wearing long curls and playing secret games, I was too intimidated to make an effort to relate to girls who wore makeup and danced with boys. So I retreated further into books and daydreams.

Books! Books were the window from which I looked out of a rather meager and decidedly narrow room, onto a rich and wonderful universe. I loved the look and feel of them, even the smell. I'm still a book sniffer. That evocative mixture of paper and ink and glue and dust never fails to bring back the twinge of excitement that came with the opening of a new book. Libraries were treasure houses. I always entered them with a slight thrill of disbelief that all their endless riches were mine for the borrowing. And librarians I approached with reverent awe—guardians of the temple, keepers of the golden treasure.

It has occurred to me to wonder if I might not have faced up to life sooner if I had been deprived of books. (I know my father worried sometimes about the amount of time I spent reading. My father, not my mother. Her first priority was that we were safely and virtuously at home, with a book or without one.) Lacking a refuge in books, would I have been forced to confront my social inadequacies and set myself to learning the skills that would have made me acceptable to my peers? Perhaps. But then I wonder if it would really have been a fair trade. Would dances and parties and inexpert kisses by pimply contemporaries have made me happier than did Mr. Rochester, Heathcliff, the Knights of the Round Table and the many

other heroes and heroic villains with whom I was intermittently in love? Who's to say? In any event, I went on reading—and suffering the daily agony of the preteen outcast.

Beyond my personal world of home and school and books and dreams, the Depression deepened. Although my father never lost his job, his salary was cut and cut again until he was finally unable to cover the mortgage payments and it was only the New Deal's mortgage relief legislation that enabled us to keep our home. Like so many other families, we lived constantly under that sword of Damocles called the "pink slip." My sisters and I, as well as many of our friends, knew about the slip of pink paper which might at any time be included in our father's pay envelope, and we knew that the result would be the disgrace of "relief lines" and perhaps actual hunger. Sometimes as I walked past the "Okie Camp" that had sprung up on a neighbor's vacant land—trying to pretend I wasn't staring at the cardboard shanties, broken down cars and ragged dirty children—I fantasized that I belonged there; that I would turn in on the dirt road and as I approached the first crumbling shanty I would see my mother in the doorway. It was a game that both intrigued and terrified me.

As the first decade of my life ended the times slowly began to get better. The Okie camps disappeared, people who had been laid off went back to work and salaries began to rise. And then one day when we turned into our driveway after a Sunday morning at church, a neighbor ran to meet us. The Japanese, she said, had attacked Pearl Harbor.

I was in my early teens during the war and I would *like* to report that I thought deeply about the issues involved and the terrible suffering that was going on around the world—but it wouldn't be true. In spite of the fact that a Japanese sub once shelled an empty field not far from where we lived, and we had occasional air raid drills in our classrooms, the war seemed distant and almost unreal. I wrote a few sentimental war poems and went on reading and dreaming. Years later when I visited Anne Frank's apartment in Amsterdam and saw the pictures of movie stars on her bedroom walls, familiar Hollywood faces of the forties, treasured by teenage girls in California as well as those in hiding in Amsterdam, I was deeply shaken. I cried not only with grief for Anne but with shame that I had known and cared so little.

By the time I was in high school my social skills had begun to improve, and I became a little less afraid of my peers. I had some good teachers and made some exciting new friends, such as Shakespeare and Emily Dickinson.

And college was wonderful. At Whittier College, a small private liberal arts school in Southern California, originally established by Quakers, I grew physically and socially as well as intellectually. I discovered contemporary authors, politics, social injustice, psychology—and boys; men, actually, as the time was the late forties and campuses were full of returned servicemen. It was a good time to be in college. I learned a lot at Whittier: facts, ideas, and essences. Many of the facts have faded, as elusive as seven times eight, but I remember that Whittier taught me how little I knew; a startling concept to any new high school graduate. And even more important—how little anyone knew. Until then I had been satisfied that all possible knowledge was pretty much in hand, and as a student my only job would be to commit it to memory. What a thrill to realize that a lot of so-called facts were actually still up for grabs, and that decision-making was a part of learning.

And one more thing I owe to Whittier—my husband, Larry Snyder. We met first in the Campus Inn where we both waited on tables, and when I first saw him he was playing the piano. Six-foot-five with curly black hair and blue eyes, Larry was a music major who was also an athlete, a charismatic extrovert who was—and still is—a natural scholar, and a small-town boy who was born with a Ulysses-like yearning for new horizons. I liked him a lot. I still do.

But I was planning to be a writer. I wanted to live in New York City, in an attic apartment, and write serious novels for serious people. It's a good thing I didn't try it. At barely twenty-one with a new college degree, I had a sketchy instinct for self-preservation and all the sophistication of a cocker spaniel puppy. New York City would have eaten me alive, and that's without even trying to guess what New York editors would have done to me. The pages that have survived from the period suggest that as a writer I still had the lively imagination of my childhood, and some feeling for the sound and sweep of a sentence. But style, theme, subject matter, and even handwriting (I still didn't own a typewriter) have a pronounced aura of puppy.

Facing up to the fact that I didn't even have the money for a ticket to New York City, I decided to be practical. So, "temporarily until I got back to ranching," I took another job—I decided to teach school. Only I was more fortunate

Larry A. and Zilpha K. Snyder, June 18, 1950.

than my poor dear father. I didn't hate my temporary job. In fact, I liked it a lot. After the first year, which was a bit traumatic until I stopped being surprised when I told the class to do something and they did it, I developed into what must have been a pretty good teacher. I taught in the upper elementary grades for a total of nine years, three of them as a master teacher for the University of California at Berkeley, during which time my classroom was almost constantly being observed by teachers in training. I found teaching to be as rewarding as it was demanding, and I would probably still be at it if I hadn't been lucky enough to have my dream-ranch become a reality when my first book was published—but that was later. And I also decided to accept Larry's offer of marriage, which was probably the best decision I ever made.

Larry and I were married in June of 1950, and the next ten years flew by. They were happy years for the most part, although I sometimes think that if they hadn't been I might not have had time to notice. During that time Larry was in graduate school at Eastman School of Music; taught for one year at Eastern Washington College in Cheney, Washington; and then, because of the Korean War, was in the air force in Texas, New York and Alaska, before returning to graduate school at UC Berkeley. In the period we moved fifteen times, I taught school in New York, Washington, Alaska and California, and we had three children. Our first child was born by emergency caesarian section in 1952 and died two days after his birth. Our daughter, Susan Melissa, was born in 1954 in Rome, New York, and our son Douglas in Alaska in 1956. There were no further additions to our family until 1966 when our foster son, Ben, came to live with us. Ben was born in Kowloon, China, and when he became a part of our family he was eleven years old and spoke no English, and three years later he was the valedictorian of his eighth-grade class. Ben is like that.

In the early sixties the dust began to settle a bit. Larry was out of school and teaching at the College of Marin north of San Francisco, and the children were in school, Doug, the youngest, in kindergarten. I was still teaching but there seemed to be a bit more time and I caught my breath and thought about writing. Writing for children hadn't occurred to me when I was younger, but nine years of teaching in the upper elementary grades had given me a deep appreciation of the gifts and graces that are specific to individuals with ten or eleven years of experience as human beings. It is, I think, a magical time—when so much has been learned, but not yet enough to entirely extinguish the magical reach and freedom of early childhood. Remembering a dream I'd had when I was twelve years old about some strange and wonderful horses, I sat down and began to write.

Now comes the hard part. I've always maintained that I would never write an autobiography. To me, writing anything other than fiction is a chore. Take away the marvelous incentive of a world yours-for-the-making, and the joy dies. Thus, I once answered when asked if I would write an autobiography, by saying, "Not unless they'd let me make it up as I went along." But then I weakened and accepted the invitation to participate in the *Something about the Author Autobiography Series,* and up to this point

I've found, to my surprise, that I've enjoyed it a great deal. But from here on it won't be so easy.

My husband says that all authors' autobiographies should be entitled *And Then I Wrote.* This, of course, has put me on my mettle to avoid, not only that phrase, but also anything even remotely resembling it while, at the same time, covering thirty-six books and a computer game. After considerable thought I've decided to rely on the appended bibliography to provide chronology, while I deal with my years as a writer in a less structured way.

One of the questions most often asked of a writer concerns how he or she managed the giant step between being "would be" and "published." Everyone has heard about the difficulties involved in selling a first book; the closets full of unpublished manuscripts, and walls papered with rejection slips. I've been known to answer such questions by blandly announcing that I sold my first manuscript to the first publisher I sent it to. It's the truth, but not, unfortunately, the whole truth; and I always go on to explain the less glorious particulars. But once when I made the initial pronouncement in a gathering of writers and before I could qualify it, someone said quite justifiably, "Stand back, everyone. I'm going to shoot her."

The truth is that I did send my first attempt to write for young people to Atheneum and it was, indeed, published there some time later. The other part of the story is what happened in between.

I was still teaching school that year and I began to write at night after a day in the classroom. I was a lousy typist and at that time I was completely unable to compose at the typewriter, so I wrote on a tablet, and my husband, whose fingers move almost as well on a typewriter as they do on the piano, typed it for me. Later, when the book was accepted, he bought me an electric typewriter and told me to get busy and learn to type as he didn't intend to make a profession of typing manuscripts.

I didn't exactly pick Atheneum because it was at the beginning of the alphabet, but it was nearly that arbitrary. It was recommended to me by our school librarian as a house

Melissa and Douglas Snyder, about 1960.

Ben and Doug (and Wotan), about 1966.

that had recently published some good fantasies. But what I received when I mailed in my manuscript—"over the transom," no agent, no introduction—was neither the rejection slip I fully expected, nor the enthusiastic acceptance of which I'd occasionally allowed myself to daydream. What I received was a long letter, two full pages, telling me what was wrong with my story. It was only at the very end that the editor, Jean Karl, stated that if I were going to be working on it some more she would like to see it again. I remember telling my husband that either she was slightly interested or I had just received the world's longest rejection slip.

Of course I was going to be working on it some more. It never occurred to me to reply, "Who the hell are you?" as one well-known author is reported to have done when an editor asked for changes in his first manuscript. It was my first attempt to write for young people, and almost the only writing I had done for ten years. I knew I had lots to learn and I was delighted that someone was willing to help.

My first version of *Season of Ponies* was, among other failings, much too short to be a book for the age level towards which it was aimed. Jean liked the ending but wanted me to lengthen and strengthen the body of the story. I did, and she liked it better, but still there were problems. It was after the third complete rewriting that the book was accepted, and I became a published writer.

Being published, I found, makes a difference. It makes a difference to all writers, but there are, I think, differences specific to the writer who is also a wife and mother. Almost no one feels called upon to honor the working hours of an unpublished wife and mother who insists on wasting large chunks of time in front of a typewriter. But once she is published, friends are somewhat more hesitant about calling up for long midmorning chats, and recruiters for the United Fund, the PTA and Faculty Wives are a little less inclined to put her on the "readily available" list.

Within my own family, however, being published made very little difference. Larry had always been encouraging and supportive, and he continued to be. And my mother, who often lived with us, continued to bring her reading or mending into my room. "Just for the company, I won't say a word." She would say, "Go right on with your writing." And I would try to, knowing that she was lonely and watching for the slightest sign that my attention was wavering and that I was, therefore, fair game. And, of course, published or unpublished, I was always fair game to the children. Rules concerning an off-limits area in the general vicinity of my typewriter during certain hours of the day were impossible to enforce in the face of such major crises as the need for financing an ice cream purchasing expedition, or the mysterious and momentous disappearance of a baseball, rollerskate, sneaker, or any one of numerous pets, including cats, dogs, hamsters, rats, snakes and one very large, very green iguana. The demand for my expertise as a pet finder was especially pressing when the snakes or iguana were involved, since grandmothers and other guests objected to coming across them suddenly in unexpected places.

But children do go to school, and after I stopped teaching there were the blessedly quiet hours of the school day in which to write, and the list of my published books began to grow, usually at the rate of one a year.

My second book evolved from the remains of a manuscript written when I was nineteen years old, a novel for adults set in a fictional town in Ventura County during the Depression. The story, lustily begun, had run into plotting problems and had dwindled off in midsentence on about the forty-fifth page, but the setting and a few of the characters still intrigued me. Knocking a dozen years off the ages of the central characters I began the book again and the result was *The Velvet Room.*

I had not been a published writer for long when I discovered a new threat to my precious time at the typewriter, one which I had not counted on. I began to get invitations to speak or lecture. Many were requests that I speak in classrooms, and these, except for the loss of writing time involved, were never any problem. I was accustomed to the classroom situation, I enjoy interacting with children, and it was a thrill to learn about their reactions to my books. But a request that I speak to an adult group was a different matter. I accepted the first one because I was asked eight months ahead of time and I didn't think they'd believe me if I said I'd already booked the date. And then it was such a long time away—perhaps the world would come to an end, or some other fortuitous circumstance would prevent me from having to face up to my commitment. But the day did arrive, preceded by many sleepless nights during which I lay awake wondering what my hosts would do when I collapsed in a dead faint at the podium. But both I and my audience of several hundred librarians managed to survive that one, the requests continued to come, and my terror when facing large bodies of librarians, teachers or writers, gradually diminished.

The Egypt Game was my fourth book, and a good one to look at as an example of the complexity of the only possible answer to a simple, and very commonly asked question; "Where do you get your ideas?" Children ask it poised on tiptoe, ready to run off and get some of their own, and adults suspiciously, as if expecting one to either: 1) Admit to having personally experienced every event

described in one's body of work, or 2) Own up to hereditary insanity. The only answer to the question is "everywhere," and without meaning to be facetious, because in any one book the idea roots are many and varied; some of them easily followed while others are fainter and more mysterious.

For example the beginning seeds of *The Egypt Game* were sown during my early childhood, as is true of a great many of my books. A fifth-grade project on ancient Egypt started me on my "Egyptian period," a school year in which I read, dreamed and played Egyptian. But my dream of Egypt was private and it was my daughter, many years later, who actually played a game very like the one in the story, after I had turned her on to the fascinating game possibilities of a culture that includes pyramids, mummies, hieroglyphic writing and an intriguing array of gods and goddesses. However the actual setting and all six of the main characters came from my years as a teacher in Berkeley. The neighborhood described in the story, the ethnic mix in the classroom, as well as the murder, were all taken from realities of our years in Berkeley. So, as I tell children who ask me if I ever write "true" stories, all of my stories have bits-and-pieces of truth—true events, true people, true facts, as well as true memories and even true dreams (the real sound-asleep kind). But the fun comes from what goes on in-between and around and over the bits-and-pieces, tying them together and making them into a story. The in-between substance is woven of imagination and that is what makes fiction fascinating, to write as well as to read.

And then there is another element, a mysterious idea source which, it seems, many writers tap from time to time, and its unexpected and unpredictable gifts provide some of the most exciting and rewarding moments in writing. One might call such exciting moments a lateral thinking breakthrough, serendipity, the light-bulb syndrome, or just sudden inspiration; an inspiration that seems to come from nowhere and to have no known roots. Whatever you call it,

Zilpha in France, 1968.

Larry and Zilpha at a party celebrating the 100th year of their house, The Gables, 1977.

it's the kind of thing that makes you look up from the keyboard and say, "Hey. Thanks a lot."

The Egypt Game came out in 1967. We were still living in Marin County while across the bay to the east, Berkeley was leading the way in a world-wide explosion of protest. To the south, in San Francisco, the Flower Children were painting gracious old Haight-Ashbury Victorians purple and living on love and LSD. And in our own neighborhood Ken Kesey's psychedelic bus was parked not three blocks away, and Janis Joplin's west coast hangout was just up the street. Larry and I marched in anti-war parades but otherwise mostly watched in wonder from the sidelines while lifestyles changed, traditions crumbled, and protest, drugs and violence became a part of American life—and our children entered their teenage years. It was not an easy time to be a parent or a writer of books for young people. *Eyes in the Fishbowl, The Changeling, The Headless Cupid,* and *The Witches of Worm* came from those years.

Also during those years Larry became the dean at the San Francisco Conservatory of Music, and we began to make almost yearly trips to Europe. In 1970 we spent a month touring France with our three children, who were sixteen, fifteen and thirteen at the time. Melissa chose the day we arrived in France to announce that she had just become a strict vegetarian; Ben, who had been working hard at being a typical American teenager, perfected an admirably authentic teenage griping technique; and Doug

showed little interest in French culture other than *patisseries,* pigeons and stray cats. With the five of us cooped up together daily in a small rental car, Larry and I came to the conclusion that early teenagers, like fine wines, do not travel well. It was not until some years later that all three of them began to tell us how much they enjoyed that summer in France and how much it had meant to them.

In 1971 Larry took a position at Sonoma State University in Sonoma County and we moved to a one-hundred-year-old-farmhouse in the country near Santa Rosa, California. Larry was anxious to get out of administration and back into music and teaching and we wanted to get our children into a quieter, more rural atmosphere. We were also eager to own horses, a goal that was quickly accomplished after the move. I was out horse shopping almost before we were unpacked.

In our old house, mysteriously like the one I'd described in *The Headless Cupid,* I finished *The Witches of Worm, The Princess and the Giants, The Truth about Stone Hollow* and the three books of the "Green-Sky" Trilogy.

Like so many of my books the trilogy's deepest root goes back to my early childhood when I played a game that involved crossing a grove of oak trees by climbing from tree to tree, because something incredibly dangerous lived "below the root." Years later when I was writing *The Changeling* I recalled the game, and in the course of embellishing it for that story, became intrigued with the idea of returning to the world of Green-sky for a longer stay. The return trip took three years and produced three more books. Initially published in 1975, 1976, and 1978, the trilogy was later reincarnated as a computer game (programmed by Spinnaker Software of Cambridge, MA).

The computer game transpired when I was contacted by a young computer programmer named Dale Disharoon. After Dale introduced me to the world of computer games, I wrote and charted, Dale programmed, and a young artist named Bill Groetzinger made marvelous graphics for a game that takes off from where the third book of the trilogy ends.

Larry and Zilpha and a camel named Moses, 1985.

Zilpha Snyder and friends, 1983.

In 1977-78, with our children grown and away from home, Larry and I spent his first sabbatical year in Europe. Larry, who is quite fluent in Russian and had done much of his graduate work on Russian music, had for some years been leading a UC Berkeley Extension tour to the Soviet Union during the summers. For his sabbatical project we traveled for seven weeks in Russia, the Baltic Republics, Poland and Czechoslovakia while he did research on contemporary music. It was an incredible trip, sometimes uncomfortable and often a bit dismaying, but never less than fascinating, and very productive in terms of Larry's project.

When we finally reached Italy we were ready to settle down, which we did for four months in a lovely villa in the Tuscan countryside between Florence and Siena. During that time we alternated trips around Italy with long days of work, in which Larry compiled his collected data and practiced the piano, and I finished a novel for adults, *Heirs of Darkness,* and began a children's book set in Italy (a sequel to *The Headless Cupid* entitled *The Famous Stanley Kidnapping Case*). "Just like Chopin and Georges Sand," Alton Raible, who has illustrated many of my books, wrote, and then added, "Without all the coughing and spitting, I hope." Our villa was part of a complex of rental units constructed from a country manor house and outlying farm buildings, and among the residents were writers, artists and academics from various countries. It was an environment

molto simpatico and friendships we made there have been important and lasting.

On returning to Sonoma County I began work on a novel for young adults. It was a story concerning a teenage boy and a magnificent buck deer, and when I began to write I had in mind a fantasy about mythical animals. But *A Fabulous Creature* turned out to be one of those novels that seem to take over and direct their own development and I soon found I was writing a story that was quite realistic and that had a bit to say about one of my pet antipathies—the whole mystique of hunting. As had happened many times before, I suddenly said, "Oh, so *that's* what I'm writing about."

That backdoor approach to themes or "messages" has been a part of the scene for me since my first book, when I thought I was basing my story's antagonist on Greek mythology and only discovered after-the-fact that I'd been writing about someone I once knew—and feared; and my unconscious theme concerned the evil that arises when selfish and insensitive use is made of a naturally dominant personality.

It worried me for a while, this rather haphazard approach to thematic material, and now and then I tried it the other way, starting a few stories with the intention of addressing a given problem. But it never turned out well. Plots went lame and characters turned into caricatures. After a while I decided that, for me at least, "messages"

Larry and Zil at the Taj Mahal, April 1998.

were best left to their own devices. I would mind my own business, which was to tell a good story and let "messages" take care of themselves. They could, and would, I found, and in more subtle and interesting ways than when marshalled by my conscious mind. A case in point were some books of mine that were endorsed by NOW (National Organization for Women). The stories in question had been written before my own consciousness had risen very far, and I'd not set out to say anything in particular about liberation or equality. But the message—that little girls can be vital and original and courageous people—found an appropriate opening, and there it was. Or when *Heirs of Darkness,* which I'd set out to write as a straightforward, one-dimensional Gothic horror story (not for children) turned into an exploration of guilt, and its relationship to the passive/masochistic personality.

As the eighties began we were still living in Sonoma County. Larry had been lured back into administration serving as Dean of Humanities and then of the School of Performing Arts at Sonoma State University—and the

pendulum of American Youth Culture had begun a dramatic swing. Liberal arts departments were shrinking, while business management and computer sciences burgeoned. Watching this new breed of hard working, practical young people, it suddenly occurred to me that some of the present teenagers were undoubtedly the offspring of the flower-child generation. And the next step was to wonder where teenage rebellion might take a child who had grown up in the "hippie" milieu. The result was another young adult novel called, *The Birds of Summer.*

Blair's Nightmare, a third book about the Stanley family and *The Changing Maze,* a picture-book fantasy illustrated by Charles Mikolaycak, were published in 1985, while Larry and I were again living for a year in Florence, Italy, while he served as director of the California State Universities' Foreign Study Program. Among the side trips we were able to make that year was a nine-day exploration of Egypt, a destination that had been high on my must-see list since I used to walk to school as Queen Nefertiti when I was ten years old.

On the way to Petra, 1999.

Following our return to the States, Delacorte Press published *And Condors Danced,* a story set at the time and place of my mother's childhood in rural Southern California. In the next few years, *Squeak Saves the Day,* a fantasy about tiny forest people, was followed by *Janie's Private Eyes,* a fourth book in the Stanley family series. *Libby on Wednesday,* a story inspired by the many talented aspiring young writers I have been privileged to meet, came out in 1990. And in 1991 there was *Song of the Gargoyle,* a story which relates the adventures of a thirteen-year-old boy and the mysterious beast who becomes his constant companion. Set as it is in the middle ages, this book required a great deal of fascinating research, including the exploration of real castles in Europe. *Fool's Gold,* a contemporary story set in the picturesque gold-rush country of California, tells the story of fourteen-year-old Rudy, whose social aplomb contrasts strangely with the mysterious attacks of abject terror that have begun to torment him. And in November of 1994, *Cat Running* was published. Cat's story again evoked childhood memories of the Great Depression and of what it meant to be the children of the nineteen-thirties. *The Trespassers,* published in 1995, is set in the Big Sur country on the California coast and involves a brother and sister who discover the secrets of a deserted mansion. In 1996 a series of slightly shorter novels center around the exploits and adventures of a group of kids who live around a cul-de-sac called Castle Court. The four Castle Court Kids titles are *The Diamond War, The Box and the Bone, Ghost Invasion,* and *Secret Weapons.* In 1997, after many requests, pleas and demands from readers for a sequel to *The Egypt Game,* I finally got around to *The Gypsy Game,* which begins with Melanie's answer to April's question, "What do you know about Gypsies?" March of 1998 saw the publication of *Gib Rides Home,* a story inspired by my father's tragic childhood and his later life as a cowboy and trainer of horses. In 1999, *The Runaways* was published. This story, set in a tiny town in the high desert, centers around the plans of three young would-be runaways. These widely diverse adventurers include Dani, who is determined to escape the desert in order to return to the beautiful redwood country from which she came; Stormy, a dyslexic whose lack of reading ability does nothing to discourage his love of stories, and the books which provide them; and Pixie, a fearless follower of uninhibited fantasy.

As we approach the new century Larry and I continue to enrich our lives by travels which, in the last dozen years, have included Japan, China, Thailand, Singapore, Java, Bali, Australia, New Zealand, as well as many countries in South America. In 1998 we were in India and Nepal; and in May of 1999, Israel and Jordan.

So there it is, the story of my life and work, and while sticking to the facts wasn't easy, or nearly as much fun as fiction, I've faithfully done so. "See Mom, no embroidering." But before I sign off there's just one more question I'd like to address. And that is *why*?

Once, some years ago during the question and answer period after a lecture, a man asked me why I wrote for children. "Do you do it for the pocket book, or just for the ego?" was the way he put it. He didn't give me any other choices, but there is another answer. The ego and the pocket book are affected, of course, at least minimally; much of the time only too minimally. But the maximum reward is simply—joy; the storyteller's joy in creating a story and sharing it with an audience.

So I write for joy, my own and my imagined audience's—but why for children? Unlike many writers who say that they are not aware of a particular audience as they write, I know that I am very conscious of mine. Sometimes I can almost see them, and they look very much like the classes I taught, and often read to. And, like those classes when the story was going well, they are wide-eyed and open-mouthed, rapt in the story and carried out of the constraining walls of reality into the spacious joys of the imagination.

I began to write for children by accident, through the fortunate accident of nine years in the classroom. But I've continued to do so because over the years I've come to realize that it's where I'm happiest. It is, I think, a matter of personal development (or lack of it, as the case may be). There are several peculiarities that I share with children which, like having no front teeth, are perhaps more acceptable in the very young, but which, for better or worse, seem to be a part of my makeup.

First of all, there is optimism. Since growth and hope are almost synonymous no one begrudges a child's natural optimism, but a writer's is another matter. It's not fashionable to write optimistically for adults, nor, I must admit, even very sensible, given the world we live in today. But my own optimism seems to be organic, perhaps due to "a bad memory and a good digestion" (a quote that I can't attribute due to the aforementioned failing).

Secondly, there is curiosity. Mine is as intense as a three-year-old's, but where a three-year-old's most obnoxious trait might be asking "Why" several hundred times a day, I am given to eavesdropping on conversations, peering into backyards and lighted windows, and even reading other people's mail if I get a chance.

And thirdly there is a certain lack of reverence for factual limitations and a tendency to launch out into the far reaches of possibility.

So I enjoy writing for an audience that shares my optimism, curiosity and freewheeling imagination. I intend to go on writing for some time, and though I may occasionally try something for adults, I will always come back to children's books, where I am happiest and most at home.

Writings

FOR CHILDREN; FICTION

Season of Ponies, illustrated by Alton Raible, Atheneum, 1964.

The Velvet Room, illustrated by A. Raible, Atheneum, 1965.

Black and Blue Magic, illustrated by Gene Holtan, Atheneum, 1966.

The Egypt Game, illustrated by A. Raible, Atheneum, 1967.

Eyes in the Fishbowl, illustrated by A. Raible, Atheneum, 1968.

The Changeling, illustrated by A. Raible, Atheneum, 1970; Guildford, Surrey: Lutterworth Press, 1976.

The Headless Cupid, illustrated by A. Raible, Atheneum, 1971; Guildford, Surrey: Lutterworth Press, 1973.

The Witches of Worm, illustrated by A. Raible, Atheneum, 1972.

The Princess and the Giants (picture book), illustrated by Beatrice Darwin, Atheneum, 1973.

The Truth about Stone Hollow, illustrated by A. Raible, Atheneum, 1974; published in England as *The Ghosts of Stone Hollow,* Guildford, Surrey: Lutterworth Press, 1978.

Below the Root (first book of "Green-Sky" trilogy), illustrated by A. Raible, Atheneum, 1975.

And All Between (second book of "Green-Sky" trilogy), illustrated by A. Raible, Atheneum, 1976.

Until the Celebration (third book of "Green-Sky" trilogy) illustrated by A. Raible, Atheneum, 1977.

The Famous Stanley Kidnapping Case, Atheneum, 1979.

Come on, Patsy (picture book), illustrated by Margot Zemach, Atheneum, 1982.

Blair's Nightmare, Atheneum, 1984.

The Changing Maze (picture book), illustrated by Charles Mikolaycak, Macmillan, 1985.

POETRY

Today Is Saturday, photographs by John Arms, Atheneum, 1969.

FOR YOUNG ADULTS; FICTION

A Fabulous Creature, Atheneum, 1981.

The Birds of Summer, Atheneum, 1983.

And Condors Danced, Delacorte, 1987.

Squeak Saves the Day, Delacorte, 1988.

Janie's Private Eyes, Delacorte, 1989.

Libby on Wednesday, Delacorte, 1990.

Song of the Gargoyle, Delcorte, 1991.

Fool's Gold, Delcorte, 1993.

Cat Running, Delcorte, 1994.

The Trespassers, Delacorte, 1995.

The Gypsy Game, Delacorte, 1997.

Gib Rides Home, Delacorte, 1998.

The Runaways, Delacorte, 1999.

Gib and the Gray Ghost, Delacorte, 2000.

OTHER FICTION

Heirs of Darkness, Atheneum, 1978; London: Magnum, 1980.

STAUNTON, Ted 1956-

Personal

Born March 29, 1956; son of Frederick William (a real estate executive and dance band leader) and Ethel Marjorie Staunton (a homemaker; maiden name, Stewart); married Melanie Catherine Browne (a visual artist); children: William. *Education:* University of Toronto, B.A., B.Ed. *Hobbies and other interests:* playing guitar, basketball, running.

Addresses

Home—46 Ward Street, Port Hope, Ontario, Canada L1A 1L5.

Career

Writer, 1983—. Musician, 1979—. Parks and Recreation Department, City of Etobicoke, Ontario, Canada, community programmer, 1974-1980; St. Michael's College Library, University of Toronto, Ontario, library technician, 1983-1984; Ministry of Consumer and Commercial Relations, Toronto, education officer, 1984-1985; full-time writer and speaker, 1985—. *Member:* Canadian Society of Children's Authors, Illustrators and Performers, Writers' Union of Canada.

Awards, Honors

Puddleman and *Taking Care of Crumley,* have been named "Our Choice" by Canadian Children's Book Centre.

Writings

PICTURE BOOKS

Puddleman, illustrated by Maryann Kovalski, Kids Can Press, 1983, revised edition illustrated by Brenda Clark, 1988.

Taking Care of Crumley, illustrated by Tina Holdcroft, Kids Can Press, 1984.

Simon's Surprise, illustrated by Sylvie Daigneault, Kids Can Press, 1986.

Miss Fishley Afloat, illustrated by Eric Parker, Kids Can Press, 1990.

Anna Takes Charge, illustrated by Michael Martchenko, Yorkdale Shopping Centre (Scarborough Town Centre, Bramalea City Centre), 1993.

JUNIOR FICTION

Morgan Makes Magic, illustrated by Bill Slavin, Formac Publishing Company, 1997.

Morgan and the Money, illustrated by Bill Slavin, Formac Publishing Company, 1998.

Hope Springs a Leak, Red Deer College press, 1998.

CHILDREN'S FICTION

Maggie and Me, Kids Can Press, 1986; revised edition illustrated by Jacqui Thomas, Penguin, 1989.

Greenapple Street Blues, Kids Can Press, 1987.

Mushmouth and the Marvel, Kids Can Press, 1988.

Great Minds Think Alike, Kids Can Press, 1989.

Taking the Long Way Home, Kids Can Press, 1992.

CHILDREN'S NONFICTION

Leigh-Burton, Maggie Della, *Grandma Burton's book: Memoirs of Earlier Days in Minnesota,* South Dakota and Saskatchewan, revised and edited by Ted Staunton, Iona Private Press, 1981.

Rodgers, John, *Birdwatching for Young Canadians,* illustrated by Ted Staunton, Douglas & McIntyre, 1982.

Contributor to books, including *Writers on Writing: Guide to Writing and Illustrating Children's Books,* edited by David Booth, Overlea House, 1989; and *Everybody's Favourites: Canadians Talk about Books that Changed Their Lives,* compiled by Arlene Perly Rae, Viking, 1997. Staunton's works have been translated into French, and produced as sound recordings.

Sidelights

Ted Staunton's work appeals to children ranging from preschool age to middle school. Audiences relate to Staunton's stories about familiar childhood experiences that contain action, humor, and authentic dialogue. Through story he delves into the nature of friendship and connects with his young audience through authentic dialogue.

Staunton infuses his writing with the uncanny ability to remember what it was like to be a kid. His first book, *Puddleman,* takes readers into the fantasy life of a preschooler named Michael who loves to play in mud—but doesn't like the real-life problems it causes. Jan Marriott writes in *Quill & Quire:* "These are all emotions and situations with which most young children can readily identify."

Staunton followed up these books with a series of stories about the everyday escapades of two grade-school chums, Maggie and Cyril. *Taking Care of Crumley,* reveals their plot to teach a lesson to Cyril's nemesis, the schoolyard bully. Using realistic playground banter, Staunton captures "the terror as well as the pleasure of ultimate social justice," according to Joan Yolleck in *Quill & Quire.*

Cyril and Maggie are back at school in *Maggie and Me,* which Nancy Gifford recommends for its "humorous tone ... dialogue and action" in her review for *School Library Journal.* Gifford noted the variety of classmates Staunton includes: "some bossy, some bullies, some leaders (Maggie), and some followers (Cyril)"—someone with whom everyone can identify.

Staunton characterizes the series with a fast pace. *Taking the Long Way Home,* the fifth in the Maggie and Cyril series, "lays each plot development on top of the previous one to make a precarious structure that will have the children [readers] holding their breath until the last scene," according to *Canadian Materials* reviewer Alison Mews. In the end, however, Staunton's popular

Wham! Something smacked into Puddleman from behind. He ran for his life. The water hissed and splattered after him and Puddleman leaped into his mud puddle.

Dirtily disguised as Puddleman, Michael terrorizes his neighborhood until his mother foils his plan in Brenda Clark's **Puddleman,** *delightfully illustrated by Ted Staunton.*

characters manage to help each other and solve their individual predicaments.

Reviewer Andre Gagnon voiced his opinion of the series in *Canadian Materials:* "Staunton's ability to build an episode with quick, funny, unforced dialogue and situations to which children can relate puts this series well above others."

Great Minds Think Alike chronicles another Maggie and Cyril episode that takes place during summer vacation. This time, Cyril worries about losing his best friend as he searches for adventure. Writing for *Quill & Quire,* critic Ann Gilmore concluded that this edition to the series is for those who "regard fairy tales as psychologically nurturing and growth-enhancing," and determined it a "wonderful addition to the genre."

Titles, such as *Simon's Surprise,* introduce readers to new characters with their own set of childhood dilemmas to solve. After being told "when you're bigger" once too often, Simon sets out to prove he's BIG enough NOW. Early one morning before his parents awaken, he decides to wash the family car by himself. In *Canadian Children's Literature (CCL),* reviewer Mary Rubio commented that the text and illustrations work together to capture his parents "dazed and dumbfounded looks," as well as "proud little Simon standing amid his mess."

Staunton's work has many rhythms. He and illustrator Eric Parker speed up the tempo in *Miss Fishley Afloat* with what *Canadian Materials* reviewer Patricia Butler calls "wacky events that take place at such a rapid pace, two readings are necessary to feel that the story has been understood." Sarah Ellis, in her review for *Quill & Quire* described the sea-faring tale as "outrageous, heaping surprise upon coincidence" and the "cartoon-style pictures are energetic and jaunty. The writing is bombastic . . . ."

Readers interested in linking Staunton to his characters don't have to look far. In *Meet Canadian Authors and Illustrators,* Staunton told Allison Gertridge: "The character of Cyril is based on me when I was in grade school. I was a very shy and retiring type like Cyril. But more than the things that happen to Cyril, it's Cyril's outlook or his desires that echo mine."

However reminiscent his books may be of his own "normal" and "stable" childhood, Staunton avoids oversimplification and overdoses of sweetness and light. "I'm not interested in writing about nice things or role models, or being cute. I'd rather explore what happens when things go slightly wrong," he told a writer for the *Canadian Children's Book Centre.* "I tend to prefer it when kids can't quite answer their own problems because, after all, who really can?"

Works Cited

Butler, Patricia L. M., review of *Miss Fishley Afloat, CM: Canadian Materials for Young People,* November, 1990, p. 272.

Canadian Children's Book Centre, 1994, pp. 280-81.

Ellis, Sarah, review of *Miss Fishley Afloat, Quill & Quire,* August, 1990, p. 14.

Gagnon, Andre, review of *Mushmouth and the Marvel, CM: Canadian Materials for Young People,* March, 1989, p. 53.

Gertridge, Allison, *Meet Canadian Authors and Illustrators,* Scholastic Canada, 1994, pp. 94-95.

Gifford, Nancy A., review of *Maggie and Me, School Library Journal,* July, 1990, p. 79.

Gilmore, Anne, review of *Great Minds Think Alike, Quill & Quire,* September, 1989, pp. 23-24.

Marriott, Jan, review of *Puddleman, Quill & Quire,* January, 1984, p. 28.

Mews, Alison, review of *Taking the Long Way Home, CM: Canadian Materials for Young Material,* November, 1992, p. 306.

Rubio, Mary, review of *Simon's Surprise, Canadian Children's Literature,* 1987, p. 105.

Yolleck, Joan, review of *Taking Care of Crumley, Quill & Quire,* November, 1984, pp. 12-13.

For More Information See

PERIODICALS

Books for Young People, October, 1988, p. 17.

CM: Canadian Materials for Young People, November 28, 1997.

Horn Book Guide, January, 1990, p. 243.

School Library Journal, August, 1985, p. 58.

Quill & Quire, August, 1986, p. 38.*

*   *   *

TATE, Richard
See MASTERS, Anthony

*   *   *

THOMAS, Abigail 1941-

Personal

Born in 1941 in Boston, MA; married Richard Rogin. *Education:* Attended Bryn Mawr College.

Addresses

Home—369 Riverside Dr., New York, NY 10025.

Career

Viking Press, former literary agent and editor; author, 1988—. Also teacher of fiction writing.

Writings

FOR CHILDREN

Wake up, Wilson Street, illustrated by William Low, Holt, 1993.
Pearl Paints, illustrated by Margaret Hewitt, Holt, 1994.
Lily, illustrated by William Low, Holt, 1994.

FICTION; FOR ADULTS

Getting over Tom: Stories, Algonquin Books (Chapel Hill, NC), 1994.
An Actual Life (novel), Algonquin Books, 1996.
Herb's Pajamas (short stories), Algonquin Books, 1998.

Contributor of short stories and poetry to numerous magazines and journals, including *Missouri Review, Santa Monica Review, Little Magazine, Ms., Paris Review,* and *Nation.*

Sidelights

New York City writer and former literary agent Abigail Thomas writes books to charm preschool and early elementary-age readers. In her 1993 work *Wake up, Wilson Street,* little Joe and his grandmother sit in a rocking chair very early one Saturday morning and observe the rhythm of daily life that unfolds on their street. In Thomas's 1994 book, *Lily,* she takes a somewhat radical approach in dealing with her young audience, giving them no identifiable character like themselves on which to attach. The title character is instead a lovable little black dog. Lily lives with Eliza in a big city, and her canine comfort is greatly disrupted when movers come to move all of Lily's familiar surroundings to rural Vermont. The young reader, noted *Booklist* contributor Stephanie Zvirin, "won't fail to respond to Lily's confusion and fear." Illustrated in rich hues by artist William Low, this title "teaches that home, even if a doghouse, is where the heart is," assessed a reviewer in *Publishers Weekly.*

Pearl Paints, another of Thomas's children's books published in 1994, follows the newfound fervor of budding artist Pearl. After receiving art supplies for her birthday, she takes up painting with such a passion that her family becomes worried. At night, Pearl even dreams about painting, and Margaret Hewitt's illustrations have Pearl envisioning the works of the masters in these passages. Only her Aunt Peg lends support, and the drama ends happily when her family approves of the fantastic mural Pearl creates on her bedroom wall. *School Library Journal* contributor Alexandra Marris found the plot of "an offhand, slapdash quality," but, like *Booklist* reviewer April Judge, deemed it an excellent way to introduce young learners to the visual arts. An interesting aside, noted by a *Publishers Weekly* reviewer, is that the illustrator Hewitt had met her husband, William Low—whom Thomas had worked with on her first two books—at a New York City art store called Pearl Paint; Thomas wrote the tale in homage to her friends.

Lily and Aunt Eliza have always lived in a small apartment in the city of Boston, and everything has always stayed in its rightful spot, just the way Lily likes it.

The soft blue couch. The big yellow chair. The bookcase by the window. And under the piano, where somedays Lily likes to chew her rubber hedgehog.

Canine Lily is dismayed when her comfortable surroundings in Boston are disrupted by a move to rural Vermont in Abigail Thomas's story of the trials of relocation. (From Lily, *illustrated by William Low.)*

Thomas has also published several collections of short fiction. *Getting over Tom* appeared in 1994, a trio of short "incredibly touching stories ... about the eventuality of love found," wrote Mary Frances Wilkens for *Booklist*. One tale revolves around two teen sisters, another deals with an unplanned pregnancy, and the third tells of a romance with a vast difference in age. All feature a character named Virginia at various life crises over three decades. "A powerful collection," noted a *Kirkus Reviews* critic, mentioning also Thomas's background as a literary agent—"the experience shows," noted the reviewer, comparing Thomas's fiction to that of writers Alice Adams and Bobbie Ann Mason for its sensitive and insightful portraits of women.

In her 1996 novel, *An Actual Life,* Thomas again introduces Virginia, married at a young age after her unexpected pregnancy. The novel is set in 1960 and unfolds as Virginia and her husband, Buddy, arrive in Buddy's home town in New Jersey. But the marriage to Buddy is a forced, unhappy one, and his unfaithfulness with an old flame from high school calls upon stores of nerve and reserve Virginia was unaware she possessed. "Thomas does a masterful job in portraying Virginia, [who] has little sense of herself," declared a contributor to *Publishers Weekly.* A *Kirkus Reviews* critic noted that while Thomas may not have based her novel on any startlingly original idea, in her hands the tale, "quietly told, resonates in a powerful way." In her *New York Times Book Review* piece, Paula Friedman found its ending "somewhat predictable," but praised Thomas's ability to evoke sympathy for Virginia's "painful feelings of jealousy and alienation."

Though *Herb's Pajamas* may sound like a children's tale, it is the third of Thomas's works of fiction for adult readers. Another collection of short stories, the common

setting is New York City's Upper West Side. The four protagonists in eighteen interrelated stories, all vary in background and motivation, share a common bond— "profound loneliness and desperation," according to *Booklist* reviewer Kathleen Hughes. A teen searches for her runaway sister, a introvert wonders why his wife has left him, and a middle-aged woman comes to terms with the death of her aged film-star mother. In the title vignette, a widowed woman's lover dies in her bed, wearing her late husband's sleeping gear. Reviewing *Herb's Pajamas* for *Library Journal*, Barbara Hoffert termed the book "a pleasing tale that never veers into bathos." *New York Times Book Review* contributor Barbara Quick praised Thomas's precise pitch in rendering each of her characters' voices, and the wit and psychological insight evident in many passages. "While no resolutions are offered, the book is, nevertheless, full of hope," wrote Quick. "We are left feeling that all these people will somehow find their way."

Works Cited

Review of *An Actual Life, Kirkus Reviews,* February 1, 1996, p. 170.

Review of *An Actual Life, Publishers Weekly,* March 11, 1996, p. 40.

Friedman, Paula, review of *An Actual Life, New York Times,* June 9, 1996.

Review of *Getting over Tom, Kirkus Reviews,* March 15, 1994, p. 337.

Hoffert, Barbara, review of *Herb's Pajamas, Library Journal,* April 15, 1998, p. 116.

Hughes, Kathleen, review of *Herb's Pajamas, Booklist,* March 1, 1998, p. 1096.

Judge, April, review of *Pearl Paints, Booklist,* December 1, 1994, p. 688.

Review of *Lily, Publishers Weekly,* February 28, 1994, p. 86.

Marris, Alexandra, review of *Pearl Paints, School Library Journal,* December, 1994, p. 87.

Review of *Pearl Paints, Publishers Weekly,* October 24, 1994, p. 60.

Quick, Barbara, review of *Herb's Pajamas, New York Times,* May 31, 1998.

Wilkens, Mary Frances, review of *Getting over Tom, Booklist,* April 15, 1994, p. 1516.

Zvirin, Stephanie, review of *Lily, Booklist,* April 15, 1994, p. 1542.

PERIODICALS

Booklist, May 1, 1993, p. 1606.

Library Journal, April 15, 1994, p. 116; April 1, 1996, p. 120.

Publishers Weekly, March 11, 1996, p. 40; January 19, 1998, p. 371.

School Library Journal, April, 1993, p. 103; August, 1994, p. 147.*

W

WISHINSKY, Frieda 1948-

Personal

Surname is pronounced "wish-in-ski"; born July 14, 1948, in Munich, West Germany (now Germany); daughter of Herman (originally a pastry chef; became a sculptor) and Mala (a housewife) Reches; married Solomon W. (Bill) Wishinsky (a family doctor), 1971; children: David, Suzanne. *Education:* City University of New York, B.A. in International Relations, 1970; Ferkanf Graduate School, Yeshiva University, M.Sc. in Special Education, 1971. *Politics:* "Independent (but usually Democrat)." *Religion:* Jewish.

Addresses

Home and office—292 Horsham Ave, Willowdale, Ontario, Canada M2R 1G4.

Career

Full-time freelance writer. Speaker at workshops on literature and writing for children. *Member:* Society of Children's Book Writers and Illustrators, Canadian Association for Children's Writers and Performers (CANSCAIP).

Awards, Honors

Nominee, Governor General's Award, Canada Council, and Tiny Torgi Award for Print Braille Book of the Year, both 1999, both for *Each One Special.*

Writings

JUVENILE

Oonga Boonga, illustrated by Sucie Stevenson, Little, Brown (Boston), 1990, illustrated by Carol Thompson, Dutton (New York), 1998, illustrated by Michael Martchenko, Scholastic Canada (Richmond Hill, Ontario), 1998.

Why Can't You Fold Your Pants Like David Levine?, illustrated by Jackie Snider, HarperCollins, 1992.
Jennifer Jones Won't Leave Me Alone!, illustrated by Linda Hendry, HarperCollins (Toronto), 1995.
Crazy for Chocolate, illustrated by Jock McRae, Scholastic Canada, 1998.
The Man Who Made Parks: The Story of Parkbuilder Frederick Law Olmsted, illustrated by Song Nan Zhang, Tundra Books (Toronto), 1999.
Each One Special, illustrated by H. Werner Zimmermann, Orca Book Publishers (Victoria, BC), 1999.
No Frogs for Dinner, illustrated by Linda Hendry, Fitzhenry & Whiteside (Markham, Ontario), 1999.
Give Maggie a Chance, ITP Nelson, 1999.

EDUCATIONAL

Airplanes, Teacher Created Materials, Inc., 1997.
Construction, Teacher Created Materials, Inc., 1997.
Farm, Teacher Created Materials, Inc., 1997.
Cars & Trucks, Teacher Created Materials, Inc., 1997.
Boats & Ships, Teacher Created Materials, Inc., 1997.
Nelson Language Arts 5, Supplementary Readings, ITP Nelson (Toronto), 1998.
Nelson Language Arts 6: Going the Distance, Choosing Peace, Supplementary Readings, ITP Nelson, 1998.
Nelson Language Arts 3, Supplementary Readings, ITP Nelson (Toronto), 1999.

Contributor of reviews, features, and profiles to "Books for Young Readers" department, *Quill & Quire.* Contributor to *Parentalk, Canadian Living, Owl Canadian Family,* and *Publishers Weekly.* Contributor to *Nelson Language Arts,* Levels 1A-1E and *Nelson Language Arts 4,* both ITP Nelson, 1998. Writer of author profiles for *Books in Canada.*

Sidelights

"I love writing probably because I've always loved reading," Frieda Wishinsky once told *SATA.* "As an only child, books were some of my best companions. Many of my happiest memories are heading home from the library laden with six books (the maximum you could

Harry's customers loved his cakes too.

"Ooh," they applauded when Harry opened the cake box.

"Ahh," they sighed as Harry turned their cake from side to side.

"A masterpiece!" they proclaimed as they carefully carried their cake home.

Young Ben, protagonist of Frieda Wishinsky's **Each One Special,** *tries to help his friend Harry, who loses his job as a cake decorator and has difficulty finding a new venture. (Illustrated by H. Werner Zimmermann.)*

take out at one time) and opening each one like a treasure. Then would come the hard part; deciding which book to read first. The choice was all mine.

"As a child I had few choices. I had to make my bed, go to school, learn multiplication tables, and do my homework. What to read, on the other hand, was up to me. My parents, immigrants from Europe, never censored my reading and so I read everything: fiction, travel books, history. I especially loved books about magic, adventure, and biographies. The "Mary Poppins" series was a particular favorite and as for biographies, I loved reading about scientists who changed the world: people like Louis Pasteur or Madame Curie. In my fantasies, I dreamed about becoming a scientist and perhaps discovering a cure for cancer or a new vaccine. (That all changed when I realized I liked the romance of science a lot more than the reality).

"Aside from the pleasure I derived from reading, I soon discovered that I liked writing, too. In seventh grade I had a teacher who introduced us to some exciting literature and gave lots of creative writing assignments. Rereading some of them now, I realize they were full of flowery phrases and elaborate sentences, but my teacher saw beyond that. On one paper he wrote: 'You know how to use words effectively. Therefore you should attempt to read and write poetry, stories, and essays in order to develop your writing talent.' His words have stayed with me all these years.

"I majored in International Relations in university. I loved history and political science and still do, but right before entering graduate school I realized that it wasn't what I wanted to do with my life. So I started to hunt for a job. I stumbled into an excellent M.S. program in Special Education and before I could fully think it through, I was headed in an entirely new area. I earned my degree and began teaching. Since then I've taught in three countries and with every age group. Teaching has been rewarding and generally a pleasure. It's also led me back into writing.

"About ten years ago, when I taught in a high school for students with very low reading abilities, I began to search for books at their reading level that would also be fun. At that time, 'high-interest/low-vocabulary books' had hit the market, but the kids and I found the stories boring. So I started to introduce them to picture books that I liked and felt were suited for any age. These books delighted me and my students. They were funny and touching and always universal in feeling. I began buying picture books and early novels with a school library budget that had never been used because no one thought these kids would ever read. Soon I was adopted as an honorary librarian by the head librarian of the school board and was invited on buying trips. On those trips, I discovered Arnold Lobel, James Marshall, Jean Fritz, Katherine Patterson, the Narnia books, *The Secret Garden* and *Tom's Midnight Garden.* And then, when I was on a two-month sabbatical with my husband in

Eugene, Oregon (where he was doing a family medicine rotation), I started to write. I haven't stopped since.

"Throughout these years of writing, I've learned that publishing is an iffy business, but I've also learned I'm persistent and that there's nothing more satisfying to me than writing for children. It's just what I want to do."

Frieda Wishinsky found success as a children's book author with her first effort, the picture book *Oonga Boonga,* which earned positive reviews for its warmhearted depiction of the havoc wrought on a young family by a fussy baby. Nothing and no one seems able to make baby Louise happy until older brother Daniel steps in to whisper the magic words of the title, bringing smiles all around. The author "adeptly captures the ordinary but magical relationship between an older and younger sibling," commented Theo Hersh in *Quill & Quire.* He also praised the "rhythmic cadence" of Wishinsky's prose. *School Library Journal* contributor Ellen Fader observed that the story's elevation of the older sibling to the role of hero would be a comfort to those feeling pushed out of the way at the birth of a new family member, and called the book "fun for all who enjoy the warmth and sweetness of a family story touched by just the right sense of silliness."

For early readers, Wishinsky wrote *Why Can't You Fold Your Pants Like David Levine?,* a humorous tale about a boy who feels unappreciated at home because his mother always compares his accomplishments unfavorably with a neighborhood boy. When he runs away from home, however, he quickly meets up with another boy, who is running away for the same reason, and the two decide to switch places, whereupon they discover that their parents really do miss them. Wishinsky returned to the picture-book genre with *Jennifer Jones Won't Leave Me Alone!,* in which a little girl's love for a little boy provides ample fodder for teasing from the boy's friends. But when Jennifer goes away for a while, the boy discovers he misses her after all, and decides to show his true feelings to Jennifer, despite what his friends might say. The book's "message about friendship and feelings is implicit rather than explicit, and the book remains light and funny," remarked Gwyneth Evans in *Quill & Quire.*

Crazy for Chocolate is an amusing adventure novel for young readers in which Anne Banks travels back through time with the help of a magical CD-ROM given to her by a local librarian in order to research a school assignment. With the help of her computer mouse, Anne clicks in and out of fun and sometimes frightening countries and historical eras in her quest for information on the history of chocolate. "Although the text of the novel is extremely simple, readers will be engaged and intrigued by the situations and difficulties Anne encounters," attested Sheree Haughian in *Quill & Quire,* and the inclusion of Anne's report at the end of the book provides appropriate closure for Wishinsky's story.

Wishinsky is also the author of *Each One Special,* a picture-book story about young Ben, whose friend the baker, Harry, is laid off from his job and quickly falls into depression until he and Ben start a new venture molding sculptures out of clay. "As a work portraying 'special' talents and warm relationships between generations, the book succeeds," concluded Mary Beaty in *Quill & Quire.*

Works Cited

Beaty, Mary, review of *Each One Special, Quill & Quire,* September, 1998, p. 66.

Evans, Gwyneth, review of *Jennifer Jones Won't Leave Me Alone!, Quill & Quire,* March, 1995, p. 77.

Fader, Ellen, review of *Oonga Boonga, School Library Journal,* May, 1990, p. 93.

Haughian, Sheree, review of *Crazy for Chocolate, Quill & Quire,* May, 1998, p. 34.

Hersh, Theo, review of *Oonga Boonga, Quill & Quire,* September, 1990, p. 20.

For More Information See

PERIODICALS

Booklist, March 1, 1990, pp. 1350-51.
Children's Book News, summer-fall, 1999, p. 7.
Kirkus Reviews, April 15, 1990, p. 588; May 1, 1999.
Publishers Weekly, February 23, 1990, p. 216.
Quill & Quire, January, 1994, p. 37.
Toronto Star, October 17, 1999.

*   *   *

WONG, Jade Snow 1922-

Personal

Born January 21, 1922, in San Francisco, CA; daughter of Hong (a manufacturer) and Hing Kwai (Tong) Wong; married Woodrow Ong (a travel agent), August 29, 1950; children: Mark Stuart, Tyi Elizabeth, Ellora Louise, Lance Orion. *Education:* San Francisco Junior College, A.A., 1940; Mills College, B.A., 1942. *Politics:* Democrat. *Religion:* Methodist.

Addresses

Office—2123-2125 Polk St., San Francisco, CA 94109. *Agent*—Curtis Brown Ltd., 575 Madison Ave., New York, NY 10022.

Career

Worked as secretary in San Francisco, CA, 1943-45; proprietor of ceramics gallery, 1946-; co-owner of travel agency, 1957-; writer. Director of Chinese Culture Center, 1978-81. *Member:* International Air Traffic Association, Norcal Pacific Area Travel Association, Museum Society (director, 1976-81). Member of California Council for the Humanities, 1975-81; member of advisory councils for China Institute of New York and Friends of the San Francisco Libraries.

Awards, Honors

Award for pottery from California State Fair, 1947; Silver Medal for craftsmanship from *Mademoiselle;* award for enamel from California State Fair, 1949; Silver Medal for nonfiction from Commonwealth Club of San Francisco, 1976, for *Fifth Chinese Daughter;* honorary doctorate of humane letters from Mills College, 1976.

Writings

Fifth Chinese Daughter (autobiography), Harper, 1950, reprinted with a new introduction by the author, illustrated by Kathryn Uhl, University of Washington Press, 1989.

The Immigrant Experience (nonfiction), Dial, 1971.

No Chinese Stranger (nonfiction), illustrated by Deng Ming-Dao, Harper, 1975.

Also author of column in *San Francisco Examiner.* Contributor to periodicals, including *Holiday* and *Horn Book.*

Sidelights

Jade Snow Wong once commented: "My writing is nonfiction based on personal experiences. So few Chinese American have published that I think it is my responsibility to try to create understanding between Chinese and Americans. In my work with ceramics and travel, I follow the same philosophy. Because I am innovative and unconventional, I am often far ahead of my time. Thirty-two years after publication, *Fifth Chinese Daughter* is still in print and used by schools everywhere. I am fluent in English, Cantonese, and have studied Mandarin since beginning my travels in the People's Republic of China. Though I don't think being a woman has been any problem, I give priority to women's responsibility for a good home life; hence, I put my husband and four children before my writing or ceramics. I also believe in serving my community and this work has taken more time than writing a book."

With the release in 1950 of her autobiography, *Fifth Chinese Daughter,* Jade Snow Wong became one of the first Chinese-American women ever to be published. When her book first appeared, Wong was praised for the candor with which she described her struggle to balance both Chinese and American influences. Wong's resolution of the conflict between the traditions of her ancestors and those of her adopted country forms the core of *Fifth Chinese Daughter.* Critics also praised the book for its preservation of a part of Chinese-American history in the first half of the twentieth century and as an engaging coming-of-age story. A second volume of autobiography, *No Chinese Stranger,* appeared twenty-five years later, offering an account of Wong's marriage, the birth of four children, the establishment of a travel agency with her husband, and a description of their 1972 trip to the People's Republic of China, among other travel narratives. Like *Fifth Chinese Daughter, No Chinese Stranger* also contains detailed instructions on

the preparation of several Chinese dishes, making it a valuable resource of information on Chinese cooking. Although both fictional and nonfictional accounts of the Chinese-American experience are more common at the end of the twentieth century than when Wong first became an author, the historical merit of, in particular, her first book, with its rare depiction of pre-World War II Chinatown in San Francisco, is considered invaluable, as is her account of the prejudice she faced, both as a Chinese American and as a woman, when she sought first education and then employment in mid-twentieth-century America.

Fifth Chinese Daughter is an "account of how a young woman of notable intelligence, good humor, and talent handled the job of dovetailing American ways with a Chinese upbringing," began a reviewer for the *New Yorker* in 1950. Wong wrote and published her first book when she was still in her twenties, and it generated much commentary. Wong responded to some of this criticism in an essay published in *Horn Book,* where she wrote, in part:

"I do not think of myself as a writer, and I am not an authority in the field of intercultural relations. I was born in San Francisco of parents who had come from China and I speak only as one individual who was raised in the old-world Chinese standards and who found outside the confines of Chinatown a new American world waiting for her. The new world was full of light and promised independence, but the path between the two worlds was untrod and, as I later found, a rough one."

Wong continued: "As I made clear in the author's note for *Fifth Chinese Daughter,* I am not saying that mine is a typical story, not even typical of the experiences of other members of my family. But I am speaking the truth as I know it, and the conservatives who have been angered at my book cannot denounce it on the grounds that it is untrue, only on grounds that the truth should not have been told,—least of all, by me."

Fifth Chinese Daughter has been continuously in print for half a century. Over the years it has gathered comparisons to Henry Adams's *The Education of Henry Adams,* as the model for an autobiographical narrative told in the third person, and to Maxine Hong Kingston's *The Woman Warrior,* published a generation after Wong's book, as an example of an utterly different portrait, in both form and content, of growing up Chinese in America. Much has been made in the years since its first publication of Wong's choice to rely on the third-person singular voice to tell her own life story, a choice the author explained in an introduction by reference to the shocking immodesty of telling a story in the first person in Chinese tradition. For Kathleen Loh Swee Yin and Kristoffer F. Paulson, writing in *MELUS* in 1982, Wong's choice to write an autobiography in the third person "effectively renders the divided consciousness of dual-heritage," and thus is at the heart of the genius of her book. "Wong's achievement ... is a foundation stone for ethnic literature, for feminist literature and for American literature," Yin and Paulson concluded. With the publication of a new edition of *Fifth Chinese Daughter* nearly fifty years after the appearance of the first, critics responded equally to the historical value of Wong's intimate and detailed description of life in San Francisco's Chinatown in the 1920s and 1930s and to her struggle to gain American-style independence and self-respect while retaining her Chinese heritage.

In *No Chinese Stranger,* Wong's second volume of autobiography, the author briefly retraces in third person the story of her upbringing and education, then, with the death of her father, turns to the first person to recount the story of forming her own family, setting up a business as a ceramicist, and then another with her travel agent husband, raising their four children, and traveling to Hong Kong, Thailand, and the People's Republic of China. Throughout, "the lively, forthright prose makes for delightful reading," contended Elizabeth A. Teo in *Library Journal.* The attractions of *No Chinese Stranger* for *Publishers Weekly* reviewer Barbara A. Bannon included the author's commentary on the San Francisco Bay Area, cooking, ceramics, and travel.

Works Cited

Bannon, Barbara A., review of *No Chinese Stranger, Publishers Weekly,* April 21, 1975, p. 45.
Review of *Fifth Chinese Daughter, New Yorker,* October 7, 1950, p. 118.
Teo, Elizabeth A., review of *No Chinese Stranger, Library Journal,* June 15, 1975, pp. 1211-12.
Wong, Jade Snow, "Growing up between the Old World and the New," in *Horn Book,* December, 1951, pp. 440-45.
Yin, Kathleen Loh Swee, and Kristoffer F. Paulson, "The Divided Voice of Chinese-American Narration: Jade Snow Wong's *Fifth Chinese Daughter,*" *MELUS,* spring, 1982, pp. 53-59.

For More Information See

BOOKS

Contemporary Literary Criticism, Volume 17, Gale, 1981.
Culley, Margo, editor, *American Women's Autobiography: Fea(s)ts of Memory,* University of Wisconsin Press, 1992, pp. 252-67.
Kim, Elaine H., *Asian American Literature: An Introduction to the Writings and Their Social Context,* Temple University Press, 1982, pp. 58-90.
Who's Who among Asian Americans, Gale, 1994.

PERIODICALS

Amerasia Journal, vol. 15, no. 2, 1989, pp. 224-26.
Booklist, September 1, 1975, p. 18.
Christian Science Monitor, March 31, 1981, p. 23.
Commonweal, November 24, 1950, p. 182.
Interracial Books for Children Bulletin, vol. 7, nos. 2-3, 1976, pp. 13-14.
Kliatt, September, 1989, p. 33.
MELUS, fall, 1979, pp. 51-71.
New York Herald Tribune Book Review, September 24, 1950.
New York Times Book Review, October 29, 1950, p. 27.*

WRIGHT, David K. 1943-

Personal

Born January 10, 1943, in Richmond, IN; son of Richard M. (a teacher) and Wilma S. (a teacher) Wright; married Grace Snyder (a teacher), June 27, 1970; children: Austin D., Monica G. *Education:* Wittenberg University, B.A., 1966. *Politics:* Independent. *Religion:* None.

Addresses

Home—452 S. 7th Ave., West Bend, WI 53095. *Office*—P.O. Box 353, West Bend, WI 53095.

Career

Chicago Tribune, Chicago, IL, copy editor, 1970-75; *Truth,* Elkhart, IN, city editor, 1975-77; *Monroe Evening Times,* Monroe, WI, editor, 1976-77; free-lance writer, 1977—. *Military service:* U.S. Army, 1966-68, served in Vietnam; became sergeant. *Member:* Member of advisory committee for public television station; publicity chair of Citizens Advocacy.

Writings

JUVENILE

War in Vietnam, Volume 1: *Eve of Battle,* Volume 2: *A Wider War,* Volume 3: *Vietnamization,* Volume 4: *Fall of Vietnam,* Children's Press, 1989.
The Story of the Vietnam Memorial, Children's Press, 1989.
(And photographer) *Canada Is My Home,* Gareth Stevens, 1992.
Vietnam Is My Home, photographs by Vu Viet Dung, Gareth Stevens, 1993.
A Multicultural Portrait of Life in the Cities, Marshall Cavendish (New York), 1994.
A Multicultural Portrait of World War II, Marshall Cavendish (New York), 1994.
A Multicultural Portrait of the Vietnam War, Benchmark (Tarrytown, NY), 1996.
Causes and Consequences of the Vietnam War, Raintree Steck-Vaughn (Austin, TX), 1996.
John Lennon: The Beatles and Beyond, Enslow (Springfield, NJ), 1996.
Arthur Ashe: Breaking the Color Barrier in Tennis, Enslow (Springfield, NJ), 1996.
P. T. Barnum, illustrated by Mike White, Raintree Steck-Vaughn (Austin, TX), 1997.
Frank Lloyd Wright: Visionary Architect, Enslow (Springfield, NJ), 1998.
Paul Robeson: Actor, Singer, Political Activist, Enslow (Springfield, NJ), 1998.

"ENCHANTMENT OF THE WORLD" SERIES

Vietnam, Children's Press, 1989.
Malaysia, Children's Press, 1988.
Brunei, Children's Press, 1991.
Burma, Children's Press, 1991.
Albania, Children's Press, 1992.

"CHILDREN OF THE WORLD" SERIES

(Editor with MaryLee Knowlton) *Czechoslovakia,* photography by Leos Nebor, Gareth Stevens, 1988.

(Editor with Knowlton and Scott Enk) *Bhutan,* photography by Yoshio Kamatsu, Gareth Stevens, 1988.

(Editor with Knowlton and Enk) *Yugoslavia,* photography by Takako Yokotani, Gareth Stevens, 1988.

(Editor with Knowlton) *India,* photography by Gareth Stevens, 1988.

(Editor with Knowlton) *Thailand,* photography by Kei Orihara, Gareth Stevens, 1988.

(Editor with Knowlton) *Jordan,* photography by Hirokawa Ryuichi, Gareth Stevens, 1988.

(And photographer) *Hong Kong,* Gareth Stevens, 1991.

(And photographer) *Singapore,* Gareth Stevens, 1991.

(And photographer) *Canada,* Gareth Stevens, 1991.

ADULT NONFICTION

The Harley-Davidson Motor Company: An Official Eighty-Year History, Motorbooks International (Osceola, WI), 1983.

(Contributor) *Great National Park Vacations,* Rand-McNally, 1987.

(With Clarence Jungwirth) *Oshkosh Trucks: 75 Years of Specialty Truck Production,* Motorbooks International (Osceola, WI), 1992.

The Harley-Davidson Motor Company: An Official Ninety-Year History, Motorbooks International (Osceola, WI), 1993.

David K. Wright examines Vietnam's history, beginning with the French occupation in 1874, and highlights the culture, geography, religion, and politics of the country. (Cover photo by Joe Smoljan.)

America's 100 Year Love Affair with the Automobile: And the Snap-On Tools That Keep Them Running, Motorbooks International (Osceola, WI), 1995.

Contributing editor of bimonthly business magazine. Writer, editor, and publisher for *Working Writers* (monthly newsletter), 1991-92.

Sidelights

David K. Wright targets young audiences with his nonfiction works covering notable Americans and the histories and cultures of numerous countries. In particular, Wright, a former U.S. soldier who served in the Vietnam War, has written several books about Vietnam. *Vietnam,* his first volume in the "Enchantment of the World" series for Children's Press, examines Vietnam's history, culture, geography, religion, and politics. Wright explores the country's history beginning with the French occupation in 1874. He details the civil war in Vietnam, which involved the U.S. military troops aiding the South Vietnamese against the invasion and subsequent take-over in 1975 by Communist North Vietnam. The author emphasizes postwar effects on Vietnam, especially environmental, and the problems associated with the flux of refugees fleeing the country. Wright includes color photographs and maps to explain various aspects of the region.

In 1989, a year after publishing *Vietnam,* Wright produced *War in Vietnam,* a four-volume set providing a more detailed account of the Vietnam conflict. In this book Wright recounts the situations leading up to the war and how the U.S. became entangled in the fighting. He discusses the effects of the war, both during and after, on the Vietnamese and U.S. soldiers and civilians. He includes discussion of American anti-war protests and the formation and actions of the Vietnam Veterans Against the War (VVAW) association. Leaders of the war are featured in separate biographies, which *School Library Journal* contributor Mary Mueller lauded as "a strong point in the books." In *War in Vietnam* Wright also reports on the country in the late 1980s. In a review for *Booklist,* Denise Wilms praised the book to be "a staple item for the history or reference shelves."

Wright once told *SATA:* "I'm successful, I think, because I'm willing to attempt any assignment. Consequently, the quality of the finished product may fluctuate. But I need to feed my family and spend lots of time at the keyboard."

Wright's willingness to be open to a variety of writing assignments becomes evident when reading his bibliography. While he takes on war and city living, investigating them from a multicultural point of view, his writing, editing, and photography talents also become immersed in exotic and faraway countries like Malasia and Burma, and covers notable figures such as Arthur Ashe, John Lennon, and Frank Lloyd Wright.

In his book *Arthur Ashe: Breaking the Color Barrier in Tennis,* Wright draws attention not only to this tennis player's struggle to compete as a black man in a sport historically all-white and inclusive, he also gives full dimension to this talented athlete as a person. He shows Ashe as a man of integrity and discipline, a man who stood up for his beliefs. Steve Matthews, reviewing this book for *School Library Journal,* recommended it as a solid detailed source for libraries. He called it a book with "special focus on the athlete's role in breaking open the white world of tennis."

John Lennon: The Beatles and Beyond details the life of John Lennon from birth, to the release of the "Beatles" recording in 1996. Marilyn K. Roberts, writing for *Voice of Youth Advocates,* praised the book's chronology which contains the "significant personal and professional points in Lennon's life." Renee Steinberg noted in her review for *School Library Journal* that the book has "double value" because both John Lennon 'and' the Beatles were discussed. Wright shows Lennon's complex nature and his development as a creative performer and political activist. Steinberg recommended the book for acquisition, reporting how "Lennon's eccentricities and keen talent come through in this thorough biography."

Works Cited

PERIODICALS

Matthews, Steve, review of *Arthur Ashe: Breaking the Color Barrier in Tennis, School Library Journal,* October, 1996, p. 142.
Mueller, Mary, review of *War in Vietnam, School Library Journal,* June, 1989, p. 131.
Roberts, Marilyn K., review of *John Lennon: The Beatles and Beyond, Voice of Youth Advocates,* February, 1997, p. 355.
Steinberg, Renee, review of *John Lennon: The Beatles and Beyond, School Library Journal,* December, 1996, p. 149.
Wilms, Denise, review of *War in Vietnam, Booklist,* June 1, 1989, p. 1727.

For More Information See

PERIODICALS

Booklist, August, 1989, p. 1972-1973; March 15, 1994, p. 1340.
Horn Book Guide, spring, 1997, p. 147; fall, 1994, p. 398; fall, 1996, p. 381.
School Library Journal, January, 1990, p. 118; September, 1991, p. 274; March, 1994, p. 234; January, 1996, p. 166.*

*   *   *

WRIGHTSON, (Alice) Patricia 1921-

Personal

Born June 19, 1921, in Lismore, New South Wales, Australia; daughter of Charles Radcliff (a solicitor) and Alice (Dyer) Furlonger; married, 1943 (divorced, 1953); children: Jennifer Mary Wrightson Ireland, Peter Radcliff. *Education:* Attended St. Catherine's College, 1932, and State Correspondence School, 1933-34.

Addresses

Home—Lohic, P.O. Box 91, Maclean, New South Wales 2463, Australia.

Career

Secretary and administrator with Bonalbo District Hospital, New South Wales, 1946-60, and Sydney District Nursing Association, New South Wales, 1960-64; Department of Education, New South Wales, assistant editor of *School Magazine,* 1964-70, editor, 1970-75; writer.

Awards, Honors

Book of the Year Award from Children's Book Council of Australia, 1956, for *The Crooked Snake;* Notable Books of the Year Award from American Library Association, 1963, for *The Feather Star;* Book of the Year Award runner-up from Children's Book Council of Australia, and Children's Spring Book Festival Award from *Book World,* both 1968, and Hans Christian Andersen Honors List award of the International Board on Books for Young People (IBBY), 1970, all for *A Racecourse for Andy;* Book of the Year Honour List award from Children's Book Council of Australia, 1974, IBBY's Honor List for Text award, 1976, *Voice of Youth Advocate's* Annual Selection of Best Science Fiction and Fantasy Titles for Young Adults, 1988, and Hans Christian Andersen Medal, all for *The Nargun and the Stars;* Officer, Order of the British Empire, 1978; Book of the Year award from Children's Book Council of Australia, and *Guardian* Award commendation, both 1978, IBBY's Books for Young People Honor List award, and Hans Christian Andersen Honors List award, both 1979, all for *The Ice Is Coming;* New South Wales Premier's Award for Ethnic Writing, 1979, selection as one of the Children's Books of the Year by Child Study Association of America, all 1979, all for *The Dark Bright Water;* Book of the Year Award high commendation from Children's Book Council of Australia, 1982, for *Behind the Wind;* Carnegie Medal Commendation, 1983, Book of the Year Award from the Children's Book Council of Australia, *Boston Globe/Horn Book* Award for Fiction, Hans Christian Andersen Medal, and *Observer* Teenage Fiction Prize, all 1984, all for *A Little Fear;* Dromkeen Medal from the Dromkeen Children's Literature Foundation, 1984, for "a significant contribution to the appreciation and development of children's literature in Australia"; chosen to deliver sixteenth annual Arbuthnot Lecture, 1985; Golden Cat Award from the Sjoestrands Forlag AB, 1986, for "a contribution to children's and young adult literature"; Hans Christian Andersen Medal, 1986, for *Moon Dark;* Lady Cutler Award, 1986, New South Wales Premier's Special Occasional Award, 1988.

Writings

The Crooked Snake, illustrations by Margaret Horder, Angus & Robertson, 1955, reprinted, Hutchinson, 1972.

The Bunyip Hole, illustrations by Horder, Angus & Robertson, 1957, reprinted, Hutchinson, 1973.

The Rocks of Honey, illustrations by Horder, Angus & Robertson, 1960, reprinted, Penguin, 1977.

The Feather Star, illustrations by Noela Young, Hutchinson, 1962, Harcourt, 1963.

Down to Earth, illustrations by Horder, Harcourt, 1965.

I Own the Racecourse!, illustrations by Horder, Hutchinson, 1968, published in the United States as *A Racecourse for Andy,* Harcourt, 1968.

An Older Kind of Magic, illustrations by Young, Harcourt, 1972.

(Editor) *Beneath the Sun: An Australian Collection for Children,* Collins, 1972.

The Nargun and the Stars (fantasy), Hutchinson, 1973, Atheneum, 1974.

(Editor) *Emu Stew: An Illustrated Collection of Stories and Poems for Children,* Kestrel, 1976.

The Ice Is Coming (first book in fantasy trilogy), Atheneum, 1977.

The Dark Bright Water (second book in fantasy trilogy), Hutchinson, 1978, Atheneum, 1979.

Night Outside, illustrations by Jean Cooper-Brown, Rigby, 1979, illustrations by Beth Peck, Atheneum, 1985.

Behind the Wind (third book in fantasy trilogy), Hutchinson, 1981, published in the United States as *Journey behind the Wind,* Atheneum, 1981.

A Little Fear (fantasy), Atheneum, 1983.

Moon Dark, illustrated by Young, McElderry Books, 1988.

Balyet, McElderry Books, 1989.

The Old, Old Ngrang, illustrated by David Wong, Nelson, 1989.

The Sugar-Gum Tree, illustrated by David Cox, Ringwood, 1991, Viking, 1991.

Shadows of Times, Random House, 1994.

Rattler's Place, illustrated by D. Cox, Ringwood, 1997, Viking, 1996.

(With Peter Wrightson) *The Wrightson List of Aboriginal Folk Figures,* Random House, 1998.

Wrightson's books have been translated into nine languages, including German, Spanish, and Norwegian. Her papers are collected at the Lu Rees Archives, Canberra College of Advanced Education Library, Australia, and the Kerlan Collection at the University of Minnesota.

Adaptations

The Nargun and the Stars was adapted as a television series by ABC-TV in 1977. *I Own the Racecourse!* was filmed by Barron Films in 1985.

Sidelights

Best known for her "Song of Wirrun" fantasy trilogy, Australian writer Patricia Wrightson is "Australia's most distinguished writer for children," according to Karen Jameyson writing in *Children's Books and Their Creators.* As John Murray noted in *Bookbird,* Wrightson's "greatest achievement has been her synthesis of the Australian pastoral with the kind of fantasy refined during the latter half of this century by Ursula Le Guin and Susan Cooper." The only Australian recipient of the Hans Christian Anderson Medal, Wrightson blends Aboriginal mythic and folk tradition with the landscape of the vast Australian landmass to create a literature peculiarly Down Under. Over the course of her four-decade career, Wrightson has proven great versatility, writing genres such as the holiday adventure, the animal story, science fiction, teen novels, and short stories. But it is for her fantasy tales that she is best known, having earned numerous awards and gained an international following for her tales that draw upon ancient Australian myths. According to Zena Sutherland and May Hill Arbuthnot in their *Children and Books,* "Wrightson has been a channel through which children of her own and other countries have learned the beauty and dignity of the legendary creatures of Aborigine mythology."

Wrightson was born in 1921, in a small country town in New South Wales. She lived on a farm with her parents and older sisters until the age of four, and her memories of those early years are vivid and pleasant. With the exception of one year spent in a suburb of Sydney, she and her family remained in the coastal river country throughout her childhood. Culturally isolated, Wrightson became an avid reader and believes that her love of books originated in her father's nightly readings from Charles Dickens. As she indicated in her essay "Becoming an Australian" for *Something about the Author Autobiography Series:* "Our school was a good one, the central school for a large district and one of the biggest in the state; but it had no library. That's how things were in those days . . . . You had your own books, and lent them to friends and borrowed theirs. We were lucky; we had, between us, a lot of books, and my father bought lots that were 'family' books, mainly for adults but good for children to prowl in." However, as Wrightson continued, "without knowing it, I began to feel dissatisfied about something, unsure about something; it was many years before I knew what, or why . . . . If you looked at all those books we had as children, and all the others that my friends had when they were children, you have to notice something strange: they were all fine books that I am glad to have known—but none of them were written by an Australian, or about Australia."

When she finished primary school, she spent one year in a boarding school before returning home to begin high school by a correspondence school for children who lived in isolated areas. She graduated when World War II began in 1939, and then went to Sydney with a friend to work in a munitions factory. By the time the war was over, she was married; however, when the marriage failed, she returned with her two children to live with her parents in the country. It was at that time that she began to think about writing books for her own children about the Australia they knew. Using her children as her initial audience, she smoothed and refined her work and finally sent the manuscript to a publisher, meanwhile continuing to work on other books. When *The Crooked Snake* was finally published, the Children's Book Council of Australia had granted it the Book of the Year Award. Together with its successors, *The Bunyip Hole, The Rocks of Honey, The Feather Star,* and *Down to Earth,* it recalls the author's own childhood in New South Wales, the country her grandfather helped pioneer.

Wrightson's first two novels, *The Crooked Snake* and *The Bunyip Hole,* "lean heavily upon the English outdoor adventure story that Arthur Ransome developed during the 1930s and 1940s," according to Murray in *Bookbird.* Already with her second novel, however, Wrightson was making use of the spirit world of the Aborigine, a theme and technique that would serve as the cornerstone of her mature work. With *The Rocks of Honey,* Wrightson approached one of her major themes: the curative power of landscape and the Aboriginal character. *The Feather Star,* on the other hand, is a holiday story, one that leaves childhood gangs and mythology behind to explore the sensitivities of an adolescent girl. Attempting sci-fi, Wrightson next wrote *Down to Earth,* the story of a Martian invasion that has already happened while no one was looking.

Wrightson was relatively unknown outside Australia until the publication of *A Racecourse for Andy,* when, according to John Rowe Townsend in *A Sounding of Storytellers: New and Revised Essays on Contemporary Writers for Children,* she "was suddenly recognized far beyond her own shores as a leading children's writer." The book centers on Andy, a mildly retarded boy who is convinced that he has "bought" the local racecourse from a derelict for three dollars. His conviction results in a conflict between the adults, who encourage the fantasy because they don't want to disappoint him, and his young friends, who realize the potential harm of deluding him. As Townsend wrote: "One wonders what way out there can be that will not deal a fearful psychological blow to Andy. But the author finds one; and it is the perfect and satisfying answer."

Critics praised Wrightson's portrayal of Andy as realistic and sensitive; she "allows us to understand him and feel his frustration," remarked Christine McDonnell in *Horn Book.* "Wrightson marks Andy's difference from the other boys with subtle indications of his behaviour, his facial expressions, his mode of speech," noted Margery Fisher in her *Who's Who in Children's Books: A Treasury of the Familiar Characters of Childhood.* Calling it "a refreshing, optimistic book," McDonnell added: "It is about the best in people, their basic goodness. It is about friendship and the responsibility friends have for each other.... But most of all, it is about Andy.... Andy is special, but his limitations can be seen as assets. Andy is innocent, and Patricia Wrightson shows us that innocence is a gift."

A deeper approximation to fantasy came in the 1972 *An Older Kind of Magic,* in which an urban setting is used as a foil to demonstrate human separation from nature. Researching this novel, Wrightson studied the beliefs of Aboriginal Australians, searching out anthropological

texts as well as oral histories to get a handle on the spirit folk of the indigenous peoples. One such spirit character is the Nargun, an ancient mass of stone, a spirit form evoked from a boulder. Such a spirit has limited mobility, and only the hint of eye or limb. Wrightson served this mythic creature up in *The Nargun and the Stars,* which tells the story of a boy and his aunt and uncle who try to protect their land from the Nargun. These huge stone figures become an aspect of the psyche of the protagonist, Simon Brent; his gradual understanding of their place in the natural scheme of things leads Simon to accept a sense of stewardship for the land. A *Times Literary Supplement* contributor commented that "the Nargun itself, described with passion, is a poetic creation, genuinely frightening and pitiful." Fisher noted that the Nargun "must be accounted one of the most remarkable myth-beings ever created," while C. S. Hannabuss, in *Children's Book Review,* indicated that "the landscape ... is a reflection and extension of the imagination." Ethel L. Heins remarked in a *Horn Book* review that the book's "essentially simple plot is worked into the rich fabric of a story that begins serenely, arches up to a great crescendo of suspense, and then falls away at the end to 'a whisper in the dark.'"

In a sense, all of Wrightson's work in the first two decades of her career was a warming up for her cycle of three books in "The Book of Wirrun." These three novels—*The Ice Is Coming, The Dark Bright Water,* and *Journey Behind the Wind*—draw on "the myths and folktales of the Aboriginals to produce a fantasy of great freshness and distinction," noted Audrey Laski in *Times Educational Supplement.* "[This]is fantasy on a grand scale, resonant in the imagination." The aboriginal boy Wirrun holds the three books together, as does the tapestry of myth and legend which serve as the background to the sequence of books. Similar to Hercules, Wirrun has tasks to perform and quests to journey on in order to save his people. In *The Ice Is Coming,* Wrightson describes a journey from the interior of Australia down the eastern seaboard to the southwest coast of Victoria. Calling it "a magnificent heroic novel," a contributor to the *Junior Bookshelf,* detailed its plot: "It is the story of how the Ninya, manlike spirits of ice, broke out of their caves in the heart of Australia and set out to create a new ice age, and how their enterprise was challenged by a young Aborigine and a Mimi, a frail spirit of the rocks." Referring to the novel as a "tale of Australian beings," Margery Fisher continued in *Growing Point:* "The relation of the various beings to the land, the central element in the complex folk-beliefs of the Aboriginals, is consistently felt through the book, not superimposed but an integral part of its argument and its setting." Rebecca Lukens, writing in the *World of Children's Books,* regarded the novel as stylistically pleasing, as well. "[Wrightson's] keen appreciation of the land, of its sounds, its wild animals and birds, its insects and its climate is apparent in the imagery rich with connotative meaning." According to Jane Langton in the *New York Times Book Review,* "Wrightson gives a sentence a gentle shove and it seems to roll over the Australian landscape, echoing down the page in patterns of sound, transforming print into vistas of haunted cliffs."

The second tale in the trilogy, *The Dark Bright Water,* Wirrun's task is to tame the water-spirits "whose wild behaviour is turning water-holes dry and making the barren desert flower," according to Donald A. Young in *Junior Bookshelf.* In the final volume, published in Australia and England as *Behind the Wind,* Wirrun comes face to face with Death, the greatest foe of all. "The fight to the death against Death is as dramatic as any combat in the chronicles of Western mythology," concluded Young.

From these novels that are set in the heart of Australia, Wrightson moved her action to the north cost for both *A Little Fear* and *Moon Dark.* The former novel features an elderly protagonist, Agnes Tucker, who runs away from a retirement home to her dead brother's remote cottage. In her attempt to recapture a pastoral idyll, she is defeated by the resentful spirit, Njimbin. Winner of a *Boston Globe-Horn Book* award for fiction, *A Little Fear* presents Wrightson's first animal character, a dog called Hector who notes the human and spirit-world action. In *Moon Dark* Wrightson features a dog that lives with an old fisherman in a remote area by the sea. When the population grows and disturbs wildlife habitats, the animals intercede by tricking the humans. "Wrightson's prose has real fairytale qualities, and when the animals act to restore ecological balance, they do so through magic," commented Donald McCaig in the *Washington Post Book World.* "Their magic owes more to Australian Aboriginal beliefs than Hans Christian Andersen."

With *Balyet,* Wrightson served up more tribal magic, this time in the guise of a centuries old Aboriginal ghost who broke a taboo of her tribe and was condemned to walk the earth forever. Balyet, however, is finally allowed to die after the intercession of a contemporary girl named Jo. Jean Kaufman, writing in *Voice of Youth Advocates,* remarked that "[t]his is a wonderfully written book, with well rounded characters and a fast pace that should keep readers interested." A critic in *Kirkus Reviews* also had high praise for the novel, calling it "Wrightson's best yet," while noting that Balyet herself was a "compelling creation" and that the novel "explores the characteristic Wrightson theme of interdependence and continuity among all creatures."

Something of a departure for Wrightson was *The Sugar-Gum Tree,* a realistic friendship story for beginning readers. Penny and Sarah have a tiff over the construction of a hideaway; Penny climbs high up into a sugar-gum tree and won't come down until the other girl apologizes. Zena Sutherland, reviewing the book in *Bulletin of the Center for Children's Books,* remarked that Wrightson, "one of Australia's most eminent writers, shows . . . that she is as adroit in realism as she is in fantasy." *Booklist's* Hazel Rochman commented that the "fine Australian writer Wrightson knows about friendship."

Returning to the more familiar grounds of fantasy fiction, Wrightson presented in *Shadows of Time* nothing less than the history of Australia as seen through the eyes of two eighteenth-century youngsters who have the magical gift of never growing old. Sarah Jane is a kitchen maid who teams up with an unnamed Aboriginal boy to run away from home, only to discover their magical gift of longevity. They remain children, ever traveling, while Australia grows up all around them. "The whole story is a meditation on the nature of time and change, and the way we exist within them," noted Gillian Cross in *School Librarian.* Cross concluded that though the novel was a demanding one, "it leaves a powerful, poetic impression." A reviewer for *Junior Bookshelf* remarked that the book was many things: "an allegory, a history of Australia, an adventure story, a guide to survival." The same reviewer was pleased to announce that the physical book itself was "built to last, and there are surely several generations of readers to come who will turn to it in love and respect."

The same can be said for the entire body of work of this remarkable novelist who has, for more than four decades, been at the center of Australian children's literature. As Wrightson once remarked to *Authors and Artists for Young Adults,* she was in many ways fortunate to have herself been born into the infancy of such a literary tradition. "I do think I've been lucky to work in Australia, for there we had no paths to follow. Most other countries had well-established paths . . . . But Australian writers, with so small a body of work behind them, could feel that the country's literature was immediately in their hands. Every story that anyone could conceive was his own new concept, not shaped or directed or limited by other people's thinking; to be worked out in his own way and for almost the first time." In her "Hans Christian Andersen Award Acceptance Speech" Wrightson also noted that even her failures were lucky: "It can't be common, in the twentieth century, for a writer to discover a hole in his nation's literature through the accident of falling into it; and then to find the missing piece through sheer need, and to have it welcomed so warmly."

Works Cited

Review of *Balyet, Kirkus Reviews,* April 15, 1989, p. 632.

Cross, Gillian, review of *Shadows of Time, School Librarian,* August, 1996, p. 121.

Fisher, Margery, *Who's Who in Children's Books: A Treasury of Familiar Characters of Childhood,* Holt, 1975, pp. 21-22, 256.

Fisher, Margery, "Special Review," *Growing Point,* December, 1977, pp. 3217-18.

Hannabuss, C. S., review of *The Nargun and the Stars, Children's Book Review,* December, 1973, pp. 180-81.

Heins, Ethel L., review of *The Nargun and the Stars, Horn Book,* August, 1974, pp. 382-83.

Review of *The Ice Is Coming, Junior Bookshelf,* February, 1978, pp. 52-53.

Jameyson, Karen, "Wrightson, Patricia," *Children's Books and Their Creators,* edited by Anita Silvey, Houghton, 1995, pp. 693-94.

Kaufman, Jean, review of *Balyet, Voice of Youth Advocates,* June, 1989, p. 119.

Langton, Jane, review of *The Ice Is Coming, New York Times Book Review,* January 28, 1978, p. 26.

Laski, Audrey, review of "The Book of Wirrun," *Times Educational Supplement,* December 23, 1983, p. 23.

Lukens, Rebecca, review of *The Ice Is Coming, World of Children's Books,* fall, 1978, pp. 63-65.

McCaig, Donald, review of *Moon Dark, Washington Post Book World,* May 8, 1988, p. 23.

McDonnell, Christine, review of *A Racecourse for Andy, Horn Book,* April, 1980, pp. 196-99.

Murray, John, "Author Spotlight-Patricia Wrightson," *Bookbird,* vol. 37, no. 1, 1999, pp. 57-61.

Rochman, Hazel, review of *The Sugar-Gum Tree, Booklist,* April 1, 1992, pp. 1458-59.

Review of *Shadows of Time, Junior Bookshelf,* April 1996, pp. 84-85.

Something about the Author Autobiography Series, Volume 4, Gale, 1987, pp. 335-46.

Sutherland, Zena, and May Hill Arbuthnot, *Children and Books,* 7th edition, Scott, Foresman, 1986, p. 232.

Sutherland, Zena, review of *The Sugar-Gum Tree, Bulletin of the Center for Children's Books,* June, 1992, p. 285.

Times Literary Supplement, November 23, 1973, p. 1434.

Townsend, John Rowe, *A Sounding of Storytellers: New and Revised Essays on Contemporary Writers for Children,* Lippincott, 1971, pp. 194-206.

Wrightson, Patricia, "Hans Christian Andersen Award Acceptance Speech," *Bookbird,* March-April, 1986.

Wrightson, Patricia, *Authors and Artists for Young Adults,* Volume 5, Gale, 1990, pp. 236-37.

Young, Donald A., "Patricia Wrightson, O.B.E.," *Junior Bookshelf,* December, 1981, pp. 235-37, 240-41.

For More Information See

BOOKS

Children's Literature Review, Gale, Volume 4, 1982, Volume 14, 1988.

de Montreville, Doris, and Elizabeth D. Crawford, *Fourth Book of Junior Authors and Illustrators,* H. W. Wilson, 1978.

Drew, Bernard A., *The One Hundred Most Popular Young Adult Authors,* Libraries Unlimited, 1996.

PERIODICALS

Australian Book Review, December-January, 1994-95, p. 59.

Best Sellers, December, 1983.

Bookbird, Number 2, 1970; April, 1984; February, 1986; June 15, 1986.

Booklist, April 1, 1989, p. 1393.

Bulletin of the Center for Children's Books, February, 1978; July-August, 1979; November, 1983; October, 1985; May, 1988; February, 1989, p. 161.

Children's Book World, July-August, 1987.

Children's Literature in Education, September, 1974; spring, 1978.

Growing Point, October, 1977; September, 1979.

Horn Book, June, 1963; June, 1965; October, 1972; February, 1978; April, 1979; December, 1980, pp. 609-17; August, 1981; August, 1982; February, 1984; January-February, 1985; January-February, 1986; September-October, 1986; March-April, 1988.

Junior Bookshelf, August, 1979; December, 1981; October, 1983.

Kirkus Reviews, September 15, 1977; March 15, 1988, p. 462; March 15, 1992, p. 402.

Magpies, May, September, 1991, p. 4; 1993, p. 37; July, 1998, p. 44.

New York Times Book Review, November 13, 1983.

Publishers Weekly, August 30, 1985; October 31, 1986; October 30, 1987; March 21, 1989; April 20, 1992, p. 57.

School Library Journal, May, 1984; December, 1985; April, 1988, p. 106; July, 1992, p. 66.

Starship: The Magazine about Science Fiction, winter-spring, 1982-83.

Times Educational Supplement, March 5, 1993, p. 12; August 9, 1996, p. 21.*

—*Sketch by J. Sydney Jones*

Y

YOLEN, Jane (Hyatt) 1939-

Personal

Also writes as Jane H. Yolen; married name Jane Yolen Stemple; born February 11, 1939, in New York, NY; daughter of Will Hyatt (an author and publicist) and Isabelle (a social worker, puzzle-maker, and homemaker; maiden name, Berlin) Yolen; married David W. Stemple (a retired professor of computer science and ornithologist), September 2, 1962; children: Heidi Elisabet, Adam Douglas, Jason Frederic. *Education:* Smith College, B.A., 1960; University of Massachusetts, M.Ed., 1976; also completed course work for doctorate in children's literature at the University of Massachusetts. *Politics:* Liberal Democrat. *Religion:* Jewish/Quaker. *Hobbies and other interests:* "Folk music and dancing, reading, camping, politics, all things Scottish."

Addresses

Home—Phoenix Farm, 31 School Street, Box 27, Hatfield, MA 01038, and Wayside, 96 Hepburn Gardens, St. Andrews, Fife, Scotland KY16 9LN. *Agent*—Marilyn Marlow, Curtis Brown Ltd., 10 Astor Place, New York, NY 10003.

Career

Saturday Review, New York City, production assistant, 1960-61; Gold Medal Books (publishers), New York City, assistant editor, 1961-62; Rutledge Books (publishers), New York City, associate editor, 1962-63; Alfred A. Knopf, Inc. (publishers), New York City, assistant juvenile editor, 1963-65; full-time professional writer, 1965—. Editor of imprint, Jane Yolen Books, for Harcourt Brace Jovanovich, 1988-1998. Teacher of writing and lecturer, 1966—; has taught children's literature at Smith College. Chairman of board of library trustees, Hatfield, MA, 1976-83; member of Arts Council, Hatfield. *Member:* International Kitefliers Association, Society of Children's Book Writers (member of board of directors, 1974—), Science Fiction Writers of America (president, 1986-88), Children's Literature Association (member of board of directors, 1977-79), Science Fiction Poetry Association, National Association for the Preservation and Perpetuation of Storytelling, Western New England Storyteller's Guild (founder), Bay State Writers Guild, Western Massachusetts Illustrators Guild (founder), Smith College Alumnae Association.

Awards, Honors

Boys' Club of America Junior Book Award, 1968, for *The Minstrel and the Mountain;* Lewis Carroll Shelf Award, 1968, for *The Emperor and the Kite,* and 1973, for *The Girl Who Loved the Wind;* Best Books of the Year selection, *New York Times,* 1968, for *The Emporer Flies a Kite; World on a String: The Story of Kites* was named an American Library Association (ALA) Notable Book, 1968; Children's Book Showcase of the Children's Book Council citations, 1973, for *The Girl Who Loved the Wind,* and 1976, for *The Little Spotted Fish;* Golden Kite Award, Society of Children's Book Writers, 1974, ALA Notable Book, 1975, and National Book Award nomination, 1975, all for *The Girl Who Cried Flowers and Other Tales;* Golden Kite Honor Book, 1975, for *The Transfigured Hart,* and 1976, for *The Moon Ribbon and Other* Tales; Christopher Medal, 1978, for *The Seeing Stick.*

Children's Choice from the International Reading Association and the Children's Book Council, 1980, for *Mice on Ice,* and 1983, for *Dragon's Blood;* Parents' Choice Awards, Parents' Choice Foundation, 1982, for *Dragon's Blood,* 1984, for *The Stone Silenus,* and 1989, for *Piggins* and *The Three Bears Rhyme Book; School Library Journal* Best Books for Young Adults citations, 1982, for *The Gift of Sarah Barker,* and 1985, for *Heart's Blood;* Garden State Children's Book Award, New Jersey Library Association, 1983, for *Commander Toad in Space;* CRABbery Award from Acton Public Library (MD), 1983, for *Dragon's Blood; Heart's Blood* was selected one of ALA's Best Books for Young Adults, 1984; Mythopoeic Society's Fantasy Award,

1984, for *Cards of Grief; The Lullaby Songbook* and *The Sleeping Beauty* were each selected one of Child Study Association of America's Children's Books of the Year, 1987; World Fantasy Award, 1988, for *Favorite Folktales from around the World;* Parents' Choice Silver Seal Award, Jewish Book Council Award, Association of Jewish Libraries Award, all 1988, Judy Lopez Honor Book, Nebula Award finalist, both 1989, and Maude Haude Lovlace Award, 1996, all for *The Devil's Arithmetic;* Golden Sower Award from the Nebraska Library Association, 1989, and Charlotte Award from New York State Reading Association, both for *Piggins.* Yolen has received several awards for her body of work, including the Chandler Book Talk Reward of Merit, 1970; LL.D. from College of Our Lady of the Elms, Chicopee, MA, 1981; Daedelus Award, 1986, for her fantasy and short fiction; Kerlan Award for "singular achievements in the creation of children's literature," 1988; Smith College Medal, 1990; Skylark Award, New England Science Fiction Association, 1990; the Regina Medal for her body of writing in children's literature, 1992; the Keen State Children's Book Award, 1998; Literary Light Award, Boston Library, 1998; and the Anna V. Zarrow Award, 1999. Thirteen of Yolen's books have been selected by the Junior Literary Guild. In addition, *The Emperor and the Kite* was named a Caldecott Medal Honor Book, 1968, for its illustrations by Ed Young, and *Owl Moon* received the Caldecott Medal, 1988, for its illustrations by John Schoenherr.

Writings

FOR CHILDREN; PICTURE BOOKS AND FICTION

The Witch Who Wasn't, illustrated by Arnold Roth, Macmillan, 1964.

Gwinellen, the Princess Who Could Not Sleep, illustrated by Ed Renfro, Macmillan, 1965.

The Emperor and the Kite, illustrated by Ed Young, World Publishing (Cleveland, OH), 1967, Philomel, 1988.

The Minstrel and the Mountain: A Tale of Peace, illustrated by Anne Rockwell, World Publishing, 1967.

Isabel's Noel, illustrated by Roth, Funk and Wagnalls (New York), 1967.

Greyling: A Picture Story from the Islands of Shetland, illustrated by William Stobbs, World Publishing, 1968, illustrated by David Ray, Philomel, 1991.

The Longest Name on the Block, illustrated by Peter Madden, Funk and Wagnalls, 1968.

The Wizard of Washington Square, illustrated by Ray Cruz, World Publishing, 1969.

The Inway Investigators; or, The Mystery at McCracken's Place, illustrated by Allan Eitzen, Seabury (New York), 1969.

Hobo Toad and the Motorcycle Gang, illustrated by Emily McCully, World Publishing, 1970.

The Seventh Mandarin, illustrated by Young, Seabury, 1970.

The Bird of Time, illustrated by Mercer Mayer, Crowell (New York), 1971.

The Girl Who Loved the Wind, illustrated by Young, Crowell, 1972.

The Girl Who Cried Flowers and Other Tales, illustrated by David Palladini, Crowell, 1974.

The Boy Who Had Wings, illustrated by Helga Aichinger, Crowell, 1974.

The Adventures of Eeka Mouse, illustrated by Myra McKee, Xerox Education Publications (Middletown, CT), 1974.

The Rainbow Rider, illustrated by Michael Foreman, Crowell, 1974.

The Little Spotted Fish, illustrated by Friso Henstra, Seabury, 1975.

The Transfigured Hart, illustrated by Donna Diamond, Crowell, 1975, Magic Carpet Books/Harcourt, 1997.

Milkweed Days, photographs by Gabriel Amadeus Cooney, Crowell, 1976.

The Moon Ribbon and Other Tales, illustrated by Palladini, Crowell, 1976.

The Seeing Stick, illustrated by Remy Charlip and Demetra Maraslis, Crowell, 1977.

The Sultan's Perfect Tree, illustrated by Barbara Garrison, *Parents'* Magazine Press (New York), 1977.

The Hundredth Dove and Other Tales, illustrated by Palladini, Crowell, 1977.

Hannah Dreaming, photographs by Alan R. Epstein, Museum of Fine Art (Springfield, MA), 1977.

The Lady and the Merman, illustrated by Barry Moser, Pennyroyal, 1977.

Spider Jane, illustrated by Stefan Bernath, Coward, 1978.

The Simple Prince, illustrated by Jack Kent, *Parents'* Magazine Press, 1978.

No Bath Tonight, illustrated by Nancy Winslow Parker, Crowell, 1978.

The Mermaid's Three Wisdoms, illustrated by Laura Rader, Collins (New York), 1978.

Dream Weaver and Other Tales, illustrated by Michael Hague, Collins, 1979, reissued as *Dream Weaver,* 1989.

Spider Jane on the Move, illustrated by Bernath, Coward, 1980.

Mice on Ice, illustrated by Lawrence DiFiori, Dutton, 1980.

Shirlick Holmes and the Case of the Wandering Wardrobe, illustrated by Anthony Rao, Coward, 1981.

The Acorn Quest, illustrated by Susanna Natti, Harper, 1981.

Brothers of the Wind, illustrated by Barbara Berger, Philomel, 1981.

Sleeping Ugly, illustrated by Diane Stanley, Coward, 1981.

The Boy Who Spoke Chimp, illustrated by David Wiesner, Knopf, 1981.

Uncle Lemon's Spring, illustrated by Glen Rounds, Dutton, 1981.

Owl Moon, illustrated by John Schoenherr, Philomel (New York), 1987.

(Reteller) *The Sleeping Beauty,* illustrated by Ruth Sanderson, Knopf, 1986.

Dove Isabeau, illustrated by Dennis Nolan, Harcourt, 1989.

Baby Bear's Bedtime Book, illustrated by Dyer, Harcourt, 1990.

Sky Dogs, illustrated by Barry Moser, Harcourt, 1990.

(Reteller) *Tam Lin: An Old Ballad,* illustrated by Mikolaycak, Harcourt, 1990.

Elfabet: An ABC of Elves, illustrated by Lauren Mills, Little, Brown, 1990.

Letting Swift River Go, illustrated by Barbara Cooney, Little, Brown, 1990.

The Dragon's Boy, Harper, 1990.

Wizard's Hall, Harcourt, 1991.

Hark! A Christmas Sampler, illustrated by Tomie dePaola, music by Adam Stemple, Putnam, 1991.

(Reteller) *Wings,* Harcourt, 1991.

All Those Secrets of the World (autobiographical fiction), illustrated by Leslie Baker, Little, Brown, 1991.

Encounter, illustrated by David Shannon, Harcourt, 1992.

Mouse's Birthday, illustrated by Degen, Putnam, 1993.

Hands, illustrated by Chi Chung, Sundance Publishing, 1993, also published as *Hands: Big Book,* 1993.

Beneath the Ghost Moon, illustrated by Laurel Molk, Little, Brown, 1994.

Honkers, illustrated by Leslie Baker, Little, Brown, 1993.

Travelers Rose, Putnam, 1993.

Grandad Bill's Song, illustrated by Melissa Bay Mathis, Philomel, 1994.

And Twelve Chinese Acrobats (autobiographical fiction), illustrated by Jean Gralley, Philomel, 1994.

Good Griselle, illustrated by David Christiana, Harcourt, 1994.

The Girl in the Golden Bower, illustrated by Dyer, Little, Brown, 1994.

Old Dame Counterpane, illustrated by Ruth Tietjen Councell, Putnam, 1994.

(Reteller) *Little Mouse and Elephant: A Tale from Turkey,* illustrated by John Segal, Simon & Schuster, 1994.

(Reteller) *The Musicians of Bremen: A Tale from Germany,* illustrated by Segal, Simon & Schuster, 1994.

The Ballad of the Pirate Queen, illustrated by Shannon, Harcourt, 1995.

Before the Storm, illustrated by Georgia Pugh, Boyds Mills Press, 1995.

(Reteller) *A Sip of Aesop,* illustrated by Karen Barbour, Blue Sky Press, 1995.

Merlin and the Dragons, illustrated by Ming Li, Dutton, 1995.

The Wild Hunt, illustrated by Francisco Mora, Harcourt, 1995.

(With daughter Heidi E. Y. Stemple) *Meet the Monsters,* illustrated by Patricia Ludlow, Walker, 1996.

Nocturne, illustrated by Anne Hunter, Harcourt, 1997.

Child of Faerie, Child of Earth, illustrated by Dyer, Little, Brown, 1997.

Miz Berlin Walks, illustrated by Floyd Cooper, Philomel, 1997.

(Reteller) *Once upon a Bedtime Story: Classic Tales,* illustrated by Councell, 1997.

The Sea Man, illustrated by Christopher Denise, Putnam, 1997.

Twelve Impossible Things Before Breakfast (short stories), Harcourt, 1997.

House, House, illustrated with photographs by the Howes Brothers and Jason Stemple, Marshall Cavendish (New York), 1998.

King Long Shanks, illustrated by Victoria Chess, Harcourt, 1998.

(Reteller) *Pegasus, the Flying Horse,* illustrated by Ming, Dutton, 1998.

Raising Yoder's Barn, illustrated by Bernie Fuchs, Little, Brown, 1998.

(Reteller) *Prince of Egypt,* Dutton, 1998.

(With Heidi E. Y. Stemple) *Mary Celeste: An Unsolved Mystery from History,* illustrated by Roger Roth, Simon & Schuster, 1999.

Moonball, illustrated by Greg Couch, Simon & Schuster, 1999.

Dinosaurs Say Goodnight, illustrated by Mark Teague, Blue Sky Press, 2000.

Off We Go! illustrated by Laurel Molk, Little, Brown, 2000.

The Book of Fairy Holidays, illustrated by Christiana, Blue Sky Press (New York), in press.

Harvest Home, illustrated by Greg Shed, Harcourt, in press.

(Compiler with Linda Mannheim) *Stretching the Truth,* illustrated by Kevin Hawkes, Blue Sky Press, in press.

"GIANTS" SERIES; PICTURE BOOKS, ILLUSTRATED BY TOMIE DePAOLA, PUBLISHED BY SEABURY

The Giants' Farm, 1977.

The Giants Go Camping, 1979.

"COMMANDER TOAD" SERIES; FICTION, ILLUSTRATED BY BRUCE DEGEN

Commander Toad in Space, Coward, 1980.

Commander Toad and the Planet of the Grapes, Coward, 1982.

Commander Toad and the Big Black Hole, Coward, 1983.

Commander Toad and the Dis-Asteroid, Coward, 1985.

Commander Toad and the Intergalactic Spy, Coward, 1986.

Commander Toad and the Space Pirates, Putnam, 1987.

Commander Toad and the Voyage Home, Putnam, 1998.

"ROBOT AND REBECCA" SERIES; FICTION

The Robot and Rebecca: The Mystery of the Code-Carrying Kids, illustrated by Jurg Obrist, Knopf, 1980, student book club edition illustrated by Catherine Deeter, Random House, 1980.

The Robot and Rebecca and the Missing Owser, illustrated by Lady McCrady, Knopf, 1981.

"PIGGINS" SERIES; PICTURE BOOKS, ILLUSTRATED BY JANE DYER, PUBLISHED BY HARCOURT

Piggins, 1987.

Picnic with Piggins, 1988.

Piggins and the Royal Wedding, 1988.

"MOLE" SERIES; FICTION, ILLUSTRATED BY KATHRYN BROWN, PUBLISHED BY HARCOURT

Eeny, Meeny, Miney Mole, 1992.

Eeny Up Above, in press.

"YOUNG MERLIN" SERIES; FICTION, PUBLISHED BY HARCOURT

Passager, 1996.

Hobby, 1996.

Merlin, 1997.

"TARTAN MAGIC" SERIES; FICTION, PUBLISHED BY HARCOURT

The Wizard's Map, 1998.

The Pictish Child, 1999.

FOR CHILDREN; NONFICTION

Pirates in Petticoats, illustrated by Leonard Vosburgh, McKay, 1963.

World on a String: The Story of Kites, World Publishing, 1968.

Friend: The Story of George Fox and the Quakers, Seabury, 1972.

(Editor with Barbara Green) *The Fireside Song Book of Birds and Beasts,* illustrated by Peter Parnall, Simon & Schuster, 1972.

The Wizard Islands, illustrated by Robert Quackenbush, Crowell, 1973.

Ring Out! A Book of Bells, illustrated by Richard Cuffari, Seabury, 1974.

Simple Gifts: The Story of the Shakers, illustrated by Betty Fraser, Viking, 1976.

(Compiler) *Rounds about Rounds,* music by Barbara Green, illustrated by Gail Gibbons, Watts (New York), 1977.

The Lap-Time Song and Play Book, musical arrangements by son Adam Stemple, illustrated by Margot Tomes, Harcourt, 1989.

A Letter from Phoenix Farm (autobiography), illustrated with photographs by son Jason Stemple, Richard C. Owen (Katonah, NY), 1992.

Jane Yolen's Songs of Summer, musical arrangements by Adam Stemple, illustrated by Cyd Moore, Boyds Mills Press, 1993.

Welcome to the Green House, illustrated by Laura Regan, Putnam, 1993.

Jane Yolen's Old MacDonald Songbook, illustrated by Rosekrans Hoffman, Boyds Mills Press, 1994.

Sing Noel, musical arrangements by Stemple, illustrated by Nancy Carpenter, Boyds Mills Press, 1996.

Milk and Honey: A Year of Jewish Holidays, illustrations by Louise August, musical arrangements by Stemple, Putnam, 1996.

Welcome to the Sea of Sand, illustrated by Laura Regan, Putnam, 1996.

Welcome to the Ice House, illustrated by Regan, Putnam, 1998.

Tea with an Old Dragon: A Story of Sophia Smith, Founder of Smith College, illustrated by Monica Vachula, Boyds Mills Press, 1998.

FOR CHILDREN; POETRY

See This Little Line?, illustrated by Kathleen Elgin, McKay (New York), 1963.

It All Depends, illustrated by Don Bolognese, Funk and Wagnalls, 1970.

An Invitation to the Butterfly Ball: A Counting Rhyme, illustrated by Jane Breskin Zalben, *Parents'* Magazine Press, 1976.

All in the Woodland Early: An ABC Book, illustrated by Zalben, Collins, 1979, Caroline House (Honesdale, PA), 1991.

How Beastly!: A Menagerie of Nonsense Poems, illustrated by James Marshall, Philomel, 1980.

Dragon Night and Other Lullabies, illustrated by Demi, Methuen (New York), 1980.

(Editor) *The Lullaby Songbook,* musical arrangements by Adam Stemple, illustrated by Charles Mikolaycak, Harcourt, 1986.

Ring of Earth: A Child's Book of Seasons, illustrated by John Wallner, Harcourt, 1986.

The Three Bears Rhyme Book, illustrated by Dyer, Harcourt, 1987.

Best Witches: Poems for Halloween, illustrated by Elise Primavera, Putnam, 1989.

Bird Watch, illustrated by Ted Lewin, Philomel, 1990.

Dinosaur Dances, illustrated by Degen, Putnam, 1990.

An Invitation to the Butterfly Ball: A Counting Rhyme, illustrated by Jane Breskin Zalben, Caroline House, 1991.

(Compiler) *Street Rhymes around the World,* illustrated by seventeen artists, Wordsong (Honesdale, PA), 1992.

Jane Yolen's Mother Goose Songbook, musical arrangements by Stemple, illustrated by Rosecrans Hoffman, Boyds Mill Press, 1992.

(Compiler) *Weather Report,* illustrated by Annie Gusman, Boyds Mills Press, 1993.

Mouse's Birthday, illustrated by Degen, Putnam, 1993.

Raining Cats and Dogs, illustrated by Janet Street, Harcourt, 1993.

What Rhymes with Moon?, illustrated by Councell, Philomel, 1993.

(Editor) *Sleep Rhymes Around the World,* illustrated by seventeen artists, Boyds Mills Press, 1993.

(Compiler and contributor) *Alphabestiary: Animal Poems from A to Z,* illustrated by Allan Eitzen, Boyds Mills Press, 1994.

Sacred Places, illustrated by David Shannon, Harcourt, 1994.

Animal Fare: Zoological Nonsense Poems, illustrated by Street, Harcourt, 1994.

The Three Bears Holiday Rhyme Book, illustrated by Dyer, Harcourt, 1995.

Water Music: Poems for Children, illustrated with photographs by Jason Stemple, Boyds Mills Press, 1995.

(Compiler) *Mother Earth, Father Sky: Poems of Our Planet,* illustrated by Jennifer Hewitson, Boyds Mills Press, 1996.

O Jerusalem, illustrated by John Thompson, Scholastic, 1996.

Sea Watch: A Book of Poetry, illustrated by Lewin, Putnam, 1996.

(Compiler and contributor) *Sky Scrape/City Scape: Poems of City Life,* illustrated by Ken Condon, Boyds Mills Press, 1996.

(Compiler) *Once upon Ice and Other Frozen Poems,* illustrated with photographs by Stemple, Boyds Mills Press, 1997.

Snow, Snow: Winter Poems for Children, illustrated with photographs by Stemple, Wordsong (Honesdale, PA), 1998.

The Originals: Animals That Time Forgot, illustrated by Lewin, Philomel, 1998.

FOR YOUNG ADULTS; FICTION

(With Anne Huston) *Trust a City Kid,* illustrated by J. C. Kocsis, Lothrop, 1966.

(Editor) *Zoo 2000: Twelve Stories of Science Fiction and Fantasy Beasts,* Seabury, 1973.

The Magic Three of Solatia, illustrated by Julia Noonan, Crowell, 1974.

(Editor and contributor) *Shape Shifters: Fantasy and Science Fiction Tales about Humans Who Can Change Their Shape,* Seabury, 1978.

The Gift of Sarah Barker, Viking, 1981.

Neptune Rising: Songs and Tales of the Undersea Folk (story collection), illustrated by Wiesner, Philomel, 1982.

The Stone Silenus, Philomel, 1984.

Children of the Wolf, Viking, 1984.

(Editor and contributor with Martin H. Greenberg and Charles G. Waugh) *Dragons and Dreams,* Harper, 1986.

(Editor and contributor with Greenberg and Waugh) *Spaceships and Spells,* Harper, 1987.

The Devil's Arithmetic, Viking, 1988.

(Editor and contributor with Martin H. Greenberg) *Werewolves: A Collection of Original Stories,* Harper, 1988.

The Faery Flag: Stories and Poems of Fantasy and the Supernatural, Orchard Books (New York), 1989.

(Editor and contributor with Greenberg) *Things That Go Bump in the Night,* Harper, 1989.

(Editor and contributor) *2041 AD: Twelve Stories about the Future by Top Science Fiction Writers* (anthology), Delacorte, 1990, reprinted as *2041,* Delacorte, 1991.

(Editor and contributor with Greenberg) *Vampires,* Harper-Collins, 1991.

Here There Be Dragons (original stories and poetry), illustrated by David Wilgus, Harcourt, 1993.

Here There Be Unicorns (stories and poetry), illustrated by Wilgus, Harcourt, 1994.

Here There Be Witches (stories and poetry), illustrated by Wilgus, Harcourt, 1995.

(Editor and contributor) *Camelot: A Collection of Original Arthurian Tales,* illustrated by Winslow Pels, Putnam, 1995.

(Editor with Greenberg and contributor) *The Haunted House: A Collection of Original Stories,* illustrated by Doron Ben-Ami, HarperCollins, 1995.

Here There Be Angels (stories and poetry), illustrated by Wilgus, Harcourt, 1996.

Here There Be Ghosts (stories and poetry), illustrated by Wilgus, Harcourt, 1998.

(With Bruce Coville) *Armageddon Summer,* Harcourt, 1998.

"PIT DRAGON" SERIES; FICTION

Dragon's Blood: A Fantasy, Delacorte, 1982, Magic Carpet Books/Harcourt, 1996.

Heart's Blood, Delacorte, 1984, Harcourt, 1996.

A Sending of Dragons, illustrated by Tom McKeveny, Delacorte, 1987, Harcourt, 1997.

FOR ADULTS; FICTION

Tales of Wonder (short stories), Schocken (New York), 1983.

Cards of Grief (science fiction), Ace Books, 1984.

Merlin's Booke (short stories), illustrated by Thomas Canty, Ace Books, 1982.

Dragonfield and Other Stories (story collection), Ace Books, 1985.

(Editor) *Favorite Folktales from around the World,* Pantheon, 1986.

Sword and the Stone, Pulphouse (Eugene, OR), 1991.

Briar Rose, Tor Books, 1992.

Storyteller, New England Science Fiction Association Press (Cambridge, MA), 1992, boxed edition illustrated by Merle Insinga.

(Editor and contributor with Greenberg) *Xanadu,* Tor Books, 1993.

(Editor and contributor with Greenberg) *Xanadu Two,* Tor Books, 1994.

(Editor and contributor with Greenberg) *Xanadu Three,* Tor Books, 1995.

The Books of Great Alta, St. Martin's Press (New York), 1997.

(Editor) *Gray Heroes: Elder Tales from Around the World,* Viking Penguin, 1998.

Not One Damsel in Distress, Harcourt, 2000.

(With daughter Heidi E.L. Stemple) *Mirror, Mirror,* Viking, 2000.

(Editor and contributor) *Sherwood: A Collection of Original Robin Hood Stories,* illustrated by Dennis Nolan, Philomel, 2000.

(With Robert J. Harris) *Queen's Own Fool,* Philomel, 2000.

"WHITE JENNA" SERIES; FICTION

Sister Light, Sister Dark, Tor Books, 1988.

White Jenna, Tor Books, 1989.

The One-Armed Queen, with music by Adam Stemple, Tor Books, 1998.

FOR ADULTS; NONFICTION

Writing Books for Children, The Writer (Boston), 1973, revised edition, 1983.

Touch Magic: Fantasy, Faerie and Folklore in the Literature of Childhood, Philomel, 1981, revised edition, August House, 2000.

Guide to Writing for Children, Writer, 1989.

(With Nancy Willard) *Among Angels* (poetry), illustrated by S. Saelig Gallagher, Harcourt, 1995.

OTHER

Also author of the play *Robin Hood,* a musical with music by Barbara Greene first produced in Boston, MA, 1967, and of the chapbook *The Whitethorn Wood.* Ghostwriter of a number of books for Rutledge Press that were distributed by other publishing houses, including *One, Two, Buckle My Shoe,* a counting rhyme book published by Doubleday, and a series of activity books. Editor of *A Plague of Sorcerers* by Mary Frances Zambreno, *Appleblossom* by Shulamith L. Oppenheim, *Jeremy Thatcher, Dragon Hatcher* by Bruce Coville, *The Jewel of Life* by Anna Kirwan-Vogel, *The Patchwork Lady* by Mary K. Whittington, *The Red Ball* by Joanna Yardley, all Harcourt, 1991. Contributor to many books, including *Dragons of Light,* edited by Orson Scott Card, Ace Books, 1981; *Elsewhere,* edited by Terri Windling and Mark Alan Arnold, Ace Books, Volume 1, 1981, Volume 2, 1982; *Hecate's Cauldron,* edited by Susan Schwartz, DAW Books, 1982; *Heroic Visions,* edited by Jessica Amanda Salmonson, Ace Books, 1983; *Faery!,* edited by Windling, Ace Books, 1985; *Liavek,* edited by Will Shetterly and Emma Bull, Ace Books, 1985; *Moonsinger's Friends,* edited by Schwartz, Blue-jay, 1985; *Imaginary Lands,* edited by Robin McKinley, Greenwillow, 1985; *Don't Bet on the Prince: Contempo-*

rary Feminist Fairy Tales in North America and England, by Jack Zipes, Methuen, 1986; *Liavek: Players of Luck,* edited by Shetterly and Bull, Ace Books, 1986; *Liavek: Wizard's Row,* edited by Shetterly and Bull, Ace Books, 1987; *Visions,* by Donald R. Gallo, Delacorte, 1987; *Liavek: Spells of Binding,* edited by Shetterly and Bull, Ace Books, 1988; *Invitation to Camelot,* by Parke Godwin, Ace Books, 1988; and *The Unicorn Treasury,* by Bruce Coville, Doubleday, 1988, and dozens more. Author of introduction for *Cut from the Same Cloth: American Women of Myth, Legend, and Tall Tale,* collected and told by Robert D. San Souci, Philomel, 1993; *Best-Loved Stories Told at the National Storytelling Festival,* National Storytelling Association, 1996; and *Fearless Girls, Wise Women, and Beloved Sisters: Heroines in Folktales from Around the World* by Kathleen Ragan, Norton, 1998. Yolen has also written songs and lyrics for folksingers, some of which have been recorded. Her papers are housed at the Kerlan Collection, University of Minnesota.

Author of column "Children's Bookfare" for *Daily Hampshire Gazette* during the 1970s. Contributor of articles, reviews, poems, and short stories to periodicals, including *Chicago Jewish Forum, Horn Book, Isaac Asimov's Science Fiction Magazine, Language Arts, Los Angeles Times, Magazine of Fantasy and Science Fiction, New Advocate, New York Times, Parabola, Parents' Choice, Washington Post Book World, Wilson Library Bulletin,* and *Writer.* Member of editorial board, *Advocate* (now *New Advocate*) and *National Storytelling Journal,* until 1989. Some of Yolen's books have been published in Australia, Austria, Brazil, Denmark, England, France, Germany, Japan, South Africa, Spain, and Sweden.

Adaptations

The Seventh Mandarin was produced as a motion picture by Xerox Films, 1973; *The Emperor and the Kite* was produced as a filmstrip with cassette by Listening Library, 1976; *The Bird of Time* was adapted into a play and was first produced in Northampton, MA, 1982; *The Girl Who Cried Flowers and Other Tales* was released on audio cassette by Weston Woods, 1983; *Dragon's Blood* was produced as an animated television movie by Columbia Broadcasting System (CBS), 1985, and shown on *CBS Storybreak; Commander Toad in Space* was released on audio cassette by Listening Library, 1986; *Touch Magic ... Pass It On,* a selection of Yolen's short stories, was released on audio cassette by Weston Woods, 1987; *Owl Moon* was produced as a filmstrip with cassette by Weston Woods, 1988, and as both a read-along cassette, 1990, and a video; *Owl Moon* was also adapted as part of the video *Owl Moon and Other Stories* produced by Children's Circle; *Piggins and Picnic with Piggins* was released on audio cassette by Caedmon, 1988; *Best of Science Fiction and Fantasy* was released on audio cassette by NewStar Media, 1991; *Merlin and the Dragons* was released on audio cassette by Lightyear Entertainment, 1991, was produced as a video by Coronet, 1991, and was released as *What's a Good Story? Merlin and the Dragon* with commentary

by Yolen; *Greyling* was released on audio cassette by Spoken Arts, 1993; *Hands* was released on audio cassette by Sundance Publishing, 1993; Beneath the Ghost Moon was produced as a video by Spoken Arts, 1996; *Wizard's Hall* was released on audio cassette by "Words Take Wines," narrated by Yolen, 1997. Recorded Books has also issued audio cassettes of three of Yolen's books: *Briar Rose, The Devil's Arithmetic,* and *Good Griselle.* Yolen is the subject of the audio cassette *The Children's Writer at Work—Jane Yolen,* produced by Real Life Productions; in addition, she is the subject of the videos *Good Conversation: A Talk with Jane Yolen,* produced by Weston Woods, and *The Children's Writer at Work,* produced by Reel Life, 1997.

Work in Progress

Many Mansions, a novel; *The Sword of the Rightful King,* a novel; *Books and the Seven Leagues,* a novel; *Wild Wings,* a book of poetry; several screenplays.

Sidelights

Dubbed "the American Hans Christian Andersen" by editor/publisher Ann K. Beneduce and "a modern equivalent of Aesop" by Noel Perrin in the *New York Times Book Review,* Yolen is considered a gifted, versatile author who has developed a stellar reputation as a fantasist while contributing successfully to many other genres. An exceptionally prolific writer, she is the creator of approximately three hundred books for children and young adults and approximately twenty-five for adults. Yolen has written fiction for young adults and adults as well as poetry, criticism, and books on the art of writing and the genre of fantasy for an adult audience. She has also edited and compiled a number of works for both younger and older readers and has also contributed to several collections and anthologies. As a writer of juvenile literature, Yolen addresses her books to an audience ranging from preschool through high school and has written works ranging from picture books and easy readers to young adult novels. She is the creator of realistic fiction, mysteries, verse, animal tales, concept books, historical fiction, humorous stories, and lyrical prose poems, as well as informational books on such subjects as kites, bells, the Shakers, the Quakers, and the environment. Several of Yolen's books have been published in series, and she is particularly well known for the "Pit Dragon" series of young adult fantasy novels in which she created a mythological world based around cockfighting dragons on an arid planet. A folksinger and storyteller, Yolen has created several works that reflect her love of music and oral folklore, including compilations of international songs, rhymes, and stories. Several of the author's books are autobiographical or incorporate elements from her life or the lives of her family, and her three children all contribute to her works—daughter Heidi as a writer and sons Adam and Jason as a musical arranger and photographer, respectively. Yolen has also worked with a number of outstanding illustrators such as Mercer Mayer, Michael Foreman, Barbara Cooney, Michael Hague, Glen Rounds, Nancy Winslow Parker, Barry Moser, Charles

In Jane Yolen's fantasy novel, Jakkin takes monumental risks when he and his dragon, Heart's Blood, infiltrate rebel forces to rescue the girl Jakkin loves. (Cover illustration by Dennis Nolan.)

Mikolaycak, Demi, Tomie dePaola, Jane Dyer, David Wiesner, Bruce Degen, Victoria Chess, James Marshall, and Ted Lewin. In addition, two of Yolen's books have received prizes from the Caldecott Medal committee: *Owl Moon* won the Caldecott Medal for its illustrations by John Schoenherr while *The Emperor and the Kite* was named a Caldecott honor book for its illustrations by Ed Young.

Yolen is perhaps best known as a writer of original folk and fairy tales and fables with a strong moral core. She has received special recognition for her literary fairy tales, works in the tradition of Oscar Wilde and Laurence Houseman that combine familiar fantasy motifs with contemporary elements and philosophical themes. As a fantasist, Yolen is noted for creating elegant, eloquent tales with deep psychological insights that evoke a timeless sense of wonder while having relevance to contemporary life. She includes figures such as dragons, unicorns, witches, and mermaids as

characters, and her stories often revolve around shape-shifters, animals who have the ability to transform into humans or humans into animals. As a writer, Yolen invests her works with images, symbols, and allusions as well as with wordplay—especially puns—and metaphors. She is considered an exceptional prose stylist whose fluid, musical writing is both polished and easy to read aloud. As a writer of nonfiction, the author is credited for capturing the spirit of her subjects as well as for the enthusiasm with which she invests her books. Although her fiction is occasionally criticized for unlikely plots and sketchy characterizations and her fairy tales are sometimes considered too mannered, Yolen is generally praised as a writer of consistent quality whose books are evocative, moving, and enjoyable. Peter D. Sieruta of *Children's Books and Their Creators* stated: "With a confident writing style and inexhaustible imagination, Jane Yolen has proven herself one of the most prolific and diverse creators in the field of children's literature." In her entry in *Twentieth-Century Children's Writers,* Marcia G. Fuchs commented: "Faerie, fiction, fact, or horrible fantasy, Yolen's lyrical and magical tales are indeed tales to read and to listen to, to share, to remember, and to pass on." Jane Langton, herself a noted writer of fantasy, stated in the *New York Times Book Review* that Yolen's fables "are told with sober strength and native wit. They are simple and perfect, without a word too much." Writing in *Teaching and Learning Literature (TALL),* Lee Bennett Hopkins toasted the author: "May the pen of Yolen never run dry. The world of children's literature has been, and will continue to be, richer for her vast talents."

Writing in the *Fourth Book of Junior Authors and Illustrators (FBJAI),* Yolen said, "I come from a long line of storytellers. My great-grandfather was the Reb, the storyteller in a small village in Finno-Russia, my father an author, my mother a mostly unpublished writer." Born in New York City, Yolen is the daughter of Will Hyatt Yolen, a writer, newspaperman, and publicist who was an international kite-flying champion, and Isabelle Berlin Yolen, a social worker whose crossword puzzles appeared in children's magazines. Writing in *Something about the Author Autobiography Series (SAAS),* Yolen remarked: "My father's family were merchants and storytellers (some called them well-off liars!). My mother's family were intellectuals. I seem to have gotten a bit of both, though not enough of either." Yolen's father publicized the sport of kite flying so successfully that, according to his daughter in *SAAS,* he "forced a renaissance in kiting that is still going on"; in 1968, Yolen published *World on a String: The Story of Kites,* a well-received informational book about the subject. The author's mother quit her job as a social worker in order to raise Jane and her younger brother, Steven; in her free time, Isabelle Yolen wrote short stories and created crossword puzzles and double acrostics. Jane spent most of her childhood in New York City. She also spent summers in Virginia, the birthplace of her mother, and lived for a year and a half in California, where her father did publicity for Warner Brothers.

Yolen told *Contemporary Authors (CA),* "I was a writer from the time I learned to write." An early reader as well as a tomboy, Yolen played games in Central Park while being encouraged in her reading and writing by her teachers. "I was," she recalled in *SAAS,* "the gold star star. And I was also pretty impossibly full of myself. In first or second grade, I wrote the school musical, lyrics and music, in which everyone was some kind of vegetable. I played the lead carrot. Our finale was a salad. Another gold star." Yolen wrote in *FBJAI,* "[I]f I had to point to my primary source of inspiration, it would be to the folk culture. My earliest readings were the folk tales and fairy stories I took home from the library by the dozens. Even when I was old enough to make the trip across Central Park by myself, I was still not too old for those folk fantasies." Yolen once told *SATA* that she read "all the Andrew Lang fairy books as a child and any kind of fairy stories I could get my hands on. I vividly remember *Treasure Island* and the Louisa May Alcott books. All of the Alcott books, *Jo's Boys,* and even the Alcott books that nobody else had heard of, became part of my adolescent reading. I read *The Wind in the Willows* and the Mowgli stories. We didn't have 'young adult' fiction, so I skipped right into adult books which tended to be very morose Russian novels—my Dostoevsky phase—then I got hooked on Joseph Conrad. Adventure novels or lugubrious emotional books are what I preferred. Then I went back into my fairy tale and fantasy stage. Tolkien and C. S. Lewis, metaphysical and folkloric fantasy." In a transcript of a speech in

Judaica Librarianship, Yolen commented that she was raised "on tales of King Arthur and Robin Hood. I was a fanatical reader of fantasy and magic, history and adventure." She also began to develop her musical abilities, singing with a friend and earning enough money by passing the hat to buy sodas and ice cream. In sixth grade, Yolen was accepted by Hunter, a girls' school for what were called "intelligently gifted" students. The author said: "With my gold stars and my writing ability, I expected to be a superior gift to Hunter. To my surprise—and horror—I was barely in the middle of my class and managed to stay there by studying extremely hard."

While at Hunter, Yolen wrote in *SAAS,* "[m]usic became a mainstay in my life." Her father, who sang and played the guitar, introduced Yolen to folk songs. She wrote in *FBJAI:* "I went him some better in learning every old English, Scottish, Irish, and Appalachian love song and ballad I ever heard." Yolen starred as Hansel in the school production of Engelbert Humperdinck's opera *Hansel and Gretel,* played the piano, and wrote songs; in addition, she became the lead dancer in her class at Balanchine's American School of Ballet. She also developed her interest in writing. In eighth grade, Yolen wrote her first two books, a nonfiction book on pirates, and a novel about a trip across the West by covered wagon. She described this work, which is seventeen pages long and includes a plague of locusts, death by snake bite, and the birth of a baby on the trail, as "a

The next morning Mama didn't get up
to make me breakfast,
and Grandma said, "Hush, let her sleep."

In her autobiographical picture book, Yolen relates her childhood memories of the time her father left the family for two years to serve in the war. (From All Those Secrets of the World, *illustrated by Leslie Baker.)*

masterpiece of economy." Her experience writing the novel helped Yolen to develop an appreciation for the short form. She wrote in *SAAS* that short stories and poetry "have remained my first loves." During her twelfth and thirteenth summers, Yolen attended Indianbrook (now Farm and Wilderness), a Quaker camp in Vermont. Here, she said, "I learned about pacifism, swimming, storytelling, mucking out horse stalls, planting a garden, and kissing, not necessarily in that order."

After returning from her second summer at Indianbrook, Yolen moved with her family to Westport, Connecticut. As a student at Staples High School, she became captain of the girls' basketball team; news editor of the school paper; head of the Jewish Youth Group; vice-president of the Spanish, Latin, and jazz clubs; a member of the school's top singing group; and a contributor to the school literary magazine. She also won a Scholastic Writing Award for one of her poems, a contest called "I Speak for Democracy," and her school's English prize. Before graduation, her class named Yolen "The Perfect Senior." A high school friend, Stella Colandrea, introduced Yolen to the Catholic Mass. "It was because of Stella's influence that I became enamored of different religions. My own Judaism and camp-discovered Quakerism were the most morally appealing, but the panoply of Catholic rites seem to have taken hold of my imagination and wind in and out of many of the elaborate religious rituals I write about in my fantasy tales. And, since I am an Arthurian buff and a lover of things medieval, knowing a bit about the church helps," Yolen wrote in *SAAS*. However, Yolen's greatest influence in high school was her cousin-in-law Honey Knopp, a pacifist and peace activist who held hootenannies at her home and gave Yolen a copy of *Journal* by George Fox, the founder of the Quaker faith. Fox later became the subject of Yolen's biography *Friend: The Story of George Fox and the Quakers.* The home that Honey Knopp shared with her husband, Burt, according to Yolen, "became my haven. Oh, I still went to basketball games and dances and parties, wisecracking with my friends and being outrageous. But Honey called out another side of me." Honey's influence is present in many of Yolen's most well-known books, such as *The Gift of Sarah Barker* and *The Transfigured Hart.*

After graduating from high school, Yolen attended Smith College, a prestigious institution for women in western Massachusetts. Going to Smith, Yolen wrote in *SAAS,* "was a choice that would, all unknowingly, change my life. It made me aware of friendships possible—and impossible—with women. It created in me a longing for a particular countryside, that of New England. It charged me with a sense of leftsidedness, of an alien or changeling awareness. And it taught me, really, about poetry and literature and the written word." At Smith, Yolen majored in English and Russian literature and minored in religion. She ran several campus organizations, authored and performed in the class musicals, and wrote her final exam in American Intellectual History in verse, receiving an A+ as her grade. She also wrote poetry: between her junior and senior year, one of Yolen's poems was published in

Poetry Digest, and her verse was also published in other small literary magazines.

Although poetry was in her soul, Yolen decided to become a journalist. During the summer between her freshman and sophomore years, Yolen worked as a cub reporter for the *Bridgeport Sunday Herald.* "It was there," Yolen recalled in *SAAS,* "I wrote my first signed pieces for a newspaper. My very first byline read 'by Joan Yolen.' I did not take it as a sign." Other vacations were spent as a junior counselor in New Jersey and working for *Newsweek* magazine as an intern; she also contributed to the *New Haven Register* and published an article on kites in *Popular Mechanics.* Yolen dismissed the idea of being a journalist when she found herself making up facts and writing stories off the top of her head; she also found that she was emotional when it came to interviewing the poor. "It became clear," she told *SATA,* "that I was a fiction writer." However, Yolen did continue her musical pursuits, writing in *FBJAI* that she "made an unhappy college career bearable by singing with a guitar-playing boyfriend at fraternity parties and mixers. We made a little money, a lot of friends, and imprinted hundreds of folk tunes on our hungry minds." After graduating from Smith, Yolen moved to New York City and worked briefly for *This Week* magazine and *Saturday Review* before launching her career as a freelance writer. She helped her father write his book *The Young Sportsman's Guide to Kite Flying* and did a number of small freelance jobs. Yolen took an apartment in Greenwich Village with two roommates. At a wild party there in the summer of 1960, she met her future husband, David Stemple, who was a friend of one of her roommates; the couple were married in 1962. Yolen has noted that one of her most popular books, *The Girl Who Loved the Wind,* is about her meeting with David, a computer expert and photographer who is Yolen's chief advisor on her books. "In it," she stated in *SAAS,* "a Persian girl is kept in a walled-in palace by an overprotective father until the day the wind leaps over the garden wall and sweeps her away into the wide, everchanging world."

Approached by an editor from the publishers Alfred A. Knopf, Yolen fibbed and said that she had a book-length manuscript ready for review. She recalled in *SAAS:* "Caught in the web of this deceit, I, who always prided myself on my honesty, realized there was nothing to do but sit down at my typewriter and get something done quickly. Children's books! I thought. They'd be quickest and easiest." Yolen soon learned that writing books for children was not as quick and easy as she first thought. She collaborated with a high school friend, illustrator Susan Purdy, on several manuscripts, none of which were accepted by the editor at Knopf. Then, Yolen and Purdy sent their manuscripts to other publishers, but with no success. In 1961, Yolen became an assistant editor at Gold Medal Books, a paperback house known for its western novels and spy thrillers. She wrote in *SAAS:* "I was famous for about a moment in publishing as the one who coined 'she was all things to two men' for some Gothic novel." Her father introduced Yolen to Eleanor Rawson, the vice-president of David McKay

The baby canoes spat out many strange creatures, men but not men. We did not know them as human beings, for they hid their bodies in colors, like parrots. Their feet were hidden, also.

And many of them had hair growing like bushes on their chins. Three of them knelt before their chief and pushed sticks into the sand. Then I was even more afraid.

Yolen's controversial picture book relates the arrival of Columbus in America from the viewpoint of a Taino Indian boy. (*From* Encounter, *illustrated by David Shannon.*)

Publishing Company. In turn, Rawson introduced the fledgling author to Rose Dobbs, the editor in charge of children's books. Yolen's first book, the nonfiction title *Pirates in Petticoats,* was accepted by Dobbs and published by McKay in 1963; Dobbs also bought Yolen's second work, *See This Little Line?,* a picture book in rhyme that was published the same year.

After leaving Gold Medal Books, where she got to know such authors as Kurt Vonnegut and Harlan Ellison, Yolen became an associate editor at Rutledge Press, a small packaging house that created books and then sold them to larger publishing companies for distribution. Yolen became a ghostwriter for Rutledge, authoring several books—often concept and activity books—that were published under different names. While at Rutledge, Yolen met Frances Keene, an editor who became head of the children's book department at Macmillan. Writing in *SAAS,* Yolen called Keene, who was to publish five of her books, "a great teacher as well as a fine editor. She taught me to trust my storytelling ability and to work against being too quick.... She also pushed me into delving deeply into folklore while at the same time recognizing my comedic talents." Yolen described her association with Keene as the "beginning of an editorial relationship that I *really* count as the start of my writing career." In 1963, Yolen became an assistant editor in the children's department at Knopf, where she met authors and illustrators such as Roald Dahl and Roger Duvoisin and learned about juvenile

literature. She formed a writers' group with such aspiring authors and editors as Jean van Leeuwen, Alice Bach, and James Cross Giblin; one of the members of the group, Anne Huston, collaborated with Yolen on *Trust a City Kid,* a realistic story published in 1966.

In 1965, the Stemples decided to spend a year traveling. For nine months, they trekked across Europe and then sailed for Israel and Greece. Yolen wrote in *SAAS* that bits and pieces "of our wanderings have already found their way into my stories." She added that "places and people we met were stored away in my memory, and months, even years, later were transformed into the magical landscape of my tales." While they were traveling, Yolen discovered that she was pregnant; Heidi Stemple arrived in 1966, shortly after her parents returned to America. David Stemple took a job at the University of Massachusetts Computer Center in Amherst, so he and Jane relocated to western Massachusetts. Adam Stemple was born in 1968 and Jason Stemple in 1970. During the late 1960s, Yolen met editor Ann K. Beneduce, whom the author described in *SAAS* as "another seminal influence in my writing life." Yolen and Beneduce, who, according to the author, "produced book after book in the handsomest way possible," worked on approximately thirty books together.

The Emperor and the Kite, a picture book that was among the first of Yolen's works to be edited by Beneduce, is the first of the author's titles to receive major awards. The story outlines how Djeow Seow, the youngest and smallest daughter of an ancient Chinese emperor, saves her father after he is kidnapped by sending him a kite to which is attached a rope made of grass, vines, and strands of her hair. Writing in *Dictionary of Literary Biography (DLB),* William E. Krueger noted that the story "is simply told in the folk tradition, with traditional motifs which provide an aura both of antiquity and of familiarity to the tale." The critic also observed the theme—"that those whom society considers deficient are capable and perhaps more proficient than others—recurs in subsequent tales." A critic in *Publishers Weekly* said that *The Emperor and the Kite* "is easily one of the most distinguished [books with Oriental backgrounds]—and distinguished proof that extravagance, intelligence, premeditated extravagance, always justifies itself." A reviewer in *Children's Book News* commented: "Here is a writer who delights in words and can use them in a controlled way to beautiful effect." In 1968, *The Emperor and the Kite* received the Lewis Carroll Shelf Award and was named a Caldecott Honor Book. Yolen received a second Lewis Carroll Shelf Award for *The Girl Who Loved the Wind,* a picture book, again illustrated by Ed Young, that was published in 1972. In this work, a widowed merchant tries to protect his beautiful daughter from unhappiness but ends up making her a virtual prisoner. The wind visits her and sings to her about life, how it is always full of change and challenges. Finally, the princess escapes with the wind into the world. Writing in *School Library Journal,* Marilyn R. Singer stated that Yolen "produced a treasure. The story has the grace and wisdom of a folk tale, the polish that usually comes from centuries of telling." Eleanor Von Schweinitz of *Children's Book Review* added that the author "has an especial gift for the invention of traditional-type tales and this is complemented by her rare ability to use language creatively. Here she has used the simple rhythms of the storyteller to conjure up the distinctive flavour of an Eastern tale." Writing in *SAAS,* Yolen said that she wrote *The Girl Who Loved the Wind* "for myself, out of my own history. But recently I received a letter from a nurse who told me that she had read the story to a dying child, and the story had eased the little girl through her final pain. The story did that—not me. But if I can continue to write with as much honesty and love as I can muster, I will truly have touched magic—and passed it on."

When she was sixteen, her aunt's sister by marriage, Honey Knopp, gave Yolen a copy of the journal of George Fox, the founder of the Quakers. "Since then," Yolen told *SATA,* "I've been interested in the Quakers." Yolen became a member of the Religious Society of Friends (Quakers) in 1971. The next year, she published another of her most well-received titles, *Friend: The Story of George Fox and the Quakers.* A biography of the seventeenth-century Englishman who founded the movement that came to be known as Quakerism as part of his own quest for religious freedom, the book is noted for portraying Fox—with his long hair and pronouncements in favor of women's rights and against war and slavery—as a kindred spirit to the young radicals of today. William E. Krueger of *DLB* called *Friend* "a quite

readable biography, interesting and, in places, quite touching, without fictionalization." Writing in *Library Journal,* Janet G. Polacheck noted: "Even where the subject is not in great demand, this beautifully written, valuable biography is an essential purchase." *The Girl Who Cried Flowers and Other Tales,* a book published in 1974, won the Golden Kite Award that year; it was also nominated for the National Book Award the next year. It is a collection of five stories that, according to a reviewer in *Publishers Weekly,* "could be called modern folk- or fairy tales, since they boast all the usual ingredients—supernatural beings, inexplicable happenings, the struggle between good and evil forces." The critic concluded that Yolen's "artistry with words … makes a striking book." A critic in *Kirkus Reviews* called *The Girl Who Cried Flowers* a "showpiece, for those who can forego the tough wisdom of traditional fairy tales for a masterful imitation of the manner." Reflective of a clear moral tone, *The Girl Who Cried Flowers* is also considered notable for suggesting the close relationship of humanity and nature. William E. Krueger of *DLB* called the book "haunting in its mythic implications" and stated that "the tone and poetic elements are Yolen's unique contributions."

All in the Woodland Early, a concept book that teaches the alphabet through the author's verses and musical score, appeared in 1978. The book outlines a little boy's hunting expedition in the woods; each letter represents the animal, bird, or insect—both familiar and unfamiliar—for which he is searching. At the end of the last verse, readers discover that the boy is gathering the animals to play with him and a little girl. Yolen also provides music to go with her words. Writing in the *Washington Post Book World,* Jerome Beatty, Jr. said: "Count on versatile Jane Yolen to invent something special and intriguing." He summed up his review by saying: "So clever! It adds another dimension to a lesson in the ABCs, does it not?" A reviewer in *Publishers Weekly* called *All in the Woodland Early* "an outstanding alphabet book," while William E. Krueger of *DLB* called it a "beautifully composed book, reminiscent of cumulative nursery rhymes…. This work exhibits Yolen's delightful handling of image, verse, and music."

In 1980, Yolen published the first of her popular "Commander Toad" series, *Commander Toad in Space.* Beginning readers that poke fun at the popular "Star Wars" films—for example, Commander Toad's ship is called the *Star Warts*—and the "Star Trek" television show, the series is usually considered a humorous and entertaining way of introducing children to literature. In *Commander Toad in Space,* the brave captain and his frog crew discover a watery planet and an evil monster, Deep Wader, who is defeated by being engaged in a sing-along. Judith Goldberger of *Booklist* stated: "Any beginning-to-read book with brave space explorers, a ship named the *Star Warts,* and a monster who calls himself Deep Wader would be popular almost by definition. The bonus here is that the adventure of Commander Toad and his colleagues is a clever spoof and really funny reading." A reviewer in *School Library Journal* called the book a "hoppy combination of good story and clever media exploitation" before concluding: "This one holds water."

In 1976, Yolen published *Simple Gifts: The Story of the Shakers,* an informational book about the history of Shakerism, a millennium religion that grew out of Quakerism but has different beliefs. In 1981, she published *The Gift of Sarah Barker,* a historical novel for young adults that is set in a Shaker community. The story features two teenagers, Abel and Sarah, who have grown up in the Society of Believers, a celibate religious community, and now find that they are sexually attracted to each other. As the young people struggle with their feelings, Yolen depicts the contradiction between the religious ecstasy of the Shakers—whose dances and celebrations gave the group their nickname—and the repressive quality of their lifestyle. Sarah and Abel decide to leave the community, but not before Sister Agatha, Sarah's abusive mother, commits suicide. Writing in *Children's Book Review Service,* Barbara Baker called *The Gift of Sarah Barker* "an absorbing tale" and a "jewel of a historical novel," while Stephanie Zvirin of *Booklist* stated: "Into the fabric of a teenage romance [Yolen] weaves complicated and disturbing—at times violent—undercurrents that add a dimension both powerful and provocative." Before writing *Sarah Barker,* Yolen interviewed some of the few remaining Shakers for background information. She also used her daughter, Heidi, who was becoming interested in boys, as the prototype for Sarah. Yolen told *SATA,* "I kept wondering how, in a Shaker community, you could keep the boys away from a girl like Heidi or keep Heidi away from the boys. I imagined a Romeo and Juliet story within the Shaker setting."

In 1982, Yolen published *Dragon's Blood: A Fantasy,* the first volume in her "Pit Dragon" series. High fantasy for young adults that incorporates elements of science fiction and is often compared favorably to the "Pern" books by Anne McCaffrey, the "Pit Dragon" series is acknowledged for Yolen's imaginative creation of a completely realized world. *Dragon's Blood* features Jakkin, a fifteen-year-old slave boy whose master is the best dragon breeder on the planet Austar IV, a former penal colony where inhabitants train and fight dragons domesticated by the early colonists. Jakkin steals a female dragon hatchling to train in secret for the gaming pits, a cockfighting ritual that contributes largely to the planet's economy. Hoping to win his freedom by raising a superior fighting dragon, Jakkin establishes an amazing mental link with his "snatchling," which he names Heart's Blood. The story ends with the dragon's first win; Jakkin—now free—learns that his master knew about his theft and that Akki, a bond girl training in medicine whom Jakkin loves, is his master's illegitimate daughter. Writing in *Horn Book,* Ann A. Flowers called *Dragon's Blood* an "original and engrossing fantasy," while Patricia Manning of *School Library Journal* said that the novel provides a "fascinating glimpse of a brand new world." Pauline Thomas of the *School Librarian* called the book "[s]plendid entertainment," adding, "the author explains little, letting the reader work out the details of geography, natural history, social structure,

and sexual mores. The result is remarkably convincing. Austar IV is a world as real as [Ursula K. Le Guin's] Earthsea . . . ."

In the second volume of the series, *Heart's Blood,* Jakkin is the new Dragon Master and Heart's Blood has given birth to five hatchlings. Jakkin becomes involved in Austar politics when he is asked to infiltrate rebel forces and rescue Akki. Becoming the pawns in a deadly game, Jakkin and Akki flee with Heart's Blood into the freezing cold of night, called Dark After. Cornered by the authorities after inadvertently blowing up a major city, the trio fight for their lives. In the battle, Heart's Blood is killed. In order to survive the freezing temperatures, Jakkin and Akki enter her carcass; when they emerge, they have been given the gift of dragon's sight—telepathy—and the ability to withstand the cold. Charlotte W. Draper of *Horn Book* stated: "Rich in symbolism, eloquent in the evocation of a culture which carries within it the seeds of its own destruction, the book stretches the reader's conception of human capability." In *A Sending of Dragons,* the third volume in the series, Jakkin and Akki avoid capture by running into the wilderness with Heart's Blood's five babies. When they enter a hidden tunnel, the group encounter an underground tribe of primitives who have discovered the way to extract metals on Austar IV. Jakkin and Akki also learn that these people, who, like them, are bonded to dragons, have developed a bloody, terrifying ritual of dragon sacrifice. At the end of the novel, Akki, Jakkin, and Heart's Blood's fledglings escape with two of the primitive community's dragons. Confronted by their pursuers from above ground, they decide to return to the city and use their new knowledge to bring about an end to the feudalism and enslavement on Austar IV. A reviewer in *Publishers Weekly* stated: "Yolen's tightly plotted, adventurous trilogy constitutes superb storytelling. She incorporates elements of freedom and rebellion, power and control, love and friendship in a masterfully crafted context of a society sick with perversion." Writing in *School Library Journal,* Michael Cart said that, like the two volumes preceding it, the particular strengths of *A Sending of Dragons* are in "the almost encyclopedic detail which Yolen has lavished upon her fully realized alternative world of Austar IV, in her sympathetic portrayal of the dragons as both victims and telepathic partners, and in the symbolic sub-text which enriches her narrative and reinforces her universal theme of the inter-dependency and unique value of all life forms."

One of Yolen's most highly acclaimed books is *The Devil's Arithmetic,* a young adult novel that was published in 1988. A time travel fantasy that is rooted in one of the darkest episodes of history, the novel features Hannah Stern, a twelve-year-old Jewish girl who is transported from contemporary New York to rural Poland in 1942 when she opens the door for Elijah during her family's Seder celebration. Captured by the Nazis, Hannah—now called Chaya—is taken to a death camp, where she meets Rivka, a spirited young girl who teaches her to fight against the dehumanization of the camp and tells her that some must live to bear witness.

When Rivka is chosen to be taken to the gas chamber, Chaya, in an act of self-sacrifice, goes in her place; as the doors of the gas chamber close, Chaya—now Hannah again—is returned to the door of her grandparents's apartment, waiting for Elijah. Hannah realizes that her Aunt Eva is her friend Rivka and that she also knew her grandfather in the camp. A critic in *Kirkus Reviews* wrote of *The Devil's Arithmetic:* "Yolen is the author of a hundred books, many of which have been praised for their originality, humor, or poetic vision, but this thoughtful, compelling novel is unique among them." Writing in *Bulletin of the Center for Children's Books,* Roger Sutton noted that Yolen's depiction of the horrors in the camp "is more graphic than any we've seen in holocaust fiction for children before." Confirming that Yolen has brought the "time travel convention to a new and ambitious level," Cynthia Samuels of the *New York Times Book Review* concluded that "sooner or later, all our children must know what happened in the days of the Holocaust. *The Devil's Arithmetic* offers an affecting way to begin." Yolen, who has said that she wrote *The Devil's Arithmetic* for her own children, stated in her acceptance speech for the Sydney Taylor Book Award: "There are books one writes because they are a delight. There are books one writes because one is asked to. There are books one writes because ... they are there. And there are books one writes simply because *the book has to be written. The Devil's Arithmetic* is this last kind of book. I did not just write it. The book itself was a mitzvah." In addition to the Taylor Award, which was given to the novel in 1989, Yolen received the Parents' Choice Silver Seal Award, the Jewish Book Council Award, and the Association of Jewish Libraries Award for *The Devil's Arithmetic,* which was also a finalist for the Nebula Award.

With *Encounter,* a picture book published to coincide with the five-hundredth anniversary of the discovery of America, Yolen created what is perhaps her most controversial work. Written as the remembrance of an elderly Taino Indian man, the story, which describes the first encounter of Native Americans with Columbus, depicts the man's experience as a small boy. The narrator awakens from a terrifying dream about three predatory birds riding the waves to see three anchored ships. Frightened yet fascinated by the strangers who come ashore, the boy tells his chief not to welcome the men, but he is ignored. The boy and several other Indians are taken aboard the ships as slaves. After he escapes by jumping overboard, the boy tries to warn other tribes, but to no avail; the Taino are wiped out. Calling *Encounter* an "unusual picture book," Carolyn Phelan of *Booklist* noted that "while the portrayal of Columbus as evil may strike traditionalists as heresy, he did hunger for gold, abduct native people, and ultimately (though unintentionally), destroy the Taino. This book effectively presents their point of view." Writing in the *New Advocate,* James C. Junhke called *Encounter* "among the most powerful and disturbing publications of the Columbus Quincentennial." Noting the "pioneering brilliance" of the book, the critic called Yolen's greatest achievement "the reversal of perspective. This book forces us to confront what a disaster it was for the

Taino people to be discovered and destroyed by Europeans. Readers young and old will fervently wish never to be encountered by such 'strangers from the sky.'" Writing in response to Junhke's review in the same publication, Yolen said, "If my book becomes a first step towards the exploration of the meeting between Columbus and the indigenous peoples—and its tragic aftermath—then it has done its work, whatever its flaws, perceived or real." The author concluded, "We cannot change history. But we—and most especially our children—can learn from it so that the next encounters, be they at home, abroad, or in space, may be gentler and mutually respectful. It is a large hope but it is, perhaps, all that we have."

Throughout her career, Yolen has woven bits and pieces of her personal history—and that of her family and friends—into her works. She was quoted in *DLB* as saying that she uses "these scraps the way a bird makes a nest and a mouse makes a house—snippet by snippet, leaf and bough and cotton batting and all." Several of the author's books are directly autobiographical. For example, *All Those Secrets of the World,* a picture book published in 1991, is set during the two years that her father was away at war. Yolen recalls how, as a four-year-old, she watched her father depart by ship. The next day, Janie and her five-year-old cousin Michael see some tiny specks on the horizon while they are playing on the beach; the specks are ships. Michael teaches Janie a secret of the world, that as he moves farther away, he gets smaller. Two years later, when her father returns, Janie whispers Michael's secret after he tells her that she seems bigger: that when he was so far away, everything seemed smaller, but now that he is here, she is big. A reviewer in *Publishers Weekly* wrote: "Yolen here relates a bittersweet memory from an important period in her childhood.... This timely nostalgic story is told with simple grace, and Janie's thoughts and experiences are believably childlike." Phyllis G. Sidorsky of *School Library Journal* called *All Those Secrets of the World* an "affecting piece without an extraneous word and one that is particularly timely today."

In 1995, Yolen published *And Twelve Chinese Acrobats,* a tale for middle graders based on family stories about her father's older brother. Set in a Russian village in 1910, the book features Lou the Rascal, a charming troublemaker who keeps getting into scrapes. When Lou is sent to a military school in Kiev, the family—especially narrator Wolf, Lou's youngest brother (and Yolen's father)—is sad. Lou is expelled from military school. Months later, he surprises everyone by bringing home a troupe of twelve Chinese acrobats he met while working in a Moscow circus. The acrobats fascinate the locals with their descriptions of an exotic world far removed from the little village. When the acrobats leave the *shtel* in the spring, Lou's father, recognizing his son's managerial ability, sends him to America to find a place for the family. Writing in *Bulletin of the Center for Children's Books,* Betsy Hearne said: "The relationship between the two brothers, Lou and Wolf, lends an immediate dynamic to the historical setting." The critic concluded that the compressed narrative, brief chapters, spacious format, large print, and "vivaciously detailed pen-and-ink illustrations dancing across almost every page [by Jean Gralley] make this a prime choice for young readers venturing into historical fiction for the first time, or, for that matter, considering a probe into their own family stories." A critic in *Kirkus Reviews* called *And Twelve Chinese Acrobats* a book "radiating family warmth, in words, art, and remembrance."

In an article for *Horn Book,* Yolen stated: "As a writer I am the empress of thieves, taking characters like gargoyles off Parisian churches, the *ki-lin* (or unicorn) from China, swords in stones from the Celts, landscapes from the Taino people. I have pulled threads from magic tapestries to weave my own new cloth." The author concluded, "Children's literature is about growth. Just as we do not put heavy weights on our children's heads to stunt their growth, we should not put weights on our writers' heads. To do so is to stunt story forever. Stories go beyond race, beyond religion—even when they are about race and religion. The book speaks to individuals in an individual voice. But then it is taken into the reader's life and recreated, re-invigorated, re-visioned. That is what literature is about." Writing in *SAAS,* Yolen mused that her life, "like anyone else's is a patchwork of past and present . . . . I can also see a pattern that might tell me my future—as long as I remain consistent. I consider myself a poet and a storyteller. Being 'America's Hans Christian Andersen' means trying to walk in much-too-large seven-league boots. I just want to go on writing and discovering my stories for the rest of my life because I know that in my tales I make public what is private, transforming my own joy and sadness into tales for the people. The folk."

Works Cited

Review of *All in the Woodland Early, Publishers Weekly,* January 11, 1980, p. 88.

Review of *All Those Secrets of the World, Publishers Weekly,* March 22, 1991, p. 80.

Review of *And Twelve Chinese Acrobats, Kirkus Reviews,* April 15, 1995, p. 564.

Baker, Barbara, review of *The Gift of Sarah Barker, Children's Book Review Service,* June, 1981, p. 100.

Beatty, Jerome, Jr., "Herds of Hungry Hogs Hurrying Home," *Washington Post Book World,* April 13, 1980, p. 10.

Cart, Michael, review of *A Sending of Dragons, School Library Journal,* January, 1988, pp. 87-88.

Review of *Commander Toad in Space, School Library Journal,* December, 1980, p. 66.

Review of *The Devil's Arithmetic, Kirkus Reviews,* August 15, 1988, p. 1248.

Draper, Charlotte W., review of *Heart's Blood, Horn Book,* April, 1984, p. 206.

Review of *The Emperor and the Kite, Children's Book News,* January-February, 1970, pp. 23-24.

Review of *The Emperor and the Kite, Publishers Weekly,* August 14, 1967, p. 50.

Flowers, Ann A., review of *Dragon's Blood, Horn Book,* August, 1982, pp. 418-19.

Fuchs, Marcia G., entry in *Twentieth-century Children's Writers,* 3rd edition, St. James Press, 1989, pp. 1075-78.

Review of *The Girl Who Cried Flowers and Other Tales, Kirkus Reviews,* July 15, 1974, p. 741.

Review of *The Girl Who Cried Flowers and Other Tales, Publishers Weekly,* July 22, 1974, p. 70.

Goldberger, Judith, review of *Commander Toad in Space, Booklist,* November 15, 1980, p. 464.

Hearne, Betsy, review of *And Twelve Chinese Acrobats, Bulletin of the Center for Children's Books,* June, 1995, p. 365.

Hopkins, Lee Bennett, "O Yolen: A Look at the Poetry of Jane Yolen," *Teaching and Learning Literature (TALL),* November-December, 1996, pp. 66-68.

Juhnke, James C. and Jane Yolen, "An Exchange on *Encounter,*" *New Advocate,* spring, 1993, pp. 94-96.

Krueger, William E., "Jane Yolen," *Dictionary of Literary Biography,* Volume 52: *American Writers for Children since 1960: Fiction,* Gale, 1986, pp. 398-405.

Langton, Jane, review of *The Hundredth Dove and Other Tales, New York Times Book Review,* November 20, 1977, p. 30.

Manning, Patricia, review of *Dragon's Blood, School Library Journal,* September, 1982, p. 146.

Perrin, Noel, "Bulldozer Blues," *New York Times Book Review,* November 8, 1992, p. 54.

Phelan, Carolyn, review of *Encounter, Booklist,* March 1, 1992, p. 1281.

Polacheck, Janet G., review of *Friend: The Story of George Fox and the Quakers, Library Journal,* June 15, 1972, p. 2245.

Samuels, Cynthia, "Hannah Learns to Remember," *New York Times Book Review,* November 13, 1988, p. 62.

Review of *A Sending of Dragons, Publishers Weekly,* October 9, 1987, p. 90.

Sidorsky, Phyllis G., review of *All Those Secrets of the World, School Library Journal,* July, 1991, p. 66.

Sieruta, Peter D., entry in *Children's Books and Their Creators,* edited by Anita Silvey, Houghton Mifflin, 1995, pp. 700-01.

Singer, Marilyn R., review of *The Girl Who Loved the Wind, School Library Journal,* March, 1973, p. 102.

Sutton, Roger, review of *The Devil's Arithmetic, Bulletin of the Center for Children's Books,* October, 1988, pp. 23-24.

Thomas, Pauline, review of *Dragon's Blood, School Librarian,* December, 1983, p. 384.

Von Schweinitz, Eleanor, review of *The Girl Who Loved the Wind, Children's Book Review,* December, 1973, pp. 172-73.

Yolen, Jane, essay in *Fourth Book of Junior Authors and Illustrators,* edited by Doris de Montreville and Elizabeth D. Crawford, Wilson, 1978, pp. 356-57.

Yolen, commentary in *Something about the Author,* Volume 40, Gale, 1985, pp. 217-30.

Yolen, "Something about the Author," *Something about the Author Autobiography Series,* Volume 4, Gale, 1987, pp. 327-46.

Yolen, transcript of acceptance speech for the Sydney Taylor Book Award, *Judaica Librarianship,* spring, 1989–winter, 1990, pp. 52-53.

Yolen, interview with Jean W. Ross, *Contemporary Authors New Revision Series,* Volume 29, Gale, 1990, pp. 463-69.

Yolen, "An Empress of Thieves," *Horn Book,* November-December, 1994, pp. 702-05.

Zvirin, Stephanie, review of *The Gift of Sarah Barker, Booklist,* May 15, 1981, p. 1250.

For More Information See

BOOKS

Authors and Artists for Young Adults, Volume 4, Gale, 1990, pp. 229-41.

Children's Literature Review, Volume 4, Gale, 1982, pp. 255-69; Volume 44, 1997, pp. 167-211.

Drew, Bernard A., *The One Hundred Most Popular Young Adult Authors,* Libraries Unlimited, 1996.

Roginski, Jim, *Behind the Covers: Interviews with Authors and Illustrators of Books for Children and Young Adults,* Libraries Unlimited, 1985.

St. James Guide to Fantasy Writers, St. James Press, 1996.

St. James Guide to Young Adult Writers, St. James Press, 1999.

Yolen, Jane, *Guide to Writing for Children,* Writer, 1989.

Yolen, *Touch Magic: Fantasy, Faerie, and Folktale in the Literature of Childhood,* Philomel, 1981.

Yolen, *Writing Books for Children,* The Writer, 1973, revised edition, 1983.

PERIODICALS

New York Times Book Review, May 17, 1998

Publishers Weekly, June 15, 1998, p. 60.

School Library Journal, March, 1998, p. 207.

Voice of Youth Advocates, December, 1997, p. 328.

—*Sketch by Gerard J. Senick*

* * *

YOUNG, James
See GRAHAM, Ian